Management

McGRAW-HILL SERIES IN MANAGEMENT

Keith Davis and Fred Luthans, Consulting Editors

Management

Seventh Edition

HAROLD KOONTZ
University of California
Los Angeles

CYRIL O'DONNELL
Deceased
University of California
Los Angeles

HEINZ WEIHRICH
Arizona State University
Tempe

McGRAW-HILL BOOK COMPANY
New York St. Louis San Francisco Auckland Bogotá Hamburg Johannesburg London Madrid
Mexico Montreal New Delhi Panama Paris São Paulo Singapore Sydney Tokyo Toronto

This book was set in Melior by Black Dot, Inc.
The editors were John F. Carleo and Elisa Adams;
the designer was Joan E. O'Connor;
the production supervisor was Phil Galea.
The drawings were done by J & R Services, Inc.
R. R. Donnelley & Sons Company was printer and binder.

Management

    56 890DODO 83

Library of Congress Cataloging in Publication Data

Koontz, Harold, date
  Management.

  (McGraw-Hill series in management)
  Includes bibliographical references and indexes.
    1. Industrial management. 2. Management.
I. O'Donnell, Cyril, date, joint author.
II. Weihrich, Heinz, joint author. III. Title.
HD31.K6   1980   658.4   79-14016
ISBN 0-07-035377-8

To Mary and Ursula

About the Authors

HAROLD KOONTZ has been active as a business and government executive, university professor, company board chairman and director, management consultant, worldwide lecturer to top management groups, and author of many books and articles. Since 1950 he has been Professor of Management at the University of California, Los Angeles, and since 1978, World Chancellor of The International Academy of Management. He is an author or coauthor of seventeen books and eighty-five journal articles, and his *Principles of Management* (now in the seventh edition as *Management*) has been translated into fifteen languages. His *Board of Directors and Effective Management* was given the Academy of Management Book Award in 1968. After taking his doctorate at Yale, Professor Koontz served as Assistant to the Trustees of the New Haven Railroad, Chief of the Traffic Branch of the War Production Board, Assistant to the Vice President of the Association of American Railroads, Assistant to the President of Trans World Airlines, and Director of Sales for Convair. He has acted as management consultant for, among others, Hughes Tool Company, Hughes Aircraft Company, Purex Corporation, KLM Royal Dutch Airlines, Metropolitan Life Insurance Company, Occidental Petroleum Corporation, and General Telephone Company. Professor Koontz's honors include being elected a Fellow of the American and the International Academies of Management, and serving as President of the American Academy of Management. He received the Mead Johnson

Award in 1962 and the Society for Advancement of Management Taylor Key Award in 1974 and is listed in *Who's Who in America, Who's Who in Finance and Industry,* and *Who's Who in the World.*

The late CYRIL O'DONNELL was educated at the University of Alberta and University of Chicago, where he received a Ph.D. in management. His last position was Professor of Business Organization and Policy and Director, Case Development Program, at the Graduate School of Business Administration, University of California, Los Angeles. He was previously chairman of the Department of Economics at DePaul University. He had extensive business and professional experience, having been affiliated with the War Labor Board and private business enterprises. Professor O'Donnell was a consultant to several domestic and foreign firms and government agencies and was an active director of several business corporations. In addition to contributing to numerous professional journals, he was the author of *Business Management, Cases in General Management,* and *The Strategy of Corporate Research.*

HEINZ WEIHRICH received his Ph.D. from the University of California at Los Angeles. Currently Professor of Management at Arizona State University, he has also taught at the University of California at Los Angeles, at INSEAD—the European Institute of Business Administration in France, and at universities in Germany and Austria. His numerous articles on management and behavioral science topics have been published in the United States and abroad. Professor Weihrich conducted the first comprehensive research study of management by objectives (MBO) as a total system of managing and coauthored *Management: An MBO Approach.* In addition to pursuing his academic interests, Professor Weihrich is active in management consulting as well as in executive and organizational development in the United States and abroad. He has more than fourteen years of business and consulting experience in the United States and Europe, working with such companies as Volkswagen, Hughes Aircraft Company, and others.

Contents

PART 6 CONTROLLING

Preface

This book presents the basics of an operational theory and science of management. While we would not pretend to put in one volume all the knowledge that might be useful to a practicing manager, we hope to present the most important portions of this knowledge in an organized and useful way. In doing so, we emphasize the essentials of management that are pertinent to the effective work of practicing managers and show how in various areas these must be looked upon as a system. We demonstrate that managing itself is a part of a larger system interacting with a manager's total environment—economic, technological, social, political, and ethical. This book also stresses that what managers do in practice must both reflect and be modified by the actual situations in which they operate and the realities they face.

While long emphasizing concepts, theory, principles, and techniques of management, beginning with the first edition in 1955, we have taken the position that managing is an art. This means that to achieve the best kind of practice, managers must apply science—the underlying organized knowledge of management—to the realities of any situation. As every practicing manager knows, there is no universal "one best way" of doing things in all instances, and the practical application of management theory and science has always recognized the importance of the realities or contingencies in a given situation. This is normal for all arts. Practicing engineers, for example, may use generally known and accepted knowledge of physics, electronics, hydraulics, or other sciences in their design of an instrument, a piece of machinery, or a building. But the actual products of their design will differ in appearance and content depending on the situations they are intended to serve.

In developing a framework in which management knowledge can be organized in a useful and practical way, we have chosen, as a primary classification, to use the functions of managers—planning, organizing, staffing, leading, and controlling. Each function, in turn, is dealt with by further breakdowns of knowledge pertaining to it. Experience has proved that any new knowledge, whether from the behavioral or quantitative sciences or from the innovations of practice, can be placed within this framework. It is hoped in this way to make a start toward developing a true management science—organized knowledge—that puts new developments into a proper perspective and makes this science useful to those who must apply it, as practitioners, to reality.

In our attempt to develop classifications of knowledge, we recognize these classifications as being nonexclusive and as requiring a systems approach. The functions of managers represent an interlocking, interacting system. Each functional area has within it a number of systems and subsystems. With eclectic inclusion of pertinent knowledge and techniques from other areas of scientific inquiry, we likewise recognize the need for interconnecting elements between these and the task of the manager. Moreover, it should be strongly emphasized that this book does not look at any enterprise and the manager's role within it as a closed social system. Even though the primary stress of the text is on the role of managers in creating and maintaining an internal environment for performance, it would be foolish indeed for managers (or the authors) not to consider their need to interact with the entire external environment in which every manager operates.

As we did in previous editions, we would like again to make certain aspects of our position clear at the outset. While we recognize that managers seldom, if ever, spend all their time and talents in managing, it is our conviction that the functions of a manager, as manager, are essentially the same whether the person is a first-level supervisor or the top executive of an enterprise. The reader will therefore find no basic distinction made among managers, executives, administrators, or supervisors. To be sure, the environment of each may differ, the scope of authority held may vary, and the types of problems dealt with may be considerably different; a person in a managerial role may also act as a salesperson, an engineer, or a financier. But the fact remains that, as managers, all who obtain results by establishing an environment for effective and efficient performance of individuals operating in groups undertake the same basic functions.

Moreover, the fundamentals related to the task of managing apply to every kind of enterprise in every kind of culture. The purposes of different enterprises may vary, but all that are organized do rely on effective group operation for efficient attainment of whatever goals they may have. It is true that many of the case examples and techniques used in this book are drawn from actual business enterprises. However, we have no intention of overlooking the fact that the same fundamental truths are applicable elsewhere.

In this edition, as in the sixth edition, we have dropped the term "principles" from the title, not because we believe that principles do not exist or are not important to management, but rather because some instructors and readers have erroneously gained the impression that the book is primarily an enumeration of principles. The book has always been more, even though identification of principles has been, and still is, regarded as a means of abstracting certain truths from an immensely complicated body of knowledge. In this new edition, in order to make much clearer the treatment of a broad science and practice of management, attempts are made throughout to identify systems elements in the field and to relate the many techniques and elements of theory to a contingency, or situational, approach.

However, we would not wish the reader to lose sight of the importance of theory and principles. Principles are used here in the sense of fundamental truths applicable to a given set of circumstances that have value in predicting results. They are thus descriptive and predictive and not prescriptive as so many have erroneously believed. An attempt has been made to cast most of these fundamental truths in the form of propositions with independent and dependent variables. In a few cases, principles are very little more than concepts. In other instances, concepts and basic truths are introduced without being elevated to the status of major principles. In any event, however, an attempt has been made to recognize the indisputable fact that clear concepts are the initial requirement of science and understanding. The structure of major principles emphasized, to the extent that they reflect fundamentals in a given area, may be referred to as "theory"—a body of related principles dealing systematically with a subject. Even though principles and theory are referred to throughout the book, the reader must not gain the impression that they are impractical. If accurately formulated and properly used, principles and theory should be eminently practical. The real test of their validity is in the crucible of practice.

There are those who object to using the term "principles" for fundamental truths not supported by elaborate and complete verification of their validity. Such persons would prefer to see these principles characterized as hypotheses. Perhaps, strictly speaking, many are. However, even far more statistically verified principles in the so-called exact sciences are virtually always regarded as subjects for further verification. Moreover, we are completely aware that the formulation of many principles made here represents essentially a preliminary attempt to codify a number of basic truths and, by their being placed in a framework believed to be logical, an attempt to move toward a theory of management. Being preliminary, these summaries are not intended as a final scheme of a theory of management. But they are believed to be a convenient and useful way of packaging some of the major truths that experience and research have found to have a high degree of credibility and predictability.

In this seventh edition, as in those preceding it, attempts have been made to respond to several major influences. One is the continuing help from comprehensive surveys of teachers and scholars who have used past editions of this book at various levels of academic and practical management education in a wide variety of universities and operating enterprises. The input of those using the English version of the book has been supplemented by that of the many others who use its fifteen foreign-language editions. Another major influence to which we have attempted to respond is the burgeoning volume of research, new ideas, and advanced techniques, especially those being applied to management from the behavioral, social, and physical sciences.

In this revision, considerable new material has been added. Many chapters have been largely or completely rewritten. In order to introduce new findings from recent research and experience, certain older material has been deleted or compressed so as to limit the length of the book. New material has been included on managing by objectives, organization development, managing the human factor, control techniques, and other topics. In the realm of theory, we discuss positive tendencies indicating possible future coalescence of the varied approaches to management.

Largely new chapters have been written on comparative and international management, strategies and policies, the nature and purpose of staffing, the selection of managers, manager and organization development, managing and the human factor, and communication. All these chapters reflect the latest findings, techniques, and thinking in their subject areas.

We have also made a number of changes to better reflect modern thinking and teaching. Part 5 is now called "Leading" instead of "Directing and Leading." We now include chapter objectives at the beginning of each chapter. Also, the cases have been placed at the end of the part to which their subject matter refers, and leading questions are placed at the end of each case. The glossary of management terms and concepts has been expanded to include many more terms of interest to students and practitioners of management.

As might be expected with a text of this kind, we are indebted to so many persons who have helped us over the quarter-century of the book's existence that a complete acknowledgment would be encyclopedic. Some scholars and managers are acknowledged in footnotes and other references to their contributions. Many managers with whom we have served in business, government, education, and other enterprises have contributed by word and deed. Thousands of managers at all levels in all kinds of enterprises in the United States and many countries throughout the world have allowed us to test ideas in executive training seminars and lectures. To the executives of various companies and other organizations with which we have been privileged to work as directors or consultants, we are grateful for the opportunities to continue the clinical practice of management. Nor should we forget the searching questions and criticisms of many of our academic colleagues throughout the world who have helped us sharpen our thinking.

In previous editions, special appreciation was expressed to a number of individuals who contributed in many important ways to the content of the book. While they are not again named here, their contributions, by shaping many parts of earlier editions, have also been important to this edition. For this edition, in particular, we would like to express our great appreciation to certain individuals who went through the sixth edition in detail and made a number of very helpful suggestions. These are Professor Keith Davis of Arizona State University, Professor Fred Luthans of the University of Nebraska, Professor Arthur G. Bedeian of Auburn University, and the late Professor Barry Richman of the University of California, Los Angeles. We wish also to acknowledge the very great assistance given us by Professor Leon C. Megginson of the University of Southern Alabama.

We wish also to thank Ms. Carol Pincus and Ms. Betty Preddy for their conscientious and intelligent work in preparing the manuscript of this edition for publication.

It is with deep regret that the senior author notes the lamented death of his respected colleague and coauthor for more than two decades, Dr. Cyril O'Donnell, who passed away in February of 1976.

Harold Koontz
Heinz Weihrich

1 The Basis of Management Theory and Science

Presentation of basic management theory, science, and techniques is the purpose and focus of this book. This presentation is based on the concept that the task of all managers is to design and maintain an environment conducive to the performance of individuals who are working together in groups toward the accomplishment of some preselected objective. This book attempts to organize and present in a practical way the fundamental knowledge underlying managing. What is said in this book is intended to apply to managers at every level in every kind of enterprise in any kind of society. Although it is recognized that the environment of managing may differ between large and small businesses, between businesses and other kinds of organized enterprises, and between differing cultures or areas of economic and social development, and therefore that many problems may vary, it is the authors' conviction that the essentials of managing are the same.

As many scholars and managers have found, the analysis of management knowledge is facilitated by a useful and clear organization of that knowledge. In this book, as a first order of classification, management knowledge is organized around the basic functions of managers—

planning, organizing, staffing, leading, and controlling. Thus, the concepts, principles, theory, and techniques are organized, as a first order, around these functions. While others might prefer a slightly different major classification, the one used here has the advantage of being comprehensive, of being divisible into enough parts to permit logical analysis, and of being practical in the sense that it portrays functions as most perceptive managers see them. Moreover, in this book this classification sharply distinguishes managerial tasks from nonmanagerial ones, such as finance, production, and marketing, and permits concentration on the basics of the job of managers, as managers.

Part 1, then, is an introduction to the science and practice of management. Chapter 1 is intended to lay the groundwork for an understanding of the nature and importance of managing as an art and of management as a developing and important science. This chapter emphasizes the difference between art and science and takes the position that managing itself is an art, but that like other practices it is an art whose practitioner will do best if he or she has an understanding of the science—organized knowledge—underlying this art. Another key point emphasized in this chapter is that all managers in all kinds of enterprises must be guided by a "surplus" goal. In other words, whatever a manager's particular objectives or mission may be, that manager has another logical and socially desirable goal—to manage so as to accomplish an objective or mission with the least inputs of material and human resources, including in the latter human dissatisfaction, or to accomplish as much of an objective or mission as possible with the resources available.

Chapter 2 is devoted to a summary of the emergence of management thought. While only a limited view of the history of management thought can be presented in a single chapter, it is hoped that the chapter will give the reader an appreciation of what earlier thinkers and researchers in the area of management said, thought, and did. Although the importance of management was recognized from earliest times as group effort became important, the major contributions to management have occurred only in the twentieth century and even more particularly in the past three decades. Even though there were many precursors to Frederick Taylor, who is credited with being the father of scientific management, he and his followers, thinking and writing early in the twentieth century, did whet the appetites of many business and government managers for more efficient operations through attempts to replace "rules of thumb" with scientific analyses and methods.

A contemporary of Taylor, the French industrialist Henri Fayol, took a different tack in his analysis of management. Fayol was the first to look on management as a total and universal activity separate from the nonmanagerial activities of a business or government agency. Because he attempted to distill basic knowledge of management, largely from his own experience, and classified that knowledge according to the functions of managers, Fayol can be looked upon as the father of operational-management theory.

Interestingly enough, the currently very popular study of human behavior in relation to management arose from the interest of early psychologists to have managers pay more attention to the human factor and thereby make scientific management work and be more fruitful.

As might be expected in this chapter, many of the currents of management thought are summarized, with attention being given to the large volume of research and thought that has come to the fore in recent years.

The varying patterns of management are treated in Chapter 3. The growing interest in management in recent years has given rise to a number of approaches to management by a variety of specialists seeking to explain the basics of management. Some of these approaches have been extremely varied and often confusing. As a matter of fact, these varying approaches, referred to by the senior author as "the management theory jungle" in 1961, are now even more numerous than they were then. However, there is some evidence, albeit fairly slight, that the various approaches are beginning to converge toward a system of thought subscribed to by the authors of this book and referred to as the "operational theory" of management. This term is meant to describe a school of thought that is "operational" in the sense that it underpins and reflects what managers actually do.

The fourth chapter of this part deals with the external environment in which managers operate. Even though this environment is very complex, being the entire external environment in which an organization acts, it is hoped that the essential elements can be effectively identified and classified according to economic, technological, social, political-legal, and ethical factors. As a part of the discussion of managing and its open-system interaction with its environment, attention is paid to the nature of social responsibility of business and nonbusiness enterprises and the technique of the social audit.

As the final chapter of this part, Chapter 5 deals with comparative and international management. There are two main thrusts to this chapter. One is the attempt to analyze the basics of management in various social and political environments. It is believed that this analysis shows the universality and transferability of management fundamentals. Another thrust is to analyze major problems encountered when a business, in particular, extends its operations into nations and societies other than that of the headquarters, or home, offices. As shown in this chapter, there are necessarily many interactions between any manager's task and the environment in which he or she operates. But there has been nothing yet disclosed that indicates any lack of applicability of the basic concepts and theory of management.

chapter 1

Management: Theory, Science, and Practice

MAJOR CHAPTER OBJECTIVES

1 To point out that the major purpose of this book is to explain and analyze the basic science, theory, and principles of management and how they relate to the practice of managing.

2 To emphasize that in all kinds of enterprises, whether business or nonbusiness organizations,[1] the logical and socially desirable aim of all managers, as managers, must be "surplus."

3 To recognize that managing as practice is an art, and that its practitioners, like those in other fields, will do best if they can understand and apply, in the light of situations, the underlying theory and science.

4 To show that concepts, theories, principles, and techniques furnish the basic elements of an operational science.

To emphasize that all managing requires a systems approach and that practice must always take into account situations and contingencies.

[1]Note that the authors here and in many other places in the book use the term "organization" in the common way as denoting an enterprise or other group operation, such as a department, a company, a government agency, a church, or any other group of persons working together. While this term often causes confusion in distinguishing between an operation or enterprise and an organization structure, we know of no other term to use, especially since the term "enterprise" is too often employed to denote a business operation. However, in the chapters in Part 3 of this book, when we use "organization" in the structural sense, we try to be clear that we are so doing.

Perhaps there is no more important area of human activity than managing, for it is the basic task of all managers at all levels and in all kinds of enterprises to design and maintain an environment in which individuals, working together in groups, can accomplish preselected missions and objectives. In other words, managers are charged with the responsibility of taking actions that will make it possible for individuals to make their best contributions to group objectives.

Ever since people began forming groups to accomplish goals they could not achieve as individuals, managing has been essential to assure the coordination of individual efforts. As society has come to rely increasingly on group effort, and as many organized groups have become large, the task of managers has risen in importance.

It is the purpose of this book to study managers and what is involved in their task—to organize and summarize the important basic knowledge that underlies their task—so that their job, so important to social progress, can be done better. As incomplete as this knowledge may be, compared with knowledge in some of the more mature sciences, like physics and chemistry, there is a considerable and rapidly developing body of knowledge—concepts, theory, principles, and techniques—underlying managing.

In concentrating on the manager in this book, we must not forget that managers never operate in a vacuum or in a system unaffected by outside influences. We are not suggesting that management or managing is a closed system unaffected by the external environment. Quite the contrary. Whether they head a government, a company, a department, or a section within an organization, managers must always take into account the many influences, both inside and outside the organization, which affect their task. Can anyone imagine a sales manager, for example, trying to administer a group of salespeople without taking into account such internal factors as the company's engineering, manufacturing, and advertising, and such external influences as economic conditions, the market, the state of technology affecting a product, applicable government regulations, the vast areas of social concerns and pressures, and the attitudes and other personality factors salespeople bring from their family, educational, and other backgrounds? Similarly, would a company president attempt to make decisions without taking into account the multitude of influences both inside and outside the company?

WHY MANAGEMENT?

Not all groups believe that they need managing. Even faculties of many colleges and universities seem to feel this way and continually emphasize the need for maintaining "collegial" management. In their desire not to be managed, they forget that effective managers—whether presidents, or deans—do everything in their power to design an environment in which professors and researchers can best perform. Certain critics of modern management feel that people would work together better and with more personal satisfaction if there were no managers. They prefer to refer to the ideal group operation as a "team" effort. They apparently do not realize that in most rudimentary form of team play, individuals playing a game have clear group goals as well as personal ones, are assigned to positions, follow play patterns, allow someone to call the plays, and follow certain rules and guidelines. Indeed, a characteristic of every effective group effort designed to attain group goals at the least cost of time, money, material, or discomfort is that it adopts the basic process, principles, and techniques of management.

Managing is essential in all organized cooperation, as well as at all levels of organization in an enterprise. It is the function not only of the corporation president and the army general but also of the shop supervisor and the company commander. In working with many enterprises and organizations, the authors have heard it said repeatedly that the "trouble" with the enterprise is the "management," meaning persons at a higher level in the organization. Even vice presidents of a company have made this observation to one of the authors, leaving only the president who was the "problem." While weaknesses and difficulties may appear at any level of management, effective and perceptive management demands that all those responsible for the work of others, at all levels and in any type of enterprise, regard themselves as managers. It is in this sense that the term is used in this book.

Thus the reader will find no basic distinction between managers and executives, administrators, or supervisors. To be sure, a given situation may differ considerably between various levels in an organization or various types of enterprise, the scope of authority held may vary, the types of problems dealt with may be considerably different, and a person in a managerial role may also be a salesman, engineer, or financier; but the fact remains that, as managers, all who obtain results by establishing an environment for effective group endeavor undertake the same functions.

Even so, those in a managerial role seldom devote all their time and talents to managing, and the organization roles which individuals fill almost invariably involve nonmanagerial duties. One has only to look at the duties and performances associated with perhaps the most complex managerial role in our society—that of the President of the United States—to realize that much of his work is nonmanagerial. Even in business corporations, company presidents find themselves doing a considerable amount of nonmanagerial work. And, as one goes down the organization ladder, the number of nonmanagerial duties tends to increase. Nevertheless, this fact of life should not detract in any way from the key significance of managing.

The Goal of All Managers

Nonbusiness executives sometimes say that top business managers have it easy—that profit is their goal. As will be elaborated in later discussions, profit is only a measure of the surplus of business income over cost. It was pointed out earlier that in a very real sense, the goal of all managers must be surplus. Their task is to establish the environment for group effort in such a way that individuals will contribute to group objectives with the least amount of such inputs as money, time, effort, discomfort, and materials. By the very definition of the task, this becomes the goal of managers. But if they were ever to know whether the efforts of those for whom they are responsible are effective and efficient—whether they are attaining goals with least costs—they obviously must know what group goals are. Not only must these goals be known to managers, and preferably to all those for whom they are responsible, but they should also be known in a verifiable way. Otherwise, managers can never measure either their own effectiveness and efficiency or the effectiveness and efficiency of their group.

Thus the goal of managers, as managers, is fundamentally the same in business and nonbusiness enterprises. It is also the same at every level. The corporation president, the city administrator, the hospital department head, the government first-line supervisor, the Boy Scout leader, the bishop, the baseball manager, and the university president or dean, all, as managers, have the same kind of goals. The purposes of their enterprise or their department may vary, and these purposes may be more difficult to define in one situation than in another, but their basic managerial goal remains the same.

IS MANAGING A SCIENCE OR AN ART?

This question is often raised. Actually, managing, like all other arts (whether medicine, music composition, engineering, baseball, or accountancy), makes use of underlying organized knowledge—science—and applies it in the light of realities to gain a desired, practical result. In doing so, practice must design a solution which will work, that is, get the results desired. Art, then, is the "know-how" to accomplish a desired concrete result. It is what Chester I. Barnard has called "behavioral knowledge."[2] Those who diagnose "by the book," or design wholly by formula, or attempt to manage by memorization of principles are almost certain to overlook practical realities. With the possible exception of formulating science itself, art is the most creative of all human pursuits. When the importance of effective and efficient group cooperation in any

[2]As Barnard said in *The Functions of the Executive* (Cambridge, Mass.: Harvard University Press, 1938), pp. 290–291: "It is the function of the arts to accomplish concrete ends, effect results, produce situations, that would not come about without the deliberate efforts to secure them. These arts must be mastered and applied by those who deal in the concrete and for the future. The function of the sciences, on the other hand, is to explain the phenomena, the events, the situations, of the past. Their aim is not to produce specific events, effects, or situations, but explanations which we call knowledge. It has not been the aim of science to be a system of technology, and it could not be such a system. There is required in order to manipulate the concrete a vast amount of knowledge of a temporary, local, specific character, of no general value or interest, that it is not the function of a science to have or to present and only to explain to the extent that it is generally significant."

society is appreciated, it is not difficult to argue that managing is the most important of all arts.

The most productive art is always based on an understanding of the science underlying it. Thus science and art are not mutually exclusive, but are complementary. As science improves, so should art, as has happened in the physical and biological sciences. Physicians without a knowledge of science become witch doctors; with science, they may be artful surgeons. Executives who attempt to manage without theory, and without knowledge structured by it, must trust to luck, intuition, or what they did in the past; with organized knowledge, they have a far better opportunity to design a workable and sound solution to a managerial problem. However, mere knowledge of principles or theory will not assure successful practice, because one must know how to use them. Since there is no science in which everything is known and all relationships are proved, science cannot be a comprehensive tool of the artist. This is true whether one is diagnosing illness, designing bridges, or managing a company.

One of the common errors in utilizing theory and science is to overlook the necessity of compromising, or blending, in order to achieve a total desired result. An airplane designer must make a compromise between weight and strength on the one hand and cost on the other. Managers may wisely assign employees more than one superior— breaking the principle of unity of command—if they are certain that this will improve the total results attained. But in disregarding principles and the other elements of science, one must calculate the cost and weigh it against the total result. The ability to compromise with the least amount of undesired consequences is the essence of the managerial art. As we will note in Chapter 3, this fact has given rise to a "contingency" or "situational" theory of mangement.

Another problem often results from the attempt to remedy a situation by applying a principle not designed to cover it. One would not apply a theory of metal stress to an engineering problem in which stresses were unimportant and the cost of material was of great significance, nor would one be likely to apply a principle of management to a problem of medical diagnosis. One of the difficulties of many management scholars and practitioners is that they try to force a principle into a situation it was not designed to explain.

Science and Management

Although the organization of human beings for the attainment of common objectives is ages old, a science of management is just now developing. Since World War II there has been an increasing awareness that the quality of managing is important to modern life, and this has resulted in extensive analysis and study of the management process, its environment, and its techniques.

Analysis of business failures made over many years by the credit analysis firm of Dun and Bradstreet has shown that a very high percentage of these failures have been due to unqualified or inexperienced management. The prominent investor journal *Forbes*, which has studied American business firms for a number of years, has found that companies succeed almost invariably to the extent that they are well managed. The Bank of America said a few years ago in its publication *Small Business Reporter*: "In the final analysis more than 90% of business failures are due to managerial incompetence and inexperience."

The importance of management is nowhere better dramatized than in the case of many underdeveloped or developing countries. Review of this problem in recent years by economic development specialists has shown that provision of capital or technology does not ensure development. The limiting factor in almost every case has been the lack of quality and vigor on the part of managers.

While the culture of present-day society is characterized by revolutionary improvements in the physical and biological sciences, the social sciences have lagged far behind. Yet, unless we can learn to harness human resources and coordinate the activities of people, inefficiency and waste in applying technical discoveries will continue. One has only to look at the incredible waste of human and material resources, in the light of the unfulfilled social objectives, to realize that the social sciences are far from doing their job of guiding social policy and action.

Certain social sciences have progressed further than others. With all its deficiencies, economics, for example, has gone far toward explaining what course of action will yield optimum output at the least expenditure of labor and capital. But economic principles assume that economic objectives can be attained through the coordination of human activity and that the enterprise, as well as groups of enterprises, will be well managed. Other social sciences, such as sociology and anthropology, have gone far toward explaining our cultural environment. Even though the foundations of these sciences suffer from incompleteness and inexactness, the theories have helped us to understand our society.

The study and analysis of management have lagged behind other sciences until recent years. Yet, as in other fields, the development of an underlying science must precede an improved practice.

Science and the Scientific Method

Science explains phenomena. It is based on a belief in the rationality of nature—on the idea that relationships can be found between two or more sets of events. The essential feature of science is that knowledge has been discovered and systematized through the application of scientific method. Thus we speak of a science of astronomy or chemistry to indicate accumulated knowledge formulated with reference to the discovery of general truths in these areas. Science is systematized in the sense that relationships between variables and limits have been ascertained and underlying principles have been discovered.

Scientific method involves determining facts through observation of events or things and verifying the accuracy of these facts through continued observation. After classifying and analyzing the facts, scientists look for and find some causal relationships which they believe to be true. Such generalizations, called "hypotheses," are then tested for their accuracy. When hypotheses are found to be supported, to reflect or explain reality, and therefore to have value in predicting what will happen in similar circumstances, they are called "principles."

Application of scientific method to the development of principles does not totally eliminate doubt. Every generalization, however proved, may be subject to further research and analysis. Even so long-standing a generalization as Newton's law of gravitation might be modified with new knowledge and phenomena. But without new facts, induction from them of significant relationships, testing of hypotheses, and development of principles, we would never understand our universe.

Principles and Causal Relationships

If principles are to explain management behavior, they should be formulated to predict results. In connection with many of the principles presented in this book, it is not explicitly stated that a certain course of action will bring "good" results. This is implied. Since principles are designed to predict results in given circumstances, the reader must be aware of what the authors regard as "good." The standard used in this book—one with which managers would certainly agree—is the efficient and effective attainment of enterprise or departmental objectives, whether economic, political, educational, social, or religious.

This includes the objective of maintaining the organized enterprise as an effective joint effort over time, that is, of providing for the survival of the group until basic goals are reached. For most enterprises, these goals are so continuing and of so long a duration that this means indefinite survival. Thus a business enterprise may have a continuing goal of producing goods or services that people want and can buy, just as an educational or religious enterprise pursues continuing goals of disciplining the mind in the acquisition and pursuit of knowledge or of furthering spiritual life.

Even though the principles as stated in this book may not always be established as complete causal propositions, the reader should interpret them as such. They can always be read in the sense that if this or that is done, the result will be more efficient and effective attainment of objectives.

Management as an Inexact Science

It is often pointed out that the social sciences are "inexact" sciences, as compared with the "exact" physical sciences. It is also sometimes indicated that management is perhaps the most inexact of the social sciences. The social sciences, and management in particular, deal with complex phenomena about which too little is known. Likewise, the structure and behavior of the atom are far less complex than the structure and behavior of groups of people, including both those inside and those outside an enterprise.

But we should not forget that even in the most exact of the exact sciences—physics—there are areas where scientific knowledge does not exist now and must be developed through speculation and hypothesis. As much as is known of bridge mechanics, bridges still fail as a result of such things as vibrations set up from wind currents. And as we move from the longer-known areas of physics into the biological sciences, we find that areas of exactness tend to diminish.

Since virtually all areas of knowledge have tremendous expanses of the unknown, people working in the social sciences should not be defeatist. A scientific approach to management cannot wait until an exact science of management is developed. Had the physical and biological sciences thus waited, we might still be living in caves.

Certainly, the observations of perceptive managers must substitute largely for the desirable laboratory-proven facts of the management scientist, at least until such facts can be determined. Statistical proof of theory and principles of management is desirable, but there is no use waiting for such proof before giving credence to principles derived from experience. After all, no one has been able to give statistical proof of the validity of the Golden Rule, but people of many religions have accepted this fundamental precept as a guide to behavior for centuries, and there are few who would doubt that its observance improves human conduct.

The earliest contributions toward viewing general management from an intellectual and scientific standpoint came from such experienced business managers as Fayol, Mooney, Alvin Brown, Sheldon, Barnard, and Urwick. Many of the concepts, propositions, and techniques offered in this book are based on the distilled experience of these and later practitioners. Admittedly, much of the research has been done without questionnaires, controlled interviews, laboratory experiments, or mathematics, but it can hardly be regarded as "armchair" or lacking in experienced observation. In recent years the burgeoning research by management scholars and practitioners has also added to the store of knowledge.

To be sure, management is an inexact science. But the questions one must ask are these: Does the use of such knowledge as is available help us understand management and aid in improving management practice now? Are we better off using such knowledge now—for guidelines in research and practice—or waiting until that perhaps distant future when the science can be "proven"? Does such knowledge help in substituting rationality for confusion? Does it increase objectivity in the understanding and practicing of management?

Principles and theory furnish the structural framework of a science. Principles are fundamental truths, or what are believed to be truths at a given time, explaining relationships between two or more sets of variables. In its purest form, a principle embodies an independent and a dependent variable. Thus in physics, if gravity is the only force acting on a falling body, it will fall at a uniformly accelerated speed (at 32.16 feet per second per second at the latitude of New York City). Or take the much less physical example of Parkinson's Law, which states that work tends to expand to fill the time available; thus work depends on time available.

March and Simon point out that propositions explaining relationships may be of various forms.[3] One type includes propositions that state the dependence of one variable on one or more dependent variables. Another type includes those which embody a qualitative, descriptive generalization about a subject, for example: "One of the important activities that goes on in an organization is the development of programs for new activities that need to be routinized for day-to-day performance."[4] As can be seen, this is little more than the concept type of proposition. A third type of proposition mentioned by these authors is one in which a particular phenomenon performs a particular function, such as: "Rigidity of behavior increases the defensibility of individual action."[5] Although all three types of the March and Simon propositions might be used to indicate principles, the most meaningful principles are those which involve causal relationships with dependent and independent variables.

Theory is a systematic grouping of interrelated principles. Its task is to tie together significant knowledge, to give it a framework. Scattered data, such as the miscellaneous numbers or diagrams typically found on a blackboard after a group of engineers have been discussing a problem, are not information unless the observer has a knowledge of the theory which explains their relationships. With this knowledge the observer can tie them together and probably comprehend what they mean. Theory is, as Homans has said, "in its lowest form a classification, a set of pigeon holes, a filing cabinet in which fact can accumulate. Nothing is more lost than a loose fact."[6]

The importance of theory to the development of organized knowledge has been dramatically indicated by the various essays of Talcott Parsons. In one, he says:

It is scarcely too much to say that the most important index of the state of maturity of a science is the state of systematic theory. This

[3]J. G. March and H. A. Simon, *Organizations* (New York: John Wiley & Sons, Inc., 1958), pp. 7–9.
[4]*Ibid.*, p. 8.
[5]*Ibid.*
[6]G. C. Homans, *The Human Group* (New York: Harcourt, Brace & World, Inc., 1950), p. 5.

includes the character of the general conceptual scheme in use in the field, the kinds and degrees of logical integration of the different elements which make it up, and the ways in which it is actually used in empirical research.[7]

Any system of principles or theory requires clarity of concepts— mental images of a thing formed by generalization from particulars. Obviously, a clear definition of a word is an elemental type of concept. Concepts are the building blocks of theory and principles. Unless concepts are clear, meaningful to those who use them, and used consistently, what may be said by one person who attempts to explain knowledge will not transfer to another in the same way. Indeed, this is one of the major difficulties with management as a science. As will be noted in Chapter 3, the same word or term does not imply the same phenomena to different people. One need only reflect on the term "organization" to see how true this is.

Principles are often referred to as being "descriptive," "prescriptive," or "normative." As might be surmised, a principle is descriptive if it merely describes a relationship between variables. A principle is prescriptive, or normative, if it is stated in such a way as to indicate what a person should do. Obviously, the principle of falling bodies, referred to above, is purely descriptive. It says nothing about whether you should jump from the top of a tall building; it is only an indication that, as far as gravity is concerned, if you do jump, you will fall at a certain speed. On the other hand, when principles are applied against some scale of values, they may be referred to as prescribing action or as being prescriptive, or normative. If the reader agrees with the thesis of the authors that it is the goal of all managers to operate in such a way as to accomplish the purposes of the organization effectively and efficiently, he or she has a value against which to apply management principles. It is consequently easy, by inserting a standard of value like efficiency in our thinking, to make management principles normative as well as descriptive.

THE NEED FOR THEORY AND TECHNIQUES OF MANAGEMENT

Obviously, knowledge of the basic principles and techniques of management can have a tremendous impact upon its practice, clarifying and improving it. Since in all fields of human cooperation, efficiency of group effort lags far behind that of machines, application of management knowledge will further human progress.

The need for a clear concept of management and for a framework of related theory and principles was recognized many years ago by such early practical scholars of management as Henri Fayol, Chester Barnard,

[7]*Essays in Sociological Theory, Pure and Applied* (Glencoe, Ill.: The Free Press, 1949), p. 17.

and Alvin Brown.[8] This need has been increasingly recognized by intelligent managers as time has gone on.

To Increase Efficiency

When management principles and techniques can be developed, proved, and used, managerial efficiency will inevitably improve. Then the conscientious manager can become more effective by using established guidelines to help solve problems, without engaging in original laborious research or the risky practice of trial and error.[9]

It is not always appreciated that only fundamentals can be learned from experience and transferred to new situations. The kind of experience on which many managers rely too heavily is only a hodgepodge of problems and solutions existing in the past and never exactly duplicated. Two management situations are seldom alike in all respects, and managers cannot assume that exact techniques applicable in one situation will necessarily work in another. However, if managers can distill experience and seek out and recognize the fundamental causal relationships in different circumstances, they can apply this knowledge to the solution of new problems. In other words, solutions become simplified if dealt with in terms of fundamentals. The value in understanding management as a conceptual scheme of concepts, principles, and techniques is that it lets one see and understand what would otherwise remain unseen. Theory and science can solve future problems arising in an ever-changing environment.

The value of knowing principles might be illustrated by several examples. We know from principles that having individuals report to more than one boss involves certain costs and disadvantages, even though the benefits of doing so may justify the costs; by knowing principles, we may be able to minimize these costs. Principles tell us that no manager can develop controls without basing them on plans, that managers must have organization authority necessary to accomplish the results expected of them, and that no manager can develop a meaningful plan without a clear idea of the goal to be accomplished and the future environment premised for its operation. While principles are, as they should be, distilled knowledge, awareness of them can help managers avoid mistakes. It is obviously wasteful for every manager to have to learn these truths from his or her own experience.

---

[8]In *General and Industrial Management* (New York: Pitman Publishing Corporation, 1949), pp. 14–15. Writing originally in 1916, Fayol bemoaned the lack of management teaching in vocational schools, but ascribed it to a lack of theory, since, as he said, "without theory no teaching is possible." Likewise, Barnard (op. cit., p. 289) deplored the lack of literature and instruction for executives and, above all, the lack of "an accepted conceptual scheme with which to exchange their thought." Alvin Brown, in *Organization of Industry* (Englewood Cliffs, N.J.: Prentice-Hall, Inc., 1947), p. vi, held that the understanding and development of the art of management must be a study "grounded in principle."

[9]As Urwick has aptly said: "And we should not forget that in the field of management our errors are other people's trials."

To Crystallize the Nature of Management

Lack of understanding of the concepts, principles, and techniques of management makes it difficult to analyze the managerial job and to train managers. Fundamentals act as a checklist of the meaning of management. Without them, the training of managers depends upon haphazard trial and error. To some extent, this will be the case until an adequate science of management has been developed. Meanwhile, in business, government, and other enterprises a considerable body of management knowledge has already come into being and serves increasingly to crystallize the nature of management and to simplify manager training.

To Improve Research

As pointed out above, all hypotheses can be used to guide research. And if research is undertaken to build further theory or otherwise to expand the horizons of knowledge, establishment of a structural framework of knowledge would appear to be useful for productive research.

In view of the rising interest in management in the past three decades and the tremendous amount of study by students and managers, better channeling of research is bound to be productive. Since management deals in part with people and since groups of people are unpredictable and complex, effective research is difficult. Management also deals with the planning of action, the devising of controls, and the grouping of activities, and progress in research in all these areas is slow and costly. The need for tested knowledge of organized enterprise is great, and anything which makes management research more pointed will help improve management practice.

To Achieve Social Goals

In a broad sense, managing coordinates the efforts of people so that individual objectives become translated into social attainments. Development of management knowledge, by increasing efficiency in the use of human as well as material resources, would unquestionably have a revolutionary impact on the cultural level of society. To illustrate this point, nations with a high material standard of living tend to have a high level of intelligence and skill in their management of business. Ample raw materials and a favorable political climate have been important in accounting for the economic productivity of the United States. Equally significant, particularly in the twentieth century, has been the relatively high quality of management.

CONTINGENCY, OR SITUATIONAL, MANAGEMENT

There has been a fairly widespread tendency for certain scholars and writers in organization theory to misunderstand the approach to management by those who emphasize the study of management and its fundamentals. They see principles and theory as a search for the one best way of doing things. For example, as recently as 1970, two scholars said:

> During the past few years there has been evident a new trend in the study of organizational phenomena. Underlying this new approach is the idea that the internal functioning of organizations must be consistent with the demands of organization task, technology, or external environment, and the needs of its members if the organization is to be effective. Rather than searching for the panacea of the one best way to organize under all conditions, investigators have more and more tended to examine the functioning of organizations in relation to the needs of their particular members and the external pressures facing them. Basically, this approach seems to be leading to the development of a "contingency" theory of organization with the appropriate internal states and processes of the organization contingent upon external requirements and member needs.[10]

In the same tone, another writer on management, one among many, appears to be concerned that basic management theory and science attempt to prescribe a one best way of doing things and do not take the situation into account. In an interesting book, this writer states:

> Above all, the situationalist holds that there is no one best way to manage. Taylor may have been right when he said there is one best way to perform a repetitive physical task, but that is not true of planning, organizing, leading, controlling, or decision making. Different organizations with different tasks and different competitive environments require different plans. No one would expect a social club, a giant corporation, and a family business to be organized in the same way. In each, the leadership style must be related to the personality of the leader and the skill, training and attitudes of the followers. Just as every human personality, and every organization is unique, so is every managerial position or situation unique.
>
> This entire book is based upon the major premise that there is no one best way to handle any of the management functions. There is no one best way to plan; there is no one best way to lead; there is no one best way to organize a group; and there is no best way to control the activities of an organization. The best concepts and techniques can be selected only after one is aware of the particular circumstances he is facing. . . .
>
> The theoretical structure of management knowledge has been developed with the one-best-way assumption as a major tenet. . . .[11]

[10]J. W. Lorsch and P. R. Lawrence, *Studies in Organization Design* (Homewood, Ill.: The Dorsey Press and Richard D. Irwin, Inc., 1970), p. 1. Note that Professor Lorsch now believes that the term "contingency" is misleading and he should have used "situational." See chap. 3, p. 84.

[11]H. M. Carlisle, *Situational Management: A Contingency Approach to Leadership* (New York: AMACOM, American Management Association, 1973), p. 7.

MANAGEMENT THEORY AND SCIENCE NEVER ADVOCATE THE ONE BEST WAY

Any practitioner of, or writer on, management—and certainly the authors of this book—would be amazed at the above statement. Management theory and science do *not advocate* the best way to do things in the light of every situation, any more than the sciences of astrophysics and chemistry, which are far more exact than management, do. Of course, the situation makes a difference. Of course, "internal states and processes of the organization" are "contingent upon external requirements and member needs." Of course, actual practice and the solution of varied problems will differ, depending on the circumstances.

This point has already been made earlier in this chapter in connection with the distinction between science and art. It will continue to be made in succeeding chapters.

Effective Managing Is Always Contingency or Situational Management

It has never been and never will be the task of theory and science to prescribe what should be done. Theory and science are intended as a search for fundamental relationships, for basic techniques, and for organization of available knowledge—all, it is hoped, based on clear concepts. How these are applied in practice depends on the situation. No one would expect physicians to give all patients penicillin regardless of their ailment. Nor would one expect engineers, although using basic principles of physics and metallurgy, to design automobiles the way they would design airplanes, or chemists to use the same formulas for mixing detergents that they would for drugs. But we would expect all these practitioners to understand and utilize in their work the science and theory underlying their practice.

In the same way, effective management is always contingency, or situational, management. The very concept of management used in this book—involving the *design* of an environment in which people working together in groups can accomplish objectives—implies this. Design presumes application of knowledge to a practical problem for the purpose of coming up with the best possible results for *that* situation. But this does not mean that the practicing manager cannot gain from knowing the concepts, fundamentals, principles, theory, and techniques of management.

Indeed, this is what managing and management are all about—the application of knowledge to realities in order to attain desired results.

MANAGING REQUIRES A SYSTEMS APPROACH

No book on management, and certainly no practicing manager, can overlook the systems approach. As was pointed out earlier and will be emphasized throughout this book, managers must always take into account a vast number of interacting influences and variables in doing their job. A manager's company, agency, department, or section represents a system. A department, for example, operates within a company system. Both it and the company operate in an industry, which is a complex system of interacting elements.

What Systems Are

Systems are neither new nor startling in their fundamentals.[12] A system has been defined in the *Oxford English Dictionary* as simply "a set or assemblage of things connected, or interdependent, so as to form a complex unity; a whole composed of parts in orderly arrangement according to some scheme or plan." To this, *The Random House Dictionary of the English Language* adds as a definition of a system "an ordered and comprehensive assemblage of facts, principles, doctrines, or the like, in a particular field of knowledge or thought."

This definition indicates that almost all life is a system. Our bodies certainly are. Our homes and universities are, as are our government agencies and our businesses. These, in turn, are interconnected with various other systems, and each has within it a number of subsystems. No one can or should disregard the network nature of the components in any company, department, problem, technique, or program. Certainly the theory and practice of management presented in this book do not.

Key Concepts of Systems Theory[13]

Other than the basic nature of systems outlined above, the major key concepts involved in systems theory may be summarized (and somewhat oversimplified) as follows:

1   A system—such as an enterprise—is more than the sum of its parts; it must be viewed as a whole.
2   Systems can be considered to be either "closed" or "open." A system is regarded as open if it exchanges information, energy, or material with its environment, as happens with biological (like people or animals) or social (like a company) systems; it is regarded as closed if it does not have such interactions with its environment (like a spring-wound alarm clock during the time it's wound).

[12]See, for example, John Dearden, "MIS Is a Mirage," *Harvard Business Review*, vol. 50, no. 1, pp. 90–99 (January–February, 1972). He makes the following point (on p. 95): "My conclusion, then, is that the systems approach is precisely what every good manager has been using for centuries. The systems approach may be new to science and to weapons acquisition, but it is certainly not new to business administration."
[13]A good summary of systems theory may be found in F. E. Kast and J. E. Rosenzweig, "General Systems Theory: Applications for Organization and Management," *Academy of Management Journal*, vol. 15, no. 4, pp. 447–465 (December, 1972). Also, as applied to social systems generally, these concepts may be found in D. Katz and R. L. Kahn, *The Social Psychology of Organizations*, 2d ed. (New York: John Wiley & Sons, Inc., 1978), particularly in chaps. 2–3.

3   For any system to be looked on as a system, it must have "boundaries" that separate it from it from its environment; thus a spring-wound alarm clock, at least until it is touched by a person winding it, represents a boundary that is closed and rigid. We may define a social system, such as a company or a department within it, as a system, but, as can be readily seen, the boundaries are not rigid, impenetrable, or closed. We can likewise look upon management as a system by creating the boundaries, as is done in this book, while recognizing, of course, that the boundaries are not closed and are often rather fuzzy.

4   Closed physical systems are subject to entropy—the tendency to "run down"; open systems, because they receive inputs from their environment, do not suffer from entropy if these inputs are at least as great as the energy the systems use plus their outputs. Indeed, most social systems, like businesses and governments, may achieve negative entropy by importing more from their environment than they use and export.

5   Thus if an open system is to survive, it must at least achieve a state in which it ingests enough inputs from its environment to offset its outputs plus the energy and materials used in the operation of the system; this is referred to by systems theorists as a "steady state" or "dynamic homeostasis," borrowing the term "homeostasis" from the biological process by which our bodies achieve constant temperature in the face of a changing environment and the concept of "dynamic" from the idea that the steady state is constantly in motion. Thus, a company will fail to survive if its inputs do not at least equal its outputs; a successful, growing business will of course have more inputs than outputs. With growth, however, we normally see an increase in the number of subsystems, as happens when divisions or departments are added.

6   As can be seen, if a system is to achieve dynamic homeostasis, or a kind of dynamic equilibrium, it must have feedback—an informational input that tells whether the system is indeed at least achieving a steady state and is not in danger of destruction. As we shall see later in this book, this is the major purpose of managerial control.

7   With the exception of the entire universe, all systems are subsystems. Putting it another way, systems have subsystems and are also a part of a suprasystem; they are hierarchical. An automobile, for example, has such subsystems as the engine, the transmission, and the starter, and when a person gets into it and drives on the highway, it becomes a subsystem in a larger system of traffic flow. A company or university has many subsystems and in turn is a part of a larger system, such as an industry or a community.

8   Open systems, and social systems in particular, tend toward increased elaboration and differentiation; in other words, the open system will, as it grows, tend to become more specialized in its elements and to elaborate its structure, often enlarging its boundaries or creating a new

suprasystem with wider boundaries. Thus, in a growing business, we see considerable differentiation and elaboration; more specialized departments are created, and elaboration of the system may occur through acquisition of sources of supply, expansion of product lines, or the creation of new sales offices or districts.

Systems theorists emphasize that open systems can achieve desired results (dynamic homeostasis, or the steady state) in various ways by means of a concept or process referred to as "equifinality." In a closed physical system, such as an automobile transmission system, elements react in a direct cause and effect way. In a social system, goals can be accomplished with varying inputs and with varying processes or methods; there is no single best way. This is nowhere more evident than in management; the Ford Motor Company and General Motors, for example, are organized in substantially different ways, and yet both are effective in producing and selling automobiles at a profit.

Social Systems Are Contrived Systems

Social systems of every kind are contrived by human beings to accomplish certain objectives. As Katz and Kahn have so well said:

> Social structures are essentially contrived systems. They are made by men and are imperfect systems. They can come apart at the seams overnight, but they can also outlast by centuries the biological organisms which originally created them. The cement which holds them together is essentially psychological rather than biological. Social systems are anchored in the attitudes, perceptions, beliefs, motivations, habits, and expectations of human beings. Such systems represent patterns of relationships in which the constancy of the individual units involved in the relationships can be very low. An organization can have a very high rate of turnover and still persist. The relationships of items rather than the items themseleves provide the consistency.[14]

Because they are contrived by human beings, the patterns of relationships can be as variable as any set of human beings and their relationships. However, over time and in every society, people develop certain attitudes, customs, and standards of behavior which become environmental forces influencing organizations within any large social system. Thus in some countries of the world bribery to get a business contract is regarded as normal and acceptable, and in others it is regarded as unethical or illegal. In some countries, cooperating with a competitor to hold prices up is acceptable conduct, while in other countries, such as the United States, this is completely unlawful.

[14]Katz and Kahn, op. cit., p. 33.

The first to see management in the context of systems was New Jersey Bell Telephone Company president Chester I. Barnard. Writing over four decades ago, Barnard saw the executive as a component of a formal organization, and the latter as a part of an entire cooperative system involving physical, biological, social, and psychological elements.[15] Barnard's inclusion of physical and biological, as well as social and psychological, elements in the system in which the manager operates is perhaps a more accurate portrayal of the managerial subsystem than the usual social psychologists' view of this subsystem as related only to the social system. To be sure, most of the interactions of a manager have to do with social and psychological forces or elements. But it is difficult not to see a manager interacting with other elements, particularly with such physical ones as money, materials, and facilities.

It is perhaps most accurate to speak of the manager's role, as Barnard did, as fitting into a total cooperative system, with elements that encompass physical (materials and machinery), biological (people as discrete beings who breathe air and need space), and social (group interactions, attitudes, and beliefs) elements. These systems may be found both within and outside the organization or system (the Exxon Corporation, the city of Los Angeles, or Joe's Country Market) where a certain manager operates.

In more recent years, the emphasis on the interconnection of physical and social elements in an organization has given rise to what is referred to as "sociotechnical systems." Obviously, all businesses, governments, universities, and other so-called organizations are sociotechnical systems, as are their divisions and subdivisions. Sometimes the systemic relationships are very close, as in the case of workers and their machines, typists and their typewriters, or even college professors and their special lecture rooms. Sometimes they are not so close, as in the case of salespeople and their offices. But the relationship always exists. There is always the danger of trying to separate too sharply the social system from the nonsocial elements of a total cooperative system.

As can be seen, each of us is involved in so many cooperative, or sociotechnical, systems and these systems interact and interconnect in so many complex ways that it is difficult to set boundaries around any activity or field of knowledge. But if we are ever to make progress in studying any field and gaining useful knowledge from it, we simply cannot contemplate the whole universe.

This is exactly where we are in the field of management and in this book. We set primary system boundaries around the task of the manager. We study this field as a system of interrelated and interconnected elements. But, as we do so, we can never regard it as a closed system. There are simply too many important and obvious elements and forces in other systems that affect managing for us to be able to do that!

[15]Chester I. Barnard, op. cit., p. 65.

**Misunderstandings in Looking at
Management as a System**

When one talks of a business enterprise or a university as a social system or considers those who manage any part of them, it is not possible to think of these and other organizations and their managers as not having—and realizing it—a significant interaction with other systems influencing them. In the light of this self-evident truth, it is surprising to any manager or theorist to find that management theory is sometimes criticized for regarding an enterprise or a department of it as a closed system. For example, two respected social psychologists have erroneously said:

> Traditional organizational theories have tended to view the human organization as a closed system. This tendency has led to disregard of differing organizational environments and the nature of organizational dependency on the environment. It has led also to an overconcentration on principles of internal organizational functioning, with consequent failure to develop and understand the processes of feedback which are essential to survival.[16]

Surely no person interested in management as a practitioner, theorist, or student could ever overlook the open-system nature of managing. Neither objectives nor plans can possibly be set in the vacuum of a closed company system. Markets, government regulations, competitors, technology, and many other elements of an enterprise environment affect plans and objectives and cannot be overlooked. Likewise, no manager with any experience with people could disregard the fact that they are products of, and are influenced by, their entire cultural environment.

It is true that in order to carve out an area of knowledge and make it manageable, operational-management theory emphasizes the functions of managers in an enterprise or department. But this theory can never disregard the impact of their environment.

The Value of the Systems Approach to Management

To say that systems are not new is not to say that modern systems thinking and new special systems approaches have not been valuable to both theory and practice. The advantage of approaching any area of inquiry or any problem as a system is that it enables us to see the critical variables and constraints and their interaction with one another. It forces scholars and practitioners in the field to be constantly aware that one single element, phenomenon, or problem should not be treated without regard for its interacting consequences with other elements.

This is nowhere better exemplified than in the case of the functions of managers. While we define and organize knowledge around the functions of planning, organizing, staffing, leading, and controlling, a moment's

[16]Katz and Kahn, op. cit., p. 34.

reflection will show how interlocked these functions are. For example, managers plan their organization structure, develop staffing programs, and base their controls on plans. And this is true in various ways with all the functions.

THE SYSTEMS APPROACH TO OPERATIONAL MANAGEMENT

An organized enterprise does not, of course, exist in a vacuum. Rather, it is mutually dependent on its external environment; it is a part of a larger system such as the economic system, the industry to which it belongs, and society. Thus the enterprise receives inputs, transforms them, and exports the outputs to the environment, as shown by the very basic model in Figure 1.1. However, this simple model needs to be expanded and developed into a system of operational management that indicates how the various inputs are transformed through the managerial functions of planning, organizing, staffing, leading, and controlling. The nature of operational management theory and the use and definition of the managerial functions are discussed in Chapter 3, pages 74–81. Clearly, any business or other organization is an open-system model with interactions between the enterprise and its external environment.

Inputs and Claimants

The inputs from the external environment—as shown in Figure 1.2—include people, capital, and managerial skills, as well as technical knowledge and skills. In addition, various groups of people make demands on the enterprise. Unfortunately, many of the goals of these claimants are incongruent with each other, and it is the manager's job to reconcile these divergent needs and goals.

Employees, for example, want higher pay, more benefits, and job security. Consumers, on the other hand, demand safe and reliable

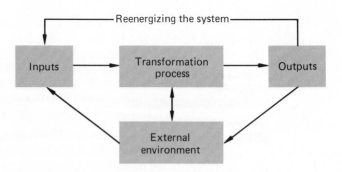

Figure 1.1 Input-output model.

products at a reasonable price. Suppliers want assurance that their products are bought. Stockholders want not only a high return on their investment but also security of their money. Federal, state, and local governments depend on taxes paid by the enterprise, but they also expect the enterprise to comply with their laws. Similarly, the community demands that enterprises be "good citizens," providing the maximum number of jobs with a minimum of pollution. Other claimants to the enterprise may include financial institutions and labor unions; even competitors have a legitimate claim for "fair play." It is clear that many of these claims are incongruent with each other, and it is management's job to integrate the legitimate objectives of the claimants.

The Managerial Transformation Process

It is management's task to transform the inputs in an effective and efficient manner to produce outputs. Of course, the transformation process can be viewed from different perspectives. Thus, one could focus on such enterprise functions as finance, production, personnel, and marketing. Writers on management, as indicated in Chapter 3, look on the transformation process in terms of their particular approach to management. Specifically, as we will see, writers belonging to the human behavior school focus on interpersonal relationships; social systems theorists analyze the transformation by focusing on social interactions; and those advocating decision theory see the transformation as sets of decisions. The authors suggest in Chapter 3 that the most comprehensive and useful approach for discussing the job of managers is to use the managerial functions as a framework (see Figure 1.2).

Communication System

Communication pervades the total managerial process: It integrates the managerial functions, and it links the enterprise with its environment. For example, the objectives set in planning are communicated so that the appropriate organization structure can be devised. To fill the roles, communication is essential in the selection, appraisal, and training of managers. Similarly, effective leadership and the creation of an environment conducive to motivation depend on communication. Moreover, it is through communication that one determines whether events and performance conform to plans. Thus, it is communication which makes managing possible.

The second function of the communication system is to link the enterprise with its external environment, where many of the claimants are. For example, one should never forget that the customer, who is the reason for the existence of virtually all businesses, is outside a company. It is through the communication system that the needs of customers are identified, which then enables the firm to provide products and services at a profit. Similarly, it is through an effective communication system that

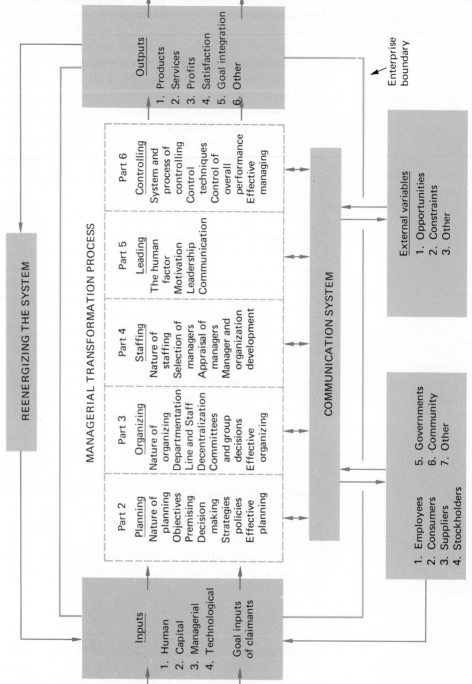

Figure 1.2 Systems approach to management.

the organization becomes aware of the competition and other potential threats and constraining factors.

External Variables

Effective managers will constantly scan the external environment. While it is true that managers may have little or no effect on changing these forces, they have no alternative but to respond to them. The nature of these forces is discussed in Chapter 4.

Outputs

It is the task of managers to secure and utilize inputs to the enterprise, transforming them through the managerial functions of planning, organizing, staffing, leading, and controlling—with due consideration of external variables—to produce outputs.

Although the kinds of outputs will vary with a specific enterprise, they usually include at least one or more of the following: products, services, profits, satisfaction, and goal integration of claimants to the enterprise. Most of them require no elaboration, and only the last two will be discussed. The organization must indeed provide many *satisfactions* if it hopes to retain and elicit contributions from its members. This pertains to the satisfaction not only of basic material needs (for example, earning money to buy food and shelter, having job security) but also of needs for affiliation, acceptance, esteem, and perhaps even self-actualization.

Another output in the model (Figure 1.2) is "goal integration." As noted above, the different claimants to the enterprise have very divergent—and often directly opposing—objectives. It is the task of managers to resolve conflicts and integrate these aims. This is not easy, as one of the earlier executives of Volkswagen discovered. Economics dictated the construction of a Volkswagen assembly plant in the United States. However, this plan was opposed by German labor, an important claimant, because of fear of the elimination of some jobs. The conflict was so deep that it contributed to executive resignation and a change in leadership. After a costly delay, the Volkswagen assembly plant was eventually built in the United States. This example indicates that the integration of goals of the various claimants to the enterprise is an important task of any manager.

Reenergizing the System

The final aspect of the operational-management systems model is that some of the outputs become inputs again. Thus, the satisfaction of employees becomes an important human input. Similarly, profits, the surplus of income over costs, are reinvested in capital goods, such as machinery and equipment, buildings, inventories of goods, tools, and cash.

1 In what fundamental way are the basic goals of all managers at all levels and in all kinds of enterprises the same?

2 Is managing a science or an art? Could the same explanation apply to engineering or accounting?

3 Look up the terms "science," "theory," and "principle" in an acceptable dictionary and determine how they are used. Compare these definitions with the usage of these terms as applied to management in this book. What advantages are there in attempting to identify science, theory, and principles in a book on management?

4 Why do management analysis and practice require a systems approach? Reviewing the key elements of systems and the systems approach, how do they apply to management? Do managers operate in an open or a closed system? How?

5 What is the contingency, or situational, approach to management? Could any explanation of management be any different? Could any manager operate in any other way?

chapter 2
The Emergence of Management Thought

MAJOR CHAPTER OBJECTIVES

1 To explain why, despite the importance of management from the earliest times of group efforts, the major development of management thinking has occurred in the twentieth century and more particularly in the past three decades.

2 To give the reader some appreciation of early contributions to management.

3 To highlight contributions of major precursors to Frederick Taylor.

4 To discuss the "scientific management" thinking of Frederick Taylor and his major followers, and to correct the mistaken notion that their search for science in management was based completely on mechanistic considerations.

5 To give special attention to the ideas of Henri Fayol and his pioneering theory that management is a universal activity to be identified and analyzed as such.

6 To outline the emergence of the behavioral sciences and the early relationship of them to scientific management.

7 To give attention to the earlier sociological approaches to management, especially the "social man" concepts of Mayo and his colleagues, and to the "social system" theory of Chester Barnard.

8 To correct the widely held and erroneous beliefs that the "classicists" regarded the human being as an "inert instrument" and that traditional theorists have looked on management as a "closed system."

9 To summarize the emergence of management thought among public administrators, business managers, the behavioralists, and the systems theorists.

Despite the inexactness and relative crudity of management theory and science, the development of thought on management dates back to the days when people first attempted to accomplish goals by working together in groups. Although management thought and research have greatly accelerated in the past three decades and although modern operational-management theory dates primarily from the early twentieth century, with the work of Frederick Taylor and Henri Fayol, there was serious thinking and theorizing about managing many years before.

While this chapter can do little more than sketch some of the high spots in the emergence of management thought,[1] it is worthwhile for persons interested in management to know something of the background of the evolution of management thought. Even limited knowledge can help one appreciate the many insights, ideas, and scientific underpinnings which preceded the upsurge of management writing during recent years. Familiarity with the history of management thought may help the reader to avoid rediscovering previously known ideas and to avoid accepting as gospel such uninformed bromides as "the classicists regarded the human being as an inert instrument."

WHY THE SLOWNESS IN DEVELOPMENT OF MANAGEMENT THOUGHT?

Considering the pressing need for the best possible management practice, it seems surprising that most of the development of management theory has been confined to the past few decades, and that business managers and others generally have been awakening to the need only since World War II. As we shall see in the following section, this does not mean that there was no concern, no theory, or no attempt to develop a science of management until this time. Indeed, many persons—mostly practitioners—attempted to bring some orderly thinking to management. But in a field of such importance, one would have expected a stronger interest in, and a much faster growth of, management thought many years ago.

For Centuries Business Was Held in Low Esteem

In pointing to some of the reasons for this delay, one cannot overlook those centuries during which business was held in low esteem. Although business institutions of insurance, credit, and marketing were developed in the Middle Ages and although these and still others were well formed by the time of the industrial revolution in the nineteenth century, business was long regarded as a degrading occupation. Aristotle's

[1]For the most comprehensive history of management thought, see Daniel A. Wren, *The Evolution of Management Thought* (New York: The Ronald Press Company, 1972). See also Claude S. George, Jr., *The History of Management Thought* (Englewood Cliffs, N.J.: Prentice-Hall, Inc., 1968).

characterization of buying and selling as "unnatural" moneymaking,[2] Adam Smith's disparaging remarks concerning businessmen,[3] and Napoleon's castigation of England as a "nation of shopkeepers" are evidences of this fact. Even in the past century, business was often regarded by the educated as a somewhat inglorious occupation. Indeed, one can say that only in the past half century has the businessman begun to hold a place of respect.

Another reason for the delay has been the preoccupation of economists with political economy and the nonmanagerial aspects of business. In their analysis of business enterprise and the development of philosophical precepts concerning business, the early economists generally followed the lead of Adam Smith, whose concern was for measures to increase the wealth of a nation; of Ricardo, whose emphasis was upon the distribution of wealth to the factors of production; and of Alfred Marshall and others, who refined some of the marginal analyses in competitive and monopolistic marketing. The modern treatment of the economics of the individual firm is largely a development of the past 50 years. Even the work of Chamberlin and Robinson, which has so changed the course of economic theory since 1933, assumed the existence of an effective business management. These preoccupations kept economists from examining the theoretical implications of the significant job of management until recent years.

One might expect that political science would have been the father of a theory of management, since the administration of programs is one of the major tasks of government and since government itself is the oldest comprehensive form of social organization. Yet, despite its obvious importance, early political theorists were slow to turn their attention to the problem of administration. They, like the early economists, were too preoccupied with policy making on a national and international level; therefore, they largely overlooked the executive process, at least until recent years. Some of the early contributions to the theory of management, nevertheless, have come from scholars in the field of public administration, and important contributions have continued to come from this source at an accelerated pace.

To some extent the delay has also been due to the tendency to compartmentalize the disciplines within the broad field of social science, as in the failure to apply the research of sociologists to the area of management. The theories of sociology concerning formal and informal organizations have only recently been applied to the functions of the

[2] In *Politics and Ethics*, Aristotle wrote: "Of the two sorts of money making, one is part of household management, the other is retail trade; the former necessary and honorable, the latter a kind of exchange which is justly censured, for it is unnatural, and a mode by which men gain from one another."

[3] In his *Wealth of Nations* (New York: Modern Library, Inc., 1917), p. 250 (a book originally published in 1776), Smith said of certain businessmen that they are "an order of men, whose interest is never the same with that of the public, who have generally an interest to deceive and even to oppress the public, and who accordingly have, upon many occasions, both deceived and oppressed it."

manager. Likewise, with the exception of certain industrial psychologists, research of psychologists in the fields of individual motivation, reactions to authority, and the meaning and analysis of leadership has extended to the area of management only in recent years.

In addition to these reasons, there was for many years a widespread belief among managers in business, government, and other organizations that management is not susceptible to theory—that management is totally an art, not, to any extent, a science.

Moreover, business owners and managers themselves have in the past discouraged the development of a theory of management. Too often their preoccupation has been with technology, price, and the balance sheet—an orientation hardly conducive to an understanding of, and inquiry into, the job of the manager.

It is interesting to note that the opening wedge to the study of management as a science was driven by the so-called scientific-management school, founded by Frederick W. Taylor.

Recent Impetus

Impetus to the development of a theory of management has come in the past half century as the result of the recognition that one missing link in the attainment of an effective enterprise system is the effective handling of human factors. The Great Depression following 1929 brought forth such symptoms of human unrest as the New Deal and national unionism, which served to alert business people that, among the deficiencies of American industrial development, perhaps the greatest was the concentration on the mere manipulation of resources. It is probably not too much to say that the upheaval of the 1930s and the attack by government and other social groups upon the institution of free private enterprise were instrumental in forcing business managers increasingly to examine the nature of their job.

World War II and the subsequent defense and space programs were of even greater importance in the development of a theory of business management. The emphasis upon production with the least cost in materials and labor focused attention on the job of the manager—at every level in an organization—as the strategic factor in accomplishing the objective. The importance of the manager increased in the postwar years. For one thing, the siphoning off of some of the best young men into military programs during the war left a shortage of promotable exployees after the war. For another thing, the technical advances which accompanied the war exaggerated the lag in managerial knowledge as compared with technical knowledge.

The decade of feverish productive activity set off by military preparation accelerated the movement toward larger and more complex business enterprises. The challenge to effective management increases as business size increases. As business methods and products become more complex and as relationships with other businesses, consumers, workers, and the government become more intricate, the need for skilled management, even in the small firm, expands materially.

In more recent years, tremendous impetus to the development of management theory and to the search for scientific underpinnings to improve practice has come from the worldwide rivalry for markets, power, and progress. This might be called the "era of supercompetition." Increasingly severe competition has resulted from such factors as (1) dissemination of technical knowledge, which has allowed an increasing number of firms and nations to compete for world markets; (2) the freeing of trade; (3) the change from sellers' to buyers' markets; (4) the increase of capital investment and capacity and the rise in the level of break-even points; and (5) the rapid rate of technological change, which can make a product obsolete or lower its costs virtually overnight.

In addition to the growth of competition from these factors, both within the United States and on an expanding world front, enterprises have been faced with cost-price squeezes. The pressure for wage and fringe increases has raised costs to a point where businesses which fail to use modern techniques of management are at the mercy of those which do. With the tendency of wages to rise faster than labor productivity, the firm which would continue to enjoy profit dares not be content to be mediocre, but must aggressively attempt to be more efficient than its competitors.

This intense rivalry applies not only to business firms. In government, universities, churches, and other enterprises, one sees forces at work which indicate that group effectiveness may be a key to continued survival. In government, the demand for public services tends to outstrip the tax resources available to support them, and the same atmosphere of pressure exists in other nonbusiness enterprises.

These forces, always important but now of such magnitude as to affect survival, have placed heavy emphasis on management effectiveness. It may be that technical know-how will become less important to the growth of higher living standards in the United States and elsewhere than the continued improvement of management. The present effort to develop management theory and science reflects this possibility.

EARLY CONTRIBUTIONS TO MANAGEMENT

Many records and ideas relating to management date from antiquity. Among these are the records of the Egyptians, the early Greeks, and the ancient Romans. In addition, there have been the experience and administrative practices of the Catholic Church, military organizations, and the cameralists of the sixteenth to the eighteenth centuries.

Management in Antiquity

Interpretations of early Egyptian papyri, extending as far back as 1300 B.C., indicate the recognition of the importance of organization and administration in the bureaucratic states of antiquity.[4] Similar records exist for ancient China. Confucius's parables include practical suggestions for proper public administration and admonitions to choose honest, unselfish, and capable public officers.[5]

Although the records of early Greece do not give much insight into the principles of management employed, the very existence of the Athenian commonwealth, with its councils, popular courts, administrative officials, and board of generals, indicates an appreciation of the managerial function. Socrates's definition of management as a skill separate from technical knowledge and experience is remarkably close to our current understanding of the function.[6]

The records of management in ancient Rome are incomplete, although it is well known that the complexity of the administrative job brought about considerable development of managerial techniques. The existence of the Roman magistrates, with their functional areas of authority and degrees of importance, indicates a scalar relationship characteristic of organization. Indeed, it is thought that the real genius of the Romans and the secret of success of the Roman Empire lay in the ability of these people to organize. Through the use of the scalar principle and the delegation of authority, the city of Rome was expanded to an empire with an efficiency of organization that had never before been observed.[7]

The Roman Catholic Church

If one is to judge by age, the most effective formal organization in the history of Western civilization has been the Roman Catholic Church. Its long organizational life has been due not only to the appeal of its objectives but also to the effectiveness of its organization and management

---

[4]See A. Lepawsky, *Administration* (New York: Alfred A. Knopf, Inc., 1949), pp. 78–81, and numerous original and secondary sources there quoted.

[5]L. S. Hsu, *The Political Philosophy of Confucianism* (New York: E. P. Dutton & Co., Inc., 1932), p. 124. For excerpts from this study as well as other sources of early Chinese works on administration, see ibid., pp. 82–84.

[6]In his discourse with Nicomachides (Plato and Xenophon, *Socratic Discourses*, book III, chap. 4, New York: E. P. Dutton & Co., Inc., 1910), Socrates is reported to have made the following observations on management: "I say that over whatever a man may preside, he will, if he knows what he needs, and is able to provide it, be a good president, whether he have the direction of a chorus, a family, a city, or an army. . . . Is it not also the duty . . . to appoint fitting persons to fulfill the various duties? . . . To punish the bad, and to honour the good. . . . Do not, therefore, Nicomachides, despise men skillful in managing a household; for the conduct of private affairs differs from that of public concerns only in magnitude; in other respects they are similar, but what is most to be observed is, that neither of them are managed without men; and that private matters are not managed by one species of men, and public matters by another; for those who conduct public business make use of men not at all differing in nature from those whom the managers of private affairs employ; and those who know how to employ them, conduct either private or public affairs judiciously, while those who do not know, will err in the management of both."

[7]For an excellent analysis of the Roman genius for organization, see J. D. Mooney, *The Principles of Organization*, rev. ed. (New York: Harper & Brothers, 1947), pp. 62–72.

techniques. Striking examples of these techniques are the development of the hierarchy of authority with its scalar territorial organization, the specialization of activities along functional lines, and the early, intelligent use of the staff device. It is remarkable that, for centuries, the successful employment of managerial techniques by the Church had virtually no influence on other organizations. In his study of this, Mooney expresses the belief that "nothing but the general neglect of the study of organization" can explain why the staff principle, so important in the organization of the Catholic Church, did not take root in other organizations until fairly recently.

Military Organizations

As might be expected, some of the more important principles and practices of modern business management may be traced to military organizations. Except for the Church, no other form of organization in the history of Western civilization has been forced, by the problems of managing large groups, to develop organization principles. Yet despite the need, military organizations failed to put much theory to use before the past two centuries.

Although military organizations remained fairly simple until recent times, being limited largely to refinements of authority relationships, they have, over the centuries, gradually improved their techniques of leadership. Early armies, even those composed of mercenaries, were often characterized by adequate morale and the complementary relationship of individual and group objectives. History is replete with examples of military leaders who communicated their plans and objectives to their followers, thereby developing what Mooney calls a "unity of doctrine" in the organization. Even as autocratic a commander as Napoleon supplemented his power to command with a careful explanation of the purpose of his orders.

Later, however, military organizations have applied other management principles. Among the most important of these has been the staff principle. Although the term "general staff" was used in the French army of 1790, and although certain staff functions have characterized military organizations for many centuries, the modern concept of general staff can be traced to the Prussian armies of the nineteenth century. This group, organized under a chief of staff, furnished specialized advice and information and supplied auxiliary services which have come to be essential features of military as well as all other types of enterprises.

The Cameralists

The cameralists were a group of German and Austrian public administrators and intellectuals who generally held, from the sixteenth to the eighteenth centuries, the same tenets as the British mercantilist and the

French physiocratic schools of political economy. They all believed that to enhance the position of a state, it was necessary to maximize material wealth. But the cameralist school alone emphasized systematic administration as a source of strength and was one of the earliest groups to do so.[8]

The cameralists believed as well in the universality of management techniques, noting that the same qualities which increased an individual's wealth were called for in the proper administration of the state and its departments. In developing management principles, they emphasized specialization of function, care in selection and training of subordinates for administrative positions, establishment of the office of controller in the government, expedition of legal processes, and simplification of administrative procedures.

PRECURSORS TO TAYLOR AND SCIENTIFIC MANAGEMENT

Although Frederick Taylor, who did his work in the early years of the twentieth century, is usually called the father of scientific management, many persons before Taylor made considerable contributions to the development of management thought. A few of these will be noted here.

James Watt, Jr., and Mathew Robinson Boulton

Perhaps the earliest users of a scientific approach to management were Watt and Boulton, sons of the pioneers who invented and developed the steam engine. These two men took over the management of the Soho Engineering Foundry in Great Britain when it was established by their fathers in 1796. Watt was in charge of organization and administration, and Boulton paid particular attention to the sales, or commercial activities. During the next decade, Watt and Boulton developed a number of management systems which are a surprise to scholars even today.

Among the many managerial techniques developed by these men for Soho were such things as market research and forecasting, planned machine layout in terms of work-flow requirements, production planning, production process standards, and standardization of product components. In the accounting and costing area, Watt and Boulton developed detailed statistical records and advanced control systems whereby they could calculate the cost and profits for each machine manufactured and for each department. In the personnel area, they developed both worker and executive training and development programs, work study, and payment by results based on work study, and such welfare programs as a sickness benefit program administered by an elected committee of employees.

[8]For one of the most scholarly analyses of cameralism, see A. Small, *The Cameralists* (Chicago: The University of Chicago Press, 1909).

One of the most successful industrialists of the early nineteenth century, Robert Owen was an outstanding pioneer of management. During the period 1800 to 1828, Owen carried out what was then regarded as an unprecedented experiment in the group of textile mills he managed in Scotland. It is not without good reason that he has been referred to as "the father of modern personnel management."

In these early years of the industrial revolution, when workers were indeed regarded as inert instruments, Owen improved working conditions in the factory, raised the minimum working age for children, reduced hours of work for employees, provided meals for employees at the factories, set up stores to sell necessities to employees at cost, and sought to improve the entire community in which his employees lived by building houses and streets and making the community and factory attractive.

But Owen was no philanthropist, no "do-gooder." His philosophy was that good personnel management pays dividends to the employer and is an essential part of every manager's job. In an instruction he wrote to his superintendents, he declared:

> Many of you have long experienced in your manufacturing operations the advantages of substantial, well-contrived and well-executed machinery. If then, due care as to the state of your inanimate machines can produce beneficial results, what may not be expected if you devote equal attention to your vital machines which are far more wonderfully constructed?[9]

Charles Babbage

Not an industrialist or a manager but primarily a professor and scientist, Babbage was a leading British mathematician who served as professor of mathematics at Cambridge University from 1828 to 1839. His scientific work both prior to and following his tenure as a professor involved continued interest in shops and factories both in Great Britain and in continental Europe.

Babbage is probably best remembered for his invention in 1822 of a mechanical calculator, which he called a "difference machine." Its basic principles were employed in accounting machines nearly a century later. He conceived an "analytical machine" in 1833 which was a computer that would follow instructions automatically and had all the basic elements of the modern computer—a memory device, a punch-card input system, an arithmetic unit, and an external memory system (through stored punch cards). It is hardly surprising that Babbage is referred to as "the father of the computer."

[9]Quoted in L. Urwick, *The Golden Book of Management* (London: Newman Neame Limited, 1956), p. 7.

From the point of view of management, however, Babbage is best remembered for his famous book *On the Economy of Machinery and Manufactures,* published in 1832. In a very real sense, Babbage was a mathematical management scientist. He was especially interested in the economics of division of labor and the development of scientific principles to govern a manager's use of facilities, materials, and labor to get the best possible results. He was impressed with the economics of division of labor, not only for manual operations but for mental activities as well.

But mathematician and scientist though he was, even he did not overlook the human element. Like Taylor, three-quarters of a century later, Babbage argued that there could be a mutuality of interest between the worker and the owner of the new factories. He argued strongly for a kind of profit sharing system by which workers could share in the profitability of factories as they contributed to productivity. He argued that workers should receive a fixed pay depending on the nature of their work, plus a share in the profits, plus bonuses for any suggestions they might make to improve productivity. However, it is true that Babbage's greatest interests and contributions were not in the broader areas of management but in the areas of costing, engineering, and incentives, based on a belief in specialization and allocation of rewards according to productivity.

Henry Varnum Poor

One of the major precursors to Taylor, who has been all but overlooked in the evolution of management thought, is Henry Varnum Poor, editor of the *American Railroad Journal* in the latter half of the nineteenth century. From this position he watched and analyzed the progress of the American railroad systems from infancy to maturity. He saw the railroads being mismanaged and occasionally plundered by the early promoters and stock manipulators. From this vantage point he came to the conclusion that what railroads needed was effective management.

Poor's recommendations in managerial matters sound exceedingly modern. He saw the need for a managerial "system" with a clear organization structure in which people were, and could be, held completely accountable—one with an adequate report communications system throughout the organization so that the top management could know what was happening—and the need for a set of operating reports summarizing costs, revenues, and rates. However, he recognized the danger that such systematization might make people feel like cogs in a machine, and his solution was to recommend a kind of leadership, beginning at the top of an enterprise, that would overcome routine and dullness by instilling in an organization a feeling of unity, an appreciation of the work, and an esprit de corps.

As one thoughtful historian has said of Poor's work, "Long before Frederick Taylor he called for a system; long before Elton Mayo he called for recognition of the human factor; and long before Chris Argyris he called for leadership to remove the rigidities of formal organization."[10]

FREDERICK TAYLOR AND SCIENTIFIC MANAGEMENT

Frederick Winslow Taylor gave up going to college and started out as an apprentice patternmaker and machinist in 1875, joined the Midvale Steel Works in Philadelphia as a machinist in 1878, and rose to the position of chief engineer after earning a degree in engineering through evening study. He invented high-speed steel-cutting tools and spent most of his life as a consulting engineer. Taylor is generally acknowledged as "the father of scientific management." Probably no other person has had a greater impact on the development of management. His experiences as an apprentice, a common laborer, a foreman, a master mechanic, and then the chief engineer of a steel company gave Taylor ample opportunity to know at firsthand the problems and attitudes of workers and to see the great opportunities for improving the quality of management.

Taylor's patents for high-speed steel-cutting tools and other inventions, as well as his early engineering consulting work, made him so well off that he retired from working for payment in 1901, at the age 45, and spent the remaining 14 years of his life as an unpaid consultant and lecturer to promote his ideas on scientific management.

Taylor's Principal Concern

Taylor's principal concern throughout most of his life was that of increasing efficiency in production, not only to lower costs and raise profits but also to make possible increased pay for workers through their higher productivity. As a young man working in machine shops, he was impressed with the degree of "soldiering" on the job, of making work, and of producing less rather than more, due primarily to the workers' fear that they might work themselves out of a job if they produced more. He saw "soldiering" as a system. From his own experience, he knew that much higher productivity was possible without unreasonable effort on the part of the workers.

Taylor decided that the problem of productivity was a matter of ignorance on the part of both management and labor. Part of this ignorance arose from the fact that both managers and workers did not know what constituted a "fair day's work" and a "fair day's pay." Moreover, he believed that both managers and workers were concerned too much with how they could divide the surplus that arose from productivity—the split in thinking between pay and profits—and not enough with increasing the surplus so that *both* owners and laborers

[10]Wren, op. cit., p. 92.

could get more compensation. In brief, Taylor saw productivity as the answer to both higher wages and higher profits, and he believed that the application of scientific methods, instead of custom and rule of thumb, could yield this productivity without the expenditure of more human energy or effort.

Taylor's Principles

Taylor's famous work entitled *The Principles of Scientific Management* was published in 1911. But one of the best expositions of his philosophy of management is found in his testimony before a committee of the House of Representatives, where he was forced to defend his ideas before a group of congressmen, most of whom were hostile because they believed, along with labor leaders, that Taylor's ideas would lead to overworking and displacing workers.[11]

There is perhaps no better way to understand Taylor's basic thinking than to read his own words in his testimony before the House committee in 1912:

> Scientific management is not any efficiency device, not a device of any kind for securing efficiency; nor is it any bunch or group of efficiency devices. It is not a new system of figuring costs; it is not a new scheme of paying men; it is not a piecework system; it is not a bonus system; it is not a premium system; it is no scheme for paying men; it is not holding a stop watch on a man and writing things down about him; it is not time study; it is not motion study nor an analysis of the movements of men; it is not the printing and ruling and unloading of a ton or two of blanks on a set of men and saying "Here's your system; go use it!" It is not divided foremanship or functional foremanship; it is not any of the devices which the average man calls to mind when scientific management is spoken of. . . .
>
> Now, in its essence, scientific management involves a complete mental revolution on the part of the workingman engaged in any particular establishment or industry—a complete mental revolution on the part of these men as to their duties toward their work, toward their fellow men, and toward their employers. And it involves the equally complete mental revolution on the part of those on the management's side—the foreman, the superintendent, the owner of the business, the board of directors—a complete mental revolution on their part as to their duties toward their fellow workers in the management, toward their workmen and toward all of their daily problems.

[11]Taylor's principal works, *Shop Management* (originally published in 1903), *Principles of Scientific Management* (published in 1911), and *Testimony before the Special House Committee* (given in 1912), are combined in one book entitled *Scientific Management* (New York: Harper & Brothers, 1947).

The great mental revolution that takes place in the mental attitude of the two parties under scientific management is that both sides take their eyes off the division of the surplus as the all-important matter, and together turn their attention toward increasing the size of the surplus until this surplus becomes so large that it is unnecessary to quarrel over how it should be divided. They come to see that when they stop pulling against one another, and instead both turn and push shoulder to shoulder in the same direction, the size of the surplus created by their joint efforts is truly astounding. They both realize that when they substitute friendly cooperation and mutual helpfulness for antagonism and strife they are together able to make this surplus so enormously greater than it was in the past that there is ample room for a large increase in wages for the workmen and an equally great increase in profits for the manufacturer.[12]

The fundamental principles that Taylor saw underlying the scientific approach to management may be summarized as follows:

1 Replacing rules of thumb with science (organized knowledge)
2 Obtaining harmony in group action, rather than discord
3 Achieving cooperation of human beings, rather than chaotic individualism
4 Working for maximum output, rather than restricted output
5 Developing all workers to the fullest extent possible for their own and their company's highest prosperity

The reader will note that these basic precepts of Taylor's are not far from the fundamental beliefs of the modern manager.

It is true that some of the techniques Taylor and his colleagues and followers developed in order to put his philosophy and principles into practice had certain mechanistic aspects. To determine what a fair day's work was and to help in finding the one best way of doing any given job, the careful study of time and motion was widely applied. Likewise, various pay plans based on output were used in an attempt to increase the "surplus" (as Taylor referred to "productivity"), to make sure that workers who produced were paid according to their productivity, and to give workers an incentive for performance. As can be seen, techniques such as these were necessary to make Taylor's philosophy work, based as it was on improving productivity, on giving people their best opportunity to be productive, and on rewarding workers for individual productivity.

It is likewise true that these techniques could be used, as they often were by many factory owners over the world, to increase labor productivity without providing ample reward, adequate training, or managerial help. But this was certainly not what Frederick Taylor had in mind.

On the contrary, throughout Taylor's written work, even though it

---

[12]*Testimony*, pp. 26–27, 29–30.

does seem to be unduly preoccupied with productivity at the shop level, runs a strongly humanistic theme. He believed that people should be carefully selected and trained and that they should be given the work they could do best. He had perhaps an idealist's notion that the interests of workers, managers, and owners could and should be harmonized. Moreover, Taylor emphasized the importance of careful advanced planning by managers and the responsibility of managers to design work systems so that workers would be helped to do their best. But, as he spoke of management, he never overlooked the fact that "the relations between employers and men form without question the most important part of this art."[13]

Followers of Taylor

Among the immediate disciples of Taylor were such outstanding pioneers as Carl Georg Barth, Henry L. Gantt, Frank and Lillian Gilbreth, and Edward A. Filene, to mention only a few. Barth was for some years a close associate of Taylor's, having worked first for him in the Bethlehem Steel Company, although during most of his later life he operated as an independent management engineering consultant. An accomplished mathematician, Barth developed many mathematical techniques and formulas that made it possible to put Taylor's ideas into practice. He was regarded as Taylor's most loyal and orthodox follower.

Gantt—like Taylor, a mechanical engineer—joined Barth and Taylor at the Midvale Steel Company in 1887. He stayed with Taylor in his various assignments until 1901, when he formed his own consulting engineering firm. Although he strongly espoused Taylor's ideas and did much consulting work on the scientific selection of workers and the development of incentive bonus systems, he was far more cautious than Taylor in selling and installing his scientific-management methods. Like Taylor, he emphasized the need for developing a mutuality of interests between management and labor, a "harmonious cooperation." In doing this, he stressed the importance of teaching, of developing an understanding of systems on the part of both labor and management, and of appreciating that "in all problems of management the human element is the most important one."

Gantt is perhaps the best known for his development of graphic methods of depicting plans and making possible better managerial control. He emphasized the importance of time, as well as cost, in planning and controlling work. This led eventually to the famous Gantt chart, which, as we shall see in Chapter 27, is in wide use today and was the forerunner of such modern techniques as PERT (Program Evaluation and Review Technique), as well as being regarded by some social historians as the most important social invention of the twentieth century.

The ideas of Taylor were also strongly supported and developed by

[13]*Shop Management*, p. 25.

the famous husband-and-wife team of Frank and Lillian Gilbreth. Frank Gilbreth gave up going to the university to become a bricklayer at the age of 17 in 1885; he rose to the position of chief superintendent of a building contractor firm 10 years later and became a building contractor on his own shortly thereafter. During this period, and quite independently of Taylor's work, he became interested in wasted motions in work; by reducing the number of bricklaying motions from eighteen to five, he made possible the doubling of a bricklayer's productivity with no greater expenditure of effort. His contracting-firm work soon gave way largely to consulting on the improvement of human productivity. After meeting Taylor in 1907, he combined his ideas with Taylor's to put scientific management into effect.

In undertaking his work, Frank Gilbreth was greatly aided and supported by his wife Lillian. She was one of the earliest industrial psychologists and received her doctor's degree in this field in 1915, 9 years after her marriage and during the period when she was involved in having and raising her celebrated dozen children (later made famous by the book and movie *Cheaper by the Dozen*). After her husband's untimely death in 1924, she carried on his consulting business and was widely acclaimed as the "first lady of management" throughout her long life, which ended in 1972 when she was 93.

Lillian Gilbreth's interest in the human aspects of work and her husband's interest in efficiency—the search for the one best way of doing a given task—led to a rare combination of talents.[14] It is therefore not surprising that Frank Gilbreth long emphasized that in applying scientific-management principles, we must look at workers first and understand their personalities and needs. It is interesting, too, that the Gilbreths came to the conclusion that it is not the monotony of work that causes so much worker dissatisfaction, but rather management's lack of interest in workers.

Another follower of Taylor was Edward A. Filene, who hired Gilbreth to help him apply scientific-management methods to his family's Boston department store. Filene's primary interest was in bringing in these devices, especially employee training and evaluation, with adequate concern for the human element in his business. As the result of his many efficiencies, as well as his imaginative management in the department store business, Filene's store became immensely successful, and he used a part of his fortune to create the Twentieth Century Fund, a famous research organization still in existence.

There were, of course, many other management pioneers who built some of their thinking and practice on the ideas and findings of Frederick Taylor. But the four mentioned here will give the reader some idea of Taylor's influence and the nature of the thinking developed by his disciples.

[14]Although the Gilbreths were known for their search of the "best way," it should be noted that they really were interested in the "best way" to do something under a given set of realities, not in every possible situation.

FAYOL: FATHER OF MODERN OPERATIONAL-MANAGEMENT THEORY

Perhaps the real father of modern management theory is the French industrialist Henri Fayol. Although there is little evidence that management scholars, either in England or in the United States, paid much heed to Fayol's work or knew much about it until the 1920s or even years later, his acute observations on the principles of general management first appeared in 1916 in French, under the title *Administration Industrielle et Générale*. This monograph, reprinted in French several times, was not translated into English until 1929; even then it was printed by the International Institute of Management at Geneva, and only a few copies were made available for sale outside Great Britain. No English translation was published in the United States until 1949, although the work of Fayol was brought to the attention of American management scholars in 1923 by Sarah Greer's translation of one of Fayol's papers, later incorporated in a collection of papers by Gulick and Urwick.[15] In this same collection, the more general aspects of Fayol's work were referred to in a paper by the British management consultant and scholar Lyndall Urwick.[16]

Thus, even though Fayol's monograph did not appear in the United States in a form for general reading until 1949,[17] and despite the fact that few in this country knew of his work until 1937—more than 2 decades after its original publication and more than a decade after the author's death—a study of Fayol's monograph, with its practical and clear approach to the job of the manager and its perception of the universality of management principles, discloses an extraordinary insight into the basic problems of modern management. Indeed, even though the thinking of certain students of management was clearly affected by Fayol long before his work was brought to the attention of the general public, one regrets that few serious students of business management had the advantage of Fayol's analysis. Most of those who later contributed to the principles of business management—such as Sheldon, Dennison, Mooney, and Barnard—show no evidence of having been familiar with the work of Fayol.

Fayol wrote as the practical man of business reflecting on his long managerial career and setting down the principles he had observed. In doing so, he made no attempt to develop a logical theory or a self-contained philosophy of management. His observations, however, fit amazingly well into the currently developing mold of management theory.

---

[15]L. Gulick and L. Urwick (eds.), *Papers on the Science of Administration* (New York: Institute of Public Administration, 1937). Fayol's paper was translated by Miss Greer as "The Administrative Theory of the State."
[16]"The Function of Administration," in ibid.
[17]H. Fayol, *General and Industrial Administration* (London: Sir Isaac Pitman & Sons, Ltd., 1949). Most of the biographical material used here has been drawn from Urwick's interesting introduction in this edition.

Fayol found that activities of an industrial undertaking could be divided into six groups: (1) technical (production); (2) commercial (buying, selling, and exchange); (3) financial (search for, and optimum use of, capital); (4) security (protection of property and persons); (5) accounting (including statistics); and (6) managerial (planning, organization, command, coordination, and control). Pointing out that these activities exist in businesses of every size, Fayol observed that the first five were well known, and consequently he devoted most of his book to an analysis of the sixth.

Because there will be occasions to refer to Fayol in the succeeding pages, it will be helpful at this point to outline briefly the contents of his remarkable monograph. The book may be divided into observations on managerial qualities and training, general principles of management, and elements of management. Fayol distinguished between principles and elements by reserving the former term for rules or guides and the latter for functions.

Managerial Qualities and Training

Fayol considered the qualities required by managers to be physical ("health, vigor, address"); mental ("ability to understand and learn, judgment, mental vigor, and adaptability"); moral ("energy, firmness, willingness to accept responsibility, initiative, loyalty, tact, dignity"); educational ("general acquaintance with matters not belonging exclusively to the function performed"); technical ("peculiar to the function"); and experience ("arising from the work proper").[18]

With insight, confirmed in more recent studies, Fayol observed that while the most important ability for a worker is technical, the relative importance of managerial ability increases as one goes up the scalar chain, becoming the most important skill for top-level executives. On the basis of this conclusion, Fayol recognized a widespread need for principles of management and for management teaching, and he decried the lack of the latter in the technical schools of his time. He held that managerial ability should be acquired as technical ability is, first in school and later in the workshop. Aware of the absence of a well-developed and accepted theory of management, he set about early in the twentieth century to provide such a theory. If later scholars of management had followed his example more assiduously, they would probably have gone far toward closing a gap which still exists today.

General Principles of Management

Noting that principles of management are flexible, not absolute, and must be useable regardless of changing and special conditions, Fayol listed fourteen, based on his experience. They may be summarized as follows:

[18]Ibid., p. 7.

1   Division of work. This is the specialization which economists consider necessary to efficiency in the use of labor. Fayol applies the principle to all kinds of work, managerial as well as technical.

2   Authority and responsibility. Here Fayol finds authority and responsibility to be related, with the latter the corollary of the former and arising from it. He sees authority as a combination of official—deriving from the manager's position—and personal—"compounded of intelligence, experience, moral worth, past service, etc."—factors.

3   Discipline. Seeing discipline as "respect for agreements which are directed at achieving obedience, application, energy, and the outward marks of respect," Fayol declares that discipline requires good superiors at all levels.

4   Unity of command. This means that employees should receive orders from one superior only.

5   Unity of direction. According to this principle, each group of activities with the same objective must have one head and one plan. As distinguished from the fourth principle, it relates to the organization of the "body corporate," rather than to personnel. (Fayol did not in any sense mean that all decisions should be made at the top.)

6   Subordination of individual to general interest. This is self-explanatory; when the two are found to differ, management must reconcile them.

7   Remuneration. Remuneration and methods of payment should be fair and afford the maximum possible satisfaction to employees and employer.

8   Centralization. Without using the term "centralization of authority," Fayol refers to the extent to which authority is concentrated or dispersed. Individual circumstances will determine the degree that will "give the best over-all yield."

9   Scalar chain. Fayol thinks of this as a "chain of superiors" from the highest to the lowest ranks, which, while not to be departed from needlessly, should be short-circuited when to follow it scrupulously would be detrimental.

10   Order. Breaking this into "material" and "social" order, Fayol follows the simple adage of "a place for everything [everyone], and everything [everyone] in its [his or her] place." This is essentially a principle of organization in the arrangement of things and people.

11   Equity. Loyalty and devotion should be elicited from personnel by a combination of kindliness and justice on the part of managers when dealing with subordinates.

12   Stability of tenure. Finding unnecessary turnover to be both the cause and the effect of bad management. Fayol points out its dangers and costs.

13   Initiative. Initiative is conceived of as the thinking out and execution of a plan. Since it is one of the "keenest satisfactions for an intelligent man to experience," Fayol exhorts managers to "sacrifice personal vanity" in order to permit subordinates to exercise it.

14 Esprit de corps. This is the principle that "in union there is strength," as well as an extension of the principle of unity of command, emphasizing the need for teamwork and the importance of communication in obtaining it.

In concluding his discussion of these principles, Fayol observed that he had made no attempt to be exhaustive, but had tried only to describe those he had had the most occasion to use, since some kind of codification of principles appeared to be indispensable in every undertaking.

Elements of Management

Fayol regarded the elements of management as its functions—planning, organizing, commanding, coordinating, and controlling.[19] A large part of his treatise is given to an examination of these functions, and his observations are, on the whole, still valid, after more than six decades of study and experience of others in the field. Throughout Fayol's treatise there exists an understanding of the universality of principles. Again and again, he points out that these apply not only to business but also to political, religious, philanthropic, military, and other undertakings. Since all enterprise requires management, the formulation of a theory of management is necessary to its effective teaching.

THE EMERGENCE OF THE BEHAVIORAL SCIENCES

During practically the same period that Taylor, Fayol, and others were concentrating on scientific management and the manager's tasks, many scholars and practitioners were thinking about, experimenting with, and writing on industrial psychology and on social theory, both of which, in many instances, were stimulated by the scientific-management movement. We can get the flavor of these developments by looking briefly at the emergence of industrial psychology, the growth of personnel management, and the development of a sociological approach to human relations and management.

Emergence of Industrial Psychology

Acknowledged to be "the father of industrial psychology," Hugo Münsterberg was trained as a psychologist, receiving his Ph.D. at the University of Leipzig in 1885. He also was trained as a medical doctor, receiving the M.D. degree at the University of Heidelberg in 1887. At the age of 29, in 1892, Münsterberg went to Harvard at the invitation of psychologist William James to take charge of the psychological laboratory and to act as professor of experimental psychology. In 1910 his interest

---

[19]Ibid., chap. 5.

turned to the application of psychology to industry, where he saw the importance of applying behavioral science to the new scientific-management movement. In his landmark book entitled *Psychology and Industrial Efficiency*, first published in 1912,[20] Münsterberg made it clear that his objectives were to discover (1) how to find people whose mental qualities best fit them for the work they are to do, (2) under what psychological conditions the greatest and most satisfactory output can be obtained from the work of every person, and (3) how a business can influence workers in such a way as to obtain the best possible results from them. Like Taylor, he was interested in the mutuality of interests between managers and workers. He stressed that his approach was even more strongly aimed at workers and that through it he hoped to reduce their working time, increase their wages, and raise their "level of life."

Münsterberg's work was supplemented by the pioneering thinking of Lillian Gilbreth, who attempted to apply early psychological concepts to the practice of scientific management in her *Psychology of Management*, published in 1914.[21] Another important early behavioral scientist who applied psychology to management was Walter Dill Scott. He received his doctorate in psychology in 1900, wrote many books on the application of psychological concepts to advertising and marketing and on the development of such personnel-management practices as effective selection, and later became president of Northwestern University.[22]

The Growth of Personnel Management

Scott's books, the tight labor market during World War II, the necessity for psychological testing of thousands of soldiers who were mobilized for the war, and the realization that caring for human assets were simply good business—an idea recognized by Robert Owen a century earlier—led to the growth of personnel management. B. F. Goodrich had formed an "employment office" in 1900; National Cash Register, a "labor department" in 1902; and Plimpton Press, one of Taylor's clients, a personnel department in 1910.[23]

Even Henry Ford, widely known as an industrial autocrat, but concerned about what workers might do in the light of their much higher wages and worried about labor turnover, established a personnel department called the "sociological department" in 1914. But perhaps the leading early industrialist to develop extensive personnel-management practices was B. Seebohm Rountree, son of the founder of the British

---

[20]Published in German in 1912 and in English in 1913 (Boston: Houghton Mifflin Company).

[21](New York: Sturgis and Walton Company.) This book was also Dr. Gilbreth's Ph.D. dissertation.

[22]Among his books were *Influencing Men in Business* (New York: The Ronald Press Company, 1911); *Increasing Human Efficiency* (New York: The Macmillan Company, 1911); and (with R. C. Clothier) *Personnel Management: Principles, Practices and Point of View* (New York: McGraw-Hill Book Company, 1923).

[23]The authors are indebted to Wren, op. cit., pp. 199–200, for these and other data used in this section.

chocolate manufacturer, Rountree & Co., Ltd., now a part of John Macintosh & Sons, Ltd. Entering his father's firm as a chemist in 1889, he became its "labor director" in 1897 and headed the company as chairman from 1923 to 1936. During the entire period from 1897, he developed many programs aimed at enhancing the status of workers. Among the many were a medical department (1904), a day continuation school (1905), a 5-day week (1919), profit sharing (1923), and such innovative practices as unemployment compensation, trained company industrial psychologists to guide both managers and workers, and provisions for canteens and recreation.

Indeed, Rountree has been referred to as "the British management movement's greatest pioneer."[24] His managerial philosophy was based on two basic principles: (1) "Whatever may be the motives which induce any given individual to engage in industry, its true basic purpose must be service to the community," and (2) "Industry is a human thing, in which men and women earn the means of life, and from which men and women are entitled to expect the means to a life worth living."[25] It is significant how much Rountree's philosophy and practices rubbed off on two other pioneers of management, Oliver Shelton and Lyndall Urwick, both of whom worked for him, and on Mary Parker Follett, who cited Rountree's firm as a model for how a company should be run. It is likewise interesting how closely they fit managerial philosophies of many modern companies of the 1970s and 1980s.

Development of the Sociological Approach to Management

In part preceding and in large part concurrent with the development of scientific management by Taylor and administrative management by Fayol, a considerable amount of thinking and research were being devoted to looking at people as products of group behavior. This is sometimes called the "social man" approach to management. Generally regarded as fathers of organization theory, or the social systems approach to management, were three outstanding scholars who wrote books and essays at the close of the nineteenth century and during the early years of the twentieth century.

One of these was the German intellectual Max Weber, whose empirical analyses of church, government, the military, and business led him to the belief that hierarchy, authority, and bureaucracy (including clear rules, definition of tasks, and discipline) lie at the foundation of all social organizations. Another was the French scholar Émile Durkheim, whose doctoral dissertation, published in 1893,[26] and subsequent writings emphasized the idea that groups, through establishing their values and norms, control human conduct in any social organization.

---

[24]Urwick, op. cit., p. 155.
[25]Ibid.
[26]*De la Division du travail social (The Division of Labor)* (Paris: F. Alcan, 1893).

The third was the French-Italian Vilfredo Pareto, who, in a series of lectures and books between 1896 and 1917, earned the right to be called "the father of the social systems approach" to organization and management.[27] Pareto viewed society as an intricate cluster of interdependent units, or elements—that is, as a social system with many subsystems. Among his many ideas was the tendency of social systems to seek equilibrium upon being disturbed by outside or inside influence. His thesis was that social attitudes, or sentiments, function to cause the system to seek an equilibrium when disturbed by these forces. He saw also that it was the task of the elite (the "ruling class") in any society to provide the leadership to maintain the social system.

Although these few words give inadequate expression of the views of the social man or social system pioneers (and space does not permit even the mention of many others), there is no question that they did have considerable influence on Elton Mayo, F. J. Roethlisberger, and others who undertook the famous experiments at the Hawthorne plant of the Western Electric Company between 1927 and 1932.[28] Earlier, from 1924 and 1927, the National Research Council made a study in collaboration with Western Electric to determine the effect of illumination and other conditions upon workers and their productivity. Finding that, when illumination was either increased or decreased for a test group, productivity improved, the researchers were about to declare the whole experiment a failure until Elton Mayo, of Harvard, saw in it something unusual and, with Roethlisberger and others, continued the research.

What Mayo and his colleagues found, based partly on the earlier thinking of Pareto, was to have a dramatic effect on management thought. Changing illumination for the test group, modifying rest periods, shortening workdays, and varying incentive pay systems did not seem to explain changes in productivity. Mayo and his researchers then came to the conclusion that other factors were responsible. They found them in the social attitudes and relationships of work groups. Changing illumination—up and down—caused increased productivity because the test group began to be noticed, to feel important. They found, in general, that the improvement in productivity was due to such social factors as morale, satisfactory interrelationships between members of a work group (a "sense of belonging"), and effective management—a kind of managing that would understand human behavior, especially group behavior, and serve it through such interpersonal skills as motivating, counseling, leading, and communicating. This phenomenon, arising basically from people being "noticed," has been known as the "Hawthorne effect."

[27]The most famous of which was his *Trattato di sociologia generale*, published in Florence in 1916, with a second edition in 1923; it may be found in English translation as *The Mind and Society: A Treatise on General Sociology* (New York: Harcourt, Brace and Company, Inc., 1935; also New York: Dover Publications, Inc., 1963).
[28]For a full description of these experiments, see Elton Mayo, *The Human Problems of an Industrial Civilization* (New York: The Macmillan Company, 1933), chaps. 3–5; and F. J. Roethlisberger and W. J. Dickson, *Management and the Worker* (Cambridge, Mass.: Harvard University Press, 1939).

What the Hawthorne studies dramatized was that humans are social—that business operations are a matter not merely of machinery and methods but also of gearing these with the social system to develop a complete sociotechnical system. These experiments led to increased emphasis on the behavioral sciences as applied to management and to the recognition that managers operate in a *social system*. It should not be inferred from this that prior to the Hawthorne experiments successful managers did not recognize the importance of the human factor, or that management theorists overlooked it. As the brief discussions earlier in this chapter clearly indicate, this is simply not true. But what the work of Mayo and his associates did underscore was the need for a greater and deeper understanding of the social and behavioral aspects of management.

CHESTER BARNARD AND SYSTEMS THEORY

Probably the most influential book in the entire field of management is the classic treatise entitled *The Functions of the Executive*, written by Chester I. Barnard in 1938.[29] A lifelong executive himself and president of the New Jersey Bell Telephone Company from 1927 to 1948, Barnard was a first-rate scholar and intellectual who was greatly influenced by Pareto, Mayo, and other faculty members at Harvard, where he occasionally lectured. His analysis of the manager is truly a social systems approach since, in order to comprehend and analyze the functions of executives, Barnard looked for their major tasks in the system where they operate.

In determining that the task of executives (by which he meant all kinds of managers) was one of maintaining a system of cooperative effort in a formal organization, Barnard addressed himself first to the reasons for, and the nature of, cooperative systems. The logic of his analysis can be seen in the steps his book follows:

1 Physical and biological limitations of individuals lead them to cooperate, to work in groups; while the basic limitations are physical and biological, once people cooperate, psychological and social limitations of individuals also play a part in inducing cooperation.

2 The act of cooperation leads to the establishment of cooperative systems in which physical, biological, personal, and social factors or elements are present (for example, Barnard would see a college class as a cooperative system, made up of such elements as the room, seats, blackboards, people as biological beings, personalities, interchange of thought, and so on). He also makes the point that the continuation of cooperation depends on effectiveness (does it accomplish the cooperative purpose?) and efficiency (does it accomplish the purpose with a minimum of dissatisfactions and costs to cooperating members?).

[29](Cambridge, Mass.: Harvard University Press, 1938.)

3   Any cooperative system may be divided into two parts: "organization," which includes only the *interactions* of people in the system, and "other elements."

4   Organizations can in turn be divided into two kinds: the "formal" organization, which is that set of consciously coordinated social interactions that have a deliberate and joint purpose, and the "informal" organization, which refers to those social interactions without a common or consciously coordinated joint purpose.

5   The formal organization cannot exist unless there are persons who (a) are able to communicate with one another, (b) are willing to contribute to group action, and (c) have a conscious common purpose.

6   Every formal organization must include the following elements: (a) a system of functionalization so that people can specialize (that is, various forms of departmentation); (b) a system of effective and efficient incentives that will induce people to contribute to group action; (c) a system of power ("authority") which will lead group members to accept the decisions of executives; and (d) a system of logical decision making.

7   The functions of the executive in this formal organization are then the following: (a) the maintenance of organization communication through a scheme of organization, plus loyal, responsible, and capable people, and a compatible executive "informal organization"; (b) the securing of esential services from individuals in the organization; and (c) the formulation and definition of purpose (that is, planning).

8   The executive functions enter the process through the work of the executive in integrating the whole and in finding the best balance between conflicting forces and events.

9   To make the executive effective requires a high order of responsible leadership; as Barnard so well emphasizes, "Cooperation, not leadership, is the creative process; but leadership is the indispensable fulminator of its forces."[30]

It is hardly any wonder that this book has had so much influence. Although the brief outline of Barnard's thesis cannot do justice to it, the book is a social systems approach, concentrating on major elements of the managerial job, containing extraordinary insights on decision making and leadership, and bearing the authority of an intellectual with exceptional executive experience.

CRITICISMS AND MISUNDERSTANDINGS OF THE CLASSICISTS

Although only a few of the leading pioneers in the development of management thought have been discussed above, any reader will be

[30]Ibid., p. 259.

surprised to hear of the various criticisms which have been aimed at the "classicists" and "traditional management theory." One reads over and over again, primarily in the writings of behavioral scientists but also in the work of other modern writers, that the classicists regarded the human being as an "inert instrument." One also reads that traditional management theory looks upon management as a closed system.

While few authors are clear as to whom they mean by the "classicists," they must at least have in mind such writers as Taylor, Fayol, Gantt, the Gilbreths, Filene, and their followers. They could hardly mean the early industrial psychologists or sociologists whose work paralleled that of such writers as Fayol and Taylor. It is hardly conceivable that they could mean Chester Barnard. As has been seen from the summaries of various management pioneers, certainly from the time of Taylor, none overlooked the human factor or treated it in a mechanical way. Moreover, the many pioneers not discussed here, such as Mary Parker Follett[31] and Lyndall Urwick,[32] took positions many years ago which agree with points made in recent years by behavioralists, understandably with greater sophistication and insight than was possible decades ago. And surely those who mislabel the classicists could not have been speaking of such leading pioneers as Lillian Gilbreth, Seebohm Rountree, or Edward Filene.

Did the Classicists Regard the Human Being as an Inert Instrument?

As for the unwarranted assertion that the classicists, whoever they were, regarded the human being as an inert instrument, one can only come to the conclusion that the critics have not read the works of those they criticize—or, what is more likely, that they confuse the early writers on management with managerial practice of a half century ago. It is true that many industrialists did pick up the techniques of scientific management, such as time and motion study, and pursued them with inadequate attention to human factors, partly because these showed a quick return in reducing costs and increasing profits. But the intelligent critic should hardly blame the classicists for what certain business practitioners did.

Did the Traditionalists Look on Management as a Closed System?

Also, it is difficult to find in the writings of the traditional management theorists, whoever they may have been, adequate evidence that they

---

[31]See, for example, her collection of papers, almost all written from 1925 to 1927, in H. C. Metcalf and L. Urwick (eds.), *Dynamic Administration* (New York: Harper & Brothers, 1941). Almost all these papers dealt with the human aspect of management. She spoke of the leader as "the man who can energize his group, who knows how to encourage initiative, how to draw from all what each has to give" (p. 247).

[32]See, for example, his many references to the human factor in his early book, *The Elements of Administration* (New York: Harper & Row, Publishers, Incorporated, 1944). See especially pp. 32–33, 49–51, 89–94.

regarded management as a closed social system. While it is true that some management theorists have concentrated on such internal aspects of management as work measurement and efficiency, effective organization structure, and internal group behavior, it is hardly true that management theorists, in general, have regarded management as a closed system. Fayol clearly recognized the importance of marketing and planning, which hardly implies dealing with a closed system. Certainly, Seebohm Rountree, with his stress on social responsibility, was thinking in open-system terms. Pareto, the original social systems theorist, recognized the disturbances that could be caused to a social system by external influences. In summary, no one from Fayol's time to the present could think of planning in the vacuum of the closed system of an enterprise. Nor could one believe that the type of organization structure used or the process of dealing with people, who necessarily bring into an enterprise cultural factors from their external environment, could ever be practically treated on a closed-system basis.

The lesson from all this is that individuals who are interested in management and in studying the hundreds of writers in this field should ask themselves a few questions: Are these bromides and shibboleths true? Who is responsible for them? Who are the "classicists" and the "traditionalists"? To fail to seek answers to such questions is to close one's mind to what people really said, thought, and did.

THE EMERGENCE OF MODERN MANAGEMENT THOUGHT

As can be seen from the preceding discussion, the development of management thought has had a fairly long history, although most of it belongs to the twentieth century. The early strands of thinking evolved around the ideas of the introduction of science into the art of managing; the study of the managerial functions; analysis of, and experimentation with, the psychological aspects of people working in organized enterprise; the study of group behavior; and the introduction of the concept of social systems.

Although it is impossible to recount the contributions of the many analyses of management, we can sketch some of the growing thinking in this important field. Some has come from public administrators, much from business managers, a great deal from the behavioralists, and in more recent years a considerable amount from the systems scientists.

Contributions of Public Administrators

Coincident with the scientific-management movement and encouraged by it, a number of scholars attempted to bring about increased efficiency in government by means of improved personnel practices and better management. One of the leading apostles of this movement was Woodrow Wilson, who, as early as 1885 and on many occasions later, sounded the call for efficient government.[33] In a quest for economy and efficiency, those interested in public administration have naturally stressed organization, personnel practices, budgetary controls, and planning; to these fields many public administrators and political scientists have made major contributions. Among these are such scholars as Luther Gulick, with his observations on government organization and his research in the application of scientific methodology to public administration,[34] as well as such other noteworthy pioneers in the field as White,[35] Gaus,[36] Friedrich,[37] Stene,[38] Dimock,[39] Simon,[40] and Merriam,[41] who have approached the field not only as practical public administrators but also as university scholars.

Contributions of Business Managers

Many of the most significant contributions to the basic field of management theory have been made by business executives including Taylor, Fayol, and Barnard. One of these early writers was Russell Robb, who in 1910, at the Graduate School of Business Administration at Harvard, gave a special group of three lectures on organization.[42] Drawing from his business experience, Robb saw organization as a tool for the efficient

[33]See, for example, Wilson's *Congressional Government* (Boston: Houghton Mifflin Company, 1885) and "The Study of Administration," *Political Science Quarterly*, vol. 2, pp. 197–222 (June 1887). Note also, with regard to developments in Great Britain, D. B. Eaton, *Civil Service in Great Britain* (New York: Harper & Brothers, 1880).

[34]See "Notes on the Theory of Organization" and "Science, Values, and Public Administration," in Gulick and Urwick, *Papers on the Science of Administration*.

[35]L. D. White, *Introduction to the Study of Public Administration* (New York: The Macmillan Company, 1939).

[36]J. M. Gaus, "The Responsibility of Public Administration," in J. M. Gaus, L. D. White, and M. E. Dimock (eds.), *The Frontiers of Public Administration* (Chicago: The University of Chicago Press, 1936), pp. 26–44; see also (with L. O. Wolcott), *Public Administration and the U.S. Dept. of Agriculture* (Chicago: Public Administration Service, 1941).

[37]C. J. Friedrich, *Constitutional Government and Politics* (New York: Harper & Brothers, 1937); see also *Responsible Bureaucracy* (Cambridge, Mass.: Harvard University Press, 1932) and "Public Policy and the Nature of Administrative Responsibility," in *Public Policy* (Cambridge, Mass.: Harvard University Press, 1940).

[38]E. O. Stene, "An Approach to a Science of Administration," *American Political Science Review*, vol. 34, pp. 1124–1137 (December 1940).

[39]M. E. Dimock, "The Criteria and Objectives of Public Administration," in Gaus, White, and Dimock, op. cit., pp. 116–133.

[40]H. A. Simon, *Administrative Behavior* (New York: The Macmillan Company, 1950); see also *Determining Work Loads for Professional Staff in a Public Welfare Agency* (Berkeley, Calif.,: University of California Bureau of Public Administration, 1941) and *Public Administration* (New York: Alfred A. Knopf, Inc., 1950).

[41]C. E. Merriam, *Political Power: Its Composition and Incidence* (New York: McGraw-Hill Book Company, 1934); see also *The New Democracy and the New Despotism* (New York: McGraw-Hill Book Company, 1939).

[42]*Lectures on Organization* (privately printed, 1910); incorporated in Catheryn Seckler-Hudson (ed.), *Processes of Organization and Management* (Washington: Public Affairs Press, 1948), pp. 99–124, 269–281.

utilization of workers and materials, a tool which had to be suited to the circumstances of each enterprise. Robb was one of the first to warn of overorganization.[43] Emphasizing the importance of definite authority, harmony, and "team play," Robb warned that too much functional specialization would result in problems of coordination.

Of the comprehensive works on management, perhaps one of the most significant is *The Philosophy of Management*,[44] written in 1923 by the scholarly British industrial consultant Oliver Sheldon. Like Fayol, Sheldon sought to formulate a theory of "management as a whole" by defining its purpose, tracing its line of growth, and spelling out the principles governing its practice. Sheldon thought of management in broad terms as including the determination of policy and the coordination of functions (administration), the execution of policy and the employment of organization (management proper), and the combination of the work of individuals or groups "with the faculties necessary for its execution" (organization).[45] Although Sheldon stressed such matters as the social responsibilities of managers and examined such functional fields of management as personnel ("labour management") and production management, many of his principles are similar to those of Fayol. One receives the impression from Sheldon's work, however, that he did not have Fayol's breadth of understanding and that, except for organization, he did not see the functions of managers as having universal application. For example, his discussion of planning revolves primarily around factory planning.[46]

Another important contribution by a businessman to the development of management theory is that of Henry Dennison, a Massachusetts industrialist whose advanced management techniques employed in the Dennison Manufacturing Company permitted him to explore the principles of management. In a book published in 1931,[47] Dennison set out to study the scientific aspects of management, particularly organization, and to ascertain whether the methods of the engineer might be applicable. In doing so, Dennison developed concepts of motivation, leadership, and teamwork and analyzed the effects of the structural factors of organization on personalities. Although Dennison did not develop a theory of management, his emphasis upon human engineering and the role of leadership made his contribution significant.

One of the most illuminating attempts to develop a logical framework

[43]Ibid., p. 45. In speaking of organization to control costs, Robb sagely remarks: "While it pays to know costs, it also pays to find out how much it costs to know costs."

[44]O. Sheldon, *The Philosophy of Management* (London: Sir Isaac Pitman & Sons, Ltd., 1923).

[45]Ibid., p. 32. It is interesting that Sheldon drew these concepts of the functions of management from an American, J. N. Shultze, in a paper read before the Taylor Society in 1919.

[46]Ibid., p. 218. Note that Sheldon defines planning as "the business of directing and controlling the processes of production to a given end."

[47]H. S. Dennison, *Organization Engineering* (New York: McGraw-Hill Book Company, 1931).

for the theory of organization is contained in the work of Mooney and Reiley.[48] Drawing upon lessons from history, particularly those furnished by church and military organizations, these authors undertook to combine the elements of organization into a logical pattern of principle, process, and effect. Starting with the principle of coordination, they moved into the concepts of scalar organization and functionalism, arriving at a total of nine principles. While the work of Mooney and Reiley has been criticized as being too doctrinaire,[49] it represents a logical approach for relating fundamental principles of organization to one another.

Another contribution by a practicing business executive is Alvin Brown's *Organization of Industry*, published in 1947.[50] This treatise is essentially an analysis of the delegation of authority, with an attempt to construct a theory of organization and a division of the managerial functions into the "phases of administration" of planning, doing, and seeing. Although Brown often refers to "responsibility" when he means authority or authority plus an assigned activity, his work is outstanding as a thorough analysis of authority delegation and an attempt to codify a number of principles of management.

Among other contributions by business and professional management people, one should not overlook the crisp reasoning and syntheses of Lyndall Urwick[51] and the pioneering work of Ordway Tead,[52] R. C. Davis,[53] and Paul Holden,[54] to mention only a few. Nor should one overlook the tremendous force which has been exerted by the Society for Advancement of Management and the American Management Association. The latter organization, particularly, has its roots in the top managerial group in this country, its members being drawn mostly from among the alert business managers who seek a scientific foundation for their jobs. The Society for Advancement of Management, another important group, is an outgrowth of the Taylor Society, and much of its early emphasis was upon the production-management aspects of general management.

The fact that so many of the major contributions to management theory have come from persons to whom the practice of management has

---

[48]First published as J. D. Mooney and A. C. Reiley, *Onward Industry* (New York: Harper & Brothers, 1931), this work later appeared with slight modifications as *The Principles of Organization* (New York: Harper & Brothers, 1939). A later edition, in 1947, appeared with only the name of Mooney as author.

[49]Lepawsky, *Administration*, p. 253.

[50](Englewood Cliffs, N.J.: Prentice-Hall, Inc., 1947).

[51]See especially *The Elements of Administration* (New York: Harper & Brothers, 1943) and *Management of Tomorrow* (New York: Harper & Brothers, 1933).

[52]*The Art of Leadership* (New York: McGraw-Hill Book Company, 1935).

[53]Especially *The Principles of Business Organization and Operation* (Columbus, Ohio: H. L. Hedrick, 1935).

[54]With L. S. Fish and H. L. Smith, *Top-Management Organization and Control* (New York: McGraw-Hill Book Company, 1951).

been a real and challenging task speaks well for the importance of the field and the realism with which it is being approached.

Contributions of the Behavioralists

Spurred on by the Hawthorne experiments of 1927 to 1932 and the awakened interest in human relations in the 1930s and 1940s, a great many behavioral scientists have taken up the study of management in recent years. As will be recalled, the Hawthorne experiments, undertaken by Mayo and Roethlisberger of the Harvard Business School, disclosed that attitudes toward workers may be more important to efficiency and productivity than such material factors as rest periods, illumination, and even money. This disclosure, as well as the more basic work done earlier by psychologists and sociologists, resulted in much academic writing by the behavioral scientists.

Although one cannot say that prior to the 1940s many sociologists, anthropologists, psychologists, and social psychologists were particularly interested in the problems of management, by now their contributions to management theory have been considerable. While those in all areas of behavioral science who have made significant contribution to management are too numerous to detail,[55] a few can be named.

Sociologists have contributed much to an understanding of the anatomy of organizations through their work on groups, cultural patterns, group cohesiveness, and cooperation. Among the sociologists who might be noted, in addition to those mentioned earlier, are Bakke,[56] Selznick,[57] Homans,[58] Dubin,[59] Dalton,[60] and Katz and Kahn.[61]

As has already been made clear by the discussion of earlier writers, psychologists have likewise contributed to management understanding through their illumination of the aspects of rational behavior and influence, the sources of motivation, and the nature of leadership. Among the many in the area of individual and social psychology who have contributed materially to management are McGregor,[62] Likert,[63] Argyris,[64]

---

[55]For an inventory of scientific findings in the behavioral sciences, but with particular reference to contributions of psychologists, see B. Berelson and G. A. Steiner, *Human Behavior* (New York: Harcourt, Brace & World, Inc., 1964).

[56]See, for example, *Bonds of Organization* (New York: Harper & Brothers, 1950).

[57]See, for example, "Foundations of the Theory of Organization," *American Sociological Review*, vol. 13, pp. 25–35 (February 1948).

[58]*The Human Group* (New York: Harcourt, Brace & World, Inc., 1950).

[59]For example, *The World of Work: Industrial Society and Human Relations* (Englewood Cliffs, N.J.: Prentice-Hall, Inc., 1958).

[60]*Men Who Manage* (New York: John Wiley & Sons, Inc., 1959).

[61]*The Social Psychology of Organizations* (New York: John Wiley & Sons, Inc., 1966 rev. ed. 1978).

[62]*The Human Side of Enterprise* (New York: McGraw-Hill Book Company, 1960).

[63]*New Patterns of Management* (New York: McGraw-Hill Book Company, 1961).

[64]For example, *Integrating the Individual and the Organization* (New York: John Wiley & Sons, Inc., 1964).

Leavitt,[65] Blake and Mouton,[66] Sayles,[67] Tannenbaum and his associates,[68] Bennis,[69] Fiedler,[70] Stogdill,[71] and Herzberg.[72]

These scholars and others have shown how human beings bring to their task aspects of behavior which the effective manager should profitably understand. After all, it is individuals and groups with which a manager is concerned, and while organizational roles are designed to accomplish group purposes, these roles must be filled by people. Likewise, as will be pointed out later, the most effective manager is a leader, and understanding how leadership emerges is a key to understanding management itself. The contributions of many of the writers noted here, as well as in other parts of this chapter, will be discussed at various points in this book.

Contributions of the Systems Scientists

As already emphasized, realization of the managerial process and environment as involving a series of systems has led to increased sophistication of management. While it is difficult to select specific contributors in this field because so many contributions have been made by physical, biological, and social scientists of a wide array of interests, a few major threads may be identified.

An outstanding contribution of the systems approach to managing came with the introduction of operations research[73] into the areas of planning and control. Through its use, management planning and control have been given the more rigorous treatment required by clear-cut goals, measures of effectiveness and mathematical models, and the attempt to develop quantified answers. Other types of problem simulation have developed with the modeling and manipulative techniques of mathematics, with speed and memory capacities of computers playing a major part. In addition, seeing plans as networks of interacting events has sharpened managerial perceptiveness in planning and control.[74]

One of the major contributors to the expansion of systems theory to

[65]*Managerial Psychology* (Chicago: The University of Chicago Press, 1958, 1964, 1972, and 1978).
[66]R. B. Blake and J. S. Mouton, *The Managerial Grid* (Houston: Gulf Publishing Company, 1964).
[67]*Managerial Behavior* (New York: McGraw-Hill Book Company, 1964).
[68]See, for example, R. Tannenbaum, I. R. Weschler, and Fred Massarik, *Leadership and Organization: A Behavioral Science Approach* (New York: McGraw-Hill Book Company, 1961).
[69]*Changing Organizations* (New York: McGraw-Hill Book Company, 1966).
[70]*A Theory of Leadership Effectiveness* (New York: McGraw-Hill Book Company, 1967).
[71]*Individual Behavior and Group Achievement* (London: Oxford University Press, 1959).
[72]See, for example, with B. Mausner and B. B. Synderman, *The Motivation to Work*, 2d ed. (New York: John Wiley & Sons, Inc., 1959) and *Work and the Nature of Man* (Cleveland: The World Publishing Company, 1966).
[73]See chap. 9.
[74]For a discussion of network planning and control, see chap. 27.

all science was von Bertalanffy[75] in 1951 and, with special reference to management, Boulding in 1956.[76] Many others have made significant contributions to various aspects of systems theory as it may apply to management. Among them one might mention the work of Katz and Kahn in social systems[77] and of Forrester in industrial systems[78] and the operations research contributions of Stafford Beer,[79] Churchman and his associates,[80] Hertz,[81] McCloskey,[82] and Morse.[83] Nor should one ever underestimate the influence of Norbert Wiener on developing and emphasizing feedback theory, which had such an influence on systems theory.[84] Likewise, the contribution of Johnson, Kast, and Rosenweig in forcefully relating systems theory to management through their early textbook should not be overlooked.[85]

FOR DISCUSSION

1   Why did the primary impetus to the development of management thought occur only in the twentieth century and even more especially during the past few decades?

2   "The classicists in management looked upon the human being as an inert instrument." Identify whom the writer of this statement must have meant by the "classicists" and analyze the accuracy of the statement.

3   "The systems approach is new, having been used or recognized in management only in the past few years." Analyze and comment on this statement.

4   Why has Frederick Taylor been called "the father of scientific management," and Henri Fayol "the father of modern operational-management theory"?

[75]"General Systems Theory: A New Approach to Unity of Science," *Human Biology*, vol. 23, pp. 303–361 (December 1961).

[76]"General Systems Theory: The Skeleton of Science," *Management Science*, vol. 3, no. 4, pp. 197–208 (April 1956).

[77]*The Social Psychology of Organizations* (New York: John Wiley & Sons, Inc., 1966 rev. ed., 1978).

[78]*Industrial Dynamics*, (New York: The M.I.T. Press and John Wiley & Sons, Inc., (revised ed., 1978).

[79]For example, *Decision and Control* (New York: John Wiley & Sons, Inc., 1966).

[80]For example, with R. L. Ackoff and E. L. Arnoff, *Introduction to Operations Research* (New York: John Wiley & Sons, Inc., 1957).

[81]See, for example, with A. H. Rubenstein, *Research Operations in Industry* (New York: King's Crown Press, 1953).

[82]See, for example, with F. N. Trefethen, *Operations Research for Management* (Baltimore: The Johns Hopkins Press, 1954).

[83]See, for example, with G. E. Kimball, *Methods of Operations Research* (New York: John Wiley & Sons, Inc., 1951).

[84]*Cybernetics* (Cambridge, Mass.: The M.I.T. Press, 1948).

[85]*The Theory and Management of Systems* (New York: McGraw-Hill Book Company, 1963).

5 To what extent and how has the development of behavioral thought tended to parallel and assist the scientific-management movement?

6 Taylor, Fayol, and other management pioneers have been accused of seeking and recommending a one best way to do everying in managing. To what extent, if at all, is this accusation correct?

7 Chester Barnard has been referred to as "the originator of the social systems approach" to management. Why might he be so regarded?

chapter 3 Patterns of Management Analysis

1 To explain the nature of the "management theory jungle" by outlining the eleven current approaches to the study, analysis, and teaching of management theory and science. These approaches are now found to be (1) the empirical, or case, approach; (2) the interpersonal behavior approach; (3) the group behavior approach; (4) the cooperative social systems approach; (5) the sociotechnical systems approach; (6) the decision theory approach; (7) the systems approach; (8) the mathematical, or "management science," approach; (9) the contingency, or situational, approach; (10) the managerial roles approach; and (11) the operational theory approach.

2 To show how the operational approach to management theory and science has a basic core of theory of its own and also draws eclectically from all the other ten approaches to management.

3 To show how the operational approach, around which this book is organized, is implemented by using the five functions of managers—planning, organizing, staffing, leading, and controlling—as a first-level classification of knowledge, and to discuss certain basic questions pertaining to each function.

4 To define the major management functions of managing and to show how each is both independent and interdependent.

5 To note and analyze certain hopeful signs indicating that there may be developing a convergence of some of the patterns of management thought.

Because of the extraordinary interest in management in recent years, a number of approaches to its analysis have developed. Their variety and the large number of persons, particularly from universities, who espouse them have resulted in much confusion as to what management is, what management theory and science are, and how management should be studied. One of the authors in 1961, called the situation "the management theory jungle."[1]

In 1961, six schools of, or "approaches" to (as it is now believed to be more appropriate to call them), management theory and science were found. As evidence that the jungle still exists and may even be becoming more dense, the authors now find eleven approaches to management. At the same time, as will be noted later, there are a few significant signs indicating that there is some convergence among the various approaches.

THE VARIOUS APPROACHES TO MANAGEMENT

Some may believe that it is no more important that there be one approach to management than that there be a single approach to psychology or trout fishing. But no one can doubt that it is important for students and managers to be able to classify and recognize the various patterns of management analysis. Management is a difficult enough field without those in it being forced to face confusion and apparent contradiction.

As we shall see in this chapter, the approach adopted in this book is best referred to as "operational"[2] since it attempts to analyze management in terms of the practical aspects of managerial knowledge. In this context, the authors believe that they analyze management in a way most useful to managers, reflecting the way they see the knowledge underlying their jobs. The authors nevertheless recognize that other analyses of management are useful and important and that contributions made by proponents of other approaches have been significant. As will be made clear after these various approaches have been discussed, the operational theory of management draws from all the material significantly pertinent to the manager's job.

Yet there can be no doubt that the management theory jungle still persists, a jungle of confusing thought, theory, and advice to practicing managers. The major sources of entanglement in the jungle are believed to be (1) varying meanings given to common words like "organization"; (2) differences in defining management as a body of knowledge; (3) wide-

---

[1]See Harold Koontz, "The Management Theory Jungle," *Journal of the Academy of Management,* vol. 4, no. 3, pp. 174–188 (December 1961). See also Harold Koontz, "Making Sense of Management Theory," *Harvard Business Review,* vol. 40, no. 4, pp. 24ff. (July–August 1962). Much of the material in these chapters has been drawn from these articles. It is interesting that the variety of approaches has even increased since these papers were written.

[2]For a discussion of the operational approach to concepts and analysis, see P. W. Bridgman, *The Logic of Modern Physics* (New York: The Macmillan Company, 1938), pp. 2–32.

spread casting aside of the findings of early practicing managers as "armchair" rather than what they were—the distilled experience and thought of perceptive individuals; (4) misunderstanding of the nature and role of principles and theory; and (5) the narrow training of many specialists in fields allied to management, made more narrow by the inability or unwillingness of many new "experts" to understand each other.

Moreover, until the past quarter century, almost all the meaningful writing was the product of alert and perceptive practitioners—for example, the French industrialist Henri Fayol, the General Motors executive James Mooney, the Johns-Manville vice president Alvin Brown, the British chocolate executive Oliver Sheldon, the New Jersey Bell Telephone president Chester Barnard, and the British management consultant Lyndall Urwick.

But the early absence of the academics from the field of management has been more than atoned for by the deluge of writings on management from our colleges and universities in the past 25 years. For example, there are now more than 100 (one of the authors could find 97 in his library) different textbooks purporting to tell the reader—student or manager—what management is all about. And in related fields like psychology, sociology, social psychology, systems sciences, and mathematical modeling, the number of textbooks which can be used to teach some aspect, usually narrow, of management is at least as large.

At the present time, we find a total of eleven clearly identified approaches to the study of management science and theory. These are (1) the empirical, or case, approach; (2) the interpersonal behavior approach; (3) the group behavior approach; (4) the cooperative social systems approach; (5) the sociotechnical systems approach; (6) the decision theory approach; (7) the systems approach; (8) the mathematical, or "management science," approach; (9) the contingency, or situational, approach; (10) the managerial roles approach; and (11) the operational theory approach.

The Empirical, or Case, Approach

The members of this school study management by analyzing experience, usually through cases. They work on the premise that students and practitioners will understand the field of management and somehow come to know how to manage effectively by studying managerial successes and failures in various individual cases.[3]

No one can deny the importance of analyzing past experience or the "how it was done" of management. But management, unlike law, is not a science based on precedent, and future situations exactly resembling those of the past are unlikely to occur. Indeed, there is a positive danger in

---

[3]For an example of this approach, see Ernest Dale, *The Great Organizers* (New York: McGraw-Hill Book Company, 1960), pp. 11–28.

relying too much on past experience and on undistilled history of managerial problem solving, for the simple reason that a technique found "right" in the past may be far from an exact fit for a somewhat similar situation in the future.

The empiricists are likely to say that, in analyzing cases or history they draw from them certain generalizations to be applied as useful guides for future thought or action. As a matter of fact, Ernest Dale, after claiming to find "so little practical value" in the principles of management approach, drew similar generalizations or criteria from his study of a number of great managers.[4]

Judging from the emphasis of the empirical approach on the study of experience, it appears that the research and thought so engendered should actually help in verification of principles. But, to the extent that the empirical approach draws generalizations of what is fundamental from research into past cases, and finds it necessary to do this to avoid exchanging meaningless and structureless experience, the empirical approach tends to be much the same as any principles approach.

The Interpersonal Behavior Approach

This approach is based on the thesis that managing involves getting things done through people and, therefore, that the study of management should be centered on interpersonal relations. The writers and scholars in this school are heavily oriented toward individual psychology and, indeed, most are trained as psychologists. Their focus is on the individual and his or her motivations as a sociopsychological being. In this school are those who appear to emphasize human relations as an art which managers, even when foolishly trying to be amateur psychiatrists, can understand and practice. There are those who see the manager as a leader and who may even equate managership and leadership, thus in effect treating all "led" activities as "managed." Others have concentrated on motivations and on leadership and have cast important light on these subjects, which has been useful to managers.

That the study of human interactions, whether in the context of managing or elsewhere, is useful and important cannot be denied. But it can hardly be said that the field of interpersonal behavior encompasses all there is to management. It is entirely possible for all the managers of a company to understand psychology and its nuances and yet not be effective in managing. One major division of a very large American company did put its managers from top to bottom through sensitivity training (called by its critics "psychological striptease"), only to find that the managers had learned much about feelings but little about how to manage. Both research and practice are finding that we must go far beyond interpersonal relations to develop a useful science of management.

[4]Ibid., pp. 11, 26–28, 62–68.

This approach is closely related to the interpersonal behavior approach and is often confused or intertwined with it. It includes those who look on management as primarily a study in group behavior patterns. It varies all the way from the study of small groups with their cultural patterns to the behavioral composition of large groups in an enterprise. The latter approach is generally called a study of "organization behavior," and the term "organization" is taken to mean the system, or pattern, of any set of group relationships in a company, a government agency, a hospital, or any other kind of undertaking. But sometimes the term "organization" is used, as Barnard employed it, to apply to the "cooperation of two or more persons"[5] and even "formal organization" as an organization with conscious, deliberate purpose.[6] Argyris even uses the term "organization" to include "*all* the behavior of *all* the participants."[7]

This approach has made many noteworthy contributions to management. The recognition of the organized enterprise as a social organism—made up in turn of many social organisms within it, subject to all the attitudes, habits, pressures, and conflicts of the cultural environment of people—has been helpful to both the theorist and the practicing manager. Among other helpful aspects are the awareness of the institutional foundations of organization authority, the influence of informal organization,[8] and such social factors as those Wight Bakke has called "bonds of organization."[9] Likewise, many of Barnard's insights, such as seeing the necessity of furnishing incentives to get members of a group to contribute their efforts toward group objectives, have brought the power of sociological understanding into the realm of management practice.

Moreover, those scholars who have concentrated on studying the behavior of members and groups in an organization and who have carried this analysis farther to show how organization behavior can become increasingly effective[10] have contributed to the science and practice of

[5]C. I. Barnard, *The Functions of the Executive* (Cambridge, Mass.: Harvard University Press, 1938), p. 65.
[6]Ibid., p. 4.
[7]*Personality and Organization* (New York: Harper & Brothers, 1957), p. 239.
[8]For a discussion of the nature of informal organization, see chap. 12 below.
[9]*Bonds of Organization* (New York: Harper & Brothers, 1950). These "bonds," or devices of organization, are identified by Bakke as (1) the functional specifications system (a system of teamwork arising from job specifications and arrangements for association); (2) the status system (a vertical hierarchy of authority), (3) the communications system, (4) the reward and penalty system, and (5) the organization charter (ideas and means which give character and individuality to the organization).
[10]See for example, F. Luthans, *Organizational Behavior* (New York: McGraw-Hill Book Company, 1973); J. D. Thompson, *Organizations in Action* (New York: McGraw-Hill Book Company, 1967); J. A. Litterer, *The Analysis of Organizations* (New York: John Wiley & Sons, Inc., 1965); W. G. Scott, *Organization Theory* (Homewood, Ill.: Richard D. Irwin, Inc., 1967); A. G. Athos and R. E. Coffey, *Behavior in Organizations* (Englewood Cliffs, N.J.: Prentice-Hall, Inc., 1968); and N. Margulies and A. P. Raia, *Organizational Development* (New York: McGraw-Hill Book Company, 1972); E. F. Huse, *Organization Development and Change* (St. Paul: West Publishing Co., 1975).

management. Even though their writing is definitely behaviorally oriented and even though they often talk of "organizations" and "organizational behavior" in rather vague terms, many of these scientists are seeing that basic management techniques and theory, such as managing by objectives, fit into their scheme of things.

Basic sociology—analysis of social and group behavior in social systems—does have great value in the study of management. But one may ask whether this is all there is to management. Is the field of behavioral sociology coterminous with management? Or are sociology and the study of group behavior an important underpinning, like psychology?

The Cooperative Social Systems Approach

The interpersonal behavioral and group behavior approaches to the study of management have increasingly focused on the study of human relationships as cooperative social systems. This is due partly to the fairly recent vogue of looking at every kind of phenomenon from a systems point of view. Although earlier pioneers in the behavioral sciences showed recognition of systems approaches to human relationships, the real pioneer was the great sociologist Vilfredo Pareto, to whom brief attention was given in the previous chapter.

But Pareto's work has apparently influenced modern social systems writings primarily through his definite influence on Chester Barnard, whose concept of cooperative social systems was discussed in the previous chapter. Barnard may therefore be most accurately regarded as "the spiritual father" of the social systems school. It will be recalled that, in seeking fundamental explanations of the management process, this thoughtful executive developed a theory of cooperation based on human limitations and in turn a theory of cooperative systems. From this, Barnard extracted those systems elements which were only social, and he referred to these relationships as "organizations."

The Barnard concept of cooperative social systems pervades the work of many social scientists who have contributed to the social systems school. For example, Herbert Simon at one time defined human organizations as "systems of interdependent activity, encompassing at least several primary groups and usually characterized, at the level of consciousness of participants, by a high degree of rational direction of behavior toward ends that are objects of common knowledge."[11] Simon and many others in recent years have seemed to expand this concept to apply to any system of cooperative and purposeful group interrelationship or behavior and have given it the rather general title of "organization theory."

The cooperative social systems approach does have real significance

[11]"Comments on the Theory of Organizations," *American Political Science Review*, vol. 46, no. 4, p. 1130 (December 1952).

to management. All managers do, of course, operate in a social system. But we do not find managers in *all* kinds of cooperative social systems. One would hardly think of a mob or a riot gang as being managed, although it would probably have a leader. We would hardly think of a cooperating group of motorists sharing a main highway as being managed. Therefore, it can be concluded that this approach is broader than management and that in practice it tends to overlook many management concepts, principles, and techniques that are important to practicing managers.

The Sociotechnical Systems Approach

A fairly new school of management identifies itself as "the sociotechnical systems approach." This approach is generally credited to E. L. Trist of the British Tavistock Institute. In studies made by Trist and his associates of production systems in long-wall coal mining in England, it was discovered that, to solve social problems, it is not enough to look only at the cooperative social system.[12] Instead, as was found in studying the problems of productivity in coal mining, the technical system (methods and machines) and how it affects and is affected by the social system must be studied. In other words, personal attitudes and group behavior are influenced by the technical system in which people work. Thus the sociotechnical systems approach views an organization as two systems—a social system and a technological system—which necessarily interact. It is claimed that organizational effectiveness, and therefore managerial effectiveness, must depend on looking not only at people and their interactions but also at the technical environment in which they operate. This school of thought would study people and social systems, and also technological systems, to make sure they are harmonious and, if they are found to be inharmonious, to see whether changes in technology could result in a more effective operating unit.

Most of the work of the sociotechnical systems analysts has concentrated on factory or other production systems. It therefore tends to be greatly oriented toward industrial engineering. It has also tended to give rise to many studies and analyses of the influence of technology on various kinds of organizations.

Although this school of thought is fairly new, it is rising in importance in the management literature, and has made considerable contributions to the field of management, it is doubtful that many experienced and perceptive practicing managers would find the idea very

---

[12]See E. L. Trist and K. W. Bamforth, "Some Social and Psychological Consequences of the Long-Wall Method of Coal Getting," *Human Relations*, vol. 4, no. 1, pp. 3–38 (1951). See also F. E. Emery, *Characteristics of Socio-Technical Systems* (London: Tavistock Institute of Human Relations, Document 527, 1959), and A. K. Rice, *Productivity and Social Organization: The Ahmedabad Experiment* (London: Tavistock Publications, 1958).

new, that technology affects individuals, groups, and organizations. The technology of oil development, production, and refining has long been known by managers in petroleum companies to materially influence how they organize and manage their companies. Likewise, the technologies of the steamship, the railroad, and the airplane have long had a tremendous impact on the social systems and their managing in transportation companies. And few people in the last 60 years would be surprised that the technology of the automobile assembly line affects social systems and enterprise management.

At the same time, as in the case of any systems approach, even though the fundamentals may not be so startling and new, the purposeful and integrated analyses of the interactions of social and technical systems make valuable contributions to the knowledge underlying effective managing. It is an important area of inquiry and research underlying managing, but it is certainly not all there is to the field of management.

The Decision Theory Approach

This approach concentrates on rational decisions—the selection, from among possible alternatives, of a course of action. Decision theorists may deal with the decision itself, with the persons or organized group making the decision, or with an analysis of the decision process. Some limit themselves essentially to the economic rationale of the decision; others regard anything that happens in an enterprise as a subject for analysis; and still others expand decision theory to cover the psychological and sociological aspects and environments of decisions and decision makers.

The decision theory school is apparently an outgrowth of the theory of consumer's choice, with which economists have long been concerned. It has arisen out of such economic considerations as utility maximization, indifference curves, marginal utility, and economic behavior under risks and uncertainties. It is therefore no surprise that most of the members of this school are economic theorists. It is likewise no surprise to find the content of this theory oriented to model construction and mathematics.

The decision theory school has expanded its horizon considerably beyond the process of evaluating alternatives. That has become for many only a springboard for examination of the entire sphere of enterprise activity, including the nature of organization structure, the psychological and social reactions of individuals and groups, the development of basic information for decisions, and the analysis of values—particularly, value considerations with respect to goals. As one would expect, when the decision theorists start with study of the small, but central, area of decision making, they are led by this keyhole look at management to consider the entire field of enterprise operation and its environment. The result is that decision theory is no longer a neat and narrow concentration on decision, but becomes a broad view of the enterprise as a social system.

There are those who believe that, since management is characterized by decision making, the future development of management theory will use the decision as its central focus and that the rest of management theory will be hung on this structural center. This may occur, and certainly the study of the decision, the decision process, and the decision maker can be much extended. Nevertheless, one wonders whether the entire area of human knowledge could not also be built around this function. For, as most decision theorists recognize, the problem of choice is individual as well as organizational, and most of pure decision theory could be applied to the existence and thinking of a Robinson Crusoe as well as the United State Steel Corporation.

The decision theory approach overlooks the fact that there is much more to managing than making decisions and that, for most managers, the actual making of a decision is a fairly easy thing—if goals are clear, if the environment in which the decision will operate can be fairly accurately anticipated, if adequate information is available, if the organization structure provides a clear understanding of responsibility for decisions, if competent people are available to make decisions, and if many of the other prerequisites of effective managing are present.

The Systems Approach

During recent years, many scholars and writers in management have emphasized the systems approach to the study and analysis of management thought. They feel that this is the most effective means by which such thought can be organized, presented, and understood.

A system is essentially a set or assemblage of things interconnected, or interdependent, so as to form a complex unity. These things may be physical, as with the parts of an automobile engine; or they may be biological, as with components of the human body; or they may be theoretical, as with a well-integrated assemblage of concepts, principles, theory, and techniques in an area such as managing. All systems, except perhaps the universe, interact with and are influenced by their environments, although we define boundaries for them so that we can see them more clearly and analyze them.

The long use of systems theory and analyses in physical and biological sciences has given rise to a considerable body of systems knowledge. It comes as no surprise that systems theory has been found helpfully applicable to management theory and science. The authors have long emphasized that an arbitrary boundary of management knowledge—as the thought underlying the managerial job in terms of what managers do—is set for the field of management theory and science to make our subject "manageable," but this does not imply a closed-system approach to the subject. On the contrary, there are many interactions with the system environment. Thus, when managers plan, they have no choice but to take into account such external variables as markets, technology, social forces, laws, and regulations. When managers design an organizational system to provide an environment for performance, they cannot help but be influenced by the behavior patterns people bring to their jobs from the environment external to an enterprise.

Systems also play an important part within the area of managing itself. There are such systems as planning systems, organizational systems, and control systems. And within these we can perceive many subsystems, such as systems of delegation, network planning, and budgeting systems.

Intelligent and experienced practicing managers and many management writers with practical experience, accustomed as they are to seeing their problems and operations as a network of interrelated elements with daily interaction between environments inside or outside their companies or other enterprises, are often surprised to find that many writers regard the systems approach as something new. To be sure, conscious study of, and emphasis on, systems have forced many managers and scholars to consider more perceptively the various interacting elements affecting management theory and practice. But it can hardly be regarded as a new approach to management thought.

The Mathematical, or "Management Science," Approach

Some theorists see managing as primarily an exercise in mathematical processes, concepts, symbols, and models. Perhaps the most widely known of these are the operations researchers, who have given themselves the title "management scientists." The primary focus of this school is the mathematical model since, through this device, problems—whether managerial or other—can be expressed in basic relationships and, where a given goal is sought, the model can be expressed in terms which optimize that goal.

To be sure, the journal *Management Science*, published by the Institute of Management Sciences, carries on its cover the statement that the Institute has as its purpose to "identify, extend, and unify scientific knowledge pertaining to management." But, as judged by the articles published in this journal and by the hundreds of papers presented by members of the Institue at its many meetings over the world, the school's almost complete preoccupation has been with mathematical models and elegance in developing solutions to certain kinds of problems. Consequently, as many critics both inside and outside the ranks of the so-called management scientists have observed, the narrow mathematical focus can hardly be called an approach to a true management science.

No one interested in any scientific field can overlook the great usefulness of mathematical models and analyses. But it is difficult to see mathematics as a school of management any more than it is a separate school of chemistry, physics, or biology. Mathematics and mathematical models are, of course, a tool of analysis, not a school of thought.

One of the so-called approaches to management thought and practice which has tended to take management academicians by storm is the contingency, or situational, approach to management. Essentially, this approach emphasizes the fact that what managers do in practice depends upon a given set of circumstances, or the "situation." Contingency management is akin to situational management, and the two terms are often used synonymously. Some scholars distinguish between the two on the basis that, while situational management merely implies that what managers do depends on a given situation, contingency management implies an active interrelationship between the variables in a situation and the managerial solution devised. Thus, under a contingency approach, managers might look at an assembly line situation and conclude that a highly structured organization pattern would best fit and interact with it. According to some scholars, contingency theory takes into account not only given situations but also the influence of given solutions on behavior patterns of an enterprise. For example, an organization structured along the lines of operating functions, such as finance, engineering, production, and marketing, might be most suitable for a given situation; however, managers using this approach should consider that it may foster patterns of group loyalty to the function rather than to the company.

As pointed out earlier, by its very nature, managerial practice requires that managers take into account the realities of a given situation when they apply theory or techniques. It has never been and never will be the task of science and theory to prescribe what should be done in a given situation. As emphasized in Chapter 1, science and theory in management do not advocate the "best way"[13] to do things in every situation, any more than the sciences of astrophysics or mechanics tell an engineer how to design a single best instrument for all kinds of applications. How theory and science are applied in practice naturally depends upon the situation.

This is saying that there is science and there is art, that there is knowledge and there is practice. These are matters that any experienced manager has long known. One does not need much experience to understand that a corner grocery store could hardly be organized like General Motors, or that the technical realities of petroleum exploration,

---

[13]Many writers who have not read the so-called classicists in management carefully have come up with the inaccurate shibboleth that classical writers were prescribing the "one best way." It is true that Gilbreth in his study of bricklaying was searching for the one best way, but that was bricklaying and not managing. Even Fayol recognized this clearly when he said, "Principles are flexible and capable of adaptation to every need: it is a matter of knowing how to make use of them, which is a difficult art requiring intelligence, experience, decision and proportion." See *General and Industrial Management* (New York: Pitman Publishing Corporation, 1949), p. 19.

production, and refining make impracticable autonomously organized product divisions for gasoline, jet fuel, or lubricating oils.

The Managerial Roles Approach

Perhaps the newest approach to management theory to catch the attention of academics and practitioners alike is the managerial roles approach, popularized by Professor Henry Mintzberg of McGill University.[14] Essentially, this approach is to observe what managers actually do and from such observations come to conclusions as to what managerial activities (or roles) are. Although there have been many researchers who have studied the actual work of managers, from chief executives to line supervisors, Mintzberg has given this approach sharp visibility.

By systematically studying the activities of five chief executives in a variety of organizations, Mintzberg came to the conclusion that executives do not act out the classical classification of managerial functions—planning, organizing, coordinating, and controlling. Instead they engage in a variety of other activities.

From his research and the research of others who have studied what managers actually do, Mintzberg has come to the conclusion that managers really fill a series of ten roles. These are:

A Interpersonal roles
  1 The figurehead role (performing ceremonial and social duties as the organization's representative)
  2 The leader role
  3 The liaison role (particularly with outsiders)
B Informational roles
  1 Receiving information about the operation of an enterprise
  2 The disseminator role (passing information to subordinates)
  3 The spokesperson role (transmitting information outside the organization)
C Decision roles
  1. The entrepreneurial role
  2. The disturbance-handler role
  3. The resource allocator role
  4. The negotiator role (dealing with various persons and groups of persons)

Mintzberg refers to the usual way of classifying managerial functions as "folklore." As we will see in the following discussion on the operational theory approach, operational theorists have used such mana-

---

[14]Especially in his award-winning article "The Manager's Job: Folklore and Fact," *Harvard Business Review*, vol. 53, no. 4, pp. 49–61 (July–August 1975), and his book *Nature of Managerial Work* (New York: Harper & Row, Publishers, Incorporated, 1973).

gerial functions as planning, organizing, staffing, leading, and controlling as the means of classifying the growing body of managerial knowledge. While the functions are believed to be real, they are not intended to classify all actual activities of managers. If Mintzberg has intended to sweep away this first-level classification (a point he has denied in conversations with one of the authors), he can hardly be taken seriously. In the first place, the sample used in his research is far too small to arrive at so sweeping a conclusion. In the second place, in analyzing the actual activities of managers—from chief executive to supervisor—any research-er must realize that all managers do some work that is not purely managerial; one would expect even presidents of large companies to spend some of their time in public and stockholder relations, in raising money, perhaps in dealer relations, marketing, and so on.

In the third place, Mintzberg should realize that many of the activities he found are evidences of planning, organizing, staffing, leading, and controlling. For example, what is resource allocation but planning? Likewise, the entrepreneurial role is certainly an element of the whole area of planning. And the interpersonal roles are mainly evidences of leading. In addition, the informational roles can be fitted into a number of the functional areas.

Nevertheless, looking at what managers actually do can have consid-erable value. In analyzing activities, an effective manager might wish to ascertain how activities and techniques fall into the various fields of knowledge reflected by the basic functions of manager. However, the roles Mintzberg identifies appear to be inadequate. Where in them does one find such unquestionably important managerial activities as structuring organization, selecting and appraising managers, and determining major strategies? Omissions such as these make one wonder whether the executives in his sample were really effective managers. It certainly opens a serious question as to whether the managerial roles approach, at least as interpreted by Mintzberg, is an adequate one on which to base a practical, operational theory of management.

The Operational Approach

The operational approach to management theory and science attempts to draw together the pertinent knowledge of management by relating it to the functions of managers. Like other operational sciences, it endeavors to put together for the field of management the concepts, principles, theory, and techniques which underpin the actual practice of managing.

The operational approach recognizes that there is a central core of knowledge about managing which exists only in management; such matters as line and staff, departmentation, the limitations of the span of management, managerial appraisal, and various managerial control tech-niques involve concepts and theory found only where managing is involved. But, in addition, this approach is eclectic in that it draws on pertinent knowledge derived from other fields. These include such things as clinical study of managerial activities, problems, and solutions; applications of systems theory, decision theory, motivation and leadership findings and theory; individual and group behavior theory; and the application of mathematical modeling and techniques. All these subjects are applicable to some extent to other fields of science, such as certain of the physical and biological sciences. But our interest in them must necessarily be limited to managerial aspects and applications.

The nature of the operational approach can perhaps best be appreciated by reference to Figure 3.1. As this diagram shows, the operational-management school of thought includes a central core of science and theory unique to management plus knowledge eclectically drawn from various other schools and approaches. As the circle is intended to show, the operational approach is not interested in all the important knowledge

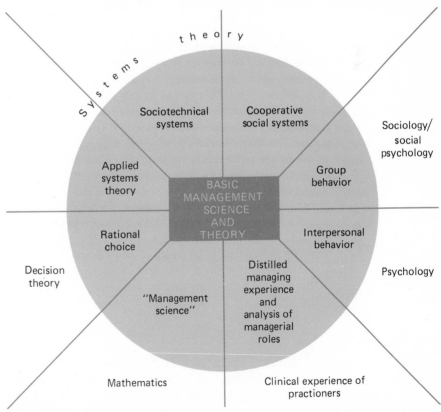

Figure 3.1 Management theory and science as a system drawing on other areas of organized knowledge. Operational-management theory and science are that part of the diagram enclosed in the circle. The figure shows how operational management theory and science have a core of basic science and theory and draw from other fields of knowledge pertinent to understanding management. Basic management is thus, in part, an eclectic science and theory.

in these various fields, but only that which is deemed most useful and relevant to managing.

IMPLEMENTING THE OPERATIONAL APPROACH

Certainly if a field of knowledge is not to become bogged down in a quagmire of misunderstandings, the first need is for definition of the field, not in sharp, detailed, and inflexible terms, but rather along lines which will give it fairly specific content. The authors have suggested that the field of management be defined in the light of the able and discerning manager's frame of reference, since theoretical science unrelated to the practical art it is designed to serve is unlikely to be productive.

Defining the Field of Management

In defining the field of management, care must be taken to distinguish between tools and content. Thus mathematics, operations research, accounting, economic theory, sociometry, and psychometrics, to mention a few, are *tools* of management, but they are not in themselves a part of its basic *content*. This is not to say that these fields are unimportant to the study and practice of management, for important contributions have come from them. Nor should we say that these fields may not further push back the frontiers of knowledge of management. But they should not be confused with the basic content of the management field.

In defining the field, it also seems imperative to draw some limits for purposes of analysis and research. If we were to call the entire cultural, biological, and physical universe the field of management, we could make no more progress than could have been made if chemistry or geology had undertaken to cover such a broad field rather than to carve out specific areas for inquiry. As pointed out above, one might say that the field of management should deal with an area of knowledge and inquiry that is manageable. In other words, knowledge of the field of management must be recognized as forming a part of, and interacting with, a larger universe of knowledge, but it need not encompass that universe.

Management Knowledge is the Operational Approach

In organizing any field of knowledge, we need a scheme of classification. Although various first-order classifications of knowledge could be used, the authors believe it is both realistic to managers and helpful to those understanding management to utilize the functions of managers— planning, organizing, staffing, leading, and controlling. Utilizing these functions as the major conceptual framework of this book, the second-order classification is to analyze all these functions essentially by asking basic questions concerning each one. These include: (1) What are the nature and purpose of each function? (2) What are the structural properties of each? (3) How is each undertaken? (4) What are the key concepts applicable to each? (5) What are the underlying principles and theory in each area? (6) What are the techniques most useful in each area? (7) What are the difficulties involved in applying basic knowledge in each? (8) How may an environment for performance be created in each?

The authors have found that even the newest ideas on management can be placed in this framework.

Because the functions of managers are used as the first-level classification of management knowledge, this approach is often called the "management process" school. Inasmuch as the management pioneer Henri Fayol first attempted to organize management knowledge around a similar set of functions, it is often called the "classical" or "traditional" school. Also, because operationalists generally believe that the fundamentals of management are universal and apply in all kinds of enterprises and in all kinds of cultures, the school is often referred to as "universalist."

But none of these appellations is strictly correct. As emphasized above, the operational school is intended to organize useful knowledge that is directly and importantly pertinent to the manager's task. It attempts to do so in a fundamental way and to separate managerial considerations from nonmanagerial ones. It also attempts to be eclectic by drawing useful and pertinent knowledge from any field that has something to offer.

The Basis of the Operational Approach

In summary, the approach used in this book is based largely on the fundamental beliefs that:

1 Managing is an operational process initially best dissected by analyzing the managerial functions.
2 If the knowledge of management is to be presented effectively, clear concepts are necessary, and the more these can be expressed in language generally used by intelligent practicing managers, the more meaningful they will be.
3 Experience with managing in a variety of enterprise situations can furnish grounds for distillation of basic truths—theory and principles—which have a clarifying and predictive value in understanding and improving practice.
4 Management techniques—ways of doing things in managing—not only belong in a basic science of management but also are important to practicing managers in their design and maintenance of an environment for performance of the persons for whom they are responsible.
5 Principles can become the focal points for useful research both to ascertain their validity and to improve their applicability.
6 Such principles, at least until disproved and certainly until sharp-

ened, can furnish essential elements of a useful theory of management.

7　Managing is an art, like medicine and engineering, that should rely on an underlying science—concepts, theory and principles, and techniques.

8　The elements of management science, such as basic principles, like those in other sciences, are nonetheless true even if a practitioner in a given situation chooses to ignore them and the costs involved in so doing or attempts to accomplish some other benefit that offsets the costs incurred. This is, of course, common in designing practical solutions to all kinds of problems.

9　While the total culture and the physical and biological universe variously affect the manager's environment, as they do in every other field of science and art, management science and theory need not encompass all knowledge in order to serve as a useful foundation of management practice.

THE FUNCTIONS OF THE MANAGER

In classifying the functions of the manager, one must distinguish clearly those of enterprise-function operation, such as selling, manufacturing, accounting, engineering, and purchasing. These differ from one enterprise to another, but the basic tasks of the manager, as a manager, are common to all.

Although the development of a theory and science of management suffers from disagreement among scholars and managers as to the classification of managerial functions, a general pattern of practice and terminology has emerged. Adopted here and used by managers in many fields, this pattern avoids artificial terminology. Thus students and managers need not learn new definitions—rather, they may use common terms with greater precision. It is also hoped that managers, using common terms with ordinary meanings, will be encouraged to adopt an increasingly scientific approach to their important task.

Although the authors believe that they have adopted the most useful method of classifying managerial functions, at least for purposes of classifying knowledge, in practice it is not always possible to place all managerial activities neatly into these categories, since the functions tend to coalesce. However, this classification is a helpful and realistic tool for analysis and understanding.

Some authorities suggest "representation" as a distinct management function. They have in mind managers who represent their firm in trade association and government relationships, with a view to modifying the external environment or committing the firm to a contractual obligation, or managers who represent their division or department in committee meetings which may affect the internal environment. There is also the larger problem of the "corporate image," which is influenced by the behavior of all employees, whether managerial or not. The authors of this book have excluded representation as a separate function, partly because it appears to be a complex made up largely of communication and of the exercise of authority (included in leading, and organizing, respectively) and partly because nonmanagers often represent an enterprise and exert influence on the corporate image.

Occasionally, scholars concern themselves about the order in which the managerial functions should be undertaken. Theoretically, planning comes first, and organizing, staffing, leading, and controlling follow. But according to this logic, an enterprise carries out only one master plan, each part of which, once completed, never has to be revised or modified. This conception is unrealistic. In practice, managers oversee many plans in various stages of execution; they are at least likely to be engaged in solving a control problem or a motivation problem at any moment in time. They move easily from one function to another and devote their attention to the most pressing issues. Managing, after all, is a systematic network and not a sequentially undertaken set of duties.

Moreover, the question of what managers actually do is really secondary to what makes an acceptable and clear first breakdown of management knowledge. As was pointed out earlier, our major concern is to organize knowledge with respect to managing, as an indispensable approach to developing a science of management. The authors believe that by utilizing the functions of managers at this first step, a logical start can be made in setting up some "pigeonholes" for classifying knowledge, recognizing, of course, that in management as in all areas of knowledge, the classification is not airtight and that there are interlocking and even overlapping elements.

Planning

Planning involves selecting objectives—and the strategies, policies, programs, and procedures for achieving them—either for the entire enterprise or for any organized part thereof. Planning is, of course, decision making, since it involves selecting from among alternatives. There are, for example, policies relating to authority, prices, and competition; programs of production, management succession, and internal audit; and procedures requiring a specific method of handling paper, products, and people.

Considerable confusion has arisen about who should plan and when. Ever since the work of F. W. Taylor, executives have toyed with separating planning from performance. The responsibility for planning cannot be completely separated from managerial performance because all managers plan, whether they are at the top, middle, or bottom of the organization structure. If, however, planning is undertaken as an advisory service to the manager in charge of performance, this small degree of separation is often highly productive.

Organizing involves the establishment of an intentional structure of roles through determination of the activities required to achieve the goals of an enterprise and each part of it, the grouping of these activities, the assignment of such groups of activities to a manager, the delegation of authority to carry them out, and provision for coordination of authority and informational relationships horizontally and vertically in the organization structure. Sometimes all these factors are included in the term "organization structure"; sometimes they are referred to as "managerial authority relationships." In any case, it is the totality of such activities and authority relationships that constitutes the organizing function.

There are several implications of this concept of organizing. In the first place, the one-man or one-woman business cannot possibly be organized. Since the owner or operator performs all the business functions, no authority is delegated. However, let the owner split off the buying activities, assign them to a subordinate, and provide coordination of activity between the buyer and himself, and the enterprise will have become organized.

A second implication is that all managers, when they decide to organize an enterprise or a department, are involved basically in the same task. Whether they be presidents, sales managers, controllers, or office managers, they will reflect the goals toward which they are striving by identifying and grouping activities essential for their accomplishment, assigning some of them to subordinates, delegating the requisite authority to accomplish results, and providing for their coordination.

The organization structure is, of course, not an end in itself but a tool for accomplishing enterprise objectives. Efficient organization will contribute to the success of the enterprise, and for this reason the application of principles is very important. But striving for a "pretty" structure, without regard for its precise use, is futile. The organization structure must fit the task—not vice versa—and must reflect any compromises and limitations imposed on the manager by people, since organizational roles must be staffed. It must also, of course, reflect the environment of the enterprise.

Staffing

Staffing involves filling, and keeping filled, the positions provided for by the organization structure. It thus necessitates defining work-force requirements for the job to be done, and it includes inventorying, appraising, and selecting candidates for positions; compensating; and training or otherwise developing both candidates and incumbents to accomplish their tasks effectively. Since this book is devoted to managers, the staffing function will be dealt with primarily as it concerns managers rather than nonmanagers, but the needs and principles involved apply in most principles involved apply in most instances to both groups. This is in no way meant to imply that the first-level supervisor is not a manager.

Leading

This function has to do with the predominantly interpersonal aspect of managing. All managers would agree that their most important problems arise from people, their desires, and attitudes, their behavior as individuals and in groups, and the need for effective managers also to be effective leaders. Since leadership implies followership and people tend to follow those in whom they see a means of satisfying their own needs, wishes, and desires, it is understandable that this area of management involves motivation, leadership styles and approaches and effective communications.

Controlling

Controlling is the measuring and correcting of *activities* of subordinates to assure that events conform to plans. Thus it measures performance against goals and plans, shows where negative deviations exist, and, by putting in motion actions to correct deviations, helps assure accomplishment of plans. Although planning must precede controlling, plans are not self-achieving. The plan guides managers in use of resources to accomplish specific goals. Then activities are monitored to determine whether they conform to planned action.

In the past, control activities generally related to the measurement of objective achievement. Such control devices as the budget for controllable expense, inspection records, and the record of labor-hours lost are generally familiar. Each has the characteristic of objective counting; each shows whether plans are working out. If abnormal deviations persist, correction is indicated. But what is corrected? Activities through persons. Nothing can be done about reducing scrap, buying according to specifications, or handling sales returns until the personal responsibility for deviations has been determined. Compelling events to conform to plans means locating the persons who are responsible for negative deviations from planned action and then taking the necessary steps to improve performance. Thus, things are controlled by controlling what people do.

Coordination, the Essence of Managership

Many authorities consider coordination to be a separate function of the manager. It seems more accurate, however, to regard it as the essence of managership, for the achievement of harmony of individual efforts toward the accomplishment of group goals is the purpose of management. Each of the managerial functions is an exercise in coordination.

The necessity for synchronizing individual action arises out of differences in opinion as to how group goals can be reached or how individual and group objectives can be harmonized. Even in the case of a church or a fraternal organization, individuals often interpret similar interests in different ways, and their efforts toward mutual goals do not automatically mesh with the efforts of others. It thus becomes the central task of the manager to reconcile differences in approach, timing, effort, or interest and to harmonize cooperative and individual goals.

The best coordination occurs when individuals see how their jobs contribute to the dominant goals of the enterprise. This implies knowledge and understanding of enterprise objectives, not just on the part of a few at the top, but by everyone throughout the enterprise. If, for example, managers are not sure whether the basic goal of their firm is profit, quality, advanced techniques, or customer service, they cannot coordinate their efforts to achieve the true objective. Each would be guided by his or her own ideas of what is in the interest of the firm or, without any such conviction, might work for self-aggrandizement. To avoid such splintering efforts, the dominant goal of the enterprise should be clearly defined and communicated to everyone concerned. And, naturally, goals of subordinate departments should be designed to contribute maximally to enterprise goals.

THE MANAGEMENT THEORY JUNGLE: POSITIVE TENDENCIES TOWARD CONVERGENCE OF THEORIES

As can be seen from the discussion above of the approaches to management theory and science, there is evidence that the management theory jungle not only continues to flourish but gets more dense, with nearly twice as many schools or approaches as were found 19 years ago. It is no wonder that useful operational-management theory and science have been so tardy in arriving. It is no wonder that we still do not have a clear notion of the scientific underpinnings of managing, nor have we been able to identify clearly what we mean by competent managers.

The varying approaches, each with its own gurus, each with its own semantics, and each with a fierce pride to protect the concepts and techniques of the approach from attack or change, make the theory and science of management extremely difficult for the intelligent practitioner to understand and utilize. If the continuing jungle were only an evidence of competing academic thought and research, it would not much matter. But when it retards the development of a useful theory and science and confuses practicing managers, the problem becomes serious. Effective managing at all levels and in all kinds of enterprises is too important to any society to allow it to fail through lack of available and understandable knowledge.

At the same time, there are signs indicating tendencies for the various schools of thought to coalesce. While the convergence is by no means complete, hope does exist that, as scholars and writers become more familiar with what managers really do and the situations in which they act, more and more of these schools or approaches will adopt, and even expand, the basic thinking and concepts of the operational school of management.

Realizing that these are only indications and signs along the road to a more unified and operational theory of management, and that there is much more of this road to travel, let us briefly examine some of these tendencies toward convergence.

Greater Emphasis on Distillation of Basics within the Empirical Approach

In reviewing the many programs utilizing cases as a means of educating managers, there appears to be much greater emphasis on distilling fundamentals than there was two decades ago. Likewise, in the field of business policy, by which term these case approaches have tended to be known, there has been increased emphasis in teaching and research on going beyond recounting what happened in a given situation to analyzing the underlying causes for what happened. One major result of all this has been a new emphasis on strategy and strategic planning. This has led many empiricists to come up with distilled knowledge that fits neatly into the operational theorist's classification of planning.

Recognizing that Systems Thinking Is Not a Separate Approach

When systems theory was introduced into the management field some two decades ago, it was hailed by many as being a new way of analyzing and classifying management knowledge. But in recent years, as people have come to understand systems theory *and* the job of managing better, two things have become increasingly clear: first, that in its essentials there is little new about systems theory and second, that practicing managers as well as the operational theorists had been utilizing its basics (although not always using the jargon) for a number of years. Nonetheless, as those in the field of operational theory have more consciously and clearly utilized the concepts and theory of systems, their attempts at developing a scientific field have been improved.

Recognizing that Situational and Contingency Approaches Are Not New or Separate Approaches to the Organization of Management Knowledge

Although perceptive and intelligent managers have not been surprised, nor have many management theorists, it is now clear that the concepts of situational or contingency management are merely a way of distinguishing between science and art—knowledge and practice. As pointed out in Chapter 1 and earlier in this chapter, these are two different things, albeit mutually complementary. Those writers and scholars who have emphasized situational or contingency approaches have done the field of management theory and practice a great service by stressing that what the intelligent manager actually does depends on the realities of a situation. But this has long been true of the *application* of any science.

That contingency theory is really "application in the light of a situation" has been increasingly recognized. This is evidenced by a recent statement of one of the founders of contingency theory, Professor Jay Lorsch of Harvard, who admitted that his use of the term "contingency" was "misleading."[15] Even he appeared to recognize that an operational-management theorist would necessarily become a situationalist when it came to applying management concepts, principles, and techniques.

Finding that "Organization Theory" Is Too Broad an Approach

Largely because of the influence of Chester Barnard and his broad concept of "organization" as referring to almost any kind of interpersonal relationships, it has become customary, particularly in academic circles, to use the term "organization theory" to refer to theory pertaining to almost any kind of interpersonal relationship. While many scholars attempted to make this field equal to management theory, it is now fairly well agreed that managing is a narrower activity and that management theory pertains only to theory related to managing. Management theory is often thought of as being a subset of organization theory, and it is now fairly well agreed that the general concept of organization theory is too broad.

This is a hopeful sign in clearing away some of the underbrush of the jungle.

The New Understanding of Motivation

As we will see in Chapter 23, the more recent researches into motivation of people in organizational settings has tended to emphasize the importance of the organizational climate in curbing or arousing motives. The oversimplified explanations of motives by Maslow and Herzberg may identify human needs fairly well, but much more emphasis must be given to rewards and expectations of rewards. These, along with a climate which arouses and supports motivation, depend to a very great extent on the nature of managing in an organization.

The interaction between motivation and organizational climate not only underscores the systems aspects of motivation but also emphasizes how motivation depends on what managers do in setting and maintaining an environment for performance. These researches move the problem of motivation from a purely behavioral matter to one closely related to and dependent upon what managers do. The theory of motivation, then, fits

---

[15]"Organization Design: A Situational Perspective," *Organizational Dynamics*, vol. 6, no. 2, pp. 2–14, at p. 2 (Autumn 1977).

nicely into the operational approach to management theory and science.

The Merging of Motivation and Leadership Theory

Another interesting sign that we may be moving toward a unified operational theory of management is the way that research and analysis have tended to merge motivation and leadership theory. As will be seen in Chapters 23 and 24, especially in recent years leadership research and theory have tended to emphasize the rather elementary propositions that the job of leaders is to know and appeal to things that motivate people and to recognize the simple truth that people tend to follow those in whom they see a means of satisfying their own desires. Thus, explanations of leadership have been increasingly related to motivation.

The blending of motivation and leadership theories has also emphasized the importance of organization climate and styles of leaders. Most recent studies and theories tend to underscore the importance of making managers effective leaders. Implied by most recent research and theory is the clear message that effective leaders design a system that takes into account the expectancies of subordinates, the variability of motives between individuals, and, from time to time, situational factors, the need for clarity of role definition, interpersonal relations, and types of rewards.

Knowledgeable and effective managers do exactly these things when they design a climate for performance, when goals and means of achieving them are planned, when organizational roles are defined and well structured, when roles are intelligently staffed, and when control techniques and information are designed to make control by self-control possible. In other words, leadership theory and research are, like motivation, fitting neatly into the scheme of operational-management theory, rather than going off as a separate branch of theory.

The New Managerially Oriented "Organization Development"

Both "organization development" and the field ordinarily referred to as "organization behavior" have grown out of the interpersonal and group behavior approaches to management. For a while, it seemed that these fields were far away and separated from operational-management theory. But many specialists in these areas are now beginning to see that basic management theory and techniques, such as managing by objectives and clarifying organization structure, fit well into their programs of behavioral intervention.

Fortunately, a review of the latest organization behavior books indicates that some authors in this field are beginning to understand that behavioral elements in group operations must be more closely integrated with organizational structure design, staffing, planning, and control. In so doing, certain members of this behavioral school of thought are beginning to see the deficiencies of the narrowness of their approach. This is a hopeful sign. It is a recognition that analysis of individual and group behavior, at least in managed situations, easily and logically falls into place in the scheme of operational-management theory.

The Impact of Technology: Researching an Old Problem

That technology has an important impact on organizational structure, behavior patterns, and other aspects of managing has been recognized by intelligent practitioners for many years. However, primarily among academic researchers, there has seemed to be in recent years a "discovery" that the impact of technology is important and real. To be sure, some of this research has been helpful to managers, especially that developed by the sociotechnical school of management. Also, while perceptive managers have known for many years that technology has important impacts, some of this research has tended to clarify and give special meaning to this impact.

Defections among "Management Scientists"

It will be recalled that in the discussion of schools of, or approaches to, management above, one of them is identified as the mathematical, or "management science," approach. The reader has also undoubtedly noted that "management science" was put in quotation marks. This was done because this group does not really deal with a total science of management, but rather with mathematical models, symbols, and elegance.

There are clear signs of defectors among the so-called management scientists, who realize that their interests go far beyond the use of mathematics, models, and the computer. These defectors exist primarily in the ranks of operations researchers in industry and government, where they are faced daily with practical management problems. A small but increasing number of academics are also coming to this realization. In fact, one of the leading and most respected academics, widely regarded as one of the pioneers in operations research, Professor C. West Churchman (in conversations with one of the authors), has been highly critical of the excessive absorption with models and mathematics and, for this reason, has even resigned from the Operations Research Society.

There is no doubt that operations research and similar mathematical and modeling techniques fit nicely in the planning and controlling areas of operational-management theory and science. Most operational-management theorists recognize this. All that is really needed is for the few "management science" defectors to become a torrent, moving their expertise and research to the service of a practical and useful management science.

Clarifying Semantics: Some Hopeful Signs

One of the greatest obstacles to disentangling the jungle has been the problem of semantics. Those writing and lecturing on management and related fields have tended to use common terms in different ways. This is exemplified by the variety of meanings given to such terms as "organization," "line and staff," "authority," "responsibility," and "policies," to mention a few. While this semantics swamp still exists and we are a long way from general acceptance of meanings of key terms and concepts, there are some hopeful signs on the horizon.

It has become rather common for the leading management texts to include a glossary of key terms and concepts, and an increasing number of them are beginning to show some commonality of meaning. Of interest also is the fact that the Fellows of the International Academy of Management, comprising some 180 management scholars and leaders from thirty-two countries of the world, have responded to the demands of members and have undertaken to develop a glossary of management concepts and terms, to be published in a number of languages and given wide circulation in many countries of the world.

Although it is too early even to hope, it does appear that we may be moving in the direction necessary for the development of a science—the acceptance of clear definitions for key terms and concepts.

FOR DISCUSSION

1. Do the various approaches to the analysis of management represent a management theory jungle, or do they simply represent an intellectual division of labor?
2. Taking each approach, other than the operational approach, identify its major elements and probable biases and show how each can be integrated into an operational approach to management.
3. To what extent is the "management science" approach truly management science?
4. Why and how is the problem of semantics so important in explaining the confusion arising from the various approaches to management? Taking any four books or articles on management that you like, ascertain what approach to management each author reflects and the extent of semantic differences between them.
5. By using the functions of the manager as a first-order classification of management knowledge, do the authors of this book consequently take a closed system approach to management?
6. How are the various functions of managers, as defined in this chapter, both independent and interdependent?
7. Why has coordination not been included as one of the major functions of the manager?
8. As you read the following chapters of this book, watch for signs of convergence of the various approaches to management theory and science. Have the authors taken too extreme a position by referring to the various approaches as the "management theory jungle"?

chapter 4 Managers and Their External Environment

MAJOR CHAPTER OBJECTIVES

1 To identify the major areas of the external environment that influence what managers do.

2 To discuss each of these external areas under the classification of economic, technological, social, political-legal, and ethical factors and to indicate how they affect managerial practice.

3 To analyze the nature of the social responsibility of managers.

4 To describe the nature and major problems of the social audit.

Although this book is designed to draw its primary boundary around the conceptual system we refer to as "management"—the knowledge underlying managerial tasks and practices—it has been made completely clear in earlier chapters that neither the field of management nor the practice of managing can be looked upon as a closed system. All managers must interact with the many environments within their departments and within the enterprise in which they operate. They must also constantly respond to and interact with a complex environment external to their enterprise.

Much of this book deals with interaction with environment inside the enterprise, but in many instances the effective manager must also deal with the outside environment. Every time managers plan, they take into account the needs and desires of members of society outside the organization, as well as needs for material and human resources, technology, and other requirements in the external environment. They do likewise to some degree with almost every other kind of managerial activity.

All managers, whether they operate in a business, a government agency, a church, a charitable foundation, or a university, must, in varying degrees, take into account the elements and forces of their external environment. While they may be able to do little or nothing to change these forces, they have no alternative but to respond to them. They must identify, evaluate, and react to the forces external to the enterprise that may affect its operations.

Later, especially in the chapters on planning, attention will be given more precisely to how managers take their environment into account. At this point, only the nature and major elements of these environments will be discussed. Obviously, if managers are to respond to their environment, they should attempt to forecast it, simply because it takes time to make changes in any organization. While managers can react when changes are apparent, it is far better that they be in a position to anticipate them. Business managers and, to a certain extent, government managers have long forecasted their economic environment so that they will be prepared for economic changes when they occur. A few but rapidly increasing number of business and other organizations have attempted to forecast their technological environment. Very few business or other organizations, however, have done much about forecasting their social, political, or ethical environment.

The relationships between the enterprise and its environment have been examined in several ways. First, the enterprise can be viewed as importing various kinds of inputs, such as human, capital, managerial, and technical. These inputs are then transformed to produce outputs, such as services and profits. A second approach in the study of the relationships between the enterprise and society is to focus on the demands and legitimate rights of different claimants, such as employees, consumers, suppliers, stockholders, governments, and the community. A third approach is to view the enterprise as operating in an external environment of opportunities and constraints, which can be classified into economic, technological, social-cultural, political, and ethical.

Any single approach by itself is insufficient. The three approaches are not inconsistent with each other; they are complementary. Thus business enterprises—and any other enterprises for that matter—are a part of a larger system. This means that events external to the firm affect all organizations. Conversely, the operations of organizations—business or nonbusiness—affect the external environment. The result is a delicate and complex relationship between business and nonbusiness enterprises and society. This chapter and the next one deal with these relationships.

THE EXTERNAL ENVIRONMENT: ECONOMIC

It is sometimes thought that the economic environment is of concern only to businesses whose socially approved mission is the production and distribution of goods and services that people want and can pay for. But it is also of the greatest importance to other types of organized enterprises. A government agency takes resources, usually from taxpayers, and provides services desired by the public. A church takes contributions from members and serves their religious and social needs. A university takes resource inputs from taxpayers, students, and contributors of various kinds and transforms these into educational and research services.

Capital

Almost every kind of organization needs capital—machinery, buildings, inventories of goods, office equipment, tools of all kinds, and cash. Some of this may be produced by the organization itself, as happens when a business builds its own machinery or a church group prepares a church supper. Cash resources may also be generated within an organization to buy capital items outside, as happens when business profits are used for this purpose or when a university collects parking fees to build parking structures. But organized enterprises are usually dependent for capital requirements on various suppliers, whose job it is to produce the many materials and other items of capital that an organization requires for its operation.

This means that all kinds of operations are dependent on the availability and prices of needed capital items. Societies vary considerably in this availability. Railroad facilities are in short supply in Brazil but in plentiful supply in the United States and the countries of Western Europe. Capital, by way of fertilizers and advanced farm machines, may be scarce and hamper farm productivity in rural Russia, but may be plentiful in rural America.

Another important input from the economic environment is the availability, quality, and price of labor. In some societies, untrained common labor may be plentiful, while highly trained labor may be in short supply. Engineers may be scarce at one time and plentiful at another, as has occurred in the ups and downs of the defense and space operations of the United States. People with doctorates in many fields may be plentiful in one society, as they were in the 1970s for many academic disciplines in the United States, but be in short supply in another, as was the case in Australia at the same time.

The price of labor is also an extremely important economic input to an enterprise. The relatively high wages in the United States and many European countries often create cost problems for producers in these countries. Many items can be produced at a lower cost in countries such as Mexico and Taiwan. It is not surprising that many products requiring high labor input are often made outside the United States.

Price Levels

The input side of an enterprise is clearly affected by price-level changes. If the prices go up fairly rapidly, as happened in most parts of the world in the 1970s, the turbulence created in the economic environment on both the input and output sides can be severe. Inflation not only upsets businesses but also has highly disturbing influences on every kind of organization through its effects on costs of labor, material, and other items.

Productivity

One cannot look merely at the impact of the availability and price of capital for enterprises; one also has to consider productivity. One of the reasons the United States has been able to compete in the world market for many years has been productivity. But there is reason for concern. A recent report from the Bureau of Labor Statistics showed the United States trailing virtually all industrialized nations in the percentage rise indexes of manufacturing output per hour. Specifically, the output per hour from 1967 (index 100) to 1975 increased 88.6 percent in Belgium, 81.7 percent in Japan, 78.0 percent in the Netherlands, 77.3 percent in Denmark, 53.3 percent in Germany, 52.8 percent in Sweden, 48.9 percent in France, 44.8 percent in Switzerland, 34.4 percent in Canada, 24.3 percent in the United Kingdom, and only 14.9 percent in the United States.[1] Surely this

---

[1] Data for all employed persons in the United States and Canada; wage earners only in Switzerland; and all employees in the other countries. Source: *News,* U.S. Department of Labor, Bureau of Labor Statistics, USDL—77-623; July 15, 1977. See also "How to Promote Productivity," *Business Week,* pp. 146–151 (July 24, 1978).

is a concern, but at the same time a challenge to increase effectiveness and efficiency of managers and the enterprise. Meeting this challenge is the aim of this book.

There are many ways to increase productivity. One approach, for example, is goal-oriented management with a focus on increased involvement, effective training, and open communication.[2] But productivity is also dependent on other factors, such as the state of technology, a topic that is discussed later.

Entrepreneurs and Managers

Another major economic input is the availability of high-quality entrepreneurs and managers. We usually think of an entrepreneur as existing only in business—as a person who sees a business opportunity, obtains the needed capital, knows how to put together an operation successfully, and has the willingness to take a personal risk of success or failure. But in a real sense we see entrepreneurial ability also as an important input in most nonbusiness operations. We have seen such entrepreneurs as Robert Gordon Sproul, for example, who was largely responsible for the growth of the University of California from a small college into a large university. We can think of Joseph Smith and Brigham Young, who founded the Mormon Church, and of President Franklin D. Roosevelt, who started the huge expansion of the federal government in the 1930s in response to his perception of human and social needs.

The availability of managers is critical for the success of an enterprise. In fact, it is frequently noted that the shortage of qualified managerial talent is a major constraint that keeps any enterprise from growing at a desired rate. Although this whole book aims at increasing managerial and personal competency, special attention is given to the development and training of managers in the section on staffing.

Government Fiscal and Tax Policy

Another important input to the enterprise is the nature of governmental fiscal and tax policies. Although these are, strictly speaking, aspects of the political environment, their economic impact on all enterprises is tremendous. Government control of the availability of credit through fiscal policy has considerable impact not only on business but also on most nonbusiness operations. Similarly, government tax policy affects every segment of our society. The way taxes are levied is also important, not only to business but to people generally. For example, if taxes on business profits are too high, the incentive to go into business or stay in it

---

[2]H. Weihrich, "What to Do about the Productivity Crisis," *The Harvest* (Productivity Institute, College of Business Administration, Arizona State University), vol. 2, no. 4, pp. 1–2 (April 1978).

tends to drop, and investors will look elsewhere to invest their capital. If taxes are levied on sales, prices will rise and people will tend to buy less. If heavy taxes are placed on real estate, people may find it too expensive to own a house and may go to cheaper and less comfortable living quarters.

Customers

One of the most important factors for success of the enterprise is customers. Without them, a business cannot exist. But to capture customers, a business must try to find out what people want and will buy. Nonbusiness enterprises have "customers" also. Universities and colleges have students and alumni to satisfy. Similarly, police, fire, and government health departments must serve the public.

To be sure, the expectations and demands of the various publics served by organized enterprises are influenced by noneconomic as well as economic factors in the environment. The principal ones are the attitudes, desires, and expectations of people, many of which arise from cultural patterns in the social environment. Nevertheless, economic factors still play a major role. People want as much as possible for the money, whether it goes to businesses, government, or charitable organizations.

It is not always easy to know what people want. For one thing, tastes change, as the automobile manufacturers found out some years ago when the once-despised Volkswagen Beetle became popular in the American market. But its success was also limited. Tastes (but also government regulations) changed again and gave rise to Volkswagen's popular Rabbit.

Another factor in the market is the appearance of substitute products. For example, publishers of magazines saw their market eroded when advertisers shifted to television. Also, people like different products. Some want a power boat, others want a sailboat, and still others do not want a boat at all. The needs of industrial buyers change as their products change, as new processes are developed, and as different equipment and materials come on the market. In the long run, any enterprise (at least in our society) has to serve the different and changing needs of customers. To do otherwise is a sure road to enterprise failure.

THE EXTERNAL ENVIRONMENT: TECHNOLOGICAL

One of the most pervasive factors in the environment is technology. It is science which provides the knowledge and it is technology that uses it. The term "technology" refers to the sum total of knowledge we have of ways to do things. It includes inventions, it includes techniques, and it includes the vast store of organized knowledge about everything from aerodynamics to zoology. But its main influence is on ways of doing things, on how we design, produce, distribute, and sell goods as well as services.

The impact of technology is seen in new products, new machines, new tools, new materials, and new services. A few of the benefits from technology are greater productivity, higher living standards, more leisure time, and a greater variety of products. Consider, for example, the great variety of cars available: subcompacts, compacts, intermediates, full-size, sports, and specialty cars. Consider also the many body styles, the various colors, and the many options in engine (sizes), transmissions (manual, automatic), and brakes (mechanical, power). In addition, one may select tinted glass, power windows, power steering, automatic speed control, air conditioning, special mirrors, vinyl roof, sun roof, and the various interior and exterior trim strips.

But the benefits of technology must be weighed against the problems associated with technological developments, such as traffic jams, polluted air and water, shortage of energy, and the loss of privacy through the application of computer technology. What is needed is a balanced approach that takes advantage of technology and at the same time minimizes some of the undesirable side effects.

Categories of Technological Change

In a general way, we know that technology has had a wide and pervasive impact, so much so that we refer to various developments as "revolutions," such as the industrial revolution of the eighteenth century or the computer revolution of the latter half of the twentieth century. But we do not always appreciate the precise developments that make up these revolutions. To better comprehend the wide scope of technological change, the following categories and examples are helpful:

1 Increased ability to master time and distance for the movement of freight and passengers: railroads, automobiles and trucks, airplanes, space vehicles (to some extent)
2 Increased ability to generate, store, transport, and distribute energy: electricity, nuclear power, the laser
3 Increased ability to design new materials and change the properties of others so that they better serve needs: steel alloys, synthetic fibers, plastics, new drugs
4 Mechanization or automation of physical processes: the large number of labor-saving devices, from Hargreaves's spinning jenny in 1770 to the largely automatic San Francisco subway system of 1976
5 Mechanization or automation of certain mental processes: the computer, which greatly expands our ability to store, manipulate, select, and supply the data
6 Extension of human ability to sense things: radar, the electron microscope, night-vision instruments
7 Increased understanding of individual and group behavior and how to deal with it: psychological bases of motivation, group behavior patterns, improved managerial techniques

8   Increased understanding of diseases and their treatment; inoculations for polio, kidney transplants, antibiotic treatment of infections

The Impact of Technology on Management

Technology always has had an important impact on managerial practice. It is a vital element in planning, both in the design of products and services and in their development, production, and distribution. Technology always has affected organization structure. For example, research conducted by Joan Woodward of 100 British manufacturing plants indicates that organization structure tends to vary with the types of technology employed. In other words, certain structures appear to be more successful with certain kinds of technology.[3] No one should be surprised that oil producing and refining companies are organized in a way that reflects the special technologies of their operations. One should expect an automobile company, with its engine, parts, and body plants and assembly lines to be organized differently from the way railroads and airlines, with their different technologies, are organized. One would also expect the staffing of organizations and leadership to vary, to some exent at least, with technology. Certainly intelligent managers have always recognized this factor.

THE EXTERNAL ENVIRONMENT: SOCIAL

In any classification of environmental elements impacting on a manager, it is extremely difficult to separate, even for discussion purposes, the social, political, and ethical environments. Conceptually, however, it is possible. The *social* environment is made up of the attitudes, desires, expectations, degrees of intelligence and education, beliefs, and customs of people in a given group or society. The *political* environment is primarily that complex of laws, regulations, and government agencies and their actions which affects all kinds of enterprises, often to a varying degree. The *ethical* environment—which could well be included as an element in the social environment—includes sets of generally accepted and practiced standards of personal conduct. These standards may or may not be codified by law, but for any group to which they are meant to apply, they sometimes have virtually the force of law.

The interweaving complexity of these environmental elements makes their study and comprehension exceptionally difficult. To forecast them so that a manager can anticipate and prepare for changes is even more difficult. Social desires, expectations, and pressures give rise to laws and standards of ethics. Social forces, including ethics, normally arise before laws are passed, since the legislative process is notably reactive in

[3]J. Woodward, *Industrial Organization: Theory and Practice* (London: Oxford University Press, 1965).

the sense that it acts when a crisis is at hand, but seldom before. Furthermore, existing laws and regulations, which are so numerous and complex that even the best-trained lawyers cannot know all of them (though they would probably know where to find them), often are brought to our attention in surprising and unusual ways. For example, until the Watergate investigation of 1974, one almost never heard of "obstruction of justice," and few persons knew of it as a felonious crime.

Social Attitudes, Beliefs, and Values

Managers of various enterprises have been critized for not being responsive to the social attitudes, beliefs, and values of particular individuals, groups, or societies. But attitudes and values are different for workers and employers, rich and poor people, college students and alumni, accountants and engineers, Californians and New Yorkers. This variety of values makes it difficult for managers to design an environment conducive to performance and satisfaction. It is even more difficult to respond to these forces when they are outside the enterprise. Yet managers have no choice but to take them into account in their decision making.

For example, in Great Britain until recent years, business ownership was regarded as highly respectable, but professional managership was not nearly so prestigious. In certain Latin countries, what people from northern Europe and the United States would think of as a bribe to obtain a business contract is regarded as a fair service charge. It is clear that any manager who moves from one social group or society to another must take into account these facts about attitudes, beliefs, and values and must consciously respond to them in some way.

Over the centuries of American social development, a number of social beliefs have evolved that are of significance to the manager. Among the most important of these are:

1 The belief that there are opportunities for people who are willing and able to work to take advantage of them
2 A faith in business and a respect for business owners and leaders
3 A belief in competition and competitiveness in all aspects of life, but particularly in business
4 A respect for the individual, regardless of race, religion, or creed
5 A respect for authority arising from ownership of property, expert knowledge, and elected or appointed political position
6 A belief in, and respect for, education
7 A faith in logical processes, science, and technology
8 A belief in the importance of change and experimentation to find better ways of doing things

It is true that these and other major beliefs have tended to erode as the country has become more populous and as social problems have forced more government involvement in everyone's life. It is also true, as usually happens in all cultures, that when people's standard of living improves, their expectations for a better life tend to increase even faster. The result is the existence of social problems, which can indeed be defined as the gap between expectations and realities. Nonetheless, the long-held American beliefs are still strong, supported as they are by the American work ethic developed by early settlers and immigrants, by a long tradition of individual rights and freedoms, and by our remarkable Constitution.

The Recent Explosion of Social Beliefs

In recent years, these long-held beliefs have been not only somewhat modified but also supplemented. The Great Depression of the 1930s and a growing sympathy for the disadvantaged have resulted in the development of a strong belief in people's right to work or to receive material assistance if they cannot get or hold a job. These and other forces have also given rise to demands for adequate health care and for the abolition of discrimination in all its forms, whether due to race, religion, political belief, age, or sex. Recent problems have also given rise to pressures for a better *quality of life*, for an environment cleansed of water and air pollution, and for more livable communities with decent housing, safe streets, efficient transportation, and better educational and cultural opportunities.

THE EXTERNAL ENVIRONMENT: POLITICAL AND LEGAL

As was pointed out earlier, the political and legal environment of managers is closely intertwined with the social environment. Laws are ordinarily passed as the result of social pressures and problems. But what is bothersome is that once passed, laws often stay on the books after the socially perceived need for them has disappeared. For example, much railroad regulation passed nearly a century ago, when railroads did pose a threat of monopoly, remains on the books in an era of sharp competition. Similarly, agricultural subsidies granted originally in the 1930s to save American agriculture are still present even though they are hardly needed in a time of agricultural prosperity. Many other examples could be given.

Political environments—the attitudes and actions of political and government leaders and legislators—do change with the ebb and flow of social demands and beliefs. The effect of the patriotic fervor of World War II on virtually every segment of American society, and even the world society, may be contrasted with the effect on government and other organizations of the disillusionment concerning the unpopular conflict in Vietnam. Many legislators who strongly supported going into Vietnam did a complete turnabout when people became disenchanted with the conflict. In many communities, strong sentiments about air and water pollution control subsided when plants that were unable to meet new standards had to be shut down. During the gasoline and oil crisis of early 1974, and again in 1979, many people had second thoughts about using high-sulfur coal and oil, about offshore drilling for oil, and even about fuel-using automobile pollution control devices.

Government affects virtually every enterprise and every aspect of life. In respect to business, it acts in two main *roles:* First, it promotes and constrains business. For example, it *promotes* business by stimulating economic expansion and development, by providing assistance through the Small Business Administration, subsidizing selected industries, giving tax advantages in certain situations, supporting research and development, and even protecting some businesses through special tariffs. Finally, government is also the biggest customer, purchasing goods and services.

The other role of the government is to *constrain* and regulate business. Every manager is encircled by a web of laws, regulations, and court decisions. Some are designed to protect workers, consumers, and communities. Others are designed to make contracts enforceable and to protect property rights. Many are designed to regulate the behavior of managers and their subordinates in business and other enterprises. There is relatively little that a manager can do in any organization that is not in some way concerned with, and often specifically controlled by, a law or regulation.

What most concerns managers and other people is that a desirable law with social objectives everyone wants may be administered by government agencies in such ways as to put people under detailed regulatory controls far beyond those foreseen when the law was enacted. The rules and regulations in such areas as discrimination, occupational safety and health, and pure foods and drugs, for example, have gone further than ever dreamed of by the legislators who voted for them. Who would have even thought that a small Midwestern college would be brought under fairly complete government control because a few students received government guaranteed loans or veterans' benefits? Or that many companies would be required to hire people with certain racial backgrounds on the basis of detailed numerical quotas? And, at the same time, be sued for discrimination against white people? Or that managers with factory guardrails 41 or 43 inches high would have to replace them with rails exactly 42 inches high? Or that the United States would be the 106th country in the world to permit marketing of a certain antibacterial drug?

The problem forced on managers by the thousands of rules and interpretations of the federal government alone is dramatized by their sheer volume. These regulations required some 60,000 pages in the *Federal Register* in 1975, a volume, allowing for the *Register's* large pages and small print, that is roughly equivalent to 400 college textbooks. It is no wonder that managers at times feel overwhelmed by government controls.

This is not to imply that many of our laws and regulations are unnecessary, even though, as noted, many become obsolete. But they do present a complex environment for all managers. Managers are expected to know the legal restrictions and requirements applicable to their actions. Thus, it is understandable that managers in all kinds of organizations, and in business and government especially, usually have a legal expert close at hand as they make their decisions.

In many areas laws are too slow to develop. For example, if one of the many businesses that contributed to the pollution of Lake Erie had gone to the great expense of eliminating the dumping of wastes into the lake, the costs would have put it at the mercy of competitors who did not go to this expense. If the city fathers of a single municipality that was polluting the lake had gone to similar expense, they would probably have had to answer to the taxpayers. Likewise, if one automobile manufacturer had produced a nonpolluting car 15 years ago and had offered it at a price a few hundred dollars higher than the prices of its competitors' models, there can hardly be a question that this company would have been at a competitive disadvantage. It took strong legislation to approach the solution of pollution problems.

Thus, not only must perceptive managers respond to social pressures but they also have the problem of foreseeing and dealing with political pressures, as well as laws that might be passed. As can be readily understood, this is not an easy matter.

THE EXTERNAL ENVIRONMENT: ETHICAL

The ethical environment is really a part of the social environment. All persons, whether in business, government, a university, or any other enterprise are concerned with ethics. In Webster's Dictionary, ethics is defined as "the discipline dealing with what is good and bad and with moral duty and obligation." Often ethical standards are enacted into laws. But ethical behavior is just and fair conduct which goes beyond observing laws and government regulations. It means adhering to moral principles, being guided by particular values, and behaving in a way people ought to act.

In a study of *Harvard Business Review* readers, it was found that most respondents favor ethical codes. However, they prefer general codes over specific codes of conduct. In fact, many of the respondents seem to suggest that ethical behavior is good for business in the long run.[4]

Some Ethical Guides for Managers

Although there is general agreement on the need for, and benefits of, ethical codes and principles, it is difficult to establish them. Father John W. Clark undertook this difficult task, and the result is a set of tentative

---

[4]S. N. Brenner and E. A. Molander, "Is the Ethics of Business Changing?" *Harvard Business Review*, vol. 55, no. 1, pp. 57–71 (January–February 1977).

statements of ethical guides. These guides are not a blueprint for solving all the problems in the complex business environment; rather they can serve as a basis for guiding behavior and for formulating ethical principles.[5]

The tentative statements are shown as a model in Figure 4.1. The "primary guides" are the foundations of the codes, the "middle guides" help to accomplish the goals of the primary guides. In order to apply the abstract norms to specific situations, judgment is necessary. This is shown in the model as the "area of prudential judgment."

Primary guides   The primary guides are broad and widely accepted by Americans. The first guide suggests that ethical actions have as their foundation the "backing of the generally accepted social institutions of the society." Business itself is such an institution, in fact an integral part of society. Business managers are thus expected to act in a way that contributes to society.

The second guide pertains to "respect for others." This respect is essential for interpersonal, mutual relationships. It implies, for example, honesty in communication and in business transactions. It also requires accepting the personal dignity, rights, and privileges of others.

The third primary guide pertains to "individual integrity." A person with integrity behaves according to ethical standards. This guide draws attention to the personal responsibility for one's own behavior and actions. Therefore, it relates to the concept of individualism based on freedom and responsibility.

The middle norms   The primary guides are the foundation for the middle norms, which are more specific. The first guide in this group pertains to

[5]The discussion of the tentative statement of ethical guides is based on J. W. Clark, S. J., *Religion and the Moral Standards of American Businessmen* (Cincinnati: South-Western Publishing Company, Incorporated 1966), chap. 7.

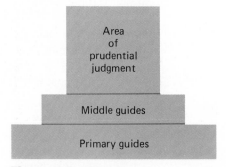

Figure 4.1   The structure of an ethical decision. [*J. W. Clark,*. Religion and the Moral Standards of American Businessmen *(Cincinnati: South-Western Publishing Co., 1966), p. 150. Reprinted by permission of the publisher.*]

executive "behavior in congruence with laws" established by legitimate civil authority. Laws are expressions of society prescribing how citizens should behave. Social institutions, such as business, are a part of society, and managers (and, of course, nonmanagers as well) are obligated to observe the laws of the land.

The second guide in the category of middle norms refers to the recognition that the power and authority of executives are held in the interest of others; in short, this guide pertains to "representative authority." This concept demands that managers must not act solely for their own personal advantage. Managers must especially refrain from actions that are in conflict with the interests they represent.

The third guide pertains to the "parity of authority and moral responsibility." The latter is an obligation to use power with integrity. Authority and power without responsibility lead to arbitrary actions. On the other hand, it is unreasonable to hold people responsible and accountable for situations which they do not have the authority or the power to change.

The final guide in the group of middle norms pertains to "private enterprise as an essential and legitimate institution" in the economic system of the United States. This guide is based on the belief that by providing individual freedom and opportunity, people will, through private enterprise, contribute to the welfare of society.

These guides, by providing theoretical norms, give executives directions in ethical decision making. To be sure, these guides are broad and still require considerable judgment in their application to specific situations. These guides are, nevertheless, a step in the right direction.

The Benefits of Ethical Codes

Ethical codes and ethical behavior can benefit all constituents of society, the enterprise itself, employees, customers, and industry.[6]

The *enterprise* may benefit from the establishment of ethical codes because it requires a review of internal and external relationships. This analysis should result in clarification of desirable and acceptable standards. Furthermore, the publication of ethical codes and their practice may serve as a sales and public relations device. Finally, effective self-regulation may prevent external controls and government actions.

Employees also benefit from ethical codes. They can expect that employee relations with the firm will be guided by ethical considerations. Moreover, the codes provide guides for managerial and nonmanagerial behavior, thus reducing uncertainties. Employees, therefore, are strengthened by the codes in their refusal to engage in unethical practices.

Customers benefit from ethical codes because they can expect that the

---

[6]The discussion of the benefits is based primarily on R. M. Fulmer, *The New Management,* 2d ed. (New York: The Macmillan Company, 1978), pp. 454–456.

business transactions will be conducted in a fair and honest manner; this, in turn, gives customers added confidence in dealing with the enterprise.

The *industry* may benefit when firms unite and agree on ethical behavior. This can raise the level of fair competition and eliminate unethical practices, especially when the sanctions are considerable. Finally, ethical codes can become the basis for professionalizing managers.

This raises the question, What factors may bring about higher ethical standards? In the study cited earlier, the two most outstanding factors, according to the respondents, are (1) public disclosure and publicity and (2) the increased concern of a better-informed public. These factors are followed by government regulations and by education to increase the professionalism of business managers.[7]

To make ethical codes effective, provisions must be made for their enforcement. Unethical managers should be held responsible for their actions. This means that privileges and benefits have to be withdrawn and sanctions have to be applied. Although the enforcement of ethical codes may not be easy, the mere existence of such codes can increase ethical behavior by clarifying what expected ethical conduct is. On the other hand, one should not expect ethical codes to solve all problems. In fact, they could create a false sense of security. To enforce codes effectively requires consistent ethical behavior and support from top management.[8]

The Causes of Confusion

There are several factors that have led us into the present state of uncertainty about ethical standards. In the first place, the successive waves of immigration have brought to the United States masses of people with widely varying practices of ethical behavior. Their cultures have not yet been wholly integrated into a *national* culture, and until this occurs, there is very little reason to anticipate any national ethical standards. In the second place, there is no recognized source of ethical standards. In nations that have a state religion, there may exist a central source of authority to teach ethical practices. In the United States, with its many cultures and religions, no one can look to a church, government, educational institution, or private association as the center of ethical teaching.

We tend to develop our ethical standards by experience and "feel." To a considerable extent that is all to the good because it assumes a certain degree of commonality of ethical standards. But care must be taken. Uncertainty concerning another's ethical standards establishes a situation in which we learn of them only through trial and error.

[7]Brenner and Molander, op. cit., p. 63.
[8]Ibid., pp. 66, 71.

Any person in business, government, a university, a church, or some other organization is aware that ethical, as well as legal, standards do differ, particularly among various nations and societies. This has long been true. For example, every nation with privately owned companies, except the United States, permits corporations to make contributions to political parties, campaigns, and candidates. In many countries of the world, payments to government officials and other persons with political influence to assure expedited or favorable handling of a business transaction are not regarded as an unethical bribe but as a proper payment for services rendered. In many cases, payments to assure the landing of a desired contract are even looked upon as a normal and acceptable way of doing business.

These problems of ethics were dramatically disclosed to the American public in the mid-1970s by the exposure of "payoffs" by many American corporations doing business in certain foreign countries. While some of these payoffs were unquestionably bribes that may not have been acceptable conduct even in these countries, many involved doing business in the common and acceptable way. It is true that some payoffs of various kinds do exist even in the United States, although they are usually illegal and certainly inconsistent with standards of ethical conduct.

The question facing responsible American business managers is, What ethical standards should they follow? There is no question of what to do in the United States, and most American executives have had to refuse the suggestion of putting money in a "paper bag." But in dealing in a country where such practices are expected and common, American executives are faced with a difficult problem. In very recent years, with the passage of laws by the United States Congress and the adoption of regulations by the Securities and Exchange Commission, not only must American firms report anything that could be called a "pay off," but also such "pay offs" and anything else that can be construed as a "bribe" are now unlawful. We have, therefore, attempted to "export" our standards of doing business, often into countries in which our competitors from other nations are not so restricted. Only time will tell whether this policy will harm the ability of American firms to compete effectively in the world market. Of course, the question always exists of whether a payment is a legitimate sales commission paid to a representative of the buyer, or a bribe.

THE SOCIAL RESPONSIBILITY OF MANAGERS

Probably no question has received more attention by business, governments, politicians, and people in general in the past few years than the question of what the social responsibility of business is. The same question, originally aimed at business, is now being addressed with increasing frequency to government agencies and their leaders, universities, nonprofit foundations, charitable organizations, and even churches. A society, awakened and vocal with respect to the urgency of social problems, is asking the managers of all kinds of organizations, particularly those at the top, what they are doing to discharge their social responsibilities and why they are not doing more.

It cannot be overlooked that various kinds of organized enterprises have different missions that have been entrusted to them by society. The mission of business is the production and distribution of goods and services. The mission of a police department is protection of the safety and welfare of the people. The mission of a state highway department is the design and construction of desired highways. The mission of a university is teaching and research. And so on.

We should not hold business managers, for example, responsible for solving all manner of social problems, any more than we should expect those responsible for a church to produce and distribute economic goods. There can hardly be any sense in making the job of business one of furnishing public school education, religious services, or the many other things, like police and fire protection, that the government provides. But business, like any other type of organized enterprise, must interact with, and live within, its environment.

To live within our environment is to take into account in our every action those elements of our surroundings which are important to us and to others. We all do this when we drive on the right side of the street, wear clothes, work for a living, vote, go to the church of our choice, or pay taxes. Some of these things we do because we get satisfaction from conforming; some we do because of social expectations; and some we do because of the pressure of codes and laws.

Whether managers achieve their missions, and how they do so, are matters of great social importance. A society deserves the accomplishment of the basic missions of approved enterprises. In striving to fulfill these expectations, managers know that they must interact with, and live within, an existing environment. This means that they must take into account every element in their surroundings that is important to their success and important to others who may be affected by the action taken. In other words, managers *respond* to their environment. This is what they must do, since the survival of their enterprises depends upon successful interaction with all environmental elements.

But to live within an environment and be reponsive to it does not mean that managers should merely assume a reactive posture in the face of stress. There is a positive aspect as well. For example, there may be a question of whether to react or a question of taking positive action intended to modify some environmental elements.

As indicated earlier in this chapter, to respond requires first of all that we know what aspects in our total environment have or will have a significant influence on our operations. Since any enterprise, whether it is a business, a university, or a government agency, cannot be expected to react very quickly to unforeseen developments, it must practice ways of anticipating them through forecasts. An alert company, for example, does not wait until its product is obsolete and sales have fallen off before coming out with a new or improved product. A government agency should not wait until its regulatory system has become obsolete and discredited before attempting another way of achieving its objectives. No enterprise should wait for problems to develop as the result of environmental forces before preparing to face them. This, as we shall see in the chapters on planning, is an essential part of the planning process.

The importance of forecasting environmental forces and being ready to respond to them can be illustrated in the case of the automobile industry and the smog problem. We can scarcely blame any individual auto maker for not doing much about the smog problem 10 or 20 years ago when buyers would almost surely not have paid an extra amount for a smog-free car, even though they bought such extras as power steering and brakes, air conditioning, and automatic transmission. But we can criticize all the manufacturers for not seeing, many years ago, the developing social forces demanding less smog, and for not getting ready, through research and development, to make the technical changes when the laws were passed in response to these social demands.

There are many instances where social forces can be enforced only by the enactment of legislation, particularly in a competitive situation. However, many managers in business and elsewhere have found it to their advantage to do something about pressing social problems. For example, many businesses have profited by filtering smokestack pollutants and selling or utilizing these recovered wastes. Some companies have made a profit by building low-cost apartments in ghetto areas. The Internal Revenue Service learned that it increased tax collection efficiency and effectiveness by simplifying or eliminating certain burdensome reports and forms. In other words, contributing to the solution of social problems does not always involve net expenses. But we may need the bludgeoning force of legislation to get improvements under way.

Even if individual managers of all types of enterprises have full freedom to act in accordance with the currently conceived social responsibilities, they may not do so because of standards applied in evaluating their performance. Managers, like everyone else, want their performance positively appraised—they seek approval. Therefore, if their success is measured in terms of profit, living within a budget, tax collection as a percentage of income, the volume of blood contributed to a blood bank, or the number of communicants in a church, managers will strive to achieve excellence in these regards. On the other hand, if success is measured in terms of pollution control, the ratio of convicts returned successfully to society, the dollar support for employees seeking university degrees, the proportion of "disadvantaged" to total number of employees, achievements in raising the productivity of subordinates, or combinations of these and similar goals, it is clear that managers will strive to achieve them.

In other words, managers will respond to socially approved values and will give priority to those held in highest esteem. It is essential, if improvement in responding to social forces is desired, to clarify these social values and forces and then, within a system of varied organizations with a variety of missions, reward managers for their success in responding to them.

The Social Audit

The discussion of social responsibility raises the question of how social performance should be evaluated. This led to the concept of the "social audit," which was first proposed in the fifties by Howard R. Bowen.[9] But it is only more recently that corporations have seriously concerned themselves with this idea. The social audit has been defined as "a commitment to systematic assessment of and reporting on some meaningful, definable domain of the company's activities that have social impact."[10]

In a survey, corporations were asked whether they had attempted to assess what was done in a series of "activity fields." A surprising 76 percent responded "yes" to the question. Although the term "social audit" was not mentioned in the question, the concept was implied. When the same corporations were asked for the *reasons* for the social audit, they responded that they wanted to examine what the company was actually doing and to appraise performance in selected areas.[11]

Another recent survey of the *Fortune* 500 firms indicated that 456 companies (91.2 percent) have made social responsibility disclosures in their annual reports.[12] Although these disclosures may not be equated with a social audit, the large number of firms making such disclosures shows a general concern of major corporations about their social responsibility.

It is rather difficult to determine *what* areas the social audit should encompass. Often the items include pollution and the hiring, training, and promotion of minorities, but there are many other areas. For example, General Electric developed a matrix which facilitates the analysis of the expectations of customers, investors, employees, communities, and other claimants in the following areas: product and technical performance, economic performance, employment performance, environment and

[9]*Social Responsibilities of the Businessman* (New York: Harper & Brothers, 1953), pp. 155–156.
[10]R. A. Bauer and D. H. Fenn, Jr., "What Is a Corporate Social Audit?" *Harvard Business Review*, vol. 51, no. 1, p. 38 (January–February 1973).
[11]Steiner, *Business and Society*, 2d ed. (New York: Random House, Inc., 1975), pp. 198–199.
[12]*Social Responsibility Disclosure—1977 Survey of Fortune 500 Annual Reports* (Cleveland, Ohio: Ernst & Ernst, 1977).

natural resources, community welfare and development, government-business relations, as well as international trade and development.[13]

Another difficulty is to determine *how* social performance should be measured. One way is to determine the amount of money an enterprise spends in selected areas. But cost alone is an inadequate measure. It does not necessarily indicate the results of social involvement. Other problems are the collection of the data and their presentation in a way that accurately reflects the social involvement of an enterprise. There is no doubt that many difficulties are associated with a social audit, but there is evidence that many companies and other organizations in the United States honestly attempt to address themselves to this challenge.

In summary, managers operate in a complex environment. They are affected by—and to some extent influence—the economic, technological, social, political, and ethical environment. The concept of social responsibility is still evolving. To determine the appropriate relationships between various organizations and society is not an easy task. Nevertheless, many corporations and organizations are making serious efforts to establish an environment beneficial to individuals, business, and society.

FOR DISCUSSION

1   Why is the environment external to an enterprise so important to all managers in carrying out their activities? Can any manager avoid being influenced by the external environment? Identify the environmental elements that are likely to be the most important for each of the following: a company president, a sales manager, a production manager, a controller, and a personnel manager.

2   Why and how is the economic environment of concern to business and nonbusiness enterprises? Can you give some examples from your own knowledge and experience?

3   How does technology affect the enterprise in general, and managing in particular?

4   What effect does the external social and political environment have on the enterprise? How do managers respond to these influences?

5   List and discuss some codes of ethics. What additional ethical codes would you recommend for your enterprise, your university, your class, your family? How should these codes be enforced?

6   What are the major social responsibilities of business managers? of government managers? Have these responsibilities changed over the years? How?

7   How would you measure the social performance of a major corporation? What are some of the difficulties in conducting a social audit? What are your recommendations to overcome these problems?

[13]Steiner, op. cit., pp. 202–203.

chapter 5 Comparative and International Management

MAJOR CHAPTER OBJECTIVES

1 To recognize the importance of effective managing for economic growth.

2 To explore the question of transferability of management knowledge and know-how to different cultural environments.

3 To explain the Farmer-Richman model of comparative management.

4 To illustrate the impact of the environment on managing in selected countries.

5 To introduce the Koontz model of comparative management, which separates environmental factors and enterprise-function elements from management fundamentals.

6 To point out the significance of universality for management research, teaching, and practice.

7 To discuss the nature and purpose of international business and multinational corporations.

8 To give special attention to managerial functions in the international context.

As the study of management has increasingly commanded worldwide interest and recognition, the question of whether management is a science with universal application has concerned scholars and practitioners alike. A real science should explain phenomena regardless of national or cultural environments. Thus, the science of mechanics knows no boundaries, providing it applies to the reality being considered. Principles of the building sciences are no different whether they are applied to a small house or a large building and whether these structures are built in the tropics or the arctic.

Unless basic management science can be useful for practitioners in varying circumstances, it is certainly suspect, for the task of an "operational" science is to organize pertinent knowledge so as to make it applicable, and thereby useful, to those who would achieve intended' results.

The authors have taken the position that management fundamentals—concepts, theory, and principles—have universal application in every kind of enterprise and at every level of an enterprise. Yet they have constantly acknowledged that the specific problems with which managers deal, the individuals and groups with which they interact, and the elements of the external environment will differ. One expects, therefore, that given techniques and approaches, even though based upon the same fundamentals, will vary in their applications because of these differences, just as engineering design will vary if a mechanical engineer is planning a bridge rather than a precise pressure-measuring instrument.

It is true that most studies of management fundamentals have been made without regard to specific external cultural environments. It is likewise true that most studies have been made against the backdrop of culturally well-developed and predominantly private enterprise societies. However, in approaching the study of comparative management, two basic questions may be posed: (1) Do management fundamentals, in contrast to specific applications and approaches, vary with external cultural differences of a social, economic, political, technological, or ethical nature? (2) To what extent should we expect managerial practice—the art of managing—to differ with variations in the external environment? These questions are addressed in the first part of this chapter. The second part deals with various characteristics of international management and multinational corporations.

A distinction can be made between *comparative* management and *international* management. The former is concerned with the *analysis* of management in different environments and the reasons that enterprises show different results in various countries. International management, on the other hand, focuses on the *operation* of international firms in host countries. It concerns managerial problems related to the flow of people, goods, and money with the ultimate aim being to manage better in situations that involve crossing national boundaries.[1]

[1] R. N. Farmer, in J. W. McGuire (ed.), *Contemporary Management—Issues and Viewpoints* (Englewood Cliffs, N.J.: Prentice-Hall, Inc., 1974), p. 302.

MANAGEMENT AS A CRITICAL ELEMENT IN ECONOMIC GROWTH

In light of the increasing concern for economic growth, it is natural for social scientists to look for underlying causes of that growth. Why does one country have a higher per-capita national income than another? Why did only fifty-five countries of the world in 1975 have a national per capita income of more than $1000 per year, while another fifty-five had a national per-capita income of $210 to $1000 per year, and thirty-one countries had a national per-capita income of $200 or less per year?[2]

Concern for Productivity and Economic Growth

Because of the disparity in national incomes and the problems caused in much of the world by incomes that do not allow for adequate subsistence, let alone the raising of cultural standards, attention to world leaders and development economists have naturally turned to the need for increasing productivity.

Until recently, the necessities for development were thought to be the transfer of technology, education, and capital. But important as these are, it is now recognized that advanced managerial know-how is probably the most critical of all elements responsible for growth.[3]

Rostow recognizes the importance of entrepreneurial skills in management and economic growth when he points out that "a small professional elite (of entrepreneurs and executives) can go a long way toward initiating economic growth."[4] Sayles expresses the same viewpoint even more strongly when he concludes that "in the world race for economic growth and for the allegiance and stability of lesser-developed sections of the globe, United States management 'know-how' is a crucial factor."[5]

These conclusions are not difficult for a person knowledgeable in management to understand. The goal of managing is to make it possible for people to operate in groups in such a way as to gain the most, in terms of objectives sought by an enterprise or a part of it, with the human and material resources available. Clearly, ineffectual managership leads to inefficient use of these resources, whether the goal of an enterprise is economic, political, or other.

Although one must grant that pure technical knowledge is necessary

---

[2]*United Nations Yearbook of National Accounts Statistics*, vol. II (New York: United Nations Department of Public Information, 1977), pp. 10–13.

[3]"Know-how" is used differently by various authors. Here it is used to connote the ability to apply knowledge effectively in practice; it therefore includes both knowledge of the underlying science and the artful ability to apply it to reality in the light of contingencies or situations.

[4]W. W. Rostow, *The Stages of Economic Growth* (Cambridge, Mass.: Harvard University Press, 1962), p. 52.

[5]L. R. Sayles, *Managerial Behavior* (New York: McGraw-Hill Book Comapny, 1964), p. 17.

for economic growth, such knowledge is fairly easily transferable between countries, and no nation long holds a monopoly on it. Even a technological development as sophisticated as that of the atomic bomb, whose secrecy was actively protected by the United States, became known in Russia, France, China, and elsewhere in less than two decades. Most advances in technology are neither as complex nor as well guarded, so that their transfer is not likely to be difficult, particularly when one realizes that in any country only a few people need to have this knowledge to make it available for use.

Environmental Factors Are Important

On the other hand, a cultural factor such as the level of education, particularly knowledge of skills, has an important impact on economic progress. Also, such cultural variables as desire for more of the products and services that a country *can* provide can be significant. Similarly constraining on economic progress are a large number of political factors, such as fiscal policy, labor regulations, business restrictions, and foreign policy. But even with these and other constraints which may limit managerial effectiveness, qualified managers can do much to bring economic progress to a society by identifying them and by designing a managerial approach or technique to take them into account.

The Need for Management Theory and Practice

Two prominent scholars of comparative management have said in respect to economic progress:

> We view management as the single most critical social activity in connection with economic progress. Physical, financial, and manpower resources are by themselves but passive agents; they must be effectively combined and coordinated through sound, active management if a country is to experience a substantial level of economic growth and development. A country can have sizeable natural and manpower resources including plentiful skilled labor and substantial capital but still be relatively poor because very few competent managers are available to put these resources efficiently together in the production and distribution of useful goods and services.[6]

The United States is generally credited as being the world leader in the development of management know-how. It is therefore not surprising that American management is regarded widely as the standard of the world and that most scholars regard the problem of comparative manage-

---

[6]R. N. Farmer and B. M. Richman, *Comparative Management and Economic Progress* (Homewood, Ill.: Richard D. Irwin, Inc., 1965), p. 1.

ment as one of transferring American management knowledge and practice to less-developed countries.

This may be a justifiable point of view, but the authors of this book do not base their belief in management universality on such a premise. After all, the earliest and most perceptive managerial insights were those of a Frenchman, Henri Fayol. Many early management pioneers were British, and other management scholars have come from a host of countries and cultures. It is the authors' position that effective management knowledge and art are not uniquely American. In their writing on management and in their experience in leading seminars for managers and scholars throughout the world, it has never been the position of the authors that their task was to export American management; rather it has been to identify and discuss management fundamentals and their application to effective managing.

IS MANAGEMENT CULTURE-BOUND?

A few scholars of management have concluded that management is culture-bound. In other words, the facts that management practices differ and that people and their environment vary are believed by some to be persuasive evidence that management theory and principles—the framework of management knowledge—are applicable only in developed societies similar to that existing in the United States. Also, there are some who believe that the structure and content of management science are not transferable and that the application of these to specific enterprise situations in the same national culture is not necessarily possible.

The Differing Views

The findings of Gonzalez and McMillan are among those often quoted to show that management is culture-bound. These scholars, on the basis of a 2-year study in Brazil, concluded that "American management experience abroad provides evidence that our uniquely American philosophy of management is not universally applicable but is a rather special case."[7] Note that these authors refer to "philosophy" and not to "science" or "theory" or "principles" and have emphasized that "that aspect of management which lacks universality has to do with interpersonal relationships, including those between management and workers, management and suppliers, management and the customer, the community, competition and government."[8]

[7]R. F. Gonzalez and C. McMillan, Jr., "The Universality of American Management Philosophy," *Journal of the Academy of Management*, vol. 4, no. 1, pp. 33–41 (April 1961), at p. 41.
[8]Ibid., p. 39.

On the basis of similar research, Oberg appears to agree with Gonzalez and McMillan and expresses doubt that the "game" of management in Brazil, being so different from that played in the United States, would permit application of management principles, useful in the United States, to Brazil.[9] It is Oberg's belief that the applicability of management principles may be limited to a particular culture or situation and that it may be fruitless to search for a common set of "principles," "absolutes," or "determinate solutions." It is even argued that since management principles appear not to be adaptable between cultures, they may not even be applicable between subcultures such as those of a rural business owner versus the manager of a large corporation within the United States.[10]

On the other hand, even those who question the transfer of managerial knowledge have admitted that it has often been successfully applied. For example, Gonzalez and McMillan, in their article indicating belief that the American philosophy of management is culture-bound, stated that:

> The science of management has reached its highest state of development in the U.S., and it is for this knowledge, this know-how, that American management is most highly respected abroad. Transferred abroad, this know-how is first viewed with skepticism. Foreign national employees and partners are slow to respond and understand the American scientific approach to management problems. However, once fully indoctrinated, they accept and support this way of doing things. The superiority of this more objective, systematic, orderly and controlled approach to problems is seen and appreciated. For the host country, for American international relations, and for the American parent firm itself the export of American managerial know-how as well as technological know-how has yielded great dividends.[11]

Harbison and Myers, in their study of management in a number of countries of the world, concluded that there is a "logic of industrialization." They indicated, moreover, that "organization building has its logic, too, which rests upon the development of management. . . . This brings us to the fundamental premise of our study: there is a general logic of management development which has applicability both to advanced and industrializing countries in the modern world."[12] While offered as a premise, their study of management in twelve foreign countries supports it.

[9]W. Oberg, "Cross-Cultural Perspectives on Management Principles," *Academy of Management Journal*, vol. 6, no. 2, pp. 129–143 (June 1963), at p. 120.
[10]Ibid., pp. 142–143.
[11]Gonzalez and McMillan, op. cit., p. 39.
[12]F. Harbison and C. A. Myers, *Management in the Industrial World* (New York: McGraw-Hill Book Company, 1959), p. 117.

Interesting and consistent findings were made in another study in which the behavior of some 3600 managers in fourteen countries was probed. This study, undertaken by Haire, Ghiselli, and Porter, found that there was a high degree of similarity in managerial behavior patterns and that many of the variations disclosed were due to identifiable cultural differences.[13] It is interesting also that Richman, in reporting on the developing interest in management in the Soviet Union in 1965, found that the evolving Soviet approach to management utilized the functions of managers—planning, organizing, coordination, control, direction, leadership, motivation, and staffing—which were essentially the same as long-held American concepts.[14] As will be pointed out below, other studies, particularly those carried on by the Comparative Management Program of the University of California, Los Angeles, also support this view.

The Problem of Semantics in Assessing the Transfer of Management

The authors of this book have attempted to give the concepts of management theory, principles, and science careful definition. In essence, "science" is organized knowledge, "theory" is a structure of fundamental concepts and principles around which knowledge in a field is organized, and "principles" are regarded as fundamental truths—or what are thought to be truths at a particular time—which can be used to describe and predict the results of certain variables in a given situation. Management "know-how," on the other hand, refers to the effective application of knowledge; it includes knowledge of the underlying science and the artful ability to apply it in a particular situation. Unfortunately, the discussion of comparative management is often unnecessarily confused by the failure to distinguish between management fundamentals and management practice.

Semantic problems cloud the transferability issue   In looking over the scant evidence on the transferability of management knowledge between countries and cultures, it is apparent that differences of opinion seem to arise largely from semantics. The concepts of "management philosophy," "management know-how," "management practice," "management theory," "management principles," and "management knowledge" are often left undefined.

The authors suggest that management "philosophy" has such a variable meaning as almost to defy definition. Strictly speaking, philosophy is the "love, study, or pursuit of knowledge," and the term is

---

[13]M. Haire, E. E. Ghiselli, and L. W. Porter, *Managerial Thinking: An International Study* (New York: John Wiley & Sons, Inc., 1966).

[14]B. M. Richman, "The Soviet Educational and Research Revolution: Implications for Management Development," *California Management Review*, vol. 9, no. 4, p. 12 (Summer 1967).

sometimes, but certainly not always, used synonymously with "science." Yet studies of comparative management sometimes use "management philosophy" to describe attitudes of managers toward such groups as consumers, stockholders, suppliers, unions, and government.[15]

If a concept of management science includes underlying basic knowledge of management and, in addition, the application of this knowledge in given situations and cultures, differences in interpretation of what a researcher finds in comparative societies would naturally exist. Likewise, if a concept of management philosophy includes not only basic management theory and principles but also beliefs related to such societal matters as ownership of property and attitudes toward individuals, one would expect the resultant concept to vary between cultures as attitudes on fundamental social matters differ. In this context, it is easy to understand how Gonzalez and McMillan could come to the conclusion that American business philosophy is culture-bound, while they admit that the export of American managerial know-how has yielded great dividends.

Clear Distinctions Essential for Assessing Transferability

The essential point is simply this: Cultural differences exist between various countries and societies, sometimes to a marked degree. There are even subcultural variations of an important nature in the same country or society. It is therefore important in any study of the transferability of knowledge to separate the *fundamentals* of management from their application to given situations.

When the distinction is made between management fundamentals, as expressed in basic concepts, theory, and principles, and management practice—the application of management fundamentals to a given situation—progress can be made in determining the extent of management universality and the transferability of managerial fundamentals. With variations in cultures, one would not expect that *application* of management fundamentals to these varied cultures would always be the same.

The importance of this distinction cannot be overlooked, particularly if basic knowledge of management in one culture is to be transferred to another. However, this does not mean that a management technique or approach that is successful in one society may not work with few, if any, changes in another society. It simply means that the manager who would succeed in a different culture should ascertain the extent of change in technique or application required to meet any existing differences. The same is true in any field of science. One would not necessarily expect an automobile designed for use in deserts or jungles to be the same as one

---

[15]A. R. Negandhi and B. D. Estafen, "A Research Model to Determine the Applicability to American Management Know-How in Differing Cultures and/or Environments," *Academy of Management Journal*, vol. 8, no. 4, pp. 309–318 (December 1967), at 312.

planned for high-speed superhighways, even though the physical science which underpins both remains the same.

THE FARMER-RICHMAN MODEL:
INTRODUCING THE EXTERNAL ENVIRONMENT

In comparing management in various countries, a model for analysis is necessary. Professors Richard N. Farmer and Barry M. Richman—two pioneers in comparative management—emphasize that environments external to the firm do affect management practices. These authors were the first to identify the critical elements in the management process and to evaluate their operation in firms in different cultures. They also described the environmental factors they considered to have a significant impact on the management process and managerial effectiveness. These factors, viewed as constraints, are classified as (1) educational variables, (2) sociological-cultural variables, (3) political and legal variables, and (4) economic variables.[16]

The Concept of Managerial Effectiveness

Hypothesizing that management of productive enterprises is directly related to the external environment in which a manager operates and that managers may at times affect this environment, Farmer and Richman believe that management practice and its effectiveness will depend to a major extent upon external environmental characteristics.

Assuming that one of the major goals of any society is productivity (even though this appears sometimes to be unrealistic), managerial effectiveness is defined as simply how well and efficiently the managers of an enterprise in a given environment accomplish enterprise objectives. If we can assume that the objective is productivity, the efficiency is given by $E = O/I$, where E is effeciency, O is output, and I is input. While this concept is clear, Farmer and Richman realize that, in measuring the efficiency of management, an analyst will encounter extremely difficult problems in measuring inputs and outputs. These include (1) the problem of uncertainty, since management decisions and practice always deal with the future; (2) the problem of clearly defining goals, since, if not so defined, outputs cannot be accurately measured, and a knowledge of efficiency becomes impossible; (3) the problem of subsystem optimization, since the conceptual ability and measuring techniques are seldom available to evaluate adequately the enterprise as a total system over time; and (4) the problem of resource mobility, since inputs, such as labor and

---

[16]R. N. Farmer and B. M. Richman, *Comparative Management and Economic Progress* (Homewood, Ill.: Richard D. Irwin, Inc., 1965). Also B. M. Richman, "Empirical Testing of a Comparative and International Management Research Model," *Proceedings of the 27th Annual Meeting of the Academy of Management,* pp. 34–65 (December 27–29, 1967).

capital, cannot be easily shifted from less profitable opportunities to more profitable ones.

Although difficulties of measuring and other deficiencies exist, there are a number of means by which the efficiency of a country or a firm's operation can be assessed. From the standpoint of a country, they include (1) the level of real per capita gross national product; (2) the rate of growth of real per capita gross national product; (3) the rate of utilization of inputs (how well are labor, capital, and land utilized?); (4) the usability of outputs (are they needed, and how usable are they?); (5) the level of competition (how much rivalry is there to force entrepreneurs to be efficient?); and (6) the adequacy and accuracy of planning (are outputs available for unwanted and unneeded items in some sections of the economy, while shortages exist in others?).

The efficiency of an individual firm may be ascertained by looking at a number of factors. One of these is profitability as measured either by the return on net worth or on assets employed. Another is how well the firm competes in export markets. A third is the output per employee, such as tons of steel. A fourth measure is the extent to which a firm utilizes its plant capacity. A fifth factor, where applicable, is the level of costs and prices and their relationship to those of another firm. A final type of measurement involves the matter of long-run innovation and whether policy and actions are optimizing short-range performance at the expense of long-range performance, or vice versa.

It does seem that these measures of management effectivness, both in a nation and within a firm, are appropriate. Fairly accurate data exist for some. Data subject to various degrees of inaccuracy exist for others. And, for still others, credible data may not currently be available. Also, there is the danger that different statistical and accounting treatments between countries and firms may be such as to make comparisons difficult or invalid.

Managerial Elements

In order to separate the elements of the management process from the external constraints of the environment, Farmer and Richman use the framework of management and most of the fundamentals outlined in this book. Thus they pick the critical elements of the management process as follows:

Planning and innovation

1.1 Basic organizational objectives pursued and the form of their operational expression.

1.2 Types of plans utilized.

1.3 Time horizon of plans and planning.

1.4 Degree and extent to which enterprise operations are spelled out in plans (i.e., preprogrammed).

1.5 Flexibility of plans.

1.6 Methodologies, techniques, and tools used in planning and decision making.

1.7 Extent and effectiveness of employee participation in planning.

1.8 Managerial behavior in the planning process.

1.9 Degree and extent of information distortion in planning.

1.10 Degree and extent to which scientific method is effectively applied by enterprise personnel—both managers and nonmanagers—in dealing with causation and furturity problems.

1.11 Nature, extent, and rate of innovation and risk taking in enterprise operations over a given period of time.

1.12 Ease or difficulty of introducing changes and innovation in enterprise operations.

Control

2.1 Types of strategic performance and control standards used in different areas; e.g., production, marketing, finance, personnel.

2.2 Types of control techniques used.

2.3 Nature and structure of information feedback systems used for control purposes.

2.4 Timing and procedures for corrective action.

2.5 Degree of looseness or tightness of control over personnel.

2.6 Extent and nature of unintended effects resulting from the overall control system employed.

2.7 Effectiveness of the control system in compelling events to conform to plans.

Organization

3.1 Size of representative enterprise and its major subunits.

3.2 Degree of centralization or decentralization of authority.

3.3 Degree of work specialization (division of labor).

3.4 Spans of control.

3.5 Basic departmentation and grouping of activities. Extent and uses of service departments.

3.6 Extent and uses of staff generalists and specialists.

3.7 Extent and uses of functional authority.

3.8 Extent and degree of organizational confusion and friction regarding authority and responsibility relationships.

3.9 Extent and uses of committee and group decision making.

3.10 Nature, extent, and uses of the informal organization.

3.11 Degree and extent to which the organization structure (i.e., the formal organization) is mechanical or flexible with regard to causing and/or adapting to changing conditions.

Staffing

4.1	Methods used in recruiting personnel.
4.2	Criteria used in selecting and promoting personnel.
4.3	Techniques and criteria used in appraising personnel.
4.4	Nature and uses of job descriptions.
4.5	Levels of compensation.
4.6	Nature, extent, and time absorbed in enterprise training programs and activities.
4.7	Extent of informal individual development.
4.8	Policies and procedures regarding the layoff and dismissal of personnel.
4.9	Ease or difficulty in dismissing personnel no longer required or desired.
4.10	Ease or difficulty of obtaining and maintaining personnel of all types with desired skills and abilities.

Direction, leadership, and motivation

5.1	Degree and extent of authoritarian vs. participative management. (This relates to autocratic vs. consultative direction.)
5.2	Techniques and methods used for motivating managerial personnel.
5.3	Techniques and methods used for motivating nonmanagerial personnel.
5.4	Supervisory techniques used.
5.5	Communication structure and techniques.
5.6	Degree and extent to which communication is ineffective among personnel of all types.
5.7	Ease or difficulty of motivating personnel to perform efficiently, and to improve their performance and abilities over time (irrespective of the types of incentives that may be utilized for this purpose).
5.8	Degree and extent of identification that exists between the interests and objectives of individuals, work groups, departments, and the enterprise as a whole.
5.9	Degree and extent of trust and cooperation or conflict and distrust among personnel of all types.
5.10	Degree and extent of frustration, absenteeism, and turnover among personnel.
5.11	Degree and extent of wasteful time and effort, resulting from restrictive work practices, unproductive bargaining, conflicts, etc.

In addition, these authors expand their listing of critical elements of the management process to include major policy areas of management planning in order to obtain a view of the policies followed by various companies. These policies are classified as those related to marketing, production and procurement, research and development, finance, and external relations. Each of these in turn is broken down into a number of elements. In the area of marketing policy, for example, channels of distribution and types and locations of customers are listed. In the area of production and procurement, policy with respect to making or buying items is one of those listed, and in the area of finance, policy with respect to distribution of earnings is an example.[17]

External Environmental Constraints

As noted above, Farmer and Richman divide external and environmental constraints into four classes: educational, sociological-cultural, legal-political, and economic.

Educational constraints   Among the major educational constraints noted are literacy level, the availability of specialized vocational and technical training and secondary education, higher education, management development programs, the prevailing attitude toward education, and the extent to which education matches requirements for skills and abilities. Mere reference to these educational factors indicates how they may support or limit effective management. Moreover, where education is inadequate, not only will economic enterprises themselves tend to suffer thereby, but political and legal systems are also likely to be poor. Even in advanced societies, where education appears to be more closely matched with requirements, there is always the phenomenon of a shortage of educational brainpower, since it is characteristic of all societies that the more that is available, the more is needed.

Sociological-cultural constraints   In the sociological-cultural area, Farmer and Richman identify a large number of factors. These include (1) the general attitude of the society toward managers (for example, is a career in the profession of medicine or law or in government regarded as a higher status than one in business management?); (2) the dominant views of authority and subordinates (for example, are subordinates expected to follow the all-knowing, paternalistic decisions of the top manager, or is participation of subordinates accepted and encouraged?); (3) the extent to which cooperation between various groups is a way of life (for example, are class structures rigid, or are the means for advancement open to a person who is capable, regardless of class affiliation?); (4) the extent of union-management cooperation; (5) the view of achievement and work (for example, does the society value economic achievement through hard work as a desirable personal trait, or is achievement in the arts or preparation for life after death regarded as paramount?); (6) the extent of

[17]For a full listing of these policy areas, the reader is referred to Farmer and Richman, op. cit., pp. 348–349.

inflexible class structure and individual mobility (for example, are individuals moved to positions on the basis of their abilities, or are they restricted by caste systems or other forms of discrimination not related to ability?); (7) the dominant view of wealth and material gain, such as attitudes toward saving and the desire for material wealth versus religious satisfaction, the "good life," or other nonmaterial stimuli; (8) the view of scientific method (for example, is the society interested in preserving traditional cultures and patterns or in following a given ideology, regardless of the logic involved or the empirical evidence and new discoveries available, or does the society understand the basic relationships between such economic factors as demand, price, wages, training, absenteeism, and turnover?); (9) the view of risk taking (for example, are nations, enterprises, and individuals willing to take reasonable risks?); and (10) the view of change (for example, do the people in a society maintain their basic faith in traditions—old ways of doing things—or do they embrace change which promises to improve productivity?).

Legal-political constraints The major legal-political constraints in an external environment have been identified by Farmer and Richman as falling into six categories: (1) relevant rules of the game, (2) defense policy and national security, (3) foreign policy, (4) political stability, (5) political organization, and (6) flexibility of law and legal changes.

There are, as one might expect, a number of legal rules in any business game. One is the general business law which provides a framework within which the firm must work. Important factors in this framework are codes of fair and effective competition, the law of contracts, and laws pertaining to trademarks, copyrights, and patents. Likewise, general laws governing society, such as those affecting health, welfare, and safety, have their effect, as automobile and pharmaceutical manufacturers, among others, in the United States are well aware.

Another legal area constraining the manager is that dealing with prices and competition. The United States has been the leader in the work of framing and enforcing laws to require a responsible level of competition, and these have had both a constraining and a constructive effect on a manager's environment. But elsewhere in the world these laws differ, ranging from those coming somewhat close to American legislation in enforcing competition to laws which permit or even encourage monopoloy or monopolistic practices.

Still another area which has a far-reaching effect on management is labor law. In most countries these laws are extremely complex. They usually apply to hours and conditions of work, use of women and minors, tenure and job security, employer responsibility for health and welfare, use of nationals, and unemployment compensation. But differences in requirements may be considerable. In the United States, for example, company managers are normally permitted to discharge or lay off an employee with little or no difficulty or cost. But in many other countries they may find it virtually impossible to do so, especially if the employee has fairly long tenure. Furthermore, in one country the cost of social benefits may be virtually nonexistent, while in another it may amount to nearly half the payroll costs.

Tax law variations are also significant. Tax regulations and the impact of taxes are different in various jurisdictions. Some may even materially affect whether a business operates as a proprietorship, partnership, or corporation. Possibilities of evasion differ considerably. It is customary for businesses in many countries to evade taxes to a great extent. This is epitomized by the statement of a foreign business owner to one of the authors that he kept three sets of books: one for the tax collector, one for the person who might wish to buy his business, and one for himself. Also, the extent of tax benefits or penalties to encourage or discourage a business obviously has a significant effect on management policy.

Another political factor affecting management is the country's policy toward defense and national security. Where huge sums are spent toward this end, as in the United States, the effect is obvious. Defense policy often has considerable impact on the allocation of labor and resources. Draft of workers and allocation and rationing of materials are cases in point.

Foreign policy also has its influence on the management of enterprises. Tariffs and quotas, economic aid, protection of local businesses by restricting foreign ownership, monetary exchange controls, and control of imports or exports are conspicuous and widespread examples. Managers always have to contend with these influences, and companies domiciled in one country and doing business in another, either through export or through license, joint venture, or wholly owned subsidiary, have special problems in dealing with them.

Still another environmental factor is the extent of political stability which a country enjoys. Where political systems and leadership are highly unstable, managers face an area of uncertainty which cannot help but materially affect their planning. Even moderate political uncertainties can have consequences. The changing policy in Great Britain with respect to nationalizing the steel industry, as Labour and Conservative elements come into and lose power, cannot help but have a detrimental effect on planning in this industry—planning which in many respects unavoidably involves commitments of a long-range and inflexible nature.

Likewise, the type of political organization has an important influence on managers. If a country is operated under a federal system, as the United States and Australia are, the environment is different from that of one operated under a highly centralized political organization, such as France. The more government levels and functions there are with power to affect a manager's operation, the more complicated the manager's task may be in meeting legal requirements. But managers are also likely to receive more local understanding of their problems in a federal system than under a highly centralized government.

Farmer and Richman further identify as an important factor in the political environment the flexibility of law—the ease with which legal changes are brought about in a society. Law is notably conservative, largely because it is designed to correct past abuses and conditions. But as conditions change, if the law itself is not flexible or cannot be changed readily, the manager may have a critical problem to deal with.

Economic constraints Farmer and Richman likewise identify a number of economic constraints which differ between countries and affect the practice of managing. Among these are the basic economic system— whether it is predominantly private or public in ownership, whether it is competitive, whether exchange is based on sound money, and the extent to which the government controls economic activities.

There are economic differences in whether the central banking system and national monetary policy work to help or to thwart managers. Does the banking system provide needed money and credit expansion as businesses grow? Does it control monetary supply to avoid unsettling inflation? Does it operate to stabilize the economy, or does it contribute to excess booms? Does it support or hinder export business? These questions are closely tied in with fiscal policy in the extent to which the public sector of an economy creates price stability, tax fluctuations, booms, and recessions. Obviously, this element of the environment of managers greatly influences their managerial policies.

Economic stability is a significant economic variable. A degree of price stability is highly desirable, since managers are required to make many fairly long-range commitments and are almost forced to rely very largely upon financial data for much of their planning and control. Utilization of production factors is an environmental matter of importance; cycles in employment of capital and land can understandably have a disturbing effect on enterprises that must use, and plan to utilize for some time, these resources. While no manager would expect perfect stability in either prices or the economy, and while managers would normally prefer a growing economy and are usually able to live with moderate price changes, uncertainty in these economic elements cannot help but hinder planning effectiveness and compel shortening the time span of decision commitment.

Since capital is the lifeblood of any business enterprise, organization of capital markets is an important environmental factor. The manager operating in an environment where capital is reasonably available has, of course, a tremendous advantage over one who operates in an environment where capital is scarce and expensive. Even in completely government-planned and government-controlled economies, this problem exists. Capital needs may be furnished as a government service, but with all the problems of restriction and bureaucratic meddling which exist.

In addition to the above economic controls, Farmer and Richman identify three all-pervasive economic constraints. One they refer to as "factor endowment"—the extent to which a country has available natural resources, adequate and useful labor, and capital which can be employed for efficient production. Another is the size of markets. Obviously, to take advantage of many of the economies of large-scale production, the size of a market open to a firm is important. Closely related are the extent to which competition exists and whether there are legal or other limitations on a manager reaching a market.

A third major pervasive economic constraint which they stress is the extent to which social-overhead capital is available, that is, the supply and quality of public utility type of services. These refer to a host of services necessary to support production, distribution, and consumption. They include transportation, communication, energy production and transmission, warehousing, and sewer and water facilities.

The Farmer-Richman Model

From their identification of the various elements of the management process and the external environment which affect the way in which a manager operates, Farmer and Richman have constructed a model. While probably subject to revision in the future, this model nonetheless distinguishes the management process from the environment of managing. In doing so, it appears to be a useful tool for evaluating management as management and for understanding what may make effective management practice differ as between varying cultures.

The model may be depicted as in Figure 5.1.

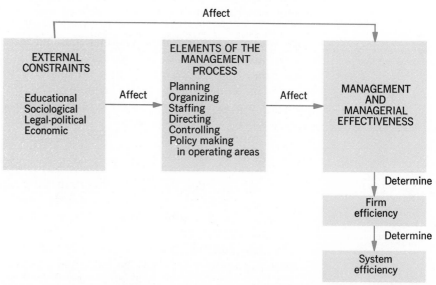

Figure 5.1 Farmer-Richman model for analyzing comparative management. *Adapted from R. N. Farmer and B. M. Richman,* Comparative Management and Economic Progress *(Homewood, Ill.: Richard D. Irwin, Inc., 1965), p. 35.*

Farmer and Richman express the belief that external conditions of the type outlined above will affect both managerial effectiveness and the elements of the management process. Managerial effectiveness will, in turn, determine a firm's efficiency and consequently the efficiency of a given country or society (a "system").

They put it in this way: If a country has a negative attitude toward education, it presents managers with staffing difficulties if a level of unavailable education is important to their operations. If a population has a negative attitude toward scientific method, staffing with people who have analytical abilities will be difficult. Or if a law against pollution of streams exists in a country, this will affect production policies and activities. A lack of an established communications system will also have an effect on the efficiency of many firms. While they may furnish their own system, this is likely to be less efficient.

Other factors may affect only the operation of the management process. The planning time horizon may be limited by political instability or rapid inflation. A paternalistic attitude toward people may influence organizational patterns by restricting delegation. Or an accounting system based on tax evasion may so contort financial data as to make managerial control information misleading. Likewise, management development and promotion may be thwarted by a caste system or racial or religious discrimination. As can be seen, these and many other cultural variables may materially influence management functions and the way a manager undertakes them.

But there is no evidence in the Farmer-Richman model or in their study of comparative management that the *fundamentals* of managing are changed by these environmental constraints. For example, the limitation of the planning horizon caused by rapid inflation does not invalidate the principle of commitment. It means only, as many Brazilian businessmen have found, that the period and means of obtaining recovery of costs plus return on investment are shortened. Nor does a level of education affect the principle of job definition, although its application in terms of a given structure of roles and provisions for incentives will vary. Also, even though a caste system or an attitude of racial or religious discrimination may not permit operation of the principle of open competition and promotion, this does not mean that the principle is untrue. It means, rather, that managerial efficiency is hampered by these external constraints, since a manager is not able to apply the principles completely.

THE KOONTZ MODEL: SEPARATING ENVIRONMENTAL FACTORS FROM MANAGEMENT FUNDAMENTALS

From the point of view of studying comparative management to determine the universality and transferability of the basics of management and thus to make a start in separating science from practice in this field, the Farmer-Richman model is not entirely satisfactory. It makes major contributions in recognizing the importance of environmental factors and in attempting to show how they affect the practice of management, but it is not as useful as it might be in dealing with the problem of transferability. Many other studies that have contributed much to an understanding of comparative management suffer from a similar deficiency.

The Need for a New Approach

There are several difficulties with the generally used models. The problem of separating the art and science of management has been noted. Also, the effectiveness of an enterprise's operation depends not only on management but also on other factors. Management knowledge does not by any means encompass all the knowledge that is utilized in an enterprise. The specialized knowledge, or science, in such basic areas of enterprise operation as engineering, production, marketing, and finance is essential to enterprise operation. Many are the enterprises that have been successful, despite poor management, because of brilliant marketing, strong engineering, well-designed and well-operated production, or astute financing. Even though it is the authors' firm judgment, based on an analysis of the histories of many companies, that effectiveness of management will ultimately make the difference between continued success or decline, at least in a competitive economy, it is still true that enterprises have for a time succeeded entirely through nonmanagerial factors. It is also probably true that if an enterprise has excellent capabilities in nonmanagerial areas, effective managing will assure its success.

In total, then, enterprise activities fall into two broad categories, managerial and nonmanagerial. Either or both can be the causal factors for at least some degree of enterprise effectiveness. Also, nonmanagerial activities will be affected by relevant underlying science or knowledge, just as managerial activities will be affected by underlying management science. Both types of activities will be affected by the availability of human and material resources and by the constraints and influences of the external environment, whether these are educational, political-legal, economic, technological, or sociological-ethical.

If the factors affecting enterprise effectiveness and the role of underlying management science are to be brought to light more clearly than has been done, it would appear that we need a model of the kind shown in Figure 5.2.

As is clear, this revised model is far more complex than those used by previous researchers in the field of comparative management. It is also believed to be far more accurate and realistic. If the purpose is to study comparative *management*, something like this must be done in order to understand and see the elements of universality in management.

The real problem is to separate not only the influence of environmen-

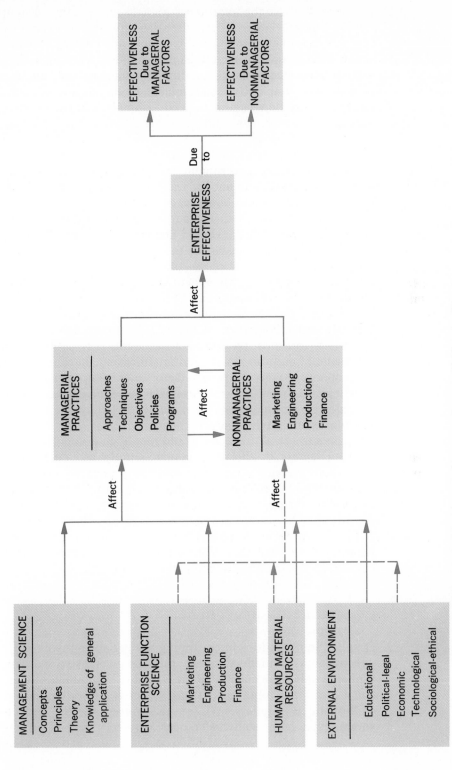

Figure 5.2 Koontz model for analyzing comparative management. *H. Koontz: "A Model for Analyzing the Universality and Transferability of Management," Academy of Management Journal, vol. 12, no. 4, pp. 415–429 (December 1969).*

tal factors but also the importance of managerial, rather than nonmanagerial, factors in determining enterprise effectiveness. This is obviously difficult. If an enterprise were in a laboratory where all input variables except managerial ones could be controlled, it would then be possible to ascribe effectiveness to the quality of managing. But this is impossible. However, if comparative management researchers would try to identify enterprise-function factors as well as they have external environment variables, a closer, even though crude, recognition of *managerial* effectiveness could be made.

This may not be as difficult as it appears. If we could take enterprises (whether business, government, or other) operating in essentially the same external environment and trace the primary causes of their effectiveness to managerial and nonmanagerial factors, we might be surprised at what would be disclosed. The authors have had the occasion to analyze several companies in the United States that had had a profitable growth, only to find in some instances that the quality of managing was rather poor and that the success—often erroneously ascribed to astute managing—was really due to genius in marketing or in engineering or to clever financial manipulation.

It will be noted that managerial attitudes are not included in the model as an independent variable. While they are recognized as very important and must be taken into account, it is believed that they are resultants of cultural factors and environment. In other words, attitudes are responses to environmental factors, not independent variables. Many sociological consultants, for example, on being asked to help change attitudes in an enterprise, have found that they cannot do so without making certain environmental changes.

The authors of this book would like to go a step further. Rather than viewing factors in the environment simply as "constraints"—a term which has a negative connotation—it is preferable to consider them as environmental "variables," which may constitute constraints or opportunities. For example, in the economic category of factor endowments, a country may be short on capital, but it may be rich in natural resources. Similarly, some laws may be restrictive for conducting business, but others may be favorable. Therefore, any environmental restraint could become an opportunity in certain situations.

EVIDENCES OF UNIVERSALITY

Despite the difficulties in separating the variables involved in enterprise effectiveness or ineffectiveness, there is persuasive evidence that the fundamentals of managing are universal. While much of this represents conclusions and opinions, it has arisen from studies and analyses of well-qualified scholars. While the studies are too numerous to be summarized here, some references may be noted. The conclusion of

Harbison and Myers that "organization building has its logic" has been noted.[18] The work of Farmer and Richman[19] covering a number of different cultures is particularly noteworthy and indicates the universality of basic management theory and principles. Likewise, the work of Negandhi points in the same direction.[20] The same kind of inferences can clearly be drawn from the work of Fayerweather on Mexico,[21] the various publications of the National Planning Association,[22] the work of Abegglen on Japan,[23] the studies of Prasad,[24] and many others.

Also, a number of studies on comparative management have been made by doctoral students. Most of these have found a high degree of universality in the application of management concepts and principles. For example, a series of studies undertaken at the University of California, Los Angeles, indicate quite persuasively that well-managed American-owned companies, operating in less developed countries, have generally shown superiority in management and economic effectiveness.[25]

The universal nature of management fundamentals is also apparent in the specialized books on administration for business, government, and other types of enterprises. While semantic differences may exist, one finds that, at the fundamental level, authors are talking about the same phenomena.

Persons like the authors who have led management seminars for various types of enterprises find that the identical concepts, theory, and principles, and often the same techniques (such as variable budgeting or management by objectives), apply with equal force in widely different

---

[18]Harbison and Myers, loc. cit.

[19]*Comparative Management and Economic Progress.* See also many other publications by the same authors, either jointly or individually presented. In a later assessment of comparative management, Farmer, for example, writes, "Management *is* universal; only the outcomes are strikingly different," in J. W. McGuire (ed.), op. cit., p. 302.

[20]See, for example, his paper "A Model for Analyzing Organizations in Cross-Cultural Settings: A Conceptual Scheme and Some Research Findings," *Comparative Administration and Research Conference* (Kent, Ohio: Kent State University (1969), pp. 55–87.

[21]J. Fayerweather, *The Executive Overseas* (Syracuse, N.Y.: Syracuse University Press, 1959).

[22]See, for example, F. Brandenberg, *The Development of Latin American Private Enterprise* (1964); T. Geiger, *The General Electric Company in Brazil* (1961); T. Geiger and W. Armstrong, *The Development of African Private Enterprise* (1961); and S. Kannappan and E. Burgess, *Aluminum Ltd. in India* (1967).

[23]*The Japanese Factory* (New York: The Free Press of Glencoe, Inc., 1958).

[24]See, for example, "New Managerialism in Czechoslovakia and the Soviet Union," *Academy of Management Journal*, vol. 9, no. 4, pp. 328–336 (December 1966).

[25]These include such unpublished dissertations as B. D. Estafen, "An Empirical Experiment in Comparative Management: A Study of the Transferability of American Management Policies and Practices into Firms Operating in Chile" (1967); A. J. Papageorge, "Transferability of Management: A Case Study of the United States and Greece" (1967); F. C. Flores, Jr., "Applicability of American Management Know-How to Developing Countries: Case Studies of U.S. Firms Operating Both in the United States and the Philippines in Comparison with Domestic Firms in the Philippines" (1967); John Jaeger, "A Comparative Management Study: Organization Patterns and Processes of Hotels in Four Countries" (1965); and Y. K. Shetty, "A Comparative Study of Manpower Management Practices in American and Indian Industrial Enterprises" (1967).

enterprise environments. Also, it is interesting that most of the basic propositions inventoried from the behavioral sciences have universal application where relevant to managerial situations.[26]

The Significance of Universality for Management Research, Teaching, and Practice

It is hoped that increasing effort will be made to separate the underlying science of management from the art of managing. This should make it increasingly possible to recognize fundamentals of universal application and transferability, thereby lifting many of the clouds that have obscured the analysis, teaching, and practice of management, and turning the jungle of management theory into orderly rows of trees at last.

Much research has been done. Teaching of basic management has greatly expanded in the past 25 years. Management practice has become far more sophisticated and effective, but only the surface of this important field has been touched. Meanwhile, a great waste of human and material resources continues through inept research, ineffective teaching, and too much seat-of-the-pants managing. It is believed that much can be accomplished through the simple, but largely unaccomplished, approach of clearly and purposively separating underlying science from its artful application to reality.

ENVIRONMENTAL IMPACT ON MANAGING IN SELECTED COUNTRIES

It may be useful to illustrate some relationships between environmental factors and both managerial and nonmanagerial activities. The matrix, Table 5.1, shows selected relationships for France, Germany, and Japan. In addition, general relationships between environmental factors and managerial functions are indicated by abbreviated notations. For example, the fact that educational variables affect planning is shown as "Ed → Pl" in Table 5.1 Similarly, the impact of economic factors on planning is indicated by "Ec → Pl."

It should be noted that the matrix is illustrative rather than comprehensive and conclusive for the selected countries. Also, this discussion is based on generalizations. There are, for example, great differences in managerial styles among French managers just as there are differences among United States managers. Furthermore, a society is not static and changes do occur over time. For instance, the traditional authoritarian

---

[26]See, for example, the inventory of propositions in J. L. Pierce, *Organizational Effectiveness: An Inventory of Propositions* (Homewood, Ill.: Richard D. Irwin, Inc., 1968); and B. Berelson and G. A. Steiner, *Human Behavior: An Inventory of Scientific Findings* (New York: Harcourt, Brace & World, Inc., 1964).

Table 5.1   The Impact of External Factors on Managerial and Enterprise Functions and Activities

Functions and activities	Environmental factors			
	Educational (Ed)	Sociological-cultural (Sc)	Legal-political (Lp)	Economic (Ec)
Managerial functions				
(a) Planning (Pl) (Objectives, strategies, policies, programs, procedures, decision making)	Ed → Pl	**Japan:** consultation in decision making; upward flow of decisions	**France:** planning within guidelines by government (Le Plan)	Ec → Pl
(b) Organizing (Or) (Structure, roles, grouping of activities, authority and responsibility, coordination)	Ed → Or	**Japan:** authority often based on seniority; respect for age	**Germany:** co-determination; worker representation on supervisory board and executive committee	Ed → Or
(c) Staffing (St) (Manpower requirements, selection, appraisal, compensation, training)	Ed → St	**Japan:** lifelong employment	**Germany:** labor participates in major staffing decisions in major firms	Ec → St
(d) Leading (Le) (Motivation, leadership, communication)	Ed → Le	**Japan:** loyalty to the firm **Germany:** benevolent-authoritarian leadership	Lp → Le **Germany:** laws requiring companies to put worker representatives on supervisory board and executive committee	Ec → Le
(e) Controlling (Co) (Standards, measurement, correction)	Ed → Co	Sc → Co	Lp → Co	Ec → Co
Enterprise functions				
(a) Engineering, research, and development (En)	Ed → En	Sc → En	Lp → En	Ec → En
(b) Production (Pr)	Ed → Pr	**Japan:** lifetime employment	Lp → Pr	**Japan** and **Germany:** emphasis on productivity
(c) Marketing (Ma)	Ed → Ma	Sc → Ma	Lp → Ma	Ec → Ma
(d) Finance (Fi)	Ed → Fi	Sc → Fi	Lp → Fi	Ec → Fi

style of German managers is slowly giving way to a more participative approach.

Despite these limitations, managers involved in international business can benefit by developing such a matrix (shown as Table 5.1) for the country in which they plan to operate. For a more sophisticated analysis, the environmental factors should be further itemized as suggested by Farmer and Richman. Similarly, the managerial functions should be broken down into key managerial activities as discussed above. This approach, then, requires (1) the identification of critical external variables, (2) a review of managerial functions and activities, and (3) the recognition of the impact of external factors on the management process and selected nonmanagerial policy areas.

France: Le Plan

In France, government planning on a national scale (legal-political environment factor) helps coordinate plans of individual industries and companies (managerial function of planning). The government's aim is to utilize most effectively the country's resources and to avoid expansion in uneconomic areas. Although governmental planning—which is also extended to regional areas—is carried out by relatively few, but competent, people, cooperation and assistance are provided by other governmental departments, employers' organizations, unions, and consumers.

The plan, which is generally revised every 5 years, attempts to obtain economic growth, price stability, a balance in foreign payments, and a favorable employment situation. Managers, then, are not only constrained by ''Le Plan'' but also aided by having a great deal of information available for preparing plans for their own enterprises.

Germany: Authority and Codetermination

In the past, and to a lesser extent today, the German cultural environment favored reliance on authority in directing the work force, although it was often benevolent authoritarianism (managerial function of leading). Even today, while managers may show concern for subordinates, they also expect obedience.

It appears almost a paradox that, on the one hand, the managerial style is characterized by considerable use of authority, while, on the other hand, labor, by law, is represented and actively involved in managing large corporations (legal-political environment). In 1951 a law was passed that provides for codetermination, which requires labor membership in the supervisory board and the executive committee of certain large corporations. Furthermore, a labor director is elected as a member of the executive committee. This position is a difficult one. Labor directors, supposedly must represent the interests of the employees and, at the same time, must make managerial decisions that are in the best interest of the enterprise.

Labor's participation in the decision-making process has contributed to relatively peaceful labor-management relations, but it also can delay vital strategic decisions. For instance, Volkswagen's management recognized long ago the need for building an assembly plant in the United States, yet this decision was delayed by labor, which feared loss of jobs. Eventually, after long and costly indecision, labor recognized that the well-being of the company is inextricably interwoven with its own well-being, and agreed to setting up an assembly plant in Pennsylvania.

Japan: Lifetime Employment and Consensus Decision Making

Japan, one of the leading industrial nations in the world, has adopted managerial practices that are quite different from those of other economically advanced countries in the Western world. This discussion focuses on two common Japanese practices: lifetime employment and consensus decision making.

Lifetime employment   Important features of Japanese management practice are lifelong employment (related to staffing function), great concern for the individual, and emphasis on seniority. Typically, employees spend their working life with a single enterprise, which in turn provides employees with security and a feeling of belonging. This practice brings the culturally induced concept of *wa* ("harmony") to the enterprise,[27] resulting in employee loyalty and close identification with the aims of the company.

However, it also adds to business costs because employees are kept on the payroll even though there may be insufficient work. Consequently, firms are beginning to question the practice of lifelong employment. Indeed, changes appear to be in the making, but they are slow—very slow.[28] What is often overlooked, however, is that this permanent employment practice, known as *nenko*, is used only by large firms. In fact, it is estimated that the job security system applies to only about one-third of the labor force.[29]

Closely related to lifelong employment is the seniority system, which provides privileges for older employees who have been with the enterprise a long time. But there are indications that the seniority system may be superceded by a more open approach that provides opportunities for advancement for young people. For example, the relatively new Sony Corporation has team leaders (a point is made not to call them supervisors) who are often 18- and 19-year old girls, with practically no age difference between these leaders and the operators they lead.

[27]"Japanese Managers Tell How Their Systems Works," *Fortune*, vol. 96, no. 5, 126–132, 136, 138 (November 1977).
[28]Ibid.
[29]T. K. Oh, "Japanese Management—A Critical Review," *The Academy of Management Review*, vol. 1, no. 1, pp. 14–25 (January 1976).

Decison making   The managerial practice of decision making is also considerably different from that in the United States. It is built on the concept that change and new ideas should come primarily from below. Thus, lower-level employees prepare proposals for higher-level personnel. Supervisors, rather than simply accepting or rejecting suggestions, tactfully question proposals, make suggestions, and encourage subordinates. If necessary, proposals are sent back to the initiator for more information.

Japanese management, then, uses decision making by consensus in which lower-level employees initiate the idea and submit it to the next higher level until it reaches the desk of the top executive. If the proposal is approved, it is returned to the initiator for implementation. Although the decision-making process is time-consuming, the implementation of the decision—because of the general consensus at various levels of management—is swift and does not require additional "selling."

An important characteristic of Japanese decision making is the great amount of effort that goes into defining the question or problem; there is a great deal of communication *before* a decision is actually made. American managers are often accused of making decisions before defining the problem. In contrast, Japanese management makes a decision only after long discussions of the issue.[30]

In summary, Japanese managerial practices are still marked (although changes are occurring) by lifetime employment, concern for the individual, emphasis on seniority, and a sense of loyalty to the firm. Furthermore, in decision making there is open communication among people at different levels of the organizational hierarchy, a great deal of collaboration, and a recognition of mutual dependence.

INTERNATIONAL MANAGEMENT AND MULTINATIONAL CORPORATIONS

The foregoing discussion indicated the impact of environmental factors on the managerial functions. While it is true that similar factors also affect domestic firms, they usually are more critical for international corporations operating in different countries. As illustrated in Table 5.2, managers involved in international business are faced with many factors that are different from those of the domestically oriented firm. Managers have to interact with employees who have different educational backgrounds and value systems; they also must cope with different legal, political, and economic factors. Thus, environments do influence the way managerial and enterprise functions are carried out.

The following discussion of international business management focuses on the interface of the parent corporation with host countries and

[30]S. Kobayashi, "The Creative Organization—A Japanese Experiment," *Personnel, vol. 47, no. 6, pp. 8–17 (November–December 1970).*

Table 5.2 Characteristics of and Practices by Domestic and International Enterprises

	Domestic enterprise (industrialized country)	International enterprise
The environment		
(a) Educational environment		
1 Language (spoken, written, official)	One	Multiple
2 Education system (quality, level, extent)	No or little constraint	Great constraint
(b) Sociological-cultural environment		
1 Values, attitudes (toward achievement, risk taking, scientific method, work)	Homogeneous	Heterogeneous
2 Social organization (authority, status, roles, institutions, .mobility, social systems)	Similar	Different
(c) Political-legal environment		
1 Political orientation (power, ideologies)	Country-centered	Transnational
2 Legal environment (laws, codes, regulations)	Fairly uniform	Different
3 National sovereignties.	One	Many
4 Government policies, regulations	Same	Different
(d) Economic environment		
1 Economic development (underdeveloped, industrialized)	At similar stages	At different stages
2 Economic system (capitalistic, mixed, Marxist)	Similar	Different
Managerial functions		
(a) Planning		
1 Scanning the environment for threats and opportunities	National market	Worldwide market
(b) Organizing		
1 Organization Structure	Structure for domestic operations	Global structure
2 View of authority	Similar	Different
(c) Staffing		
1 Sources of managerial talent	National labor pool	Worldwide labor pool
2 Manager orientation	Often ethnocentric	Geocentric

Table 5.2 Cont.

	Domestic enterprise (industrialized country)	International enterprise
Managerial functions		
(d) Leading		
1 Leadership and motivation	Influenced by similar culture	Influenced by many different cultures
2 Communication lines	Relatively short	Network with long distances
(e) Controlling		
1 Reporting system	Similar requirements	Many different requirements
Enterprise functions		
(a) Engineering and production		
1 State of the art, technology	Similar technology	Different levels of technology
(b) Marketing		
1 Consumer needs and preferences	Local market	Global market
(c) Financing		
1 Sources, capital transfer	Primarily domestic	Global

on the managerial functions of planning, organizing, staffing, leading, and controlling within the international context. Although the discussion emphasizes large multinational corporations, it usually applies also to international firms of various sizes.

The Nature and Purpose of International Business

International business involves transactions across national boundaries. This requires the transfer of goods, services, technology, managerial knowledge, and capital to other countries. Although business has been conducted on an international scale for many years, it has gained greater visibility and importance in recent years through the growth of large multinational corporations.

The interaction of a firm with the host country can take many forms. One is the *exportation* of goods and services. Another form is through *licensing agreements* for producing goods in another country. Still another form of interaction is the use of *joint ventures* with firms in host countries. The parent company may also engage in *management contracts* that provide for operating foreign companies. Finally, multinationals may set up wholly owned *subsidiaries* or *branches* with production facilities in the host country. Thus, in developing a global stragegy, an international firm has many options.

Unifying effects   The contact between the parent firm and the host country is affected by several characteristics; some are unifying, others have potential for conflicts. Unifying influences occur when the parent company provides and shares technical and managerial know-how, thus assisting the host company in the development of human and material resources. Moreover, the parent corporation and the firm in the host country may find it advantageous to be integrated into a global organization structure. Whatever the interaction, policies must provide for equity and result in benefits for both the parent firm and the host company. Only then can one expect a long-lasting relationship.

Potentials for conflict   Other factors can cause conflicts between the parent firm and the host country. In the comparative-management discussion, attention was drawn to the many environmental constraints. Nationalistic self-interest may overshadow the benefits obtained through cooperation. Similarly, sociocultural differences can lead to breakdowns in communication and subsequent misunderstandings. Also, a large multinational firm may have such an overpowering economic effect on a small country that the host country feels overwhelmed. Some international corporations have been charged with obtaining excessive profits, hiring the best local people away from local firms, and operating contrary to social customs.[31] Thus, the international corporation must develop social and diplomatic skills in its managers in order to prevent or resolve such conflicts.

The Multinational Corporations

Multinational corporations (MNC) have their headquarters in one country, but their operations are in many different countries. In its early stages, international business was conducted with an *ethnocentric* outlook; that is, the orientation and type of operation was based on that of the parent company. In contrast, the modern multinational corporation has a geocentric orientation. This means that the total organization is viewed as an interdependent system operating in many countries. The relationships between headquarters and subsidiaries are collaborative, with communication flowing in both directions. Furthermore, key positions are filled by managers of different nationalities. In short, the orientation of the multinational corporation is truly international and goes beyond a narrow nationalistic viewpoint.

[31]For a more extensive discussion of criticisms see R. H. Mason, "Conflicts Between Host Countries and the Multinational Enterprise," *California Management Review*, vol. 17, no. 1, pp. 5–14 (Fall 1974).

Who are the multinationals? There are scores of small and medium-sized firms operating in different countries. Many may not have production facilities abroad, but engage primarily in exporting goods and services. The focus of this discussion, however, is on large multinational corporations.

Most people are familiar with the names of large United States multinationals such as IBM, Colgate-Palmolive, Exxon, National Cash Register, General Motors, and General Electric. Yet multinationals are not only an American phenomenon. The ten largest non-United States firms and their headquarters countries, ranked in terms of 1977 net sales, were as follows: Royal Dutch/Shell Group (Netherlands, Britain); British Petroleum (Britain); National Iranian Oil (Iran); Unilever (Britain, Netherlands); Phillips (Netherlands); Fiat (Italy); Veba (Germany); Daimler-Benz (Germany); Volkswagen (Germany); and Compagnie Française des pétroles (France).[32]

Advantages of multinationals Multinational corporations have several advantages over firms that have a domestic orientation. Obviously, the MNC can take advantage of business opportunities in many different countries. They also can utilize capital markets throughout the world. In fact, largely in response to the needs of the 450 largest multinationals, a stateless financial system was created about two decades ago. This would include such leading institutions as the International Bank for Reconstruction and Development and the Inter-American Development Bank. This supranational banking system has grown to at least $400 billion, providing easy access to the world capital markets.[33]

The large MNCs also can recruit management and other personnel from a worldwide labor pool. Moreover, multinational firms benefit by being able to establish production facilities in countries where the products can be produced most effectively and efficiently. Finally, companies with worldwide operations sometimes have better access to natural resources and materials that may not be available to domestic firms.

Challenges for the multinationals The advantages of multinational firms must be weighed against the challenges and risks associated with operating in foreign environments. One problem is the increasing nationalism in many countries. Years ago, developing countries lacked managerial, marketing, and technical skills. Consequently, they welcomed the multinationals. But the situation is changing, with people in developing countries acquiring those skills. In addition, countries not only become aware of the value of their natural resources, but they also become more skilled in international negotiations. Finally, multinationals must main-

---

[32]"The Industrial Nations Lag Again in Profits," *Business Week*, p. 82 (July 24, 1978).
[33]"Stateless Money—A New Force on World Economics," *Business Week*, pp. 76–85 (August 21, 1978).

tain good relations with the host country, which may prove difficult because governments frequently change, and corporations must deal with and adapt to these changes.

THE MANAGERIAL FUNCTIONS IN INTERNATIONAL BUSINESS

Considerable evidence exists to show that management fundamentals are applicable in different countries, different cultures, and different environments. However, specific problems occur in international business that affect the *practice* of the managerial functions of planning, organizing, staffing, leading, and controlling (see Table 5.2 for an overview).

Planning in the Multinational Corporation

Planning requires setting objectives and then selecting strategies, policies, programs, and procedures for achieving them. In doing this, a critically important activity for the MNC is the assessment of opportunities and threats in the external environment. This is a complex task, even for a domestic enterprise; but it becomes more intricate when many different, ever-changing world markets must be scanned.

Analyzing the external environment according to educational, sociocultural, legal-political, and economic factors may be a first step in developing a profile of the environment. This, of course, helps planners identify the critical external variables and estimate the probable impact on managerial and nonmanagerial functions.

External threats and opportunities must be matched against internal strengths and weaknesses of the firm. For example, a poor educational system makes it difficult to find qualified personnel. Similarly, cultural orientation toward time will affect planning. Specifically, culturally induced attitudes that emphasize a short-time perspective will not be conducive to long-range or strategic planning. Finally, political and economic instability in a country will discourage long-term commitment of resources.

Thus, long-range objectives and development of strategies, policies, programs, and procedures for achieving them are influenced by external factors that are even more difficult to forecast for the international firm operating in a world environment than for the domestic enterprise operating in only one country.

Organizing the Multinational Corporation

In order to achieve corporate objectives, organizational structures must be established. Many alternatives are available. An enterprise may, for example, establish a vice-presidential position at corporate headquarters with responsibility for the *international division*. An alternative is to organize according to *geographical* areas. For example, managers may be put in charge of regions such as North America, Latin America, Europe, Africa, and the Far East. Still another way of grouping organizational activities is according to *product lines*. For instance, at corporate headquarters, managers may be put in charge of a product line which is marketed worldwide. The truly multinational firm may integrate domestic and international business into a *global structure* which gives similar importance to domestic and foreign business activities.

Each structure has advantages and disadvantages which are further discussed in Chapter 13. At this point it is important to realize that for the large multinational corporation any one structure may be insufficient, and different organizational designs may have to be mixed depending on the environmental and task demands.

Staffing in the Multinational Corporation

The positions identified in the organization structure must be filled by qualified persons. This involves staffing—determining work-force requirements, evaluating the existing human resources, and recruiting, selecting, appraising, training, and compensating managers.

Sources of managerial talent Staffing the multinational firm requires consideration of national boundaries. Basically, managers of the MNC can be classified in three ways. First, managers may be *nationals* selected from the country in which the headquarters is located. These expatriates (with home-country nationality) are chosen to represent and manage the enterprise abroad. These managers, because of their experience, are usually familiar with the parent company's policies and operations.

Second, a firm may select managers who are nationals of the *host country*. These managers are well aware of the country's environment, its education system, its culture, its legal and political processes, and its economic environment. They usually are familiar with local customers, suppliers, government officials, behavioral characteristics of employees, and the public in general.

The third source for managerial personnel consists of *third-country nationals*. These are managers who have a different nationality from either the country of the parent company or the host country. Such managers may have gained experience by working at the company headquarters as well as in different countries. Thus, they would have developed behavioral flexibility that eases their adaptation to different cultures. These managers may be truly transcultural.

Trends in staffing the multinational corporation Each of the three sources for managers has advantages and disadvantages, and a firm may use a variety of combinations,[34] but a few factors that influence the trend

[34]For a detailed discussion, see S. B. Prasad and Y. K. Shetty, *An Introduction to Multinational Management* (Englewood Cliffs, N.J.: Prentice-Hall, Inc., 1976), pp. 97–99.

in staffing the multinationals are worth noting. First, the cost of sending United States managers abroad has increased, partly due to the declining value of the United States dollar in the 1970s. Second, people in the host countries are now better prepared to assume responsible managerial positions. Finally, employing nationals of the host country can improve the relations with that country. Consequently, as far as American firms are concerned, the trend is toward employing more host-country nationals than managers from the parent company.

Leading in the Multinational Corporation

Leading involves motivating and communicating. It requires exerting leadership by inducing employees to contribute to enterprise objectives.

Motivating and leading demand an understanding of employees and their cultural environment. For instance, participative management may work well in the United States, but may cause confusion among employees in another country with a tradition of autocratic rule.

Communication is often a problem in multinational firms with subsidiaries and affiliates in countries where different languages are spoken. Even a firm with operations in a country where English is the primary language may encounter communication problems because of the distance between headquarters and the subsidiary. To be sure, communication technology has greatly improved the transmission of information, yet a telephone call is still not quite the same as a visit and a person-to-person discussion.

Controlling in the Multinational Corporation

Controlling—the measurement and correcting of performance to assure that events conform to plans—is an essential managerial function that is influenced by several environmental factors unique to international enterprises. First, revenues, costs, and profits are measured in different currencies. Second, the ratios between currencies are subject to considerable fluctuations. Third, accounting practices and financial reporting often differ from country to country. For example, accounting procedures may have to satisfy the demands of tax authorities of the host country as well as the government of the parent firm. The procedures should also satisfy stockholders in various countries, agencies in charge of regulating securities, and banks. Procedures must also be suitable to meet the internal requirements of the firm. To develop a procedure that meets all these demands at the same time is extremely difficult. Finally, and partly due to the complex nature of measurement, there is a time lag in the measurement of performance which may delay detecting deviations from standards and the initiation of corrective action. In all, these few examples indicate that controlling the international corporation is considerably more difficult than monitoring a domestic operation.

1 Why is management quality a crucial factor in economic growth? Can a country thrive economically with poor or average management?

2 From your knowledge of any foreign country, outline the major elements of its culture that would, in your judgment, influence the kind of management you would expect in a typical firm.

3 Analyze and discuss the strengths and weaknesses of the Farmer-Richman model of comparative management.

4 Take an enterprise—whether business or nonbusiness—with which you are familiar and apply the Koontz model to see if its success or failure is due to managerial or nonmanagerial factors.

5 What are the advantages of multinational corporations? What challenges must they meet? Give examples.

6 What are likely to be the differences between the operation of a domestic firm and a multinational corporation? Select five characteristics and discuss their importance.

7 How does the material in this chapter fit the situational or contingency approach to management?

8 In accepting or rejecting the concept of universality of management theory, do you agree that separation of fundamental management knowledge from its application to practice is a useful and logical approach for comparative management?

CASES FOR PART 1:
THE BASIS OF MANAGEMENT

1 Hart Electronics

Hart Electronics, Incorporated, was built up in the early 1960s to design and manufacture special instruments for the Apollo moon landing program. Its founders were two eminent physicists, Dr. Smith Lane and Dr. Raymond Morey. Adequately financed by Robert Hart, well-known multimillionaire, the two founders soon attracted a large group of scientists who developed acceleration instruments and test equipment useful in space programs and in airborne missile systems. Within a few years, they found themselves as the designers and producers of entire space control systems. Within 10 years the company prospered and reached $100 million in annual sales with some 2000 employees.

The company was not well organized and managed during its rapid growth, but, because of its new and imaginative products, it did succeed in making reasonable profits. However, as it grew, competition came into the field and Mr. Hart became worried about the company's ability to market and produce efficiently. On discussing this problem with his consultant, Mr. Hart was told that the top scientists in managerial positions running the company must learn to become more effective managers. As this point, he asked the consultant to start a management development program. With the approval of the company's top officers, who felt compelled to follow the suggestions of their major owner, a management development committee was established with the consultant as chairperson. The committee's task was to design and implement a development program for the company. The consultant was given a committee comprising the company's financial vice president, director of personnel, and two top scientific leaders who headed major divisions of the company.

At the first meeting of the committee, the two top scientists were clearly unsympathetic with the program, feeling with some justification that a company with such a rapid and successful growth could hardly need any management training. One of them, obviously trying to stop the whole program, said at the start of the meeting: "How can we even be talking about instituting a management development program? No one has even been able to tell me what management is. I have heard it said that it is getting things done through people. If that is all it is, I have been doing this in my work for years. How can we be taking our time to develop a program of any meaning for something as simple as this?"

1   Does the scientist have an accurate idea of what managing is?
2   Exactly how would you respond to him and convince him of the desirability of having a management development program?

2 The Atomic Research Laboratory

A senior management professor in one of our large universities was invited to lead a special seminar for the top 200 managers and their assistants of one of the nation's largest atomic energy research and development laboratories. This laboratory was spending nearly $200 million per year of United States government funds.

As the professor was getting into her subject and introducing the nature and importance of management theory and techniques for improving the quality of managing, a pleasant, sandy-haired gentleman (who was unknown to the speaker but turned out to be head of the laboratory and a Nobel Prize winner) arose from his seat and said:

"Professor, we are very interested in what you have to say and there may even be some intellectual content in it. But, for your benefit and the benefit of those gathered here, I would like to say that, while management may apply to General Motors, Lockheed Aircraft, Hughes Aircraft Company, the Bell Telephone System, and even to many government agencies such as the Internal Revenue Service, it does not apply here. We are scientists and researchers, and we do not need or want management."

The professor was understandably taken aback, and, since it was shortly after April 15 and she had just paid her income taxes, she was also irritated.

1 Suppose that you were the professor leading the seminar. What would you have said at this point?
2 Explain why an intelligent top scientist would have made such a statement?

3 Carlton Plywood Company

The Carlton Plywood Company is a medium-sized company in the Pacific Northwest that buys logs, peels them, and makes plywood, which is marketed through independent sales agents. Frank Carlton, now 55 years old, inherited the company from his father, who founded it 40 years ago. With his astute ability to buy logs, anticipate market trends, and run an efficient operation, Frank Carlton built the company to an annual sales level of $10 million, with profits after taxes averaging $750,000, with 200 stockholders (although he and his family hold 60 percent of the stock), and with some 300 employees in three mills. His son James, having just graduated from a business school with an M.B.A. degree, joined his father as assistant to the president, with the plan that he would become president in a few years, when his father took early retirement.

After a few weeks in his new position, James told his father that he must modernize his management style and manage the company more in accordance with the new theories of contingency management. His father listened patiently and with great expectations as James explained that the company should not be managed and organized in accordance with "classical" theories—that there was no best way to organize it, to develop or carry out plans, or to promote and compensate employees. Instead, the company should be managed by taking into account contingencies, that is, the various situations which exist from time to time.

Frank Carlton then questioned his son as to what he would have done differently over the past 30 years, pointing out that the plywood industry had always been subject to many variables, such as changing prices and availability of logs, price and demand variables of finished plywood as markets changed (especially as demand for plywood for housing and commercial construction and for exports to Japan changed so often), and large variations in labor rates and availability of skilled labor from year to year. He asked his son how the new contingency theory would change what he was doing and what he had been doing.

1   If you were Frank Carlton, what would you have answered James when he said that the company should not be managed according to "classical" theory, and that there is no one best way to manage?
2   How would you apply contingency theory? How would it change the way effective managers, who may never have heard about contingency theory, carry out their jobs?

4   The Systems Approach to Management

An upper-level executive of one of America's best-managed companies retired early from his position and became a lecturer in management in one of the nation's business schools. One of the concepts he continually heard discussed by his younger colleagues was that the modern manager must learn and take a systems approach to managing. Impressed by this apparently new idea, he seriously asked each of these academic colleagues what executives would do differently if they adopted the systems approach.

Without exception, the replies seem to assume that the "traditional" executives were incompetent. He discovered that utilizing the systems approach was exactly what every good manager had been doing for years. Whether a program involved marketing of a new product, expansion of plant facilities, managerial appraisal, reorganization, or the many other areas in which managers are called to take action, the systems approach was precisely what good managers had long been doing, and it was therefore not new to management.

1   What does it mean "to take a systems approach" to managing? List at least six key concepts of systems theory.
2   Identify important variables in a systems model of managing. Describe the relationships among these variables.
3   How useful, do you think, are the systems concepts for managers? What are the advantages and limitations of systems theory?

5   The Paragon Radar Corporation

The Paragon Radar Corporation was organized in 1955. It was managed by three engineers who formerly worked for the McDonnell Aircraft Company. They were instrumental in developing a radar capable of handling transmissions over distances far beyond those formerly permitted by the curvature of the earth. The Paragon people were adequately financed and decided upon a market policy of dealing only with government agencies, especially the Air Force, Navy, Army, and NASA. The budgets of these agencies grew steadily as the years passed, and business was very good.

The Paragon people did not have a marketing department in the usual sense of this term. The heads of each department were expected to develop their own business. Consequently, the engineers would keep in close touch with their counterparts in the several agencies, help them identify their needs, help them sell these needs to their relevant policy-making executives and contracting officers, and write the proposal as soon as the request came through.

As the decade of the 1970s began, the federal government drastically cut back the budget for the Department of Defense and NASA. Business was scarce and hard to get. The Paragon people bid more and more contracts with less and less success. This state of affairs became the subject of a staff meeting at the corporate level.

"Ladies and Gentlemen," said the president, "you all know the causes for the decline in our business. The corporation is gradually approaching a precarious posture. We do have excellent technical abilities, and there are still some $75 billion being spent on national defense so our potential is still there. I have pointed out to the department heads that you must get new business if you are to remain part of the organization. It seems that my words have fallen on unhearing ears. But I assure you that I am really serious. The time has come when we either get well or be acquired by another firm."

James Simpson, one of the department heads, spoke up, saying, "You may think that there is something lacking in my loyalty, but I really believe that we are not organized in an effective way to do what we must do. In the good years we did very well. Business was good, our bids were highly successful, indeed so much so that department managers would turn down business if the technical content did not interest them. Now that we need business we don't have the contacts. The way we have approached the problem no one is responsible for getting business: we all are, but no one can say how much. Authority is widely diffused. We all share the blame and yet no one accepts it."

The members of the staff were shocked. The president had the good sense to let time run on while each examined his or her position. One member eventually reached for his alibis. "I don't view the matter in that light. Here we have been successful for going on two decades, we get business like other aerospace companies do, and you can't expect a department head to accept and work on a contract that he is not interested in. You know, the defense business is not like selling soap."

"I know," said Simpson. "I used to believe that too. Recently I have been looking at the management literature to see if there is some principle we have overlooked. These chaps seem to be saying that the best results occur when a man has a definite objective to achieve, when he is personally held responsible for achieving it, when he has the authority to make decisions that must be made in order to bring in the business. We operate this way in everything except marketing. Why is this an exception?"

The meeting adjourned at this point. The president said he would reexamine the matter and try to bring in a proposal at the next meeting. Two weeks later, and after many hours of study and consultation, he opened the regular staff meeting with an announcement.

"Ladies and gentlemen," he said, "I think it is time we stop fighting management principles; let's use them for our own benefit. I think we should have a 'business-getting' activity centralized in the hands of one person and reporting to me. We might call the function 'Advanced Program Development,' for semantic purposes. I visualize this activity comprising three functions. One would be staffed by engineers with marketing ability, another with engineers who will write the proposals, and another with market research capability. The head of this whole group would be responsible for bringing in new business and would have the necessary decision-making authority. The head would be expected to run a right shop. I do not want an expanding bureaucracy. We will borrow technical people as needed from the operating departments. In order that the technical people in the new department will not grow stale and useless, I feel that whoever is head of a proposal committee should be made program manager when and if the contract is secured. Thus, I can see a great deal of lateral movement among the engineers in all our activities."

The proposal was so revolutionary that no one could be expected to take a position on its feasibility. The staff was dismissed with the injunction to study it and bring back suggestions that would make it more viable.

1   Do you believe that the president's proposal for an "advanced program development" department would work in Paragon? What do you see to be the strengths and weaknesses of this proposal?
2   Can you suggest anything else that could be done to solve Paragon's problem?

6   LMT, Incorporated

Frank W. Bates was president of LMT, Incorporated, a large company making wheels, brakes, springs, radios, and other components for the automobile manufacturing companies. The firm also had a division taking part in developing and manufacturing components for the space program. The space program activities of LMT were in a division headed by a general manager, Julia Sanders. Her personnel manager, Lewis Lemke, recommended that the way to develop managers at all levels in the division was to give them courses and exercises in psychology and human relations. He made the point that, after all, managing is a "people" problem, and the only way people can be good managers is to thoroughly understand themselves and their fellow managers and employees.

Ms. Sanders, impressed with this idea, told Mr. Lemke to go ahead with the program. The personnel manager did so with great energy and thoroughness. After a few years, every manager from top to bottom of the division had gone through a number of courses and exercises to make them understand themselves and other people as well as the entire area of human relations.

But then Ms. Sanders found that the quality of management in the division had not improved, even though it was clear that people did better understand people. In fact, it became apparent that, in terms of performance, the other divisions of LMT were doing far better than the space division. President Bates had also noted this and asked Ms. Sanders to explain how her division developed managers. After hearing the nature of the program, Mr. Bates said, "I wonder if you have been on the right track."

1   What do you think of the space division's approach to training managers in the essentials of management?

2   If you were Mr. Bates, what would you suggest that Ms. Sanders should have done?

7   Consolidated Computers, Inc.

James Pruitt was ushered into the president's office. Three months ago he had been appointed manager of the first foreign plant of Consolidated Computers, Inc. He appeared to be the ideal person for this assignment, as a proven division manager of many talents. He was an innovator and very much interested in a foreign appointment. Now he was calling on his superior just before catching the plane for Riyadh.

"I wanted to talk to you," the president began, "about some issues you will be facing when you reach Saudi Arabia. I guess you might call what I want to say a matter of my search for a business philosophy. We have not had to experience here the new issues that you will face, and we simply do not have a set of policies and procedures to cover such matters. Perhaps out of your experience we can move in that direction in case we later establish our operations in other countries.

"I am not concerned about your encountering new principles of management. They are universal, you have developed great skill in applying them to domestic operations, and I have no doubt about your skill in applying them in a foreign environment. You will soon discover, however, that managing is different abroad precisely because the cultural environment is so different.

"I think our best position is to realize that we are going into Saudi Arabia as a guest. We each need the other at this time, but there may come a time when their political forces will require us to give up ownership of our plant. It is up to you to develop the rapport with all interested parties which will most benefit our long-run interests.

"Since all of your employees will be, or soon will be, Saudis, it is vital to learn as quickly as possible something about their culture. Perhaps your best move is to perfect your skill in the use of their language and really learn to think and act as a native. I am not sure anyone from the United States can do this. You and I were raised in the folds of Western civilization, which has very different institutions and behavioral patterns from those you will encounter in the Near East. For instance, does one adhere to the ethical principles of the Saudis or to our own? Do they have the same trust and reliance on people that we do? Will they always react as we here are accustomed? Is social responsibility thought of in the same terms? What intentions and actions on your part will be well received by your suppliers, customers, competitors, and public figures?

"You know, I suppose that what is really on my mind is that we don't really know at what point there may be a conflict in our two cultures, and when that is discovered, what choice you will make."

1   If you were James Pruitt, how would you go about finding what the local business customs in Saudi Arabia are? What other environmental factors would you look for? How would you respond to them?

2 Suppose you found that it is customary not to lay off employees when work slackens. What would you do?

3 Suppose you found that it is normal business practice to give government employees a small amount of money when they help your people to get something through a department or clear up some paperwork jams. Would you do the same thing? Why, or why not?

8 The Social Responsibility of Business

In a conference held in Washington to consider the social responsibility of business managers, among the many statements made were the following:

By a leader of a consumer group: "The trouble with business managers is that they talk a lot about social responsibility but they do little or nothing about it. Look at the problem of air-polluting smog caused by automobiles that our manufacturers have produced. Look at the problem of energy shortages caused by businesses with their manufacture and sale of energy-eating air conditioners, electrical appliances, and automobiles. Look at the unwillingness of our oil companies to find more oil and gas, on the excuse that they cannot afford to do so, especially when the government rightly limits the prices of oil and gas. Look at the problems of poverty and unemployment caused by the unwillingness of business to pay higher wages and hire more people. I could mention more things, but they all add up to an unwillingness of business managers to meet their social responsibilities."

By a prominent economist: "There is one and only one social responsibility of business—to use its resources and engage in activities designed to increase its profits, so long as it stays within the rules of the game, which is to say, engages in open and free competition, without deception or fraud. Few trends could so thoroughly undermine the very foundations of our free society as the acceptance by corporate officials of a social responsibility other than to make as much money for their stockholders as possible."

By a corporation president: "We speak constantly of the social responsibility of business. Why not speak also of the social responsibility of our governments, our hospitals, our universities, and our other organizations? Our federal, state, and local governments spend around 40 percent of our nation's entire spendable income; are they socially responsible in taking so much from all of us and then often spending even more than they take in? Many of our cities with poor sewage disposal systems are polluting our oceans, lakes, and rivers. Our hospitals are charging, for a little room, from $175 to $300 per day for their portion of health care; is this being socially responsible? Our universities continue to increase the costs of education every year and show no signs of increasing their productivity; is this being socially responsible? And so on. No, ladies and gentlemen, social responsibility is not a business manager problem. It is far more."

1 What do you see to be the social responsibility of business managers?

2 How does this problem fit into the need for managers in nonbusiness as well as business enterprises to take into account their total external environment?

3 How should managers meet their social responsibilities?

2 Planning

The reader is now familiar with the nature and development of basic management theory and has been introduced to the five essential managerial functions: planning, organizing, staffing, leading, and controlling. The following six chapters on planning form Part 2 of this book.

Planning is not only the most basic of all management functions, since it involves selecting from among alternative future courses of action, it also determines how the four other functions of the manager will be implemented. Thus a manager organizes, staffs, leads, and controls in order to assure the attainment of goals according to plans.

Planning involves selection of enterprise and departmental objectives as well as determination of the means of reaching them. It is thus a rational approach to preselected objectives. Since this approach does not take place in a vacuum, good planning must consider the nature of the future environment in which planning decisions and actions are intended to operate. In other words, planning must involve an open-system approach to managing.

In the first chapter of this part, the reasons for planning and the general kinds of plans are explained. The logical process of planning is discussed, and attention is given to such practical matters as the length of time for which a manager should plan.

This is followed by a chapter on objectives, the determination of which decides the basic nature of total planned action. Utilizing a hierarchy and network of derivative goals, a host of supporting plans are then developed by the component units of the organization.

In Chapter 7, the reader should come to appreciate (1) the importance in any enterprise of having verifiable objectives; (2) how objectives in any enterprise relate to one another in a hierarchical and interconnective way; and (3) the nature, process, benefits, and weaknesses of programs of managing by objectives.

Plans are made to operate in the future. Therefore, a key part of planning is the establishment of clear planning premises. To ensure coordination among all managers who make plans in a given organization, these premises should be used by all concerned. Premises spell out the "stage" of the expected key future events which, it is believed, will exist when plans operate. They are the expected environment of plans. Chapter 8 gives the reader a clear view of "premising" in management, including methods of making these important planning determinants clear to enterprise planners and all managers who make decisions.

Chapter 9 analyzes the decision-making process, which is at the heart of planning. Decisions are essential to planning since they represent that part of the process where a selection of a course of future action is made. As a matter of fact, until a decision is made to embark on a certain course of action, we really do not have plans, but rather planning proposals and studies. Therefore, decision making is treated in the planning section of this book rather than elsewhere. Decision making, like all planning, requires a systems approach; more specifically, since decisions are made in the light of environmental factors, it calls for an open-system approach. As will be seen, among the major developments in decision making are the increasing use of the research methodology long used in the physical sciences, the employment of decision trees and probabilities, and a greater reliance on mathematical modeling, which is central to operations research.

Policy formulation and strategy are the subjects of Chapter 10. Policies, written or unwritten, may be thought of quite simply as guides to thinking in decision making. They enable all managers in an organization to make consistent decisions that contribute to the achievement of goals in an orderly way. Strategies are broad overall conceptions of enterprise operation. They constitute a general program of action, including the deployment of resources to attain ultimate objectives; thus they include the selection of major goals and overall policies that indicate what the enterprise is trying to achieve or to become. Since both policies and strategies are designed to guide thinking and action, they are dealt with in the same chapter.

The development and implementation of strategies are of top importance to all kinds of enterprises and to business in particular. In Chapter 10, the authors hold that the actual development of clear strategies depends upon asking the right questions in order to identify the best possible course of action in the light of an organization's strengths and weaknesses and the opportunities presented by the environment in which it operates. Suggestions are also made in this chapter with regard to how to implement strategies as well as develop them.

Chapter 11 deals with some of the major considerations involved in putting plans into action, such as coordination of plans, communication for planning, and the importance of getting participation in making plans. The problems of limitations in plans and the difficulties encountered in making plans operate effectively are analyzed, and suggestions are offered as to the major elements necessary for an effective planning environment.

It should be emphasized that the planning function of managing is the area where innovation plays a key part. Some scholars and practitioners consider innovation a separate function of managing. However, since all managing deals with change (it is often said that to manage is to manage change), this necessarily implies innovation. Nevertheless, while the introduction of something new is inherent in the entire field of management, we believe that innovation is especially implied in planning.

6

chapter

The Nature and Purpose of Planning

In designing an environment for the effective performance of individuals working together in groups, the most essential task is to see that purposes and objectives, and methods of attaining them, are clearly understood. If group effort is to be effective, people must know what they are expected to accomplish. This is the function of planning. It is the most basic of all the managerial functions. It involves selecting from among alternative future courses of action for the enterprise as a whole and for every department or section within it. It requires selecting enterprise objectives and departmental goals and determining ways of achieving them. Planning thus provides a rational approach to preselected objectives. It strongly implies managerial innovation and ability to create something new.

As Billy E. Goetz[1] said years ago, planning is "fundamentally choosing," and "a planning problem arises only when an alternative course of action is discovered." In this sense, it is essentially decision making, although, as will be seen, it is also much more. Planning presupposes the existence of alternatives, and there are few decisions for which some kind of alternative does not exist—even when it comes to meeting legal or other requirements imposed by forces beyond the manager's control.

Planning is deciding in advance what to do, how to do it, when to do it, and who is to do it. Planning bridges the gap from where we are to where we want to go. It makes it possible for things to occur which would not otherwise happen. Although the exact future can seldom be predicted and factors beyond control may interfere with the best-laid plans, unless there is planning, events are left to chance. Planning is an intellectually demanding process; it requires the conscious determination of courses of action and the basing of decisions on purpose, knowledge, and considered estimates.

An important aspect of the managerial revolution of the past three decades has been a tremendous interest in planning by all forms of enterprise—business, government, educational, and others. Note that this strong interest in planning is primarily a recent phenomenon, although in areas such as factory operations, production planning has been stressed for many years. Production managers discovered early that without planning, their mistakes showed up within days, as production lines came to a halt because of a misfit part or the absence of a needed component. Also, well-managed companies have long planned to meet cash needs before their checks bounced. But, generally speaking, planning as a widely recognized and actively pursued managerial function is a fairly recent development.

Now, nearly everyone plans. Enterprises of all kinds plan further into the future, plan more aspects of their operations, plan less by intuition or hunch, and lean more heavily on forecasts and analyses. In fact, a few years ago, McKaye-Shields and Associates, an economic consulting firm

[1]*Management Planning and Control* (New York: McGraw-Hill Book Company, 1949), p. 2.

advising the Hughes Aircraft Company's policy committee, stated that the development of business planning has been as revolutionary a movement as the technological revolution or the revolution in expansion of income.

We are in an economic, technological, social, and political era in which planning, like the other functions of managers, has become requisite for enterprise survival. Change and economic growth bring opportunities, but they also bring risk, particularly in an era of worldwide rivalry for markets, resources and influence. It is exactly the task of planning to minimize risk while taking advantage of opportunities.

With all the interest in planning and all the sense of urgency brought about by modern supercompetition, there is danger that planning can become merely a costly fad, not very useful, and even disillusioning. To plan well, to make plans that will succeed, planning—again, like the other managerial functions—must take place in a context of fundamental theories, principles, and techniques. Many failures in planning have been caused by a lack of understanding of the fundamentals.

THE NATURE OF PLANNING

The essential nature of planning can be highlighted by the four major aspects of planning: contribution to purpose and objectives, primacy of planning, pervasiveness of planning, and efficiency of plans.

Contribution to Purpose and Objectives

The purpose of every plan and all derivative plans is to facilitate the accomplishment of enterprise purpose and objectives. This principle derives from the nature of organized enterprise, which exists for the accomplishment of group purpose through deliberate cooperation. This was emphasized by Goetz when he said:

> Plans alone cannot make an enterprise successful. Action is required; the enterprise must operate. Plans can, however, focus action on purposes. They can forecast which actions will tend toward the ultimate objective . . . which tend away, which will likely offset one another, and which are merely irrelevant. Managerial planning seeks to achieve a consistent, co-ordinated structure of operations focused on desired ends. Without plans, action must become merely random activity, producing nothing but chaos.[2]

Primacy of Planning

As shown in Figure 6.1, since *managerial operations in organizing, staffing, leading, and controlling are designed to support the accomplish-*

---

[2]Ibid., p. 63.

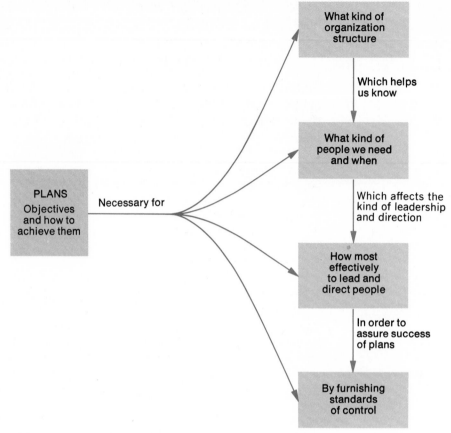

Figure 6.1 Planning precedes all other managerial functions.

ment of enterprise objectives, planning logically precedes the execution of all other managerial functions.

Although all the functions intermesh in practice as a system of action, planning is unique in that it establishes the objectives necessary for all group effort. Besides, plans must be made to accomplish these objectives before the manager knows what kind of organization relationships and personal qualifications are needed, along which course subordinates are to be directed and led, and what kind of control is to be applied. And, of course, all the other managerial functions must be planned if they are to be effective.

Planning and control are especially inseparable—the Siamese twins of management. Unplanned action cannot be controlled, for control involves keeping activities on course by correcting deviations from plans. Any attempt to control without plans would be meaningless, since there is no way for people to tell whether they are going where they want to go—the task of control—unless they first *know* where they want to go—the task of planning. Plans thus furnish the standards of control.

Pervasiveness of Planning

Planning is a function of all managers, although the character and breadth of planning will vary with their authority and with the nature of policies and plans outlined by their superiors. It is virtually impossible so to circumscribe their area of choice that they can exercise no discretion, and unless they have some planning responsibility, it is doubtful that they are truly managers.

Recognition of the pervasiveness of planning goes far in clarifying the attempt on the part of some students of management to distinguish between policy making (the setting of guides for thinking in decision making) and administration, or between the "manager" and the "administrator" or "supervisor." One manager, because of his authority delegation or position in the organization, may do more planning or more important planning than another, or the planning of one may be more basic and applicable to a larger portion of the enterprise than that of another. However, all managers—from presidents to supervisors—plan. The supervisor of a road gang or a factory crew plans in a limited area under fairly strict rules and procedures. Interestingly, in studies of work satisfactions, a principal factor found to account for the success of supervisors at the lowest organization level has been their ability to plan.[3]

Efficiency of Plans

The efficiency of a plan is measured by the amount it contributes to purpose and objectives as offset by the costs and other unsought consequences required to formulate and operate it.[4] A plan can contribute to the attainment of objectives, but at too high or unnecessarily high costs. This concept of efficiency implies the normal ratio of input to output, but goes beyond the usual understanding of inputs and outputs in terms of dollars, labor-hours, or units of production to include such values as individual and group satisfactions.

Many managers have followed plans, such as in the acquisition of certain aircraft by airlines, where costs were greater than the revenues obtainable. There have actually been some aircraft with which an airline found it could not make money. Companies have inefficiently attempted

[3]See, for example, D. Katz et al., *Productivity, Supervision and Morale among Railroad Workers* (Ann Arbor: Survey Research Center, Institute for Social Research, University of Michigan, 1951).
[4]The authors are indebted to Chester I. Barnard for having so clearly pointed out the applicability of concepts of effectiveness and efficiency to systems of human cooperation. See *The Functions of the Executive* (Cambridge, Mass.: Harvard University Press, 1938), pp. 19–20.

to attain objectives in the face of the unsought consequence of market unacceptability, as happened when a motor car manufacturer tried to capture a market by emphasizing engineering without competitive advances in style. Plans may also become inefficient in the attainment of objectives by jeopardizing group satisfactions. The new president of a company that was losing money attempted quickly to reorganize and cut expenses by wholesale and unplanned layoffs of key personnel. The result in fear, resentment, and loss of morale led to so much lower productivity as to defeat his laudable objective of eliminating losses and making profits. And some attempts to install management appraisal and development programs have failed because of group resentment of the methods used, regardless of the basic soundness of the programs.

TYPES OF PLANS

The failure of some managers to recognize the variety of plans has often caused difficulty in making planning effective. It is easy to see that a major program, such as one to build and equip a new factory, is a plan. But what is sometimes overlooked is that a number of other courses of future action are also plans. Keeping in mind that a plan encompasses any course of future action, we can see that plans are varied. They are classified here as purposes or missions, objectives, strategies, policies, rules, procedures, programs, and budgets. The nature of these may be expressed as a hierarchy, as shown in Figure 6.2.

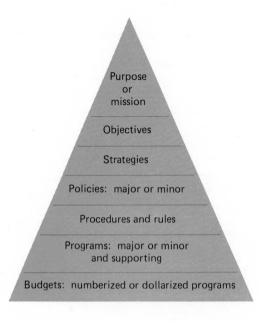

Purpose
or
mission

Objectives

Strategies

Policies: major or minor

Procedures and rules

Programs: major or minor
and supporting

Budgets: numberized or dollarized programs

Figure 6.2 The hierarchy of plans.

Every kind of organized group operation has, or at least should have, if it is to be meaningful, a purpose or mission. In every social system, enterprises have a basic function or task which is assigned to them by society. The purpose of businesses generally is the production and distribution of economic goods and services. The purpose of a state highway department is the design, building, and operation of a system of state highways. The purpose of the courts is the interpretation of laws and their application. The purpose of a university is teaching and research. And so on.

Although this book does not do so, sometimes distinctions are drawn between purposes and missions. While a business, for example, may have a social purpose of producing and distributing economic goods and services, it may accomplish this by fulfilling a mission of producing certain lines of products. The mission of an oil company like Exxon is to search for oil and to produce, refine, and market petroleum and a wide variety of petroleum products, from diesel fuel to chemicals. The mission of the Du Pont Company has been expressed as "better things through chemistry," and Kimberly-Clark (noted for its Kleenex trademark) regards its business mission as the production and sale of paper and paper products.

It is true that in some businesses and other enterprises the specific purpose or mission often becomes fuzzy. In some of the larger conglomerates, such as Litton Industries, a product line mission does not appear to exist. However, many of the conglomerates have regarded their mission as "synergy,"[5] which is accomplished through the combination of a variety of companies. Some businesses never make clear to themselves or their organizations what their purpose or mission is, and many nonbusiness enterprises have likewise not always made this clear. It would, for example, be difficult to get a very clear notion of the mission of the Department of State, the Department of the Interior, or the Interstate Commerce Commission, to mention a few. Even some nonprofit foundations seem to the observer to have an obscure mission. One cannot help but wonder, for example, what the mission of the very large Ford Foundation is.

It can hardly be doubted that a clear definition of purpose or mission is necessary in order to formulate meaningful objectives. While every business should know the answer to the question, What is our business and what should it be? Many business executives have difficulty finding the answer.

[5]Synergy is the phenomenon in which elements added together produce a result that is greater than the mere addition involved. It is adding 4 and 2 and getting 7. For example, when Western and Continental airlines planned a merger in 1979, studies showed that the combined airline would make more profit than merely adding together the profits of each. This was due to certain efficiencies in the use of equipment, in staffing passenger terminals, in being able to offer more thorough service, and other factors.

The correct approach requires, first, that a business defines who its customers are and what their attitudes and expectations are. This is a simple approach, but it often poses difficulties, as the railroads apparently found when they realized that they had too long looked upon themselves as being in the railroad business rather than the transportation business. However, every kind of enterprise in a society should know who its customers are and what they expect. Nonbusiness enterprises, in a very real sense, also have customers. Is not the public the "customer" of government agencies, and are not the parishioners the "customers" of a church?

It is sometimes thought that the mission of a business, as well as its objective, is to make a profit. It is true that every kind of enterprise must have, as was pointed out in the first chapter, a "surplus"—in business, "profit"—goal or objective if it is to survive and do the task society has entrusted to it. But this basic objective is accomplished by undertaking activities, going in clear directions, achieving goals, and accomplishing a mission.

Objectives

Objectives, or goals, are the ends toward which activity is aimed. They represent not only the end point of planning, but the end toward which organizing, staffing, leading, and controlling are aimed. While enterprise objectives constitute the basic plan of the firm, a department may also have objectives. Its goals should naturally contribute to the attainment of enterprise objectives, but the two sets of goals may be entirely different. For example, the objective of a business might be to make a certain profit by producing a given line of home entertainment equipment, while the goal of the manufacturing department might be to produce the required number of television sets of a given design and quality at a given cost. These objectives are consistent, but they differ in that the manufacturing department alone cannot assure accomplishing the company's objective.

The nature of objectives and their relationship to planning are discussed in the following chapter. It is enough to emphasize here that objectives, or goals, are plans and that they involve the same planning process as any other type of planning, even though they are also end points of planning. A sales goal, for example, cannot be guessed at or wished for; it must be determined in the light of purpose and circumstances. Likewise, a plan to accomplish a certain sales goal will have within it, or as derivatives of it, project or departmental goals.

Strategies

For years the military used "strategies," or "grand plans," to mean plans made in the light of what it believed an adversary might or might not do.

While the term "strategies" still usually has a competitive implication, it has been increasingly used to reflect broad overall concepts of an enterprise operation. "Strategies," therefore, most often denote a general program of action and an implied deployment of emphasis and resources to attain comprehensive objectives. Anthony defines them as resulting from "the process of deciding on objectives of the organization, on changes in these objectives, on the resources used to attain these objectives, and on the policies that are to govern the acquisition, use, and disposition of these resources."[6] And Chandler defines a strategy as "the determination of the basic long-term goals and objectives of an enterprise, and the adoption of courses of action and the allocation of resources necessary to carry out these goals."[7]

Thus, a company may have an objective of profitable growth at a certain percentage per year. Supportive of this might be a determination that the company will be of a certain kind, such as a transportation company rather than a railroad company, or a container company rather than a paper box manufacturer. A strategy might include such major policies as to market directly rather than through distributors, or to concentrate on proprietary products, or to have a full line, such as General Motors decided to have years ago for its automobile business.

The purpose of strategies, then, is to determine and communicate, through a system of major objectives and policies, a picture of what kind of enterprise is envisioned. Strategies show a unified direction and imply a deployment of emphasis and resources. They do not attempt to outline exactly how the enterprise is to accomplish its objectives, since this is the task of countless major and minor supporting programs. But they are a useful framework for guiding enterprise thinking and action. This usefulness in practice and importance in guiding planning do, however, justify their separation as a type of plan for purposes of analysis.

As a matter of fact, most strategies, particularly in business, do fit the traditional military concept by including competitive considerations. In the 1950s and later, the German Volkswagen Company, for example, selected the strategy of offering on the highly competitive American market a low-priced and small car getting high mileage per gallon of fuel, easy to drive in congested areas, and easy to park, in order to meet a demand by consumers who were not being served in these respects by native manufacturers. In this strategy were all the elements of the traditional military concept: (1) competitors, (2) a market not large enough to satisfy all competitive manufacturers, and (3) a gap that offered an adversary an opportunity. But even this kind of strategy is not entirely an independently separate type of plan because it is actually a combination

[6]R.N. Anthony, *Planning and Control Systems: A Framework for Analysis* (Boston: Division of Research, Harvard Business School, 1965), p. 24.
[7]A. D. Chandler, Jr., *Strategy and Structure* (Cambridge, Mass.: The M.I.T. Press, 1962), p. 13.

of objectives (to secure a given market share), a major policy (produce ánd market a small, low-priced car), and various programs (for example, exporting and marketing).

Policies

Policies, also, are plans in that they are general statements or understandings which guide or channel thinking and action in decision making. One can hardly refer to all policies as "statements," since they are often merely implied from the actions of managers. The president of a company, for example, may strictly follow—perhaps for convenience rather than as policy—the practice of promoting from within; the practice may then be interpreted as policy and rigorously followed by subordinates. In fact, one of the problems of all managers is to make sure that subordinates do not interpret as policy minor decisions which they make without intending these decisions to serve as precedents.

Policies delimit an area within which a decision is to be made and assure that the decision will be consistent with and contributive to objectives. Policies tend to predecide issues, avoid repeated analysis, and give a unified structure to other types of plans, thus permitting managers to delegate authority while maintaining control. For example, a certain railroad has the policy of acquiring industrial land to replace all acreage sold along its right of way. This permits the manager of the land department to develop acquisition plans without continual reference to top management, which is nevertheless furnished with a standard of control.

Policies ordinarily have at least as many levels as organization, ranging from major company policies through major departmental policies to minor or derivative policies applicable to the smallest segment of the organization. They may also be related to functions—such as sales and finance—or merely to a project—such as that of designing a new product with materials to meet a specified competition.

The varieties of policies are legion. Examples are department policies to hire only university-trained engineers or to encourage employee suggestions for improved cooperation, and company policies to promote from within, to conform strictly to a high standard of business ethics, to compete on a price basis, to insist on fixed rather than cost-plus pricing.

Being guides to thinking in decision making, it follows that policies must allow for some discretion. Otherwise, they would be rules. Too often policies are established as a kind of Ten Commandments which leave no room for discretion. Although the discretion area, in some instances, is quite broad, it can be exceedingly narrow. For example, a policy to buy from the lowest of three qualified bidders leaves for discretion only the question of which bidders are qualified; a requirement to buy from a certain company, regardless of price or service, is a rule.

Because policies are so often misunderstood, the authors have selected examples from a company's policy manual. It will be noted in each case that there is an area for a person in a decision-making capacity to use discretion. The following are interesting examples:

1 **Gifts from suppliers.** Except for token gifts of purely nominal or advertising value, no employee shall accept any gift or gratuity from any supplier at any time. (What is "token" or "nominal"?)

2 **Entertainment.** No officer or employee shall accept favors or entertainment from an outside organization or agency which are substantial enough to cause undue influence in his selection of goods or services for the company. (What is "substantial" or "undue"?)

3 **Outside employment.** It is improper for any employee to work for any company customers, or for any competitors, or for any vendors or suppliers of goods or services to the company; outside employment is further prohibited if it: (a) results in a division of loyalty to the company or a conflict of interests, or (b) interferes with or adversely affects the employee's work or opportunity for advancement in the company. (What is meant by a "division of loyalty," "conflict of interest," or "adversely"?)

4 **Pricing.** Each territorial division manager may establish such prices for the products under his control as he deems in the division's interest so long as (a) these prices result in gross profit margins for any line of products which are consistent with his approved profit plan; (b) price reductions will not result in detrimental effects on prices of similar products of another company division in another state or country; and (c) prices meet the legal requirements of the state or country in which the prices are effective. (What are "consistent," "detrimental," or "legal requirements"?)

The area of discretion in most of these policies is fairly general. However, in the pricing policy shown, the discretion area is fairly specifically defined. Likewise, in the outside employment policy, that portion dealing with employment with any vendors or suppliers leaves no discretion and is, consequently, a rule.

Policy should be regarded as a means of encouraging discretion and initiative, but within limits. As shown in Figure 6.3, the amount of freedom possible will naturally depend upon the policy, which in turn reflects position and authority in the organization. The president of a company with a policy of aggressive price competition has a broad area of discretion and initiative in which to interpret and apply this policy. The district sales manager abides by the same basic policy, but the interpretations made by the president, the vice president for sales, and the regional sales manager become derivative policies which narrow his scope to the point where, for example, he may be permitted only to approve a special sale price to meet competition not exceeding a 10 percent reduction.

Making policies consistent and integrated enough to facilitate the realization of enterprise objectives is difficult for many reasons. First,

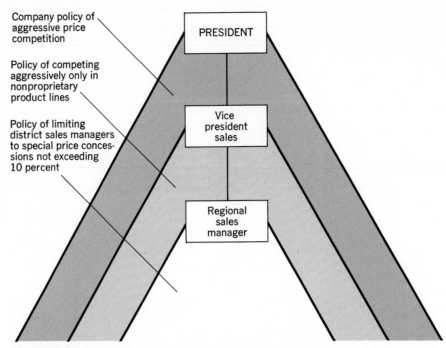

Company policy of
aggressive price
competition

Policy of competing
aggressively only in
nonproprietary
product lines

Policy of limiting
district sales managers
to special price conces-
sions not exceeding
10 percent

Figure 6.3 How policies may be successively limiting.

policies are too seldom written and their exact interpretations too little known. Second, the very delegation of authority that policies are intended to implement leads, through its decentralizing influence, to widespread participation in policy making and interpretation, with almost certain variations among individuals. Third, it is not always easy to control policy because *actual* policy may be difficult to ascertain and *intended* policy may not always be clear.

Procedures

Procedures are plans in that they establish a customary method of handling future activities. They are truly guides to action, rather than to thinking, and they detail the exact manner in which a certain activity must be accomplished. Their essence is chronological sequence of required actions.

    Their pervasiveness in the organization is readily apparent. The board of directors follows many procedures quite different from those of the supervisors; the expense account of the vice president may go through quite different approval procedures from that of the salesperson; the procedures for carrying out vacation and sick leave provisions may vary considerably at various levels of organization. But the important fact is that procedures exist throughout an organization, even though, as one might expect, they become more exacting and numerous in the lower levels, largely because of the necessity for more careful control, the economic advantages of spelling out actions in detail, the reduced need for discretion, and the fact that routine jobs lend themselves to obtaining greater efficiency through prescription of what is thought to be the one best way.

As in other types of plans, procedures have a hierarchy of importance. Thus, in a typical corporation, one may find a manual of "Corporation Standard Practice" outlining procedures for the corporation as a whole; a manual of "Division Standard Practice"; and special sets of procedures for a department, a branch, a section, or a unit.

Procedures often cut across department lines. For example, in a manufacturing company, the procedure for handling orders will almost certainly encompass the sales department (for the original order), the finance department (for acknowledgment of receipt of funds and for customer credit determination), the accounting department (for recording the transaction), the production department (for order to produce or authority to release from stock), and the traffic department (for determination of the shipping means and route).

The relationship between procedures and policies may best be indicated by a few examples. Company policy may grant employees vacations; procedures established to implement this policy will schedule vacations to avoid disruption of work, set methods and rates of vacation pay, maintain records to assure each employee a vacation, and provide means of applying for the vacation. A company may have a policy of shipping orders quickly; particularly in a large company, careful procedures will be necessary to assure that orders are handled in a specific way. Company policy may require clearance by the public relations department of public utterances of its employees; to implement this policy, procedures must be established to obtain clearance with a minimum of inconvenience and delay.

Rules

Rules are plans in that they are required actions which, like other plans, are chosen from among alternatives. They are usually the simplest type of plan.

Rules are frequently confused with policies or procedures. A rule requires that a specific and definite action be taken or not taken with respect to a situation. It is thus related to a procedure, in that it guides action, but it specifies no time sequence. As a matter of fact, a procedure could be looked upon as a sequence of rules. A rule, however, may or may not be part of a procedure. For example, "no smoking" is a rule quite unrelated to any procedure; but a procedure governing the handling of orders may incorporate the rule that all orders must be confirmed the day they are received. This rule allows no deviation from a stated course of action and in no way interferes with the procedure for handling orders. It is comparable to a rule that all fractions over half an ounce are to be counted a full ounce or that inspectors in the receiving department must count or weigh all materials and compare these against the purchase order. The essence of a rule is that it reflects a managerial decision that certain action be taken—or not be taken.

Rules should be carefully distinguished from policies. The purpose of policies is to guide thinking in decision making by marking off areas of discretion. Although rules also serve as guides, they allow no discretion in their application. Many companies and other organizations think they have policies when they really spell out rules. The result is confusion as to when a person may use his or her judgment, if at all. This can be dangerous. Rules and procedures, by their very nature, are designed to repress thinking and should of course be used only when we do not want people in an organization to use their discretion.

Programs

Programs are a complex of goals, policies, procedures, rules, task assignments, steps to be taken, resources to be employed, and other elements necessary to carry out a given course of action; they are ordinarily supported by necessary capital and operating budgets. Programs may be as major as that of an airline to acquire a $400 million fleet of jets or the 5-year program embarked upon by the Ford Motor Company several years ago to improve the status and quality of its thousands of supervisors. Or they may be as minor as a program formulated by a single supervisor in a parts manufacturing department of a farm machinery company to improve the morale of workers.

A primary program may call for many derivative programs. For example, an airline program to invest in new jets, costing many millions of dollars for the aircraft and the necessary spare parts, requires many derivative programs if the investment is to be properly used. A program for providing the maintenance and operating bases with spare components and parts must be developed in detail. Special maintenance facilities must be prepared, and maintenance personnel trained. Pilots and flight engineers must also be trained, and, if the new jets mean a net addition to flying hours, flight personnel recruited. Flight schedules must be revised, and ground station personnel trained to handle the new airplanes and their schedules, as service is expanded to new cities in the airline's system. Advertising programs must give adequate publicity to the new service. Plans to finance the aircraft and provide for insurance coverage must be developed.

These and other programs must be devised and effected before any new aircraft are received and placed in service. Furthermore, all these programs necessitate coordination and timing, since the failure of any part of this network of derivative plans means delay for the major program with consequent unnecessary costs and loss of revenues. Some of the programs, particularly those involving hiring and training of personnel, can be accomplished too soon as well as too late, since needless expense results from employees being available and trained before their services are required.

Thus one seldom finds that a program of any importance in enterprise planning stands by itself. It is usually a part of a complex system of programs, depending upon some and affecting others. This interdependence of plans makes planning very difficult. The results of poor or inadequate planning are seldom isolated, for planning is only as strong as its weakest link. Even a seemingly unimportant procedure or rule, if badly conceived, may wreck an important program. Coordinated planning requires extraordinarily exacting managerial skill. It truly requires the most rigorous application of systems thinking and action.

Budgets

A budget as a plan is a statement of expected results expressed in numerical terms. It may be referred to as a "numberized" program. As a matter of fact, the financial operating budget is often called a "profit plan." It may be expressed either in financial terms or in terms of labor-hours, units of product, machine-hours, or any other numerically measurable term. It may deal with operations, as the expense budget does; it may reflect capital outlays, as the capital expenditures budget does; or it may show flow of cash, as the cash budget does.

Since budgets are also control devices, the principal discussion of them is reserved for the chapters on control. However, *making* a budget is clearly planning. It is the fundamental planning instrument in many companies. A budget forces a company to make in advance—whether for a week or 5 years—a numerical compilation of expected cash flow, expenses and revenues, capital outlays, or labor- or machine-hour utilization. The budget is necessary for control, but it cannot serve as a sensible standard of control unless it reflects plans.

Budgetary planning does vary considerably in its accuracy, extent of detail, and ways of developing budgets. Some budgets are made to vary with possible levels of output of an enterprise; these are called "variable" or "flexible" budgets. Another approach that has been widely (but not always successfully) used by government agencies has been referred to as "program budgets." The idea behind this type of budgeting is that each agency and department of it will identify program goals sought, then develop detailed planning programs needed to meet these goals, and finally "numberize" or "dollarize" the needed programs. It is easy to see that this kind of budget, where it is done well, goes far in forcing a fairly detailed and complete degree of planning. Still another type of budgeting, which really combines variable and program budgeting, has been given the attractive name "zero-based budgeting." In this approach, the objectives sought and the work found necessary for their accomplishment are put up in "work packages" as though the budget planner were starting from the beginning, or "base zero." The impetus to make planning more complete may be readily seen from this approach.

As a matter of fact, the principal advantage of budgeting is that it makes people plan; and because it is usually in the form of numbers, it forces definitives of planning.

THE IMPORTANCE OF PLANNING

The planning function has four important goals: to offset uncertainty and change, to focus attention on objectives, to gain economical operation, and to facilitate control.

To Offset Uncertainty and Change

Future uncertainty and change make planning a necessity. Just as the navigator cannot set a course once and forget about it, so the business manager cannot establish a goal and let the matter rest. The future is seldom very certain, and the further in the future the results of a decision must be considered, the less the certainty. An executive may feel quite certain that within the next month orders, costs, productive capacity, output, cash availability, and other factors of the environment will be at a given level. A fire, an unforeseen strike, or an order cancellation by a major customer could change all this; but in the short run this is unlikely. However, as this manager plans further in advance, his or her certainty about the internal and external environment diminishes, and the rightness of any decision becomes less sure.

Even when the future is highly certain, some planning is usually necessary. In the first place, there is the necessity of selecting the best way in any situation to accomplish an objective. With conditions of certainty, this becomes primarily a mathematical problem of calculating, on the basis of known facts, that course which will yield the desired result at the least cost. In the second place, after the course has been decided, it is necessary to lay out plans so that each part of the organization will know how to contribute toward the job to be done.

Even when trends indicating change are easily discernible, difficult planning problems arise. The manufacture of automobiles is a case in point. The change away from large, fuel-inefficient cars to light, fuel-efficient ones did not take place overnight. The manufacturer had to determine what percentage of production should be assigned to smaller cars and what to larger cars and how to retain efficient production of both lines. However, the manufacturer could have chosen an entirely different course. Once satisfied about the certainty of the change, the firm might have deliberately sacrificed large-automobile business in order to concentrate on the design and development of small, fuel-efficient cars, with the hope of becoming the leader among small-automobile manufacturers.

When trends are not easily discernible, good planning can be even more difficult. Many executives underestimated, or did not appreciate soon enough, the significance of inflationary prices, rapidly increasing interest rates, and the energy crisis of the early 1970s, with the result that they were not ready for certain market and material shifts and the increased costs that occurred. Even the long concern with air and water pollution did not reach urgent proportions until the late 1960s and the early 1970s.

To Focus Attention on Objectives

Because all planning is directed toward achieving enterprise objectives, the very act of planning focuses attention on these objectives. Well-considered overall plans unify interdepartmental activities. Managers, being typically immersed in immediate problems, are forced through planning to consider the future and even consider the periodic need to revise and extend plans in the interest of achieving their objectives.

To Gain Economical Operation

Planning minimizes costs because of the emphasis on efficient operation and consistency. It substitutes joint, directed effort for uncoordinated, piecemeal activity, even flow of work for uneven flow, and deliberate decisions for snap judgments.

The economy of planning is plainly seen at the production level. No one who has watched the assembly of automobiles in one of the larger factories can fail to be impressed with the way that the parts and subassemblies come together. From one overhead conveyor system comes a body and from others various appurtenances. Exactly the right engine, transmission, and accessories fall into place at the exact appointed time. This implies extensive detailed planning without which the manufacture of automobiles would be chaotic and impossibly costly. Although every manager sees the imperative economy of planning at the production level, planning of equal or sometimes greater importance in other areas is occasionally left to chance and too great individual discretion.

To Facilitate Control

Managers cannot check on their subordinates' accomplishments without having goals and programs against which to measure. There is no way to control without plans to use as standards. Moreover, as we shall see in later chapters on control, controlling, like planning, must look to the future. As a top executive told one of the authors, "After I leave my office at 5 o'clock in the evening, I will not care what happened today, for I

Figure 6.4 Steps in planning.

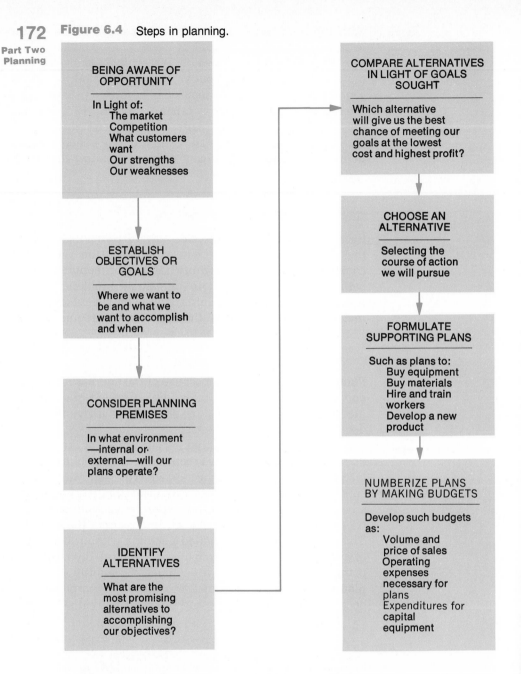

BEING AWARE OF
OPPORTUNITY

In Light of:
    The market
    Competition
    What customers
    want
    Our strengths
    Our weaknesses

ESTABLISH
OBJECTIVES OR
GOALS

Where we want to
be and what we
want to accomplish
and when

CONSIDER PLANNING
PREMISES

In what environment
—internal or
external—will our
plans operate?

IDENTIFY
ALTERNATIVES

What are the
most promising
alternatives to
accomplishing
our objectives?

COMPARE ALTERNATIVES
IN LIGHT OF GOALS
SOUGHT

Which alternative
will give us the best
chance of meeting our
goals at the lowest
cost and highest profit?

CHOOSE AN
ALTERNATIVE

Selecting the
course of action
we will pursue

FORMULATE
SUPPORTING PLANS

Such as plans to:
    Buy equipment
    Buy materials
    Hire and train
    workers
    Develop a new
    product

NUMBERIZE PLANS
BY MAKING BUDGETS

Develop such budgets
as:
    Volume and
    price of sales
    Operating
    expenses
    necessary for
    plans
    Expenditures for
    capital
    equipment

cannot do anything about it; I will only care about what will happen tomorrow or the next day or next year, because I can do something about it." Perhaps this is an extreme position, but it emphasizes the point that effective control is that which looks to the future.

Although the steps in planning are presented here in connection with major programs such as the acquisition of a plant or a fleet of jets or the development of a product, essentially the same steps would be followed in any thorough planning. As minor plans are usually simpler, certain of the steps are more easily accomplished, but the following practical steps are of general application. These steps are diagramed in Figure 6.4. Obviously, the discriminating manager would not use $100 worth of time to make a decision worth 50 cents, but what is shocking is to see 50 cents worth of time used to make a planning decision involving millions of dollars.

1. Being Aware of Opportunity

Although preceding what is usually considered to be actual planning, the awareness of an opportunity is the real starting point for planning.[8] It includes a preliminary look at possible future opportunities and the ability to see them clearly and completely, a knowledge of where we stand in the light of our strengths and weaknesses, an understanding of why we wish to solve uncertainties, and a vision of what we expect to gain. Setting realistic objectives depends on this awareness. Planning requires realistic diagnosis of the opportunity situation.

2. Establishing Objectives

The first step in planning itself is to establish objectives for the entire enterprise and then for each subordinate unit. Objectives specifying the results expected indicate the end points of what is to be done, where the primary emphasis is to be placed, and what is to be accomplished by the network of strategies, policies, procedures, rules, budgets, and programs.

Enterprise objectives should give direction to the nature of all major plans which, by reflecting these objectives, define the objectives of major departments. Major department objectives, in turn, control the objectives of subordinate departments, and so on down the line. The objectives of lesser departments will be better framed, however, if subdivision managers understand the overall enterprise objectives and the implied derivative goals, and if they are given an opportunity to contribute their ideas to them and to the setting of their own goals.

[8]The word "problem" might be used instead of "opportunity." But, in the view of the authors, a state of disorder or confusion and a need for a solution to gain a given goal can more constructively be regarded as an opportunity. In fact, the authors know of a very successful and astute company president who does not permit his colleagues to speak of problems, but only of opportunities.

A second logical step in planning is to establish, obtain agreement to utilize, and disseminate critical planning premises. These are forecast data of a factual nature, applicable basic policies, and existing company plans. Premises, then, are planning assumptions—in other words, the expected environment of plans in operation. As was discussed in Chapter 4, the external environment of an enterprise can be quite complex. Even the internal environment of an organization must be carefully considered when plans are drawn up. The premising step leads to one of the major principles of planning: *The more individuals charged with planning understand and agree to utilize consistent planning premises, the more coordinated enterprise planning will be.*

Forecasting is important in premising: What kind of markets will there be? What quantity of sales? What prices? What products? What technical developments? What costs? What wage rates? What tax rates and policies? What new plants? What policies with respect to dividends? How will expansion be financed? What political or social environment? Planning premises include far more than the usual basic forecasts of population, prices, costs, production, markets, and similar matters.

Some premises forecast policies not yet made. For example, if a company has no pension plan and no policy with respect to one, planning sometimes must premise whether such a policy will be set and, if so, what it will contain. Other premises naturally grow out of existing policies or other plans. For example, if a company has a policy of paying out no more than 3 percent of its profits, before taxes, for contributions and if there is no reason to believe that this policy will be changed, the policy becomes a planning premise. Or, if a company has made large investments in special-purpose fixed plant and machinery, this becomes an important planning premise.

A difficulty of establishing complete premises and keeping them up to date is that every major plan, and many minor ones, becomes a premise for the future. The plan to establish a factory in Kansas City, for example, becomes a premise for plans in which plant location is important. Similarly, it would make little sense for a Denver local bus line to premise future plans on Florida markets. And when an airline equips its long-haul routes with one type of aircraft for which it builds maintenance and overhaul facilities, this becomes a critical premise for other plans.

As one moves down the organization hierarchy, the composition of planning premises changes somewhat. The basic process will be the same, but old and new major plans will materially affect the future against which managers of lesser units must plan. A superior's plans affecting a subordinate manager's area of authority become premises for the latter's planning.

Because the future environment of plans is so complex, it would not be profitable or realistic to make assumptions about every detail of the future environment of a plan. Therefore, premises are, as a practical matter, limited to those which are critical, or strategic, to a plan, that is, those which most influence its operation.

It would be surprising if all members of a company's management at all levels agreed independently about the company future. One manager might expect world peace to last 10 years; another, world war for the same period. One manager might expect prices to go up 10 percent in 5 years; another, 50 percent; and another might expect prices to drop.

Lack of planning coordination, through use by managers of different sets of premises, can be extremely costly. The use of consistent premises should, therefore, be agreed upon. A single standard for the future is necessary for good planning, even though this standard includes several sets of premises, with the instruction that different sets of plans be developed on each. Some companies, for example, customarily develop plans in prospect of both peace and war, so that, regardless of what occurs, the company will be ready. Obviously, however, a plan actually put into operation for any future period can use only one set of premises if coordination of its elements is to be achieved.

Since agreement to utilize a given set of premises is important to coordinated planning, it becomes a major responsibility of managers, starting with those at the top, to make sure that subordinate managers understand the premises upon which they are expected to plan. It is not unusual for chief executives in well-managed companies to force top managers with differing views, through group deliberation, to arrive at a set of major premises that all can accept. But whether they are acceptable to all or not, no chief executive can afford to chance a situation where lieutenants are planning their portions of the company's future on substantially different premises.

The importance of premising is illustrated by the case where a company president, believing that planning should start from the bottom, issued instructions that all departments should develop their own budgets and submit them to him. When he received them, he was surprised and dismayed to find that the budgets did not fit, and he had a complex of inconsistent plans on his hands. Had he been aware of the importance of premises, he would never have asked for budgets without first giving his department heads their guidelines.

4. Determining Alternative Courses

The third step in planning is to search for and examine alternative courses of action, especially those not immediately apparent. There is seldom a plan for which reasonable alternatives do not exist, and quite often an alternative that is not obvious proves to be the best.

The more common problem is not finding alternatives, but reducing the number of alternatives so that the most promising may be analyzed.

Even with mathematical techniques and the computer, there is a limit to the number of alternatives that may be examined. It is therefore usually necessary for the planner to reduce by preliminary examination the number of alternatives to those promising the most fruitful possibilities or by mathematically eliminating, through the process of approximation, the least promising ones.

5. Evaluating Alternative Courses

Having sought out alternative courses and examined their strong and weak points, the fourth step is to evaluate them by weighing the various factors in the light of premises and goals. One course may appear to be the most profitable but require a large cash outlay and a slow payback; another may be less profitable but involve less risk; still another may better suit the company's long-range objectives.

If the only objective were to maximize profits in a certain business immediately, if the future were not uncertain, if cash position and capital availability were not worrisome, and if most factors could be reduced to definite data, this evaluation should be relatively easy. But typical planning is replete with uncertainties, problems of capital shortages, and intangible factors, and so evaluation is usually very difficult, even with relatively simple problems. A company may wish to enter a new product line primarily for purposes of prestige; the forecast of expected results may show a clear financial loss; but the question is still open as to whether the loss is worth the gain in prestige.

Because the number of alternative courses in most situations is legion and the numerous variables and limitations are involved, evaluation can be also exceedingly complex. Due to these complexities, the newer methodologies and applications of operations research and analysis, discussed in Chapter 9, are helpful. Indeed, it is at this step in the planning process that operations research and mathematical and computing techniques have their primary application to the field of management.

6. Selecting a Course

The fifth planning step, selecting the course of action, is the point at which a plan is adopted—the real point of decision making. Occasionally an analysis and evaluation of alternative courses will disclose that two or more are advisable, and the manager may decide to follow several courses rather than a single course.

7. Formulating Derivative Plans

At the point where a decision is made, planning is seldom complete, and a sixth step is indicated. There are almost invariably derivative plans required to support the basic plan. In the case where an airline decided to acquire a fleet of new planes, this decision was the signal for the development of a host of derivative plans dealing with the hiring and training of various types of personnel, the acquisition and positioning of spare parts, the development of maintenance facilities, scheduling and advertising, financing and insurance.

8. Numberizing Plans by Budgeting

After decisions are made and plans are set, the final step to give them meaning, as indicated in the discussion above on types of plans, is to numberize them by converting them to budgets. The overall budgets of an enterprise represent the sum total of income and expenses, with resultant profit or surplus, and budgets of major balance sheet items such as cash and capital expenditures. Each department or program of a business or other enterprise can have its own budgets, usually of expenses and capital expenditures, which tie into the overall budget.

If done well, budgets become a means of adding together the various plans and also important standards against which planning progress can be measured. As such, budgets will be discussed below in connection with managerial control.

THE PLANNING PROCESS: RATIONAL APPROACH

As seen in the planning steps outlined above, planning is simply a rational approach to accomplishing an objective. The process can be illustrated as shown in Figure 6.5. In this diagram, progress (toward more sales, more profits, lower costs, and so forth) is on the vertical axis, and time is on the horizontal axis. x indicates where we are (at t_o), and y where we want to be—a goal for the future (at t_n). Since we ordinarily have to study where we are in advance of t_o, particularly with the lag of accounting and statistical data, we may actually have to start our study of the future at x_1 (at t_n). The line xy indicates the decision path which will take us from x to y.

If the future were completely certain, the line xy would be relatively easy to draw. However, in actuality, a myriad of factors in the environment in which a plan is to operate may push events away from or toward the desired goal. These are the planning premises. Again, because we cannot forecast or consider everything, we try to develop our path from x to y in the light of the most critical premises.

The essential logic of planning applies regardless of the time interval between t_o and t_n, whether 5 minutes or 20 years. However, the clarity of premises, the attainability of goals, and the lessening of other planning complexities are almost certain to be inversely related to the time span.

Decision making may be the easiest part of planning, although it involves techniques of evaluation and approach and considerable skill in

Figure 6.5 Progress, time, and critical planning premises.

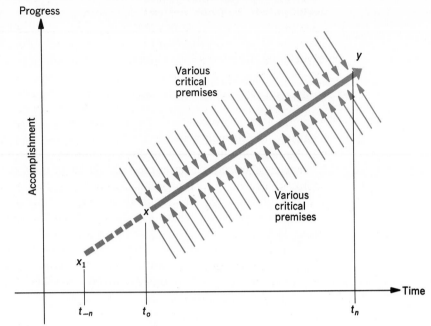

applying these. The real difficulties arise primarily from sharpening and giving meaning to objectives (preferably verifiable), spelling out and giving meaning to critical premises, seeing the nature and relationship of the strengths and weaknesses of alternatives, and communicating goals and premises to those throughout the enterprise who must plan.

THE PLANNING PERIOD:
LONG-RANGE PLANNING

Shall plans be for a short period or a long one? How shall short-range plans be coordinated with long-range plans? These questions suggest a multiple horizon of planning—that, in some cases, planning a week in advance may be ample and that, in others, the desirable period may be a number of years. Even within the same firm at the same time, various planning periods may exist for various matters.

The National Industrial Conference Board, reporting on a survey of business planning some years ago disclosed,[9] as might be expected, that businesses varied considerably in their planning periods. In some instances, long-range plans were confined to 2 years, while in others they

[9]"Industry Plans for the Future," *Conference Board Business Record,* vol. 9, pp. 324-328 (August 1952).

spanned decades. But 3 to 5 years appeared to be most common for long-range planning, and few companies planned less than a year in advance. Later surveys showed more companies engaging in long-range planning, with the planning period being extended. A survey made by McGraw-Hill in 1956 disclosed that the number of large firms laying plans 3 to 5 years in advance had doubled in the prior few years and that even small and medium-sized companies were increasingly undertaking long-range planning.[10] Approximately one-third of the companies interviewed had established their formal long-range planning programs in the previous 2 or 3 years. However, an increasing number of companies were laying their plans on forecasts of a future 10 to 20 years ahead.

Long-range planning has continued to increase until today it is almost a badge of alert management to have some kind of long-range, or corporate, planning department. In 1962, a study by the American Management Association reported that 5 years seemed to be the norm of long-range planning,[11] although planning periods ranging to 25 years and more did exist. In analyzing case studies, the AMA report concluded that companies seemed to base their period on a future that can reasonably be anticipated. Yet, as late as 1973, a study made for the Planning Executives Institute and involving a sample of nearly 400 firms disclosed that 86 percent of the firms having long-range plans used a time period of 3 to 5 years, and only 1 percent planned for longer than 10 years.[12] Moreover, it was surprising that 19 percent of the firms surveyed had no long-range plans.

The Commitment Principle

There should be some logic in selecting the right time range for company planning. In general, since planning and the forecasting that underlies it are costly, a company should probably not plan for a longer period than is economically justifiable; yet it is risky to plan for a shorter period. The answer as to the right planning period seems to lie in the "commitment principle": *Logical planning encompasses a period of time in the future necessary to foresee, as well as possible, the fulfillment of commitments involved in decisions made today.*

Perhaps the most striking application of this principle is the setting of a planning period long enough to anticipate the recovery of costs sunk in a course of action.[13] But since other things than costs can be committed for

---

[10]"In Business, Everyone's Looking Ahead," *Business Week*, p. 113 (Jan. 5, 1957).

[11]Stewart Thompson, *How Companies Plan*, Research Study No. 54 (New York: American Management Association, 1962), pp. 23–31.

[12]R. M. Fulmer and L. W. Rue, *The Practice and Profitability of Long-Range Planning* (Oxford, Ohio: The Planning Executives Institute, 1973), p. 18.

[13]As a matter of fact, in the first edition of this book this was referred to as the "recovery-of-cost" principle. See Harold Koontz and Cyril O'Donnell, *Principles of Management* (New York: McGraw-Hill Book Company, 1955), p. 442.

various lengths of time and because a commitment to spend often precedes an expenditure and may be as unchangeable as sunk costs, it seems inadequate to refer to recovery of costs alone. Thus a company may commit itself, for varying lengths of time, to a personnel policy, such as promotion from within or retirement at age 65, or to other policies or programs involving commitments of direction and not immediately measurable in terms of dollars.

One can readily grasp the logic of planning far enough in the future to foresee, as well as possible, the recovery of capital sunk in a building or a machine. Since capital is the lifeblood of an enterprise and is normally limited in relation to the firm's needs, its expenditure must be accompanied by a reasonable possibility of recovering it, plus a return on investment, through operations. For example, when Lever Brothers sank $45 million into a new factory on the West Coast, they, in effect, decided that the detergent business would permit the recovery of this investment over a period of time. If this period was 20 years, then logically the plans should have been based upon a projection of business for such a time. Of course, as will be discussed presently, they might have introduced some flexibility and reduced their risk (as they did) by spending extra funds to make the plant useful for other purposes.

What the Commitment Principle Implies

What the commitment principle implies is that long-range planning is not really planning for future decisions but rather planning for the future impact of *today's* decisions. In other words, a decision is a commitment, normally of funds, direction of action, or reputation. And decisions lie at the core of planning. While studies and analyses precede decisions, any type of plan implies that some decision has been made. Indeed, a plan does not really exist as such until a decision is made. Under these circumstances, then, the astute manager will recognize the validity of gearing longer-term considerations into present decisions. To do otherwise is to overlook the basic nature of both planning and decision making.

Application of the Commitment Principle

There is no uniform or arbitrary length of time for which a company should plan or for which a given program or any of its parts should be planned. An airplane company embarking on a new commercial jet aircraft project should probably plan this program some 12 years ahead, with 5 or 6 years for conception, engineering, and development and as many more years for production and sales in order to recoup total costs and make a reasonable profit. An instrument manufacturer with a product already developed might need to plan revenues and expenses only 6 months ahead, since this may represent the cycle of raw material acquisition, production, inventorying, sales, and collection of accounts.

But the same company might wish to see much further into the future before assuming a lease for specialized manufacturing facilities, undertaking a program of management training, or developing and promoting a new product.

If a commitment appears to a manager to be for a longer period than he can foresee with reasonable accuracy and if it is not feasible to build enough flexibility at reasonable cost into a plan, the manager may decide arbitrarily to shorten his period of commitment. In many cases, particularly those involving capital expenditures, the actual recovery of cost is determined by accounting or tax practices. In these cases it is possible to decide (regardless of whether the tax authorities would agree for tax purposes) to write off an investment faster than would normally be the case. A West Coast aerospace company president was faced a few years ago with the purchase of some special purpose machinery for performance under a government contract. The machinery would normally be written off in 10 years, but, in his opinion, the contract would probably last only 2 years, and the machinery had no apparent use for other purposes. He argued correctly and logically (but not successfully) with government contracting officers that he should be allowed to include in his costs a 2-year write-off of the machinery. By doing so, he would shorten the commitment period for a highly inflexible investment to the length of time in which he could foresee fulfillment of his commitments.

The planning period will be longer or shorter depending upon the extent to which flexibility can be built into the plan. Thus, a company might be willing to lease a factory for 10 years, even though it is impracticable to plan for longer than 3, because of the possibility of subleasing on a 1- or 2-year notice. But where there is no practicable flexibility, or where flexibility is too costly, it is desirable to plan for the entire period of commitment. This almost surely explains why certain major oil companies have led the nation's business management in the excellence of their long-range planning and the many years they have been doing it, since there is probably no investment quite so inflexibly committed as that of developing an oil field, building piplines, and constructing refinery facilities.

Although this principle indicates that various plans call for various planning periods, those used are often compromises. The short range tends to be selected to conform to quarters or a year because of the practical need for making plans agree with accounting periods. The somewhat arbitrary selection of 5 years or so for the long range is often based on the belief that the degree of uncertainty over longer periods makes planning of questionable value.

Comprehensive Planning

As the commitment principle indicates, then, there may be different time spans for any plan and planning decision, depending on the nature of the

Figure 6.6 Planning areas and time periods. Various management decision areas typically involve planning ahead for differing periods of time. These periods also vary according to the kind of business. For instance, a large public utility may plan new power-production plants 25 or 30 years into the future, while a small garment manufacturer may plan new production facilities only 1 year ahead.

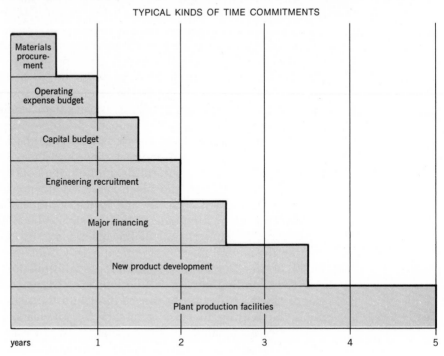

TYPICAL KINDS OF TIME COMMITMENTS

Materials procurement

Operating expense budget

Capital budget

Engineering recruitment

Major financing

New product development

Plant production facilities

years   1   2   3   4   5

commitment involved. Therefore, it has never been logical to look at short-range, medium-range, and long-range planning as essentially different processes. As pointed out above, planning is planning, regardless of the time span of the commitment involved.

As a result, an increasing number of companies and other organizations have been characterizing their major enterprise planning effort as simply "comprehensive" or "strategic" planning. This makes considerable sense because the core of major overall planning is setting major objectives and determining the basic direction to be taken in accomplishing them. It is likely, therefore, that such planning is comprehensive in nature and heavily oriented to strategic planning.

Coordination of Short-Range and Long-Range Plans

Often short-range plans are made without reference to long-range plans. This is plainly a serious error. The importance of integrating the two can hardly be overemphasized, and no short-run plan should be made unless it contributes to the achievement of the relevant long-range plan. Many of the wastes of planning arise from decisions on immediate situations that fail to consider their effect on more remote objectives.

Sometimes these short-range decisions not only fail to contribute to a long-range plan but actually impede or require changes in the long-range plan. For example, if a small company accepts a large order without reckoning the effect on productive capacity or cash position, it may so hamper its future ability to finance an orderly expansion as to require a complex reorientation of its long-range program. Or, in another company, the urgency of obtaining small additions to plant may utilize vacant property so haphazardly as to thwart its longer-range use as the site for a large new plant. In other instances, the decision of a plant superintendent to discharge workers without adequate cause may interfere with the company's longer-range objective of developing a fair and successful personnel program.

Responsible managers should continually scrutinize immediate decisions to ascertain whether they contribute to long-range programs, and subordinate managers should be regularly briefed on company long-range plans so that they will make consistent short-range decisions. It is far easier to do this than to correct inconsistencies, especially since short-term commitments tend to engender further commitments along the same line.

Flexibility in Planning

The above discussion has indicated that the commitment principle must be considered in the light of flexibility of planning. If plans can be changed to meet future requirements which either were not or could not be foreseen, the planning period can be shorter than otherwise would be the case. Because of future uncertainties and possible error in even the most expert forecast, the ideal of planning is to be flexible—the ability to change direction when forced to do so by unexpected events, without undue cost.

Building flexibility into plans: the flexibility principle   *The more that flexibility can be built into plans, the less the danger of losses incurred by unexpected events; but the cost of flexibility should be weighed against the risks involved in future commitments made.*

The flexibility principle applies to the *building into* plans of a practical ability to change direction. As in the case noted above in the discussion of the commitment principle, Lever Brothers did actually spend some $5 million in extra construction cost in building a soap and detergent factory so that it could, if the company later decided to do so, be changed into a chemical manufacturing plant. It is not unusual, also, for companies to spend more for movable partitions than for fixed partitions in office buildings to maintain the flexibility of more easily changing space arrangements. Likewise, a company introducing a new product might use temporary tooling rather than more expensive permanent tooling, even though manufacturing costs are increased thereby, in order to avoid the risk of larger losses if the product does not succeed on the market.

To many managers, flexibility is the most important principle of planning. The ability to change a plan without undue cost or friction, to detour, to keep moving toward a goal despite changes in environment or even failure of plans, has great value. Flexibility is critical when the commitment is great and cannot be discharged in a short time (for example, in retrieving outlays for major capital facilities plus a return). But it is almost invariably true that built-in flexibility involves costs, and the most inflexible plan is likely to be the least costly if later events prove that the ability to change direction was unnecessary.

Flexibility is possible only within limits. In the first place, a decision cannot always be put off long enough to assure its rightness. This is exemplified by the decision of the Mobil Oil Company to build a refinery in the Pacific Northwest. The financial point of no return was reached several years before the management could be completely certain that this would be an economical venture.

In the second place, built-in flexibility of plans may be so expensive that the benefits of hedging may not be worth the cost. Whether a company spends extra money to modify a special purpose plant so that it can be used for other purposes, if the original program is not successful, will depend on the costs of doing so and the risks to be avoided. Some companies have felt, as apparently the top management of Montgomery Ward did for several years after World War II, that they could buy flexibility by keeping their resources in that most flexible of all assets—cash—only to have a competitor step forward with aggressive expenditures and capture much of the market.

A striking case of this was Montgomery Ward. Under the leadership of Sewell Avery, it built up cash reserves exceeding $250 million by 1953, but saw its share of business fall from 40 percent in 1942 to 28 percent in 1952. Sears, Roebuck, on the other hand, under the leadership of Robert E. Wood, adopted an expansionist program and increased its share of the business from approximately 50 to 66 percent in the same period. Sears also increased its profits relative to Ward's. Although Sears stock rose during this period, that of Ward fell. Had a depression occurred during this immediate postwar period, however, Montgomery Ward would have been in an excellent position to capitalize on its liquidity, and Sears might have been in a very vulnerable position.

A third major limit to building flexibility into plans is the fact that there are often cases where flexibility either cannot be built into plans at all, or can be only with such great difficulty as to be impracticable. A special purpose machine may be useful only to produce or package a particular product, and to change it for other uses would be impracticable. An oil refinery can hardly be used for any other purpose than refining petroleum, and there is no reasonable possibility of doing anything to make it useful for any other purpose. These should be compared with a typical manufacturing plant or warehouse that might be used for a number of purposes.

Reviewing plans regularly: the principle of navigational change *The more planning decisions commit for the future, the more important it is that a manager periodically check on events and expectations and redraw plans as necessary to maintain a course toward a desired goal.* Unlike the flexibility principle, which applies to the adaptability built into plans themselves, this principle applies to flexibility in the planning process. Built-in flexibility does not automatically revise plans; the manager, like the navigator, must continually check the course and redraw plans to meet a desired goal.

After two decades of intensive education, it is now fair to say that managers are becoming quite sophisticated in planning. They used to feel that a plan committed them to an invariable course of action. Now they understand that managers manage the plan; they are not managed by it.

PLANNING INVOLVES AN OPEN-SYSTEM APPROACH

As emphasized in the first chapter, practitioners must necessarily take into account interactions with their total environment in every aspect of managing. Managing is not, nor could it be, a closed-system approach to enterprise operation. This is nowhere more apparent than in the theory and practice of planning.

Objectives must obviously be set in the light of the economic, technological, social, political, and ethical elements of an enterprise environment. Planning premises represent a clear recognition that plans cannot be constructed, nor decisions made, in the vacuum of an internal system. The interfaces and interactions of plans with every element of the conditions and influences surrounding an enterprise are indeed many and complex. While certain scholars criticize what they think they see as a closed-system approach of operational-management theory, they can hardly do so with an awareness of what management is. And practicing managers with even the slightest knowledge of their task can hardly disregard the milieu in which they operate.

FOR DISCUSSION

1 "Planning is looking ahead, and control is looking back." Comment.
2 If planning involves a rational approach to selected goals, how can one include goals or objectives as a type of plan?

3 Using the concepts of policies and procedures, draw up a statement of policy and devise a brief procedure which might be useful in implementing it. Are you sure your policy is not a rule?

4 If all decisions involve commitments and if the future is always uncertain, how can a manager guard against costly mistakes?

5 Taking a planning problem which is now facing you, proceed to deal with it in accordance with the steps involved in planning outlined in this chapter.

6 Using an example of a planning decision with which you are familiar, show to what extent, and how, the principles of commitment, flexibility, and navigational change apply to it.

7 "Planning theory illustrates the open-system approach to management." Comment.

chapter 7 Objectives

As set forth in the previous chapter, objectives are the ends toward which enterprise activities are aimed—the end points of planning—even though they cannot be taken as given, but require considerable planning to establish them. Often, distinctions are made between objectives, goals, and targets. An "objective" is sometimes thought of as the end point of a management program, whether stated in general or specific terms, while the implication of "goal" or "target" is almost invariably one of specific quantitative or qualitative aims. However, because clear distinctions tend not to be made uniformly by writers and practitioners, these terms are generally used interchangeably in this book.

As pointed out in Chapter 1, all managers have, logically and morally, a "surplus" goal, to operate so that the group for which they are responsible will achieve its objectives with the minimum of expenditure of human and material resources or will achieve as much as possible with the resources at its command.

This is, of course, the advantage of profit in business enterprise. It is actually a surplus of revenues over expenses in an enterprise whose purpose is the production and sale of goods and services desired by consumers. Government managers often say that they are at a disadvantage in comparison with business, that they have no profit by which to gauge their success. While it is true that government agencies, except for those in a quasi-business operation, do not have a profit objective in the conventional sense of the term, it is nonetheless true that they should have a surplus goal.[1] In other words, whatever the purpose entrusted by society to a government agency, it is reasonable to expect that those who manage it should achieve the purpose with a minimum of resources, with as much "surplus" as possible. A chief of police, for example, has the duty to obtain as effective a police protection service as possible with the human and material means available.

Likewise, except for those managers who have profit responsibility for an integrated operation, managers of parts of businesses do not have responsibility for profits in the normal sense of the term. Nevertheless, each of their operations—from marketing director to machine-shop supervisor—should have clear objectives and the obligation to accomplish them in a "surplus" way.

If surplus is to have any practical significance in management, the objectives of any enterprise, or of any department or section of it, must be verifiable. An objective is verifiable if, at some target date in the future, we can look back and say with certainty, "Yes, it was accomplished" or "No, it was not." Otherwise, there can be no measure of effectiveness since we cannot know whether we are accomplishing a vague objective. Nor can there be any measure of efficiency unless we know output as well as input.

[1]See, for example, the excellent discussion of the role of objectives for nonprofit enterprises by D. D. McConkey, *MBO for Nonprofit Organizations* (New York: AMACOM, American Management Association, 1975).

For far too many years and still for too many business firms and most nonbusiness enterprises, it has been customary to say something like: "It is our objective to make a fair profit while making and selling a quality product and being a good citizen in the community." As nice as this sounds, it is a virtually meaningless objective since no one can know whether it is being accomplished. Or one may say, as is often said, that the objective of a university is "to discover new knowledge and disseminate knowledge." This objective is likewise not very meaningful and does not make possible the operation of a surplus objective by a manager or, for that matter, by a professor.

ENTERPRISE PURPOSE AND OBJECTIVES

The surplus goal of managers still leaves open the question of what the purpose of an enterprise is and what the objectives of an enterprise and its departments are in contributing to this purpose. The purpose of business is production and marketing of economic goods and services; of government, the fulfillment of such social needs as security and welfare; of a university, research and teaching; of a church, administering to religious needs; and so on. But to accomplish these purposes, a number of enterprise objectives may be necessary and, in turn, a number of supporting goals by departments and sections.

Objectives Form a Hierarchy

As shown in Figure 7.1, objectives can be structured as a hierarchy. The purpose of a business might be to furnish low-cost and convenient transportation to the average person. Its mission might be to produce,

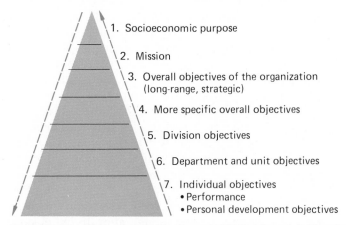

1. Socioeconomic purpose
2. Mission
3. Overall objectives of the organization (long-range, strategic)
4. More specific overall objectives
5. Division objectives
6. Department and unit objectives
7. Individual objectives
   • Performance
   • Personal development objectives

Figure 7.1 Hierarchy of objectives. *H. Weihrich and J. Mendleson,* Management: An MBO Approach *(Dubuque, Iowa: William C. Brown Co., 1978), p. xi. Reprinted by permission of the publisher.*

market, and service automobiles. These aims are in turn translated into general objectives or strategies, such as designing, producing, and marketing a low-cost, fuel-efficient, and reliable automobile.

At the next level of the hierarchy the objectives in key result areas can be stated. These are the areas in which performance is essential for the success of the enterprise. Although there is no complete agreement on what the key result areas of a business should be—and they may differ for various enterprises—Peter F. Drucker suggests the following:

> Market standing; innovation; productivity; physical and financial resources; profitability; manager performance and development; worker performance and attitude; public responsibility.[2]

Some examples of such objectives are the following:

Profitability: To obtain 10 percent return on investment by the end of calendar year 1985.

Productivity: To increase the number of units of product X by 7 percent without an increase in cost or reduction of current quality level by June 30, 1981.

These objectives have to be further translated into division, department, and unit objectives down to the lowest level of the organization.

Objectives Form a Network

Both objectives and planning programs normally form a network of desired results and events. A company or other enterprise is a system. If goals are not interconnected and mutually supportive, people very often pursue paths that may seem good for their own function but may be detrimental to the company as a whole.

In considering goals and plans as a network, it is sometimes overlooked that they are seldom linear, that is, where one objective is accomplished, it is followed by another, and so on. It is almost universal that goals and programs are interlocking in a network fashion. Figure 7.2 depicts the interlocking network of contributory programs (each of which has appropriate objectives) that constitute a total new product program. Moreover, as can be readily appreciated, each of the interconnected programs shown could itself be broken down into an interlocking network. Thus the product research program shown in Figure 7.2 as a single event might involve within it a network of such subsidiary goals and programs as development of preliminary schematic design, development of a rough working model, simplifying electronic and mechanical elements, packaging of the design, and other events.

[2]*The Practice of Management* (New York: Harper & Brothers, 1954), p. 63.

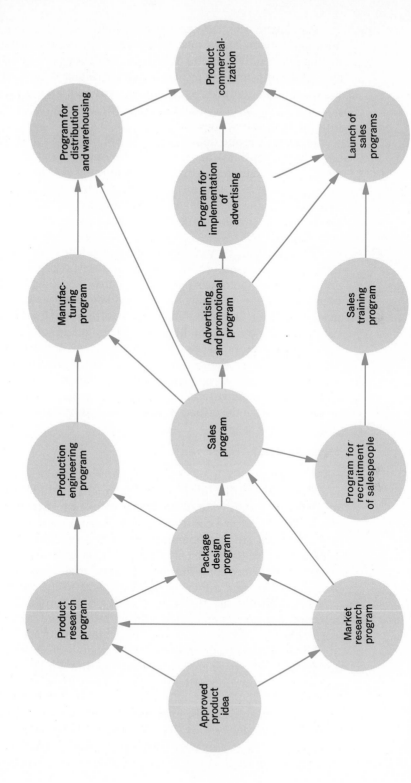

Figure 7.2 Network of programs constituting a typical new-product program.

As can be seen, the network of goals and programs places a heavy burden on managers in making sure that the components fit one another. Fitting is not only a matter of having the various programs performed, but also of timing their completion, since undertaking one program often depends upon completion of another. Thus, in Figure 7.2 it would not be possible to undertake a package design program until the nature of the product was determined.

It is easy for one department of a company to set goals that may seem entirely appropriate for it, only to be operating at cross-purposes with another. The manufacturing department may find its goals best served by long production runs, but this might interfere with the marketing department's desire to have all products in the line readily available, or the finance department's goal to maintain investment in inventory at a certain level.

The problem of making a network effective is difficult enough in itself. But it is compounded by the necessities of organization structure and such other factors as personality considerations. While we may try to organize units in an enterprise around key result areas, this is not always possible. Other factors might be controlling, such as technology (an oil company simply cannot have an integrated gasoline division separate from motor oils or asphalt) or personnel attitudes (research engineers seldom like to see themselves as a part of the marketing organization).

It is bad enough when goals do not support and interlock with one another. It is tragic when they interfere with one another. What is needed, as one executive described it, is a "matrix of mutually supportive goals."

Multiplicity of Objectives

Objectives are, of course, many. Even broad major enterprise objectives are normally multiple. A business might include among its overall objectives a certain rate of profit and return on investment; emphasis on research to develop a continuing flow of proprietary products; developing publicly held stock ownership; financing primarily by earnings plowback and bank debt; distributing products in foreign markets; assuring competitive prices for superior products; achieving a dominant position in an industry; and adhering in all respects to the value of our society.

Similarly, to say that the objective of a university is research and education is not enough. It would be much more accurate (but still not verifiable) to state its objectives in the areas of attracting highly qualified students; offering basic training in the liberal arts and sciences as well as in certain professional fields; granting the Ph.D. degree to qualified candidates; attracting a highly regarded faculty; discovering and organizing new knowledge through research; and operating as a private school supported principally through tuition and gifts of alumni and friends.

Likewise, at every level in the hierarchy of objectives, goals are likely to be multiple. It is exactly this fact that has caused some management specialists concern. It is believed by some that a manager cannot pursue effectively more than a few objectives. Edward Schleh, prominent management consultant, has stated that "no position should have more than two to five objectives" at one time.[3] His argument is that too many objectives before a manager tend to take the drive out of their accomplishment and may unduly highlight minor objectives to the detriment of major ones.

There is something to what Schleh says, but his number seems too arbitrary and too few. It is true that minor goals should not be given the status of important objectives unless we are dealing with a low-level job. It would hardly be useful for an upper-level manager to make much of such lesser objectives as meeting callers, attending meetings, or answering correspondence. There are certain things which any manager is expected to do and these need not be made into specific and special objectives. Goals are not conceived of as dealing with every facet of a person's job. They should not be confused with activities.

Even if routine matters are excluded, it seems that there is not any specific maximum number of objectives. To be sure, if there are so many that none commands adequate attention, planning will be ineffective. At the same time, it does seem possible that managers might pursue simultaneously as many as ten or fifteen significant objectives. This depends in turn on how much they do themselves and how much they can assign, thereby limiting their role to one of assigning, supervising, and controlling.

Long-Range and Short-Range Objectives

If planning is to be effective, there must be an integral relationship between short-range and long-range objectives.

Long-range plans, drawn to specifications of objectives, are notably more speculative for distant years than for the immediate future. This means that plans for the fifth year of a 5-year plan are much more uncertain than those for the first, less certain than those for the fourth, and so on. Short-range objectives, usually to be realized in the first year of a long-range plan, are likely to be both comprehensive and specific. The approach should always be from the distant (fifth) year to the present, and not vice versa, because what is to be done the first year must provide a foundation for what is to be done each successive year, and this can only be guaranteed if short-range plans are part of the long-range plan.

The selection of short-range objectives proceeds from an evaluation of priorities relating to long-range objectives. Some things simply need to be done first, either because they are a prerequisite to doing other things or because of lead time considerations. For instance, as a new firm is established, raising capital for fixed and operating expenses is likely to be a prime objective and may be the sole short-run objective. If so, short-range objectives visualized for succeeding periods might be hiring

---

[3]*Management by Results* (New York: McGraw-Hill Book Company, 1961), p. 22.

managers for engineering, production, and sales; leasing space and equipment; and staffing the organization. At the same time, if a long lead time is necessary, say, for installing a piece of specialized equipment, then writing specifications and placing .the order would also be a short-range objective.

Thus, for short-range objectives to help achieve intermediate and long-range objectives, it is necessary to draw a plan for accomplishing each objective and to combine these into a master plan for review in terms of logic, consistency, and practicality.

THE DEVELOPMENT OF MANAGING BY OBJECTIVES

One of the most interesting developments that has swept across the management scene in the past decade has been the inauguration of programs of managing by objectives, or results.[4] As basic as objectives are to planning and to all managing, it is one of the remarkable phenomena of human history that only in recent years have a significant number of those responsible for managing our various enterprises come to realize the simple truth that if objectives are to be actionable, they must be clear and verifiable to those who pursue them.

No one can accomplish an ambiguous goal. People must know what their goals are, what actions contribute to the attainment of these goals, and when they have been accomplished. As basic as developing and accomplishing verifiable goals are, they are nonetheless difficult in practice. Too few managers who speak of managing by objectives are really doing so effectively, and it is a fairly rare nonbusiness operation that is even attempting to do so.

Early Impetus to MBO

It is not strictly accurate to identify any one person as the originator of an approach that emphasizes objectives because common sense has told people for many centuries that groups and individuals expect to accomplish some end results. However, there have been certain individuals who have long placed emphasis on management by objectives and, by doing so, have given impetus to its development as a system.

One of those is Peter Drucker. In 1954, he acted as a catalyst by emphasizing that "objectives are needed in every area where performance and results directly and vitally affect the survival and prosperity of the business" and "the performance that is expected of the manager must be derived from the performance goals of the business, his results must be

---

[4]Some of the material on objectives in the following sections is drawn from Harold Koontz, *Appraising Managers as Managers* (New York: McGraw-Hill Book Company, 1971), chaps. 3–4.

measured by the contribution they make to the success of the enterprise."[5] This in turn requires "management by objectives" and "control by self-control."

At the same time, if not indeed earlier than Drucker, the General Electric Company laid out the elements of managing by objectives in its extensive planning for reorganization in 1954.[6] The company pointed out at that time:

> Decentralization of managerial decision-making requires that objective goals and objective measurements of progress toward these goals be substituted for subjective appraisals and personal supervision. Through a program of objective measurements, managers will be equipped to focus attention on the relevant, the trends, and on the future. To the extent, therefore, that we are able to develop sound, objective measurements of business performance, our philosophy of decentralizing authority and responsibility will be rendered more effective.[7]

The company implemented this philosophy of appraisal by identifying key result areas and undertaking considerable research on their measurement. However, there is no evidence that it was actually placed in operation by a program of appraising performance against verifiable objectives as we know it today. Nonetheless, the report reflects a pioneering approach to the problem.

The Appraisal Approach to MBO

In 1957, Douglas McGregor, in his classic paper criticizing trait-appraisal systems for requiring "the manager to pass judgment on the personal worth of subordinates," thereby "playing God,"[8] made a strong plea for appraising on the basis of preset objectives. McGregor's concern was with the then (and largely now) conventional appraisal methods which emphasized personal characteristics. He saw in appraisal against objectives a means of making evaluations constructive and placing the emphasis where it ought to be, on performance rather than on personality. Its main advantage, according to McGregor, would be to stimulate development of subordinates and give them means for greater motivation.

Considerable impetus toward emphasizing objectives was also given by Edward Schleh's stimulating book *Management by Results*. He

---

[5]*The Practice of Management* (New York: Harper & Brothers, 1954), pp. 63, 101. In conversation with one of the authors, Drucker gave credit for the concept to the late Harold E. Smiddy, then of General Electric.

[6]See especially *Professional Management in General Electric* (New York: The General Electric Company, 1954), book 3, "The Work of the Professional Manager," pp. 24–28, 38–42, 113–132.

[7]Ibid., p. 113.

[8]"An Uneasy Look at Performance Appraisal," *Harvard Business Review*, vol. 35, no. 3, pp. 89–94 (May–June 1957).

suggested that "management objectives state the specific accomplishment expected of each individual in a specific period of time so that the work of the whole management group is soundly blended at a particular moment of time" and that "objectives should be set for personnel all the way down to each foreman and salesman and, in addition, to staff people such as accountants, industrial engineers, chemists, etc.[9] Schleh recommended that delegation be by results expected and appraisals geared to the same standard.

Singling out the basic contributions of Drucker, General Electric, McGregor, and Schleh may be unfair to their many predecessors and successors. Although they were not thinking of objectives as a means of appraisal, Henri Fayol emphasized objectives, Lyndall Urwick built much of his management writing around accomplishment of objectives, and Chester Barnard made purpose the distinguishing feature of formal organizations—all of these men—and others of the so-called classicists—many years before 1954. However, much of the early emphasis on objectives and on management by objectives in the many books and articles published even in the 1960s and much of the practice then and now have failed to refine the concept to require a network of *verifiable* objectives.

It is true that interest in developing a more objective and performance-oriented system of appraising managers gave major impetus to the modern growth of total management by objectives. As interest in appraisal shifted from personality to performance and the search for objectivity in appraisal grew, it was natural and normal that attempts should be made to develop more verifiable objectives throughout the enterprise structure. In some enterprises managing by objectives has become an entire system and philosophy of managing.

The Motivation Approach to MBO

Writers, consultants, and practitioners soon recognized that MBO was a means of integrating individual needs and organizational demands. Individuals become active participants in the managerial process, which motivates people at all levels to contribute to the success of an enterprise.

Another aspect at this stage of development of MBO is the concern not only for organizational goals, but also for personal growth objectives. As everyone now knows, learning does not stop with finishing school. Rather, it is a continuing process which is facilitated by the inclusion of personal development objectives in the MBO process.

Today, managers are better educated than ever before. They want to be involved; they demand participation in decisions; they want more control over their job and their life; and they want to contribute to the objectives of the enterprise. Management by objectives helps to satisfy these needs because it not only clarifies and communicates organizational

[9]Op. cit., pp. 18–19.

aims but also is based on a philosophy that emphasizes participation and self-control. Thus, MBO provides a high degree of independence and a way of integrating individual needs and organizational demands—and this means motivation.

Long-Term View in MBO

In the appraisal and motivational approaches to MBO, the focus tends to be on short-term objectives. This orientation, unfortunately, may result in undesirable managerial behavior. One may pursue short-term aims but ignore the long-term health of the enterprise. Recognizing these shortcomings, several writers now include strategic planning in their MBO approach.[10]

The Systems Approach to MBO

Certainly MBO has undergone great changes from performance appraisal, to being an instrument for motivating individuals, and finally to serving as a way of integrating strategic planning into the MBO process.[11] But the development of MBO must not stop at this stage. More recently, MBO has been viewed as a system. For example, George S. Odiorne considers MBO a system of managerial leadership.[12] Similarly, Anthony P. Raia and Dale D. McConkey discuss the systematic relationships of many key managerial activities.[13]

One of the early research studies that investigated MBO as a comprehensive system of managing indicates that most key managerial activities can and should be integrated with the MBO process. The degree of integration, however, differs for individual activities. It was found, for example, that the highest degree of integration of MBO with managerial functions was in controlling, planning, and directing. But several key managerial activities in staffing and organizing also were well integrated into the MBO process. These findings indicate that MBO, to be effective, has to be viewed as a comprehensive system. In short, it must be considered a way of managing, and not an addition to the managerial job.[14]

---

[10]See, for example, J.W. Humble, *Improving Business Results* (Maidenhead, England: McGraw-Hill Publishing Company, 1968) and A.P. Raia, *Managing by Objectives* (Glenview, Ill.: Scott, Foresman and Company, 1974).

[11]The various approaches to MBO constitute a kind of "jungle." How to untangle it is discussed by H. Weihrich in "An Uneasy Look at the MBO Jungle: Toward a Contingency Approach to MBO," *Management International Review*, vol. 16, no. 4, pp. 103–109 (1976).

[12]*Management by Objectives* (New York: Pitman Publishing Corporation, 1965).

[13]Raia, op. cit., chap. 2; McConkey, op. cit., chap. 1.

[14]H. Weihrich, "A Study of the Integration of Management by Objectives with Key Managerial Activities and the Relationship to Selected Effectiveness Measures," unpublished doctoral dissertation, University of California, Los Angeles, 1973. Also, a model of the systems approach to MBO is discussed by H. Weihrich in "A New Approach to MBO—Updating a Time-Honored Technique," *Management World*, vol. 6, no. 4, pp. 6–12 (April 1977).

As is eminently clear, a system of managing or appraising managers by verifiable objectives is a reflection of the purpose of managing itself. Without clear objectives, managing is haphazard and random, and no individual and no group can expect to perform effectively or efficiently unless a clear goal is sought.

Quantitative Objectives

It has been noted that to be meaningful, objectives must be verifiable. The easiest way to get verifiability is to put goals in quantitative terms. Instead of saying a goal is to make a profit, we should say that it is to make $10 million in profit after taxes in 1980 by selling $200 million worth of products—with $40 million in product line A, $60 million in product line B, $20 million in product line C, and $80 million in product line D—at a gross profit margin of 33 percent, a net profit before taxes on sales of 10 percent, and a return on stockholders' equity of 18 percent.

The goals of a manufacturing manager might be to produce 2 million units at a total direct cost of $100 million and period costs not to exceed $33 million,[15] to reduce scrap from 2.5 to 2.0 percent, to keep factory labor turnover under 4 percent per month, or to purchase and install a given type of plant equipment at a cost not to exceed $3 million by December 15, 1980.

Similar quantitative goals could be made for other positions on down the line. Even a packaging line supervisor in a given month might have goals to package 500 cases of product per hour, with a labor cost not to exceed 5 cents per case, and with a scrap loss not in excess of 1 percent. The district sales manager might have objectives of selling in his district 25,000 cases of merchandise in a month with a sales volume of $750,000 and to have each member of the sales force make an average of six calls per day. Or a personnel manager might have a department goal to recruit 100 persons of various specific qualifications each month, to hold exit interviews with each departing employee within 1 day of separation, and to reduce clerical costs in the department by 4 percent.

Qualitative Objectives

Unfortunately, many goals cannot be reasonably quantified. In fact, there is danger in attempting to push numbers too far since the specious accuracy of numbers in many areas can lead managers astray. There is the danger that numbers and mathematics may even tend to replace managing. Moreover, there are too many worthwhile goals that are not quantifia-

---

[15]Under modern direct cost accounting, costs that vary in some way with volume are referred to as "direct" costs; those which vary with time are called "period" costs.

ble; and the higher one goes in the management structure, the more objectives are likely to be qualitative.

Qualitative goals can, for the most part, be made verifiable, although admittedly not with the complete degree of accuracy possible in quantitatively stated objectives. For example, a training manager may have a goal to develop and implement a certain new program of training with specified characteristics by a certain date. Or a company controller may be charged with devising, with the cooperation of affected line managers, a program of variable budgeting by a certain date, with expense variations spread over volumes of sales outputs from $350,000 to $650,000 per month. The manufacturing manager might have, as one objective, the development and installation of a certain program of equipment realignment by a given date. Likewise, the head of research and development might have an objective of completing the design of a new product with certain specifications by a certain date.

Sometimes it is said that qualitative objectives are gauged by the standard of "how well," and quantitative objectives by "how much." To some extent this is true, but the authors' experience is that any qualitative goal can be made highly verifiable by spelling out the characteristics of the program or other objective sought and a date of accomplishment. If it can be said, for example, that an objective is "to make more effective use of personnel recruitment services," it can almost as easily be said "to make more effective use of personnel recruitment services by (1) requiring all unfilled positions below a certain level to be submitted to the personnel department; (2) having the personnel department develop a program (with certain specified characteristics) for publicizing its approaches and services within the company by June 30; and (3) having the personnel department develop and implement a program of regular follow-up on candidates recommended to line managers by May 1."

Verifiability Is the Key

It should be abundantly clear at this point that verifiability is the key to operational objectives.

One of the interesting experiences one of the authors has had was in working with a government agency to install a program of management by verifiable objectives. In this uncommon and admirable case, many of the department heads' objectives were qualitative. In asking, as a first step, that these managers come up with objectives, it was not surprising to find many like the following:

Informing more people of available health services

Utilization of personnel methods designed to secure and retain high-caliber public employees

Select and organize a staff in such a way as to best accomplish the departmental objective

Eliminate all possible time now wasted in unproductive action

Refine and manage the work program

Establish an ongoing program for data processing personnel

One must recognize that, particularly in some departments of typical government agencies, setting verifiable objectives is extremely difficult. Nevertheless, as each department manager was asked the simple question, "At the end of the year how will you know whether this objective has been accomplished?" or "How will your subordinates know when they are accomplishing an objective?" a little thought made it possible to develop highly verifiable objectives. For example, the general objective on health services became one "to increase the utilization of public health services during the fiscal year by 15 percent (as measured by the number of persons using the services) through specific programs of (1) developing three decentralized medical clinics; (2) establishing night clinics in two locations; and (3) geographically consolidating various preventive health services." Each program included enough specific characteristics and even quantitative data so that the objectives became highly verifiable and meaningful to the department manager and his or her subordinates.

Budgetary Objectives and Other Objectives

It is sometimes argued that all a manager really needs is a well-planned and well-constructed budget—that this will furnish all the objectives required. The argument is that if a budget is based on sound planning premises, including especially a credible sales forecast and an acceptable level of profit, all the department managers need to do is to meet the budget, item by item.

It is true that a good budget, like a clear and accurate profit and loss statement and balance sheet, is a summary, in numerical terms, of what a business or other operation does. It is true, too, that any well-constructed financial summary can be a "window" through which the plans and activities of managers can be seen if the observer looks far enough.

But more is needed in practice. Budget figures are resultants of plans and expected performance. They have meaning only when backed by actionable plans and programs. The end points of each plan must be some goal toward which actions are aimed.

Thus a marketing department might have a goal to accomplish sales of $20 million in a given year. To do this, however, programs must be made for pinpointed market research, for developing sales promotions with certain characteristics by a certain time, for launching advertising programs with certain features during a given period, and for specific deployment and preparation of the field sales force. In each of these areas, too, the organizational subcomponents should have plans and objectives to contribute toward the accomplishment of the various programs. In addition, the marketing area plans and objectives normally need to be supported by coordinate supporting programs in such areas as new product development, purchasing, production, shipping, warehousing, costing, and pricing.

Without a workable network of plans and objectives, budget figures themselves tend to be wishes or guesses. Yet, no one would exclude the meeting of budget commitments from a manager's set of objectives.

THE PROCESS OF MANAGING BY OBJECTIVES

The practical importance of objectives in management can perhaps be seen best by summarizing how managing by objectives should work in practice. This is shown in Figure 7.3. The ideal is a system that starts at the top of an enterprise and has the active support of the chief executive, for whom verifiable goals are also set. While objective setting should start at the top, it is not imperative that it do so. It can start at a division level, at a marketing manager level, or even lower. This has happened. For example, in one company the system was first started in a division where it was carried down to the lowest level of supervision with an interlocking network of goals. Under the personal leadership and tutelage of the division general manager, it succeeded in areas of profitability, cost reduction, and improved operations. Soon, some other division managers and the chief executive became interested in and attempted to implement similar programs. In another case, the head of an accounting section started to develop a system for her group; her success not only gave her recognition (and promotion) but served as an entrance point for the entire company to embark on a program.

As in all planning, one of the critical needs is the development and dissemination of consistent planning premises. No manager can be asked to set goals or establish plans and budgets without guidelines. Planning premises will be discussed in the following chapter.

Preliminary Setting of Objectives at the Top

Given appropriate planning premises, the first step in setting objectives is for the top manager concerned to determine what he or she perceives to be the most important goals for the enterprise to achieve in a given period ahead. These can be set for any period—a quarter, a year, 5 years, or whatever is felt desirable in given circumstances. In most instances they are set to coincide with the annual budget. But this is not necessary and often not desirable. Certain goals should be scheduled for accomplishment in a much shorter period and others for a much longer period. Also, typically as one goes down the line in an organization, goal accomplishment of managers tends to have a shorter time span. It is seldom feasible or wise for first-level supervisors, for example, to set many annual goals

Figure 7.3 The system of managing and appraising by objectives. *H. Koontz, Appraising Managers as Managers (New York: McGraw-Hill Book Company, 1971), p. 78.*

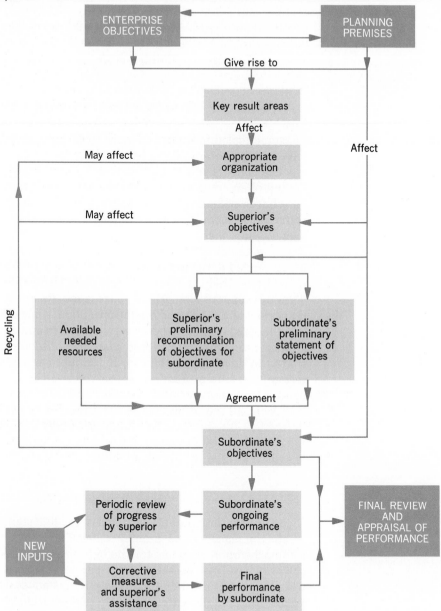

since their goal span on most operating matters, such as cost or scrap reduction, rearrangement of facilities, or instituting of special personnel programs, is likely to be shorter and may be accomplished in weeks or months.

The goals set by superior managers must be looked upon as being preliminary, based on an analysis and judgment of what can and should be accomplished by the organization in a period of time and taking into account its strengths and weaknesses in the light of available opportunities. They must be regarded as tentative and subject to modification as the entire chain of verifiable objectives is worked out by subordinates. It is foolish to push top-management-dictated objectives down the throats of subordinates since forced objectives can hardly induce an indispensable sense of commitment. Most managers also find in the process of working out goals with subordinates both problems to be dealt with and opportunities they could not have previously known.

In the setting of objectives, the manager also established measures of what will indicate goal accomplishment. If verifiable objectives are developed, these measures, whether in dollars of sales or profits, percentages, cost levels, or program execution, will normally be built into the objectives.

Clarification of the Organizational Roles

Often overlooked in installing and operating programs of managing by objectives is the relationship between results expected and the location of responsibility to achieve them. Ideally, every goal and subgoal should be some one person's clear responsibility. Analysis of the organization structure in terms of results expected will often show areas of fuzziness where clarification or reorganization is called for. Sometimes it is impossible to mold an organization so that a given objective is some one person's responsibility. In setting goals for launching a new product, for example, careful coordination will normally be required of the managers of research, marketing, and production. These separate functions can be largely centralized by putting a product manager in charge. But, if this is not desirable, at least the specific parts of each coordinating manager's contribution to the total program goal can and should be clearly identified.

Setting of Subordinates' Objectives

After making sure that pertinent general objectives, strategies, and planning premises are disseminated to subordinates, superiors can then proceed to work with them in setting their objectives. Superiors normally first give subordinates their preliminary thinking on the goals believed to be feasible for the company or the department they manage, and then ask what goals subordinates believe they can accomplish, in what time period, and with what resources.

The superior's role at this point is extremely important. Questions the superior should ask include: What can you do? How can we improve your operation to help me improve mine? What stands in the way, what obstructions keep you from a higher level of performance? What changes can we make? How can I help? It is amazing how many things that obstruct performance can be removed and how many diamonds of constructive ideas can be dredged from the experience and knowledge of subordinates.

Superiors must also be patient counselors, helping their subordinates develop consistent and supportive objectives and being careful not to set goals that are impossible or highly improbable of attainment. Human nature tends to be the same. We are likely to believe that anything can be accomplished a year hence, but much less by tomorrow. And one of the things that can kill a program of managing by objectives is to allow managers to set up "blue sky" objectives that they cannot reasonably be expected to accomplish.

At the same time, goal setting by subordinates does not mean that people do whatever they want to do. Superiors must listen to, and work with, their subordinates, but in the end they must take responsibility for approving goals for subordinates. Their judgment and final approval must be based upon what is reasonably attainable with "stretch" and "pull," what is fully supportive of upper-level objectives, what is consistent with goals of other managers in other functions, and what goals will not be inconsistent with the longer-run objectives and interests of the department and company.

Goals and Resources

One of the major advantages of setting up a careful network of verifiable goals and a requirement for doing it effectively is the opportunity to tie in the need for capital, material, and human resources at the same time. All managers at all levels require these resources to accomplish their goals. By relating these to the goals themselves, superiors are better able to see the economics of allocating them. It helps to avoid what is the bane of any upper-level manager's existence—the "nickel and diming" by subordinates who need "one more" technician or engineer or "one more" piece of equipment, each of which in isolation is easy for them to sell to their boss and difficult for the superior to refuse.

Recycling Objectives

As indicated, setting objectives can hardly be done by starting at the top and dividing them up. Nor should they be started from the bottom. What is required is a degree of recycling. This is indicated by the arrows in Figure 7.3. Top managers may have an idea as to what their subordinates should set as objectives—and those who report to top managers an idea about their own subordinates' objectives—but the process of goal setting as outlined above will almost certainly change these preconceived goals as the contributions of subordinates come into focus. Thus, setting objectives is not only a joint process but also one of interaction which will require recycling. For example, a sales manager may set a goal to achieve much higher sales of a product than had been believed possible. In this event, goals of manufacturing and finance departments will surely be affected.

Guidelines for Setting Objectives

The foregoing discussion indicates that setting objectives is indeed a difficult task. It requires intelligent coaching by the superior and extensive practice by the subordinate to meet the criteria for good objectives.

The list of objectives should not be too long, yet should cover the main features of the job. Objectives should be verifiable, should state the time when they are to be achieved, and, if possible, indicate the quality of objectives and the cost in achieving them. Furthermore, objectives should present a challenge, indicate priorities, and promote personal and professional growth and development. These and other criteria for good objectives are summarized in Table 7.1. Practicing managers and persons aspiring to a management position may benefit by testing their objectives against the criteria shown in the checklist.

Table 7.1 Checklist for Manager Objectives

1. Do the objectives cover the main features of the job? * ☐
2. Is the list of objectives too long? If so, can some objectives be combined? ☐
3. Are the objectives verifiable, i.e., does one know at the end of the period whether or not they have been achieved? ☐
4. Do the objectives indicate
   (a) quantity? (how much) ☐
   (b) quality? (how well, or specific characteristics) ☐
   (c) time? (when) ☐
   (d) cost? (at what cost) ☐
   (e) If qualitative in nature, are objectives nonetheless verifiable? ☐
5. Are the objectives challenging, yet reasonable? ☐
6. Are priorities assigned to the objectives (ranking, weighting, etc.)? ☐
7. Does the set of objectives also include
   (a) improvement objectives? ☐
   (b) personal development objectives? ☐
8. Are the objectives coordinated with other managers and organizational units? Are the objectives consistent with the objectives of the superior, the department, the company? ☐
9. Are the objectives communicated to all who need to be informed? ☐
10. Are the short-term objectives consistent with long-term aims? ☐
11. Are the assumptions underlying the objectives clearly identified? ☐
12. Are the objectives expressed clearly, and in writing? ☐
13. Do the objectives provide for timely feedback so that any necessary corrective steps can be taken? ☐
14. Are the resources and authority sufficient for achieving the objectives? ☐
15. Have the individuals who are expected to accomplish objectives been given a chance to suggest their objectives? ☐
16. Does the individual have control over aspects for which he or she is assigned responsibility? ☐

*Mark "+" if the objectives meet the criteria.
Mark "−" if the objectives do not meet the criteria.

OBJECTIVES FOR STAFF POSITIONS[16]

It is sometimes believed that meaningful objectives can be established only for line managers since they have direct responsibility for some phase of operating results. If we consider staff positions, wherein the responsibility is to advise and counsel line managers, we may ask whether objectives can be set for them since the staff's primary job is to help people in line positions succeed in their jobs.

The authors believe that objectives can be set for any position in an enterprise. As a matter of fact, in some cases this has been done. In the Radio Corporation of America, for instance, an active program has been applied to staff personnel for some years. While most staff objectives in this company could not be placed in quantitative terms, staff projects (even though advisory) were established in qualitative terms, indicating characteristics and target completion dates. Many involved "developing a method," or "conducting a study," or "finding the cause of" some problem. Thus, most staff objectives, while verifiable, were qualitative.

The experience at RCA showed that some staff people even stated many quantitative objectives, such as "In 1980 I will save the company $—— through evaluation of new materials" or "Develop a cost reduction program by June 30, 1980, that will reduce plant operating expenses by $——." To be sure, none of these staff individuals had the authority to implement any of these programs. They did, however, take the position that they had failed to meet an objective if the program they recommended to operating managers was not good enough to be implemented and result in targeted savings.

One research study in a large bank indicated similarities and differences in the application of MBO to line and staff.[17] Respondents were asked whether they were in (1) a line, (2) a staff, or (3) a line and staff position. No attempt was made to define the terms. The third alternative was designed to identify those persons who might be uncertain about their position or who were in a position that was a combination of both line and staff. The third question facilitated the exclusion of this group, providing greater "purity" in, and distinction between, the remaining two groups used for the analysis of the data.

The findings showed that there were statistically significant differences between line and staff (with line scoring higher in all instances) on all the following items:

The liking for the MBO program

The applicability of MBO to the job

---

[16]The nature of "line" and "staff" is discussed in chap. 14.
[17]This discussion is taken from H. Weihrich and S. N. Tingey, "Management by Objectives—Does It Apply to Staff?" *Industrial Management*, vol. 18, no. 1, pp. 24–29 (January–February 1976). Material used by permission.

The usefulness of MBO in carrying out the job

The degree of clarity of what is expected of the respondents

The extent to which people in the department work together as a team

But there were *no* statistically significant differences for line and staff in respect to

The satisfaction with the MBO program

The degree of clarity of the objectives of the superiors of line and staff respondents

The clarity about the overall objectives of the company

The extent of cooperation between departments of line and staff respondents and other departments of the company

The findings in this organization indicate that in applying MBO, attention should be given to the special nature of staff functions. It is not suggested that MBO cannot be used for staff, but rather that the task requirements are different, which may have an impact upon the effectiveness of MBO. Perhaps the wise administrator should not expect the same results from MBO when applied to staff as one normally expects from line. Simply being aware of the differences between line and staff will not guarantee success, but it will make it possible to anticipate problems for staff positions and to take positive steps to overcome them.

BENEFITS OF MANAGING BY OBJECTIVES

Because managing by objectives has excited the interest of managers throughout the world, particularly in business enterprises, and even though there has been far more talk than effective action, it might be helpful to summarize the major benefits and weaknesses of the system. The potential of managing and appraising managers by objectives is very great. But there is the danger that, through misapplication, the system might degenerate into a management fad or gimmick.

Better Managing

One could summarize all the advantages of formalizing managing by objectives by saying that it results in much improved managing. Actionable objectives cannot be established without planning, and results-oriented planning is the only kind that makes sense. It forces managers to think of planning for results, rather than merely planning activities or work. To assure that objectives are realistic, it also requires managers to think of the way they will accomplish given results, the organization and personnel they will need to do it, and the resources and assistance they will require. Also, there is no better incentive for control and no better way to know standards for control than a set of clear goals.[18]

Clarifies Organization

Another major benefit of managing by objectives is that it tends to force clarification of organizational roles and structures. To the extent possible, key result areas should be translated into positions that carry responsibility for goal accomplishment.

Companies that have effectively embarked on these programs have often discovered organizational deficiencies. The most common is finding that results accomplishment requires giving major consideration to the first principle of delegation of authority—delegation by results expected. As an executive of Honeywell is reported to have said: "There are two things that might also be considered fundamental creed at Honeywell: decentralized management is needed to make Honeywell work and management by objectives is needed to make decentralization work."

Elicits Commitment

One of the great advantages of managing by objectives is that it elicits commitment for performance. No longer are people just doing work, following instructions, and waiting for guidance and decisions; they are now individuals with clearly defined purposes. They also have had a part in actually setting their objectives, they have had an opportunity to put their ideas into planning programs, they understand their area of discretion—their authority—and they have, it is hoped, been able to get positive help from their superiors to assure that they can accomplish their goals.

These are the elements that make for a feeling of commitment. People become willing and enthusiastic masters of their own fate.

Helps Develop Effective Controls

In the same way that managing by objectives sparks more effective planning, it also aids in developing effective controls. Control, it will be recalled, is measuring activities and taking action to correct deviations from plans in order to assure desired accomplishment. As will be pointed out in a later discussion of management control, one of the major

---

[18]For example, one study indicated that over half the advantages mentioned by the 278 respondents pertain to such aspects of planning as goals and goal setting, planning in general, organization objectives, giving directions, setting priorities, and decision making. For a detailed discussion see H. Weihrich, "Management by Objectives: Does It Really Work?" *University of Michigan Business Review*, vol. 28, no. 4, pp. 27–31 (July 1976).

problems is knowing what to watch. A clear set of verifiable goals is the best guide to knowing.

WEAKNESSES IN MANAGING BY OBJECTIVES

With all its advantages, a system of managing by objectives has a number of weaknesses and shortcomings. Some are found in the system. Others are due to shortcomings in applying it.

Failure to Teach the Philosophy

As simple as managing by objectives may seem, there is much to be understood and appreciated by managers who would put it into practice. This requires patient explanation of the entire program, what it is, how it works, why it is being done, what part it will play in appraising managerial performance, and above all, how participants can benefit.

Failure to Give Goal Setters Guidelines

Managing by objectives, like any other kind of planning, cannot work if those who are expected to set goals are not given needed guidelines. Managers must know what corporate goals are and how their activity fits in with them. If corporate goals are vague, unreal, or inconsistent, it is virtually impossible for managers to tune in on them.

They also need planning premises and a knowledge of controlling enterprise policies. People must have some assumptions as to the future, some understanding of enterprise policies affecting their area of operation, and an awareness of the nature of objectives and programs with which their goals interlock in order to plan effectively. Failure to fill these needs can result in a fatal vacuum in planning.

Goals Are Difficult to Set

It should not be overlooked that truly verifiable goals are difficult to set, particularly if they are to have the right degree of "stretch" or "pull," quarter in and quarter out, year in and year out. This may not be much more difficult than any kind of effective planning, although it will probably take more study and work to establish verifiable objectives that are formidable but attainable than to develop most plans, most of which tend only to lay out work to be done.

Goals Tend to Be Short-Run

In almost all systems of operating under management by objectives, goals are set for the short term, seldom for more than a year, and often for a quarter or less. There is clearly the danger of emphasizing the short run, perhaps at the expense of the longer range. This means, of course, that superiors must always assure themselves that current objectives, like any other short-run plan, are designed to serve longer-range goals.

The Dangers of Inflexibility

As has happened with other types of plans, and budgets particularly, managers often hesitate to change objectives during a period of time, normally a year. While goals may cease to be meaningful if they are changed too often and do not represent a well-thought-out and well-planned result, it is nonetheless foolish to expect a manager to strive for a goal that has been made obsolete by revised corporate objectives, changed premises, or modified policies.

Failure to Ensure a Network of Goals

In the obsession to set goals, there is ever the danger that one person's objectives may be inconsistent with those of another. The production manager's goals for low cost might be nonsupportive to the marketing manager's goal of product availability or quality, or the financial manager's of low inventory. An enterprise is a system. If goals, like all other plans, are not interconnected and mutually supportive, people will tend to pursue paths that seem best for their own operations but may be detrimental to the company as a whole.

The ensurance of a network of mutually supportive goals is not easy. First, it requires seeing planning programs as a network of program elements. In the second place, action is required to see that individual goals and their program fit the desired niche in a network. This necessitates careful definition of end-result areas, dissemination of consistent planning premises, and careful review of the various goals by those responsible for them. This in turn makes desirable group discussions to assure that the network is in fact being woven together.

Setting Arbitrary Goals

One of the sure causes of failure is for the boss to set arbitrary goals for subordinates. While superiors must take final authority for approving the objectives of those who report to them, if they force goals on subordinates, they will destroy the feeling of commitment on the part of those who must achieve them. As a matter of fact, arbitrary and pressured goals represent one of the major causes of complaint expressed by managers, particularly at the middle and lower levels.

Arbitrary goal setting is not only self-defeating but also foolish. The superior who does it is deprived of the intelligence, experience, and often the know-how of problem solution that subordinates almost always have. Experience with cooperative goal-setting sessions has led most of us to have considerable respect for the useful knowledge that often lies at lower levels in an organization.

Failure to Insist on Verifiability

Requiring that goals be verifiable, whether in a quantitative or qualitative way, is probably the major key to a successful program of managing by objectives. To be verifiable, as pointed out earlier, an objective must be such that, at some targeted date in the future, a person can look back and know whether he or she did or did not accomplish it.

Yet, it is surprising how many programs that pass as managing by objectives are grounded on fuzzy goals. Such objectives as "to be alert to customers' needs and qualified to serve them," or "to keep credit losses to a minimum," or "to improve the effectiveness of the personnel department" are all but meaningless, since no one can answer accurately at a given point of time whether they have been achieved. With a little work and thinking, any goal can be made verifiable in either quantitative or qualitative terms. The authors of this book have never encountered in business, government, or other enterprises an objective that cannot be made verifiable. Certainly, without verifiability MBO can slip into an exercise in pious wishes and generalities with little meaning for managing or for appraising performance.

Overinsistence on Numbers

In many otherwise strong programs, one finds an over-insistence on numbers—quantitative objectives—in order to make the approach rigorously verifiable. But there are too many important objectives that simply cannot be expressed in numbers. For example, many of the important elements of a new product research program, a sales and advertising program, or one for making personnel services more important cannot be meaningfully quantified.

Yet, by spelling out features of these programs and emphasizing due dates for the various parts, goals can be made verifiable.

Use of Inapplicable Standards

Another error, particularly when used for appraisal, is the use of inapplicable standards for performance. In one large company, the headquarters office has set desired performance standards applicable to all parts of the company throughout the United States. Thus, the manager in Southern California is gauged against the same standards as the manager in North Dakota or Georgia.

A moment's reflection indicates that such national standards in a far-flung operation would probably not be equally applicable to managers operating in dissimilar markets and environments. In this case, they almost certainly are not. What has been the result? Frustration, resistance, no real sense of commitment, and playing the numbers game with the bosses and the system. It is true in this company, as it is almost universally, that when managing becomes a numbers game, self-preserving and reasonably intelligent subordinates can beat their bosses at the game.

Failure to Provide Adequate Review, Counseling, and Control

There is always the danger in a system of managing by objectives that, once objectives are agreed upon, progress toward goal accomplishment will not be adequately monitored by the superior. One of the major advantages of using objectives is that a person has a charter for accomplishment, the appropriate resources and discretion are allocated, and any subordinate can be given a high degree of freedom to work toward goal achievement. One would not expect a superior to meddle or constantly look over a subordinate's shoulder. By the same token, however, a superior should not sit back and assume that everything is going well and not check on progress until the date of goal achievement is due.

Superiors as well as subordinates should have regular information available to them as to how well a subordinate's goal performance is progressing. Superiors should regularly review progress through this information and through personal consultation, and should make themselves available for counseling to help subordinates in meeting goals. This is not, and should not be, taking over tasks from subordinates. It is merely following through with the job of manager. Most subordinates will welcome follow-up, counseling, assistance with their problems, and aid in removing obstructions to their successful performance.

EXPERIENCE WITH MANAGING BY OBJECTIVES

Although managing by objectives is basic common sense and has been installed by large numbers of business and nonbusiness enterprises around the world, there are real questions as to how effective these programs have been. It can be said that where managing by objectives works well, it works exceedingly well, and the benefits noted above have been achieved. But too many enterprises only *think* they have managing by objectives when they adopt their programs. Experts in the field estimate that from 20 to 40 percent of the programs are reasonably successful.

In one study of *Fortune* magazine's list of the 500 largest American industrial companies, it was found that only 45 percent of the 403 companies responding to a questionnaire survey, or 188 companies, indicated that they had managing-by-objectives programs.[19] Further study revealed that only 10 companies felt they had a highly successful application of managing by objectives, and another 88 companies said they had a moderately successful program. In analyzing the questionnaire responses, the authors of the study concluded that reasonably effective programs were in effect in 36 companies. In other words, out of an original total of 188 companies with such programs, only 19 percent were rated as successful. This represents less than 10 percent of the largest industrial companies in the United States.

The disappointing success rate of managing-by-objectives programs is a reflection of some of the weaknesses and dangers pointed out above. Managing by objectives clearly should not be undertaken without a sizable commitment of time and effort on the part of the management group in an enterprise, from the chief executive down to the first-line supervisors. The program must also be fitted into a strong managerial environment of the kind outlined in this book. It is necessary, too, that all those involved, particularly managers, understand the program, its purposes, and its requirements. Just as planning is the foundation of managing and objectives are the end points of planning, an effective program of managing by objectives must be woven into an entire pattern and style of managing. It cannot work as a separate technique standing alone. It must, indeed, be a part of the whole managing process.

FOR DISCUSSION

1   To what extent do you believe that managers you have known have a clear understanding of their objectives? If, in your opinion, they do not, how would you suggest that they go about setting them?
2   Make a list of goals you wish to achieve in the next 5 years. Are they verifiable? Are they attainable?
3   Some people object to defining long-term goals because they think it is impossible to know what will happen during the long term. Do you believe that this is an intelligent position to take?
4   Take any program of any kind that you would like to see accomplished and draw a network of contributing programs and goals necessary for its accomplishment.
5   If goals of a company are multiple, how can all of them be optimized?

---

[19]Fred E. Schuster and Alva F. Kindall, "Management by Objectives—Where We Stand—A Survey of the Fortune 500," *Human Resource Management*, vol. 13, no. 1, pp. 8–11 (Spring 1974).

6 "The only planning tool we need in this company is the budget. If everyone meets his budget, we need nothing else, and management by objectives would be an unnecessary frill." Comment.

7 Why do you suspect that although so many business enterprises talk about and introduce programs of management by objectives, the actual record of performance under these has been so poor?

chapter 8

Premising: Essential Step in Planning

MAJOR CHAPTER OBJECTIVES

1. To discuss the nature and importance of premising in assuring effective planning.
2. To analyze types of premises and show how they furnish the environment of plans.
3. To show how environmental forecasting is a major key to premising and to analyze the major kinds of environmental forecasts.
4. To give special attention to the sales forecast and show how it is both a premise and a resultant of plans.
5. To suggest some guidelines to assure the effectiveness of premising.

In Chapter 4, we discussed the fact that managers at all levels and in all kinds of organizations must respond to, react to, and live within their external environment. The major elements of this environment were identified as economic, technological, social, political and legal, and ethical. Attention was given to the nature of these environments, their importance to managers, and how the alert and perceptive manager must take these environments into account in making planning decisions.

In addition to reacting to external environmental factors, managers responsible for making decisions must also be alert and respond to internal environmental factors. There are many of these, varying from the prejudices and attitudes of owners and top executives to the fact that most organizations have made commitments for land, buildings, equipment and machinery, product or service development, or marketing and advertising. This is clear in all kinds of businesses. But it is also clear in many nonbusiness enterprises, such as a university, a municipal fire department, or a nation's navy. All these things must be taken into account as background factors when plans are being made, to ensure that decisions taken "fit."

One of the essential and often overlooked steps in effective and coordinated planning is premising—the establishment of, and agreement by planners to utilize, consistent premises critical to plans under consideration. Planning premises, it will be recalled, are the anticipated environment in which plans are expected to operate. They include assumptions or forecasts of the future and known conditions that will affect the operation of plans, such as prevailing policies and existing company plans that control the basic nature of supporting plans.

A distinction should immediately be drawn between forecasts that are planning premises and forecasts that are translated into future expectancies, usually in financial terms, from actual plans developed. For example, a forecast to determine future business conditions, sales volume, or political environment furnishes premises on which to develop plans. However, a forecast of the costs or revenues from a new capital investment translates a planning program into future expectations. In the first case, the forecast is a prerequisite of planning; in the second, the forecast is a result of planning.

At the same time, plans themselves and forecasts of their future effects often become premises for other plans. The decision by an electric utility to construct a nuclear generating plant, for example, creates conditions that give rise to premises for transmission line plans, and other plans necessarily dependent upon the generating plant being built.

PREMISING: THE ENVIRONMENT OF PLANS

Premising is the formal recognition in the planning process that plans operate in an environment, both internal to the enterprise and external. It thus emphasizes the long-known fact that managing is an open-system approach to organized activities. While it is true that until fairly recently businesses and other enterprises may have given primary attention to economic and demographic factors in their environment and too little to technological, social, political, and ethical factors, all alert and perceptive managers now are aware of all elements of the environment that might affect the operation of their plans.

It is not enough to be responsive to the *present* environment. Plans operate in the future. Therefore, effective managers anticipate the environment in which their plans *will* operate. This means, of course, that it is necessary to forecast what those elements in the environment affecting any given plans will be. As is sometimes said, the successful manager is not one who just responds to changes as they occur but one who will, rather, forecast change and take appropriate action. Clearly, those who foresee the critical changes that will affect given plans have a far better chance of being successful than those who either cannot or will not.

This does not mean that everything can be predicted, nor does it mean that prediction is an infallible science. In fact, many scientists shy away from predicting the future on the basis that this is not dealing with what is known. Many things that affect a future are known—a plan already made that requires derivative plans, the vast array of organized knowledge of an imperishable nature, and some of the implications of current world forces. But these are not enough. There are in addition short- and long-range economic, technological, social, political, and even ethical changes that will affect what will or can be done in a near or far future.

Some of these are quite predictable, such as population growth and changes in the gross national product. Some are credibly predictable, such as price levels, population shifts, and certain technological developments. Others may not be reasonably predictable, such as the Arab states' oil embargo early in 1974, the discovery of penicillin, the fast rise in interest rates between 1972 and 1974, or the extensive cheapening of the dollar in world markets during the late 1970s.

Increasing awareness of the impact of the future environment has led to a developing science referred to as "futurism"—the attempt to forecast changes in the various elements of the environment with skill and preceptiveness through the use of the most sophisticated available techniques. In a real way, this approach represents an extension of the much earlier attempts to base future population growth on science, rather than on hunches, and on the development of national economic predictions that have come so far in the past three decades. More recently, futurism has made strides in technological forecasting and is moving on to the social and political elements of the environmental spectrum.

TYPES OF PREMISES

Planning premises may be classified as those which are external and those which are internal to the enterprise, or they may be regarded as those which are quantitative and those which are qualitative. In addition, premises differ in the degree that they are within the control of an enterprise.

External and Internal Premises

As implied above, one is likely to think of most premises as those arising from the outside world, because they usually cause the most difficulty. External premises may be classified into three groups: the general environment, which includes economic, technological, political, social, and ethical conditions; the product market, which includes conditions influencing demand for product and services; and the factor market, which has to do with land, location, labor (not the least of which is labor unions), materials, parts, and capital. As can be seen, these groups are not completely separable, since there are interactions between them.

Likewise, it can be seen that internal premises include such things as capital investment in plant and equipment, strategies, policies, major programs already decided, the developed and approved sales forecast, a given organization structure that is unlikely to change, and the many other elements that will influence the nature of plans.

Quantitative and Qualitative Premises

Occasionally, managers forget that planning premises may be qualitative as well as quantitative. They are referred to as "quantitative" when they can be put in numbers, whether in dollars, labor hours, square feet of space, machine hours, or units of product.

Of equal importance are the many qualitative factors normally encountered. These cannot be expressed numerically, but they are significant elements in the planning scene. Among the many examples are prestige in a product line (which might eventually have a tangible effect on sales and profits), local opinion of a certain plant as a desirable or undesirable neighbor, political stability or attitude of a city or state toward taxes, emotional impact of a certain personnel policy among employees, or the receptivity of style factors by potential customers. There are many, many areas of a manager's environment that even the best market, attitudinal, or other kinds of research cannot make quantitative.

Degree of Controllability

Premises may also be classified by the degree to which they are controllable by an enterprise. There are noncontrollable premises, such as population growth, future price levels, political environment, tax rates and policies, and business cycles. There are semicontrollable premises, such as a firm's assumptions as to its share of the market, the character of labor turnover, labor efficiency, company price policy, and even industry legislative policy. And, finally, there are controllable premises, decided largely by company management and involving policies and programs such as expansion into new markets, the adoption of an aggressive research program, or the site for headquarters offices.

ENVIRONMENTAL FORECASTING: KEY TO PREMISING

As the influence on plans of the entire environment outside the enterprise has come increasingly to be recognized, forecasting of the environment has risen in importance. As mentioned above, this has given rise to an embryonic science referred to as "futurism."

If the future could be forecast with accuracy, planning would be relatively simple. Managers would need only to take into account their human and material resources and their opportunities, compute the optimum method of reaching their objective, and proceed with a high degree of certainty toward it.

Fayol speaks of *prévoyance* as the essence of management.[1] This looking ahead, according to Fayol, includes both assessing the future and making provision for it.

As a matter of fact, more than a half century ago Fayol referred to plans as syntheses of various forecasts, whether short-term or long-term, special, or otherwise.[2] It is interesting, in this connection, that Fayol recommended yearly forecasts and 10-year forecasts, the latter being revised at least each 5 years and oftener if proved necessary by the yearly ones. Furthermore, each forecast was to include a wide variety of subsidiary or elemental forecasts, composed of such data as capital, output, production costs, sales, and selling price, as well as other factors.

In practice, forecasts vary considerably in length, breadth of coverage, and quality, from little more than a manager's hunch to a detailed analysis of the future made by competent experts. Some enterprises need forecasts of long periods, and others may be able to operate effectively with very short-term forecasts. Furthermore, some managers who need expert forecasts may be unable to afford more than the information that grows out of their reading of economic and other predictions in numerous journals plus their own judgment of the situation.

---

[1]Henri Fayol, *General and Industrial Management* (New York: Pitman Publishing Corporation, 1949), p. 43. In this translation, the term is translated as "foreseeing."
[2]Fayol emphasized this usage in an interview published in the *Chronique sociale de France* in January 1925, quoted in Urwick's foreword to *General and Industrial Management*, p. xi.

The need for adequate forecasting is apparent from the key role it plays in planning. But it has values aside from this use. In the first place, the making of forecasts and their review by managers compel thinking ahead, looking to the future, and providing for it. Also, the very act of forecasting may disclose areas where necessary control is lacking. For example, in a report submitting the results of a pessimistic forecast to his key executives, a president of a large company said: "The declining profit in this forecast is disappointing, but it is my impression that every forecast extending beyond a year has shown profits less than we have been able to procure as the result of determined efforts by all members of our management team. This picture should not dishearten us but should stimulate our efforts to improve it."

Forecasting, especially where participated in throughout the organization, may help to unify and coordinate plans. By focusing attention on the future, it assists in bringing a singleness of purpose to planning.

Even though much emphasis is placed on forecasting, it must be recognized that all forecasts are subject to a degree of error, since the best analyses or judgments cannot result in true clairvoyance. Guesswork can never be omitted from forecasts, although it can often be reduced to a minimum. Managers often expect too much from forecasts and fail to recognize the unavoidable margin of error which must exist in any prophecy. They also occasionally neglect to examine the underlying assumptions of a forecast to determine whether these are supported by facts, reasonable estimates, or accurate reflection of policies and plans.

Informed and intelligent "guesstimates" made by experienced business executives and technicians are often extraordinarily prophetic. A clairvoyant quality is a rare gift, but many experienced managers have developed it, and where it exists, it is an excellent supplement to the work of the forecaster. However, what may appear to be a clairvoyant quality may really be the conceptual and computing ability of an exceptional mind.

Economic Forecasting

Fairly reliable economic premises can be obtained from the well-considered forecasts of employment, productivity, national income, and gross national product that have been available to planners for a number of years. Among the more prominent of these are those made regularly by the President's Council of Economic Advisers, the Wharton School (University of Pennsylvania), Econometric Model, the University of Maryland Interindustry Forecasting Model, the U.C.L.A. Forecasting Project, the coordinative work of the Conference Board Forum, and the many forecasts of university and bank economists. In fact, there is no shortage of national and even regional economic forecasts. The major problem the planner has is which to use, although, as a matter of fact, the better-known forecasts do have a record of surprising consistency and accuracy.[3]

Most economic forecasts are derived from calculating gross national product, the total of which is not difficult to estimate if acceptable forecasts of population, productivity increases, unemployment percentage, and average workweek are available. But problems do occur in estimating such components of gross national product as government purchases, personal consumption expenditures, business fixed and inventory investment, residential construction, and other investments. Greater difficulties occur as each of the elements is further broken down. In addition, of course, forecasts of gross national product need to take into account price-level changes, which, with persistent inflation over the years, can be very important to the planner.

After studying broad forecasts of national and regional economic trends, a company should translate them into their impact on its industry and on itself. This requires two basic estimating procedures. In one, the analyst moves downward from national data to industry group forecasts and perhaps to individual industries. In the other, referred to as a "bottom up" approach, the analyst moves upward from individual company data and summaries of industry plans to the national economic forecast.

As broad as typical national and regional economic forecasts are, it is interesting how many companies have found that their business relates fairly well, sometimes with a lag or lead time correction, to national data. A medium-sized company, for example, whose business was closely associated with the home construction industry, found a highly reliable correlation of its sales with housing starts, adjusted for an 8 months' lag from starts to sales. A pharmaceutical company, after studying forecasting techniques and indicators of all kinds, found somewhat to its surprise that national consumers' disposable expenditures correlated very well with its sales pattern.

What have been needed are refined breakdowns of basic economic data that serve to forecast better the markets in which a company is operating. One of the most promising approaches is the development of input-output tables. These show the relationships of industries to one another and their sharing of gross national product by calculating the purchases and sales made between industries. While some work on input-output analysis has been done by industrial and regional specialists, these lack the accuracy and usefulness of an analysis on a national scale.

Developed by Professor Wassily W. Leontief of Harvard, input-output tables were first roughly utilized by him in 1945 and served to forecast the impending large demand in the postwar period for steel and other raw

---

[3]An interesting long-term forecast is *The U.S. Economy in 1990* (New York: The Conference Board, 1972).

materials. The federal government issued input-output tables for 1947 several years later. Unfortunately, because of lack of government appropriation, no analyses were again available until 1964. At that time, input-output tables for the year 1958 were published and, shortly thereafter, were updated to 1961 and 1963.[4] Since that time data have continued to be updated, with some reports being issued annually and others from time to time. Many companies have made such studies for certain areas.[5]

The availability of this powerful tool for forecasting is an encouraging development for business which now can have the derivative effects of national production and income factors reflected in their impact on a given industry.

There are, nonetheless, a tremendous number of industry studies available through government and industry sources, of both a forecast and a historical nature. Most federal government departments with a business interest publish economic material useful for forecasting, as do trade associations, trade publications, banks, private research organizations, and professional associations. Certainly, in most industries, the manager who wants industry data can tap many sources.[6]

Technological Forecasting

One of the more interesting aspects of premising has been the rapid increase of interest in recent years in technological forecasting. Since the pace of technological change is so great and since new products and processes may be keys to a company's future plans, an increasing but still small number of companies are emphasizing regular and complete technological forecasts affecting their industry. In fact, developing premises from such forecasts may be as important to the company's planning and its future as are political, economic, or social premises.

Those companies which have gone far in developing planning premises from their technological forecasts have tended to be high-technology enterprises. What has been done in these instances is to encourage members of their technical staffs to be alert to future developments; to make frequent contacts with suppliers and customers with development staffs; to think in terms of the impact of current scientific

[4]Wassily W. Leontief, "Proposal for Better Business Forecasting," *Harvard Business Review*, vol. 42, no. 6, pp. 166–182 (November–December 1964).

[5]See, for example, M. F. Elliott-Jones, "An Introduction to Input-Output Analysis"; M. Godfrey, "Some Neglected Aspects of Foreign Trade Revealed through I-O Analysis"; and G. H. Blackett, "Measuring Raw Material Needs to the Year 2000," all in *Conference Board Record*, vol. 8, no. 1, pp. 16–28 (January 1971). See also M. F. Elliott-Jones, *Input-Output Analysis: A Nontechnical Description* (New York: The Conference Board, 1971), and M. F. Elliott-Jones, *Economic Forecasting and Corporate Planning* (New York: The Conference Board, 1973). See also D. L. Hurwood, E. S. Grossman, and E. Bailey, *Sales Forecasting* (New York: The Conference Board, 1978), chap. 8.

[6]Reichard reported over a decade ago that the federal government spends over $100 million each year on statistical data collection. See R. S. Reichard, *Practical Techniques of Sales Forecasting* (New York: McGraw-Hill Book Company, 1966), pp. 103–110.

developments on the future state of technology; and to develop orderly forecasts of how these developments affect the company's products, processes, or markets. Executives who have asked their research and development staffs to undertake such an assignment have been pleasantly surprised at the enthusiasm with which these forecasts were prepared and presented. They have apparently found that scientists and engineers like to be a part of, and contribute to, basic company planning. These executives have also reported, not at all surprisingly, that these forecasts have been extraordinarily helpful in improving company planning.

Even smaller companies without research and development staffs can successfully make such a forecast and include the future technological environment in their planning premises. A few scientists or engineers in a company, if encouraged, can do much to present an orderly picture of the company's technological environment. And many nontechnically qualified people, as well as those with special technical qualifications, can understand much of the technical literature in a periodical or report in the company's field. Moreover, suppliers especially and often major customers are willing to pass on to discerning owners and managers of small businesses the results of their research and engineering ideas, if this will make them larger-volume customers or more alert suppliers.

One of the attempts to make technological forecasting more accurate and meaningful is the use of what is known as the Delphi technique, named after the oracle at Delphi in ancient Greece. While it smacks somewhat of hunch and judgment, or the brainstorming fad of a few years ago, it is much more. And having been developed by Olaf Helmer, prominent RAND Corporation mathematician, and his colleagues, it has a degree of scientific respectability and acceptance not enjoyed by other judgment approaches.

Forecasting with the Delphi technique The Delphi technique involves several steps. First, a panel of experts on a particular problem area is selected, usually from both inside and outside an organization's ranks. The experts are asked—anonymously, so that they will not be influenced by others—to make a forecast as to what they think will happen, and when, in various areas of new discoveries or developments. For example, the panel may be asked when reliable weather forecasts will be available, when a cancer cure will be accomplished, or when and how economically feasible desalination of seawater will occur. Then the answers are compiled, and the composite results are fed back to the panel members. With this information at hand, but still with individual anonymity, further estimates of the future are made, and this process may be repeated several times. When a convergence of opinion begins to occur, the results are then used as an acceptable forecast.[7] Note that the purpose of the

[7] For a good example of the reporting of an actual Delphi technique forecast, see H. Q. North and D. L. Pyke, "Probes of the Technological Future," *Harvard Business Review*, vol. 47, no. 3, pp. 69–81 (May–June 1969).

successive opinions and feedback is not to force the experts to compromise, but rather by bringing additional informational inputs to bear, to make opinions more informed. It is thus hoped, and experience has verified this hope, that an informed consensus among experts will be arrived at.

Miscellaneous forecasting methods There are, of course, other methods used to forecast the state of technology. One, referred to as "opportunity-oriented," looks at the future and raises the question of whether a certain product may be made obsolete by a new development—and, if so, what development—or whether there is any technological breakthrough that might be expected which would solve a problem seen to exist in the development of a certain product. For example, the opportunity-oriented forecast might look at the possible development of an atomic power plant for an automobile and ask whether certain known limitations will probably be solved and when. Or one might forecast when economic desalination of seawater will occur.

Another approach has been referred to as the "goal-oriented" forecast. In this case, a decision is made to reach a certain goal, the technological needs for accomplishing it are identified, and analysis is made as to when, and perhaps how, these might be accomplished. Thus, after a decision was made to put a man on the moon by 1970, the technological requirements of so doing were identified, and time and resource estimates were made as to how and when each could be solved.

Still other techniques of technological forecasting follow time-honored hypotheses that knowledge expands exponentially, and it is possible to project when a certain technological development is likely to occur. For example, in illumination technology one can plot the growth of lumens per watt on a logarithmic scale from Edison's first lamp in 1880 to the fluorescent lamp in 1940 in almost a straight line.

The important thing is not necessarily the methods and approaches to technological forecasting. It is rather the fact that its need is being perceived, and serious and useful attempts are being made to predict the state of the art in an increasing number of fields. This can certainly lead to planning premises of an important and useful nature. However, there is danger that technological forecasts are not being as integrated into planning as they should be. But this is a danger in all premising, and special effort must be made to assure that all premises are, in fact, used as a background for decisions.

Social and Political Forecasting

Except for the long experience with demographic forecasting, there has not been much attention paid to forecasting social, political, and ethical trends in society, despite the fact that these are extremely important areas of premising. To be sure, a few companies have done meaningful work in this area. A major oil company over two decades ago was regularly making forecasts of political environments in the foreign countries where it was planning for oil exploration. Another company, concerned with worldwide transportation potentials, found that, particularly for certain parts of the world such as India and central Africa, they really had to make cultural forecasts because needs for transportation facilities were found to be responsive to various cultural levels. A few companies have come to the authors' attention in which continuing and formalized forecasts and analyses have been made of the combined social, political, and ethical environments expected in areas where they produce or market.

This important area has not received the attention it should. However, there are increasing signs that it will. The problems of pollution, of certain aggrieved minorities, of lawlessness and crime, and of highway safety have burst on the world's consciousness with almost surprising pressures. Surely we cannot really blame the automobile manufacturers for smog, but we might criticize them for not anticipating social pressures for eliminating pollution and therefore for not being more ready with technological solutions of the auto's contribution to air pollution some years ago.

Experience with technological forecasting has certainly opened the door to a wider spectrum of prediction of the social and political elements of the environment. One might well expect some of the same techniques that have been useful in technological prediction to be applicable to forecasting these other areas. An indication of what may be in store was given by the establishment of the Institute for the Future in 1969, a tax-exempt, nonprofit, nonmilitary research organization supported by a number of major business corporations and by the Conference Board in particular. Its purpose is environmental forecasting in all its aspects so that business may be able to anticipate future events with more confidence and include them in its planning premises. Likewise, the World Future Society was founded in 1966 to encourage research in, and exchange views on, "futurology"; it publishes a journal called *The Futurist.*

As the importance of social and political pressures on all kinds of enterprises comes to be increasingly appreciated and as more companies and agencies come to the realization that to be effectively responsive, managers must forecast, social and political forecasting will certainly be done widely. Indeed, in another decade or two it could be that this kind of forecasting will be done as generally as economic forecasting.

THE SALES FORECAST: KEY PLAN AND PREMISE[8]

One of the major planning premises in the typical business enterprise is the sales forecast. To a considerable extent it underlies various new

[8]For a thorough study of sales forecasting techniques, see N. L. Hurwood, E. S. Grossman, and E. Bailey, op cit.

product, production, and marketing plans, and it also reflects conditions of the marketplace which are external to the firm. Because it sets the framework on which most internal plans are constructed, it must be regarded as the dominant planning premise, at least of a business enterprise. Even though its use has been noteworthy in business, the idea of basing planning on a forecast of the market has much in common with nonbusiness enterprises. Certainly a university must be concerned in its planning with its student "market"; a government welfare department must gear its plans to meet expected caseloads; and church plans must be influenced by the number of communicants expected in an area.

Nature and Use

The sales forecast is a prediction of expected sales, by product and price, for a number of months or years. It is, then, a kind of pro forma sales portion of the traditional income statement for the future. With a sales forecast over a long enough period in which it has some confidence, management can usually do a good job in forecasting profits and cash flow. The revenue side of the future is usually the most difficult to forecast and the least subject to positive control by the firm. Given the revenue outlook, the firm can at least decide what it can afford to spend for operations. Moreover, since most operating expenses are within the control of managers to a major degree, the forecast of expenses can be more accurate than a forecast of revenues.

In any case, it is the sales forecast that is the key to internal planning. Business and capital outlays and policies of all kinds are made for the purpose of maximizing profits from expected sales. Although there are some enterprises that need to pay little attention to sales (for example, the small-city water company or the government defense contractor with a long-term order that has little chance of being canceled or modified), it is a rare business that can overlook the market for long. Even the farmer, who, operating under support prices, may have a guaranteed market for a certain product for a coming year, can hardly ignore market influences as they affect succeeding years or alternative crops.

Since the sales forecast is so important a tool, there is scarcely a company that should not take the time and trouble to make the best one its resources will permit. Even the company with a fairly large backlog of orders for custom-made goods that need not go on the shelf as inventory requires such a forecast. One of the authors recalls a company that measured its future sales simply by the size of the total sales backlog. Although this backlog remained high, the managers were surprised to find one day that it was for a limited number of products for delivery over so long a period that the total dollar amount of the backlog would not permit capacity operation of the machinery and workforce then being employed.

Smaller companies often make the mistake of believing that sales forecasts are too expensive and of overlooking the variety of sources of data available at little or no cost. The purchasing agent, members of the sales staff, the treasurer, and the production manager are among those who may possess bits and pieces of information, which, gathered together, could make an acceptable forecast. Moreover, the wide range of information available from government and industry sources is neither difficult nor expensive to obtain.

An indicator of the increasing importance being attached to planning is the rapid rise of sales forecasting in the past two decades. Although better-managed companies long realized the value of good sales forecasting, the experience of World War II and the shortage years that followed led most managers to plan on the basis of maximum production rather than on the requirements of the market. With the return of normal business and strong competition, along with greater attention to the managerial job itself, managers have found that planning success depends largely upon the ability to forecast sales.

There has been a real swing away from the less formal methods, such as the managerial hunch, to more formal methods. It is now a rare company that does not regularly make a sales forecast.

Methods of Sales Forecasting

Methods utilized in sales forecasting may generally be classified as the jury of executive opinion method, the sales force composite method, users' expectation method, statistical methods, and deductive methods.

Jury of executive opinion method   The jury of executive opinion method is perhaps the oldest and simplest method of making sales forecasts, since it merely combines and averages the views, many of which may be little more than hunch, of top managers. In most cases, the final estimate is an opinion of the president, based upon a consideration of the opinions of other officers; in other cases, the poll of opinion leads to a rough kind of average estimate. In some cases, the process amounts to little more than group guessing; in other cases, it involves the careful judgment of experienced executives who have studied the underlying factors that influence their company's sales.

This method has the advantage of ease and simplicity; it allows for pooling of experience and judgment; and it need not require the preparation of elaborate economic studies and statistics. An advantage not often cited is that, by forcing top managers to make an estimate, it may put pressure on them to develop pertinent data. On the other hand, such a method has serious drawbacks; forecasts are based on opinion rather than on facts and analyses; averaging opinions reduces responsibility for accurate forecasting; and forecasts are not usually broken down into products, time periods, or organizational units.

Sales force composite method One of the commonly used methods of sales forecasting is to obtain from line salespeople and sales managers their combined view as to expected sales. The usual technique is to ask salespeople to forecast sales for their districts and have these estimates reviewed by the regional sales manager and then by the head-office sales manager. Sometimes salespeople are given guides in the form of company planning premises as to business conditions generally, and often the salespeople's estimates are reviewed by the product specialists, such as the company brand, sales, and advertising managers.

This method is based on the belief that those closest to the sales picture have the best knowledge of the market. Other advantages ascribed to this method are that it places forecasting, initially at least, in the hands of those who must make good on the forecast; it gives a broad sample that makes the total forecast more valid; and it allows an easy breakdown by product, customer, or territory.

On the other hand, the sales force composite method suffers from the fact that salespeople and often even sales executives are apt to be poor forecasters for any period except the immediate future, since they tend to give primary weight to present conditions. Where forecasts are desired for more than the short range, sales personnel normally are at a loss to make sound forecasts because of lack of knowledge of basic social, political, and economic trends. Moreover, under certain conditions—particularly where the forecasts are used for quota purposes—sales personnel incline to pessimism, while in other instances—especially when salespeople want more liberal allowances for expenses, promotion, or advertising—they are inclined to be rather optimistic. Furthermore, since sales forecasting is not their primary responsibility, sales personnel may neither be adept at it nor give it the time and thought necessary.

At the same time, most companies have found that forecasts submitted by the sales organization are useful and valuable inputs into the company forecasting effort. It has been found that, when the sales force composite method is properly cross-checked by various other methods, such as review by head-office marketing and sales experts and constant check by salespeople of their estimates of past performance against actual results, it has furnished surprisingly good forecasts.

Users' expectation method Many companies, particularly those serving industrial customers in industries composed of a small number of companies or where a few large companies are dominant, find it useful to base their forecasts on expected purchases by these customers. Clearly, if a company can obtain an adequate and reliable information sample of what its customers will buy, even though the actual orders are not in hand, it will have a good basis upon which to develop a sales forecast.

The users' expectation method has clear advantages where other ways of forecasting are inadequate or where the company cannot make a systematic forecast on its own, such as in small companies with limited resources for forecasting; in cases of new products where the market is known; or instances where a supplier is dependent on plans of major customers. This method is obviously difficult to use in cases where customers are numerous, not easily located, or uncooperative. It is also subject to the difficulty of being able to accurately assess customer expectations, since the best of these are usually estimates of needs, and not commitments.

Statistical methods   The most generally relied upon approach to sales forecasting is the application of various statistical methods. As mathematical techniques have improved and the electronic computing machine has come into wider use, so have statistics. These statistical methods may be divided into trend and cycle, correlation analysis, and use of mathematical formula or model.

In approaching forecasting through an analysis of trends and cycles, the analyst summarizes a pertinent series of data that reflect dollar or unit sales, units per thousand population, or other basic indicators of sales volume. On the basis of these data the forecast is projected by extrapolation. This analysis is based on the assumption that "what is past is prologue" and that a trend will continue unless something happens to it. It is then up to the analyst to judge whether that "something" will happen. In fact, it is important to the user of a forecast to know whether it represents a mere projection of past trends or a real forecast of what the forecaster expects *will* happen.

The statistical method most widely used is correlation analysis, the measurement of the relationship between company sales and one or more other factors. What is usually desired is a close correlation between sales and some broad national index that can be used with a reasonable degree of accuracy, such as gross national product, national income, or consumers' disposable income. Such correlation, either directly or with a lag or lead of a given time period, can give a company a useful and highly reliable basis for sales forecasting.

Virtually every forecaster has found some accurate correlations in using this method. Many companies have found that *their* sales, aside from industry sales, bear a close relationship to some national index. The problem for the forecaster is, of course, to study the various relationships, with their leads and lags, to find one or more which serve as indicators of the company's sales.

The third statistical method, one which usually grows out of finding either a trend or correlation analysis relationship, is to develop a mathematical formula to depict the relationship of a number of variables to the company's sales. Often, sales for an individual company are subject to a number of variables. If the relationship of these can be ascertained with reasonable accuracy or if credible assumptions can be made to fill in statistical gaps, a mathematical model very useful to the forecaster can be constructed. Thus, the B. F. Goodrich Company found that total replacement passenger car tire sales was given by taking the number of cars in use over 2 years, multiplying by 4, correcting for the amount of wear tires receive, and further correcting by a factor giving effect to improved tire quality (found to be 1 percent per year).

Although statistical methods are good for sales forecasting from the standpoint of reliability, they are often subject to certain drawbacks. They require research and the use of statistically trained help, which may be costly. It is not always possible to find reliable trends, correlations, or mathematical relationships. Many defense subcontractors have found, for example, that their sales potential is closely related to such vague factors as defense strategy, the course of a conflict, individual program expenditure level, and advances in the art of the industry, none of which bears a reliable correlation with predictable national or industry data. There is also a danger that managers may rely too heavily on statistical relationships and the results,implied and thereby miss significant changes which intelligent judgment would have appraised. In any statistical method, it must be realized that the past is used only as a *basis* for prediction and that the future does not necessarily reflect the past.

Deductive methods   No forecaster should overlook the opportunity to apply judgment and draw intelligent deductions from facts and relationships. Generally, what is involved is to find out what the present situation is, where the sales are, and why, and then to analyze deductively, by resort to both objective factors and subjective judgments, the factors underlying sales. Although the indications so developed may be put into a mathematical model or merely left as an imprecisely correlated conglomeration of facts and value judgments, they are often a useful check on results arrived at through more scientific methods.

After all, the state of the art of forecasting is such that independent, and often apparently intuitive, appraisal of the sales picture by an intelligent and experienced brain is still an input that no forecaster should overlook. This method has sometimes been referred to as the "lost horse" technique, based upon the old gag about the best way to find a lost horse: Go to where the horse was last seen and ask yourself where you would go if you were a horse.

Combination of Methods

In practice, there is a tendency to combine sales forecasting methods. This is as it should be. The importance of the final forecast for all aspects of company planning makes desirable a forecast system in which every possible input can be utilized. What warms forecasters' hearts and gives them a feeling of reliability is to find that several different forecast indicators, based upon independent approaches and data, all point to the same result. And, even if they do not, the disparity may serve as a warning that a single approach may have overlooked an essential factor.

Sales Forecasting in Practice

To understand sales forecasting techniques, one might examine some typical examples of what companies do.

One large company approaches forecasting by having a staff prepare a forecast of general business conditions referred to as an "assumption about the future." From this premise of the external business environment is projected a forecast of product sales. The staff takes into account the various factors, both external and internal, that might bear upon sales—such as prices, production capacities, markets, technological changes, competition, and sales promotion plans—and combines them to bring about the forecast.

The basic assumptions for the future are arrived at by the staff after consideration, with upper managers, of forecasts of gross national product, disposable income, price indexes, and other basic economic conditions. Then, before the forecast is finished, a series of meetings are held with sales and other company personnel to make sure that all factors have been properly considered. Conferences are also held with staff specialists in production, advertising, research, costs, and pricing. After the forecast weathers these discussions, it goes to the finished products committee of the company, which includes several vice presidents. When this committee has approved or modified the sales forecast, it then becomes a guide for all managers in planning their budgets and operations.

In another typical case, the initial forecast is made by the salespeople in the field for each of their territories and then modified by the product managers and the sales vice president to correct for known optimism or pessimism of certain salespeople. A second forecast is prepared by the company's economists after careful study of economic and market statistics, based on a combination of historical series and judgment of future conditions as they might affect the company's sales. Supplementing these two forecasts, sampling techniques are used to determine actual markets for their products, as disclosed by plans and practices of industrial and other customers. With these three forecasts, prepared independently, top management holds a conference at which the various predictions are appraised and modified. The resulting forecast becomes the basis for company planning and operations.

Another variant found in practice is for the company, as in the previous example, to have three sets of sales forecasts prepared. One set is prepared by industry specialists in home-office sales departments, another set by the commercial research department, and still another by the

Figure 8.1   A procedure for sales forecasting.

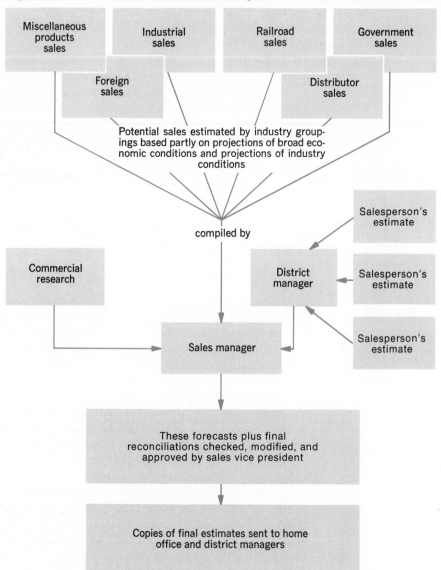

Miscellaneous products sales — Industrial sales — Railroad sales — Government sales — Foreign sales — Distributor sales

Potential sales estimated by industry groupings based partly on projections of broad economic conditions and projections of industry conditions

compiled by

Salesperson's estimate

Commercial research

District manager — Salesperson's estimate

Salesperson's estimate

Sales manager

These forecasts plus final reconciliations checked, modified, and approved by sales vice president

Copies of final estimates sent to home office and district managers

salespeople in the field. These sets are submitted to the sales manager, who presents all three, plus a forecast that reconciles differences, to the sales vice president, who, in turn, checks or modifies the reconciled forecast and submits an approved forecast as the planning basis for company operations.

This procedure can be shown in Figure 8.1.

Since so many failures occur in planning and planning coordination through poor premising, special attention should be given to this step in planning. It is difficult enough to identify the factors in a future environment that will affect a manager's plans. But it is also difficult, once these have been identified, to get consistent and meaningful planning premises actually used in practice.

Selecting Premises

Simply because managers cannot identify and keep in mind all the factors in the future that might affect the course of plans, they limit themselves to those premises which are critical or strategic for them. In making this selection, they consider those which bear materially on their programs. For most enterprises and their managers, these are likely to include national and regional gross product and income and their various elements, such as defense spending, housing and other construction, saving, and consumers' disposable income. In most businesses at least, the movement of the business cycle is a critical factor, and it is difficult to see how price movements can fail to be a significant premise for almost all enterprises. Likewise, population growth and movement have virtually universal importance.

On the other hand, there are many premises of strategic importance to one enterprise and not to another. For an airline, the availability of certain types of aircraft has specific importance. To a steel company, the trends of commercial construction or automobile production may be especially significant, but they may not be an important premise to a toy company. Likewise, in a closely regulated industry such as the airlines or railroads, the policies of regulatory commissions are strategic, while a toothpaste manufacturer may be concerned only with fair trade regulation.

The top managers of every enterprise, and to a certain extent every manager within it, should select their own premises. This basic question should be asked and answered: What factors in the environment, whether external or internal, will influence most the course of plans for which I am responsible?

Alternative Premises for Contingency Planning

Because the future cannot be foreseen with accuracy, it is usually good planning to have alternative sets of premises and plans based upon contingencies so widely varying that no single plan can encompass them all—alternative plans based on such widely varying assumptions as war, peace, peace with large defense spending, full employment, prosperity, depression, recession, rising prices, falling prices, or other major political or economic events. In ideal business planning, alternative plans should be ready whenever basic premises change materially. However, at one time or another decisions that make planning less flexible must be made. A time comes when the manager can no longer wait to order construction of a new plant, hire and train a new staff of specialists, or embark upon a sales promotion campaign. When such decisions are made, the range of alternative plans narrows, as do the premises upon which they are based.

Assuring Consistent Premises

While there can be no doubt of the desirability of consistent premises if plans are to fit one another and contribute most effectively to desired objectives, assuring that premises are consistent is not easy. Perhaps the best way of making sure is to have the planning staff at headquarters and divisional levels recommend critical planning premises applicable to an enterprise or a division to the appropriate top executive. Having a staff with this responsibility can give a fair assurance that the premises will represent study and analysis and that they will be internally consistent. Having the top executive approve these premises, usually after consultation with his or her lieutenants, will assure that the assumptions selected and formulated will be the ones on which the enterprise or division is willing to stake its future.

Communicating Premises

Even after planning premises have been carefully developed and approved, there is always the question of how to communicate them to the number of persons who, by their decision-making authority, participate in the planning process. Like all communications problems, this is difficult. But at least with something to communicate, the problem is easier. A problem arises, too, from the fact that many premises, especially those based on strategy or major programs of competitive impact, may understandably be regarded as confidential.

One of the first requirements of effective premise communication is to analyze all managers' "need to know," interpret this broadly rather than narrowly, and make sure that premises important for their planning are made available to them. There may be a risk of leaks in confidential information, but it is normally better to take this risk than to have uninformed subordinates making planning decisions. What often happens is that the competitor knows a company's strategy and major programs, but its own subordinate managers charged with effectuating this strategy or developing supportive plans do not.

Some companies have found it wise to develop and disseminate to those who need it a manual of planning premises, incorporating assumptions with wide application to planning. These will, of course, be kept current as premises change. They should also be supplemented by the practice of having superiors develop and distribute supplementary planning premises of special concern for managers reporting to them whenever a budget proposal or program recommendation is requested and whenever a major program assignment is made. It is fatal for a manager to assume that premising is no longer necessary after a program has been approved or a major decision made. The fact is that until one gets down to the nuts and bolts of actions, decisions have to be made, and better decisions will be made if the person responsible has a clear picture of the environment in which the decision is expected to operate.

FOR DISCUSSION

1 Take a major decision problem facing you and outline the more critical planning premises surrounding it. How many of these are matters of knowledge, and how many are matters of forecast? How many are qualitative, and how many are quantitative? How many are within your control?

2 A sales forecast is often regarded both as a plan and as a premise. Comment.

3 Identify major premises which, in your judgment, the Ford Motor Company would need in order to forecast its sales of automobiles for the next 2 years.

4 Can objectives, policies, and procedures be premises in planning?

5 Examine how uniform premises aid in coordination of plans.

6 How should premises be developed and communicated?

7 Exactly how would you apply the Delphi technique to premising the major social problems a company will face in the next 10 years?

chapter 9 Decision Making

Decision making—the selection from among alternatives of a course of action—is at the core of planning. A plan cannot be said to exist unless a decision—a commitment of resources, direction, or reputation—has been made. Until that point, we have only planning studies and analyses. Managers sometimes see decision making as their central job because they must constantly choose what is to be done, who is to do it, and when, where, and occasionally even how it will be done. Decision making is, however, only a step in planning, even when done quickly and with little thought or when it influences action for only a few minutes. It is also part of everyone's daily living. A course of action can seldom be judged alone because virtually every decision must be geared in with other plans. The stereotype of the finger-snapping, button-pushing managerial mogul fades as the requirements of systematic research and analysis preceding a decision come into focus.

DECISION MAKING AS A KEY STEP IN PLANNING

In outlining and discussing the steps in planning in Chapter 6, we were really considering decision making as a major part of planning. As a matter of fact, given an awareness of an opportunity and a goal, the core of planning is really a description of the decision process. Thus, in this context, decision making might be thought of as (1) premising, (2) identifying alternatives, (3) the evaluation of alternatives in terms of the goal sought, and (4) the choosing of an alternative, that is, making a decision. As will be noted, the discussion of decision making in this chapter, although emphasizing the logic and techniques of choosing a course of action, really places decision making as one of the steps in planning.

Rationality and Decision Making

Effective decision making requires a *rational* selection of a course of action. But what is rationality? When is a person thinking or deciding rationally? It is often thought to be problem solving, and a problem has sometimes been defined as a state of confusion, uncertainty, or chaos. However, if a person's *goal* is confusion, uncertainty, or chaos in a situation, obviously no problem exists and no need for a decision would arise.

It can be seen, therefore, that certain conditions must be met before we can say that people are acting or deciding rationally. In the first place, they must be attempting to reach some goal that could not be attained without positive action. Second they must have a clear understanding of alternative courses by which a goal could be reached under existing circumstances and limitations. Third, they must have the information and the ability to analyze and evaluate alternatives in the light of the goal sought. And, finally, they must have a desire to come to the best solution by selecting the alternative that best satisfies goal achievement.

Complete rationality can seldom be achieved, particularly in the area of managing. In the first place, since no one can make decisions for the past, decisions must operate for the future, and the future almost invariably involves uncertainties. In the second place, all the alternatives that might be analyzed to reach a goal can hardly be recognized because in most cases there are many ways of achieving a goal. In most instances not all alternatives can be analyzed, even with the newest available analytical techniques and computational facilities, because there are so many.

What a manager must settle for is limited rationality, or what has been called "bounded" rationality. In view of the very great limits to being completely rational in practice, it is not surprising that managers sometimes allow their dislike of risk—the desire to "play it safe"—to interfere with the desire to reach the best solution. This was referred to by Herbert Simon as "satisficing," picking a course of action that is satisfactory or "good enough" under the circumstances. Although it is true that many managerial decisions are made with a desire to "get by" as safely as possible, it is believed that most managers do attempt to make the best decisions they can within the limits of rationality and in the light of the size and nature of risks involved in uncertainty.

DEVELOPING ALTERNATIVES

Assuming known goals and clear planning premises, the first step of decision making is the development of alternatives. It is rare for alternatives to be lacking for any course of action; indeed, a sound adage for the manager is that if there seems to be only one way of doing a thing, that way is probably wrong. In such a case, the manager probably has not forced himself or herself to consider other ways, which is necessary if the decision is to be the best possible.

One of the authors was with a firm that desperately needed certain capital equipment to build up its production to the point where reduced costs and expanded markets would turn losses into profits. Losses had so depleted the company's capital and credit that the equipment desired apparently could not be financed. The single available course of action seemed to be to do nothing, but this would assure bankruptcy. The officers of the company therefore sought out alternatives. A manufacturer was found who had the needed equipment, which he had not been able to sell and which had been financed by some banks. Inquiry of the banks disclosed that they would let the manufacturer sell the equipment on a basis of monthly payments, without down payment, and accept two-name paper instead of the single-name notes they then held. In addition, a competitor of the firm needing equipment had new equipment on order and offered to sell, on a no-down-payment basis, its older machines. Hence, in an apparently hopeless situation, two promising alternatives were found.

The ability to develop alternatives is often as important as selecting correctly from among them. On the other hand, ingenuity, research, and perspicacity will often unearth so many choices that they cannot be adequately evaluated. The decision maker needs help in this situation, and this, as well as assistance in choosing the best alternative, may be found in the concept of the limiting or strategic factor.

THE PRINCIPLE OF THE LIMITING FACTOR

A limiting factor is one which stands in the way of accomplishing a desired objective. If these factors are clearly recognized, managers will confine their search for alternatives to those which will overcome the limiting factors. For instance, in the above example of the manufacturing enterprise, the objective was to turn a loss into a profit. The means for doing this was to acquire some capital equipment. The limiting factor was the lack of cash and credit. Consequently, the company's alternatives were confined to those which would overcome the limiting factor. Its search was unerring, direct, and successful.

From the consideration of this and numerous similar examples there emerges the principle of the limiting factor: *In choosing from among alternatives, the more an individual can recognize and solve for those factors which are limiting or critical to the attainment of the desired goal, the more clearly and accurately he or she can select the most favorable alternative.*

Chester I. Barnard recognized the importance of this principle when he pointed out:

> The analysis required for decision is in effect a search for the "strategic factors." . . . The theory of the strategic factor is necessary to an appreciation of the process of decision, and therefore to the understanding of organization and the executive functions as well as, perhaps, individual purposive conduct. As generally as I can state it, this theory is as follows:
>
> If we take any system, or set of conditions, or conglomeration of circumstances existing at a given time, we recognize that it consists of elements, or parts, or factors, which together make up the whole system, set of conditions, or circumstances. Now if we approach this system or set of circumstances with a view to the accomplishment of a purpose, and only when we so approach it, the elements or parts become distinguished into two classes: those which if absent or changed would accomplish the desired purpose, provided the others

remain unchanged, and these others. The first kind are called limiting factors, the second, complementary factors.[1]

The discovery of the limiting factor or facts may not be easy, since these are often obscure. For example, if a company were considering a profit sharing program, the limiting factors might be tax deductibility and the attitude of employees toward the plan. In deciding whether to expand operations, a company might find its limiting factor to be availability of capital, the diseconomies of size, or the attitude of the government antitrust authorities.

The search for, and recognition of, limiting factors in planning never ends. For one program at one time, a certain factor may be critical to the decision; but, at a later time and for a similar decision, the limiting factor may be something relatively unimportant in the earlier planning. Thus, a company might decide to acquire new equipment when the limiting factor was capital availability, only to have the limiting factor become delivery or, later, the training of people to operate the equipment.

THE BASIC PROCESS OF EVALUATION

Once appropriate alternatives have been isolated, the next step in planning is to evaluate them and select the one that will best contribute to the goal. This is the point of ultimate decision making, although decisions must also be made in the other steps of planning—in selecting goals, in choosing critical premises, and even in selecting alternatives.

Quantitative and Qualitative Factors

As we approach the problem of comparing alternative plans for achieving an objective, we are likely to think exclusively of the quantitative factors. These consist of things which can be measured, such as various types of fixed and operating costs and the time and cost associated with ancillary services. No one would question the importance of this analysis, but it would be dangerous to the success of the venture if intangible factors in the situation were ignored. These are the unmeasurable elements such as

---

[1]C. I. Barnard, *The Functions of the Executive* (Cambridge, Mass.: Harvard University Press, 1938), pp. 202–203. Note that Barnard states that he has borrowed the term "strategic factor" from John R. Commons. As one of the authors' students put it, when a person's automobile fails to operate, there are two basic choices. The person might disassemble it part by part, lay all the parts out on a canvas, check each part, replace doubtful parts, reassemble it in accordance with manufacturer's specifications and prints, and put gasoline and oil in it, and it would run. Or the person might try to locate the limiting factor and then merely replace an ignition wire. As homely as this example is, it emphasizes the fact that many problem solvers, often very intelligent individuals, tend to be "automobile disassemblers" in their attempt to solve a problem. They are content only when they have looked at and analyzed every possible variable. Doing this may take days or months.

the quality of labor relations, the risk of technological change, or the international political climate. There are all too many instances where the best of quantitative plans were destroyed by an unforeseen war, a fine marketing plan was made inoperable by a long transportation strike, or a rational tax plan was hampered by an economic recession. These illustrations point up the importance of giving attention to both quantitative and qualitative factors in the comparison of alternatives.

To evaluate and compare the intangible factors in a planning problem and make decisions from them, the analyst must first recognize them and then determine whether a reasonable quantitative measurement can be given them. If not, the analyst should find out as much as possible about them, perhaps rate them in terms of their importance, compare their probable influence with the results disclosed from evaluation of the quantitative factors, and then come to a decision. This decision may give predominant weight to a single intangible.

Such a procedure is, in effect, deciding upon the weight of the total evidence. Although it involves fallible personal judgments, few business decisions can be so accurately quantified that judgment is unnecessary. Decision making is seldom so simple. It is not without some justification that the successful executive has been cynically described as a person who guesses right.

Evaluating Alternatives: Marginal Analysis

The evaluation of alternatives may utilize the techniques of marginal analysis, wherein the additional revenues from additional costs are compared. Thus, where the objective is to maximize profits, this goal will be reached when the additional revenues and additional costs are equal.

Marginal analysis can be used in comparing factors other than costs and revenues. For example, to find the optimum output of a machine, one could vary inputs against outputs until the *additional* input equals the *additional* output. This would then be the point of maximum efficiency of the machine. Or the number of subordinates reporting to a manager might conceivably be increased to the point where incremental savings in costs, better communication and morale, and other factors equal incremental losses in effectiveness of control, leadership, and similar factors.

Perhaps the real usefulness of the marginal approach to evaluation is that it accentuates the variables in a situation and deemphasizes averages and constants. Whether the objective is optimum profits, stability, or durability, marginal analysis will help show the way.

Evaluating Alternatives: Cost Effectiveness Analysis

An improvement or variant on traditional marginal analysis is cost effectiveness, or cost benefit, analysis. It is a technique of weighing alternatives where the optimum solution cannot be conveniently reduced to dollars or some other specific measure, as in the case of marginal analysis, which is, in actuality, a traditional form of cost-benefit analysis. Special attention was drawn to it in deciding upon programs in the Department of Defense under Robert McNamara, who drew from the work of the RAND Corporation on the economics of defense projects.[2]

In its simplest terms, cost effectiveness is a technique for choosing from among alternatives to identify a preferred choice when objectives are far less specific than those expressed by such clear quantitites as sales, costs, or profits. For example, defense objectives may be so unspecific as those to deter or repel enemy attack; social objectives may be to reduce air pollution or retrain the unemployed; and business objectives may be to participate in social objectives through a program of training unemployables.

This does not mean that objectives may not be given some fairly specific measures of effectiveness. In a program with the general objective of improving employee morale, for example, effectiveness may be measured by such verifiable factors as turnover, absenteeism, or volume of grievances and also supplemented by such subjective inputs as the judgment of qualified experts. Or a program for selecting a military airplane may be verifiably quantified in part by considering bomb carrying load, speed, and maneuverability, but supplemented by judgment of military strategists on how effective it might be in meeting tactical requirements in combat.

The major features of cost effectiveness are concentration on output from a program or system, weighing the contribution of each alternative against its effectiveness in serving desired objectives, and comparison of costs of each in terms of its effectiveness. This was the reasoning that apparently led to the selection of the F-111 combat airplane some years ago for both the Navy and the Air Force. As erroneous as some may believe this decision to have been, and while the Defense Department clearly recognized that the airplane was not optimum for either service, its effectiveness, in light of estimated costs of undertaking two combat aircraft programs, especially when resources were needed for other defense requirements, was thought to be such as to justify the single aircraft program.

Although it involves the same steps as any planning decision, the major features that distinguish cost effectiveness are: (1) objectives are normally output- or end-result-oriented and usually imprecise; (2) alternatives ordinarily represent total systems, programs, or strategies for meeting objectives; (3) the measures of effectiveness must be relevant to objectives and set in as precise terms as possible, although some may not be subject to quantification; (4) cost estimates are usually traditional and normal, but may include nonmonetary as well as monetary costs, even

---

[2]See C. J. Hitch and R. N. McKean, *Economics of Defense in the Nuclear Age* (Cambridge, Mass.: Harvard University Press, 1960).

though the former may be eliminated by expressing them as negative factors of effectiveness; and (5) decision criteria, while definite but not usually as specific as highest profits, may include achieving a given objective at least cost, attaining it with resources available, or providing for a trade-off of cost for effectiveness, particularly in the light of the claims of other objectives.

Cost effectiveness can be made most systematic through the use of models and other operations research techniques, to be described present-ly. Cost models may be developed to show cost estimates for each alternative, and effectiveness models to show the relationship between each alternative and its effectiveness. Then, synthesizing models combin-ing these results may be made to show the relationships of costs and effectiveness for each alternative. As illustrated in Figure 9.1, this can show how much effectiveness can be bought for a certain cost for each alternative and how much effectiveness can be had for any alternative for any given cost.

To understand cost effectiveness better, it might be well to refer to Figure 9.1. The model shown there depicts four alternatives: A_1, A_2, A_3, and A_4. These could be four different types of military aircraft being considered for procurement. At various cost levels (C_1, C_3, and C_2) different levels of effectiveness (E_1, E_3, and E_2) are assumed to be found. These levels of effectiveness could be a measure of a number of factors, such as speed, payload, range, and maneuverability.

The purpose of cost effectiveness analysis is to relate an effectiveness measure to various costs. The model indicates that, at E_1 and C_1, alternative A_1 is the most cost effective. At E_2 and C_2, alternative A_4 is the most cost effective. And A_3 is the most cost effective at cost C_3.

It should be noted that the most costly alternative is not always the most effective, particularly when effectiveness is measured by various factors. For example, an airplane with supersonic speed might be the most effective when only speed is considered, but when speed *and* maneuvera-

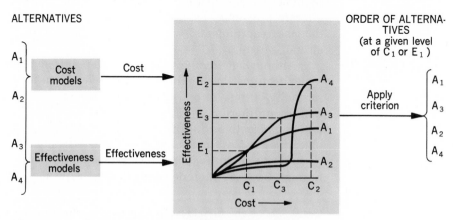

Figure 9.1 The structure of cost effectiveness analysis.

bility are considered, a slower and less costly airplane might be more effective and certainly more cost effective.

All cost effectiveness analysis does (and the model in Figure 9.1 implies this) is to force the decision maker to see various alternatives in light of their effectiveness versus their costs. If most decisions were as simple as those implied from the marginal principle of elementary economics (the most profitable price lies at the point where marginal cost and marginal revenue are equal), life would be much easier for the decision maker. But, unfortunately, most decisions are far more complex.

Planning under Dynamic Conditions

Analysis of economic forces under static conditions is useful only to isolate the effects of uncertainty and thereby develop further tools for analysis. Static conditions do not exist in practice, and planning is therefore undertaken under conditions of change and uncertainty. It is this dynamic character of the environment that makes planning difficult.

The central problem under dynamic conditions is the accuracy of a planner's estimate of the future. Since the future is uncertain—although the degree may vary widely as among products, markets, geographic and political areas, and times—when managers estimate a future situation, they necessarily make certain assumptions as to what will happen. As they weigh their contingencies in one way or another, they obtain different results. Suppose, for example, that a manager was planning a new plant and felt that 10 years were needed to recover costs. One might estimate the future with respect to markets, prices, labor costs, material costs, utilization of plant, labor efficiency, taxes, and other factors. Suppose further that six possible situations were estimated as being most likely to occur, created out of different sets of assumptions as to the future. These might bring completely different estimates of net profits, as shown in Figure 9.2.

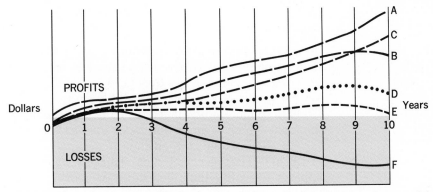

Figure 9.2 Accumulated profits from new plant on the basis of six estimates of the future.

As might be expected, all estimates for the first year or two are fairly close together, since the manager can be more certain of short-term than long-term results. But as the planning period is extended, this or that contingency makes the estimates of accumulated profits vary from high, as in forecast A, through bare break even (E), to projected loss (F).

Several observations may be made concerning this simplified model of planning under conditions of change and uncertainty. In the first place, the tools of marginal analysis are useful in arriving at these various estimates of possible situations. In each set of contingencies assumed, planners would attempt to maximize profits by assuring themselves that additional costs are compensated for by additional revenues and that, within the limits of divisibility of units of production, no opportunity for maximizing profits by increasing or reducing costs or revenues has been neglected.

In the second place, Figure 9.2 emphasizes the fact that the uncertainties over time, plus the alternatives available to accomplish results under each set of uncertainties, give alternative possibilities astronomical in number. Managers must have some means of limiting their analysis to probable situations. In most cases, this is done by judgment and test. If they can calculate their profits on basic estimates of what is most likely to occur, they will limit the alternative projections to a few most probable ones. At this point, a decision is likely to be based upon a weighing of the risks and benefits to be expected from these few probabilities, in the light of underlying uncertainties, the resources of the firm, and the ability and willingness to assume the risks involved.

BASES FOR SELECTION AMONG ALTERNATIVES

In selecting from among alternatives, managers have three bases for decision open to them—experience, experimentation, and research and analysis.

Experience

Reliance on past experience probably plays a larger part than it deserves in decision making. Experienced managers usually believe, often without realizing it, that the things they have accomplished and the mistakes they have made furnish an almost infallible guide to the future. This attitude is likely to be more pronounced the more experience a manager has had and the higher in an organization he or she has risen.

To some extent, the attitude that experience is the best teacher is justifiable. The very fact that managers have reached their positions appears to justify their decisions. Moreover, the reasoning process of thinking problems through, making decisions, and seeing programs succeed or fail does make for a degree of good judgment (at times bordering on the intuitive). Many people, however, do not profit by their errors, and there are managers who seem never to gain the seasoned judgment required by modern operations.

There is danger, however, in relying on one's past experience as a guide for future action. In the first place, most human beings do not recognize the underlying reasons for their mistakes or failures. In the second place, the lessons of experience may be entirely unsuitable to new problems. Good decisions must be evaluated against future events, while experience belongs to the past.

On the other hand, if experience is carefully analyzed rather than blindly followed and if the *fundamental* reasons for success or failure are distilled from it, it can be useful as a basis for decision analysis. A successful program, a well-managed company, a profitable product promotion, or any other decision that turns out well may furnish useful data for such distillation. Just as no scientist hesitates to build upon the research of others and would be foolish indeed to duplicate it, managers can learn much from others.

Experimentation

An obvious way to decide upon alternatives is to try them and see what happens. Such experimentation is used in scientific inquiry. It is frequently argued that it should be employed more often in enterprise and that the only way a manager can make sure a plan is right—especially in view of the intangible factors—is to try the various alternatives to see which is best.

However, as Newman has pointed out, "The experimental techniques should be utilized as a last resort after other planning techniques have been tried."[3] It is likely to be the most expensive of all techniques, especially where heavy expenditures in capital and personnel are necessary to try a program and where an enterprise cannot afford to prosecute vigorously several alternatives. Besides, there may be doubt after an experiment has been tried as to what it proved, since the future may not duplicate the present.

On the other hand, there are many decisions which cannot be made until the best course of action can be ascertained with experiment. Even reflections on experience or the most careful research may not assure the manager of a correct decision. This is nowhere better illustrated than in planning a new airplane. The manufacturer may assiduously draw from personal experience and that of other plane manufacturers and of new plane users. Engineers and economists may make extensive studies of stresses, vibrations, fuel consumption, speed, space allocations, and other factors. But all these studies do not give every answer to questions about

[3]W. H. Newman, *Business Policies and Management*, 2d ed. (Cincinnati: South-Western Publishing Company, Incorporated, 1949), p. 601.

the flying characteristics and economics of a successful plane; therefore, some experimentation is almost always involved in the process of selecting from alternatives. Ordinarily, a prototype airplane is constructed and tested, and, on the basis of these tests, production airplanes are made on a somewhat revised design.

Experimentation is used in other ways. A firm may test a new product in a certain market before expanding its sale nationwide. Organizational techniques are often tried in a branch office or plant before being applied over an entire company. A candidate for a management job may be tested in the job during the incumbent's vacation.

Research and Analysis

The most generally used and certainly a most effective technique for selecting from alternatives, when major decisions are involved, is research and analysis. This approach entails solving a problem by, first, comprehending it. It thus involves a search for relationships between the more critical variables, constraints, and premises that bear upon the goal sought. In a real sense it is the pencil and paper (or, better, the computer and printout) approach to decision making. It has many advantages for weighing alternative courses of action.

In the second place, the solution of a planning problem requires that it be broken into its component parts and the various tangible and intangible factors studied. Study and analysis are likely to be far cheaper than experimentation. Hours of analytical time and reams of paper usually cost much less than trying the various alternatives in practice. In the example of building airplanes mentioned above, if careful research did not precede the building and testing of prototype subassemblies and the final assembly, one can hardly imagine the costs that would result.

A major characteristic of the research and analysis approach is to develop a model simulating the problem. Thus we often make models of buildings, in the form of extensive blueprints or three-dimensional renditions. We test models of airplane wings and missiles in a wind tunnel. But the most useful way is likely to be a simulation of the variables in a problem situation by mathematical terms and relationships. Being thus able to conceptualize a problem is a major step toward its solution. The physical sciences have long relied on mathematical models to do this, and it is encouraging to see this method being brought into the area of managerial decision making.

OPERATIONS RESEARCH AND PLANNING

One of the most comprehensive research and analysis approaches to decision making is operations research, or, as it is sometimes called, "operations analysis" or "management science." These terms, although sometimes given an aura of mystery by their mathematically inclined proponents, apply to the growing practice of employing the systems methodology of the physical sciences to management decision making.

To a considerable extent, operations research is a product of World War II, although its antecedents in scientific method, higher mathematics, and such tools as probability theory go back far beyond that period. The accelerated growth of operations research in recent years has followed the whole trend of applying the methods of the physical scientist and the engineer to economic and political problems. It has also been made possible by the development of rapid computing machines, particularly those using electronics, since much of the advantage of operations research depends upon the economical and feasible application of involved mathematical formulas and the use of data with complex relationships.

The Concept

There are almost as many definitions of operations research as there are writers on the subject. As applied to decision making, where the term was originally used, the most acceptable definition is that operations research is "the application of scientific method to the study of alternatives in a problem situation, with a view to providing a quantitative basis for arriving at an optimum solution in terms of the goals sought." Thus the emphasis is on scientific method, on the use of quantitative data, on goals, and on the determination of the optimum means of reaching the goal. In other words, operations research might be called "quantitative common sense."

Operations research, like accounting analyses or correlation analyses, does not provide decisions, but develops quantitative data to help managers make decisions. In most situations, analyses cannot be so complete or conclusive that they constitute the decision. However, in a production planning or transportation problem, the goals may be so clear, the input data so definite, and the conclusions so workable as to point positively to the optimum solution.

Some operations researchers insist that with this tool the activities of any enterprise must be viewed as a *total system*, in contrast to the usual attempts to solve isolated problems. In addition, it is often claimed that operations research requires the team approach in the solution of problems, that is, the use of a variety of talents, such as those of the mathematician, the business specialist, the psychologist, the engineer, and the accountant. Although these conditions may be desirable, neither seems to be essential to using operations research.

All top managers would appreciate having a problem area completely analyzed and its solution related to every other problem in their operation, but they recognize the practical difficulties, if not the impossibility, of doing so. It does not seem realistic for the operations research experts to overlook the usefulness of their techniques in solving limited problems within a larger enterprise system. Even a total enterprise is a subsystem of a larger system. And suboptimization within an enterprise may be better than no system optimization. Also, the use of a team of experts with various outlooks on a problem, while often useful, cannot be said to be essential in all cases.

The Essentials

Attempts have long been made to solve management problems scientifically, but operations researchers have supplied an element of orderliness and completeness by their approach. They have emphasized defining the problem and goals, carefully collecting and evaluating data, developing and testing hypotheses, determining relationships between data, developing and checking predictions based on hypotheses, and devising measures to evaluate the effectiveness of a course of action.

Thus the essential characteristics of operations research as applied to decision making may be summarized as follows:

1. The emphasis on models—the logical representation of a reality or problem. These may, of course, be simple or complex. For example, the accounting formula "assets minus liabilities equals proprietorship" $(A - L = P)$ is a model, since it represents an idea and, within the limits of the terms used, symbolizes the relationship among the variables involved.

2. The emphasis on goals in a problem area and the development of measures of effectiveness in determining whether a given solution shows promise of attaining the goal. For example, if the goal is profit, the measure of effectiveness may be the rate of return on investment, and every proposed solution will arrange the variables so that the end result can be weighed against this measure. Some variables may be subject to control by the manager; others may represent uncontrollable factors in the system.

3. The attempt to incorporate in a model the variables in a problem, or at least those which appear to be important to its solution.

4. Putting the model with its variables, constraints, and goals in mathematical terms so that it may be clearly perceived, subjected to mathematical simplification, and readily utilized for calculation by substitution of quantities for symbols.

5. The attempt to quantify the variables in a problem to the extent possible, since only quantifiable data can be inserted into a model to yield a finite result.

6. The attempt to supplement quantifiable data with such usable mathematical and statistical devices as the probabilities in a situation, thus making the mathematical and computing problem under uncertainty workable within a small and perhaps insignificant margin of error.

Of all these essentials, perhaps the basic tool and major contribution of operations research has probably been the construction and use of conceptual models for decision making. There are many types of these. Some assert logical relationships between variables. Models may be referred to as "simulative" or "descriptive" if they are designed only to describe the relationship of elements in a situation. The models useful for planning are referred to as "decision" or "optimizing" models, designed to lead to the selection of a course of optimum action among available alternatives. While their purpose is to arrive at an "optimum" solution, they do, of course, simulate the problem area.

In order to construct a decision model, it is necessary to express in some kind of terms the goals sought, to set forth the relationships of the variables as they influence these goals, and then to express these mathematically to yield the optimum answer in terms of goals.

In typical management problems, there is usually a large number of variables. In fact, in some problems the variables are so numerous and their relationships so complex as to defy mathematical expression. The use of a model is illustrated in the determination of the economic quantity of a product for a company to order.[4] The major variables here are the requirements for the product for a year, the unit cost, the inventory carrying cost, the setup cost per order, and the order quantity. The model so derived, expressed in terms of the measure of effectiveness—economic order quantity—is as follows:

$$Qe = \sqrt{\frac{2\ RS}{I}}$$

where

Qe = economic order quantity

R = total yearly requirements

S = setup costs

I = inventory carrying cost per item

Experienced business planning analysts will recognize the ingredients of a decision model as those considerations they have long applied in coming to a recommendation for a course of action. They know that in the process of evaluation, the various courses of action are weighed against the objectives sought. In fact, long before the term "operations research" came into use, planning analysts constructed a model in the form of forecasts of costs, revenues, and profits. Even though they often did not develop a mathematical formula and hence probably restricted their analysis to a small number of most attractive alternatives, they tested for profitability. They were also aware that, whatever the results of their

---

[4]For an illustration of a number of models and an explanation of model construction, see C. W. Churchman, R. L. Ackoff, and E. L. Arnoff, *Introduction to Operations Research* (New York: John Wiley & Sons, Inc., 1957).

quantitative tests, they had to temper their recommendations with consideration of intangibles. Indeed, this is the difficulty with many operations researchers. In order to make their model useful (to them), they may leave out certain critical variables that cannot be quantified. This practice, especially if the omissions are not called to the attention of the practicing manager, has often led to distrust of the technique.

Procedure

Applying operations research involves six steps similar to those discussed in Chapter 6, on planning (see pages 173-177).[5]

1   Formulate the problem   As in any planning problem, the operations researcher must analyze the goals and the system in which the solution must operate. That complex of interrelated components in a problem area, referred to by operations researchers as a "system," will be recognized as comprising mainly the environment of a decision and representing planning premises. This system may comprehend an entire business operation or be limited to planning production for presses and lathes. It is still, however, an interconnected complex of functionally related human or material components. Obviously, unless the problem is greatly simplified by rigorous application of the principle of the limiting factor, the more comprehensive the system, the more complex the problem.

Since the purpose of formulating the problem is to determine the optimum course of action from among various alternatives, measures of effectiveness, as well as goals, must be clearly defined. Moreover, in a typical operations research problem, it is desirable to take into account as many goals as necessary and feasible. For example, in a production and distribution planning problem, the decision maker will probably wish to minimize operating costs, minimize investment in inventory, satisfy a level of consumer service, and optimize the use of capital investments. To measure effectiveness in reaching these goals and to formulate the problem so that multiple objectives can be satisfied on an optimum basis—particularly in the light of a variety of inputs—can become a very complex conceptual and computational matter. The simplest approach is to use certain goals as constraints by saying, for example, the goal is minimum costs while maintaining a certain minimum level of customer service or a maximum level of inventory.

2   Construct a mathematical model   The next step is to formulate the problem as a system of relationships in a mathematical model. For a single goal, where at least some variables are subject to control, the general form of the operations research model may be stated as follows:

$$E = f(x_i, y_j)$$

[5]Ibid., pp. 12–15. The authors have drawn much of their material for this section from this classic book.

where

E = measure of effectiveness of system

x_i = controllable variables

y_j = variables beyond control

The above model may be classified as either an optimizing model or a simulation model. When using it as an optimizing model, values inserted for the uncontrollable variables (y_j) and the controllable variables (x_i) are manipulated to optimize the measure of effectiveness (E). For example, suppose that a marketing manager wishes to optimize total sales dollars. The model to do so might include such uncontrollable variables as competitors' prices, gross national product, or price-level changes, and the controllable variables might be comprised of such variables as number of salespeople, commissions allowed, product prices, and advertising expenditures.

Although all models are intended to simulate reality, what are usually called "simulation models" are those where users give the model a set of values for the controllable variables and assume a set of values for the uncontrollable variables. By using one or more sets of values for the uncontrollable variables (because often they cannot be known), users can compute various E's until they find one they believe to be satisfactory. In this event, of course, there is no way of knowing whether an *optimum* solution has been found. However, the visibility obtained can be very important. Often an optimizing model cannot be used because of lack of known input data, the difficulty of accurately simulating reality (at least the important elements of reality), and the fact that it may be very complex and difficult to build.

3 Derive a solution from the model In arriving at a solution, there are two basic procedures. In the analytical procedure, the researcher employs mathematical deduction in order to reach, as nearly as possible, a mathematical solution before inserting quantities to get a numerical solution. This can be an exceedingly important contribution to complex decision making. Variables may be reduced or restated in terms of common variables. Certain variables (for example, sales) may appear in a number of places in a model and may be factored out or reduced. In other cases, a series of mathematical equations may be consolidated and simplified. The result of this analytical procedure is to place a complex series of relationships into as simple a mathematical form as possible. In addition, this analysis may disclose, mathematically, that certain variables are unimportant to a reasonable solution and may be dropped from consideration.

The second procedure is referred to as "numerical." In this, the analyst simply "tries" various values for the variables subject to control to see what the results will be and from this develops a set of values which seems to give the best solution. The numerical procedure varies from pure trial and error to complex iteration. In iteration, the analyst undertakes successive trial runs to approach an optimum solution. In some complex cases, such as the iterative procedures used in linear programming, rules have been developed to help analysts more quickly undertake trials and identify the optimum solution when it is reached.[6]

4 Test the model Because a model, by its very nature, is only a representation of reality and because it is seldom possible to include all the variables, models should usually be tested. This may be done by using the model to solve a problem and comparing the results so obtained with what actually happens. These tests may be carried out by using past data or by trying the model out in practice to see how it measures up with reality.

5 Provide controls for the model and solution Because a once-accurate model may cease to represent reality, because the variables believed to be beyond control may change in value, or because the relationships of variables may change, provision must be made for control of the model and the solution. This is done in the same way any control is undertaken, by providing means for feedback so that significant deviations can be detected and changes made. In many complex models, such as those used for production or distribution planning, the effect of the deviations must be weighed against the cost of feeding in the correction or against the usually greater cost of revising the entire program. As a result, the researcher may decide not to correct the model or the inputs.

6 Put the solution into effect The final step is to make the model and the inputs operable. In anything but the simpler programs, this will involve revision and clarification of procedures so that the inputs (including control feedback information) are available in an orderly fashion, and this, in turn, often requires reorganization of an enterprise's available information. What many users of operations research have found as a major stumbling block is that no one is willing to undertake the hard work of revising the nature of basic information. Accounting and other data normally available in a company are often not adequate to the requirements of successful operations research. Many managers, intrigued with the possibilities of operations research, wish that some of the research effort of experts, now so widely employed in constructing elegant models, could be channeled toward information reorganization.

Other problems in putting the solution into effect involve getting people to understand, appreciate, and use the techniques of operations research and deciding such questions as what computing facilities to use, and how, and how the information outputs are to be made useful and understandable to those responsible for decisions. In this connection,

[6]For a clear application of this procedure, as applied to the simplex technique in linear programming, see the explanation in ibid., pp. 304–316.

operations researchers would do the manager a real favor by frankly admitting the type and margin of uncertainty in their solution.

All this is to say that operations researchers are not nearly done with their task when their model is reduced to paper and tested. Mathematical gymnastics may be interesting to the pure philosopher, but the manager must make a responsible decision, and the operations researcher who would be useful to managers must be more than a mathematical gymnast.

Operations Research and Simulation

Simulation through the use of models is sometimes regarded as one of the most powerful tools available for effective management planning and control. Not that simulation itself is new. Managers have long used it in training through role playing, teaching business policy through cases, and testing airplane models in a wind tunnel. War games, long used by the military, and the more recently popular business games are examples of situations in which individuals are given a kind of experience through simulating reality.

The technique of simulation through use of mathematical models and the computer not only is relatively new but also has interesting promise for the decision maker. To the extent that a management problem can be reasonably simulated by the construction of a model, a manager can test the results of any proposed individual course of action that much better. As a consequence, no modern manager, faced with a difficult or complex decision, should overlook the possibility of simulation. Even with its limitations, it might show results of a decision which a manager had not anticipated, and this may be a great deal less costly way to experiment than through making decisions which are found later to have been monumental mistakes.

As in the case of any model, a simulation need not be mathematical. But, in the typical business problem, the important variables and constraints are usually so numerous and the relationships so complex that mathematics and the computer are normally necessary. The cases where simulation can pay off through inexpensive experimentation are numerous. To mention a few, it is relatively easy to test a program for inventory control, to experiment with proposed programs of quantity discounts, or to simulate a new production line. While active use of simulation appears to be only in its infancy, the advantages appear to be very great. Even if there are considerable uncertainties, intelligent simulation of a course of action can at least give a manager some visibility of the size and nature of risks entailed in a decision.

A Case of Operations Research in Practice: Distribution Logistics

One of the most interesting ways that some companies use operations research in practice may be seen in the case of what has been called a "distribution logistics" model. Essentially, this is a model which treats the entire materials flow system of a business—from sales forecast through purchasing and processing of materials and inventorying them to shipping finished goods to a company's sales warehouses—as a single system. The purpose is usually to develop a model that will show what to do to get the lowest costs for the entire system while still meeting needs for a desired customer service level by having required products on hand and by doing so within certain limitations of inventory of goods. Such a model gathers into one system a large mass of relationships and information so as to show the best way of doing things at any time to have the lowest costs. In such a model, it is entirely possible that shipping, manufacturing, or any single area of cost, looked upon alone, will not be lowest, but the entire system of operation will be.

Without going into the complex mathematics necessary to make a distribution logistics system work, it might be diagrammed as shown in Figure 9.3. To see the model as a common-sense diagram is to see the problem; most managers can leave the job of putting the model in mathematical form to the operations research and model-building specialists.

This figure shows the relationships between the goal desired, the input variables and limits, and the expected outputs. The company represented by this model is a consumer goods company with a fairly broad line of products, a number of plants (some producing the whole line, others producing only part of the line), a number of finished-goods warehouses, and national distribution to grocery chains and wholesalers. It will be noted that customer service standards (that is, maximum time permitted between receipt and shipment of an order) are here inserted as a constraining input.

That the mathematics of this model would be exceedingly complex can be appreciated when it is known that the company had a line of 200 products (including sizes), 16 plants, 60 warehouses, and 70 sales districts. Also, this system would require fast feedback for control, adequate inventories to meet unforeseen contingencies, good sales forecasting, and regional distribution managers able to override the system by quick change of local plans if schedules are not accurate enough to meet local sales needs.

A fully developed distribution logistics system is a fine instrument of planning and control. By arriving at lowest *total* costs in a broad area of operation, the system might show it would be cheaper to use more expensive transportation on occasion rather than to carry high inventories. Or it might show that production at less than economic order quantities would be justified in order to get better transportation or warehousing utilization or to meet customer service standards with limited inventories.

Moreover, such a system gives managers a means of control which a separate set of unconnected plans could not. By seeing how activities interlock and by setting up a system of interrelated plans, planning for the

Figure 9.3 Distribution logistics model.

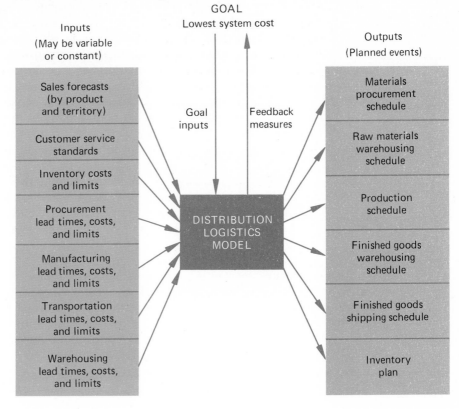

GOAL
Lowest system cost

Inputs
(May be variable
or constant)

Outputs
(Planned events)

Goal
inputs

Feedback
measures

Sales forecasts
(by product
and territory)

Customer service
standards

Inventory costs
and limits

Procurement
lead times, costs,
and limits

Manufacturing
lead times, costs,
and limits

Transportation
lead times, costs,
and limits

Warehousing
lead times, costs,
and limits

DISTRIBUTION
LOGISTICS
MODEL

Materials
procurement
schedule

Raw materials
warehousing
schedule

Production
schedule

Finished goods
warehousing
schedule

Finished goods
shipping schedule

Inventory
plan

entire production and distribution system can be obtained. That this could not be done on such a scale without mathematics and electronic computing is beyond question. But what is interesting, in the experience of one of the authors, is that where distribution logistics has been undertaken intelligently and patiently, its costs of operation have not been really high, while the benefits, although difficult to measure accurately, have been extraordinary.

To be sure, even such a broad distribution logistics system is not a system of a total business enterprise, but it does apply to a considerable part of the total business operation. And it applies to those parts where the inputs can be quantified with a reasonable degree of accuracy.

Special Tools

Although the construction of decision models is perhaps the central tool of operations research, it is interesting that various mathematical and scientific techniques, generally developed in the study of the physical sciences, have had applications to the study of management problems.

Probability theory   This important statistical device is based upon the inference from experience that certain things are likely to happen in accordance with a predictable pattern. For example, if a coin is tossed a hundred times, it is probable, although by no means certain, that it will fall heads fifty times. However, the deviations from such a probability are within a fairly predictable margin, and consequently the probability becomes a workable substitute for data otherwise unknown. In an enterprise problem, where probabilities can be substituted for unknowns, the margin of error in the solution, although not removed, is limited. As will be noted in our discussion of decision trees and preference theory below, probability plays a major role in the techniques.

Game theory   Although far too complicated to describe here, this tool is based upon the premise that a man or woman seeks to maximize gain and minimize loss, that he or she acts rationally, and that an opponent or competitor will be similarly motivated. Under these circumstances, game theory attempts to work out an optimum solution in which an individual in a certain situation can develop a strategy which, regardless of what an adversary does, will maximize gains or minimize losses. Even though the mathematical development of game theory has not proceeded beyond the stage of the most simple competitive situations and there is little evidence that it has been very useful in actual planning, future development of this theory may have a remarkable impact on the scientific approach to strategic planning in competitive situations.[7]

Queuing, or waiting-line, theory[8]   This theory uses mathematical tech-

[7]One of the most interesting and elementary expositions of game theory may be found in J. D. Williams, *The Compleat Strategyst* (New York: McGraw-Hill Book Company, 1954).
[8]For example, in the simplest example of a queuing system with one queue and one servicing station and where arrivals are random and reasonably described by the Poisson distribution, there exists a constant λ (independent of queue length, time, or any other property of the queue) such that the probability of an arrival during an interval Δt (where Δt is very small) is given by $\lambda \Delta t$. Or

Probability {arrival between time t and $t + \Delta t$} = $\lambda \Delta t$

If n is a discrete random variable representing the number of arrivals in a fixed interval of time T, the frequency distribution of n is described by

$$fT(n) = \text{probability } \{n \text{ arrivals in time } T\} = \frac{(\lambda T)_e{}^{n-\lambda T}}{n!}$$

Therefore, if T were to represent the distribution of intervals between arrivals (also a random variable), the density function for T or $g(T)$ would be an exponential distribution of

$$g(T) = \lambda e_{-\lambda T}$$

Similarly, the probability of turning out a finished unit (i.e., completing service at the station in the interval Δt (where Δt is small) is given by the formula

Probability {service completed between t and $t + \Delta t$} = $\mu \Delta t$

niques to balance the costs of waiting lines versus the costs of preventing waiting lines by increased service. It is based on the premise that although delays are costly, the cost of eliminating them may be even more costly. One of its interesting applications, often used as an example, was the case of the New York Port Authority, which used queuing theory to solve a problem involving the number of toll stations at the entrance to bridges and tunnels. Through the application of this operations research device, the Authority found it could reduce waiting lines and, at the same time, reduce the number of toll stations.

Linear programming[9]   A technique for determining the optimum combination of limited resources to obtain a desired goal, linear programming is one of the most successful applications of operations research. It is based upon the assumption that a linear, or straight-line, relationship exists between variables and that the limits of variations can be determined. For example, in a production shop, the variables may be units of output per machine in a given time, direct labor costs or material costs per unit of output, number of operations per unit, and so forth. Most or all of these

---

Where μ is a constant, then the random variable s, representing the time it takes to complete service in a unit, can be defined by the probability function

$$g(s) = \mu e^{-\mu s}$$

For this simple single-station, single-queue model with Poisson arrivals (mean arrival rate λ) and exponential service times (mean service time μ), the probability of having n units in the system (i.e., in queue and being serviced) at any one time is given by

$$P_n = \left(1 - \frac{\lambda}{\mu}\right)\left(\frac{\lambda}{\mu}\right)^n$$

where $n \geqq 0$ and $\mu > \lambda$

A simple explanation of queuing theory may be found in many books. See, for example, M. Sasieni, A. Yaspan, and L. Friedman, *Operations Research: Methods and Problems* (New York: John Wiley & Sons, Inc., 1959), chap. 6.
[9]A linear program, in its general form, can be expressed as follows:

Objective function

$$P = C_1X_1 + C_2X_2 + C_3X_3 + \cdots + C_nX_n = \text{Max}$$

Subject to

$$a_{11}X_1 + a_{12}X_2 + a_{13}X_3 + \cdots a_{1n}X_n = b_1$$

$$a_{21}X_1 + a_{22}X_2 + a_{23}X_3 + \cdots a_{2n}X_n = b_2$$

$$a_{31}X_1 + a_{32}X_2 + a_{33}X_3 + \cdots a_{3n}X_n = b_3$$

$$a_{m1}X_1 + a_{m2}X_{2a} + a_{m3}X_3 + \cdots a_{mn}X_n = b_m$$

where $X_1 = 0$, $i = 1, 2, \cdots, n$

may have linear relationships, within certain limits, and by solving linear equations, the optimum in terms of cost, time, machine utilization, or other objectives can be established. Thus, this technique is especially useful where input data can be quantified and objectives are subject to definite measurement. As one might expect, the technique has had its most promising use in such problem areas as production planning, shipping rates and routes, and the utilization of production and warehouse facilities to achieve lowest overall costs, including transportation costs. Because it depends on linear relationships and many decisions do not involve these or cannot be accurately enough simulated, newer and more complex systems of nonlinear programming have come into use.

Servo theory This is another important contribution of operations research to management problems. Originally used in the design of automatic or remotely controlled systems (for example, the thermostat), the feedback principle, by which information is fed back to correct for deviations, has become an important aspect of control. The dynamic characteristics of problems emphasize the necessity for correcting for changes in the inputs in a mathematical model. The servo theory has important implications for managerial control.

Other Tools

There are, of course, many other tools of operations research. *Symbolic logic*, by which symbols are substituted for propositions or even programs, has led to a sharper analysis of complicated and sometimes ambiguous problems. *Information theory* has sharpened the evaluation of the information flow within a given system. *Value theory* assigns numerical significance to the value of alternative tangible choices. *Monte Carlo methods* put random occurrence in models to simulate such occurrences as machine breakdown or customer arrivals.

Limitations

In the enthusiasm for the potentialities of operations research, its limitations should not be overlooked. So far, it has not been used to solve as many managerial problems as its potentiality would imply.

In the first place, one is faced with the sheer magnitude of the mathematical and computing aspects. The number of variables and interrelationships in many managerial problems, plus the complexities of human relationships and reactions, apparently calls for a higher order of mathematics than nuclear physics does. The late mathematical genius John von Neumann found, in his development of the theory of games, that his mathematical abilities soon reached their limit in a relatively simple strategic problem. However, it can also be said that managers are a long way from using the mathematics now available.

In the second place, although probabilities and approximations are being substituted for unknown quantities and although scientific method is quantifying factors heretofore believed to be impossible to quantify, a major portion of important managerial decisions involve qualitative factors. Until these can be quantified, operations research will have limited usefulness in many areas, and selections between alternatives will continue to be based largely on nonquantitative judgments.

Related to the fact that many management decisions involve unmeasurable factors is the lack of information inputs to make this tool useful in practice, even though the information desired might be obtained. By conceptualizing a problem area and constructing a mathematical model to represent it, variables are disclosed on which information, not now available, is required. What is needed is far more emphasis by those interested in the practical applications of operations research toward developing this needed information. At times it appears that if the same intelligence now devoted to the building of models and their mathematical manipulation were applied by specialists to developing information inputs, the applications of operations research would be greatly accelerated.

Still another limitation concerns bridging the gap between managers and trained operations researchers. Managers, in general, lack a knowledge and appreciation of mathematics, just as mathematicians lack comprehension of managerial problems. This is being dealt with, to an increasing extent, by the business and management schools and, more often, by organizations—private or public—with operations researchers in their staff groups. But this gap is still the major cause of slowness in using operations research.

One of the outstanding specialists in operations research reported a few years ago in a rather pessimistic tone concerning the actual use of this important tool.[10] He had his graduate students write to the authors of cases reported in the journal *Operations Research*, over the first 6 years of its publication, with a view to determining the extent to which recommendations of the studies had been carried out by practicing managers. He reported that there was not sufficient evidence in any case that the recommendations had been accepted. However, in recent years much more, but still fairly little, use is being made of this technique. This same pioneer, Professor C. West Churchman, as was pointed out in Chapter 2, has been highly critical of the undue concentration of operations researchers on model elegance.

NEWER APPROACHES TO DECISION MAKING UNDER UNCERTAINTY

Supplementing the systematic analysis of operations research in analyzing problems, a number of newer techniques have come into use to

[10]C. W. Churchman, "Managerial Acceptance of Scientific Recommendations," *California Management Review*, vol. 7, no. 1, pp. 31–38, at p. 33 (Fall 1964).

improve the quality of decision making under the normal conditions of
uncertainty. Among the most important of these are risk analysis,
decision trees, and preference theory.

Risk Analysis

All intelligent decision makers dealing with uncertainty like to know the
size and nature of the risk they are taking in choosing a course of action.
This is one of the deficiencies in using the traditional approaches of
operations research for problem solving. Many of the inputs into a model
are merely estimates, and other are based upon probabilities. The
ordinary practice is for staff specialists to come up with "best estimates."
But these might be like saying that the best estimate is that, on a given roll
of the dice, the number 7 is more likely to come up than any other
number, even though there is only a 1 in 6 chance that it will.
Consequently, to give a more precise view of risk, new techniques have
been developed.

Virtually every decision is based on the interaction of a number of
critical variables, many of which have an element of uncertainty but,
perhaps, a fairly high degree of probability. Thus, the wisdom of
undertaking the launch of a new product might depend upon the critical
variables of expense of introduction, cost of production, capital investment required, price obtainable, total market for the product, and share of
market obtainable by it. A best estimate might be made that the new
product has a high (say, 80 percent) chance of yielding a return of 30
percent on the total investment made in it.

But suppose that further analysis of each critical variable shows that
the introduction, operating, and investment costs each have a 90 percent
probability of being accurate, the price estimate a 70 percent chance of
being correct, and the market quantity estimate a 60 percent probability of
being correct. In this case, the calculated probability of the entire program
estimate being right would almost certainly be less than 80 percent;
exactly how much less would depend upon the values of each variable
and the extent to which probabilities less or more than 80 percent would
affect costs or revenues. It can be said, however, that the probability of *all*
the estimates of the various critical variables being correct is only 30.6
percent (.90 × .90 × .90 × .70 × .60).

Risk analysis attempts to develop for every critical variable in a
decision problem a probability distribution curve. Usable ones can be
derived by asking each specialist who estimated a variable to gauge what
the range and probability of each variable is. For example, the sales
manager might be asked to estimate what the probability would be of a
selling price exceeding or falling below the best estimate, and by how
much. No matter how judgmental these estimates might be, a range of
values and probabilities will be better than a single best estimate. With the

aid of computer programs that have been developed, a range of expectancies for the "rightness" of any total estimate can be made.[11]

In the example of the new product investment program noted above, the range of probabilities for a return on investment might turn out as follows:

Rate of return (percent)	Probability of achieving at least rate shown
0	.90
10	.80
15	.70
20	.65
25	.60
30	.50
35	.40
40	.30

Given such data as these, a manager is better able to assess the probability of accomplishing a "best estimate" and can see the chances that he might have if he is satisfied with a lesser return. He can also see that he has a 10 percent chance of even losing on his original investment and other costs on the project. Had the risk analysis shown a 50 percent chance of making the 30 percent return on investment, but a 25 percent probability of losing a considerable amount, he might even decide that undertaking the project would not be worth the risk.

Decision Trees

One of the best ways to analyze a decision is to use so-called decision trees, which make it possible to see directions that actions might take from various decision points and the decision points relating to it in the future. Obviously useful because adequate information is seldom available to make a confidently accurate decision at a given time, the tree depicts future decision points and possible chance events, usually with a notation of the probabilities of the various uncertain events happening.

For example, one of the common problems that occurs in business is to decide, when a new product is introduced, whether to tool up for it in a major way so as to assure production at the lowest possible cost or to undertake cheaper temporary tooling involving a higher manufacturing cost but lower capital losses if the product does not sell as well as estimated. In its simplest form, a tree showing the decision a manager faces in this situation might be similar to that in Figure 9.4.

As can be seen, the tree shows the manager in what direction the

[11]For an example of how this works out with investment analysis, see D.W. Hertz, "Risk Analysis in Capital Investment," *Harvard Business Review*, vol. 42, no. 1, pp. 95-106 (January–February 1964).

Figure 9.4 Decision tree without probabilities.

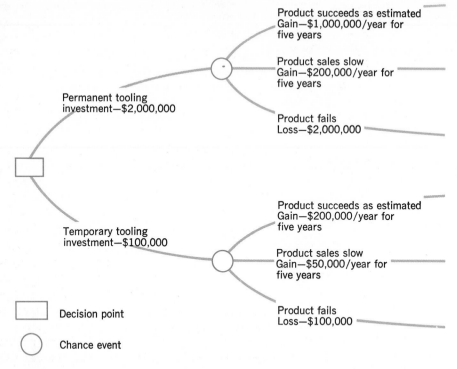

Permanent tooling
investment—$2,000,000

Product succeeds as estimated
Gain—$1,000,000/year for
five years

Product sales slow
Gain—$200,000/year for
five years

Product fails
Loss—$2,000,000

Temporary tooling
investment—$100,000

Product succeeds as estimated
Gain—$200,000/year for
five years

Product sales slow
Gain—$50,000/year for
five years

Product fails
Loss—$100,000

☐ Decision point

◯ Chance event

chance events are and what their values in terms of profits and losses are for each of the two tooling alternatives. But it is not enough to provide the visibility a person would like to have in order to decide between going for permanent tooling or more conservative temporary tooling. What is needed is an assessment of the probabilities of each course of possible events. If the probability that product sales will be as much as estimated is 60 percent, that they will be slow is 20 percent, and that the product may fail to sell is 20 percent, the manager's decision can be greatly helped. Using these probabilities, we can see that there is a 60 percent chance that an investment of $2 million will yield a net profit of $1 million per year for the assumed product life of 5 years and a similar chance that an investment of $100,000 will yield a net profit of $200,000 per year. Taking into account these probabilities, the $2 million investment has a predicted worth of $600,000 per year for the 5 years of product life assumed, and the $100,000 temporary tooling alternative a worth of $120,000 per year for 5 years. On considerations of rate of return on investment only, the temporary tooling approach would seem to be preferable. But, depending on the availability of capital, a 30 percent return on $2 million over 5 years would normally be regarded as greatly preferable to a 120 percent return on $100,000 over the same years.

There is also the possibility that if we drew a decision tree for a longer period and took into account a further chance event such as that one or more competitors would enter the market, thus putting a squeeze on prices and volume, the larger investment might look much better. With the same basic probabilities mentioned and the further probability that a vigorous competitor would enter the field, a more farsighted and complete decision tree might look like that in Figure 9.5.

As the model indicates, by calculating the value of each probability over a 5-year assumed product life (and disregarding the cost of interest and the discounting of future income), the total probability-modified return on the permanent tooling would be $1,918,000, and on the temporary tooling $360,000. While on percentage return on investment the temporary tooling approach still looks better, the higher total profits expected plus the possibility of a product life exceeding 5 years and considerations of better meeting competition might indicate that the permanent tooling program would probably be preferred. Whether this course is taken, however, would depend in large part on the extent to which the decision maker might prefer to avoid the risk of investing $2 million before a product proved itself on the market.

As chance events increase, the decision tree becomes more complicated, and the compounding of various probabilities makes the solution much more difficult. In many real-life cases a computer may even be necessary to calculate them. Also, in real life, the tree would show various decision points in the future. For example, the firm might have open the option, in case it initially followed the temporary tooling approach, to invest later in permanent tooling (at the loss of the $100,000 for temporary tooling) if product demand justified doing so. Also, it might make a decision later to reduce price, adopt a new marketing strategy, or develop a substitute improved product.

What is significant about the decision-tree approach is that it does several things for alert and intelligent decision makers. In the first place, it makes it possible for them to see at least the major alternatives open to them and the fact that subsequent decisions may depend upon events of the future. In the second place, by incorporating probabilities of various events in the tree, it is possible to comprehend the true probability of a decision leading to results desired. The "best estimate" often turns out to be quite risky.

A significant number of managers and companies have become interested in, and have explored potential applications of, decision trees. However, only a few companies have apparently used this approach to any important extent for very long. Nevertheless, growing interest in it in recent years leads some to believe that its probable use presages a new era of sharper decision making. One thing is certain: Decision trees and similar decision techniques do force replacement of broad areas of judgment with focus on the critical elements in a decision, thrust into the

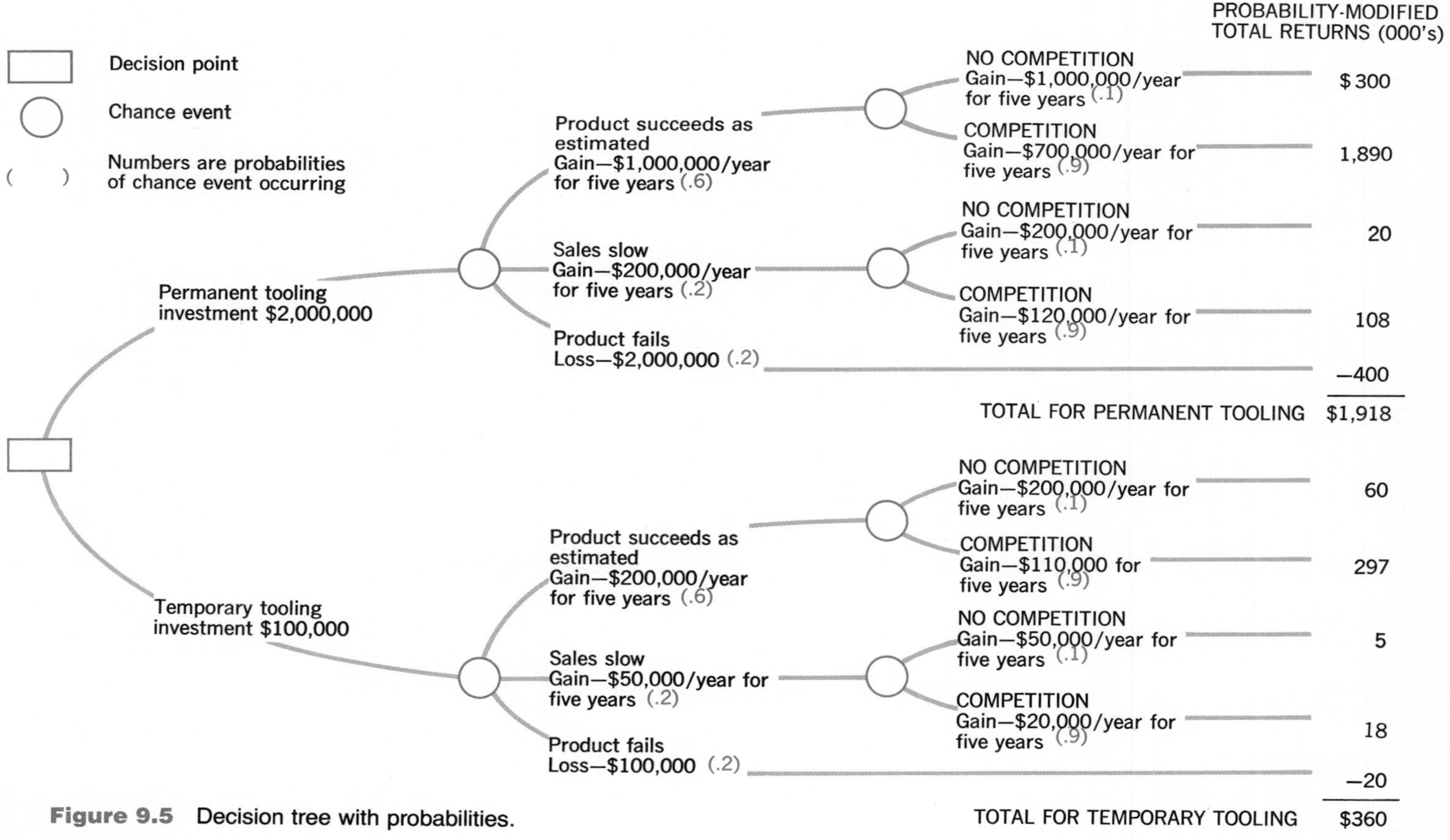

Figure 9.5 Decision tree with probabilities.

open premises often hidden in judgment, and disclose the steps in reasoning by which decisions under uncertainty are made. Some executives, long accustomed to using broad judgment, even resent these methods because they do these very things.

Preference Theory

One of the interesting and practical supplements of modern decision theory is the work that has been done and the techniques developed to supplement statistical probabilities with analysis of individual preferences in the assumption or avoidance of risk. While referred to here as "preference theory," it is more classically denoted "utility theory." Purely statistical probabilites, as applied to decision making, rest upon the questionable assumption that decision makers will follow them. It might seem reasonable that if we had a 60 percent chance of a decision being the right one, we would take it. But this is not necessarily true, since the risk of being wrong is 40 percent and a manager might not wish to take this risk, particularly if the penalty for being wrong is severe, whether in terms of monetary losses, reputation, or job security. If we doubt this, we might ask ourselves whether we would risk, say, $40,000 on the 60 percent chance that we might make $100,000. We might readily risk $4 on a chance of making $10, and gamblers have been known to risk much more on a lesser chance of success.

Therefore, in order to give probabilities practical meaning in decision making, we need better understanding of the individual decision maker's aversion to, or acceptance of, risk. This varies not only with people but also with the size of the risk, with the level of managers in an organization, and according to whether the funds involved are personal or belong to a company.

Higher-level managers are accustomed to taking larger risks than lower-level managers, and their decision areas tend to involve larger elements of risk. A company president may have to take risks of great size in launching a new product, in selecting an advertising program, or in selecting a vice president, while a first-level supervisor may have risk taking limited to hiring or promoting low-skilled workers or approving vacation times for subordinates.

Also, it can hardly be denied that the same top managers who may make a decision involving risks of millions of dollars for a company or government agency in a given program with a chance of success of, say, 75 percent would not be likely to do that with their own personal fortunes, at least unless they were very large. Moreover, the same manager willing to opt for a 75 percent risk in one case might not be willing to in another. Furthermore, a top executive may go for a large advertising program where the chances of success are 70 percent, but might not decide in favor of an investment in plant and equipment unless the probabilities for success were higher. In other words, attitudes toward risk vary with events, as well as with people and positions.

While we do not know much about attitudes toward risk, we do know that some people are risk averters in some situations and gamblers in others and that some people have by nature a high aversion to risk, and others a low one. The typical risk or preference curve may be drawn as in Figure 9.6. This set of curves shows both risk averter's and gambler's curves as well as what is referred to as a "personal" curve. The latter, of course, implies that most of us are gamblers when small stakes are involved, but soon take on the role of risk averters when the stakes rise.

Since most managers, understandably influenced by the dangers of failure, tend to be, to some extent, risk averters and do not, in fact, play the averages, it can be readily seen that statistical probabilities are not good enough for practical decision making. Indeed, as one researcher pointed out after having studied business executives' attitudes toward risk, "Our managers are not the takers of risk so often alluded to in the classical defense of the capitalistic system."[12]

Although it may be true that too many managers are risk averters and thereby miss opportunities, the fact is that few are players of pure statistical averages, at least in important decisions. Therefore, individual preference curves should be substituted for statistical probabilities in decision trees. This can be done, at least roughly, by assessing a manager's willingness to take risks in a variety of real or hypothetical situations and by developing his or her own preference curve. But even if this is not done systematically, there is certainly an important advantage for those who recommend a course of action to a superior in being aware of the effect of a manager's attitude toward risk in making decisions.

[12]R. O. Swalm, "Utility Theory: Insights into Risk Taking," *Harvard Business Review*, vol. 44, no. 6, pp. 123–136 (November–December 1966).

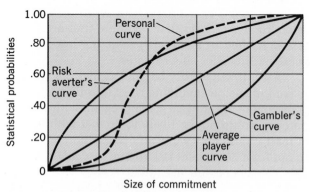

Figure 9.6　Typical preference curves.

EVALUATING THE IMPORTANCE
OF THE DECISION

Since managers not only must make correct decisions but also must make them as needed and as economically as possible, and since they must do this often, guidelines to the relative importance of decisions are useful. Decisions of lesser importance need not require thorough analysis and research, and they may even safely be delegated without endangering an individual manager's basic responsibility. The importance of a decision also depends upon the extent of reponsibility so that what may be of practically no importance to a corporation president may be of great importance to a section head.

Size or Length of Commitment

If a decision commits an enterprise to heavy expenditure of funds or to an important personnel program, such as a program for management appraisal and training, or if the commitment can be fulfilled only over a long period, such as designing and constructing a new chemical plant, it should be subjected to suitable attention at an upper level of management.

Flexibility of Plans

Some plans can be easily changed; some have built into them the easy possibility of a future change of direction; and others involve action difficult to change. Clearly, decisions involving inflexible courses of action must carry a priority over those easily changed.

Certainty of Goals and Premises

If goals and premises are fairly certain, a decision resting on them tends to be less difficult than where they are highly uncertain.

Quantifiability of Variables

Where the goals, inputs, parameters, and variables can be accurately quantified, as with definite inputs in a production machine shop, the importance of the decision, other things remaining the same, tends to be less than where the inputs are difficult to quantify, as in pricing a new consumer product or deciding on its style.

Human Impact

Where the human impact of a decision is great, its importance is high. The decision should be rated up in terms of importance, since no action contemplated for a group of people can afford to overlook its acceptance by the group.

THE POLITICS OF DECISION MAKING

Politics has been defined as the art of the possible. Good managers must be sensitive in their decision making to what they *can* do. It is not enough that a decision be logical and point to the best way of reaching a goal. The beliefs, attitudes, and prejudices of people must often be taken into account.

A few years ago, in one of the nation's major defense companies, the top management approved a commercial research project, largely to assuage the feeling of key scientific and engineering personnel that weapons development was unsocial and offered little long-range security to them. Further study disclosed both lack of resources to complete the project and a large commercial company already entrenched in the field. Faced by these facts, the board of directors decided to abandon the project, but the president considered abandonment unthinkable without adequately preparing the key people involved. Following a program for providing complete information on the project and on the available alternatives to a committee of these key people, the president was able to obtain their unanimous support for abandoning the project, when *they too* saw the practical logic of doing so.

The political environment of decisions thus rests largely on communication and is favorable when all those involved are well informed about their particular planning area. While the "need to know" has limits, the limits should be set as broadly as company or national security and the costs of information will permit. Much carping at the "stupidity" of top management decisions is eliminated when they are explained to people affected by them. Furthermore, such information helps subordinate managers make implementing decisions.

Political problems of decision making often disappear with widespread participation in planning. The widest possible participation—whether in the form of consultation, contribution of analyses, or whatever—is the best assurance that good decisions will be reached and plans intelligently and enthusiastically administered.

Recently, the idea has been advanced by some scholars that the participative approach, which is well known as a useful and motivational device, might be expanded.[13] Participation is, therefore, seen as going beyond consulting and advising and becoming an actual sharing of the decision-making process. Some even see this as the ultimate socialization

---

[13]See L. E. Preston and J. E. Post, "The Third Managerial Revolution," *Academy of Management Journal*, vol. 27, no. 3, pp. 476–486 (September 1974).

of enterprise operations, with the traditional decision-making role of managers being superseded by participant control.[14]

It is true that the more intelligent managerial decision makers will tend to rely increasingly on greater participative influence, not only from subordinates but also from the social groups and forces outside a department or the entire enterprise. With their subordinates, managers recognize that, as in the case of effective programs of managing by objectives, they have much to gain by way of knowledge of problems and solutions and by way of commitment through such participation. But few managers would regard complete decision sharing as a viable practice in view of the great dangers of weakening personal responsibility for decisions and of coming to a conclusion when many people are involved.

THE SYSTEMS APPROACH AND DECISION MAKING

Decisions cannot, of course, usually be made in a closed-system environment. As emphasized in the previous chapter on planning premises, many elements of the environment of planning lie outside the enterprise. In addition, every department or section of an enterprise is a subsystem of the entire enterprise; managers of these organizational units must be responsive to the policies and programs of other organization units and of the total enterprise. Moreover, people within the enterprise are a part of the social system, and their thinking and attitudes must be taken into account whenever a manager makes a decision.

Furthermore, even when managers construct a closed-system model, as they do with operations research optimizing models, they do so simply to have a workable problem to solve. But in doing so, they make certain assumptions as to environmental forces that importantly influence their decision, they enter inputs into their calculations as they are or appear to be at any given time, and they would logically change the construction of their model when forces and developments beyond the boundaries of their system model so require.

To say that managers take into account the various elements in the system environment of their problem does not mean, however, that they abdicate their role as decision makers. Someone must decide a course of action from among alternatives. Even though that person does take into account all sorts of events and forces in the environment of a decision, this does not mean that he or she democratizes the decision process by taking a vote from subordinates or the many other persons who may have some immediate or remote interest in the decision.

[14]See, for example, H. G. Hunt, *Interpersonal Strategies for System Management: Applications of Counseling and Participative Principles* (Monterey, Calif.: Brooks/Cole Publishing Company, 1974), and J. K. Galbraith, *Economics and the Public Purpose* (Boston: Houghton Mifflin Company, 1973).

1 Why is experience often referred to not only as an expensive basis for decision making but also a dangerous one? How can a manager make best use of experience?

2 In a decision problem you now know of, how and where would you apply the principle of the limiting factor?

3 Taking the above decision problem, whether the variables are quantifiable or not, apply operations research methodology to it in as simple form as you can. What does this do for your understanding of the problem? Does it help you solve it?

4 Take the decision problem and draw a decision tree for it.

5 Could you conceptualize an operations research problem in broad terms without the use of mathematics?

6 "Decision making is the primary task of the manager." Comment.

7 How does risk aversion affect your own life? Given a situation involving risk, can you draw your preference curve?

8 How does the systems approach help in understanding decision making?

chapter 10

Strategies and Policies

MAJOR CHAPTER OBJECTIVES

1 To understand what policies and strategies are and how they usually develop.

2 To describe the basic types of strategies and policies.

3 To show how strategies may be implemented in practice.

4 To suggest guidelines to help make strategies and policies effective in practice.

As was indicated in Chapter 6, strategies and policies are closely related. Strategies, it will be recalled, denote a general program of action and a deployment of emphasis and resources toward the attainment of comprehensive objectives. Especially when thinking of major strategies of an enterprise, they imply objectives, the deployment of resources to attain these objectives, and the major policies to be followed in using these resources. Policies were identified as guides to thinking in decision making. They assume that when decisions are made, these will fall within certain boundaries. Policies do not require action, but are intended to guide managers in their decision commitments when they do make decisions.

As will be recalled, the essence of policy is the existence of discretion. Strategy, on the other hand, concerns the direction in which human and material resources will be applied in order to maximize the chance of achieving a selected objective.

Certain major policies and strategies may be virtually coextensive. A policy to develop only new products that fit into a company's market structure or one to distribute only through retailers may be an essential element of a company's strategy for new product development or marketing. One company may have a policy of growth through acquisition of other companies, while another may have a policy of growing only by expanding present markets and products. While these are policies, they are all essential elements of major strategies. In such cases, perhaps the way to draw a meaningful distinction is to say that policies will guide thinking in decision making—if a decision is made—while strategies imply that an enterprise has made the decision to commit resources in a given direction.

It is sometimes said that there is a policy-making level of management and an administrative or operating level. This is not strictly true. Not all policy making is reserved for top management. To be sure, the higher a manager is in an organization structure, the more important his or her role in policy making is likely to be. And top managers do have the major role in making overall policies for a company or other enterprise. This is understandable since the purpose of policies is to guide decision making by subordinates. Even though managers at lower levels mainly carry out policies determined by their upper-level superiors, they may occasionally make policies on their own to guide themselves and their subordinates.

SOURCES OF STRATEGIES AND POLICIES

To understand how strategies and policies come about in a typical organization, it might be well to review their major sources. These may be classified as originated, appealed, implied, and externally imposed.

Originated

The most logical source of strategy or policy is top management, which originates it for the express purpose of guiding subordinates in their operations. Originated strategy or policy flows basically from the objectives of the enterprise, as these are defined by the top executive authority. These may be broad in scope, allowing key subordinates to give them clearer definition, or they may be promulgated so completely as to leave little room for definition and interpretation. The extent to which they are centralized or decentralized is obviously dependent upon the extent to which authority is concentrated or dispersed.

Characterizing a strategy or policy as originated does not necessarily imply that it is imposed by command. Many are the adroit managers who originate them and obtain compliance by making unobtrusive suggestions. In fact, some skillful managers originate strategy or policy and secure compliance by allowing subordinate managers to leave a conference believing that they themselves originated it. But often a strategy or policy is imposed upon subordinates with a force and clarity that permit no deviation. Thus, a company president might originate a policy of using sales agents on a commission basis, rather than full-time sales people, by merely making indirect suggestions along this line to a sales manager; or, in another instance, the president might be positive and blunt in stating a policy that the company will not engage in price-cutting to make a sale.

Appealed

In practice, perhaps most policy and even some strategies stem from appeal of exceptional cases up the hierarchy of managerial authority. If occasions for decision arise for executives who do not know whether they have sufficient authority or how the matter should be handled, they may appeal to their superior. As appeals are taken upward and decisions are made on them, a kind of common law is established. Precedents develop and become guides for future managerial action.

Policies or strategies developed from appeals are sometimes incomplete, uncoordinated, and confused. If decisions are made on a given set of facts without regard for their possible effects on other aspects of the operation, or if unintended precedents develop from them, the resulting policies may not guide the thought and action of subordinates as really desired by top managers. Moreover, policies, or even strategies, may be formulated that the top executives do not even know about. For example, in one company there existed a long-time strategy of marketing strictly on a quality basis and never engaging in price-cutting. In a particularly strong competitive period, the chief executive gave the sales manager the right to cut prices to meet some aggressive competition. After permitting this on several occasions, he found that he had, for all intents and purposes, changed the company's marketing strategy to that of being an industry price-cutter.

The aimless formulation of policy or strategy arising from appeals, caused by management's not having in mind a clear reason or goal, explains in part why it is usually so difficult to know exactly what policies exist. As analysts have come to find out in attempting to compile policy manuals, many managers simply do not know company policy in many areas. This arises partly because policy formulation is by nature complex and partly because many managers dislike to meet issues until forced to do so and thereby delay policy making until a body of precedent from individual decisions accumulates.

Appealed strategy or policy may be foresighted and internally consistent, especially if managers realize that their decision constitutes a strategy or a policy. However, when they find themselves constantly making these by appeal, they might well ask whether they have left too large an area to chance and whether their subordinates have really understood what they may have had in mind.

Implied

It is not unusual for policy and even strategy to develop from actions which people see about them and believe to constitute them. Employees will readily understand what is real policy if they work for an enterprise that has published policies to produce high-quality goods, to maintain plant cleanliness, or to promote from within, and yet permits the contrary action. Its real policies, or the lack of them, are implied.

Different circumstances account for the development of implied strategy or policy. It may be that stated strategy or policy is simply not put in practice. It may be that the enterprise states a certain strategy or policy in order to create a desired image, but is unable or unwilling to enforce it. It is suspected that in most cases, implied strategies or policies develop where no clear strategy or policy exists. Decision makers will adopt their own guidelines as they interpret the actions of their superiors.

For example, the top managers of a certain company earnestly solicited new product ideas, especially from its marketing and engineering groups. The response was generous. Each idea was subjected to complex investigatory procedures and was judged by conservative standards. Most were rejected, and no explanations were made. Even key people in the firm came to believe that it was company policy to confine new products to low-risk items. This imputed policy, which was quite contrary to what the firm really wanted, became the guideline for new product decisions.

Externally Imposed

To a rapidly increasing extent, strategy or policy is being externally imposed by government, trade unions, and trade associations. Whether in the form of direct regulation, the competition of government-owned or government-supported business, or the many conditions for accepting government aids or contracts, the result is to circumscribe and dictate many aspects of strategy or policy. Strong national unions, operating through collective bargaining and detailed labor contracts, have also imposed policy upon managers. Besides, thousands of local, regional, and national associations have their effect in varying degrees on policy. Other social groups—such as church, school, fraternal, social, and charitable organizations—may also mold or dictate an enterprise's strategy or policy.

STRATEGIES AND POLICIES GIVE DIRECTION TO PLANS

As indicated above, it is the key function of strategies and policies to give a unified direction to plans. In other words, they influence where an enterprise is trying to go. But, standing alone, they do not assure that a company or other organization will, in fact, go where it wants to go.

Strategies and Policies Furnish the Framework of Plans

Strategies and policies do furnish the framework for plans by channeling operating decisions and often predeciding them. It follows, then, that *the more strategies and policies are carefully developed and clearly understood, the more consistent and effective will be the framework of plans.* If this framework really exists and if this principle is actually followed in practice, consistency in action and efficiency in the employment of resources would replace much of the conflict in action and the dissipation of resources which often occurs. For example, if a company has a major policy of developing only new products that fit its marketing organization, it will avoid wasting energies and resources on new products that do not meet this test.

The Need for Operational Planning: Tactics

To be effective, strategies and policies require operational plans, increasing in detail until the enterprise gets down to the "nuts and bolts" of its operations. In other words, to use the military term "tactics" (the action plans by which strategies are executed), a strategy may be good, but fail through poor execution. For example, the immensely successful Volkswagen Company attempted to enter the medium-sized luxury-car market in part by planning to produce a luxury rotary-engine car. But the Wankel engine on the expensive R-80 NSU model car was inadequately engineered, and the company lost millions of dollars as a result.

Likewise, as General Robert E. Wood, who came to the helm of Sears,

Roebuck in 1924, found when he developed the strategy of centralizing purchasing and merchandising but decentralizing operations through a large number of retail department stores, it took years of careful operational planning to make this strategy effective. Changing the company from a predominantly centralized mail-order operation to a large retail-store chain with some centralized control at headquarters but considerable decentralized control at the store level required a large number of qualified managers. General Wood found that it took 10 years of careful operational planning to find and develop the needed store managers.

Strategy and Policy Affect All Areas of Managing

The influence of strategies and policies on actual planning is, of course, extensive and considerable. However, strategies and policies also have a great effect on other areas of managing. For example, major strategies and policies will naturally influence organization structure and, through this, other functions of the manager. In his extraordinary analysis of the history of some of the nation's largest companies, Chandler depicts in detail how strategy affected organization structure.[1] In the Du Pont Company, the organization around product lines, with centralized control, followed the strategy of product diversification. It did essentially the same in General Motors. However, in Du Pont the strategy of diversification was dictated by the need to use resources made surplus by the post-World War I decline in the explosives business. In General Motors, on the other hand, the strategy was one of integration and expansion of a disparate group of many companies acquired by W. C. Durant in his formation of the company during the two decades before 1920. While the strategies of these two companies were based on different premises and situations, they led to essentially the same organization structures.

THE BASIC TYPES OF STRATEGIES AND POLICIES

Although as generally used the term "strategies" implies broad, overall direction for the planning and operation of a business or other kind of enterprise, it should not be overlooked that there are several basic types. The most important are, indeed, major overall strategies and policies. But there are also supporting, or derivative strategies and policies, and one finds also some that may be regarded as minor. In addition, most enterprises have a composite of strategies and policies. Moreover, in view of possible changes in the environment in which plans are expected to operate, some may be of a contingency nature.

---

[1]Alfred D. Chandler, Jr., *Strategy and Structure* (Cambridge, Mass.: The M.I.T. Press, 1962). In this excellent historical study, the author analyzes the history of Du Pont, General Motors, Standard Oil Company (New Jersey), and Sears, Roebuck and shows how in each case organization structure followed and reflected strategy.

Major strategies and policies are those which give a unified direction to an entire enterprise and imply a commitment of resources. Of course, they should all be supportive of the enterprise's mission or purpose. In a business, there are likely to be dominant strategies and policies in the areas of marketing, the development of new products, financial resources, human resources, and capital facilities. In a military operation, the major strategies and policies are likely to be those involving the availability and deployment of personnel and equipment.

In other words, major strategies and policies are those which give the primary shape to an enterprise in its accomplishment of purpose. If a company has a basic marketing strategy, as the Procter and Gamble Company does, to presell consumers through heavy advertising and sales promotion, this will dictate various other supporting strategies. Because of the heavy investment in advertising and promotion, it is clear that new products must be carefully developed and tested and must meet consumer needs and demands. It is also clear that a company cannot be a price-cutter so that it can afford to spend money on advertising and promotion.

Derivative, or Supporting, Strategies and Policies

In any enterprise there is a need for various strategies and policies that depend on, and are supportive to, major strategies and policies and yet act as guides to thinking and action and give support to unified planning in certain areas. For example, a supporting policy in the Procter and Gamble Company is to place overall planning responsibility for a product in the hands of an advertising brand manager and have it understood by all concerned, including the sales department, that the function of all departments is to follow the lead of the brand manager.

In another company, which had a major strategy of being product leader in the air-filtration business for industrial and commercial applications, the strategy of the market research department was to search out areas of unfilled customer needs, and the strategy of the product research laboratories was to keep in the forefront in technological development in their areas, in part by keeping close contact with certain of the sophisticated filter material manufacturers.

Minor Policies and Strategies

There may be many minor strategies and policies in a typical enterprise. Office managers may follow a strategy of leasing filing cases and typewriters when they cannot get capital expenditures approved for these items. Supervisors may develop a policy in their units of occasionally allowing workers with good attendance records to take short periods of time off with pay for personal errands. Other examples of minor strategies and policies come easily to mind. They do give direction and guidance to decision making and action, but they are certainly not of overall importance to a company, and they may not even be supportive to a company's major strategies or policies.

Composite Strategies and Policies

Most enterprises have a composite of strategies and policies. In other words, they have no single strategy or policy, but rather a group of strategies and policies. Thus the typical business, as noted above, will have strategies and policies in the areas of marketing, new products, finance, human resources, and capital facilities.

For example, a company might plan to diversify through having a variety of specialized products in the consumer textile field. It may also have a strategy of achieving this diversification through well-selected acquisitions, obtained by an exchange of shares of stock. This in turn may be closely related to a strategy of aggressive consumer marketing and the maintenance of high profit margins to support high share prices. Another policy important to this effort might be to select and train highly qualified and entrepreneurially oriented managerial personnel and reward them extensively through bonuses based on company growth and profits. Because of its strategic emphasis on growth by acquisition, the company might also have a product strategy of improving present products and keeping them up to date, rather than developing new products. The important thing is that these strategies and policies are consistent, that is, that they "fit."

Contingency Strategies

The alert business, army, or other kind of enterprise will be well advised to develop, and have ready for implementation, contingency strategies. In other words, in case the environment in which enterprise plans are designed to work is not accurately forecast and assessed and if the strategy developed therefore becomes obsolete or otherwise unsuitable, a contingency strategy should indicate in what direction the enterprise should then go. For example, the appliance discount stores had a strategy of selling a wide variety of trademarked items at a considerable discount. After a fairly long period of success, some of these stores did not have an alternative strategy when the large department stores offered similar discounts plus the advantages of reputation, consumer credit, many locations in large cities, and more complete servicing facilities.

Planning for alternative strategies is simply good planning. There are almost always unexpected contingencies. The business or other organization that knows what it will do if things change—that has answered the question of "what if" with solid contingency plans—will understandably be on a more solid road to success.

Strategies and Policies Vary in Practice

Although the essential elements of the process of making strategies and policies may be the same and although their role in giving direction and framework to plans are of a universal application, their content and approach may differ widely. Just as no theory or set of principles, even though universal in nature, results in any single best way, there is not necessarily a single best strategy or major policy for all enterprises. As in other areas of managing, these depend on the situation or the contingencies involved.

We can find many examples in business. Avon has built a successful company on the marketing strategy of using a large cadre of women who sell cosmetics directly to users. Another successful cosmetics firm, Revlon, has built its success on a strategy of advertising and marketing through stores, along with strong product planning and brand-name identification. Ford has followed a strategy of organizing its automotive business around functional departments, while General Motors has used product divisions. Both companies have been successful, even though they use different strategies.

All that this means, as the systems theorists say, is that systems may be characterized by "equifinality." In other words, there may be different ways to achieve success, even in the same industry.

THE SPECIAL IMPORTANCE OF STRATEGIES[2]

It is widely agreed that the development and communication of strategy are among the most important activities of top managers. As Ross and Kami, in their insightful book on the lack of success of many large companies in the United States, have said, "Without a strategy the organization is like a ship without a rudder, going around in circles. It's like a tramp; it has no place to go."[3] Indeed, they ascribe most business failures to lack of strategy, or the wrong strategy, or lack of implementation of a reasonably good strategy. They conclude from their study that without an appropriate strategy effectively implemented, failure is a matter of time.

With all their admitted importance, there have been many disillusionments concerning strategies, their development, and implementation. The concept of what strategies are is often of little value and even meaningless, even though the term may be constantly mouthed by academics and executives. As one prominent consultant declared, particularly with respect to strategic planning, "In the large majority of

---

[2]Much of this section is drawn from Harold Koontz, "Making Strategies Planning Work," *Business Horizons*, vol. 19, no. 2, pp. 37–47 (April 1976).

[3] J. E. Ross and M. J. Kami, *Corporations in Crisis: Why the Mighty Fall* (Englewood Cliffs, N.J.: Prentice-Hall, Inc., 1973), p. 132.

companies, corporate planning tends to be an academic, ill-defined activity with little or no bottom-line impact."[4]

Many corporate chief executive officers have brushed strategic planning aside by such statements as "strategic planning is basically just a plaything of staff people," or "Strategic planning? A staggering waste of time."[5]

The authors have seen a number of companies and even some government agencies that have tried strategic planning, only to wallow in generalities, unproductive studies, and programs that do not get into practical operation. In one large company, a far too patient president watched a succession of top planning officers and their staffs founder for 12 years, until his patience was finally exhausted and he insisted on practical action.

Disillusionment with strategic planning seems to result from failure to understand fully (1) what strategies are and why they are important, (2) how strategies fit into the entire planning process, (3) how to develop strategies, and (4) how to implement strategies by bringing them to bear on current decisions.

Areas of the Major Kinds of Strategies

For a business enterprise certainly, and with some modification for other kinds of organizations as well, the major strategies which give an overall direction to a company are likely to be in the following areas.

New or changed products and services A business exists to furnish products or services of an economic nature. In a very real sense, profits are merely a measure—albeit an important one—of how well a company serves its customers by doing so.

Marketing Marketing strategies are designed to guide planning in getting products or services to customers, to get them to buy, and to reach them.

Growth Growth strategies give direction to such questions as how much growth and how fast, where, and how.

Financial Every business, and for that matter any nonbusiness, enterprise must have a clear strategy as to how to finance its operations. There are various ways of doing this and usually many serious limitations.

Organizational This kind of strategy has to do with the type of organizational pattern an enterprise will use. It answers such practical

[4]L. V. Gerstner, "Can Strategic Planning Pay Off?" *Business Horizons,* vol. 15, no. 6, pp. 5–16 (December 1972).
[5]Ibid., p. 5.

questions as how centralized or decentralized decision-making authority should be, what kinds of departmental patterns are most suitable, whether to develop integrated, profit-responsible divisions, the use of matrix organization structures, and effective design of staff. Naturally, organization structures should furnish the system of roles and role relationships that help people to accomplish objectives.

Personnel Major strategies in the area of human resources and relationships may be of a wide variety. They deal with such topics as union relations, compensation, selection, recruitment, training, and appraisal, as well as strategy in special areas such as job enrichment.

Public relations Strategies in this area can hardly be independent but must support other major strategies and efforts. They must also be designed in the light of the company's type of business, its closeness to the public, its susceptibility to regulation by government agencies, and similar factors.

REQUIREMENTS FOR DEVELOPING EFFECTIVE STRATEGIES

For developing major strategies of any kind, there are a number of key requirements. Without meeting them, a company's strategic planning program is likely to be meaningless or even incorrect.

Corporate Self-Appraisal

Corporate Self-Appraisal essentially involves asking these two questions: What is our business? What kind of business are we in? These simple questions are not always easy to answer, as many businesses have found out.[6] The classic case is the railroad industry that too long overlooked the fact that its companies were in the transportation business, not just the railroad business. Glass bottle manufacturers in the United States almost missed their opportunities by seeing themselves for too long as glass bottle makers rather than liquid container manufacturers, while plastic and metal containers came to be used in many applications in place of glass. Likewise, many believe that steel companies have too long held the belief that they are steelmakers rather than firms in the structural materials business, which includes many materials not made of steel.

To answer questions about its identity, a company must look at itself as a total entity, analyzing strengths and weaknesses in each functional area—marketing, product development, production and other operations

---

[6]As a matter of fact, many nonbusiness enterprises could and should ask this style of question. Universities could gain insights as could virtually every government agency.

areas, finance, and public relations. It must focus attention on its customers and what they want and can buy, on its technological capabilities, and financial resources. In addition, note must be made of the values, aspirations, and prejudices of top executives.

In assessing strengths, weaknesses, and limitations, an enterprise must, of course, be realistic. In doing so, however, there is danger of overstressing weaknesses and underestimating strengths. History is replete with examples of companies that have spent so much effort shoring up weaknesses that they did not capitalize on their strengths. To be sure, weaknesses should be corrected to the extent possible. But identifying strengths and taking advantage of them in formulating strategies offer the most promise.

Assessing the Future Environment

Since strategies are intended to operate in the future, the best possible estimate of the future environment is necessary. If a company can match its strengths with the environment in which it plans to operate, opportunities can be detected and taken advantage of.

To assess the future environment we must forecast it. In general, modern businesses do a fairly good job of forecasting economic developments and markets, although there can be many errors and uncertainties. Not many would have forecast the price impact of the oil-producing nations' cartel and the extent of inflation in recent years. A few companies have found rewarding results in forecasting technological changes and developments. Some companies, such as those in highly regulated industries, have even forecast political environments, particularly what actions affecting them a government body will probably take and when. But only recently have companies, research institutes, and government agencies even started to attempt any broad forecasting of social attitudes and pressures.

Clearly, the better an enterprise can foresee its total environment, the better it can prepare for the future through establishing strategies and supporting plans to take advantage of its capabilities in the light of the environment. However, experience to date indicates that, except for economic and market forecasts, it has been difficult to get the forecast and assessment of other environmental factors into practical use. While this can be done through an active and effective program of being sure that planning premises are developed and actually used as the background for decision making, this is one of the areas of planning that has not been done especially well.

An important element of any future environment, of course, is the probable action of competition. Too often, however, we premise our planning on what competition has been doing and not on what competitors may be expected to do. Planners can never assume that their competitors are asleep.

If strategies are to be developed and effectuated, we need organizational arrangements assuring effective planning. Staff assistance is important for forecasting, establishing premises, and making analyses. But there is a danger of establishing a planning staff and thinking that planning exists when all we have are planning studies, and not the decisions based on them.

To avoid ivory-towered and useless staff efforts, several things are needed. A planning staff should be given the tasks of developing major objectives, strategies, and planning premises and submitting them to top management for review and approval. It should be given the responsibility for disseminating approved premises and strategies and for helping operating people to understand them. Also, before major decisions, especially those of a long-range or strategic impact, are made, the staff group should be given the task of reviewing them and making recommendations. As can be seen, taking these steps can force decision makers to consider environmental factors and can keep the advisers from becoming a detached and impractical group.

Another major organizational device is the regular, formal, and rigorous review of planning programs and performance, preferably by an appropriate committee. This has long been done in well-managed divisionalized companies where division general managers are called in before a top executive committee. And perhaps it should be done at lower levels. Doing so has the advantage of forcing people to plan, of making sure that strategies are being followed by programs, and, where strategies do not exist or are unclear, making this deficiency apparent.

Assuring Consistent Strategies

One of the important requirements of effective strategic planning is to make sure that strategies are consistent, that they "fit" each other. For example, one medium-sized company had a successful sales record as the result of a strategy of putting out quality products at lower prices than its larger competitors, who had done their selling through heavy and expensive advertising. Pleased with this success, and after adding to its product line through acquisitions, the company then embarked on an additional strategy of trying to sell through heavy advertising, with disastrous effects on profits.

The Need for Contingency Strategies

Because every strategy must operate in the future and the future is always subject to uncertainty, the need for contingency strategies cannot be overlooked. If a regulated telephone company, for example, has some of its services suddenly opened to competition (this did happen recently in the United States when other companies were allowed to furnish telephone facilities that were once the monopoly of the telephone companies) and adopts a strategy of aggressive competition, on the assumption that regulatory commissions will allow competitive pricing, the strategy will become inoperative if the commissions do not actually allow such pricing. Or if a company develops a strategy based on a certain state of technology and a new discovery materially changes the technological environment, it is faced with a major change.

Where events might occur to render a strategy obsolete, and they often can without warning, it is wise to develop a contingent strategy based on a different set of premises. These are the "what-if" kinds of strategies, supported by contingency plans that can be put into effect quickly and avoid much of the crisis management we see so often.

DEVELOPING MAJOR STRATEGIES

To develop strategies in any area, we must ask certain questions. To get the right answers, the right questions must be asked. While no prescribed set of strategies can be formulated that will fit all organizations and situations, certain key questions can be asked that will help any company to discover what its strategies should be.

To show how the right questions can lead to answers, it is proposed here to raise some key questions in only two major strategic areas: new products and services and marketing. A little thought can result in devising key questions for other major strategic areas.

Products or Services

One of the most important areas is new products or services since these, more than any other single factor, will determine what a company or other enterprise is or will be. The key questions in this area may be summarized as follows.

What is our business? This classic question might also be phrased in terms of what is *not* our business. It is also well to ask: What is our *industry*? Are we a single product or product-line industry, such as shoes or furniture? Or are we a process industry, such as chemicals or electronic components? Or are we an end-use industry, such as transportation or retailing?

Who are our customers? To further identify what kind of business we are in and to give meaning to a product or service strategy, this is an especially key question. Peter Drucker has long said that the purpose of a business is to "create a customer," although he could hardly have meant to create customers without regard to profits. In answering this question, it is important to avoid too great an attachment to *present* customers and products. The motion picture industry did this at first when home television appeared on the market and was seen as a threat to movie theaters. Industry leaders fought television for years until they realized that their business was entertainment and their customers wanted motion pictures both in theaters and on television. They then found one of their most lucrative markets in renting old movies to television and in using their studios and other facilities for producing television shows.

What do our customers want? An effective strategy must be based on knowing what customers want. Do they want price, value, quality, availability, service? The success of the Hughes Tool Company, for example, has been based largely on making a shrewd analysis of what oil- and gas-well drillers wanted and furnishing them the exact drill bit they wanted, of a high quality, in the place the bit was needed, and with adequate service to support the product. Likewise, International Buiness Machines leadership in business computers has in large part been due to knowing what its customers wanted and needed, supplying it, maintaining advancement of product design, having a family of computers, and running a strong service organization.

How much will our customers buy at what price? This is a matter of what customers *think* they are buying; what they consider value, and what they will pay for it will determine what a business is, what it should produce, and whether it will prosper. Being able to answer this kind of question, particularly after identifying a business and who its customers really are, will be a major key to a product or service strategy.

Do we wish to be a product leader? This may seem to be a question with an obvious answer. But it is not. In developing and marketing their products, some companies owe their success to being a close second in product leadership. The product leader will often have an advantage in reaching a market first, but such a company may incur heavy costs of developing and attempting to market products which do not become commercial successes as well as those which do. One of the major airlines, for example, prided itself for years on being the leader in acquiring and putting into service new aircraft. But after undergoing extensive "debugging" of several new planes, and suffering financial losses as a result, the company adopted the strategy of letting someone else be the leader and of becoming a close second.

Do we wish to develop our own new products? Here again, a company must address itself to the question of whether it is better for it to develop its own new products, whether it should rely on innovation by competitors to show the way, or whether it should lean heavily on product development by materials suppliers. In the chemicals field, for example, such innovative raw materials producers as Du Pont and Dow Chemical discover new chemical compositions and then cast about to ascertain where they can be used in new products. Companies without adequate resources to mount a strong product research program can often find a gold mine of product ideas in the development of such suppliers.

What advantages do we have in serving customer needs? This is a difficult and important question. Most companies like to have a product or service that competitors cannot very easily duplicate. Some larger companies look only for products that require a high capital investment in tooling and machinery, heavy advertising, strong engineering, expensive service organizations, and similar characteristics that tend to discourage the entry of smaller competitors into a market. Many larger companies also purposefully keep out of products with small volume markets that can be manufactured and marketed by small companies, believing that the small operator can offer a personalized service and incur lower overhead costs than the larger company.

What of existing and potential competition? In deciding on a product strategy, it is important to realistically assess the nature and strength of existing competition. If a competitor in a field has tremendous strength in new products, marketing, and service, as International Business Machines has had in the computer field, a company should carefully consider whether it has a chance to enter the field effectively. Even the very large RCA Corporation found it had to swallow a loss of some $450 million after unsuccessfully attempting to compete with IBM with a head-on strategy.

How far can we go in serving customer needs? Product strategy formulation must consider this question. There are often important limitations. One is, of course, financial, and a company must consider whether it has the financial resources to support necessary product research, manufacturing facilities, inventory and receivables, advertising and marketing, and a requisite service competence.

Legal limitations may also be important, as Procter and Gamble found when it was forced by the antitrust laws to divest itself of its acquisition of the Clorox Company (makers of household bleach). Or, as certain pharmaceutical companies have found when they have been held up in introducing new drugs by the Food and Drug Administration.

Other important limitations may be found in the availability of suitably competent managers and other personnel. Thus, Ford, a well-managed automobile company, had difficulties in managing Philco, primarily a radio and television company. Litton Industries apparently found itself beyond its managerial abilities in running a shipbuilding subsidiary.

What profit margins can we expect?   A company naturally wants to be in a business where it can make an attractive profit. One of the keys is the gross profit margin, that profit above operating expenses which will carry overhead and administrative expenses and yield a desired profit before taxes.

What basic form should our strategy take?   In formulating a product or service strategy, a company should determine the direction it wishes to go in terms of intensive or extensive product diversification. If it follows an *intensive* strategy, it might move in the direction of market penetration—going further in present product markets. Or it might decide on one of market development—going into markets it has not been in. Thus, Reynolds Aluminum years ago expanded into such consumer products as aluminum kitchen wrappings. Or a company might concentrate on developing, improving, or changing products it already has.

If a company follows an *extensive* product strategy, it has three basic directions to go. First, it might concentrate on *vertical integration*. If it is a retailing company it might, as Sears, Roebuck has done so much, go into making the products it sells. Or, if it is a manufacturing company, it might go into retailing, as Sinclair Paints has done. Second, a company might diversify extensively by *link diversification*, going into products utilizing existing skills, capacities, and strengths. Lever Brothers, for example, has done this for many years by expanding its operations to a large number of products marketed through grocery stores. A third kind of extensive strategy is *conglomerate diversification*, going into not necessarily related products with the hope of getting synergistic advantages from combining such skills and strengths as marketing, new product development, management, and financial resources. The difficulty with this strategy, as many conglomerates have found out, is that too rapid and too varied a program of acquisition can lead to situations that cannot be effectively and profitably managed.

Marketing

Marketing strategies are closely related to product strategies. These must be supportive and interrelated. As a matter of fact, Drucker regards the two basic business functions as *innovation* and *marketing*. It is true that a business can hardly survive without at least one of these and preferably both. A company can succeed by copying products, but it can hardly succeed without effective marketing. And, as the world has become increasingly competitive, it is true that marketing has become the tail that wags the company dog.

In this area, as in products and services, certain questions can serve as guides for establishing a marketing strategy.

Where are our customers and why do they buy?   This question is really asking who our customers are, whether they are large or small buyers, whether they are end-users or manufacturers, where they are geographically, where they are in the production–ultimate-user system, and why they buy. These are difficult but important questions. Xerox answered some of them cleverly and effectively when it saw its customers not as copy machine buyers but rather as purchasers of convenient low-cost copies. As a result of its leasing program and charging on a per copy basis, this company has had a phenomenal success. Likewise, the Farr Company, one of the nation's most innovative and successful air filter companies, has effectively marketed its engine air filters for locomotives and trucks by the strategy of seeing its real customers as the ultimate users rather than the equipment manufacturers. By getting large railroads and trucking companies to specify its filters on new equipment, Farr, in effect, forced equipment manufacturers to buy and install its filters.

How do customers buy?   Some customers buy largely through specialized distributing organizations, as is so much the case with medical and hospital supplies. Some buy through dealer organizations, as with automobiles. Others are accustomed to buying directly from manufacturers, as in the case of major defense procurement, large equipment buyers, and most raw material users in such fields as chemicals, electronic components, and steel products, though even in these cases, specialized distributors and processors may be important for certain buyers and at certain times.

How is it best for us to sell?   There are a number of approaches to selling. Some companies rely heavily on preselling through advertising and sales promotion. Procter and Gamble, for example, owes much of its success to a strategy of preselling customers through heavy advertising and sales promotion expenditures (said to average 20 percent of every sales dollar). At the same time, a much smaller company in the soap and detergents field, the Purex Corporation, had great success in selling its liquid and dry detergents through the appeal of lower consumer prices and higher profit margins for retailers. Other companies may find their best sales strategy to sell on the basis of technical superiority and direct engineering contacts with customers.

Do we have something to offer that competitors do not?   The purpose of product differentiation is, of course, to make buyers *believe* we have something different and better than similar products offered by competitors, whether in fact we do or not. It is also often possible to build a marketing strategy on having some feature in a product or service that is different, regardless of the significance of the difference. This may be an attractive innovation in product design or quality, as in the case of Sylvania's push-button television sets. Or it might be an innovation in service, such as American Motors' all-inclusive automobile warranty a few years ago. Obviously, what every marketer wants is something for which a claim of uniqueness may be made in order to obtain a proprietary position.

Do we wish to take legal steps to discourage competition? There are many things a company can do to discourage competition, other than to run afoul of the antitrust or fair trade laws. Mere size and the ability to finance expensive specialized machinery and tools, or a geographically spread sales and service organization are among these. The success of the Hughes Tool Company in oil drilling bits and that of International Business Machines in the computer field fall into this category. But even medium-sized companies can discourage very small would-be competitors in the same way. Or a company's marketing strategy might be helped by innovative advertising and product image, which will entrench a company in a market and discourage competition.

Do we need, and can we supply, supporting services? A company's effectiveness in marketing can be greatly influenced by the degree of need for supporting services, such as maintenance, and the ability to supply them. The slowness of certain foreign-made automobiles to get a position in the American market was often caused by the lack of dealer repair services. Mercedes-Benz, for example, had difficulty in making much of a dent in this market until the company was able to establish service capabilities in at least the larger cities of the United States. Packard Bell enjoyed a strong position in television in the Western states some years ago because of its strong service organization in this area; and because of this, for years limited sales to that area. The major telephone companies, the Bell System and General Telephone, have recently developed a strategy of marketing industrial and commercial switchboard systems against the rising competition of special equipment manufacturers by emphasizing their capability to give prompt and competent maintenance service.

What is the best pricing strategy and policy for our operation? The strategy and policy adopted with respect to pricing are naturally important to any marketing strategy. But a variety of strategies can be used: Suggested list prices, quantity and other discounts, delivered or FOB, seller's place-of-business prices, firm prices, or prices with escalation, the extent of down payments with orders, or prices that vary with labor and material costs are among the wide number of variations. How goods or services are priced may be a matter of custom in a market, a marketing tool of a supplier, a matter of achieving price stability versus price-cutting, or may reflect the understandable desire of a producer to guard against losses from uncertainty, as in the case of "time and material" contracts.

It is one thing to develop clear and meaningful strategies. It is another matter, and one of very great practical importance, to implement strategies effectively. It appears that, if strategic planning is to be operational, certain steps must be taken to implement it.

Strategies Should Be Communicated to All Key Decision-Making Managers

It naturally does little good to formulate meaningful strategies unless they are communicated to all those managers who are in a position to make decisions on programs and plans designed to implement them. Nothing is communicated unless it is clear to the receiver. Strategies may be clear to the executive committee and the chief executive who participate in making them. But they should be in writing, and enough meetings should be held by top executives and their subordinates to make sure that strategies are understood by those who must make programs to implement them.

Planning Premises Must Be Developed and Communicated

The importance of planning premises has been emphasized earlier. Premises critical to plans and decisions must be developed and disseminated to all managers in the decision-making chain with instructions to generate programs and make decisions in line with them. Too few companies and other organizations do this. But if it is not done and if premises do not include key assumptions about the entire spectrum of the environment in which plans will operate, decisions are likely to be based on personal assumptions and predilections. The result is almost certain to be a collection of uncoordinated plans.

Action Plans Must Contribute to and Reflect Major Objectives and Strategies

Action plans are tactical or operational programs and decisions, whether major or minor, that take place in various parts of an organization. If they are not made to reflect desired objectives and strategies, vague hopes or useless statements of strategic intent result. If care is not taken in this area, then certainly strategic planning is not likely to have a bottom-line impact.

There are various ways of making sure that action plans do contribute. If every manager understands strategies, he or she can certainly review the program recommendations of staff advisers and line subordinates to see that they contribute and are consistent. It might even be well, at least in major decisions, to have them reviewed by an appropriate small committee, such as one including a subordinate's superior, the superior's superior, and a staff specialist. This would lend an aura of formality to the program decision, and important influences on implementation of strategies might become clear. Budgets likewise should be reviewed with objectives and strategies in mind.

Strategies Should Be Regularly Reviewed

Even carefully developed strategies might cease to be suitable if events change, knowledge becomes more clear, or it appears that the program environment will not be as originally thought. Thus, strategies should be reviewed from time to time, certainly not less than once a year for major strategies and perhaps more often.

Consider Developing Contingency Strategies and Programs

Where considerable change in competitive factors or other elements in the environment might occur, and it is impracticable to develop strategies and programs to cover such contingencies, strategies for such contingencies should be formulated. No one, of course, can wait until a future is certain to make plans. Even where there is considerable uncertainty and events may occur that make a given set of objectives, strategies, or programs obsolete, we have no choice but to proceed on the most credible set of premises we can come up with. But this does not mean that we need find ourselves totally unprepared if certain possible contingencies do occur.

Make Organization Structure Fit Planning Needs

The organization structure with its system of delegations should be designed as much as possible to support the accomplishment of goals and the making of decisions to implement strategies. It is best, if it can be done, for one person to be responsible for the accomplishment of each goal and for implementing strategies in achieving this goal. In other words, end-result areas and key tasks should be identified and assigned to a single position as far down the organization structure as is feasible. Since this sometimes cannot be done, there may be no alternative but to utilize a form of matrix organization. But, where this is done, the responsibilities of the various positions in the matrix should be clearly spelled out.

In an organization structure, also, the role of staff analysts and advisers should be so defined and used that staff studies and recommendations enter the decision system at the various points where decisions are actually made. Unless this is done, we end up with independent staff work of no value for planning.

Even where we may have a workable system of objectives and strategies and their implementation, it is easy for it to fail unless responsible managers continue to teach their nature and importance. This may seem like a tedious process and unnecessary repetition, but learning can be ensured in no other way. Teaching does not mean necessarily formal meetings or seminars. Rather, much of the necessary teaching can take place in the day-to-day consideration and review of planning proposals and in the review of performance as superiors undertake their normal control functions.

Create a Company Climate That Forces Planning

As mentioned earlier, people tend to allow problems and crises that arise today to postpone effective planning for tomorrow. Therefore, as is discussed in the following chapter, the only way to ensure that planning of all kinds will be done, and especially the implementation of strategies, is to utilize devices and techniques that force planning.

Strategic planning can be made to have a bottom-line impact. Effective top managers can ensure this if they develop strategies carefully and take pains for their implementation. In fact, if a company or any other kind of organization is to be successful over a period of time, it really has no other alternative.

FOR DISCUSSION

1 How can you distinguish between strategies and policies?
2 Why are these types of plans especially important?
3 It has been found that most middle managers are anxious for a business or other organization to develop and publish clear policies. Can you see any reasons why this should be the case?
4 Are strategies and policies as important in a nonbusiness enterprise (such as a labor union, the federal Department of State, a hospital, or a city fire department) as in a business? Why and how?
5 Why are contingency strategies important?
6 How would you go about formulating a company's major strategies?
7 How can strategies be effectively implemented?

chapter 11 Making Planning Effective

No one would deny the importance of good planning in any kind of enterprise and every department of it. Without planning there is no place for the enterprise to go, for the simple reason that no one knows where it is intended to go. Yet, despite the obvious importance of planning, it is still perhaps the least well done part of managing and the cause for many managerial failures.

Without attempting to be Monday morning quarterbacks, we might mention a few well-publicized disasters caused by poor or ineffective planning. Penn Central, at one time the largest railroad in the United States following the merger of the Pennsylvania and New York Central railroads in 1968, was apparently a profitable railroad in 1969. Its stock sold at $86 per share that year, but the railroad went bankrupt in 1970 and its shares dropped to as little as $1 shortly thereafter. Analysis of this disaster disclosed that the merger of the two railroads was never planned or accomplished. Also, the company adopted a questionable strategy of putting its money into diversified businesses, including real estate, amusement parks, sports teams, hotels, coalfields, and refineries while the quality of its railroad operations went down hill. It apparently forgot to ask the question of what business it was really in.

The great RCA company, long a national leader in electronics, stubbed its toe and took a loss of $450 million in 1971 when it decided to get out of the computer business. The company found that a strategy to meet IBM head on, to mimic IBM and even undersell it, could not work without RCA's having a strong commitment to the computer business and plans to build up a sales and service organization, as well as a full line of business computers, that could meet IBM's exceptional strengths in this field.

Even Rolls Royce, Great Britain's most prestigious company, went bankrupt in 1971 as the result of unrealistic planning for a new engine for Lockheed's Tri-Star airplane. As one highly regarded newspaper, the *Manchester Guardian*, said at that time, "To the British the Rolls Royce bankruptcy was like hearing that Westminster Abbey had become a brothel." The major cause of this disaster was held to be due to planning to build an engine that was twice as powerful as the company had ever built, planning on using new materials that had never been tried in commercial jets, and planning a development cost for the engine of $156 million, but that turned out to be more than four times this amount.

These and dozens of other planning failures could be recounted.[1] And within the many departments and activities of all kinds of companies, government agencies, universities, churches, and other organizations, planning shortcomings and failures are commonly found.

---

[1] For an interesting analysis of a number of planning failures, see J. E. Ross and M. J. Kami, *Corporate Management in Crisis: Why the Mighty Fall* (Englewood Cliffs, N.J.: Prentice-Hall, Inc., 1973).

There are many reasons why people fail in planning other than the obvious one that planning requires commitments to be made today for an uncertain future, and events often do not turn out as we expect. Among the most important of the reasons for ineffective planning, the following may be summarized.

Lack of commitment to planning Despite the avowed interest in planning, there is too ·often a lack of real commitment to planning by managers—from the very top down to the lowest-level supervisor. There is a natural tendency to let today's problems push aside planning for tomorrow's opportunities. It is almost certainly true that most people would rather "fight fires," "meet crises," or "kill snakes" than plan, largely because such activities seem more important and are more interesting, and rapid-fire decision making without having to think is more fun. This means that everywhere in management we need a climate that forces people to plan.

Confusion of planning studies with plans As pointed out in previous chapters, nothing is a plan unless it includes a decision of some kind. Yet, many organizations and people believe they have planning when all they have are planning studies.

Failure to develop and implement sound strategies As we found in the previous chapter, strategies are the kind of plans that give unified direction to an enterprise's planning efforts. Without a sound strategy, which is often the case, plans go in the wrong direction. Moreover, unless a strategy is implemented by action plans, it becomes only a statement of wishes and hopes.

Lack of meaningful objectives or goals Planning cannot be effective unless goals are clear (do people understand them?), attainable (can they be accomplished?), actionable (can action be developed to achieve them?), and verifiable (will we know whether we have accomplished them?). Like supporting plans, goals must be defined in the light of our strengths and weaknesses and the many internal and external environmental forces that may influence their achievement.

Tendency to underestimate the importance of planning premises If plans and decisions in an organization are to be consistent, that is, to fit one another, they must be made in the light of uniform and generally understood planning premises.

Failure to see the scope of plans Some managers get so wrapped up in developing major and minor programs that they neglect seeing that there are other types of plans: missions or purposes, objectives or goals, strategies, policies, rules, procedures, and budgets as well as programs. All must involve analysis and decision making and must be implemented if a system of planning is to be complete.

Failure to see planning as a rational process   As pointed out in Chapter 6, planning is a practical exercise in rationality. It requires clear goals, a knowledge of alternatives, an ability to analyze alternatives in the light of goals sought, information, and a desire to come up with the best possible answer.

Excessive reliance on experience   Experience, as has been indicated, is likely to be a dangerous teacher simply because what happened in the past is not likely to fit a future situation.

Failure to use the principle of the limiting factor   It will be recalled that this principle requires that managers search out those factors in a problem situation which make the most difference in the solution and then deal primarily with them, since, in most problem situations, there are so many variables that no one can solve for all of them.

Lack of top management support   Planning is not likely to be very effective if top managers do not believe in it, encourage it, and make the necessary decisions that will allow their subordinates to make their plans. Nevertheless, as will be indicated below (see p. 304), subordinates can do something about this.

Lack of clear delegation   It is obviously very difficult for people to plan if they do not know what their job is, if they are unaware of how their job relates to others in an organization, and if they do not have clear authority to make decisions.

Lack of adequate control techniques and information   Since the task of managerial control is to follow up on plans and to assure that plans are actually succeeding, planning can hardly be very effective unless people responsible for them know how well they are working. As noted in the earlier discussion of the functions of managers, controls are closely related to plans. This area of management will be discussed in Part 6 of this book.

Resistance to change   Planning implies something new. It means change. It is well known that people resist change. As the great nuclear physicist Edward Teller once said: "In all my scientific explorations, the most inert material I have ever discovered is the human mind—with one exception, a group of human minds." Managers therefore may be said to deal with the most change-resistant material known to science.

The reasons why people tend to fail in planning emphasize the practical difficulties encountered in planning and disclose that effective planning is not easy. It is hoped that recounting these problems will show people why a knowledge of the essentials of management in this area can help them to be better planners. There is probably no way that a person can prove to be more valuable to an organization than to have an ability to plan effectively.

At the same time, as good as a person may be in planning, a number of limits to planning make this undertaking difficult. While these limits should not interfere with bending every effort to plan, awareness of them can help remove many of the frustrations in effective planning.

Difficulty of Accurate Premising

A limiting factor in planning is the difficulty of formulating accurate premises. Since the future cannot be known with accuracy, premising is subject to a margin of error. Fortunately, this disability can be narrowed as forecasting techniques advance and as an enterprise gives more attention to the total environment of plans.

One way of reducing the risks involved in future uncertainties is to engage in contingency planning by having alternative sets of premises and alternative plans based on them so that unexpected circumstances can be readily reflected in action. Another is to be ready with detours in planning to allow for unforeseeable events. The latter provides flexibility, which may take the form of utilizing plant facilities for an operation not originally intended, or shifting an advertising program in accordance with a revised sales policy, or radically changing a product line.

Such flexibility is, however, possible only within limits. In the first place, an enterprise cannot always put off a decision long enough to make sure of its rightness. In the second place, built-in flexibility may be so costly that the probable benefits are not worth the expense. Or a company may keep so financially liquid in preparing for the right opportunity that the advantages are in substantial measure offset by missing opportunities for expansion.

Problem of Rapid Change

Another limiting factor in planning arises from social dynamics. In a complex and rapidly changing industry, the succession of new problems is often magnified by complications that make planning most difficult. The planning problem in the first few years of expansion in the aircraft industry during World War II—when the growth of the industry from that of a few small businesses to that of very large companies was coupled with an exceptionally complex and rapidly changing product—was almost beyond comprehension.

Essentially the same kind of difficulty has existed in many other enterprises. The growth of the electronics industry after 1948, the space program expansion in the 1960s, the space and defense slowdown in the 1970s, and the energy crisis of recent years are noteworthy examples of highly dynamic situations in which planning has been exceedingly difficult. One might contrast planning in these areas with that of such stable businesses as a local water utility in New England.

Although all businesses are subject to some change, the degree of instability and complexity caused by social dynamics varies considerably from industry to industry and among firms within an industry. Even in a dynamic industry, however, many problems are of a recurring nature. In every new problem, there may be the same elements. A well-developed pricing formula may apply to widely different situations. Likewise, problems of manufacture and utilization of plant and machinery may

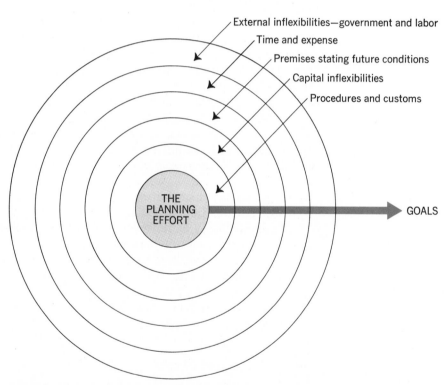

Figure 11.1 Limitations on planning effort. A manager's plans are directed at achieving goals. But a planning effort usually encounters limitations. Procedural inflexibilities within the enterprise often make it difficult to plan efficiently. Investment in fixed capital tends to limit a manager's area of choice. Premises usually present a whole series of limitations. Time and expense required for effective planning are also limiting elements. And there are many limitations imposed on managers by external factors such as government regulations and labor rules.

have common elements despite differences in product. If the *common elements* in problems are sought out and separated, planning in a dynamic situation can be simplified.

Internal Inflexibilities

Major internal inflexibilities that may limit planning are related to human psychology, policies and procedures, and capital investment.

Psychological inflexibility One of the important internal inflexibilities is psychological. Managers and employees may develop patterns of thought and behavior that are hard to change. A company may be so imbued with a tradition for operating flamboyantly or expensively that a program of retrenchment is difficult to achieve. In other cases, particularly in old, established businesses, people develop patterns of thought that are resistant to change. Managers and employees may eschew new methods, new products, and organization changes. Or close government regulation may bring about an attitude of running the business so as to avoid breaking the law rather than to seek efficiency.

Managers are often frustrated in instituting a new plan simply by the unwillingness or inability of people to accept the condition of change. This is a difficult planning limitation to overcome. To do so requires patient selling of ideas, careful dissemination of information, aggressive leadership, and intentional development of a tradition of change among the members of the organization.

Policy and procedural inflexibility Closely allied to psychological inflexibilities are those inherent in policies and procedures. Once established, these become ingrained in the enterprise, and changing them becomes difficult. A way of doing things, a chain of reports or invoices, or the routine of employees in following procedure may often be hard to modify. During World War II, an aircraft company developed from a small operation to one of fourteen divisions and some 200,000 people. Procedures, paperwork, and controls were developed for this large, far-flung operation. When the war ended and the company shrank to two divisions and 25,000 people, the wartime procedures lingered on. So drastic was the change in scale that a complete revamping of procedures was needed for guiding research and development, manufacture, and servicing of customers. Yet this would have required major overhaul of many aspects of operations and was believed to be impracticable.

One of the most convincing evidences of bureaucracy, whether in business or government, is the existence of complicated procedures designed to avoid mistakes. Progressive planning requires an environment of change, with some reasonable degree of freedom and willingness to assume the risks of mistakes; this is prevented in an enterprise bound by the straitjacket of policy and procedural inflexibilities.

Capital investment In most cases, once capital is invested in a fixed asset, the ability to switch courses of future action becomes limited, and the investment itself becomes a planning premise. Similar inflexibilities also exist where investment is sunk in items other than what is normally regarded as fixed assets. An investment in training of a particular kind or in building up a certain customer reaction to a product—through advertising, packaging, or otherwise—may become sunk. Unless the company can reasonably liquidate its investment or change its course of action or unless it can afford to write off the investment, these irretrievable costs may block the way of change. Although it may be a good axiom to disregard sunk costs in planning, their existence does influence planning.

Externally Imposed Inflexibilities

The manager has little or no control over externally imposed inflexibilities because they are related to the social, technological, geographic, and economic environment. Whether these are subject to fast or slow change, they do stand in the way of planning. Three major external inflexibilities are briefly described below.

Political climate Every enterprise, to a greater or lesser degree, is faced with inflexibilities of the political climate existing at a given time. If the local, state, or national government actively regulates business or if the national government adopts a high tariff or otherwise restricts trade, this must be taken into account in planning. Tax, antitrust, and fair trade policies also cause inflexibilities. Moreover, the basic attitude of government, as reflected in investigations of business practices, has significant effects. Furthermore, now that government has become business's largest customer, the procurement policies and programs of government agencies may cause rigidities in planning.

Labor organization The existence of strong unions, particularly those organized on a national basis, tends to restrict freedom in planning. The numerous wage and working condition provisions of union contracts and the influence of union policies on employee productivity and attitudes must be taken into account. In addition to being important environmental influences, they often give rise to definite inflexibilities. In the railroad industry, for example, management and unions entered into agreements in 1936 providing specific restrictions in the form of dismissal compensation and preservation of job rights. These agreements have been given the standing of law by the policy of the Interstate Commerce Commission of requiring such labor safeguards as a condition for approval of combinations or abandonments. The more recent resistance of the railroad brotherhoods to elimination of unneeded firemen on locomotives and changing obsolete rules is also a case in point.

Technological change   The rate and nature of technological change also present external limitations upon planning. There are perhaps few things as unyielding as the state of technological development. Not that technology does not change—of course, it changes rapidly, and one new development begets another. But at any given time, the status of technical progress is relatively inflexible. The full use of the solution to a technical problem may depend upon solution of a problem that has not been solved. In developing an electronic fire control system, for example, guiding a projectile toward a target may be well understood and it may be possible to engineer the necessary circuits, but inadequate development of a single component may delay accomplishment of the entire plan.

Time and Expense

The effort that could be spent on forecasting, evaluation of alternatives, development of derivative plans, or other aspects of planning is almost limitless, the only effective brake being the cost to the firm and the time available to the manager.

From the standpoint of expense, the underlying principle applicable to planning is simple: No firm should spend more on planning than the value of the expected benefits. But the application of this principle is more complex, for a manager cannot easily know how much planning will be worth its cost. There are useful guides to planning expense, however.

In the first place, a large firm can almost certainly engage in more thorough planning than a small one because the ratio of planning expense to operating expenses or to capital resources will be small.

In the second place, the more detailed planning becomes, the more expensive it will surely be. In modern engineering and production planning, a small project may receive the same attention as a large one. One of the authors recalls a project, undertaken by a large aircraft manufacturer, in which a minor modification of an airplane took some 3000 work-hours of engineering and production planning for a job requiring 50 direct work-hours, when, had the job been done on a relatively unplanned basis, the planning time could have been reduced to some 30 work-hours, with only a doubling of the direct work-hours involved.

In the third place, the further into the future plans are projected, the more costly they are likely to be. If long-term forecasts are to be more than informed guesses and if long-term plans are to be worked out more than in outline form, the cost of investigation and of fitting plans together, with a tolerable margin of error, is likely to be fairly high.

In addition to the restriction placed on planning by sheer expense, available time is a limiting factor. There comes a time when a decision must be taken, a course selected, and plans translated into action. Whether ready or not, managers may be forced to move. However, adequate planning done well in advance reduces the occasions when a manager may be forced into making snap decisions under the pressure of crises or the necessity for fighting business fires.

ESTABLISHING A CLIMATE

In a period of change and worldwide rivalry, planning becomes a matter of great urgency for those who manage the resources of an enterprise or a nation. It is critical that every manager establish a climate for planning.

Planning Must Be Forced

Every superior manager should remove obstacles to planning and try to establish a climate in which subordinates must plan. This involves, at each level of management, setting goals, establishing and publicizing applicable significant planning premises, involving all managers in the planning process, reviewing subordinate plans and their performance, and assuring appropriate staff assistance and information. All this adds up to recognizing that planning will not occur unless it is forced and the facilities to undertake it are made available.

Planning Should Start at the Top

Logically, basic goals from which others stem must be companywide, and therefore these must be set at the top management level. The example and drive of top management are the most important single force in planning. When top management rigorously reviews subordinates' programs, it naturally stimulates planning interest throughout an enterprise.

While the most effective planning should start at the top and receive the support of managers at that level, this does not mean that subordinates can do nothing. There is something to encouraging an "upward push" as well as a "downward press"; superiors may be pushed into setting goals and premises and approving plans if a well-reasoned program is presented to them. Top managers often want to make decisions and guide planning, but simply do not have the time, knowledge, or assistance from their subordinates to do so. Top managers have wistfully pointed out to the authors that they would like more subordinates to present solutions rather than problems. Certainly, no subordinate should be unduly critical of a superior without having come up with his or her program, recommended it, pressed for it, and been able to defend it.

Planning Must Be Organized

Good organization structure—through appropriate grouping of activities and clear delegation of authority—establishes an environment for performance. Managers must be held responsible for planning within their area of authority. What is sometimes neglected is sufficient staff assistance. While managers cannot let staff assistants make the decisions for which they are responsible, most managers could improve their planning if they had help in gathering information and in its analysis.

Good planning organization, then, implies that planning and doing cannot be separated. In other words, there is no practicable way that a manager can make decisions without taking part in planning since decision making is central to the planning process. Yet one often sees in all types of enterprises special planning staffs working to develop programs which never become operative simply because those responsible for decisions make commitments without regard to such planning proposals. A planning staff is just that. Its task is to advise and assist those in an operating-line position to make formal plans.

To avoid the error of separating planning from doing, it would seem wise for managers to consult their planning staff by putting proposed decisions of any importance before it for the staff's analysis and recommendations—*before* they make a decision. Also, the planning staff should be required to be knowledgeable concerning the realities of the situation on which its advice is sought. This means close informational contact with those who actively operate an enterprise, in place of the ivory-tower situation one often finds with such staffs. If staff advice in planning can be intermeshed with staff contact with reality and if there is a clear recognition that decision making itself is central to planning and a plan is only a study or proposal until a decision has been made, the dangerous tendency in practice to separate planning from doing can be avoided.

Planning Must Be Definite

Although some planning cannot be entirely definite, it need not even then represent little more than wishing. The need for verifiable goals has been repeatedly emphasized in this book, as has the requirement for a network of derivative goals throughout the structure of programs and organization. Also, the critical premises against which to make planning decisions must be definite; vague or nonexistent strategies and policies are an invitation to unstructured, uncoordinated planning. Plans can eventually be made definite, include specific steps of action, and be translatable into needs for people, materials, and money. As has been indicated, the budget, by quantifying plans, may force this kind of definiteness. There are few areas of planning in which—if the larger problem can be divided into steps or component parts—managers cannot see what they must do, how long it should take, and how much it should cost. Recent experience in planning research and development projects, by breaking them down into a series of definite interrelated parts, has resulted in a marked increase in definite and meaningful planning.

Goals, Premises, Strategies, and Policies Must Be Communicated

Perhaps the greatest single cause of uncoordinated planning is managers' lack of understanding of their goals and of the critical planning premises. which affect their areas of planning. Likewise, high on the list of basic causes of planning failures is the lack of understanding of company strategies and policies in the area where a manager makes decisions. Where these situations exist, no amount of logical ability or analysis will lead managers to a decision which supports and coordinates with the other plans of the enterprise.

Yet communication is a difficult process. It is most difficult either when there is nothing to communicate or when what is available is general, vague, or inapplicable to a manager's planning problems. Until enterprise managers have attempted to make sure that clear goals, premises, and policies are communicated to those who must have them, they are not doing what they can and should do to establish an environment for effective planning.

The Importance of Planning Participation

The best planning is likely to be done when managers are given an opportunity to contribute to plans affecting the areas over which they have authority. A good way of assuring adequate knowledge of plans, with the extra dividend of loyalty to them, is to have as many people as possible participate in planning. Plans are more likely to be enthusiastically and intelligently executed under these circumstances.

Participation in all planning affecting managers' areas of authority at any level, through their being informed, contributing suggestions, and being consulted, leads to good planning, loyalty, and managerial effectiveness. Yet one may ask how, in a large plant, the hundreds of supervisors and superintendents and the sales and other managers can be consulted. One cannot imagine the top managers of the Ford Motor Company, for instance, consulting with their thousands of subordinate managers on plans for a new line of cars.

Even so, there are means for wider participation by subordinate managers in planning for their departments. As was pointed out in the earlier discussion of management by objectives, participation of subordinates with superiors is a key element in making this program work. Not only does this participation improve the quality of objectives and their contribution to the superior's goals, but it also elicits clarity in planning and a sense of commitment in subordinates. Having the planning staff spend time with key subordinate managers in developing plans and in encouraging these managers in turn to discuss plans with their subordinates is another means of increasing participation. In some companies, this practice has produced excellent results.

Planning committees are a further means. Although committees have limited value as managers, their appropriate use at various levels and points of the organization structure can improve communication by transmitting planning information, by obtaining suggestions, and by encouraging participation. They must be skillfully handled to avoid wasting time, but they can pay handsome dividends in helpful advice, improved understanding of objectives and problems, and loyalty.

Another means of increasing participation is what has been called "grass roots" budgeting. Instead of a budget for operations or capital expenditures being prepared at the top or departmental level, the smallest organization units prepare their budgets and submit them upward. Naturally, to be effective, these units must be aware of objectives, policies, and programs which affect their operations; they must, above all, be given clear planning premises; and they must be furnished factors enabling them to convert work load into requirements for personnel, material, and money. If these budget requests are reviewed and coordinated by departmental management and if the budget makers are required to defend their budgets, this means of planning participation becomes real and purposeful. There probably exist no greater incentive to planning and no stronger sense of participation than those created in having managers develop, defend, and sell a course of action over which they have control and for which they bear responsibility.

Still another helpful means employed successfully in some companies is the management club, an organization of all members of management from the president to the line supervisor, which, in a large company, may be broken up into divisional or territorial clubs. At a specified number of meetings during the year the company president or a team of top managers conducts a meeting at which the planning and thinking of this top echelon are candidly reported to the club and questions are answered. The authors have noted that in several companies where this device has been tried, the lower-management group has responded avidly and has gained a strong feeling of unity with top management. Even the dullest financial matters thus become vital, and the most complicated plan is interesting. What many top managers overlook is the simple fact that the rank and file of managers have a strong interest in enterprise planning because their work is of paramount importance in their lives.

Long-Range Planning Must Be Integrated with Short-Range Plans

Managers often focus attention on very short-range ("tomorrow") planning, if they plan at all, and regard long-range planning as not affecting this area of responsibility. Part of this difficulty stems from a lack of appreciation of what long-range decisions should cover. The commitment principle gives a practical guide to this problem. As applied to the usual business enterprise, those areas which are likely to involve long-range decisions are (1) new product selection and development; (2) marketing channels and strategies; (3) facilities, particularly major capital facilities; (4) cash, particularly in a growing business; and (5) people and organization. Obviously, there are few day-to-day decisions not concerned with at least one of these, and successful planning cannot exist when short-range plans and decisions do not contribute to, or fit in with, longer-range planning.

Planning Must Include Awareness and Acceptance of Change

Change is always necessary for enterprise survival. Yet, since people resist change, it must be an objective of managers to build in their organizations an awareness of change, an ability to forecast it, and a welcoming attitude toward it.

The distilled experience of the president of a large American company sheds light on this subject:

Change is more acceptable when it is understood than when it is not.

Change is more acceptable when it does not threaten security than when it does.

Change is more acceptable when those affected have helped create it than when it has been externally imposed.

Change is more acceptable when it results from an application of previously established impersonal principles than it is when it is dictated by personal order.

Change is more acceptable when it follows a series of successful changes than when it follows a series of failures.

Change is more acceptable when it is inaugurated after prior change has been assimilated than when it is inaugurated during the confusion of other major change.

Change is more acceptable if it has been planned than if it is experimental.

Change is more acceptable to people new on the job than to people old on the job.

Change is more acceptable to people who share in the benefits of change than to those who do not.

Change is more acceptable if the organization has been trained to accept change.[2]

CREATIVITY

In a fast-changing, competitive environment, creativity and innovation are a necessity for the modern organization. Although creativity facilitates the total managerial process, it is especially useful in planning. For

---

[2]R. M. Besse, "Company Planning Must Be Planned," *Dun's Review and Modern Industry,* vol. 74, no. 4, pp. 62–63 (April 1957).

example, generating and examining alternative courses of actions, as well as developing new products, can be facilitated through a systematic approach to creativity.

What Is Creativity?

At times, a distinction is made between creativity and innovation. Specifically, the term "creativity" often refers to the ability and power to develop new ideas. "Innovation," on the other hand, usually means the use of these ideas. In an organization, this can mean a new product, a new service, or a new way of doing things. Although this discussion centers on the creative process, it is implied that organizations not only generate new ideas, but also translate them into practical applications.

The Need for Creativity

Creativity and imagination are important parts of American life. Some time ago *The New Yorker* magazine went even further, stating, "Ideas are what the United States are made of." Furthermore, in a progressive society, a weakness in the ability to produce new ideas not only may hamper an individual's advancement but also can be disastrous for the firm. Free competition requires a continuous development of new products, inventions, and new designs. Creative thinking is so important that General Electric has its own Creative Engineering Program. Although some people feel that ideas should be not only new but also useful, others maintain that creativity should not be measured by the resulting product but rather by the way an individual approaches the problem. The latter view, however, might not be feasible for most business situations. Nevertheless, several companies maintain laboratories where the emphasis, at least in the short run, is on basic research rather than on application.

Techniques to Enhance Creativity

Creative thoughts are often the fruits of extensive efforts, and several techniques are available to nurture those kinds of thoughts, especially in the decision-making process. Some techniques focus on group interactions; others focus on individual actions. As illustrative of the various techniques, two of the most popular are brainstorming and synectics.

Brainstorming   One of the best-known techniques to facilitate creativity has been developed by Alex F. Osborn, who has been called "the father of brainstorming."[3] The purpose of this approach is to improve problem

---

[3]A. F. Osborn, *Applied Imagination*, 3d rev. ed. (New York: Charles Scribner's Sons, 1963).

solving by finding new and unusual solutions. In the brainstorming session, a multiplication of ideas is sought. The rules are:

1. No ideas are criticized.
2. The more radical the ideas are, the better.
3. The quantity of idea production is stressed.
4. The improvement of ideas by others is encouraged.

Brainstorming, which emphasizes group thinking, was widely accepted after its introduction. However, the enthusiasm was dampened by research which showed that individuals could develop better ideas working by themselves than when working in groups. Additional research, however, showed that in some situations the group approach may work well, specifically when the information is distributed among various people and when a poorer group decision is more acceptable than a better individual decision. Also, the acceptance of new ideas is usually greater when the decision is made by the group charged with its implementation.[4]

Synectics Originally known as the Gordon technique, after its creator, William J. Gordon, this system was further modified and became known as synectics.[5] In this approach, the members of the synectics team are carefully selected for their suitability to deal with the problem, a problem which may involve the entire organization.

The leader of the group plays a vital role in this approach. In fact, only the leader knows the specific nature of the problem. This person narrows and carefully leads the discussion without revealing the actual problem itself. The main reason for this approach is to prevent the group from reaching a premature solution to the problem. The system involves a complex set of interactions from which a solution emerges—frequently the invention of a new product.

The Creative Manager

All too often it is assumed that most people are noncreative and have little ability to develop new ideas. This assumption, unfortunately, can be detrimental to the organization, for in the appropriate environment virtually all people are capable of being creative, even though the degree of creativity varies considerably among individuals.

---

[4]I. Summers and D. E. White, "Creativity Techniques: Toward Improvement of the Decision Process," *The Academy of Management Review*, vol. 1, no. 2, pp. 99–107 (April 1976).
[5]W. J. J. Gordon, "Operational Approach to Creativity," *Harvard Business Review*, vol. 34, no. 6, pp. 41–51 (November–December 1956); and W. J. J. Gordon, *Synectics* (New York: Harper & Brothers, 1961).

Generally speaking, creative people are inquisitive and come up with many new and unusual ideas; they are seldom satisfied with the status quo. Although intelligent, they not only rely on the rational process but also involve the emotional aspects of their personality in problem solving. They appear to be excited about solving a problem, even to the point of tenacity. Creative individuals are aware of themselves and capable of independent judgment. They object to conformity and see themselves as being different.

Unquestionably, creative people can make great contributions to the enterprise. At the same time, however, they may also cause difficulties in organizations. Change, as any manager knows, is not always popular. Moreover, change frequently has undesirable and unexpected side effects. Similarly, eccentric ideas, pursued stubbornly, may frustrate others and inhibit the smooth functioning of the organization. Finally, creative individuals may be disruptive to the organization by ignoring established policies, rules, and regulations.

In conclusion, the creativity of most individuals is probably under-utilized in many enterprises. Yet, unusual innovations can be of great benefit to the firm. Consequently, individual and group techniques can be effectively used to nurture creativity, especially in the area of planning. But, creativity is not a substitute for managerial judgment. It is the manager who must determine and weigh the risks involved in pursuing unusual ideas and translating them into innovative practices.

FOR DISCUSSION

1 Analyze any planning project with which you are familiar (whether in your personal life, your college, any social organization with which you are associated, or any business you know or have read about) and determine (1) whether any difficulties or failures occurred; (2) why they happened; and (3) what, if anything, could have been done to avoid them.

2 A company president tried to get a total company planning program underway, even appointing a vice president-planning. After 12 years, he found that his managers throughout the company were still not doing effective planning but were making decisions on problems as they came up. Are there any reasons that you might suspect caused this apparent failure in his planning program?

3 How can a company plan in an orderly way for "business as usual" and at the same time for a contingency such as a major fire or the outbreak of war?

4 In organizing for long-range planning, the typical corporation has a central long-range planning staff. But it is generally recognized that planning is the task of operating managers and that they must each

take responsibility for their plans and their execution. Can these kinds of approaches be reconciled in practice?

5 The job of good planning is to meet change successfully. How would you undertake to meet this problem in the light of the many inflexibilities and uncertainties involved in planning?

6 Show in what ways application of the major principles of planning clarifies the methods and approaches used in planning.

Some management scholars speak disparagingly of principles of management, but it nonetheless seems worthwhile to identify certain fundamentals that pinpoint essentials of management. Despite the fact there is far more to management than knowing principles, emphasizing key abstractions from a vast body of knowledge can help give greater meaning to this knowledge.

Although a complete set of empirically proved, interrelated principles has not been discovered and codified, experience and observation of planning indicate certain fundamental planning principles. As has been indicated earlier, management cannot progress as a science without a systematic theory. This, in turn, requires a conceptual scheme in which to arrange principles, not only for the benefit of the manager, but also as indicators of research areas. After all, one of the values of a conceptual scheme is that it makes visible what might otherwise remain unseen.

Major planning principles can be grouped around those dealing with (1) the purpose and nature of planning, (2) the structure of plans, and (3) the process of planning.

The Purpose and Nature of Planning

The purpose and nature of planning may be summarized by reference to the following principles:

Principle of contribution to objectives The purpose of every plan and all derivative plans is to facilitate the accomplishment of enterprise objectives.

Principle of primacy of planning Planning logically precedes the execution of all other managerial functions.

The Structure of Plans

Two major principles dealing with the structure of plans can go far in tying plans together, making derivative plans contribute to major plans, and assuring that plans in one department harmonize with those in another.

Principle of planning premises The more individuals charged with planning understand and agree to utilize consistent planning premises, the more coordinated enterprise planning will be.

Principle of strategy and policy framework The more strategies and policies are clearly understood, the more consistent and effective will be the framework of enterprise plans.

Within the process of planning, there are four principles, the understanding of which can help in the development of a science of planning.

Principle of the limiting factor

In choosing from among alternatives, the more individuals can recognize and solve for those factors which are limiting or critical to the attainment of the desired goal, the more clearly and accurately they can select the most favorable alternative.

The principle of the limiting factor is the essence of decision making. The key to decision making is to solve the problem posed by alternatives, if possible, by seeking out and solving for the limiting, or strategic, factor. To do otherwise is not only to sacrifice time and expense in examining every facet of a problem but also to risk giving too much weight to factors not critical to the decision.

The commitment principle

Logical planning covers a period of time in the future necessary to foresee, through a series of actions, the fulfillment of commitments involved in a decision.

Principle of flexibility

The more that flexibility can be built into plans, the less the danger of losses incurred through unexpected events, but the cost of flexibility should be weighed against its advantages.

Principle of navigational change

The more planning decisions commit for the future, the more important it is that managers periodically check on events and expectations and redraw plans as necessary to maintain a course toward a desired goal.

The commitment principle and the principles of flexibility and navigational change are aimed at a contingency approach to planning. Although it makes sense to forecast and draw plans far enough into the future to make reasonably sure of meeting commitments, often either it is impossible to do so or the future is so uncertain as to make the fulfillment of commitments subject to undue risk.

The principle of flexibility deals with that ability to change which is built into plans. The principle of navigational change, on the other hand, implies reviewing plans from time to time and redrawing them if that is indicated by changed events and expectations. As is apparent, unless plans have built-in flexibility, navigational change is difficult or costly.

CASES FOR PART 2

1 Eastern Electric Corporation

Margaret Quinn, the president of Eastern Electric Corporation, one of the large electric utilities operating in the eastern United States, had long been convinced that effective planning in the company was absolutely essential to success. For more than

10 years she had tried to get a company planning program installed without seeing much result. Over this time she had consecutively appointed three vice presidents in charge of planning and, although each had seemed to work hard at the job, she noticed that individual department heads kept going their own ways. They made decisions on problems as they came up, and they prided themselves on doing an effective job of "fighting fires."

But the company seemed to be drifting, and individual decisions of department heads did not always jibe with each other. The executive in charge of regulatory matters was always pressing state commissions to allow higher electric rates without having very much luck, since the commissions felt that costs, although rising, were not justified. The head of public relations was constantly appealing to the public to understand the problems of electric utilities, but electric users in the various communities felt that the utility was making enough money and that the company should solve its problems without raising rates. The vice president in charge of operations, pressed by many communities to expand electric lines, to put all lines underground to get rid of unsightly poles and lines, and to give customers better service, felt that costs were secondary to keeping customers off his back.

When a consultant called in at the request of Ms. Quinn looked over the situation, he found that the company really was not planning very well. The vice president-planning and his staff were working hard making studies and forecasts and submitting them to the president. There they stopped, since all the department heads looked on them as impractical paperwork that had no importance for their day-to-day operations.

1   If you were the consultant, what steps would you suggest to get the company to plan effectively?
2   What advice would you give the company as to how far in the future to plan?
3   How would you suggest to the president that your recommendations be put into effect?

2 Developing Verifiable Goals

The division manager had recently heard a lecture on management by objectives. His enthusiasm, kindled at that time, tended to grow the more he thought about it. He finally decided to introduce the concept and see what headway he could make at his next staff meeting.

He recounted the theoretical developments in this technique, cited the advantages to the division in its application, and asked his subordinates to think about adopting it.

It was not as easy as everyone had thought. At the next meeting, several questions were raised.

"Do you have division goals assigned by the president to you for next year?" the finance manager wanted to know.

"No, I do not," the division manager replied. "I have been waiting for Corporate to tell me what is expected but they act as if they will do nothing about the matter."

"What is the division to do, then?" the manager of production asked, rather hoping that no action would be indicated.

"I intend to list my expectations for the division," the manager said. "There is not much mystery about them. I expect $30 million in sales, a profit on sales before taxes of 8 percent, a return on investment of 15 percent, an ongoing program in effect by June 30, with specific characteristics I will list later, to develop our own future managers, completed development work on our XZ model by the end of the year, and employee turnover stabilized at 5 percent."

The staff was somewhat stunned that their superior had thought through to these verifiable objectives with such clarity and assurance. They were also surprised about his sincerity in wanting to achieve them.

"During the next month I want each of you to translate these objectives into verifiable goals for your own functions. Naturally they will be different for finance, marketing, production, engineering, and administration. However you state them, I will expect them to add up to the realization of the division goals."

1 Can a division manager develop verifiable goals, or objectives, when they have not been assigned to him by the president? How? What kind of information or help do you believe is important for the division manager to have from headquarters?

2 Do you believe the division manager was going about setting goals in the best way? What would you have done?

3 Managing by Objectives

"Managing by objectives is nothing new here," said Commissioner Henry A. Bishop of the Metropolis Police Department. "We have always had important objectives toward which every one in my department strives. Our job is to maintain law and order, firmly but fairly; to protect human lives and property; and to be the conscience and spirit of the general welfare of the millions of people who call our city home. All the officers in this department know these objectives and know that they must work toward them. If they do not, they will be replaced. I recognize that in a manufacturing concern you can measure objectives by profits, sales, costs, and product output. We can't, of course, do that for we are a service operation. But this does not mean that we are not managing by objectives. Ask anyone in my department!"

1 Is Commissioner Bishop engaging in managing by objectives? What, if anything, is missing?

2 What would you suggest the commissioner do?

4 Wilkinson Book Company

George Wilkinson was founder of a publishing company specializing in accounting books. Through personal ability to convince good authors that he could give their books special attention and the ability of three key associates to sell teachers on using the books, the company prospered and grew very fast. Its sales rose from $50,000 the first year to $5 million three years later. The editing, production, and sales staffs grew almost as fast.

But the company was having problems. Uncertainty and confusion began to exist in the company. New people were making decisions to the best of their ability, but many of them did not fit together. One of Mr. Wilkinson's key associates suggested that the company ought to have better planning and certainly needed clear policies to guide decision making, but the president was unimpressed. His response was that if he took time off to plan and develop policies today, he might not have a company tomorrow, and that he had no choice but to spend his time meeting today's problems as they came up.

1 If you were one of the newer managers in the company and had taken a course in the basics of management, what would you say to Mr. Wilkinson?
2 Outline exactly how you would show him that planning and policy making are important to the company if it is to grow effectively.

5 Olympic Toy Company

"I expect every manager in my department to act completely rational in every decision he makes," declared Lee Johnson, vice president of marketing for the Olympic Toy Company. "Every one of us, no matter what his position, is hired to be a professional rationalist and I expect him not only to know what he is doing and why he is doing it, but to be right in his decisions. I know that someone has said that a good manager needs only to be right in more than half of his decisions. But that is not good enough for me. I would agree that you may be excused for occasionally making a mistake, especially if it is a matter beyond your control, but I can never excuse you for not acting rationally."

"I agree with your idea, Lee," said Jill Goldberg, his advertising manager, "and I always try to be rational and logical in my decisions, but would you mind helping me be sure of this by explaining just what acting rationally is?"

1 Explain how the vice president of marketing might describe what is involved in making rational decisions.
2 If Jill Goldberg then declares that there is no way she can be completely rational, what would you suggest as a reply?

6 The Growing Savings and Loan Association

A large savings and loan association with offices throughout the state had a problem many financial institutions would like to have: It was very successful and growing. But top executives recognized that the management system used in the past was insufficient to cope with the new demands. Consequently, the president called a meeting to discuss the future direction of the company.

Soon the need for a planning system became evident. However, since the firm never did systematic planning, the managers did not know how to go about developing a planning system. Therefore, the president thought of hiring a consultant. The vice president concerned with finances argued against the hiring of such a consultant. She said, "We have been successful in the past without outside help and I doubt whether the benefits of the consultant would outweigh his high fees."

"Furthermore," she contended, "the firm's budgetary process is a planning system and as such is sufficient."

The president, however, overruled the vice president of finance and contacted a consultant to design a strategic planning system and integrate it with management by objectives. The vice president of finance wondered what this comprehensive system would be like.

1   Assuming that you were the consultant, how would you convince the vice president of finance about the value of strategic planning?
2   How would you go about evaluating the external environment? What factors would you consider? What is the importance of these factors for the savings and loan association?
3   How would you go about assessing the internal environment of the firm?
4   What kind of planning system would you suggest? Draw a planning model that shows the important variables and their relationships.

7 Penn Central Transportation Company

One of the most shocking failures of American history was the bankruptcy of the Penn Central in 1970, only 2 years after a merger was completed between two of the country's largest Eastern railroads, the New York Central and the Pennsylvania Railroad. During the short period of 2 years its stock dropped from a high of $86.50 per share to $5.50 and to $1 per share shortly thereafter, and many thousands of investors in bonds as well as stocks lost most of their investment. And this was in a company once regarded as one of the largest and most promising in the United States!

Many causes have been ascribed to this failure. Among these are the cost and revenue problems of most Eastern railroads, obsolete and costly labor practices, accounting deficiencies that did not accurately disclose earnings or cash flows, the foolish policy of deferring railroad maintenance, poor service to shippers and passengers, paying out cash dividends when cash losses were occurring in operations, and "gross mismanagement."

However, many financial analysts believe that the fundamental cause of Penn Central's failure was the company's strategy of diversification. It is stated by these analysts that the company lost sight of its business and that the top executives became intent on making Penn Central a conglomerate. It is true that the company did invest heavily in real estate, amusement parks, construction companies, coal fields, hotels, pipelines, oil refineries, investment companies, and even some sports teams.

When one of the most vocal critics who declared that "diversification disease" was the cause of Penn Central's fiasco was asked what the company's strategy should have been, the only reply he could readily make was, "That is something I would have to study in some depth."

1   What was the business of Penn Central? Should it have been changed? Identify the mission or purpose of the firm.
2   What opportunities and threats can you identify in the external environment?

3 What were the internal strengths and weaknesses of the firm?
4 What strategy would you have recommended for Penn Central?

8 Semiconductors, Inc.

Semiconductors, Inc. (SI) is one of the many electronics firms in the West. The firm has been reasonably successful in the past. It now recognizes the threat of Japanese competition. John Henderson, the president, realizes that one of the keys to success in this industry is to be a high-technology innovator. Consequently, he asked the consultant, Martin Rich, to analyze the organization's suitability for becoming a successful high-technology firm.

The consultant's presentation of findings is as follows:

1 The firm's objectives are mostly for 1 year and pertain primarily to operations.
2 Managers are not rewarded for activities that may be beneficial in the long run. Instead, bonuses are based on the achievement of short-term objectives.
3 Managers, generally speaking, are good "fire fighters," but little effort is expended to *prevent* problems from occurring.
4 There is little team effort. Each manager focuses on his or her own task.
5 Managers are mostly concerned about the internal operation and care little about the external environment.

The president listened carefully to the report by the consultant. In fact, the findings confirmed his impression of the organization. But the important point was, What should be done now to overcome these problems?

1 What factors would you consider in assessing the external environment?
2 How would you develop a strategic plan and objectives. Write a mission statement. Give examples of overall company objectives.
3 What would you do to encourage managers to work in teams toward long-range objectives?

9 International Motor Company

Gilbert Brown, the president of International Motor Company (IMC), leaned back in his chair and reflected on the success of his firm, which produces and distributes medium-sized cars. This afternoon at a meeting with distributors from various parts of the world, Mr. Brown was urged to introduce new models to satisfy the changing demands of the customers.

The president, who had an engineering background, recognized the implications of the suggestions by the distributors. It would require greater investments in research and development. Furthermore, the changes in the highly automated production line would be very costly indeed. Also, having a greater variety of models would require stocking many more spare parts. Depending on the kinds of changes, mechanics also might need to be retrained.

Reflecting on previous staff meetings, the president realized that sales or marketing people, always wanted a greater variety of models but never acknowledged the costs involved in changing models. After all, the company had been extremely successful with just a few models. Consequently, the president decided against the introduction of new models. Instead, he considered improving the current models and reducing the cost and price. He felt that what the customer really wants is value. Nevertheless, to test his judgment, the president asked a consultant for an opinion.

1 How would you state the mission of the enterprise?
2 What do you think are the opportunities and threats in the external environment?
3 How would you go about evaluating the strengths and weaknesses of the firm? What factors are critical for success or failure?
4 It is often said that to be successful, an organization must be an open system. What does this mean, and how does it apply to this case?

10 King's Supermarkets

King's Supermarkets was a chain of twenty-five highly successful supermarkets located in medium-sized cities in New England, New York, and New Jersey. It had always been the company's policy to have only one leading store in each of a number of cities of approximately 25,000 to 50,000 population. In each city, the best possible location was sought out and very large stores were developed with attractive buildings, large parking lots, and complete product lines of food and food-related products sold at advertised competitive prices. Although the company had had to close a few poorly located markets over the years, it relied almost entirely for cities and locations on the instincts of the founder-president, Walter King. The company's record of profits indicated that his judgment had been generally correct over the 25 years since he had opened his first market.

After Walter King's daughter Donna graduated from the university with a degree in business administration and joined the company as assistant to the president, the researching of new city locations was made one of her major assignments. Ms. King felt that the techniques of operations research might be applied to this problem. She pointed out that there must be a "best" city and a "best" location for expansion at any given time and for the future, if only this could be discovered. She insisted that all a company needed to do is to clarify its goals, identify the constraints such as cash available, existing competition, and distance from company warehouses, and look at such variables as cost of real estate, money costs, market size and characteristics, local labor markets, and local taxes and regulations; and then put these into a model to come up with a means of identifying the best location.

Her father and the other officers of the company maintained that operations research might be all right for an oil company, a large aerospace company, or even a large bank, but it was too complicated an approach and there were too many intangibles in a matter of a supermarket location. Moreover, for 25 years the company had been successful in relying on the president's judgment, and anyway, neither Mr. King nor any of the other top officers or managers understood advanced mathematics. In addition, they felt that they wanted no part of a company where such major decisions were made by a computer. They pointed out strongly that they were merchandisers and not computer experts.

Ms. King was not convinced. She was sure that operations research would greatly help in such decisions. But she did not know what to do under the circumstances.

1 Making any assumptions you wish, show Ms. King and her father how operations research might apply in this case.
2 Draw a rough diagram which shows what factors should be included in an operations research model.

11 Bartlett Drug Company

Richard Spencer was marketing manager of the cosmetics division of the Bartlett Drug Company. The company was well known as a leader in new proprietary drug and toiletry products and had a good record of profitability. The cosmetics division had been especially successful in men's toiletries and cosmetics and in the introduction of new products. It always based its new product development on market research with respect to what would appeal to men and, after almost invariably test marketing a new product in a few selected cities, launched it with a heavy advertising and sales promotion program. It had hoped in this way not only to get a large initial share of the market but also to become so well entrenched that competitors, who soon copy a successful product, would not dislodge them from their market share.

After being cautioned by the president on the necessity of watching costs more carefully, the division manager became increasingly concerned with two opposing factors in his marketing strategy: (1) test marketing of new products (offering them for sale first in a few test cities with area advertising and sales programs) tended increasingly to give competitors advance information on new products, and certain competitors had been able to copy a product almost as soon as Bartlett could offer it nationally and profit thereby from Bartlett's advertising, and (2) national advertising and sales promotion expenses were increasing so fast that a single major product failure would have an important impact on division profits, on which his annual bonus was being primarily determined. On the one hand, he recognized the wisdom of test marketing, but he disliked the costs and dangers involved. On the other hand, he hardly wished to take an unknown risk on embarking on a national program until a test showed that the product did in fact have a good market demand. Yet he wondered whether all products should be test-marketed.

Richard Spencer was asked to put this problem to his marketing department subordinates and ask them what should be done. To give the strategy some meaning, he used as a case in point the company's new men's hair spray and conditioner, which had been developed on the basis of promising, although preliminary, market research. He asked his sales manager whether he thought the product would succeed and what he thought his "best estimate" of sales would be. He also asked his advertising manager to give some cost estimates on launching the product.

Larry Hodgson, division sales manager, thought awhile and said he was convinced the product was a winner and that his best estimate would be sales of $5 million per year for at least 5 years. Harriet Jackson, the advertising manager, said that the company could launch the product for a cost of $2 million the first year and some $500 thousand per year thereafter. She also pointed out that the test-marketing program would cost $200 thousand, of which half would be saved if these test cities were merely a part of a national program, and would delay the national program for 6 months. But she warned Spencer that test marketing would save the gamble of so much money on the national promotion program.

At this point, Lucy Armstrong, the new marketing research manager, suggested that the group might come to a better decision if they used a decision tree.

Richard Spencer looked at his subordinate curiously and said: "What is that? How would we do that? How would that help us in a problem like this?"

1   Explain what a decision tree is and why and where it is used.
2   Draw one that you believe might fit this case.

12 The Roberts Company

The Roberts Company was founded in 1938 with four partners, one of whom was the inventor of a special product and technique for laying wall-to-wall carpeting without using tacks. Although the carpet layers of the world were reluctant to change their long practice of tacking carpets down, through hard work and demonstration of the method to carpet layers the four partners were able to obtain acceptance of their product as the standard way of laying carpet in the following 20 years. Not only was their original product a great success, but the company became the world's leader in furnishing tools for laying and stretching carpeting. They also developed and marketed a special adhesive for carpet laying and seaming and later expanded this line to a product for adhering plastic laminates in kitchens, bathrooms, furniture, and elsewhere. In addition, the company expanded its operations in the construction industry through such special products as steel folding doors for closets and wardrobes, steel door frames, and other items. Moreover, they took their products to many foreign countries, where they were able to establish highly profitable wholly owned subsidiaries to manufacture and sell products developed in the United States.

In deciding on future product diversification, and not wishing to become a conglomerate, it was determined that much effort and motion would be saved if energies in designing new products and considering acquisitions could be channeled within a clear product strategy. In formulating this strategy, the company considered, among other things, the following features:

1   The company had very strong marketing ability on a national and international basis in the carpet accessories field.
2   It had only regional (western United States) marketing in its building material products.
3   Its marketing ability and coverage in adhesives in the floor covering field were good, but were both specialized and limited in other adhesive applications.

4   Its overseas subsidiaries were well managed and operated in Canada, England, Holland, Sweden, Australia, and New Zealand.

5   While its size and resources could not be compared with those of the very large adhesive, chemical, and building material companies, in its special fields it was large, with $40 million of annual sales and ample resources from earnings and a receptive common stock public market; the company therefore felt that it could spend far more than its smaller competitors for marketing and specialized capital equipment.

6   Much of the specialized capital equipment used by the company was designed and built by its own engineers.

7   While a leader in some of its fields, particularly in floor-covering accessories, the company was subject in these areas to many small and vigorous local competitors.

So that both new product and acquisition programs could be effectively pursued, the board of directors asked the president to recommend a product strategy for the company at its next meeting.

1   Summarize for the president the nature of strategies and how he might go about developing a new product strategy for Roberts.

2   What product strategy would you suggest to the Roberts Company under the facts and circumstances given?

3 Organizing

In order for people to work effectively toward accomplishing goals, a structure of roles must be designed and maintained. This is the area of knowledge involved in the managerial function of organizing.

In this part, the authors are concerned with the theory underlying the structuring of organizations. Chapter 12 stresses the need for a formal system of roles to facilitate achievement of enterprise objectives. Although emphasis is placed on structuring roles, this does not imply that a manager disregards people. Quite the contrary. Roles are designed for people to fill. Practical organizers are often faced with situations in which they must allow for the limitations, strengths, availability, and interests of people. Furthermore, in speaking of role structuring, there is no implication that any role need be restrictive. It may be as narrow as the defined task of an assembly line worker or a bank teller, or as broad, with a considerable area of discretion, as that of a company president or research scientist.

Chapter 12 also makes the point that formal organization is necessary because there is a limit to the number of workers that can be effectively supervised by one individual. This limit, known as the "span of management," does not consist of a specific number that is universally applicable. Rather, in any given situation, many underlying factors determine the number of persons a manager can supervise.

Chapter 13 deals with activity groupings in organization structures. To understand the material presented in Chapter 13 quickly and with the least effort, it is important to note that grouping has two aspects. One has to do with the basic forms of departmentation which experience and logic have shown to be useful. The advantages and disadvantages of each of these forms, along with their special uses in practice, are discussed. The second aspect of grouping has to do with guides for assigning activities to existing departments within a structure. The authors suggest that while most tasks are assigned on the basis of similarity to those in an existing department, other criteria may be advantageous.

This chapter also points out that the traditional forms of departmentation, such as departmentizing by function, territories, or product, have recently been expanded to include basic forms built around, and supporting, marketing. The reader will find special emphasis given to matrix organization structures, primarily the two-dimensional matrix of project or product overlaying functional organization, but also newer forms that add a third dimension—market managing—or even more dimensions to the matrix. As indicated in this chapter, as responsibility for end results becomes more important, matrix forms are likely to be increasingly used.

Chapter 14 analyzes two basic kinds of formal relationships that may exist in an organizational role and points out reasons for confusion between the two. If readers remember that a "line" relationship is one in which responsibility exists for the performance of subordinates and that a "staff" role involves only the making of recommendations or the offering of advice, they need not be disturbed by the complex reasoning behind these concepts. This differentiation applies even to those hybrid functional authority positions which have some staff characteristics and some line characteristics.

Chapter 15 analyzes problems of delegation and authority dispersion in an enterprise. As management has become better understood and as enterprises have grown, it has become almost fashionable to decentralize authority. While authority must be dispersed in an organization structure, the degree and kind of decentralization are sources of difficulty and misunderstanding. The chapter undertakes to analyze the factors behind proper decentralization or centralization, with a view to developing some theoretical and practical bases for this important organizational area. The authors believe that neither centralization nor decentralization should be regarded as desirable or undesirable trends in and of themselves, but that the actions of an enterprise in this area must be determined by studying actual circumstances and needs in every case. Centralization and decentralization are, after all, simply means of structuring roles for achieving desired goals.

The committee or group management form of organization is given special attention in Chapter 16. Uses and abuses and advantages and disadvantages are discussed with emphasis on methods of making group management devices more effective.

Of the various types of committees that exist, the committee as a plural executive or as a form of group management is especially important. The outstanding example of a plural executive in practice is the board of directors. The chapter notes that the group form of management, when used to make decisions in place of a single manager, is open to special dangers. These dangers as well as other problems and defects are discussed, and suggestions are made to help boards or other forms of group management be more effective.

In the final chapter, organization practice is analyzed from an overall point of view. This chapter on making organizing effective puts special emphasis on applying structural organizational theory in given situations.

The chapter also outlines common mistakes people make in designing and implementing organization structures. The importance of planning organization structures is stressed, and suggestions are made for avoiding the problems caused by inflexibility or by undesirable conflict, through clarification of organizational arrangements and relationships. Also, since this is the final chapter in Part 3, it ends with a summary of major principles of organizing which have been found to be valid and helpful to the organizer.

chapter **12** Nature and Purpose of Organizing

1   To clarify the meaning of "organization structure" and "organizing" as used in this book and to draw a distinction between formal and informal organization.

2   To emphasize that the purpose of an organization structure is to establish a formal system of roles that people can perform so that they may be helped in working together to achieve enterprise objectives.

3   To show how organization structures and their levels are caused by the limitations of span of management and to show how the exact number of people a manager can effectively supervise depends on a variety of underlying variables and situations.

4   To make clear that the application of structural organization theory must necessarily take into account situations and that principles and theory do not imply that there is a single best way to organize.

It is often said that good people can make any organization pattern work. It has even been said that ambiguity in organization is a good thing in that it forces teamwork, since people know that they must cooperate to get anything done. However, there can be no doubt that good people and those who want to cooperate will work together most effectively if they know the part they are to play in any collaborative endeavor and how their roles relate to one another. This is as true in business or government as it is in football or baseball. To design and maintain these systems of roles is basically the managerial function of organizing.

For an organizational role to exist and to be meaningful to people, it must incorporate (1) verifiable objectives, which, as already indicated in the previous part, are the task of planning; (2) a clear concept of the major duties or activities involved; and (3) an understood area of discretion, or authority, so that the person filling it knows what he or she can do to accomplish results. In addition, to make a role operational, provision should be made for needed information and other tools and resources necessary for performance in a role.

It is in the sense of a "structure of roles" that formal organization is conceived. It is within this connotation that we think of organizing as the grouping of activities necessary to attain objectives, the assignment of each grouping to a manager with authority necessary to supervise it, and the provision for coordination horizontally and vertically in the enterprise structure. An organization structure should be designed to clarify the environment so that everyone knows who is to do what and who is responsible for what results; to remove obstacles to performance caused by confusion and uncertainty of assignment; and to furnish a decision-making communications network reflecting and supporting enterprise objectives.

Essentially, organization grows out of the human need for cooperation. As Barnard emphasized,[1] human beings are forced to cooperate to achieve personal goals because of physical, biological, psychological, and social limitations. Cooperation can be more productive and less costly, in most instances, with some kind of organization structure.

It should be noted that "organization" is a loosely used word with many management theorists. Some would say "it includes *all* the behavior of *all* participants."[2] Others would equate it with the total system of social and cultural relationships. Still others refer to an enterprise, such as the United States Steel Corporation or the Department of Defense, as an "organization." But for most practicing managers, the term implies a formalized intentional structure of roles or positions. It is used that way in this book. Certainly most managers believe they are organizing when they establish such a structure.

[1] *The Functions of the Executive* (Cambridge, Mass.: Harvard University Press, 1938), chaps. 6, 7, 9.

[2] C. Argyris, *Personality and Organization* (New York: Harper & Brothers, 1957), p. 239.

FORMAL AND INFORMAL ORGANIZATION

Taking the lead from Barnard and from the discoveries of the Hawthorne experiments,[3] many management people distinguish between formal and informal organization.

Formal

People, their behavior, and their association belong to a large system of social relationships of which a single formally organized enterprise is but a subsystem. Barnard referred to an organization as "formal" when the activities of two or more persons were *consciously* coordinated toward a given objective. He found that the essence of formal organization is conscious common purpose and that formal organization comes into being when persons (1) are able to communicate with one another, (2) are willing to act, and (3) share a purpose. This definition is far broader than that used in this book, and few managers adopt it. In the first place, it covers any kind of group action with a common purpose and could apply to activities such as a card game or car pool, which are certainly not regarded by practitioners as formal organizations. In the second place, it goes beyond our goal-activity-authority concept. No formal organization, as typically designed, can cover *all* human enterprise relationships. If role definition and authority lines map the course of responsible action and decision making, they are doing all that was ever intended.

As Wilfred Brown declared, after managerial experience of many years and after participating in one of the most thorough research projects on organizational life ever undertaken:

> Thus, I personally believe that the more formalization that exists, the more clearly we will know the bounds of discretion which we are authorized to use, and will be held responsible for, and [that] prescribed policies make clear to people the area in which they have freedom to act. Without a clearly defined area of freedom there is no freedom. This, in fact, is a very old story reaching down through the history of mankind: there is no real freedom without laws.[4]

---

[3]The importance of human behavior independent of the structural considerations of formal enterprise organization was brought out by the researches of Elton Mayo and F. J. Roethlisberger at the Hawthorne Works of the Western Electric Company, beginning in 1927. For a comprehensive account of the experiments, see F. J. Roethlisberger and W. J. Dickson, *Management and the Worker* (Cambridge, Mass.: Harvard University Press, 1939).

[4]"What Is Work?" *Harvard Business Review*, vol. 40, no. 5, p. 127 (September–October 1962). The research referred to is that undertaken first by the Tavistock Institute of Human Relations, London, in cooperation with Brown's Glacier Metal Company, Ltd., and after a few years by the company alone. This research project, started in 1948, is reported in Wilfred Brown, *Exploration in Management* (New York: John Wiley & Sons, Inc., 1960).

Unquestionably, some of the concern about the restrictive dangers in formal organization arises from poor organization practice. There should be room for discretion, for taking advantage of creative talents, and recognition of individual likes and capacities in the most formal of organizations. Yet to assume that individual effort in a group situation can be unchanneled is to overlook the basic realities of any group activity.

There is nothing inherently inflexible about formal organization. On the contrary, if the manager is to organize well, structure must furnish an environment in which individual performance, both present and future, contributes most effectively to group goals.

Although the attainment of goals must be the reason for any cooperative activity, we must look further for principles to guide the establishment of effective formal organization.

Principle of unity of objective   *An organization structure is effective if it facilitates the contribution of individuals in the attainment of enterprise objectives.*[5] The application of the principle of unity of objective implies, of course, the existence of formulated and understood enterprise objectives. If the objective is make a profit over a period of time, then the organization pattern that helps to accomplish this conforms to the principle of unity of objective. Whatever the goals, or derivative goals, organization structure and action must be measured against the criterion of effectiveness in meeting them.

Principle of efficiency   *An organization structure is efficient if it facilitates accomplishment of objectives by people* (that is, is effective) *with the minimum unsought consequences or costs* (going beyond the usual thinking of costs entirely in such measurable items as dollars or labor-hours). Even though financial or material unit costs are important in measuring organizational efficiency, the principle of efficiency as employed here encompasses such matters as individual and group satisfactions. To an employee, an efficient organization structure is likely to be one that operates without waste or carelessness and makes for work satisfaction, has clear-cut lines of authority and proper exaction of responsibility, allows appropriate participation in problem solving, gives provision for security and status, and furnishes an opportunity for personal development and competitive pay rates.

The principle of efficiency must be applied judiciously. Too often, in establishing an organization structure, managers see the savings possible in setting up a service department, for example, without ascertaining the

---

[5]Urwick referred to this as "the principle of objective," one of ten principles of organization. See his *Notes on the Theory of Organization* (New York: American Management Association, 1952), pp. 18ff. Barnard (op. cit., pp. 19ff.) refers to this principle as a matter of "effectiveness" in organization, making the point that an organization is effective, although not necessarily efficient, when it gains its objective.

complementary costs outside the department. For example, all activities dealing with the compilation of statistics may be assigned to a central department; although this may produce statistics at low cost, their value may decline even more because they do not suit the needs of managers. Also, a customary way for the inexperienced efficiency engineer to save money is to establish secretarial pools. While these sometimes work efficiently, there are many occasions where efficient secretarial work is done at the cost of hours of executive time spent waiting for needed stenographic work to be done.

Efficiency may become a vague and variable criterion. One manager may measure efficiency by profit, while another may measure it in terms of survival, business status, public service, or business expansion. Or a company president may impatiently drive toward cost, market, and profit goals by tactics that create morale problems for subordinates and eventual losses for the business.

However the standards of efficiency are applied, the principle of efficiency underlies the measurement of any organization structure. Difficulties may be encountered in selecting an appropriate standard. Thus one person may criticize the overlapping of activities in certain government departments, while another may feel that this overlapping is a necessary cost of gaining protection against the danger inherent in concentration of power. A president of a business may be criticized as inefficient in pressing too slowly for organizational changes, when his slowness may be justified by the benefits of having subordinates learn for themselves the advantages of such changes and voluntarily embrace them more completely.

Informal

Barnard regarded as informal organization any joint personal activity without conscious joint purpose, even though possibly contributing to joint results. As thus defined, all manner of groups fall within the sphere of informal organization, including an airplane load of passengers and people walking down a street. Pursuing this thinking, informal organizations—relationships not appearing on an organization chart—might include the machine-shop group, the water cooler clique, the production engineering group, the sixth floor crowd, the Friday evening bowling gang, and the morning coffee "regulars."

An inquiry into why and how these informal organizations exist is a special study in social psychology. A manager knows that these interpersonal relationships are important in managing. If it were not for the fact that they are so dynamic in terms of the nature of the group, the number in the group, the actual personnel involved, what the group is concerned with, its changing leadership, and the continuing process of formation and dissolution, managers might be tempted more consciously and specifically to take informal organizations into account as they formally organize or change the organization. This, however, they cannot do. They are reduced to keeping aware of the informal organization, avoiding antagonizing it, and using it as they lead and direct subordinates.

THE TERM "DEPARTMENT"

"Department" designates a distinct area, division, or branch of an enterprise over which a manager has authority for the performance of specified activities. A department, as the term is generally used, may be the production division, the sales department, the West Coast branch, the market research section, or the accounts receivable unit. In some enterprises, departmental terminology is loosely applied; in others, especially larger ones, a stricter terminology indicates hierarchical relationships. Thus a vice president may head a division; a director, a department; a manager, a branch; and a chief, a section. This relationship of terminology to status is often found in the federal government, where, in the typical executive department, the hierarchy runs from office or bureau to divisions, branches, sections, units, and subunits.

Indeed, in an enterprise requiring successive subordinate groupings, exact definitions may become imperative, since certain designations carry connotations of authority, prestige, and salary. If the vice president of production heads a "division," the vice president in charge of sales will hardly be satisfied to head a "department." Some large organizations tend to run out of appropriate designations; then they invent such terms as "group," "activity," or "component."

ORGANIZING AS A PROCESS

In looking at organizing as a process, it is apparent that several fundamental inputs must be considered. In the first place, the structure must reflect objectives and plans because enterprise activities derive from these. In the second place, the structure must reflect the authority available to enterprise managers; this depends upon such social institutions as private property, representative government, and the host of customs, codes, and laws that both restrict and sanction individuals in operating a business, a church, a university, or any group venture. Authority in a given organization is, then, a socially determined right to exercise discretion; as such, it is subject to change.

In the third place, organization structure, like any plan, must reflect its environment. Just as the premises of a plan may be economic, technological, political, social, or ethical, so may be those of an organization structure. The structure must be designed to work, to permit contributions by members of a group, and to help people gain objectives efficiently in a changing future. In this sense, a workable organization structure can never be either mechanistic or static.

Fourth, the organization must be staffed with people. Obviously, the activity groupings and authority provisions of an organization structure must take into account people's limitations and customs. This is not to say that the structure must be designed around individuals instead of around goals and accompanying activities. But an important consideration—often a constraining factor for the organization architect—is the kind of people who are to be employed. Just as engineers consider the performance strength and weaknesses of materials going into their projects, so must organizers consider their materials— people.

By Logic

There is a fundamental logic to organizing. Application of logical method to this process, in the light of the inputs outlined above, indicates the following steps: (1) establishment of enterprise objectives; (2) formulation of derivative objectives, policies, and plans; (3) identification and classification of activities necessary to accomplish these; (4) grouping these activities in the light of human and material resources available and the best way of using them; (5) delegating to the head of each group the authority necessary to perform the activities; and (6) tying these groupings together horizontally and vertically, through authority relationships and information systems.

This logical process does not imply—as so many critics have declared it does—extreme occupational specialization, which in many instances makes labor uninteresting, tedious, and unduly restrictive. There is nothing in organizing itself that dictates this. To say that tasks should be specific is not to say they must be limited and mechanical. Whether or not they should be broken down into minute parts—as on a typical assembly line—or be broad enough to encompass the design, production, and sale of a machine is for the organizer to consider in light of the total results desired. In any organization, jobs can be defined to allow little or no personal discretion or the widest possible area of discretion, as a pure detail of operation or as the most creative of activities.

All Practice Is Based on Contingencies and Situations

It should be made clear at the outset that all managerial practice, whether in organizing or elsewhere, must reflect situations and contingencies encountered. A theory of organizing, comprising concepts, principles, techniques, and approaches, never implies that there is one best way of organizing a variety of enterprises, any more than a theory of mechanics implies that there is one best kind of machine to serve all purposes. Yet it is strange and unintelligible to anyone familiar with practice to find scholars criticizing structural organizational theory as "recommending" a single best way.

In the first place, theory never recommends; it only explains. In the second place, every kind of organization structure depends on the situation it is designed to serve and the contingencies faced. This is, of course, what practice is all about. But, as pointed out earlier in this book, practitioners of management will surely do a better job of designing an appropriate structure if they understand underlying theory and use it as a diagnostic and guiding tool to create a structure that will best serve needs in given circumstances.

According to Drucker

In both logic and practice, the organization process outlined here is similar to that emphasized by Peter Drucker,[6] who finds three ways to determine the kind of structure needed in a specific enterprise: activities analysis, decision analysis, and relations analysis. Drucker believes in finding out what an enterprise actually does—in terms of concrete activities necessary to attain objectives, rather than adopt such preconceived general headings as "engineering" or "selling."

Drucker points out that only by rigorous activities analysis can managers find out what work has to be performed, what work belongs together, and how each activity should be emphasized in the organization structure. His decision analysis determines what kinds of decisions are needed, where in the organization structure they should be made, and how each manager should be involved in them. By "relations analysis" Drucker means knowing the contribution to programs that each manager must make, with whom to work, and what contribution other managers must make. This approach, then, is in accordance with what sound management practice has long recognized as logical and practical.

Organizing is, then, a process by which the manager brings order out of chaos, removes conflicts between people over work or responsibility, and establishes an environment suitable for teamwork. Implicit also is recognition of the human factor—that jobs must be designed to fit people, with all their strengths and weaknesses, and that people must be encouraged through their roles to contribute effectively to enterprise goals.

BASIC ORGANIZATION QUESTIONS

In this book, the authors have found it useful to analyze the managerial function of organizing by answering, in this and succeeding chapters, the following questions:

[6]See *The Practice of Management* (New York: Harper & Brothers, 1954), pp. 194–201.

1 What determines the span of management and hence causes levels of organization?
2 What determines the basic framework of departmentation, and what are the strengths and weaknesses in the basic forms?
3 What determines whether activities should be assigned to a given department in this basic framework?
4 What kinds of authority relationships exist in organizations?
5 How should authority be dispersed throughout the organization structure, and what determines the extent of this dispersion?
6 What place do committees have in organization?
7 How should the manager make organization theory work in practice?

The answers to these questions form a basis for a theory of organizing. When considered along with similar analyses of planning, staffing, leading, and controlling, they are offered as an operational approach to management.

ORGANIZATION LEVELS AND THE SPAN OF MANAGEMENT

While the reason for organizing is to make human cooperation effective, we find the cause of levels of organization in the limitations of the span of management.[7] In other words, because there is a limit to the number of persons a manager can supervise, even though this limit varies depending on situations, the result is the existence of organization levels.

That the problem of span of management is as old as organization itself is apparent from the passages of the Bible dealing with Moses' organizing the exodus of the Israelites. The difficulties that Moses met and the departmentation he employed to meet them are recounted in Exodus 18:17–26, in which it is recorded that Moses' father-in-law, noting that Moses was spending so much time supervising so many individuals, advised him as follows:

> The thing thou doest is not good. Thou will surely wear away, both thou and this people that is with thee: for this thing is too heavy for thee; thou art not able to perform it thyself alone. Hearken now unto my voice, I will give thee counsel. . . . Thou shalt provide out of the people able men . . . and place such over them [the people], to be rulers of thousands, and rulers of hundreds, rulers of fifties, and rulers of tens. And let them judge the people at all seasons; and it shall be, that every great matter they shall bring unto thee, but every small matter they shall judge: so shall it be easier for thyself, and they shall bear the burden with thee. If thou shalt do this thing, and God

[7]In much of the literature of management, this is referred to as the "span of control." Despite the widespread use of this term, since the first edition of this book in 1955 the authors have preferred to use "span of management," since the span is one of management and not merely of control, which is only one aspect of the managing practice.

command thee so, then thou shall be able to endure, and all this people shall also go to their place in peace.

Moses thereupon followed his father-in-law's advice, with the result that he:

> . . . chose able men out of all Israel, and made them heads over the people, rulers of thousands, rulers of hundreds, rulers of fifties and rulers of tens. And they judged the people at all seasons: the hard causes they brought unto Moses, but every small matter they judged themselves.

How Wide a Span?

In every organization it must be decided how many subordinates a superior can manage. Students of management have found that this number is usually four to eight subordinates at the upper levels of organization and eight to fifteen or more at the lower levels. For example, the prominent British consultant Lyndall Urwick found "the ideal number of subordinates for all superior authorities . . . to be four," and "at the lowest level of organization, where what is delegated is responsibility for the performance of specific tasks and not for the supervision of others, the number may be eight or twelve."[8] An experienced military observer has stated that he believes the proper number to range between three and six, with three likely to be best near the top of an organization, and six near the bottom.[9] Others find that a manager may be able to manage as many as twenty to thirty subordinates.[10]

In actual experience, one finds a wide variety of practices, even among admittedly well-managed enterprises. General of the Army Dwight D. Eisenhower had three immediate line subordinates when he was Supreme Commander of the Allied Expeditionary Forces in World War II, and none of these had more than four line subordinates. Yet, at the same time, the Army Chief of Staff had reporting to him and his deputies at least fifteen major line and staff officers. In the General Motors Corporation in 1978, the president had reporting to him three executive vice presidents, but one group vice president had eight persons reporting to him. The

---

[8]Lyndall Urwick, "Axioms of Organization," *Public Administration Magazine* (London), pp. 348–349 (October 1955). However, in other writings, Urwick modified this position by saying that "no person should supervise more than five, or at the most, six, direct subordinates *whose work interlocks*." See *Notes on the Theory of Organization* (New York: American Management Association, 1952), p. 53 (emphasis in quotation added).

[9]Sir Ian Hamilton, *The Soul and Body of an Army* (London: Edward Arnold [Publishers] Ltd., 1921), p. 229.

[10]J. C. Worthy, "Men, Management, and Organization," *Proceedings, Fifth Personnel Management and Industrial Relations Seminar* (Los Angeles: University of California at Los Angeles, Oct. 30, 1951; mimeographed). The term "subordinates" referred to in this section excludes personnel such as staff or administrative assistants, secretaries, clerks, and stenographers.

president of a railroad generally regarded as one of the best managed in the industry had in 1978 ten top executives reporting to him, and one of these had eleven subordinates. Yet the head of another large carrier, not regarded as so well managed, had only seven major subordinates. The president of one well-managed department store had four key executives, none of whom had more than five subordinates, while an equally large and successful store showed twelve key executives reporting to the president and an equally large number of subordinates reporting to most of them.

In a survey of 100 large companies made by the American Management Association,[11] the number of executives reporting to the presidents varied from one to twenty-four, and only twenty-six presidents had as few as six or less subordinates. The median number was nine. In forty-one smaller companies surveyed, twenty-five of the presidents supervised seven or more subordinates, and the median was eight. Comparable results were found by White in a study of sixty-six companies and in other studies.[12] In a much more narrowly based study, using a random sample, Fisch, on the other hand, discovered a tendency among very large companies (those with over $1 billion of sales) for a span of management at the top to be more than twelve, with the span tending to be smaller as the company size decreases.[13]

In a very real sense, none of these studies is truly indicative of the span of management actually practiced. For one thing, they measure the span only at or near the top of an enterprise. This is hardly typical of what the span may be throughout the enterprise, particularly since every organizer has experienced the tremendous pressure for a large number of the functions of an enterprise to report to the top executive. It is probably that spans below the top executive are much narrower. Indeed, analysis of more than 100 companies of all sizes made by one of the authors discloses a much narrower span in the middle levels of management than at the top.

In addition, the fact that apparently well-managed companies have, between them and certainly within them, widely varying spans indicates that merely counting what is actually done is not enough to establish what a span *ought* to be. And this is true even if it could be assumed that, through trial and error, each company has reached an optimum. It may prove only that underlying conditions vary.

---

[11]As summarized in *Business Week*, pp. 102–103 (Aug. 18, 1951). Healey found similar variations in his study of 409 manufacturing companies in Ohio, although the median was six subordinates. See J. H. Healey, *Executive Co-ordination and Control* (Columbus: Ohio State University Press, 1956), p. 66.

[12]K. K. White, *Understanding the Company Organization Chart* (New York: American Management Association, 1963), pp. 60–61. Similar results were shown in H. Stieglitz and C. N. Wilkerson, *Corporate Organization Structure* (New York: The Conference Board, 1968), and in A. R. Janger, *Corporation Organization Structure: Financial Enterprise* (New York: The Conference Board, 1974).

[13]G. G. Fisch, "Stretching the Span of Management," *Harvard Business Review*, vol. 41, no. 5, pp. 80–81 (September–October 1962).

There is a tendency to regard organization and departmentation as ends in themselves and to gauge the effectiveness of organization structures in terms of clarity and completeness of departments and department levels. Division of activities into departments and hierarchical organization and the creation of multiple levels are not completely desirable in themselves.

In the first place, levels are expensive. As they increase, more and more effort and money are devoted to managing, because of the additional managers, staffs to assist them, and the necessity of coordinating departmental activities, plus the costs of facilities for such personnel. Accountants refer to such costs as "overhead," or "burden," or "general and administrative," in contrast to so-called direct costs. Real production is accomplished by factory, engineering, or sales employees, who are or could logically be accounted for as direct labor. Levels above the "firing line" are predominantly staffed with managers and assistants who are not directly productive and whose cost it would be desirable to eliminate, *if that were possible.*

In the second place, departmental levels complicate communication. An enterprise with many levels has greater difficulty communicating objectives, plans, and policies through the organization structure than the firm in which the top manager communicates directly with lowest-level employees. Omissions and misinterpretations occur as information passes down the scalar chain. Levels also complicate communication from the "firing line" to the commanding superiors, which is every bit as important as downward communication. It has been well said that levels are "filters" of information.

Finally, departments and numerous levels complicate planning and control. The plan that may be definite and complete at the top level loses coordination and clarity as it is subdivided and elaborated at lower levels. Control becomes more difficult as levels and managers are added, while at the same time the complexities of planning and difficulties of communication make this control more important.

Operational-Management Position

The so-called classical school approach to the span of management has tended to deal with generalizations embodying specific numbers of subordinates for an effective span. Empirical data do give support to the classical school consensus of an upper- and top-level span from three to seven or eight subordinates.[14] However, modern operational-management theorists have taken the position that there are too many underlying variables in a management situation to conclude that there is any particular number of subordinates which a manager can effectively

[14]A consensus as found by Healey, op. cit., pp. 11–14.

supervise.[15] It is concluded that there is a limit to the number of subordinates a manager can effectively supervise, but the exact number will depend upon underlying factors, all of which affect the difficulty and time requirements of managing.

In other words, the dominant current view is to look for the causes of limited span in individual situations, rather than to assume that there is a widely applicable numerical limit. If one can look at what it is that consumes the time of managers in their handling of their superior-subordinate relationships, and also ascertain what devices can be used to reduce these time pressures, the analyst has an approach that will be helpful in determining the optimum span in individual cases and also a powerful tool for finding out what can be done to extend the span without destroying effective supervision. There can be no argument that the costs of levels in supervision are such as to make it highly desirable for every individual manager to have as many subordinates as can be *effectively* supervised.

GRAICUNAS'S THEORY OF SUBORDINATE-SUPERIOR RELATIONSHIPS

In a paper first published in 1933, French management consultant V. A. Graicunas[16] analyzed subordinate-superior relationships and developed a mathematical formula based on the geometric increase in complexities of managing as the number of subordinates increases. Although the formula may not be applicable to a given case, it focuses attention upon the central underlying problems of the span of management perhaps better than any other device. Graicunas's theory identifies three types of subordinate-superior relationships: (1) direct single relationships, (2) direct group relationships, and (3) cross-relationships.

Types of Subordinate-Superior Relationships

Direct single relationships, easily understood and recognized, relate the superior directly and individually with his or her immediate subordinates. Thus if A has three subordinates—B, C, and D—there are three direct single relationships.

Direct group relationships exist between the superior and each possible combination of subordinates. Thus a superior might deal with

---

[15]The authors of this book have taken this position since its first edition. Also see H. Stieglitz, *Corporate Organization Structures*, Studies in Personnel Policy, No. 183 (New York: National Industrial Conference Board, Inc., 1961), p. 8.

[16]"Relationship in Organization," *Bulletin of the International Management Institute* (Geneva: International Labour Office, 1933), in L. Gulick and L. Urwick (eds.), *Papers on the Science of Administration* (New York: Institute of Public Administration, 1937), pp. 181–187.

one subordinate, with a second in attendance; with all subordinates; or with various combinations of them. If A has three subordinates, these relationships include:

B with C

B with D

C with B

C with D

D with B

D with C

B with C and D

C with B and D

D with C and B

Although it may be objected that the relationship when A deals with B, with C in attendance, is no different from that when A works with C, with B in attendance, Graicunas implies a difference. In any case, three additional direct group relationships could have been included, as when A consults equally with BC, BD, and BCD, furnishing a different psychological situation from any of those noted above.

Cross-relationships are created when subordinates must deal with one another. For B, C, and D, Graicunas gives six cross-relationships:

B to C

B to D

C to B

C to D

D to B

D to C

From the analysis of direct single, direct group, and cross-relationships, Graicunas developed the following formula to give the number of all possible types of subordinate-superior relationships requiring managerial attention: Where n equals the number of subordinates, the number of all kinds of relationships will be represented by

$$n(2^n/2 + n - 1) \quad \text{or} \quad n[2^{n-1} + (n - 1)]$$

The results of this formula are shown in Table 12.1.

Table 12.1 Possible Relationships with Variable Number of Subordinates

Number of subordinates	Number of relationships
1	1
2	6
3	18
4	44
5	100
6	222
7	490
8	1,080
9	2,376
10	5,210
11	11,374
12	24,708
18	2,359,602

Significance of the Formula

The rapid rise in the number of relationships with the increase in number of subordinates is startling. Mathematically, but as will be seen below not necessarily in practice, executives with four subordinates, by adding a fifth, increase the *possible* relationships for which they are responsible by 127 percent (from 44 to 100). Clearly, executives must think twice before they increase the number of their subordinates, even though this mathematical truism does not prove they should not do so.

The usefulness of the formula is weakened because it does not deal with frequency or severity (in terms of time demands) of relationships. Their total possible number is probably less important to a manager (as Graicunas recognized) than their frequency and their demands on his or her time.

The Graicunas theory emphasizes the complexity of managing more than a few subordinates. Yet any managerial action that will reduce the number and frequency of relationships requiring managers' attention can increase their span of management and thereby reduce the costs and inefficiencies of an undue number of departments.

FACTORS DETERMINING THE FREQUENCY AND TIME IMPACT OF RELATIONSHIPS

In searching for the answer as to how many subordinates a manager can effectively control, one discovers that—aside from such personal capacities as comprehending quickly, getting along with people, and commanding loyalty and respect—the most important determinant is the manager's ability to reduce the frequency and time impact of superior-subordinate relationships. This ability naturally varies with managers and their jobs, but seven general factors materially influence the number and frequency of such relationships.

Subordinate Training

The better the training of subordinates, the less the impact of necessary superior-subordinate relationships. Well-trained subordinates require not only less time of the manager but also fewer contacts with their superior.

Training problems increase in new and more complex industries. Managers in the railroad industry, for example, would—after a long development of railroad technology—tend to be more completely trained than those in the aerospace industry. Similarly, the rapid changes in policy and procedures in the complex electronics and missile industries would increase training problems.

Delegation of Authority

Although training procedures enable managers to reduce the frequency and severity of time-consuming relationships, the principal cause of the heavy time burdens of such relationships is to be found in poorly conceived and confused organization. The most serious symptom of poor organization affecting the span of management is inadequate or unclear authority delegation. If a manager clearly delegates authority to undertake a well-defined task, a well-trained subordinate can get it done with a minimum of the superior's time and attention. But if the subordinate's task is not one that can be done, if it is not clearly defined, or if the subordinate does not have the authority to undertake it effectively, either the task will not be performed or the manager will have to spend a disproportionate amount of time supervising and guiding the subordinate's efforts. Certainly, superior managers, by delegating, hope to assign more of this time-consuming burden than they assume through supervision.

Planning

Much of the character of a subordinate's job is defined by the plans to be put into effect. If these plans are well defined, if they are workable within the framework of operations, if the authority to undertake them has been delegated, and if the subordinate understands what is expected, little of the superior's time will be required. Such is often the case with a production supervisor responsible for largely repetitive operations. Thus, in one large-volume work-clothing manufacturer's plant, production supervisors operated satisfactorily with as many as sixty or seventy subordinates.

On the other hand, where plans cannot be drawn accurately and where subordinates must do much of their own planning, their decisions may require considerable guidance. However, if the superior has set up clear policies to guide decisions and has made sure they are consistent with the operations and goals of the department, and if the subordinate understands them, there will certainly be fewer demands on the superior's time than there would be if these policies were indefinite, incomplete, or not understood.

Rate of Change

Obviously, certain enterprises change much more rapidly than others. The rate of change is important in determining the degree to which policies can be formulated and the stability of formulated policies maintained. It may, indeed, explain the organization structure of companies—railroad, banking, and public utility companies, for example—operating with wide spans of management or, on the other hand, the very narrow span of management used by General Eisenhower during World War II.

The effect of slow change on policy formulation and on subordinate training is dramatically shown in the organization of the Roman Catholic Church. This organization, in terms of durability and stability, can probably be regarded as the most successful in the history of Western civilization. Yet the organization levels are few: in most cases, bishops report directly to the Pope, and parish priests to bishops, although in a few instances bishops report to archbishops. Thus, there are generally only three levels in this worldwide organization and a consequent wide span of management at each level. Even though it is unquestionably too broad, this extraordinarily wide span is apparently tolerable, partly because of the degree of training possessed by the bishops and even more because the rate of change in the Church has been exceedingly slow. Changes in procedures or policies are developments of decades, and objectives have remained the same over almost two millennia.

Use of Objective Standards

A manager must find out, by either personal observation or use of objective standards, whether subordinates are following plans. Obviously, good objective standards, revealing with ease any deviations from plans, enable the manager to avoid many time-consuming relationships and to direct attention to exceptions at points strategic to the successful execution of plans.

Communication Techniques

The effectiveness with which communication techniques are used also influences the span of management. Objective standards of control are a kind of communications device, but many other techniques reduce the frequency of superior-subordinate relationships.

If every plan, instruction, order, or direction has to be communicated by personal contact and every organization change or staffing problem handled orally, the manager's time will obviously be heavily burdened. Some executives use "assistant-to" positions or administrative staff personnel as a communications device in helping to solve their problems with key subordinates. Written recommendations by subordinates, summarizing pertinent considerations, frequently expedite decision making. The authors have seen busy top executives widen their span of management by insisting upon summary presentation of written recommendations, even when these involved enormously important decisions. A carefully reasoned and presented recommendation helps the executive reach a considered decision in minutes, when even the most efficient conference would require an hour.

An executive's ability to communicate plans and instructions clearly and concisely also tends to increase a manager's span. The subordinate who, after leaving a superior's desk or receiving a memorandum of instructions, is still in doubt as to what is wanted or what has been said is sure to increase the relationships that will sooner or later require the manager's attention. One of the pleasures of being a subordinate is to have a superior who can express himself or herself well. A manager's casual, easy style may please subordinates, but where this easiness degenerates into confusion and wasted time, the effect is sharply to reduce the effective span of management and often morale as well.

Amount of Personal Contact

In many instances in management, face-to-face relationships are necessary. Many situations cannot be completely handled by written reports, memorandums, policy statements, planning documents, or other communications not calling for personal contact. The executive may find it valuable and stimulating to subordinates to meet and discuss problems in the give-and-take of a conference. There may also be problems of such political delicacy that they can be handled only in face-to-face meetings. This is also true when it comes to appraising people's performance and discussing it with them. And there are other situations where the best way of communicating a problem, instructing a subordinate, or getting a direct "feel" as to how people really think on some matter is to spend time in slow personal contact.

One wonders, however, whether the high percentage of executive time spent in conferences and committees might be reduced somewhat by better training, better policy making and planning, clearer delegation, more thorough staff work, better control systems and objective standards, and, in general, better application of sound principles of management.

One wonders, also, whether much of the time spent in personal contact might not be much better spent in thought and study.

At the other extreme of management, many companies seem somewhat unaware of how newer personnel techniques affect first-line supervisors, many of whom appear to have spans far beyond their abilities to handle. Merit rating, insurance programs, grievance procedures, and other personnel matters now requiring the supervisor's time in face-to-face relationships have perhaps reduced the traditionally wide span of first-line supervisors. This is not to say that these innovations are not worth their cost, but the span-of-management limitations must be evaluated in the light of these factors.

WIDE VERSUS NARROW SPANS

Limitations affecting the span of management are what create levels in organizations: the larger the enterprise or the narrower the spans, the greater the number of levels, other things being equal.

Organization structure laden with departments and levels causes complexity and losses. Experience with large organizations proves to anyone the frustrations of "layering," whereby authority, suggestions, questions, and instructions must flow up and down the chain of command. Although some of this may be allayed by understanding that requests for information need not follow the line of command, decision making—in which authority is required and used—does need to.

The Sears, Roebuck Studies

An interesting study of the effect of organization levels on enterprise efficiency was made some years ago by Sears, Roebuck and Company.[17] In the course of this study, the operations of two groups of B stores (150 to 175 employees) in towns of approximately the same size were analyzed. In one group the managers had organized their stores with an assistant manager and some thirty merchandise managers in charge of departments. In the other group the stores were organized with an extra level of management between store managers and department heads. Analyses of sales volume, profit, morale, and lower-management competence all indicated that the stores with the "flat" type of organization were superior on all scores to those more conventionally organized.

The results—clearly violating the classical numerical limitations of span of management—were traced to several factors. The principal one appeared to be that managers having a large number of subordinate

[17]J. C. Worthy, "Organization Structure and Employee Morale," *American Sociological Review*, vol. 15, pp. 169–179 (April 1950).

managers reporting to them had no alternative but to delegate adequate authority to these subordinates, who were thereby enabled to make important decisions. This not only improved their morale but, because of the pressure placed on them to perform, also actually improved the quality of their performance. By being forced to manage, they learned to manage. By the same token, store managers, knowing that they had to delegate considerable authority, took greater care in selecting, guiding, and training subordinates and also adopted efficient methods of objective control. In addition, the Sears study revealed that reducing the length of channels vastly improved communication between managers and subordinates, despite the large number of subordinates.

Flat versus Tall Structures

The matter of desirable spans of management and their effect on flat versus tall organization structures has been subjected to continued research by various behavioral scientists and has raised questions concerning the desirability of the wide spans indicated by the Sears, Roebuck studies.[18] In general, these later studies show no greatly significant performance difference between flat and tall structures. It appears that, in experimental work, the advantages of flat structures, such as faster information flow and individual satisfaction, were often offset by the advantages of narrower spans in faster and more effective problem resolution.[19]

However, the experimental study of Carzo and Yanouzas showed that groups operating under a relatively tall organization structure showed "significantly better performance than groups operating under the flat structure."[20] This was believed to be due to the fact that, with narrower spans, group members were able to evaluate decisions more frequently, and a more orderly decision process was possible.

These studies support conclusions of the authors in this book. It is difficult to generalize on wide or narrow spans of management since there are so many underlying variables to be considered. There are advantages to one and advantages to the other. The result is that the practitioner must seek balance, or compromise, to obtain the best total results in the light of the realities of a given situation.

---

[18]The considerable volume of research is well summarized in R. Carzo and J. N. Yanouzas, "Effects of Flat and Tall Organization Structures," *Administrative Science Quarterly*, vol. 14, no. 2, pp. 178–191 (June 1969).
[19]Although, in one study, the time required to make decisions was found to be better in somewhat flatter organizations structures. See H. R. Jones, Jr., "A Study of Organization Performance for Experimental Structures of Two, Three and Four Levels," *Academy of Management Journal*, vol. 12, no. 3, pp. 351–365 (September 1969).
[20]Carzo and Yanouzas, op. cit., p. 191.

There has been a considerable volume of research by behavioral scientists interested in the operation of small groups.[21] Although this research is interested in the operation of small groups, whether formally organized or not, and in such considerations as group cohesiveness, individual satisfaction, performance, and leadership, it does have some relevance to the problem of span of management. In a very real sense, managers and their immediate subordinates represent small groups. It is therefore interesting to see what light this research casts on the problem of span.

A number of interesting findings have come from these studies. In general, it has been found that group cohesiveness is best with approximately five members; fewer members do not provide enough interaction for cohesiveness, and many more than five tend to result in the breakdown of the groups into subgroups, or cliques. As might be expected, smaller groups tend to generate more individual satisfaction than larger ones, largely because of the greater opportunities for participation and the better chance of understanding group goals. Likewise in decision making, it has been shown that groups of five take less time than larger groups. However, studies have shown that a larger group may be able to solve a greater variety and a greater complexity of problems because of the probability that a greater variety of skills will be available. On the other hand, these same studies have indicated that as group size increases, the problems of coordination and reaching a consensus become more difficult, particularly where a problem solution sought has no clear or objective answer. Furthermore, small-group studies have shown that as groups become larger, the demands on the leader become more exacting and complex, and the group soon welcomes more directive and highly structured leadership.

A review of small-group research and other behaviorial investigations led House and Miner to conclude:

> The implications for the span of control seem to be that (1) under most circumstances the optimal span is likely to be in the range of 5 through 10; (2) the larger spans, say 8 through 10, are most appropriate at the highest, policy-making levels of an organization, where greater resources for diversified problem-solving appear to be needed (although diversified problem-solving without larger spans may well be possible); (3) the breadth of effective spans of first line supervisors is contingent on the technology of the organization; and

---

[21]This research is well summarized in R. J. House and J. B. Miner, "Merging Management and Behavioral Theory: The Interaction between Span of Control and Group Size," *Administrative Science Quarterly*, vol. 14, no. 3, pp. 451–464 (September 1969).

(4) in prescribing the span of control for specific situations, consideration must be given to a host of local factors such as desirability of high group cohesiveness, the performance demands of the task, the degree of stress in the environment, task interdependencies, the need for member satisfaction, and the leadership skills available to the organization.[22]

OPERATIONAL APPLICATION OF UNDERLYING-VARIABLES APPROACH

If, as the authors of this book believe, the number of subordinates that a manager can effectively supervise is not an exact number applicable generally but depends on underlying variables, it follows that managers should look at these variables for an answer to the span problem. Fortunately, such an experiment was undertaken a few years ago by the Lockheed Missiles and Space Company.[23]

The Underlying Variables

In the Lockheed program, the company identified a number of critical variables underlying the span of management. While the program applied only to the middle-management group, where spans were found to be quite narrow (three to five), and while the underlying variables are not the same as those outlined by the authors above, there are many similarities. The company utilized for its analysis the following variables:

1 Similarity of functions. This factor referred to the degree to which functions performed by the various components or personnel reporting to a manager were alike or different.
2 Geographic contiguity. This factor referred to the physical locations of units or personnel reporting to a superior.
3 Complexity of functions. This factor referred to the nature of the task done and the department managed.
4 Direction and control. This factor referred to the nature of personnel reporting to a superior, the amount of training required, the extent to which authority could be delegated, and the personal attention needed.
5 Coordination. This factor was related to time requirements of keeping

---

[22] Ibid., pp. 461-462.

[23] For a report on this program see H. Koontz, "Making Theory Operational: The Span of Management," *The Journal of Management Studies*, vol. 3, no. 3, pp. 229–243 (October 1966). See also, on the same problem, H. Stieglitz, "Optimizing the Span of Control," *Management Record*, vol. 24, no. 9, pp. 25–29 (September 1962), and C. W. Barkdull, "Span of Control: A Method of Evaluation," *Michigan Business Review*, vol. 15, no. 3, pp. 25–32 (May 1963).

Table 12.2 Degrees of Supervisory Burden within Span Factors (numbers show relative weighting)

Span factor					
Similarity of functions	Identical	Essentially alike	Similar	Inherently different	Fundamentally distinct
	1	2	3	4	5
Geographic contiguity	All together	All in one building	Separate building, one plant location	Separate locations, one geographic area	Dispersed geographic areas
	1	2	3	4	5
Complexity of functions	Simple repetitive	Routine	Some complexity	Complex, varied	Highly complex, varied
	2	4	6	8	10
Direction and control	Minimum supervision and training	Limited supervision	Moderate periodic supervision	Frequent continuing supervision	Constant close supervision
	3	6	9	12	15
Coordination	Minimum relation with others	Relationships limited to defined courses	Moderate relationships easily controlled	Considerable close relationship	Extensive mutual non-recurring relationships
	2	4	6	8	10
Planning	Minimum scope and complexity	Limited scope and complexity	Moderate scope and complexity	Considerable effort required guided only by broad policies	Extensive effort required; areas and policies not charted
	2	4	6	8	10

an organizational unit keyed in with other divisional or company wide activities.

6 Planning. This factor was designed to reflect the importance, complexity, and time requirements of the planning functions of managers and their organization units.

Degree of Supervisory Burden within Span Factors

After identifying the underlying variables related to the span of management, the company spread each of them over a spectrum of five degrees of difficulty. For each span factor, also, weightings were given to reflect relative importance. The degrees and weights of the span factors are shown in Table 12.2.

It is worth noting that the weight values in these span factors were based on an analysis of 150 cases at the middle-management and department-director levels. They were also checked against a number of comparative cases, the measuring standard being those organizational units which were regarded on the score of both reputation and performance as being well managed. Even though the weightings and values applied can be criticized as representing pseudoscience, there is evidence that they were developed with care. Moreover, as in so many measurements applied to life, the breaking down of factors and assigning values to them did help in clarifying issues and giving visibility to the problem being analyzed.

Correction for Organizational Assistance

After each position had been evaluated and the total of values from factor weightings had been added, corrections were made by application of a reducing factor to each score to take into account the amount of organizational assistance that a manager had. Thus, a direct-line assistant with responsibility for certain portions of a manager's operations resulted in the application of a factor of 0.70, and a staff assistant in administering, planning, or controlling resulted in the application of a reducing factor of 0.75 or 0.85. First-line supervisors with four lead people would have a factor of 0.40 applied to their score.

The Supervisory Index

After scores for a given manager's position had been calculated and had been corrected by the organizational-assistance factor, they were compared with a standard. The suggested supervisory indexes are shown in Table 12.3. These were developed by using as a standard the cases of organizational units with wider spans, which were generally considered to be effectively organized and managed. Thus individual managers could compare their own span factor ratings with the suggested standard span to determine whether they were below or above standard.

Results

Results from this experimental program were interesting. Even though the program was not completely adopted in the company and was not too

Table 12.3 Suggested Supervisory Index

Total span factor weightings	Suggested standard span
40–42	4–5
37–39	4–6
34–36	4–7
31–33	5–8
28–30	6–9
25–27	7–10
22–24	8–11

strongly pressed, there is evidence that it did lead to a widening of the span of management in the middle-management area and to the elimination of one complete level of supervision, with a consequent reduction in supervisory costs. Despite the rather crude methods necessarily used, by identifying the problem through looking at underlying variables and by making personnel in managerial posts aware of these, significant results were attained. The program thus indicates that material rewards in practice can follow the application of theory to real problems, even where methods are not completely proved and basic data are inexact.

Udell's Empirical Study

In an empirical study limited to marketing managers, J. G. Udell found considerable support for the hypothesis that certain underlying variables influence the span of management.[24] He found, in particular, that spans tended to be larger when (1) supervisors had assistants, (2) subordinates worked closely together geographically, (3) functions supervised were similar, (4) clearly written communication was used, and (5) subordinates were experienced.

THE NEED FOR BALANCE

There can be no doubt that, despite the desirability of flattening organization structures, the span of management is limited by real and important restrictions. Managers may have more subordinates than they can manage, even though they delegate authority, carry on training, formulate plans and policies clearly, and adopt efficient control and communication techniques. It is equally true that as an enterprise grows, the span-of-management limitations force an increase in organization levels.

What is required, of course, is a more precise balancing, in a given situation, of all pertinent factors. Widening spans and reducing levels may be the answer in some cases; the reverse may be true in others. One must balance *all* the costs of adopting one course or the other—not only the financial costs, but also costs in morale, personal development, and the attainment of enterprise objectives—in short, all the advantages and disadvantages. In military organization, perhaps the attainment of objectives quickly and without error would be most important; in department store operation, on the other hand, the long-run objective of profit may be best served by forcing initiative and personal development at the lower levels of the organization.

Much misunderstanding concerning the span of management has arisen from confusion. There is a tendency to regard the "theoretical"

---

[24]"An Empirical Test of Hypotheses Relating to Span of Control," *Administrative Science Quarterly*, vol. 12, no. 13, pp. 420–439 (December 1967).

limits of effective span as being a fixed number of approximately three to seven or eight subordinates.[25]

The correct principle of span of management is that *there is a limit in each managerial position to the number of persons an individual can effectively manage, but the exact number in each case will vary in accordance with the effect of underlying variables and their impact on the time requirements of effective managing.* This basic principle does exist, has not been superseded, and is useful in guiding managers toward ably managing more subordinates and simplifying organization.

FOR DISCUSSION

1   Since people must occupy organization positions and an effective organization depends on people, it is often said that the best organization arises when a manager hires good people and lets them do a job in their own way. Comment.

2   A formal organization is often conceived of as a communications system. Is it? How?

3   Construct a diagram depicting the formal organization of some enterprise or activity with which you are familiar. How does this help or hinder the establishment of an environment for performance?

4   Using the same enterprise or activity as in the above question, chart the informal organization. Does it help or hinder the formal organization? Why?

5   Some 750 line bishops and some 1200 other persons have been found to report directly to the Pope. Urwick and other writers seem to say that at top levels the number should not exceed six. At one time in the Bank of America organization over 600 bank managers reported to the chief executive officer. How do you fit these facts with the idea that there is a limit to the number of subordinates a manager can supervise?

6   At Lockheed Missiles and Space Company an attempt has been made to determine the span of management by an arithmetic formula. Do you think this approach can be adopted in other enterprises? How?

7   How would you determine the optimum span of management in a given situation?

8   Does the application of principles recommend, as many critics insist, a tall organization structure with a limited span of management?

9   How does the span of management illustrate contingency, or situational, theory?

[25]For a summary of the opinions of various authorities, see Healey, op. cit., pp. 11–15.

chapter 13 Basic Departmentation

MAJOR CHAPTER OBJECTIVES

1 To identify the basic patterns of traditional departmentation and analyze the advantages and disadvantages of each in various uses.

2 To show that service departments, often classified as staff departments, have their own special problems and needs as legitimate departments in their own right.

3 To analyze matrix organizations, particularly as they have been used in engineering and marketing, and outline steps that can be taken to avoid dangers of disunity of command.

4 To make clear that there is no best pattern of departmentation to use and that responsible managers must select patterns that will assist in accomplishing enterprise objectives in the light of the particular situation they face.

5 To identify and analyze the major guides applicable in deciding where within a department activities should be placed.

The limitation on the number of subordinates that can be directly managed would restrict the size of enterprises if it were not for the device of departmentation. Grouping activities and employees into departments makes it possible to expand organizations to an indefinite degree. Departments, however, differ with respect to the basic patterns used to group activities. The nature of these patterns, developed out of practice, and their relative merits are dealt with in the following sections.

At the outset it should be emphasized that there is no single best way of departmentalizing applicable to all organizations or all situations. What works best for General Motors may not work best for Ford or for Exxon. What pattern will be used will depend on given situations and what managers believe will yield the best results for them in the situation they face.

DEPARTMENTATION BY SIMPLE NUMBERS

Departmentation by simple numbers was once an important method in the organization of tribes, clans, and armies. Although it is rapidly falling into disuse, it still has certain applications in modern society.

The simple-numbers method of departmentalizing is achieved by tolling off undifferentiated persons who are to perform certain duties at the direction of a manager. The essential fact is not what these people do, where they work, or what they work with, but that the success of the undertaking depends only upon having the requisite number of bodies.

Even though a quick examination may impress an investigator with the number of people departmentized on a work-force basis, the usefulness of this organizational device has declined with each passing century. For one thing, labor skills have increased. In America the last stronghold of common labor is agriculture, and even here it is restricted more and more to the harvesting of fewer and fewer crops as farming operations become larger and more specialized.

A second reason for the decline of the work-force basis of departmentizing is that groups composed of specialized personnel are frequently more efficient than those based on mere numbers. The reorganization of the defense forces of the United States on this basis is a case in point. Many ways have been found to combine men skilled in the use of different types of weapons into single units. For instance, the addition of artillery and tactical air support to the traditional infantry division makes it a much more formidable fighting unit than if each was organized separately.

A third and long-standing reason for the decline of departmentation by numbers is that it is useful only at the lowest level of the organization structure. At the middle- and higher-management levels activities tend to be grouped on a basis other than similarity. As soon as any other factor besides pure human energy becomes important, the simple-numbers basis of departmentation fails to produce good results.

DEPARTMENTATION BY TIME

One of the oldest forms of departmentation, normally used at lower levels of organization, is to group activities on the basis of time. The use of shifts is common in many enterprises where for economic or technological reasons the normal workday will not satisfy needs. Except for problems of supervision and the question of efficiency and cost of "swing" and "graveyard" shifts, this form causes few managerial problems.

DEPARTMENTATION BY ENTERPRISE FUNCTION

The grouping of activities in accordance with the functions of the enterprise is a widely accepted practice. It embodies what enterprises typically do. Since all undertakings involve the creation of utility and since this occurs in an exchange economy, the basic enterprise functions consist of production (creating utility or adding utility to a good or service), selling (finding customers, patients, clients, students, or communicants who will agree to accept the good or service at a price), and financing (raising and collecting, safeguarding, and expending the funds of the enterprise). It has been logical to group these activities into such typical departments as production, sales, and finance.

Often, these particular terms do not appear in the organization chart. First, there is no generally accepted terminology: manufacturing enterprises employ the terms "production," "sales," and "finance"; a wholesaler is concerned with such activities as "buying," "selling," and "finance"; and a railroad is involved with "operations," "traffic," and "finance."

A second reason for variance of terms is that basic activities often differ in importance: hospitals have no selling departments; churches, no production departments. This does not mean that these activities are not undertaken but merely that they are unspecialized or of such minor importance that they are combined with other activities.

A third reason for the absence of sales, production, or finance departments on many organization charts is that other methods of departmentation may have been deliberately selected, the functional basis being, after all, merely one way to organize. Those responsible for the enterprise may decide upon a product, customer, territorial, or marketing-channel basis.

Functional departmentation is the most widely employed basis for organizing activities and is present in almost every enterprise at some level in the organization structure. When it is partially used, one function may be found—usually the finance department—beside or above a department based upon product, customer, or territory.

The characteristics of the selling, production, and finance functions of enterprise are so widely recognized and thoroughly understood that they are the basis not only of departmental organization but also most often of primary departmentation. The primary level is the first level in the organization structure below the chief executive. The designation is made without consideration of the major or minor nature of the departments or the basis for grouping enterprise activities. Whenever activities are grouped into major functional departments, they will naturally be located in the organization structure at the primary level, while minor, or derivative, functional departments may be found almost anywhere below the first echelon.

Major Functional Departments

The term "major" is often used to identify departments with large budgets, many employees, or an importance related to the very existence of the enterprise. Large budgets and many employees are obviously independent of the types of departmentation. The major functional departments in any organization structure are those which carry on its *characteristic activities.*

Without exception, every organization is engaged in creating utility in goods or services, exchanging this wealth at a price for purchasing power, and managing the cash flow which is entailed in the operation. This means that every organization has a production, sales, and financing function. Of course, not everyone may use these terms. A university produces educational services, attracts students, and finances its operations; a religious organization provides services, attracts worshipers, and also finances its operation. Lawyers offer services to their clients for a price; public accountants likewise provide services for a fee.

In each case, the services proffered are often divided between major departments. A university will offer services within groups of activities that may be called liberal arts, engineering, law, medicine, and business. A church may divide its services under such heads as general worship service, Sunday school, and missions. If special departments covering any of these activities are not organized, it may mean that the state of the market does not require the exertion of maximum effort.

Derivative Functional Departments

Derivative functional departments are established when the manager of any functional division feels that his or her span of management is too broad. For instance, when an enterprise is small, the production manager may have only workers as subordinates. With the expansion of activities it

Table 13.1   Derivative Functional Departments of Typical Organization Structures

Primary functional department	Derivative functional departments
In a manufacturing organization	
Production	Manufacturing:
	Fabrication
	Assembly
	Tooling
	Purchasing
	Production control:
	Scheduling
	Materials control
	Quality control
Sales	Selling:
	Selection
	Training
	Operation
	Advertising
	Sales promotion
Finance	Capital requirements
	Fund control
	Disbursements
	Credit
	Accounting
In a department store operation	
Publicity	Advertising
	Display
	Media public relations
Merchandising	Buying (organized by product line):
	Budgeting
	Merchandise control
	Sales promotion
	Sales force
General superintendent	Supplies
	Customer service
	Store protection
	Warehousing
	Receiving, marking, delivery
Finance	Financial management:
	Cash control
	Credit
	Accounting
In a wholesale organization	
Sales	Buying (organized by product line):
	Budgeting
	Merchandise control
	Sales promotion
	Sales force
General superintendent	Warehousing:
	Receiving
	Will call
	Shipping
	Stockroom

Table 13.1 *(Continued)*

Primary functional department	Derivative functional departments
In a wholesale organization	
Finance	Money management
	Credit and collections
	Accounting
In a service organization (airline)	
Operations	Engineering:
	New equipment
	Modification of equipment
	Communications engineering
	Maintenance
	Line maintenance
	Overhaul
	Ground operations:
	Station management
	Food and commissary
	Flight operations:
	Flying
	Communications
	Dispatching
Traffic or sales	Administration:
	Reservations
	Schedules
	Tariffs
	Sales:
	Passenger sales
	Cargo sales
	Sales promotion
	Advertising:
	Direct mail
	Newspaper and periodical
	Radio and television
Finance	Financial management:
	Cash control
	New financing
	Foreign exchange
	Accounting:
	Revenue
	Disbursements
	General ledger

may be necessary to split off the buying function and place a purchasing agent in charge. The new purchasing unit is a derivative functional department; it would appear on an organization chart at the second level, if production is a primary division. A typical grouping of functional activities into derivative departments is suggested in Table 13.1

Advantages

The most important advantage of functional departmentation is that it is a logical and time-proven method. It is also the best way of making certain

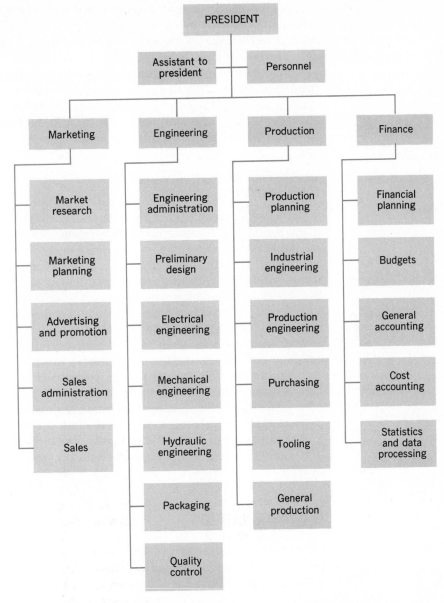

Figure 13.1 Typical functional organization grouping (manufacturing company).

that the power and prestige of the basic activities of the enterprise will be defended by the top managers. This is an important consideration among functional managers, for they see on every side the encroachments of staff and service groups, which sometimes threaten the security of the principal line executives. Another advantage is that functional departmentation follows the principle of occupational specialization, thereby making for efficiency in the utilization of the work force. Still other advantages are that it simplifies training and, because the top managers have end-results responsibility, furnishes a means of tight control at the top.

Disadvantages

In spite of the advantages of functional departmentation, there are times when the claims of other methods seem even stronger. The size of the geographic area over which an enterprise operates may call for territorial production experts, and salespeople, growing up in specialized departments, often have difficulty seeing the business as a whole, and coordination between them is frequently difficult to achieve.

Through this type of differentiation, they develop attitudes and other behavioral patterns involving loyalty to a function and not to the enterprise as a whole. Such "walls" between functional departments are common and require considerable efforts toward integration.

Another disadvantage is that only the chief executive officer can be held responsible for profits. In small firms, this is as it should be, but in large firms the burden becomes too heavy for one person to bear. What is perhaps most important is that since the first *general* managerial position is that of the president or the executive vice president, the functionally organized company is not the best training ground for promotable top management employees.

DEPARTMENTATION BY TERRITORY

Departmentation based on geographic area is a rather common method for physically dispersed enterprises. The principle is that all activities in a given area or territory should be grouped and assigned to a manager.

Extent of Use

Territorial departmentation is especially attractive to large-scale firms or other enterprises whose activities are physically or geographically spread. A plant may, however, be local in its activities and still assign the guards in its security department on a territorial basis, placing two men, for instance, at each of the south and west gates. Department stores assign floorwalkers on this basis, and it is a common way to assign janitors, window washers, and the like. Business firms resort to this method when similar operations are undertaken in different geographic areas, as in automobile assembly, chain retailing and wholesaling, and oil refining. Large life insurance companies like Prudential and Equitable have realized advantages in having a main headquarters in the East and another headquarters in the West. Many government agencies—the Internal Revenue Service, the Federal Reserve Board, the federal courts, and the Postal Service, for example—adopt this basis of organization in their efforts to provide like services simultaneously across the nation.

Reasons for Use

Although it is important for the enterprise considering territorial departmentation to base its decision on the right reasons, frequently the choice is made for the wrong reasons.

The wrong reasons   Poor communication facilities are often advanced as a reason for territorial departmentation. At one time, this reason was good, and in many parts of the world it still is. In general, communication is now so easy that this reason is less forceful. With telephone, telegraph, and television, an associate many miles away can sometimes be reached more quickly than the person in the next office.

The need for taking prompt action in a given area is also cited as a good reason for territorial departmentation. The assumption is that local officers will be prompt. They may not be. Nor is so-called ease of coordination and control on a local basis sufficient reason for territorial grouping. Fumbling will give poor results, whether perpetrated by local officers or by central office managers.

Further, those who advocate area grouping for the above reasons miss the point, developed in the next section, that not all the enterprise activities are actually associated on a territorial basis anyway. Concentrating attention on those which are locally grouped overlooks the serious management problems created when different organizational methods are employed simultaneously at headquarters.

The right reasons   Territorial departmentation is proper when its purpose is to encourage local participation in decision making and to take advantage of certain economies of localized operation. Many enterprises, as a matter of policy, avoid local participation in some or all phases of their activities. On the other hand, the managers of many firms, with great or little fanfare, do their very best to encourage it.

The firm that makes allowances for local elements in a situation will find many opportunities to do so. Those which can tie in their product with such local phenomena as fishing facilities, skiing opportunities, sunbathing, or the occurrence of smog can use local appeals in their advertising. Sometimes supplies are ordered on a local basis, as when managers of chain retail stores tie in with local businesses for construction, supplies, and services.

Sales managers look with favor upon the local recruitment of salespeople. Familiar with area factors that outsiders would have to learn, such persons are not required to uproot their families and are presumed to know how to deal with area customers. The quality of people recruited elsewhere may be better, but they will require adjustment to local factors.

Although the great improvements in communication have largely eradicated differences in custom, style, and product preferences, many enterprises still consider these differences important enough to treat on a local basis. If it is enterprise policy to heed local factors, territorial departmentation can provide the area with a manager who has the prestige essential for getting results. Middle- and high-level managers may not be ready to listen to the complaints of a distant sales employee, but they will listen to the representations of a regional executive. Finally, good as mechanical and electronic communication is becoming, there is really nothing that takes the place of face-to-face discussion. A deeper and fuller understanding is achieved, both about the person and about the subject matter being discussed.

The economic reasons for selecting territorial departmentation concern the cost of getting things done. Plants for the manufacture and assembly of parts may be located so as to reduce transportation costs. The proper location of warehouse facilities will reduce the time required for delivery, a factor that may affect booking the order. Any arrangement of sales routes to reduce traveling during the best hours for sales will likewise reduce the expense of distribution.

The district, region, or branch has long been recognized as an excellent training ground for managers. It is made to order for giving them essential experience at a place in the organization structure and at a time in their careers most valuable to them and least risky for the firm. This is not to say that a firm should organize territorially in order to permit subordinate managers to gain essential experience, but it is a factor to consider in deciding upon the type of departmentation.

Advantages

The three primary functional areas of enterprise activity may be analyzed from the point of view of the proper reasons for regional grouping. In the production department, the proposal for organizing on a regional basis would involve establishing plants, to be engaged in manufacturing, mining, refining, or assembling the *same* product, in various areas. By catering to local factors, the production activity would gain certain advantages; the good will produced by providing jobs for local labor, for instance. But the chief gains would be economic: lower freight rates and perhaps lower rent and labor costs.

The advantages of territorial organization of sales activity are primarily economy and effectiveness. Sales personnel with a localized territory can spend more of their time in sales and less in travel. Also, they can be closer to customers and get to know their needs better and, in so doing, serve customers better. Being closer permits them to know what the market is, what its preferences are, and what marketing strategy is most likely to succeed. Perhaps of all enterprise activities, sales is most likely to be organized on a territorial basis.

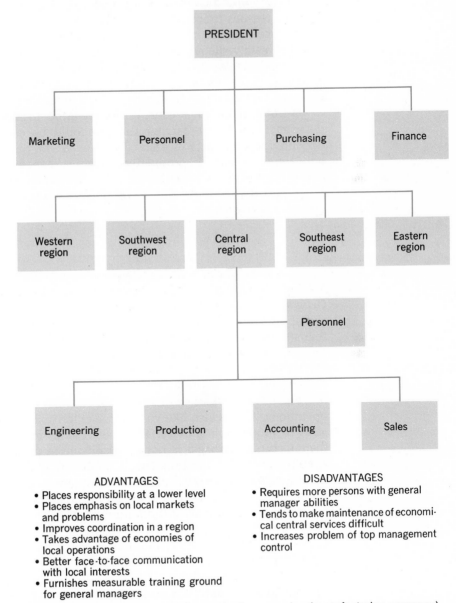

ADVANTAGES
- Places responsibility at a lower level
- Places emphasis on local markets and problems
- Improves coordination in a region
- Takes advantage of economies of local operations
- Better face-to-face communication with local interests
- Furnishes measurable training ground for general managers

DISADVANTAGES
- Requires more persons with general manager abilities
- Tends to make maintenance of economical central services difficult
- Increases problem of top management control

Figure 13.2 Typical territorial organization grouping (manufacturing company).

The span of management is also an important factor in such practices. The grouping of activities on an area basis may mean establishing a thousand districts, the managers of which cannot report directly to the general sales manager. Since that span of management may be limited to eight or ten subordinates, a thousand managers would have to report to about a hundred superiors at the branch level, who would in turn report to ten or so regional managers. Three territorial *levels* within the sales department would thus be established.

The reasons for area departmentation apply with little or no force to the finance function of enterprise. The development of sources of funds and their safety, disbursement, and control—typical activities of a finance department—enjoy few gains from catering to local factors. On the other hand, the economies of centralization of these activities are so pronounced that virtually all enterprises strive for them.

Neither is there a general rule relating to the level within the department at which territorializing should be considered. Decisions depend upon the facts in each case. It would be purely a coincidence if both the sales and the production activities reaped net advantages from area grouping at the same levels. Also, the likelihood that all derivative functional departments should be departmentized on an area basis is extremely remote.

Disadvantages

There are, however, definite disadvantages in organizing territorially. Most of them are the same as those found with product departmentation. Geographic departmentation requires more persons with general managerial abilities, clearly increases the problem of headquarters control, and tends to lead to duplication of many services which could be performed centrally in a functional organization.

Especially at the top level, general managers of territorial divisions understandably want to have their own purchasing, personnel, accounting, and other services so that they can be truly responsible for profitable operations. This is also likely to be true of territorial departmentation of a sales or production activity. The district sales manager or the Midwest manufacturing manager is not unreasonable in preferring not to rely on central services at headquarters. Sometimes, it is feared, headquarters managers worry unduly about this apparent duplication of service functions and are concerned more with what they cost than how they help a territorial manager to perform more effectively.

DEPARTMENTATION BY PRODUCT

The grouping of activities on the basis of product or product lines has long been growing in importance in multiline, large-scale enterprises.

It has been an evolutionary process. Typically, the enterprises adopting this form were originally organized functionally. With the growth of the firm, production managers, sales and service managers, and engineering executives encountered problems of size. The managerial job became intolerably complex, and the span of management limited their ability to increase the number of immediate subordinate managers. At this point, reorganization on a product division basis was indicated. This strategy permits top management to delegate a division executive extensive authority over the manufacturing, sales, service, and engineering functions that relate to a given product or product line and to exact a considerable degree of profit responsibility from each of these managers.

Advantages

Product or product line is an important basis for departmentation because it facilitates the employment of specialized capital, makes easier a certain type of coordination, and permits the maximum use of personal skills and specialized knowledge. For instance, the sales effort of a particular person may be most effective when confined to lubricants, or conveyors, or power plants, each of which is best sold by the expert thoroughly familiar with the product. Where the potential volume of business is high enough to employ fully such salespeople, the advantages of product departmentation are significant.

This basis of grouping activities also permits, although not exclusively, the employment of specialized capital goods. If production of an item, or closely related items, is sufficiently large to employ specialized facilities fully, strong pressure will be felt for product departmentation in order to realize economic advantages in manufacturing, assembly, or handling.

If it is important for activities relating to a particular product to be coordinated, then product departmentation may be preferred. Better timing and customer service can thus sometimes be provided. If sales and engineering effort also emanates from the plant, cooperation with production can be exceptionally good. Other factors that may reduce this advantage will be considered presently.

Finally, profit responsibility can be exacted from product department managers. Where they supervise the sales, production, engineering, service, and cost functions, they may be required to achieve predetermined profit goals. They share the responsibility of producing a profit along with other similarly organized groups and thus enable a general manager to evaluate more intelligently the contribution of each product line to total profit.

In considering this advantage, however, care is essential if oversimplification is to be avoided. Even product line managers may be saddled with heavy overhead costs, allocated from the expense of operating the

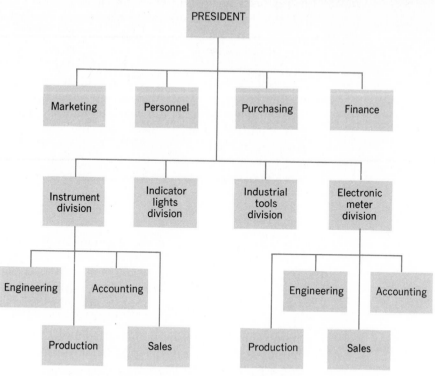

ADVANTAGES
- Places attention and effort on product line
- Places responsibility for profits at the division level
- Improves coordination of functional activities
- Furnishes measurable training ground for general managers
- Permits growth and diversity of products and services

DISADVANTAGES
- Requires more persons with general manager abilities
- Tends to make maintenance of economical central services difficult
- Presents increased problem of top management control

Figure 13.3 Typical product organization grouping (manufacturing company).

general office, perhaps a research division, and frequently many service divisions.

Accountants will recognize the similarity of these problems to those attendant upon establishing profit centers within primary functional departments or to those accounting procedures designed to identify the responsibility of product lines within functional divisions for generating costs. In these cases the amount of guesswork in making allocations is simply greater than in the case of true product departmentation.

The product basis for grouping activities can be successful in all functional areas except industrial relations and finance. In the former, where the enterprise must deal with a single national union and especially with its national officers, it is usually essential that administration be centralized. This permits the employment of skilled managers to negotiate with unions and to make authoritative interpretations of the company wide agreement. The centralization of authority over finance enables top managers to economize in the use of a very scarce resource and, by this means, hold the enterprise together.

All other functions can be successfully organized on a product basis. Such a well-known grouping as Buick, Cadillac, Chevrolet, and other divisions of General Motors rests upon the product basis. The buyers who report to the merchandise manager of a department store are known by their product lines. Hospitals departmentize on the basis of such services as surgery and radiology, and relief organizations include such "product" departments as food, clothing, shelter, and medical care. Examples of derivative product departments are shown in Table 13.2.

Sales managers of enterprises that manufacture numerous items group them on the basis of their similarity. Wholesalers do the same thing; for example, they might have a linen department, a period furniture grouping, or an electronics department, including condensers, capacitors,

Table 13.2 Derivative Product Departments of Typical Organization Structures

Primary product department	Derivative product departments
A meat packer (production department)	
Dairy and poultry	Butter, cheese, hatcheries, ice cream, eggs, poultry, dried milk
Beef, lamb, and veal	Calf buying, cattle buying, lamb buying, hides and skins, wools
Branch-house provision (functional department)	Casing, hog buying
By-products	Hides and fats, cleanser, gelatin, glue, industrial oils, soap and glycerine, tallow
Plant food	Insecticides and fungicides, phosphate rock
Agricultural research	Canned foods, margarine, table-ready meats, vegetable oil, dog and cat food
A container manufacturer (sales department)	
Food industries	Processed food, prepared food, coffee, dairy
Drug and chemical	Pharmaceutical and proprietary, household and chemical, prescription
Closure and plastics	
Beverage industries	Beverage, brewery, liquor
An insurance company (finance department)	
Investment (a functional derivative)	Mortgages, private placements, public utility, transportation, industrial, government

transistors, and similar items. This departmental structure permits the sales force to gain a broad and deep product knowledge. A commercial bank, too, is quite likely to subdivide its loan activities into commercial, industrial, and personal loans, and its investment activities into securities, real estate, and trusts.

Disadvantages

The disadvantages of product departmentation are virtually identical with those encountered in territorial departmentation. They include the necessity of having more persons with general managerial abilities available, the dangers of increased cost through duplication of central service and staff activities, and the problem of maintaining top management control. The latter becomes especially important because a product division manager is, to a very great extent, in the same position as the chief executive of a single product line company. Enterprises that operate with product divisions take care, as the General Motors Company has, to place enough decision making and control at the headquarters level so that the entire enterprise does not disintegrate into divisions.

CUSTOMER DEPARTMENTATION

The grouping of activities to reflect a paramount interest in customers is commonly found in a variety of enterprises. Customers are the key to the way activities are grouped when the things an enterprise does for them are managed by one department head. The industrial sales department of a wholesaler who also sells to retailers is a case in point. However, customer departmentation is seldom used as a major or first-level organization structure. We find it, instead, below the top level.

There are close decisions to be made in separating some types of customer departments from product departments. For instance, in the great central cash markets for agricultural products, the loan officers of commercial banks frequently specialize in fruit, vegetables, and grain, even to the point where they will make loans only on wheat or oranges. This is a clear case of customer departmentation since loan service is provided by type of customer. On the other hand, a grouping such as sales, manufacturing, engineering, and cost accounting, all of which are concerned with serving a single customer type, such as public utilities, would be likely to be called "functional departmentation" even though the special customer is identifiable.

Extent of Use

Customer departmentation is utilized in many types of enterprises. Business owners and managers frequently arrange activities on this basis to cater to the requirements of clearly defined customer groups, and educational institutions offer regular and extension courses to serve different groups of students.

Reasons for Use

The special and widely varied needs of customers for clearly defined service impel many suppliers to departmentize on this basis. The manufacturer who sells to both wholesalers and industrial buyers frequently finds that the needs of the two outlets can best be met by specialized departments. The wholesaler requires a product of dependable quality, available on a continuous reorder basis and suited to the ultimate consumer. The industrial buyer wants a product that will save money, which frequently calls for high quality, plus a service that includes survey of needs, installation and repair of the product, and the specific training of employees.

Nonbusiness groups follow similar practices. The extension work of universities is arranged, with respect to time, subject matter, and sometimes instructors, to appeal to an entirely different group of students from those who attend on a full-time day basis. The operations of a community chest drive are arranged on the basis of different "customer" classifications. And departments of the federal government are set up to care particularly for farmers, business people, industrial workers, the elderly, and others.

Employment in Functional Departments

Customer departmentation is often found useful for grouping the sales activity of those firms which cater to different classes of customers. For instance, it is not unusual for a manufacturer with only an industrial market to divide customers into large and small accounts. On the other hand, manufacturers may not develop derivative customer departments in their production function. A manufacturer of typewriters does not specialize production facilities in terms of university students and insurance company customers. Even when the manufacture of standard and electric typewriters is separated, the resulting departmentation is on a product and not on a customer basis.

Independent wholesalers and retailers combine their sales and production functions and then subdepartmentize them according to product. Sometimes, however, they organize customer departments. For instance, department stores often carry similar merchandise in the bargain basement and on an upper floor, organizing the two departments under two buyers. This is customer departmentation, since it assumes that different income groups patronize the two areas.

The financial departments of manufacturers, wholesalers, and retailers have no need for customer departmentation, since they are operated with a view to the welfare of the enterprise rather than to the needs of customers.

Disadvantages

Customer departmentation is not enjoyed without certain drawbacks. There is, for instance, the difficulty of coordination between this type of department and those organized on other bases, with constant pressure from the managers of customer departments for special treatment.

Another disadvantage is the possibility of underemployment of facilities and employees specialized in terms of customer groups. In periods of recession some customer groups may all but disappear, for example, machine-tool manufacturers; in periods of expansion the unequal development of customer groups is characteristic.

MARKETING-ORIENTED DEPARTMENTATION

Newer forms of basic departmentation involve organizing an enterprise around markets served or around marketing channels used. While both these approaches to departmentation are designed to emphasize marketing and make it more effective, they do have some differences. Organizing around marketing channels involves making an organization structure reflect the ways a company reaches an ultimate customer, whether that is through wholesale channels direct to grocery stores or direct to supermarkets, through channels designed to serve hardware stores, or through those that reach drugstores. Market-centering organization, on the other hand, groups activities to support marketing efforts in such key markets as hospitals, aerospace companies, computer operations, and brokerage firms.

Both approaches may sound like customer departmentation, and they are similar. However, the essential considerations in these marketing-oriented forms are the marketing channel and the market.

The Purex Corporation, for example, found some years ago, when it moved from a functional to a divisional organization, that neither product nor territorial departmentation patterns would work. Various soaps and detergents moved to the ultimate customer through the grocery supermarkets as well as through drugstores and drug chains. On investigating these channels it was found that the ways of doing business, the kinds of buyers, and the methods of sales and promotion were so different in grocery markets and in drug chains and drugstores that it was wise to establish a grocery products division and drug and toiletries division. While this may sound like product departmentation, it was not. The grocery products division manufactured the various soap and detergent items that were marketed through the drug and toiletries division.

These innovations in basic departmentation are, in a way, not surprising. As all kinds of economic enterprises, and even some noneconomic enterprises, have moved into a worldwide era of supercompetition, one could expect that marketing considerations might be dominant in setting up organization structure. For companies whose marketing requirements fit in with product or territorial departmentation, the more traditional forms work adequately. But for some companies whose product divisionalization has been based on technical production factors and not on marketing, a shift in organization may be desirable. The Du Pont Company learned this some years ago when marketing considerations led the company to consolidate their Orlon, Nylon, and Dacron Divisions into one Textile Fibers Division. Likewise with the reorganization of Westinghouse in recent years, divisions were methodically organized primarily around marketing channels rather than products. As in the case of the Purex Corporation, where a given product is best marketed through different marketing channels and it has seemed wise to divisionalize around these channels, the decision is then made on which division will manufacture a given product for another division.

The more purely market-centered approach to organizing has grown in importance as businesses have become more marketing-oriented. Data processing operations of International Business Machines Corporation have been segmented organizationally according to such key markets as supermarkets and hospitals. The Xerox Information Systems Group has organized around various copier markets. Hewlett Packard has organized sales and service around electrical manufacturing and aerospace markets. Other companies have taken similar steps. This means, of course, that organizational patterns must respond to situations since it is the task of the organization structure to help in making possible the kind of performance desired.

Advantages

The advantages of market-oriented departmentation are not difficult to perceive. In this day of trying to reach customers through effective selling, good marketing is the name of the game for most business enterprises. There is even some merit in being more concerned than we are with our "markets" in government, education, and churches. Eventually, it is the different publics served by government, by colleges and universities, and by churches that must be served, and served efficiently and effectively, if such organizations are to survive.

Disadvantages

But market-oriented organization does have its problems. One usually needs a manager with strong entrepreneurial skills to head up the division or department. There may be duplication of many top organization services, such as sales, advertising, accounting, purchasing, and personnel. Duplication and confusion may arise in product research and development activities, as well as in manufacturing, as the market-oriented managers demand special attention and service. The demands for market and other information are likely to be greater and more costly. For these reasons, departmentizing on a market-oriented basis does not mean that all activities necessary for producing for, and serving, a given market will be included. Economics is likely to demand that companies centralize such activities as accounting, production, engineering, purchasing, and even sales.

PROCESS OR EQUIPMENT DEPARTMENTATION

The grouping of enterprise activities about a process or a type of equipment is often employed by manufacturing establishments. Such a basis of departmentation is illustrated in a paint or electroplating process grouping or in the arrangement in one plant area of punch presses or automatic screw machines. People and material are brought together in such a department in order to carry out a particular operation.

One of the common examples of equipment departmentation is the existence of electronic data processing departments. As such installations have become more expensive and complex, with ever-increasing capacities, they have tended to be organized in a separate department. While it has become rare that a medium-sized or an even smaller company does not have such a department, and virtually all major divisions of larger companies have such installations, changes in technology have, to some extent, given rise to a degree of decentralization. Computer stations connected to an enterprise's central computer or an outside one under a time-sharing or leasing basis, minicomputers, and electronic desk computers have tended to slow the growth of centralized computer departments. However, major data processing departments will unquestionably continue to exist and to be placed fairly high in the organization structure.

The purpose of such departmentation is to achieve economic advantages, although it may also be required by the nature of the equipment involved. For example, a large computer requires heavy specialized capital since it may not be possible to utilize economically small units of this apparatus.

SERVICE DEPARTMENTS

Although often thought of as "staff" departments rather than a kind of departmentation, service departments are essentially a grouping of activities which might be carried on in other departments but are brought together in a specialized department for purposes of efficiency or control, or both. Thus, service departments should accurately be regarded as a form of departmentation. Typical of service departments found in both business and nonbusiness enterprises are personnel (especially recruiting, training, and personnel records), accounting, purchasing, plant maintenance, statistical reports, electronic data processing, and typing pools. As can be seen, in each case the activities—which could be done in the various departments using these services—are gathered together for efficiency or control, or both.

The nature and desirability of service departments can be illustrated by several examples. It would be possible to have every division, department, or section of an organization do its own accounting; but we have found that accounting can be done more efficiently and with a higher degree of accuracy and control if put in a specialized department. Likewise, supervisors and their employees in a factory could do their own maintenance of machines and electrical appliances; but it has proved to be more efficient to have a group of specialists do these things. It can be seen that in the accounting, personnel, and purchasing departments, specialized grouping of activities has advantages for both efficiency and control. In the case of plant maintenance, statistical reports, electronic data processing, and secretarial pools, the reason for consolidating activities is most likely to be expense savings, rather than control.

Being staffed by specialists, most service departments naturally tend to be used to provide expert advice for operating people. They are consequently often referred to as staff departments. But, as we shall see in the following chapter, they are not really staff departments since their *primary* function is to carry on *activities* needed in an enterprise. Although referred to as "service" departments here, some enterprises call them "facilitating," "auxiliary," or "support" departments.

Some Major Problems in Service Departments

Three major problems have been encountered in service department organization and operation. They may be summarized as follows:

Efficient inefficiency It is easy to see that, in many instances, by consolidating activities, money can be saved. By having a single department in a company or other organization do all the statistical reports, it can be readily shown that the reports will be done at the lowest cost. However, we may get low-cost reports that do not really meet the information needs of managers who are to use them. We can save money by having all training handled by a personnel department. But often managers may not get people trained in what they think is necessary, and they may pay no attention to their important responsibility for developing the people who report to them. Similarly, as efficiency experts roam through an office and see a few secretaries reading newspapers or working crossword puzzles, they can swiftly come to the conclusion that money would be saved by putting all secretaries in a pool and letting all managers take their work to the pool. But what may be overlooked is the time lost and the cost incurred by a high-priced manager's or professional specialist's taking secretarial work to a pool and waiting hours or days to get it back.

Therefore, with a service department we sometimes get a high degree of efficiency in that department, but at a greater cost to the people the department is designed to serve.

The desire to exercise control   Service department people sometimes forget that their task is to serve others and wish to take control over an activity. In one company, the purchasing people refused to order the exact equipment and parts that engineers wanted, feeling (as was sometimes true) that they knew best what the engineers needed; the result was not only friction but, in too many cases, the ordering of items that did not fit an engineer's needs for a specific use or quality. In another company, the personnel department took upon itself not only the task of recruiting and giving managers a list of prospects from which they could choose, but of actually hiring people the personnel specialists thought were best and forcing them on managers.

The problem of adequate service   Service department managers often have a difficult time. If they set up their department with enough people and equipment to meet all demands for service, they are likely to be accused of being wasteful "empire builders." If, on the other hand, they try to run an efficient department, they may not be able quickly to meet all requests for service; then they are accused of being just plain "no good!" In fact, it is often said that a "service department manager's lot is not an easy one, and no service department manager can be 'loved.'"

How to Utilize Service Departmentation Wisely

That the use of specialized departments to serve other parts of an organization is important, no one can deny. Some guidelines to help using service departments wisely are the following:

Never overlook that their task is service   As simple as this guideline is, the problems noted above, especially that of efficient inefficiency, dramatize this need. In the first place, people in service departments must be continually taught this attitude. In the second place, those who create and expand service departments should not be so carried away with the possibility of saving a few dollars by getting along without several secretaries, clerks, drafters, mechanics, or trainers that they overlook the effect on the efficiency and effectiveness of those who require the service.

Place department as close to point of service as possible   One of the tendencies in large organizations is to centralize service activities so much that a service department is too far away from the people being served. This has happened in many instances with electronic data processing. Because of the huge capacity and great expense of the modern computer system, many organizations have established large computer installations to serve a number of operations over the country. It is true that the large computer can do the work and that the various plants, sales offices, and division headquarters may reach it through a terminal. But there are many occasions where special reports and information, not having been planned for, cannot be easily made available to individual managers who need them. The result is that many companies and government agencies have chosen to decentralize at least a portion of their computer operations closer to the point where they are used.

It may even be wise, as many organizations have found, to have a fairly large number of service departments reporting to local managers when they can more readily give these managers the service they need. Also, if a service operation is on the using manager's budget, the resulting greater degree of tolerance for service priorities and costs is not at all surprising.

Charge service costs to users   One way of making sure that people will be reasonable in their requests for service from a specialized department is to charge users with the costs of their service requirements. When costs, even of a central service, are charged to users, it is interesting to note how the number of needless requests for service declines.

Never overlook the possibilities of using outside services   Often enterprises can save money by hiring outside specialists to handle their service needs. This is sometimes done for plant machinery maintenance. Many companies and government agencies have found it cheaper and more satisfactory to contract their cleaning and janitorial work to independent firms. Also, it is not all unusual to utilize executive and personnel recruiting firms to handle many of an organization's job openings. Often, outside firms can do service work at lower costs because they are not subject to the wage and salary structures and fringe benefits that a company or government agency may be required to meet. Also, in many areas, outside firms are able to keep a larger pool of highly skilled talent on hand to meet special problems than a particular enterprise would find it advantageous to maintain.

MATRIX ORGANIZATION

One of the interesting and increasingly used forms of organization is variously referred to as "matrix" or "grid" organization or "project" or "product" management, although, as will be noted presently, pure project management need not imply a grid or matrix. The essence of matrix management, as one normally finds it, is the combining of functional and

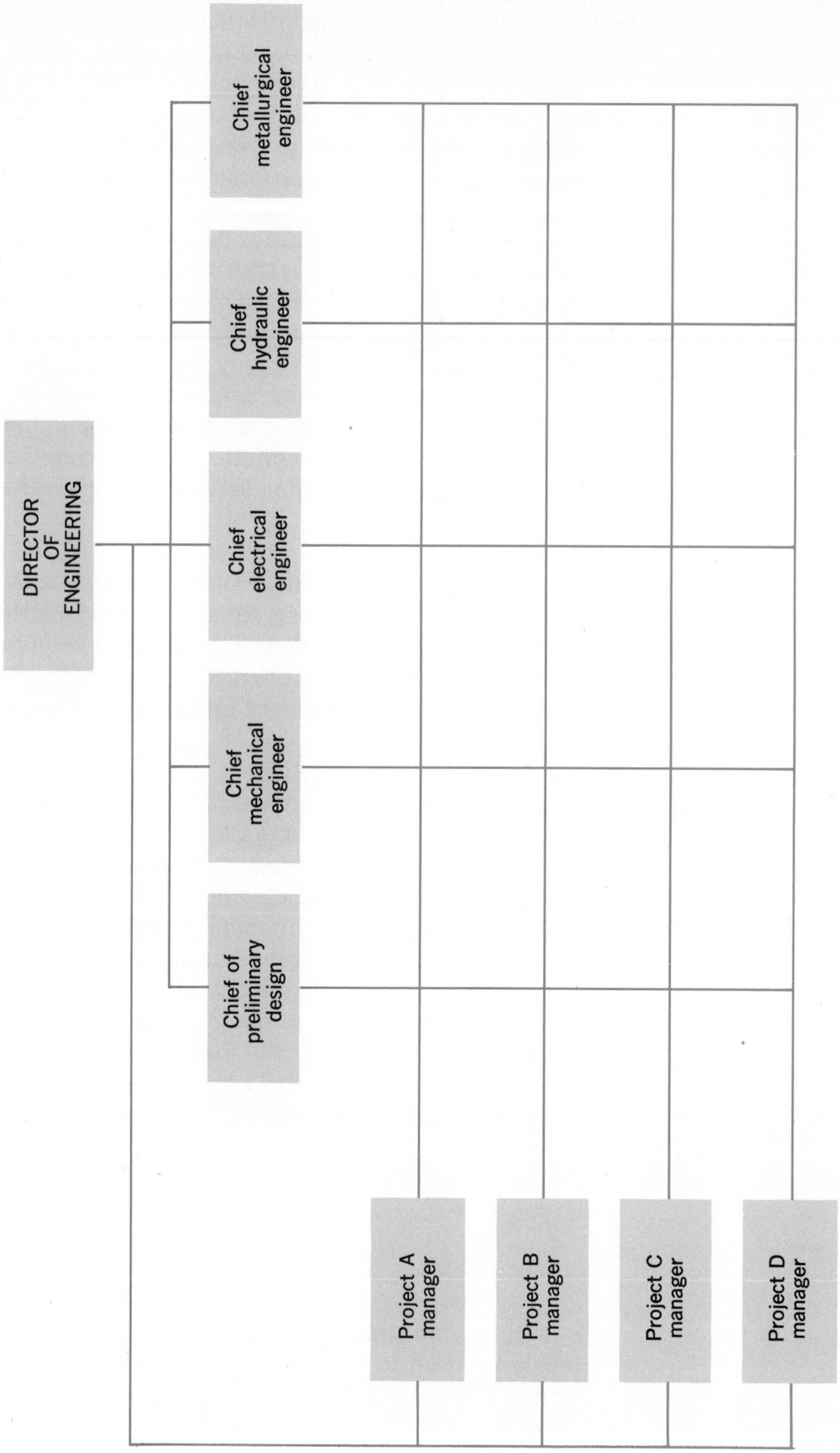

Figure 13.4 Matrix organization in engineering.

product forms of departmentation in the same organization structure. As is shown in Figure 13.4, which depicts matrix organization in an engineering department, there are functional managers in charge of engineering functions with an overlay of project managers responsible for the end product—a project. While this form has been common in engineering and research and development, it has also been widely used, although seldom drawn with a matrix, in product marketing management and, more recently, with an implied three-dimension matrix, in a combination of product and market management.

Why Matrix Management is Used

Matrix management really represents a compromise between functional and product departmentation. As companies and customers have become increasingly interested in end results, that is, the final product or completed project, there has been pressure to establish responsibility in someone to assure such end results. Of course, this could be accomplished by organizing along traditional product department lines. This is often done, even in engineering, where a project manager is put in charge of all the engineering and support personnel to accomplish an entire project. This kind of organization is depicted in Figure 13.5.

But full project organization may not be feasible for a number of reasons. In engineering, for example, the project may not be able to utilize certain specialized personnel or equipment full time; a solid-state physicist may be needed only occasionally, and the project might need only part-time use of an expensive environmental test laboratory or a prototype shop. Also, the project might be of relatively short duration. While there is no *logical* reason why an organization structure should not be changed daily or monthly, there is the practical reason that people, particularly highly trained professionals, simply will not tolerate the insecurity of frequent organization change. Another reason why pure project organization may not be feasible is that highly trained professionals (and some that are not so highly trained) generally prefer to be allied organizationally with their professional group. They feel more at home; they feel that their professional reputation and advancement will be better served by belonging to such a group than by being allied with a project; and they believe that if their superiors are professionals in the same field, they will be more likely to appreciate their expertise at times of salary advances, promotions, or layoffs. This is true not only of engineers and scientists but also of lawyers, accountants, and university professors.[1]

The reasons for existence of a matrix organization in commercial or industrial product management may be somewhat different. In a soap and detergent company, for example, the top management may want individu-

---

[1]Very few professors, for example, want to be known as members of the undergraduate, M.B.A., or Ph.D. faculties; they would rather be known as members of the accounting, finance, or management theory department.

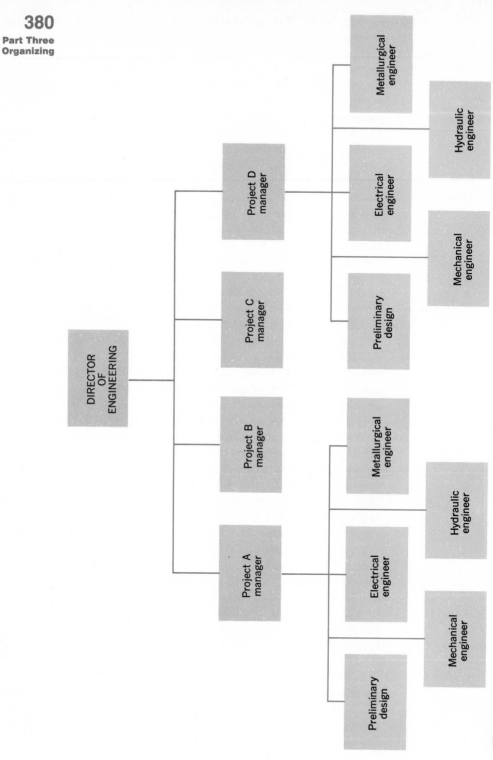

Figure 13.5 Project organization in engineering.

al responsibility for profit to exist for a given product or brand. If the company had only one product or brand, there would obviously be no problem; the chief executive would have profit responsibility. If the company could organize through the use of an integrated (research, marketing, manufacturing) product division, then the division manager would have profit responsibility. But where, as in a multiproduct soap and detergent company, technology and economics dictate that the company will not have separate manufacturing facilities or sales forces for each product, the only way to get a degree of profit responsibility is to overlay, in some way, a product manager with responsibility for profit for a given brand or product.

Variations in Practice

There are many variations of the project or product manager in practice, in addition to the pure product department. In some cases, the project or product managers have no authority to tell any functional department to do anything. In these cases, they may be only information gatherers on how their project or product is proceeding, reporting to a top executive when significant deviations from plans occur. Their role might be that of a persuader, using knowledge and personality to get results. Obviously, these roles have some very serious drawbacks, particularly if the manager without any organization power whatsoever is actually held responsible for end results. There can be no wonder that turnover among such position holders has been high.

Another variation in practice is to simply draw the grid or matrix showing certain managers in charge of functional departments and others in charge of projects or products. This is usually intended to convey a pure case of dual command. The results, as experience has shown, are predictable. If something goes wrong with a project or product, it is often difficult for a top superior to know whose fault it is and where the difficulties really lie. A superior faced with this kind of situation would do just as well not to know that the deviation exists, since if responsibility cannot be traced, little can be done to correct the problem. Also, in such cases, there tend to arise the usual friction, buck passing, and confusion one would expect from disunity of command.

Solution in Engineering and Research and Development

The more sophisticated companies in high-technology industries that have found no alternative to matrix management have solved the problem largely by clarification of the authorities and responsibilities of the functional and project managers. Project managers are normally given authority over the integrity of a total design; they usually have the contact with the customer, although in many instances this will be passed on to the marketing department; they are given authority over budget and in this case become essentially buyers of services from the functional managers; and they are given the authority to work out schedules and priorities for their projects with the functional departments. On the latter point, if they cannot work out priorities because of the claims of other project managers and if they and the other project managers cannot compromise these, then the matter of priorities goes to a higher authority, usually the manager who has primary responsibility for relationships with all customers.

Under this system of clarification, functional managers are given authority over the people in their area and over the integrity of engineering or research work done by them. Thus, between the project manager and the functional manager, much of the problem of disunity of command is eliminated, although there still may be a degree of conflict and uncertainty in such borderline areas as total project design accuracy and integrity.

Solution in Product Management

Although the Procter & Gamble Company and Libby, McNeil & Libby have successfully used product management in the marketing of their products for over 40 years and although other prominent companies like Lever Brothers and General Foods have used it for many years, most of the development of its use has occurred in the past two decades.[2]

As might be expected, the term "product manager" is used in many ways, varying from its application to the general manager of an integrated product division to its use for little more than a staff assistant in the marketing head's organization who gathers information and makes recommendations. But a matrix form of organization does not occur until product managers have some degree of authority over functional departments that do not report to them.

Research on the degree of authority granted to product managers shows that in most companies they may be held, to some degree, responsible for the success of the brands of products assigned to them, but may be given either little or no authority to accomplish these results; they may also be assigned the ambiguous role of "charming persuader."[3] It is interesting that this promising organizational device, aiming as it does in a functionally organized company toward giving someone responsibility for end results, should follow the history of ambiguity and lack of authority experienced for years in engineering.

[2]See R. M. Fulmer, "Product Management: Panacea or Pandora's Box?" *California Management Review*, vol. 7, no. 4, pp. 63–74 (Summer 1965).
[3]See for example G. H. Evans, *The Product Manager's Job* (New York: American Management Association, 1964); B. C. Ames, "Payoff from Product Management," *Harvard Business Review*, vol. 41, no. 6, pp. 141–152 (November–December 1963); K. Knight, "Matrix Organization—A Review," *Journal of Management Studies*, vol. 13, no. 2, pp. 111–113 (May 1976); and C. C. Martin, "Projectionated Organization," in *Project Management: How To Make It Work* (New York: AMACOM, 1976), pp. 63–100.

However, a number of companies have begun to solve this problem of authority in a way to make this a real and reasonably workable matrix organization. One of the best solutions is that used by Procter & Gamble for many years. In this company a brand manager (located in the advertising department, since the company has long had a policy of preselling through advertising and promotion) derives authority in an interesting way. The brand manager develops the plan for a brand, covering not only advertising but also use of the field sales force, research assistance, packaging, and manufacturing programs, and then negotiates with the various functional departments for the part they will play in the program and the costs involved. After such a comprehensive brand program is developed, it goes up the line in the company until it and other brand programs are finally approved by the chief executive. Then, armed with such an approved plan, the brand manager hardly needs any other authority. While the organization chart would not show a grid, the fact is that one exists through authority derived from plans approved at the top.

Multidimensional Matrix Organizations

Up to this point, our discussion has dealt with matrix organizations with two dimensions: project or product managers overlaying functional organization patterns. These are the most common matrix forms. But other dimensions have been added to the matrix in many companies.

The most usual third dimension of a matrix is to superimpose over the product and functional departments a market manager as well as a brand or product manager. With product managers, the focus of effort and attention is primarily on the product. This is especially suitable for companies like the soap and detergent firms that have a number of established products serving various segments of a given end-user market. However, some companies have products that can serve many markets, some of which, at least, are fairly far from the products manager's normal concern. For example, Durez Division of Hooker Chemicals Company has long been a leader in developing, manufacturing, and marketing plastics materials used primarily in automobile and electric parts. But a market-oriented manager discovered that the same materials, with little modification, could serve the plastic liquid container market.

By having a market manager whose major responsibility and interest are to search out various markets a company's products might fit, a company may discover many opportunities for profitable expansion. Companies can hardly expect a product manager to search out these opportunities since that manager's job is to market a given product or product line to an existing market.

To introduce the broader approach of a market manager is, of course, to add a third dimension to the matrix. Doing so understandably causes problems which may lead to confusion and even to wasteful rivalry between product and market manager. But, as in the case of uncertainties and possible friction between product or project managers and functional managers, clarification of roles and authority is essential. This clarification can go far toward reducing potential for friction in its three-dimension structure of product-market-functional manager.

In some instances, people have found that even three dimensions are not enough to care for demands for specialized responsibility. For example, in the Dow-Corning Corporation, makers of chemicals and plastics, a four-dimension matrix organization is used.[4] In addition to the normal matrix form overlaying product managers over functional departments, Dow-Corning has overlaid this matrix with "business" managers and geographic area managers.

The key to the four-dimension matrix of Dow-Corning is the establishment of "business" managers and "business" boards. For each of its ten business areas, Dow-Corning maintains a full-time business manager and a special business board that functions as needed. The business managers are those who are put in charge of an area of the business, such as plastics material. They are responsible for this area of business, much like individual owners of businesses, and report directly to corporate top management. The boards are usually made up of representatives from research, marketing, manufacturing and technical service and development, plus cost and economic evaluation specialists. Top management executives assign responsibility to every position on the multidimensional matrix and attribute much of the success of this complex system to the use of a companywide program of managing by objectives.

Matrix Organization and the Future

With increased emphasis on end results and goal accomplishment, there can hardly be any doubt that increasing use will be made of some form of matrix organization, especially since it is often not possible to give a single manager direct line authority over all the activities necessary to accomplish major end results. This trend is also a recognition of the fact that programs represent interacting networks and systems.

But if modern managers are to meet the challenge involved in matrix organization and get the results desired, they must step up better than they have to the task of clarifying authorities. As noted earlier, good people may make an ambiguous structure work, but they can certainly work better where roles are clarified.

WHAT IS THE BEST PATTERN OF DEPARTMENTATION?

One student reviewing this chapter criticized it for discussing the various types of departmentation and explaining the advantages and disadvantag-

[4]W. C. Groggin, "How the Multidimensional Structure Works at Dow-Corning," *Harvard Business Review*, vol. 52, no. 1, pp. 54–65 (January–February 1974).

es of each, but recommending no definite course of action. She said that if she were a manager and needed a reference for the "one best method," this chapter would not tell her what to do. She declared that it was like going to a candy store and seeing many kinds from which to choose but not knowing which to pick.

This is true. As was said at the beginning of this chapter, there is no one best way of departmentizing applicable to all organizations and all situations. Managers must determine what is "best" by the situation they face—the jobs to be done and the way they should be done, the people involved and their personalities, the technology employed in the department, the users being served, and other internal and external environmental factors in the situation. However, by knowing the various patterns, their advantages, disadvantages, and dangers, practicing managers should be able to design an organization structure most suitable for their particular operations.

Departmentation Should Facilitate Achieving Objectives

Departmentation is not an end in itself, but is simply a method of arranging activities to facilitate the accomplishment of enterprise objectives. It is not even an unmixed good, for the separation of activities on any basis creates problems of coordination that are difficult to solve. Each method has its advantages and disadvantages. Consequently, the process of selection involves a consideration of the relative advantages of each type at each level in the organization structure. In all cases the *central question* concerns the type of organizational environment that the manager wishes to design and the situation being faced. In the discussion of the alternative methods of departmentation it was made clear that each method yields certain gains and that the achievement of parallelism in the intermediate departmentation of the functional divisions is not a proper organizational objective.

Mixing Departmentation

Another point to be highlighted concerns the mixing of departmentation within a functional area. For instance, a wholesale drug firm has grouped the buying and selling activities relating to beverages in one product department, but has grouped, on the same level, all other selling activities on a territorial basis. A manufacturer of plastic goods has territorialized both the production and sale of all its products except dinnerware, which is a product department. A functional department manager may, in other words, employ two or more bases for grouping activities on the same organizational levels. Such practices may be justified on logical grounds because the objective of departmentation is not to build a rigid structure, balanced in terms of levels and characterized by consistency and identical bases. The purpose is to group activities in the manner which will best contribute to achieving enterprise objectives. If variety of bases does this, there is no reason why managers should not take advantage of the alternatives before them.

The logic of this view is frequently ignored by the specialized organization service or staff departments in large-scale enterprises, whether of a public or a private nature. For some reason, possibly aesthetics or control, it is often insisted that all departmentized activities below the primary level of organization be grouped in exactly the same manner. For instance, the organization structure of the Internal Revenue Service at the regional and district levels is exactly the same, despite tremendous variation in district sizes. Firms with multiplants often organize them in the same way; thus, the same departments will be found in virtually all stores of Sears, Roebuck and Company.

The aesthetic reason for identical organization structure of similar enterprise groupings is really not at all persuasive. The organization planner may think it "looks better," but this is a poor reason for organizing in a particular way. The matter of control, however, is quite different. There may be very important reasons for comparing the operation of similarly organized plants, stores, and agencies. They all may be comparable profit centers; their managers can be more readily compared within this organization structure. Even though these, and others, are important arguments for similarity of organization structure, it must be remembered that no one organizes to control; people organize to produce efficiently and effectively. If the latter purpose is sacrificed for the former, the cost of control is too great to bear.

The Principle of Division of Work

The mixing of departmentation in practice is, then, merely a reflection of the operation of the principle of division of work. Originally noted by Fayol as the first of his fourteen principles of management, it might be stated as follows: *The more an organization structure reflects the tasks or activities necessary to attain goals and assists in their coordination, and the more roles are designed to fit the capabilities and motivations of people available to fill them, the more effective and efficient an organization structure will be.*[5] It concerns what has been called the primary step in organization, the determination and establishment of "the smallest number of dissimilar functions into which the work of an institution may be divided."[6] As Fayol indicated, this is the principle of specialization; it

[5]Henri Fayol, *General and Industrial Administration* (New York: Pitman Publishing Corporation, 1949), p. 20. It should be pointed out that the authors' list of principles of organization vary from those of Fayol. A number of them are essentially the same, such as Fayol's principles of division of work, authority and responsibility, unity of command, unity of direction, centralization (balance), and scalar chain. Other Fayol principles apply to such managerial functions as direction. Still other principles expressed by Fayol, such as equity, initiative, and esprit de corps, seem to refer only to problems of leadership or characteristics of planning, control, or direction and are therefore not included in the authors' list.
[6]H. A. Hopf, *Organization, Executive Capacity, and Progress* (Ossining, N.Y.: Hopf Institute of Management, 1945), p. 4.

is the *division of work to produce more and better work with the same effort.*[7]

It should be emphasized that division of work—in the sense of occupational specialization—is an *economic* principle and *not* a management principle. In other words, it has been found in many cases that when work is specialized, people learn the task more easily and perform it more effectively. It may well be that in many cases, work has been overspecialized, with resultant loss of both motivation and a sense of accomplishment. Job enlargement may often be a highly desirable thing. But organization designers have to work within certain economic and other conditions. Given these, their primary task is to design a structure of roles which will help individuals contribute to objectives. Not that they should remain silent if they feel that other considerations, such as occupational specialization, force an unworkable organization structure from the standpoint of staffing it. But the *management organization* principle of division of work implies that given a system of tasks required economically to achieve enterprise goals, the better an organization structure reflects a classification of these tasks and assists in their coordination through creating a system of interrelated roles, and the more these roles are designed to fit the capabilities and motivations of people available to fill them, the more effective and efficient the organization will be.

GUIDES FOR INTRADEPARTMENTAL ORGANIZATION

Over and above the macroproblems of departmentation, operating managers are frequently both concerned and baffled about where, within a department, particular activities should be placed. The techniques and principles of departmentation provide no answer to questions as those of whether customer claims should be the responsibility of the legal department, whether competition between activities should be encouraged or discouraged, and whether executive interest in the activity should influence where the work should be done. There are two general guides which managers may wish to follow in settling problems of these types.

Assignment by Similarity of Activity

The practice of grouping together similar activities is both apparent and logical. Its wide usage emphasizes the need for understanding its advantages and the bases upon which it rests.

The search for a basis of classifying activities that leads to the association of those which are similar eventually brings organizers to the skills of people. At first, they may be persuaded that the important element is the object to which labor is applied. But that which results from labor depends upon the skills applied to it. After determining what

---

[7]Fayol, loc. cit.

needs to be done and what skills are required, the organizer can then group them under such heads as typing, chemical analysis, process engineering, and accounting. In this way, people who perform similar activities can be grouped in one department, and the advantages of occupational specialization can be realized.

Several illustrations of this procedure may be cited. Research engineers, salespeople, file clerks, and machine schedulers are commonly grouped in the research and development department, sales department, general office, and production control department, respectively. Sometimes it is also convenient to group together people who operate similar equipment or who undertake the assembly of a product. However, the fact that similar activities are not always combined suggests that there are some limitations in practice. We find that diversity as well as similarity may be grounds for grouping activities.

Guides for Assignment by Intimate Association[8]

The association of activities merely on the grounds that they are diverse would, of course, be foolish. The diversity must of a particular kind, and there must be very good reasons for using it as a basis for grouping. Such reasons are found in the guides for assignment by intimate association, which occurs when diverse activities are so closely related to the achievement of departmental purposes that they are carried out most effectively when grouped in the same organizational unit.

Most use   This guide suggests that an activity for which managers have the most use should normally be assigned to them. Such functions as traffic, process engineering, and purchasing are sometimes located in the production departments. For example, in manufacturing establishments, the traffic function, which includes such activities as the purchase of transportation services, the use of equipment for transporting materials to the plant, in-plant movement of materials, and warehousing, may be assigned to the production manager. Since his department uses traffic services much more than others do, he would endeavor to manage them efficiently. Other departments are not thereby deprived of the service, for the production manager can operate it for the benefit of all departments.

Cost accounting may be assigned to the manufacturing department rather than to the accounting department, on the grounds that it is most used there. Likewise, computer operations are often assigned to the controller's department on the basis that much of their time is devoted to processing accounting information.

---

[8]The original systematic examination of the issued involved in assigning activities was made by the late L. C. Sorrell, "Organization of Transportation and Traffic Activities," *Traffic World*, vol. 46, nos. 24–25 (November–December 1930). The authors have followed Dr. Sorrell's approach.

Executive interest   An activity may be assigned to a particular manager if he or she is especially interested in it and has the capacity to direct it intelligently. In many manufacturing and service enterprises, for example, real estate activities are assigned to the general counsel's office. A manufacturing company may have many real estate leases and a fair number of real estate sales and purchases. These are often not important enough to justify establishing a separate functional department, nor do they logically belong in any existing department. The problem is solved by assigning them to that executive who has an interest in them—most likely because of the extensive legal and contractual work involved, the chief legal officer.

Observation of practice shows other interesting examples. In a small company, the personnel activity was given to the controller, not because it fitted in with accounting activities, but because that person was interested in the field and was also regarded as available to handle it. In another company, stockholder relations were separated from public relations and assigned to the chairman of the board because of personal interests in the area. In still another case, the chairman was assigned the task of developing international operations for the same reason.

Competition   Often a desired activity does not flourish because various executives fear it, because its possibilities are not recognized, or because it fails to receive vigorous direction. The cure for a wilting activity is sometimes the application of the guide of competition. For instance, American universities attempted, in the early 1920s, to meet the growing demand for business instruction by offering a few courses in such fields as corporation finance, marketing, and accounting in their departments of economics. Since there were few economists with much interest in, or knowledge of the subject matter, there was definite hostility in the departments toward such instruction. The insistent demand was met by splitting off business from economics courses and establishing a competitive department. Since then, departments of business administration have achieved equal stature and have often surpassed the parent department in facilities, budgets, and number of students.

Encouraging competition between departments, divisions, and other units enables the firm to make comparisons that greatly aid in control. For instance, similar measures of efficiency can be applied to the domestic and foreign sales departments of a multinational company. From such records as costs of sales, gross profit per net sales dollar, and sales per dollar of effort, the president is able to compare the relative efficiency of managers operating similar and somewhat competitive divisions.

Suppressed Competition   As its title implies, this guide is the exact reverse of the one that encourages competition and, naturally, is applicable under a different set of conditions. As the advantages to be reaped from competition become fully realized, the president of the firm may feel a growing need for greater coordination between two functions, for more cooperation and less competition. To achieve this, one need only change the place in the organization structure where the two activities are coordinated.

A good example of organizing along this guideline, as well as a case of departmentizing in accordance with marketing channels, was the action the Du Pont Company took when it combined its Nylon, Orlon, and Dacron Divisions. It found that the competition of these three divisions for the same market was not in the best interests of the company as a whole. Many other companies with product divisions have found that where once-healthy competition turns into destructive and inefficient rivalry between parts of the same company, combination of the parts under a single manager may be the best cure.

Policy control Policies may be variously interpreted. General intentions—such as to compete on a price basis, not to advertise on Sunday, or never to sue a customer—rarely encounter differences of managerial opinion, but other policies, such as those relating to credit, customer claims, and returned goods, may suffer from a lack of clear specifications, permitting variations in interpretation. In such instances, it might be important that the policy be enforced by that manager who would best reflect the firm's intentions.

The customer claims activity of department stores, for example, is generally recognized as necessary and important. The typical policy relating to this function is one of fairness to the store and to the customer. But the very vagueness of what fair dealing is makes possible sincere but widely different attitudes. If customer claims are assigned to the merchandising manager, this person's interpretations may favor the customers because of a desire to keep their good will and continued patronage; furthermore, the merchandising manager is in a position to shift any blame for the cost of the activity to department buyers. If the activity is placed in the buying departments, however, the buyers will be torn between pleasing the customer and taking the blame for buying the unsatisfactory product in the first place, and there may be as many interpretations of policy as there are buyers. The accounting department, finally, might administer the activity on a coldly factual basis that would alienate both customers and department buyers. All these alternatives have been tried in independent department store operations. Since each might endanger the original policy, it is a growing practice to assign the activity to the general superintendent, the official in charge of the store building, receiving and delivery, warehousing, and safety. Many store executives feel that this manager is in the best position to execute the claims policy in the way it was originally designed.

The important point is that activities should be assigned to that manager who will interpret policy in a way satisfactory to those drafting it. It is their *intention* which needs to be reflected in policy applications. So important are the virtues of accuracy and consistency that policy control often can be vital to enterprise welfare.

Lack of a clean break Sometimes difficulties are encountered in assigning activities that would logically be placed in separate departments but are, for some conflicting practical reason, best undertaken together. In a sense, this is a perennial problem that arises the moment an enterprise is organized.

Students of independent department store operations are frequently surprised to learn that a department manager, called the "buyer," is responsible for *both* purchasing and selling merchandise. The assignment of both activities to the buyer results from the close relationship of sales volume to what is bought for resale, and when one manager is assigned both activities, it is easy to fix responsibility for results.

In the responsibility for operations of an airline at an airport, similar problems exist. People at the counter sell tickets and deal with customers—a task that logically belongs to the sales department. But they also check baggage—a task that belongs to the ground service or operations department. It would obviously be difficult to separate these functions organizationally, with the result that they are usually combined under the airline's station manager, who normally reports to the operating department but may take necessary guidance from the sales department.

These illustrations emphasize the fact that arbitrary decisions to divide control of an activity may be impractical, resulting in unworkable assignments of parts of functions to several managers. If for any reason the activities in question refuse to break clean, even though their nature may make such a break appear logical, the appropriate guide is to avoid forceful separation.

Separation The successful operation of enterprises of all types requires that certain activities be undertaken purely as a check upon the effectiveness and propriety with which functions are carried out. They should almost invariably be assigned to a manager independent of the executive whose work is being evaluated.

Manufacturing firms, for example, commonly provide for quality control of purchased materials and goods in various stages of production. This activity could clearly be subverted if its personnel were responsible to the purchasing agent or the plant superintendent.

Similar issues are involved in the employment of an outside auditor and in the separation of accounting from the finance function. The certification of financial records could hardly be made by a subordinate in the finance department. And since accounting activities are useful checks upon the treasurer, who controls the enterprise funds, it is not good practice to have the chief accountant reporting to the treasurer, or vice versa.

The concept of separation—that if an activity is designed as a check on another activity, the individual charged with the former cannot report to the department whose activity he or she is expected to evaluate—is a valuable and invariable rule.

Functional interest Functional interest, although it does not have the general applicability of other guides, is useful in grouping activities that are closely related in terms of purpose. For instance, a publicity manager may be assigned such functions as institutional advertising and publicity. These are functionally related because both concern the impact on the general public of the firm's policies, practices, and personnel. In the General Motors Corporation, for example, the Motors Holding Division, a division whose responsibility is handling new-dealer financing, is attached to the marketing staff, rather than the financial staff, for the obvious reason that marketing has a strong functional interest in the area. Likewise, one often finds the company cafeteria a responsibility of the personnel department.

FOR DISCUSSION

1 Sociologists tell us that organization is "a social invention." What do you think they mean? Do they imply that there is a "right" and "wrong" way to organize? What test of whether an organization structure is "right" would you suggest?

2 Why do most small companies use functionally organized departments?

3 Why do most large department stores and supermarket chains organize their stores on a territorial basis and then organize the internal store units by products? Give examples from your own experience.

4 If you were a manager of electronic data processing in a company, a hospital, or a government agency, how would you make sure you had an effective and efficient service department?

5 Some managers feel that a firm should not "mix up" its basic departmental forms. Would you agree with them? What is your opinion of an organizational philosophy of requiring all activities to be organized in the same manner?

6 Why are so many federal government agencies organized primarily on a territorial basis?

7 How is a typical engineering or research and development department likely to be organized? Why?

8 Do you see any relationship between managing by objectives and matrix organization and the way in which the former may result in increased use of matrix organization?

9 How does this chapter illustrate contingency, or situational, management?

10 What becomes of the guides to assignment of activities if an enterprise "organizes around people"?

11 It has been argued that guides to the assignment of activities are conflicting and therefore inappropriate. How would you respond to this?

chapter 14

Line and Staff Authority Relationships

The patterns of departmentation have been discussed. We now consider another essential organization question: What kind of authority do we find in an organizational structure? The question has to do with the nature of authority relationships—the problem of line and staff.

Without authority—the power to exercise discretion in making decisions—properly placed in managers, the various departments cannot become smoothly working units harmonized for the accomplishment of enterprise objectives. Authority relationships, whether perpendicular or horizontal, are the factors that make organization possible, harness departmental activities, and bring coordination to an enterprise.

LINE AND STAFF CONCEPTS

Much confusion has arisen both in literature and among managers as to what line and staff are; as a result, there is probably no area of management which causes more difficulties, more friction, and more loss of time and effectiveness. Yet line and staff relationships are important as an organizational way of life, and the authority relationships of members of an organization must necessarily affect their part in the operation of the enterprise.

One widely held concept of line and staff is that line functions are those which have direct responsibility for accomplishing the objectives of the enterprise and that staff refers to those elements of the organization that help the line to work most effectively in accomplishing the primary objectives of an enterprise. Those who hold to this view almost invariably classify production and sales (and sometimes finance) as line functions, and purchasing, accounting, personnel, plant maintenance, and quality control as staff functions.

The confusion arising from such a concept is immediately apparent. It is argued that purchasing, for example, merely helps in achieving the main goals of business in the sense that, unlike the production departments—such as heat treating or parts assembly—it is not directly essential. But is purchasing really any less essential to the gaining of company objectives? Could the company not store up heat-treated or assembled parts and get along without these departments as well as it could without purchasing? And could not the same question be raised as to other so-called staff and service departments, such as accounting, personnel, and plant maintenance? Moreover, there is probably nothing that could stop satisfactory production and sale of most manufactured goods more completely than the failure of quality control.

The Nature of Line and Staff Relationships

A more precise and logically valid concept of line and staff is that they are simply a matter of relationships. In line authority, one finds a superior with a line of authority running to a subordinate. As Mooney so aptly recognized, this gradation of authority is found in all organizations as an uninterrupted scale or series of steps.[1] Hence this hierarchical arrangement has been referred to as the "scalar principle" in organization: *The more clear the line of authority from the ultimate authority for management in an enterprise to every subordinate position, the more effective will be responsible decision making and organized communication.* In many large enterprises, the steps are long and complicated, but even in the smallest, the very act of organization introduces the scalar principle.

The nature of line authority, therefore, becomes apparent from the scalar principle as being that relationship in which a superior exercises

[1]J. D. Mooney, *Principles of Organization* (New York: Harper & Brothers, 1947), pp. 14–15.

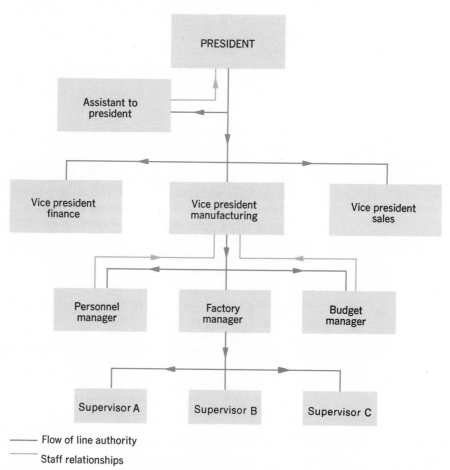

——— Flow of line authority

‒ ‒ ‒ Staff relationships

Figure 14.1 Line and staff authority relationships. Note: In certain instances such as personnel and budgets, these departments often have operating activities in addition to purely staff responsibilities.

direct supervision over a subordinate—an authority relationship in direct line or steps.

The nature of the staff relationship is advisory. As Mooney has stated,[2] staff is auxiliary, and although "it may suggest that the structure of organization is like a double-track railroad, consisting of line and staff as two coordinate functions . . . there could be no more erroneous conception." For, as he points out:

> The structure of organization is single track only, and can never be anything else. What is known in military organization as line is synonymous with what we have called the scalar chain, and there can be but one chain of line authority. Any duty in organization that cannot be identified as an actual link in the scalar process is an auxiliary function, adhering to the line like sidings along the main track. This means that every staff function must adhere to the line in some dependent relation, and could not otherwise exist. If we find in staff organization a counterpart of the same scalar gradations that appear in the line, this is implicit in the fact of its adherence. It must of necessity follow the gradations of that to which it adheres.[3]

Line and Staff: Relationship or Departmentation?

Frequently, line and staff are regarded as types of departments. Although it is true that a department may stand in a predominantly line or staff position with respect to other departments, line and staff are distinguished by their authority relationships and not by what they do.

The public relations department, for example, being primarily advisory to the top executives, may be thought of as a staff department. But within the department are line relationships; the director will stand in a line authority position with respect to his or her immediate subordinates. On the other hand, the vice president in charge of production may be regarded as heading a line department. His job is not *primarily* advisory to the chief executive officer. If, however, he counsels the chief executive on overall company policy, his relationship becomes one of staff. Within the production department there may be many subordinates and among them a number having an advisory role and, therefore, having a staff relationship to the whole department or any of its parts.

When one looks at an organization structure *as a whole*, the general character of line and staff relationships for the total organization emerges. Certain departments are predominantly staff in their relationship to the entire organization. Other departments are primarily line.

Figure 14.2 portrays the skeletal organization of a manufacturing

[2]Ibid., pp. 34–35.
[3]Ibid., p. 35.

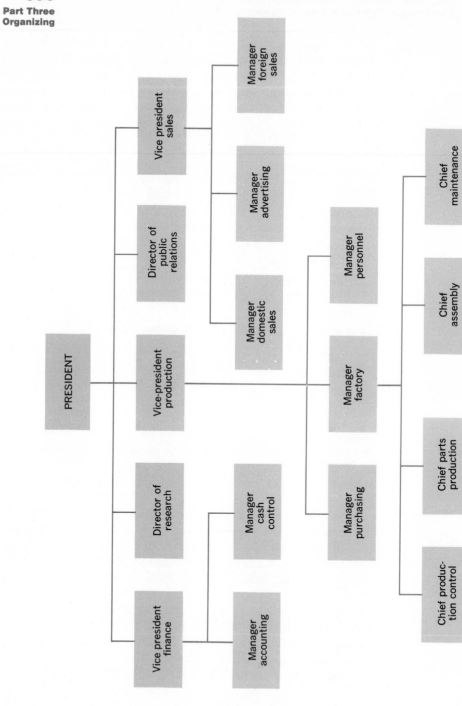

Figure 14.2 So-called line and staff organization of a typical manufacturing company.

company. The activities of the director of research and the director of public relations are apt to be mainly advisory to the mainstream of corporate operations and are consequently often considered staff activities. The finance, production, and sales departments, which have activities generally related to the main corporate functions, are ordinarily considered line departments.

Although it is often convenient and correct to refer to one department as a line department and another as a staff department, *their activities do not so characterize the departments. Line and staff are characterized by relationships and not by departmental activities.* Should research be a principal function of the company—as in aerospace manufacturing, where the engineering or research department produces ideas for sale to military and commercial customers—it will stand in an operating relationship to the organization as a whole and take on the authority characteristics of a factory department in a typical manufacturing enterprise.

Some of the tendency to regard line and staff as types of departments arises from confusing service departments with line and staff. Service departments represent a grouping of *activities* for the purpose of control or economy arising from specialization. Thus, purchasing, accounting, or certain personnel activities may be separated from other departments and grouped in service departments. As service departments, they are auxiliary to the principal operations of sales or production. Because service departments are composed of specialists, their advice is usually sought by company managers, and, at such times, they stand in a staff relationship to the rest of the company. Nevertheless, the line authority within these departments is as real as that in a production or sales department.

Line and Staff: Specialization of Managerial Functions?

Although recognizing the inherent nature of line and staff as one of authority relationships, many students of management have attempted to distinguish between them on the grounds that they represent a specialization of managerial functions. Some express the distinction by asserting that it is the line executive's function to *act* and the staff executive's function to *think*.[4]

The implied distinction between line and staff in terms of a division

[4] L. Gulick, "The Theory of Organization," in L. Gulick and L. Urwick (eds.), *Papers on the Science of Administration* (New York: Institute of Public Administration, 1937), p. 31. Gulick observed that "when the work of the government is subjected to the dichotomy of 'line' and 'staff' there are included in staff all those persons who devote their time exclusively to the knowing, thinking, and planning functions, and in the line all the remainder who are thus concerned with the doing functions. . . . Obviously those in the line are also thinking and planning, and making suggestions to superior officers. They cannot operate otherwise. But this does not make them staff officers. Those also in the staff are *doing* something; they do not merely sit and twiddle their thumbs. But they do not organize others, they do not direct or appoint personnel, they do not issue commands, they do not take responsibility for the job. Everything they suggest is referred up, not down, and is carried out, if at all, on the responsibility and under the direction of a line officer."

of managerial functions may possibly be traced to Frederick W. Taylor's attempt to separate planning from performance. He advocated the division of the functions of foremen into eight groupings and these, in turn, into a planning level and a performance level.[5] This principle has never had wide application in industry or been regarded as workable, for it involves division of managerial functions. The fact is that managers cannot manage unless they have the authority to plan, organize, lead, staff, and control, although the degree to which they may be called upon to engage in these several functions can vary. However, as will be noted below, many instances of functional authority do have a flavor of Taylor's functional foremanship.

Staff officers do *assist* line officers in carrying out their managerial functions. They often specialize in planning assistance and may also assist in other managerial functions. On every hand, one can see departments engaged actively in planning, in examining organizational problems, in drawing up instructions or commands for the use of superiors, and in making analyses. These are truly staff activities, not because they represent planning instead of performance, but because they represent counsel and assistance.

It is thus often stated that staff officers are assigned an "authority of ideas," and line officers an "authority to command."[6] Although this appraisal can be helpful in dramatizing these relationships, it must not be taken to mean a splitting of the managerial functions. Managers may benefit greatly by ideas, but they cannot delegate their job.

Importance of Understanding Line and Staff

In view of the confusion about line and staff, the distinction is sometimes assumed to be meaningless. It has been argued that these are obsolete concepts, carried into industry from military organization, and that modern firms have obliterated them by new organizational devices so that they no longer have any meaning.

The distinction seems important, however, as a way of organizational life. Superior and subordinate alike must know whether they are acting in a staff or line capacity. If in a staff capacity, their job is to advise and not command; their line superiors must make the decisions and issue instructions through the scalar chain.

A case in point is that of a competent young staff assistant, with

[5]F. W. Taylor, *Shop Management* (New York: Harper & Brothers, 1911), p. 99. Taylor believed that efficiency would be gained if the job of the shop foreman were subdivided among the following bosses and duties: (1) order of work and routing, (2) instruction, (3) time and cost, (4) gang boss, (5) speed boss, (6) repair boss, (7) inspector, and (8) disciplinarian. He thus distinguished planning and performance levels, placing the first three functions on the planning level and the remainder on the performance level.
[6]E. Petersen and E. G. Plowman, *Business Organization and Management*, rev. ed. (Homewood, Ill.: Richard D. Irwin, Inc., 1948), p. 259. A similar idea is expressed by Mooney (op. cit., p. 34), who notes that "the line represents the authority of *man*; the staff, the authority of *ideas*."

unusual industrial experience as controller and internal auditor of several large business enterprises, who was hired by the executive vice president of an expanding company. The assistant's charge was clear—to bring to the attention of the executive vice president means and plans for reducing costs of operations, expending scarce capital wisely, and achieving growth in an orderly fashion. But some uncertainty must have existed in his mind as to whether he was limited to a staff position or whether he had line authority from the executive vice president to see that these things were done. In any event, he gathered together many statisticians, production efficiency experts, planners, economists, budgetary control personnel, and organization specialists. With their help, he readily and accurately discovered numerous places where costs could be reduced, production and service improved, management bettered, and money efficiently expended; yet the entire program failed, and the executive vice president was forced to abandon it. The reason was simple: The assistant had not understood that he was to act in a staff capacity—that he could not force his findings and policy determinations on unwilling line executives, but instead was expected to sell his ideas to them. The line executives resented the intrusion of this staff officer, as well they might have, since he was, in effect, stripping from them their power to manage. The result was not only complete lack of cooperation by the line officers but also their insistence that the assistant be replaced. Faced with a choice between supporting his chief line lieutenants and supporting a staff officer who had not confined his activities to investigation and recommendations, the executive vice president could only favor the line operating officers.

Many other examples could be given of the importance of understanding line and staff relationships. Not only must staff executives recognize that their job is to counsel, but also line executives must not confuse such counsel with the power to make decisions. Authority to manage must rest with executives who stand in a line relationship with their subordinates. Failure to understand this is a common cause of friction.

DEVELOPMENT OF THE STAFF CONCEPT

The staff concept is probably as old as organization itself. Since organization almost certainly developed first in political and military areas of social activities, the first traces of staff are found there. Mooney found that the pure staff function of the boule of ancient Athens was to prepare measures for the consideration of the ecclesia and that the early Roman senate first exercised a pure staff function, but later changed to a line function.[7] In the age of feudalism, too, and on to the present, the

[7]For his excellent description of organization in antiquity, see ibid., chap. 7; chaps. 8–20 include other pertinent material; chaps. 14, 17, and 18 deal with the development of staff.

importance of staff counsel has always been recognized, even though the emphasis of early organization was clearly on the development of line relationships.

Application of the Staff Principle in the Catholic Church

Mooney found that the use of staff provides one of the "most notable lessons" furnished by the long history of Catholic Church organization, where staff service has taken forms unknown in many other areas. The most obvious instance is in the central administration of the Church, consisting of two major organizations, the Sacred College and the Roman Curia. During the entire history of these institutions, they have been regarded as advisory to the Pope, who delegates none of his final authority to them and has no obligation to adopt their advice.

One of the institutionalized organization principles of the Catholic Church has been described by Mooney as "compulsory staff service." This principle operates to force superiors to *listen* to their subordinates. While the line decision rests with superiors, they cannot refuse to listen. This principle—at least as old as the Rule of St. Benedict, promulgated in the sixth century—originally required the abbot of a Benedictine monastery to consult the elder monks, even on minor matters, and is now applied to some extent throughout the Church.

Another interesting principle Mooney calls "staff independence." In Catholic organization, staff advisers are often independent of superiors with respect to both tenure and position. Advice is thus unweakened by the fact of dependence. As Mooney so well reflects on the lack of this in military, civic, and business organization: "The weakness of many forms of staff service is that the counselor is dependent on the man whom he counsels, and hence is subject to the danger of sinking to the level of a 'yes' man."[8]

The Army General Staff

Although the staff concept can hardly be called a military invention, the terms "line" and "staff" appear to have had their origin in military organization. The modern concept of the army general staff is usually traced to the seventeenth century, when emphasis was placed upon a staff of experts by Gustavus Adolphus of Sweden. The Mark of Brandenburg is given credit for the evolution of the general staff organizations of the Prussian and German armies. The Prussian general staff, as organized by Scharnhorst in the early nineteenth century, was a completely organized advisory service coordinated under a single head, the chief of staff. Scharnhorst saw the dangers of separation of line and staff personnel and

[8]Ibid., p. 122.

required that, periodically, all staff officers assume line duty and all line officers be given staff assignments.

As a result of the brilliant report of Secretary of War Elihu Root in 1902, the American army adopted the general staff device that is the basis of its organization today. Root's report is a classic on the need for a general staff with no other duties than gathering information, presenting alternative plans, and preparing the details of selected plans.

Staffs in Business

Widespread use of staff in American business developed only in the twentieth century, particularly after the Great Depression of 1929 to 1932. The emphasis on planning and control (with their requirements for information), the growing complexities of labor relations, the expansion of government regulations, and the difficult legal and accounting problems arising from tax legislation have argued for staff assistance. The development has been accelerated by the growth of large business, in which the problems of managing approach those of any army and require specialized information of a breadth and complexity unknown to smaller operations.

The proliferation of staffs in business takes many forms. Few indeed are the top managers who do not have staff assistants in law, taxes, accounting, and perhaps research. Executives of large companies add staff assistants in public relations, personnel, engineering, or planning. Staff assistants are so widely used that a sales or production manager may have from one to a half dozen. In large-scale enterprises, for example, the sales managers may have staff persons separately assigned to such activities as the selection and training of salespeople, sales strategy, research, quotas, budgets, traffic, and warehousing. Moreover, some large companies are reminiscent of the army general staff. In the General Motors Corporation, for example, there exists a staff of eleven key managers—each in charge of a staff group devoted to such important activities as marketing, engineering, design, personnel, and environmental activities—plus financial and legal staffs.

On the other hand, many corporation presidents studiously avoid having many staff assistants or staff departments, choosing instead to have staff people report to the managers in the major line departments. Their purpose is to place the staff assistance at the point in the line where it can best be used and to avoid undermining the line officers by concentrating too much staff assistance at the top level.

FUNCTIONAL AUTHORITY

Functional authority is the right which an individual or department may have delegated to it over specified processes, practices, policies, or other matters relating to activities undertaken by personnel in departments other than its own. If the principle of unity of command were followed without exception, authority over these activities would be exercised by their line managers, but numerous reasons—including lack of special knowledge, lack of ability to supervise processes, and danger of diverse interpretations of policies—explain why they occasionally are not allowed to exercise this authority. In such cases, line managers are deprived of this limited authority. It is delegated by their common superior to a staff specialist or a manager in another department.

Functional authority is not restricted to managers of a particular type of department. It may be exercised by line, service, or staff department heads, more often the latter two, because they are usually composed of specialists whose knowledge becomes the basis for functional controls.

Development of Functional Authority

The successive steps by which a line manager is deprived of authority over particular activities make an interesting study. Pure staff specialists offer advice or recommendations to their line superiors, who may issue them as instructions to be filtered down the organization hierarchy. The first modification of this relationship may occur when the superior delegates authority to the staff person to transmit information, proposals, and advice directly to the former's subordinates. For example, a personnel assistant might be permitted to transmit directly to operating department heads information and advice on the handling of labor grievances. Obviously, this saves the president time and trouble and expedites the spread of the information.

A second modification might be to allow the staff specialist to consult with operating managers and show them how the information should be used or put into effect. For instance, the personnel assistant might be asked to advise line personnel on procedures to eliminate mishandling of grievances. It will clearly be advantageous to all concerned if the staff can instruct the persons responsible for this activity. Here, there is no question of ordering them; the agreement of the line executive concerned is needed. Should this not be forthcoming, appeals can be made to a common superior to issue the requisite instructions. Even with the variations outlined above, the specialist is still operating wholly in a staff capacity.

The transition to functional authority is accomplished when the assistant is delegated specific authority to *prescribe* processes, methods, or even policy to be followed in all subdivisions of either staff or operating departments. The personnel assistant, for example, who once could only advise, now may be given limited authority to supervise a special function or process of the line organization. Personnel assistants no longer merely advise their superiors or the line organization concerning handling grievances. Now, they may issue instructions *prescribing* procedures. Or, to use another example, a corporation controller may be given authority to prescribe the kind of accounting records to be kept by the sales and manufacturing departments.

By limiting this authority to function, the factory manager (handling labor grievances in accordance with procedures prescribed by the personnel manager) and the sales manager (keeping records according to instructions of the controller) are still primarily subject to the orders, supervision, and control of their line superiors. The extent of their control by the staff officer is governed by the latter's functional authority.

Functional Authority Delegation

Functional authority can perhaps be better understood if it is regarded as a small slice of the authority of the line superior. A corporation president, for example, has complete authority to manage the corporation, subject only to limitations placed by such superior authority as the board of directors, the corporate charter and bylaws, and government regulations. In the pure staff situation, the advisers on personnel, accounting, purchasing, or public relations have no part of this authority, their duty being merely to offer counsel. But when the president delegates authority to these advisers to issue instructions directly to the line organization, as shown in Figure 14.3, that right is called "functional authority."

As illustrated, the four staff and service executives have functional authority over the line organization with respect to procedures in the fields of accounting, personnel, purchasing, and public relations. What has happened is that the president, feeling it unnecessary that such specialized matters be cleared through him, has delegated line authority to staff assistants to issue their own instructions to the operating departments. Likewise, of course, subordinate managers can use the same device, as when a factory superintendent sets up cost, production control, and quality control supervisors with functional authority to prescribe procedures for the line operating supervisors.

Functional Authority as Exercised by Operating Managers

Operating department heads sometimes have good reason to control some method or process of another line department. For example, the vice president in charge of sales may be given functional authority over the manufacturing executives in scheduling customer orders, packaging, or making service parts available.

Where a company is organized along product lines, the exercise of functional authority over the product division managers by other executives is rather commonplace. All functions of sales, production, finance, or other operating functions may be placed under a division or product manager. In this case, certain top line officials in charge of a major function of the business might not have a direct line of authority over the

Figure 14.3 Functional authority delegation.

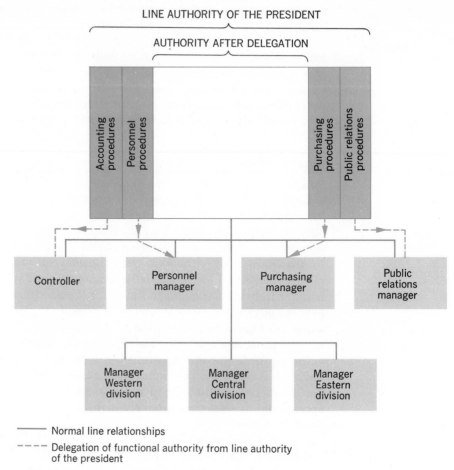

LINE AUTHORITY OF THE PRESIDENT

AUTHORITY AFTER DELEGATION

Accounting procedures

Personnel procedures

Purchasing procedures

Public relations procedures

Controller

Personnel manager

Purchasing manager

Public relations manager

Manager Western division

Manager Central division

Manager Eastern division

——— Normal line relationships

- - - - Delegation of functional authority from line authority of the president

product managers. But, to make sure that sales or financial policy is properly followed in the divisions, these officers may be given functional authority, as illustrated in Figure 14.4.

The Area of Functional Authority

Functional authority should be carefully restricted. Such authority of the purchasing manager, for example, is generally limited to the procedures to be used in divisional or departmental purchasing. When these managers conduct certain purchasing activities of an overall company nature, they are acting as heads of service departments. The functional authority of the personnel manager over the general line organization is

Figure 14.4   Functional authority of line departments.

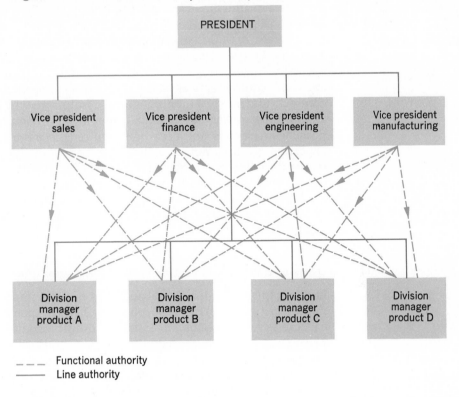

— — — Functional authority
———— Line authority

likewise ordinarily limited to the prescription of procedures for handling grievances, for sharing in the administration of wage and salary programs, and for handling vacation procedures and matters of a similar nature.

Functional authority is usually limited to the area of "how" and sometimes "when" and seldom applies to "where," "what," or "who." The reason for this limitation is not found in any logical demarcation between normal line authority and functional authority, since the latter can be made to apply to any aspect of operations. It is rather that the functionalization of authority, if carried to extremes, would destroy the manager's job. Whenever managers lose their authority to plan, organize, staff, lead, and control the activities within their department, they can no longer manage.

To some extent, this occurs when a staff or line executive has functional authority over some part of another manager's job. Even when the personnel manager requires the factory manager to follow seniority in layoffs or to grant employees definite pay and vacation allowances, he or she is interfering with some of the factory manager's prerogatives. When the accounting department requires district sales managers to file their expense accounts in a certain form, it is, to some extent, interfering with the authority of the general sales manager.

Therefore, well-managed concerns recognize that functional authority should be used sparingly and only where a real necessity exists. This necessity comes from both outside and inside influences. On the outside are such requirements as those of government agencies and labor union contracts that must be interpreted and administered by specialists. On the inside some matters are of such importance or complexity that the best possible grade of uniform action is required, necessitating in turn that the expert be given sufficient authority to carry out desired procedures. A rather thin line sometimes divides what should be controlled by the expert and what should be under the jurisdiction of the operating manager. Where there is doubt, good practice would seem to favor limiting the area of functional authority so that the operating manager's position is not weakened.

Unity of Command and the Flow of Functional Authority

Limiting the area of functional authority is, then, important in preserving the integrity of a managerial position. If a company had, as some do, executives with functional authority over procedures in the fields of personnel, purchasing, accounting, traffic, budgets, engineering, public relations, law, sales policy, and real estate, the complications of authority relationships could be great indeed. A factory manager or a sales manager might have, in addition to an immediate line superior, five, ten, or even fifteen functional bosses. Although much of the multiplication of command is unavoidable because of the demands for specialist prescription in complex areas, it is obvious that it can precipitate serious, and frequently intolerable, confusion and dispersal of responsibility.

Some semblance of unity of command can be maintained by requiring that the line of functional authority not extend beyond the first organization level below that of the manager's own superior. Thus, in Figure 14.5 the functional authority of the personnel or public relations director should not extend beyond the level of the vice presidents in charge of finance, sales, and manufacturing. In other words, functional authority should be concentrated at the nearest possible point in the organization structure to preserve, as much as possible, the unity of command of the line executives.

This principle is often widely violated. Top managers with functional authority sometimes issue instructions directly to personnel throughout the organization. Where the policy or procedure determination is so important that there must be no deviation, both the prestige of the top manager and the necessity for accurate communication may make it necessary and wise to issue such instructions. Issuing them to the responsible line subordinate, as well as to the functional counterpart at

Figure 14.5 Line and functional authority.

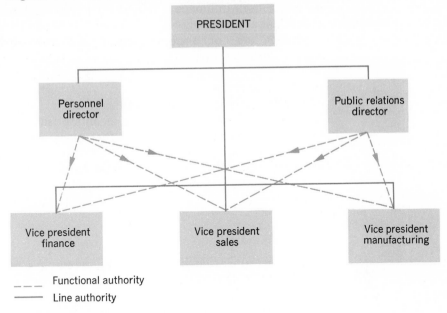

___ Functional authority

___ Line authority

the lower level, may not seem harmfully to increase the multiplicity of command. As will be noted later, there are forces of centralization of authority that may make this kind of exercise of functional authority unavoidable.

Lack of Clarification in Practice

It is surprising how many companies, even those otherwise well managed, fail to define the exact nature of the functional authority that a manager may have. Analysis by the authors of authority delegations in a large number of companies shows that adequate clarification in this area is rare. Most companies seem satisfied to say, for example, that the division managers are "administratively" responsible to the president, but "functionally responsible in accounting and similar matters" to the controller. This is an open invitation to confusion, compounded of ambiguity, lack of careful meaning and understanding, and the unsurprising tendency of specialists to see everything in a company through their own eyes. As a company controller once told one of the authors, "I realize that my authority in accounting matters throughout the company is limited; all I insist on approving is anything with a dollar sign attached."

The lack of clarification in the area of functional authority has been found in a number of studies. Studies of personnel managers, for example, have shown varying perceptions of their authority as between themselves and their staff, their superior, and the various areas of the company subject to their influence.[9] Likewise, a study of company controllers with functional authority showed a high degree of confusion to exist between controller and noncontroller groups, and even within the controllers' departments, as to what the authority of the controller really was.[10] Other studies have shown the extensiveness of this lack of clarity and the conflict it engenders.[11]

Particularly in the light of the wide use and apparent inevitability of functional authority in all kinds of enterprises, lack of clarification is difficult to understand. It is true that many people can accommodate themselves to lack of clarity or work themselves through it by trial and error or persuasion. But if it is important to place functional authority in a position, it would appear to be a waste of time and resources not to make it clear.

Clarifying Functional Authority

Almost certainly the best means of avoiding some of the problems, confusions, and frictions of functional authority is to make sure it is clarified. Thus it is not enough to say that a divison or plant manager is "administratively responsible" to a line superior and "functionally responsible" to the controller. If controllers, like a few the authors have known, regard their functional authority over accounting matters to extend to all expenditures of funds, there is a built-in situation for undue conflict through multiplication of command. Or if personnel managers interpret their delegation to cover anything concerned with people, the conflict potential is obvious. Likewise, if operating managers regard controllers as being "staff," with no authority even to prescribe the form and nature of a company's accounting system, controllers cannot discharge their responsibility.

In order to obtain clarity, it is imperative that the exact functional authority delegated to a manager or to a department be spelled out clearly. This is necessary not only from the standpoint of the bearer's use and understanding of this specialized type of authority but also for those operating managers who are on the receiving end. An example of one company's attempt to define the authority of the vice president and

---

[9]See, for example, W. French and D. Henning, "The Authority-Influence Role of the Functional Specialist in Management," *Journal of the Academy of Management*, vol. 9, no. 3, pp. 187–203 (September 1966); D. E. McFarland, *Cooperation and Conflict in Personnel Administration* (New York: American Foundation for Management Research, 1963); even J. A. Belasco and J. A. Arlutto, while professing to find that line-staff conflicts in this area are less severe than usually believed, did find that "there may be a high conflict over 'how' the agreed-upon role is performed." See "Line and Staff Conflicts: Some Empirical Insights," *Academy of Management Journal*, vol. 12, no. 1, pp. 469–477 (December 1969).

[10]See R. McIntire, "Functional Authority in the Controller's Position," Ph.D. dissertation, University of California, Los Angeles, 1971.

[11]See, for example, R. Golembiewski, *Organizing Men and Power* (Chicago: Rand McNally & Company, 1967).

controller is the following specific delegations to that officer, which were thoroughly discussed with him and his subordinates and with key operating managers and their subordinates over whom he was expected to exercise such authority:

1 Authority to prescribe the corporate chart of accounts and the divisions' charts of accounts so far as they are supportive to, and necessary for, the corporation chart of accounts; authority to direct the development and maintenance of necessary procedures to ensure the integrity of the company's accounts and statements; authority to see that the company's accounting policies and procedures are followed in the divisions.

2 Authority to prescribe policies and procedures in the handling of cash, including banking arrangements, methods of handling receipts and disbursements, and the requirements for bonding throughout the company.

3 Authority to prescribe policies, standards, and procedures with respect to inventory control matters which affect the integrity of accounting records.

4 Authority to prescribe the necessary form, procedures, and timing for the preparation and submission of profit plans.

5 Authority to require from the various divisions and departments of the company financial, accounting, and statistical reports and forecasts in a form and at times believed to be necessary for proper company planning and control.

6 Authority to approve the selection of the chief accounting officer of any division or affiliate.

7 Authority to prescribe and undertake a program of internal auditing of financial, cash, credit, and accounting transactions and an audit of corporate and divisional financial and accounting policies and procedures.

LINE AND STAFF IN PRACTICE

The essential character of line and staff relationships becomes readily apparent in the study of well-managed enterprises. Although the semantics of management occasionally mislead the student (and, more often, those managing and being managed), a clear statement of authority relationships will identify the kind of authority—whether it be line, staff, or functional authority.

An Example: The Position of Treasurer

In one instance, one of the nation's leading management consulting firms spelled out the treasurer's authority in a fast-growing enterprise with territorial divisions for major line operations and a staff of top executives to control overall policy as follows:

> The Treasurer has line authority over and is responsible for directing activities of such personnel as he requires to establish system policies and procedures for the functions under his jurisdiction and to administer system treasury and accounting functions which are reserved for his department. He has no direct line authority over the day-to-day activities of accounting personnel in the divisions and regions except as specifically delegated by the president. He is responsible for developing and interpreting budgeting, accounting, and financial policies to the divisions and regions, for assisting these organizations in carrying out such policies, and for satisfying himself that such policies are correctly and ably administered in the field.
>
> At the request of division managements, or voluntarily when system welfare is materially concerned, the Treasurer shall make recommendations concerning the employment, promotion, dismissal, or change in compensation of supervisory personnel engaged in activities within his functional responsibility. Final action on such matters shall be taken by division managements when mutual agreement has been reached with department heads concerned.[12]

This general description of authority is supplemented by a list of duties making clear that the treasurer's major assignments are establishing budgetary policy and procedures, instituting accounting policies and procedures for maintaining division records, and such other procedures as might be necessary for the discharge of his duties. The description makes clear the line, staff, and functional authority relationships of the treasurer who has line authority over a particular department, staff relationship to top and divisional managers, and functional authority to require the major operating departments, the divisions, to follow good budgeting and accounting procedures.

Unavoidability of Functional Authority

In virtually every large enterprise, and in many smaller enterprises, some delegation of functional authority to staff departments seems unavoidable. Even though a manager may abhor and try to avoid this hybrid combination of line and staff authority, most major staff departments have some functional authority. This practice is due largely to the necessity for expert interpretation of policy and for formulation of procedures by specialists, which in turn results from the need for varying degrees of uniformity in accounting, labor, public relations, and other activities.

Of course, line executives could maintain the separation of line and

---

[12]From a confidential organization report by a major management consulting firm.

staff authority relationships in the organization structure if they were to insist on issuing all the instructions relating to matters required by specialized staff assistance. As a matter of fact, some corporation and division executives have done so. However, in most enterprises, either this taxes the line managers' span of management unduly or, if they automatically accept their staff's recommendations, it makes the apparent avoidance of functional authority a meaningless pretense. It is always good practice for the person actually making decisions to be plainly identified.

STAFF AND THE SMALL BUSINESS

Since the staff type of department represents a refinement in specialization resulting from division of labor, the appearance of staffs is usually proportional to the size of the enterprise. Just how large a business firm must be before it will gain by regrouping certain activities into staff departments cannot be stated generally. However, it need not be very large before it feels the necessity for specialized assistance on such matters as taxation, government procurement, personnel policy and procedures, accounting, financing, contracts and legal matters, and even management itself. The web of government, union, and other controls and complexities in which even the small business finds itself has blurred many of the old, sharp distinctions between the small and larger business.

Even without being able to develop extensive staff departments, the small company can benefit from staff assistance in many ways. Indeed, in the present economic, social, and political environment, the price of error in such matters as the determination of costs and taxes, the maintenance of good labor relations, the meeting of environmental regulations, and planning and control is so great that the small firm cannot afford to do without the best possible counsel. Heads of companies of thirty or even fewer employees can frequently afford a general staff assistant. No matter how small the company, one of its essential costs is for legal and tax advice on a retainer, hourly, or job basis. Any company can receive accounting counsel at a moderate cost from its auditing firm, and audit of a company's books is usually a necessity in connection with income taxes and bank loans. Other advisory services include those of bankers and those relatively untapped but available resources in universities and colleges. Just as medical schools contribute to the community, so can university staffs be available, at a reasonable cost, to small businesses in such areas as engineering, accounting, economics, and management. The small corporation, furthermore, can use its board of directors as a source of advice and assistance. Sitting on boards of directors has attractions for individuals challenged by the opportunity for interesting service and for strengthening the free enterprise system.

In the small firm managers often operate in both line and staff capacities. The production manager may be the president's chief adviser on present and future costs and even on product design. The treasurer or controller may be the counselor on taxes, prices, and the availability of materials, or wage levels. But this fact does not change the essential nature of line and staff relationships, which is the same in small as in large firms. However, a staff organization suitable for the General Motors Corporation would bankrupt even a medium-sized company. Thus, one of the arts of good managing is to tailor the application of the various management devices to the resources available. This is, of course, to say that practice depends on situations and contingencies.

LIMITATIONS IN USING STAFF

Although staff specialists are necessary to an enterprise and can do much to make it successful, the nature of staff authority and the difficulty of understanding it lead to certain limitations in practice. Knowing these, both the line executive who is creating a staff and the staff personnel may be able to employ this desirable device effectively.

Danger of Undermining Line Authority

Staff personnel are often viewed with skepticism by operating executives, who see in them a high potential for harm. Observation of the fortunes of staff departments in many enterprises gives evidence that their prestige ebbs and flows. Too frequently, a president brings in a staff executive, clothes that person with authority (frequently very vague), and commands all other managers to be cooperative. The proposals of the staff specialist are received by the president with enthusiasm, and pressure is brought to bear upon the managers involved to put them into effect. What is actually taking place here is that the authority of the department managers is being undermined; yet, grudgingly and resentfully, the proposals will be accepted because all will recognize the high tide of the staff specialist's prestige. A continuation of this situation might harm or even destroy operating departments. Capable managers, not willing to submit to indignity or wait until the tide ebbs, would be snapped up by competitors, and the operating departments would gradually fall into inept hands. The denouement would be for the board of directors to fire the president or, as is more probable, for the president to discharge the staff specialist.

These operating departments represent the main line of the enterprise, and their heads gain a degree of indispensability. If staff advisers forget that they are to counsel and not to order, if they overlook the fact that their value lies in the extent to which they strengthen line managers, and if—worse yet—they should undermine line authority, they risk becoming expendable. If there is a supernumerary in an organization, it is likely to be the too energetic staff assistant.

A personnel manager recently extended her service activities and advisory functions to encompass control over the actual staffing and much of the supervision of subordinates in line departments. For a time, the line managers welcomed this assistance with their personnel problems. But when they realized they no longer controlled their subordinates and when the personnel manager was unwilling to relinquish control, the resultant outcry forced the president to request the resignation of the personnel manager.

Lack of Responsibility of Staff

Advisory departments only propose a plan. Others must make the decision to adopt it and put it into operation. This creates an ideal situation for recrimination and the shifting of blame. The staff will claim that it was a good plan and that it failed because the operating manager was inept, uninterested, or intent on sabotage. The manager who must make the plan work will claim that it was a poor plan hatched by inexperienced and impractical theorists.

Thinking in a Vacuum

The argument that a staff position gives the analyst time to think is appealing, but it overlooks the possibility of thinking in a vacuum. The weakness of impracticality has resulted, in business and government alike, in friction, loss of morale, and sabotage.

Another weakness in the assumption that analysts and specialists must be set off from line departments in order to think is the implication that operating managers are without thinking ability. They may, indeed, be without specialized knowledge, but this can be furnished them by able staff assistants. Good operating managers can analyze plans, see long-range applications, and spot fatal weaknesses far better than most staff assistants. An intelligent manager will not delegate managerial functions, and it is fatal to managership to strip away real responsibility for activities such as planning and to assign them to a staff assistant.

Management Complication

Few would deny the importance of maintaining unity of command. It is not easy for a department head to be responsible to two or three people; at the worker level it may be disastrous to attempt multiple responsibility. Some disunity in command may be unavoidable, since functional authority relationships are often unavoidable. But a manager should remain aware of the difficulties of multiple authority and should either limit them—even at the cost of some uniformity or loss of the fruits of specialization—or else carefully clarify them.

Furthermore, too much staff activity may complicate the line executive's job of direction and control. A corporation president may be so busy dealing with the recommendations of a large number of staff assistants and straightening twisted lines of authority that time and attention may not be available for operating departments; or the business may become so oriented to making policy and setting procedures that there is little time left to make shoes or give transportation service.

MAKING STAFF WORK

Observation of many business, government, educational, and other enterprises leads the authors to the belief that the line-staff problem is not only one of the most difficult that organizations face but also the source of an extraordinarily large amount of inefficiency. Solving this problem requires high managerial skill, careful attention to principles, and patient teaching of personnel.

Understanding Authority Relationships

Before the problems of line and staff can be solved, the nature of their authority relationships must be understood. So long as line and staff are regarded as groups of people or are confused with groupings of activities—as when service departments are confused with staff—this understanding is lacking. It must be recognized and emphasized that line and staff are relationships and that most managerial jobs have elements of both.

All managers and their subordinates should understand the purpose of their tasks and whether and when they operate in a line or in a staff capacity. This understanding must be accompanied by inculcation of the idea that line relationship means making decisions and acting on them, while staff relationship implies only the right to assist and counsel. The line may tell, but the staff must sell.

Making Line Listen to Staff

If staff counsel and advice are justifiable at all, the reason must be found in the complexities of enterprise operation and the need for assistance either from experts or from those freed from more pressing duties to give such assistance. Obviously, if staff help is not used, it would be prudent to abolish it. Line managers should realize that the competent staff assistant offers suggestions to aid and not to undermine or criticize. Although most line-staff friction probably arises from ineptness or overzealousness on the part of staff people, trouble also arises because line executives too carefully guard their authority and resent the very assistance they need.

Line managers should be encouraged or forced to consult with staff. Enterprises would do well to adopt the practice of compulsory staff assistance wherein the line must *listen* to staff. In General Motors, for example, product division managers consult with the staff divisions before proposing a major program or policy to the top executive and finance committees. They may not be *required* to do so, but they are likely to find that this results in smoother sailing for their proposals; if they can present a unified front with the staff division concerned, there will unquestionably be a better chance for the adoption of their proposals.

Keeping Staff Informed

Common criticisms of staff are that specialists operate in a vacuum, fail to appreciate the complexity of the line manager's job, or overlook salient facts in making recommendations. To some extent, these criticisms are warranted because specialists cannot be expected to know all the fine points of a manager's job. Specialists should take care that their recommendations deal only with matters within their competency, and the operating manager should not lean too heavily on a recommendation if, as is often the case, it deals only partially with a problem.

Many criticisms arise because staff assistants are not kept informed on matters within their province. Even the best assistant cannot advise properly in such cases. If line managers fail to inform their staff of decisions affecting its work or if they do not pave the way—through announcements and requests for cooperation—for staff to obtain the requisite information on specific problems, it cannot function as intended. In relieving their superiors of the necessity for gathering and analyzing such information, staff assistants largely justify their existence.

Completed Staff Work

Many staff persons overlook the fact that to render the most and best assistance, their recommendations should be complete enough to make possible a simple positive or negative response by the line manager. Staff assistants should be problem solvers and not problem creators. They create problems for managers when their advice is indecisive or obscure, when their conclusions are erroneous, when they have not taken into account all the facts or consulted the persons seriously affected by the proposed solution, or when they do not point out to managers the pitfalls as well as the advantages in a recommended course of action.

Completed staff work implies presentation of a clear recommendation based upon full consideration of a problem, clearance with persons importantly affected, suggestions about avoiding any difficulties involved, and, often, preparation of the paperwork—letters, directives, job descriptions, and specifications—so that a manager can accept or reject the proposal without further study, long conferences, or unnecessary work. Should a recommendation be accepted, thorough staff work provides line managers with the machinery to put it into effect.

Understanding staff authority lays the foundation for an organizational way of life. Wherever staff is used, its responsibility is to develop and maintain a climate of favorable personal relations. Essentially, the task of the staff assistant (or "assistant-to") is to make the responsible line manager "look good" and to help him or her do a better job. A staff assistant should never attempt to assume credit for an idea. Not only is this a sure way of alienating line colleagues, but operating managers who accept the idea actually do bear responsibility for their action.

Even under the best of circumstances, it is difficult to coordinate line and staff authority, for people must be persuaded to cooperate. Staff persons must gain and hold the confidence of their colleagues. They must keep in close touch with the operating departments, know their managers and staffs, and understand their problems. They must, through precept and example, convince their line colleagues that their prime interest is the welfare of operating managers, and they must deprecate their own contributions while embellishing those of the persons they assist. People in a staff capacity have "arrived" when line executives seek their advice and ask them to study their problems.

THE NEUTRAL AND INFERIOR POSITION OF STAFF

Some writers on the subject of line-staff relationships have expressed concern about the "inferior" status of staff and service personnel as compared with line employees.[13] The limited research studies do seem to reflect this status relationship, but one may doubt that its existence is anything more than an ongoing assessment of organizational truths. The earlier discussion of staff-line relationships in this chapter did not make the assumption that staff plays an inferior part in the management process; quite the contrary, the authors of this book view the status of staff or specialized service personnel with their educational levels and expertise as equal in most cases to that of the personnel who occupy line operating positions. On the other hand, the authors are fully aware that the staff and service functions have often suffered in esteem when compared with operations. It is not that this discrimination is deserved; it is that line managers who sell short their staff or service people are exhibiting a personal bias or a lack in their knowlege of line-staff relationships. One has only to ask what those in a line capacity would do without the assistance of staff.

It would appear then, that it is not the classical or operational approach to management that has projected staff in an inferior role; it has

---

[13]P. J. Browne and R. T. Golembiewski, "The Line-Staff Concept Revisited: An Empirical Study of Organizational Images," *Academy of Management Journal*, vol. 17, no. 3, pp. 406–417 (September 1974).

merely reflected the facts as seen by line managers. If indeed there is an inferior-superior relationship to be observed in organizational life, it can most clearly be seen in the relationship of supervisors to middle managers and of these to top managers. And this situation is not to be decried on the grounds of egalitarianism; it is an organizational fact of life common among human beings everywhere.

FOR DISCUSSION

1 Select four articles or books in which the terms "line" and "staff" are used. How are they defined? To what extent do the concepts you find agree or disagree with those in this book?

2 Why has there been a conflict between line and staff for so long and in so many companies? Can this conflict be removed?

3 Take as examples a number of positions in any kind of enterprise (business, church, government, or elsewhere). Classify them as line or staff.

4 If the task of a person in a purely staff position is to offer advice, how can a person receiving this advice make sure that it is competent, independent, and true?

5 How many cases of functional authority in organization have you seen? Analyzing a few, do you agree that they could have been avoided? If they could have been, would you have eliminated them? If they could not have been avoided or you would not have wanted to eliminate them, how would you remove any possible difficulties which might arise?

6 If you were asked to advise a young college graduate who has accepted a staff position as assistant to a factory manager, what suggestions would you make?

chapter 15 Decentralization of Authority

MAJOR CHAPTER OBJECTIVES

1 To explore the nature of delegation of authority and of centralization and decentralization of authority in organization structures.
2 To identify principles underlying delegation of authority and important factors underlying the practice of delegation.
3 To explain the factors that normally determine the degree of decentralization that can and should be undertaken in various circumstances.
4 To suggest means of assuring the degree of decentralization desired, with special emphasis on the importance of clarifying delegations.
5 To emphasize the special importance of obtaining balance in authority centralization and decentralization in practice.

Organization authority, it will be recalled, is merely the degree of discretion conferred on people to make it possible for them to use their judgment. Whether authority should be concentrated or dispersed throughout the organization is a question not so much of *what kind* as of *how much* authority. Decentralization is a fundamental aspect of delegation; to the extent that authority is not delegated, it is centralized. Absolute centralization in one person is conceivable, but it implies no subordinate managers and therefore no structured organization. Consequently, it ·can be said that some decentralization characterizes all organizations. On the other hand, there cannot be absolute decentralization, for if managers should delegate *all* their authority, their status as managers would cease, their position would be eliminated, and there would, again, be no organization. Centralization and decentralization are therefore tendencies; they are qualities like "hot" and "cold."

As one management writer has explained, the degree of decentralization is greater:

1   The greater the number of decisions made lower down the management hierarchy.
2   The more important the decisions made lower down the management hierarchy. For example, the greater the sum of capital expenditure that can be approved by the plant manager without consulting anyone else, the greater the degree of decentralization in this field.
3   The more functions affected by decisions made at lower levels. Thus companies which permit only operational decisions to be made at separate branch plants are less decentralized than those which also permit financial and personnel decisions at branch plants.
4   The less checking required on the decision. Decentralization is greater when no check at all must be made; less when superiors have to be informed of the decision after it has been made; still less if superiors have to be consulted before the decision is made. The fewer people to be consulted, and the lower they are on the management hierarchy, the greater the degree of decentralization.[1]

"Centralization" has been used to describe tendencies other than the dispersal of authority, as in centralization of performance (discussed below on pages 437–438). This is a problem of geography: a business characterized by centralized performance operates in a single location or under a single roof. Centralization often refers, furthermore, to departmental activities; service divisions centralize similar or specialized activities in a single department. But when centralization is discussed as

---

[1]E. Dale, *Planning and Developing the Company Organization Structure*, Research Report No. 20 (New York: American Management Association, 1952), p. 107.

an aspect of management, it refers to delegating or withholding authority and the authority dispersal or concentration in decision making.

Although closely related to delegation of authority, decentralization is more: It reflects a philosophy of organizing and managing. It requires careful selection of what decisions to push down into the organization structure and what to hold at or near the top, specific policy making to guide the decision making, selection and training of people, and adequate controls. Indeed, a policy of decentralization affects all areas of management and can be looked upon as an essential element of a managerial system. In fact, without it, managers could not use their discretion to meet the ever-present and ever-changing situations they face.

DELEGATION OF AUTHORITY

The primary purpose of delegation is to make organization possible.[2] Just as no one person in an enterprise can do all the tasks necessary for accomplishment of group purpose, so it is impossible, as an enterprise grows, for one person to exercise all the authority for making decisions. As was shown in Chapter 12, there is a limit to the number of persons managers can effectively supervise and for whom they can make decisions. Once this limit is passed, authority must be delegated to subordinates, who will make decisions within the area of their assigned duties.

How Authority Is Delegated

Authority is delegated when decision-making power is vested in a subordinate by a superior. Clearly, superiors cannot delegate authority they do not have whether they are board members, presidents, vice presidents, or supervisors. It is equally clear that superiors cannot delegate all their authority without, in effect, transferring their position to their subordinates.

The entire process of delegation involves:

1 The *determination* of results expected

2 The *assignment* of tasks

3 The *delegation* of authority for accomplishing these tasks

4 The *exaction* of responsibility for their accomplishment

In practice, it is impossible to split this process, since expecting a person

---

[2]For one of the best and most detailed treatises on the process of delegation, see Alvin Brown, *Organization of Industry* (Englewood Cliffs, N.J.: Prentice-Hall, Inc., 1947), chaps. 2–12.

to accomplish goals without the authority to achieve them is meaningless, as is the delegation of authority without knowing for what end results it will be used. Moreover, since responsibility cannot be delegated, the boss has no practical alternative but to exact responsibility from subordinates for completing the assignment. In other words, holding subordinates responsible to their superiors for using delegated authority to accomplish expected results must be regarded as a part of the process of delegation. Furthermore, since responsibility is an obligation subordinates owe to their superiors, it cannot be delegated by subordinates to anyone else. Their obligation runs to their superiors and to no one else.

Clarity of Delegation

Delegations of authority may be specific or general, written or unwritten. If the delegation is unclear, a manager may not understand the nature of the duties or the results expected. The job assignment of a company controller, for example, may specify such functions as accounting, credit control, cash control, financing, export-license handling, and preparation of financial statistics, and these broad functions may even be broken down into more definite duties. Or a controller may be told merely that he or she is expected to do what controllers generally do.

Specific written delegations of authority are extremely helpful both to the manager who receives them and to the grantor, who will thereby more easily see conflicts or overlaps with other positions. Delegators will also be able better to isolate those things for which a subordinate can and should be held responsible.

One top executive claims he never delegates authority but merely tells his subordinate managers to take charge of a department or plant and then holds them responsible for doing so. This particular executive is actually making an extremely broad delegation of authority—that of full discretion to operate as the subordinates see fit. However, in too many cases where such nonspecific delegations are made, subordinates are forced to feel their way and—by testing through practice what the superior will stand—define authority delegation by trial and error. Unless they are very familiar with top company policies and traditions, know the personality of the boss, and exercise sound judgment, they may be placed at a disadvantage. An executive will do well to balance the costs of uncertainty against the effort to make the delegation specific.

On the other hand, there are those who argue that, especially in the upper levels of management, it is too difficult to make authority delegations specific and that the subordinate, robbed of flexibility, will be unable to develop in the best way. Sometimes, particularly for new top jobs, delegations cannot be very specific, at least at the outset. If a large company establishes for the first time a traffic manager to coordinate transportation activities at its various plants, the president may be unclear about the amount of authority called for. But this situation should be remedied as soon as possible. One of the first duties of the new appointee should be a description of the job and clearance of the description with the superior and, ideally, with those other managers on the same level whose cooperation is necessary. Otherwise, organizational frictions, unnecessary meetings and negotiations, jealousies, and numerous other disadvantages are likely to follow. Too many top executives believe they have a happy team of subordinates who do not need specific authority delegations, when, in fact, they have a dissident group of frustrated managers jockeying for position.

The fear that specific delegation will result in inflexibility is best met by developing a tradition of flexibility. It is true that if authority delegations are specific, a manager may regard his or her job as a staked claim with a high fence around it. But this attitude can be eliminated by making necessary changes in organization structure an accepted and expected thing. Much of the inflexibility of definite delegations comes from managerial laziness and failure to reorganize often enough for the smooth accomplishment of objectives.

Splintered Authority

Splintered authority exists wherever a problem cannot be solved or a decision made without pooling the authority delegations of two or more managers. Thus, when the superintendent of plant A sees an opportunity to reduce costs through a minor modification in procedures in Plant B, his authority cannot encompass the change. But if the superintendents of the two plants can agree upon the change and if it affects no other equal or superior manager, all they need do is pool their authority and make the decision. Individually, their authority is said to be "splintered." In day-to-day operations of any company, there are many cases of splintered authority, and probably many managerial conferences are held because of the necessity of pooling authority to make a decision.

As may readily be seen, such problems can be handled by merely referring the decision upward until one person can make it. In the case of the two plant superintendents, it might lie within the authority of the vice president in charge of manufacturing. However, in many cases, the splinters of authority, although far down in the organization, exist in departments that have their common superior only in the office of the president. For example, one of the authors observed the solution of a problem involving a Western railroad with headquarters in Chicago. The problem was relatively minor, but a decision on it in Los Angeles required the consolidated authority of the traffic department, the operating department, and the public relations department. It could have been referred up the line by each of the managers to the president's office, where sufficient authority for making the decision was concentrated. But if such decisions were always handled by upward reference, the president's office would be swamped. In this case, the managers of the three departments in the Los Angeles office met briefly, pooled their delegated authority, and quickly made the decision.

Splintered authority cannot be wholly avoided in making decisions. However, recurring decisions on the same matters may be evidence that authority delegations have not been properly made and that some reorganization is required.

Recovery of Delegated Authority

All delegations of authority are subject to recovery by the grantor. It is a characteristic of authority that original possessors do not permanently dispossess themselves of this power by delegating it. Just as, in the political area, the right of Americans to change or revoke the Constitution and thus redistribute rights is unchallenged, so, in the area of enterprise operation, the right of a superior manager to recover authority is unquestioned.

Reorganization inevitably involves some recovery and redelegation of authority. A shuffle in organization means that rights are recovered by the responsible head of the firm or a department and then redelegated to managers of new or modified departments, so that the head of a new department may receive the authority formerly held by other managers. For example, when a reorganization takes quality control away from the works manager and assigns it to a new manager of quality control reporting to the vice president in charge of manufacturing, the vice president has recovered some of the authority formerly delegated to the works manager and has redelegated it, with or without modification, to the new quality control executive.

PRINCIPLES OF DELEGATION

The following principles are guides to delegation of authority. Unless carefully recognized in practice, delegation may be ineffective, organization may fail, and the managerial process may be seriously impeded.

Principle of delegation by results expected   Since authority is intended to furnish managers with a tool for so managing as to gain contributions to enterprise objectives, *authority delegated to an individual manager should be adequate to ensure the ability to accomplish results expected.* Too many managers try to partition and define authority on the basis of the rights to be delegated or withheld, rather than looking first at the goals to be achieved and then determining how much discretion is necessary to achieve them. In no other way can a manager delegate authority in accordance with the responsibility exacted. Often a superior has some idea, vague or fixed, as to what is to be accomplished, but does not trouble to determine whether the subordinate has the authority to do it. Sometimes the superior does not want to admit how much discretion it takes to do a job and is likewise reluctant to define the results expected. Perhaps it is no wonder that it has become common in enterprises to speak erroneously of delegating "responsibilities."

Delegation by results expected implies that goals have been set and plans made, that these are communicated and understood, and that jobs have been set up to fit in with them. It also demonstrates that planning is a prerequisite to all the tasks of management and that the managerial functions in practice coalesce into a single activity.

Principle of functional definition   To develop departmentation, activities must be grouped to facilitate the accomplishment of goals, and the manager of each subdivision must have authority to coordinate its activities with the organization as a whole. This gives rise to the principle of functional definition: *The more a position or a department has clear definitions of results expected, activities to be undertaken, organization authority delegated, and authority and informational relationships with other positions understood, the more adequately the individuals responsible can contribute toward accomplishing enterprise objectives.* To do otherwise is to risk confusion as to what is expected of whom. This principle—which is a principle of both delegation and departmentation—although simple in concept, is often difficult to apply. To define a job and delegate authority to do it requires, in most cases, patience, intelligence, and clarity of objectives and plans. It is obviously difficult to define a job if the superior does not know what results are desired.

Scalar principle   As pointed out in the previous chapter, the scalar principle refers to the chain of direct authority relationships from superior to subordinate throughout the organization. Ultimate enterprise authority must always rest somewhere. *The more clear the line of authority from the top manager in an enterprise to every subordinate position, the more effective will be the responsible decision making and organization communication.* The scale is described by Fayol as

> . . . the chain of superiors ranging from the ultimate authority to the lowest ranks. The line of authority is the route followed—via every link in the chain—by all communications which start from or go to the ultimate authority. This path is dictated both by the need for some transmission and by the principle of unity of command, but it is not always the swiftest. It is even at times disastrously lengthy in large concerns, notably in governmental ones.[3]

A clear understanding of the scalar principle is necessary for proper organization functioning. Subordinates must know who delegates author-

[3]Henri Fayol, *General and Industrial Administration* (New York: Pitman Publishing Corporation, 1949), p. 14.

ity to them and to whom matters beyond their own authority must be referred. Although the chain of command may be safely departed from for purposes of information, departure for purposes of decision making tends to destroy the decision-making system and undermine managership itself.

Authority level principle   Functional definition plus the scalar principle gives rise to the authority level principle. Clearly, at some organization level authority exists for making decisions within the competence of an enterprise. Therefore, the authority level principle would be: *Maintenance of intended delegation requires that decisions within the authority competence of individuals be made by them and not be referred upward in the organization structure.* In other words, managers at each level should make whatever decisions they can in the light of their delegated authority, and only matters that authority limitations keep them from deciding should be referred to superiors.

A fairly common complaint of top executives is that while they know the importance of delegating downward, they are concerned with the practice of subordinates delegating "upward." In other words, as chief executives have pointed out to the authors, they assign a problem only to find it in a few days or weeks back on their desks. The answer to this situation is, of course, not to permit these problems to come upward. If discretion to make a decision is properly delegated, the superior must resist the temptation to make it. Subordinates have a way of quickly detecting bosses who are willing to make decisions that should have been made by those reporting to them.

It is obvious from the authority level principle that if managers wish to make effective authority delegations and thereby to be relieved from some of the burden of decision making, they must make sure that delegations are clear and that the subordinate understands them. Moreover, they will do well to avoid the temptation to make decisions for subordinates.

Principle of unity of command   A basic management principle, often disregarded for what are believed to be compelling circumstances,[4] is that of unity of command: *The more completely an individual has a reporting relationship to a single superior, the less the problem of conflict in instructions and the greater the feeling of personal responsibility for results.* In discussing delegation of authority, it has been assumed that—except for the inevitable instances of splintered authority—the right of discretion over a particular activity will flow from a single superior to a subordinate. Although it is possible for a subordinate to receive authority from two or more superiors and logically possible to be held responsible by all of them, the practical difficulties of serving two or more masters are obvious. An obligation is essentially personal, and authority delegation

---

[4]Note in chap. 14 the case of functional authority.

by more than one person to an individual is likely to result in conflicts in both authority and responsibility.

The principle of unity of command is useful in the clarification of authority-responsibility relationships. A president, for example, does not normally divide sales activities among sales, manufacturing, public relations, finance, accounting, and personnel, with no single person responsible for them. Instead, since sales is a cohesive activity, assignment is made to the sales manager. Unity of command would not exist if, instead of a single sales manager, the president appointed an executive committee to run the department. To force every major subordinate in the sales department to owe full obligation to each committee member rather than to one manager would produce confusion, buck passing, and general inefficiency. Similarly, it is undesirable to have several managers assign duties to one employee, who would then be obligated to each of the several bosses.

Principle of absoluteness of responsibility Since responsibility, being an obligation owed, cannot be delegated, no superior can escape, through delegation, responsibility for the activities of subordinates, for it is the superior who has delegated authority and assigned duties. Likewise, *the responsibility of subordinates to their superiors for performance is absolute, once they have accepted an assignment and the right to carry it out, and superiors cannot escape responsibility for the organization activities of their subordinates.*

Principle of parity of authority and responsibility Since authority is the discretionary right to carry out assignments and responsibility is the obligation to accomplish them, it logically follows that the authority should correspond to the responsibility. From this rather obvious logic is derived the principle that *the responsibility for actions cannot be greater than that implied by authority delegated, nor should it be less.* This parity is not mathematical, but, rather, coextensive, because both relate to the same assignments. The president of a firm may, for example, assign duties, such as buying raw materials and machine tools and hiring subordinates in order to meet certain goals, to the manufacturing vice president. The vice president would be unable to perform these duties without being given enough discretion to meet this responsibility. Nor should one, on the other hand, have more authority than the responsibilities call for. Managers often try to hold subordinates responsible for duties for which they do not have the requisite authority. This is, of course, unfair. Sometimes sufficient authority is delegated, but the delegant is not held responsible for its proper use. This is, obviously, a case of poor managerial direction and control and has no bearing upon the principle of parity.

Managers are sometimes said to be given authority to do that for which they cannot be held responsible; thus, a sales manager is given authority to sell, but cannot be responsible for making people buy. However, the sales manager has the authority to use certain material and human resources to obtain sales wherever possible. Here, parity consists of his or her responsibility as an executive for managing the sales force in the best possible way, equated with the authority to sell.

THE ART OF DELEGATION

Most failures in effective delegation occur not because of lack of understanding of the nature or principles of delegation but because of inability or unwillingness to apply them in practice. Delegation is, in a way, an elementary act of managing. Yet studies made of managerial failures almost invariably find that poor or inept delegation is at or near the top of the list of causes. Much of the reason for this lies in personal attitudes toward delegation.

Personal Attitudes toward Delegation

Although charting an organization and outlining managerial goals and duties will help in making delegations and knowledge of the principles of delegation will furnish a basis for it, certain personal attitudes lie back of making real delegations.

Receptiveness An underlying attribute of the manager who would delegate authority is a willingness to give other people's ideas a chance. Decision making always involves some discretion, and this means that a subordinate's decision is not likely to be *exactly* that which a superior would have made. The manager who knows how to delegate must have a minimum of NIH ("not invented here") factor and must be able not only to welcome the ideas of others but also to help others and to compliment them on their ingenuity.

Willingness to let go The manager who would effectively delegate authority must be willing to release the right to make decisions to subordinates. A great fault of managers who move up the executive ladder—or of the pioneer who has built a large business from the small beginnings of, say, a garage machine shop—is that they want to continue to make decisions for the positions they have left. The authors have seen corporate presidents and vice presidents insist upon confirming every purchase or the appointment of every laborer or secretary, not, perhaps, realizing that doing so took time and attention from far more important decisions.

Where size or complexity forces delegation of authority, managers should realize—even if their superiors must go out of their way to teach them—that there is a kind of law of comparative managerial advantage, somewhat like the law of comparative economic advantage that applies to trade between nations. Well known to economists and logically indisputable, the law of comparative economic advantage states that a country's wealth will be enhanced if it exports what it produces most efficiently and imports what it produces least efficiently, even though it could produce such imports more cheaply than any other nation. Likewise, managers will enhance their contribution to the firm if they concentrate on tasks that contribute most to the firm's objectives and assign to subordinates other tasks, even though they could accomplish the latter better themselves. This is hard to practice, but failure to do so defeats the very purpose of delegation.

Willingness to let others make mistakes   Although no responsible manager would sit idly by and let a subordinate make a mistake that might endanger the company or the subordinate's position in the company, continual checking on the subordinate to assure that no mistakes are ever made will make true delegation impossible. As everyone makes mistakes, a subordinate must be allowed to make them, and their cost must be charged to investment in personal development.

Serious or repeated mistakes can be largely avoided without negating delegation or hindering the development of the subordinate. Patient counseling, asking leading or discerning questions, and careful explanation of objectives and policies are among the tools available to the superior who would delegate well. None of these involves discouraging subordinates by intimidating criticism, harping on shortcomings, or hovering over them.

Willingness to trust subordinates   Closely allied to willingness to let others make mistakes is willingness to trust subordinates. Superiors have no alternative to trusting their subordinates, for delegation implies a trustful attitude between the two. This is sometimes hard to come by. The superior may put off delegation with the thought that subordinates are not well-enough seasoned, that they cannot handle people, that they have not yet developed judgment, or that they do not appreciate all the facts bearing on a situation. Sometimes these considerations are true, but then the superior should either train subordinates or else select others who are prepared to assume the responsibility. Too often, however, bosses distrust their subordinates because they do not wish to let go, do not delegate wisely, or do not know how to set up controls to assure proper use of the authority.

Willingness to establish and use broad controls   Since superiors cannot delegate responsibility for performance, they should not delegate authority unless they are willing to find means ("feedback") of assuring themselves that the authority is being used to support enterprise or department goals and plans. As will be noted in later chapters, the establishing of effective controls is one of the more difficult arts of management. Obviously, controls cannot be established and exercised unless goals, policies, and plans are used as basic standards for judging the activities of subordinates. More often than not, reluctance to delegate and to trust subordinates lies in the planning deficiencies of the superior and an understandable fear of loss of control.

Guides for Overcoming Weak Delegation

Unclear delegations, partial delegations, pseudodelegations, delegations inconsistent with the results expected, and the hovering of superiors who refuse to allow subordinates to use their authority are among the many widely found weaknesses of delegation of authority.

Combine with these weaknesses untrained, inept, or weak subordinates who go to their bosses for decisions and subordinates who will not accept responsibility, plus lack of plans, planning information, and incentives, and the failure of delegation is partly explained. All that this means, as is so generally the case in managing, is that delegation does not stand alone, but is a systems phenomenon. But most of the responsibility for weak delegation lies with superiors and, primarily, with top managers. In overcoming these errors—and emphasizing the principles outlined above—the following five guides are practical in making delegation real:

1 Define assignments and delegate authority in the light of results expected. Or, to put it another way, grant authority to make possible the accomplishment of goal assignments.

2 Select the person in the light of the job to be done. This is the purpose of the managerial function of staffing and should be borne in mind, since qualifications influence the nature of the authority delegated. Although the good organizer will approach delegation primarily from the standpoint of the task to be accomplished, in the final analysis, staffing as a part of the total system of delegation cannot be ignored.

3 Maintain open lines of communication. Since the superior does not delegate all authority or abdicate responsibility and since managerial autonomy therefore does not exist, decentralization should not lead to insulation. Because plans change and decisions must be made in the light of changing conditions, delegations tend to be fluid and to be given meaning in the light of such changes. This means that there should be a free flow of information between superior and subordinate, furnishing the subordinate information with which to make decisions and to interpret properly the authority delegated. Delegations, then, do depend on situations.

4 Establish proper controls. Because no manager can relinquish responsibility, delegations should be accompanied by techniques to make sure the authority is properly used. But if controls are not to interfere with delegation, they must be relatively broad and designed to show

deviations from plans rather than interfere with detailed actions of subordinates.

5 Reward effective delegation and successful assumption of authority. It is seldom sufficient to suggest that authority be delegated, or even to order that this be done. Managers should be ever watchful for means of rewarding both effective delegation and effective assumption of authority. Although many of these rewards will be pecuniary, the granting of greater discretion and prestige—both in a given position and in promotion to a higher position—is often even more of an incentive.

FACTORS DETERMINING THE DEGREE OF DECENTRALIZATION OF AUTHORITY

Managers cannot ordinarily be for or against decentralization of authority. They may *prefer* to delegate authority, or they may like to make all the decisions. A well-known despot in a certain large enterprise in this country, who would like to make all the decisions, finds that he cannot. Even the autocrat in a smaller enterprise is often forced to delegate some authority.[5]

Although the temperament of individual managers affects the extent of authority delegation, other factors also affect it. Most of these are beyond the control of the individual manager. One may resist their influence, but no successful manager can ignore them.

Costliness of the Decision

Perhaps the overriding factor determining the extent of decentralization is, as in other aspects of policy, the criterion of costliness. As a general rule, the more costly the action to be decided, the more probable it is that the decision will be made at the upper levels of management. Cost may be reckoned directly in dollars and cents or in such intangibles as the company's reputation, competitive position, or employee morale. Thus, an airline decision to purchase airplanes will be made at top levels, while the decision to purchase desks may be made in the second or third echelon of an operating department. Quality control in drug manufacturing, where a mistake might endanger lives, to say nothing of the company's reputation, would normally report at a high level, while the quality inspection in toy manufacturing might report much lower.

The fact that the cost of a mistake affects decentralization is not

[5]*Business Week*, pp. 182–194 (Sept. 6, 1952), ran a feature story on the president of a $50 million-a-year rayon converter who apparently disproves "what the books say" by not delegating decision making. Yet, even though he made a surprising number of detailed decisions, the article quotes him as disposing of callers by saying, "See my advertising manager" or "Talk to Marty."

necessarily based on the assumption that top managers make fewer mistakes than subordinates. They may make fewer mistakes, since they are probably better trained and in possession of more facts, but the controlling reason is the weight of responsibility. As already discussed, delegating authority is not delegating responsibility; therefore, managers typically prefer not to delegate authority for crucial decisions.

On the other hand, this concept must be applied cautiously and, in large companies, sparingly. Some managers fear to delegate *any* authority for decision making, exaggerating the dangers and costs of mistakes by subordinates. Overburdened managers may incur greater costs from delay or indecision than they hope to avoid by withholding decision-making rights. Although it cannot be proved statistically, experience supports the conclusion that it may cost more to centralize too much authority, thereby permitting subordinates to drift without clear-cut decisions, than it would to risk subordinates' mistakes.

The need for top control depends on the kind of decision. In the typical large business, top managers may reasonably feel that they cannot delegate authority over the expenditure of capital funds. In General Motors Corporation, the financial aspects of that company's operations are centralized under an executive vice president, who reports to the chairman or vice chairman of the board of directors rather than to the president. This is a living example of the importance of centralization in this area.

Uniformity of Policy

Another, and somewhat related, factor favoring centralization of authority is the desire to obtain uniform policy. Those who value consistency above all are invariably in favor of centralized authority, since this is the easiest road to such a goal. They may wish to ensure that customers will be treated alike with respect to quality, price, credit, delivery, and service; that the same policies will be followed in dealing with vendors; or that public relations policies will be standardized.

Uniform policy also has certain internal advantages. For instance, standardized accounting, statistics, and financial records make it easier to compare relative efficiencies of departments and keep down costs. The administration of a union contract is facilitated through uniform policy with respect to wages, promotions, vacations, dismissals, and similar matters. Taxes and government regulation entail fewer worries and chances for mistakes with uniform policies.

Yet many enterprises go to considerable length to make sure that some policies will not be completely uniform. When a firm organizes on a product or territorial basis, it obviously prefers at least some nonuniformity in certain policies affecting the operations of these divisions. Many companies encourage variety in all except major matters, hoping that out of such nonuniformity may come managerial innovation, progress, competition between organizational units, improved morale and efficiency, and a supply of promotable managers.

Economic Size

The larger the enterprise, the more decisions to be made; and the more places in which they must be made, the more difficult it is to coordinate them. These complexities of organization may require policy questions to be passed up the line and discussed not only with many managers in the chain of command but also with many managers at each level, since horizontal agreement may be as necessary as vertical clearance.

Slow decisions—slow because of the number of specialists and managers who must be consulted—are costly. To minimize this cost, authority should be decentralized whenever feasible. Indeed, the large enterprise that prides itself on the right kind of decentralization is recognizing the inevitable, although the extent and effectiveness of decentralization may differ widely among companies, depending largely upon the quality of their management.

Diseconomies of large size may be reduced by organizing the enterprise into a number of units. Considerable increases in efficiency are likely to result from making the unit small enough for *its* top executives to be near the point where decisions are made. This makes possible speedy decisions, keeps executives from spending time coordinating their decisions with many others, reduces the amount of paper work, and improves the quality of decisions by reducing their magnitude to manageable proportions.

Exactly what this size is cannot be arbitrarily stated. Some managers believe it to be 1000 persons, others believe it to be closer to 100 or 250, and some would hold that 2500 employees can be grouped into manageable divisions, each with considerable decentralized authority. In any case, there is evidence that where the unit exceeds a certain size, the distance from top to bottom may impair the quality and speed of decision making.

Also important to size is the character of the unit. For decentralization to be thoroughly effective, the unit must possess a certain economic and managerial self-sufficiency. Functional departments such as sales or manufacturing or engineering cannot be the independent unit that product or territorial departments of the same size can be, encompassing as they do nearly all the functions of an enterprise. It therefore follows that if the uneconomic aspects of size are to be reduced, it is preferable to departmentize along product, territorial, or distribution channel lines.

In the zeal to overcome the disadvantages of size by increasing the number of decision-making units, certain shortcomings of decentralization should be avoided. When authority is decentralized, a lack of policy uniformity and of coordination may follow. The branch, product division, or other self-sufficient unit may be so preoccupied with its objectives as to lose sight of those of the enterprise as a whole. What headquarters executive has not had the feeling that a division or a branch is at times "running away with the company"? Independence may mean, too, that the talents of top line and staff officials and specialists—whose experience and training are expensive business assets—are not sufficiently used by subordinate managers in the decentralized units.

History of the Enterprise

Whether authority will be decentralized frequently depends upon the way the business has been built. Those enterprises which, in the main, expand from within—such as Marshall Field and Company and International Harvester Company—show a marked tendency to keep authority centralized, as do those which expand under the direction of the owner-founder. The Ford Motor Company was, under its founder, an extraordinary case of centralized authority; Henry Ford, Sr., prided himself on having no organizational titles in the top management of the company except that of president and general manager, which he held, insisting, to the extent he could, that every major decision in that vast company be made by himself.

On the other hand, enterprises that represent amalgamations and consolidations are likely to show, at least at first, a definite tendency to retain decentralized authority, especially if the unit acquired is operating profitably. To be sure, this tendency not to rock the boat may be politically inspired rather than based on pure managerial consideration. Certainly, the claim of autonomy of the once-independent units is especially strong, and a full managerial generation may have to pass before the chief executive of the amalgamation dares materially to reduce the degree of decentralization.

In some cases the first influence of an amalgamation may be toward increased centralization. If the controlling group wishes to put in its own management or take immediate advantage of the economies of combined operation, the requirements of policy uniformity and quick action may necessitate centralization at least as a first step.

Management Philosophy

The character of top executives and their philosophy have an important influence on the extent to which authority is decentralized. Sometimes top managers are despotic, brooking no interference with the authority and information they jealously hoard. At other times, top managers keep authority not merely to gratify a desire for status or power but because they simply cannot give up the activities and authorities they enjoyed before they reached the top or before the business expanded from an owner-manager shop.

Some people find decentralization a means to make big business work. In those cases, top managers may see decentralization as a way of organizational life that takes advantage of the innate desire of people to create, to be free, and to have status. Many successful top managers find in it a means to harness the desire for freedom to economic efficiency, much as the free enterprise system has been responsible for this country's remarkable industrial progress. As an example of this attitude General Robert E. Wood, former chairman of the board of Sears, Roebuck and Company, said:

> We complain about government in business, we stress the advantages of the free enterprise system, we complain about the totalitarian state, but in our industrial organizations, in our striving for efficiency, we have created more or less of a totalitarian organization in industry—particularly in large industry.[6]

Retaining efficiency and discipline in these large organizations and yet allowing people to express themselves, to exercise initiative, and to have some voice in the affairs of the organization is the greatest problem large organizations have to solve.

Desire for Independence

It is a characteristic of individuals and of groups to desire a degree of independence. A region may resent various aspects of absentee control. Observe the hostility of the Chicago Board of Trade and the Chicago newspapers toward the absent managers of its railroads during the 50 years prior to World War I, the resentment felt by local banks at the establishment of twelve Federal Reserve banks with many powers over local banking operations, and the frequent exasperation of branch managers with their head offices.

Individuals may become frustrated by delay in getting decisions, by long lines of communication, and by the great game of passing the buck. This frustration can lead to dangerous loss of good people, to jockeying by the office politician, and to resigned inertia by the less competent seeker of security.

Availability of Managers

A real shortage of managerial talent would limit the extent of decentralization of authority, since dispersal of decision making assumes the availability of trained managers. But too often the mourned perennial scarcity of good managers is used as an excuse for centralizing authority; executives who complain that they have no one to whom they can

---

[6]Quoted in Dale, op. cit., p. 116.

delegate authority are often trying to magnify their own value to the firm or are confessing a failure to develop subordinates.

There are managers, also, who believe that a firm should centralize authority because it will then need very few good managers. One difficulty is that the firm that so centralizes authority may not be able to train managers to take over the duties of the top managers, and external sources must be relied upon to furnish any necessary replacements.

The key to safe decentralization is adequate training of managers. By the same token, decentralization is perhaps the most important key to training. Many large firms whose size makes decentralization a necessity consciously push decision making down into the organization for the purpose of developing managerial talent because they feel that the best training is actual experience. Since this usually carries with it chances for mistakes by the novice, it is good practice to limit, at least initially, the importance of the decisions so delegated.

Control Techniques

Another factor affecting the degree of decentralization is the state of development of control techniques. One cannot expect a good manager at any level of the organization to delegate authority without some way of knowing whether it will be used properly. Not knowing how to control often explains unwillingness to delegate authority and makes valid the belief of some managers that it takes more time to unmake mistakes or oversee a job than it would to do the job themselves.

Coupled with the manager's need to understand and use appropriate control techniques is the state of their development. Improvements in statistical devices, accounting controls, and other techniques have helped make possible the current trend toward extensive managerial decentralization. Even the most ardent supporters of decentralization, such as General Motors, Du Pont, and Sears, could hardly take so favorable a view without adequate techniques to show management, from the top down, whether performance is conforming to plans. To decentralize is not to lose control, and to push decision making down into the organization is not to abdicate responsibility.

Decentralized Performance

This is basically a technical matter depending upon such factors as the economies of division of labor, the opportunities for using machines, the nature of the work to be performed (thus, a railroad has no choice but to disperse its performance), and the location of raw materials, labor supply, and consumers. Although this kind of decentralization may be geographic or physical in nature, it influences the centralization of authority.

Authority tends to be decentralized when performance is decentralized, if for no other reason than that an absentee headquarters manager is unable to manage, although there are exceptions. For example, some of the large chain store enterprises are characterized by widely decentralized performance, and yet the local manager of a store may have little or no authority over pricing, advertising and merchandising methods, inventory and purchasing, or product line, all of which may be controlled from a central or regional office. The head of a local manufacturing plant of a large organization may have little authority beyond the right to hire and fire, and even in these cases action may be circumscribed by company policy and procedure and by the authority of a centralized personnel department. At the same time, the decentralization of performance limits the ability to centralize authority. The most despotic top manager of a national organization cannot supervise the San Francisco plant as closely as could be done if it were adjacent to the New York headquarters.

It does not follow that when performance is centralized, authority is centralized. True, authority can be more easily centralized if performance is, and if a company wishes tight control over decision making, centralized performance will aid this. But there are too many other factors to give geographic concentration a controlling influence in centralization. Here, again, what is done depends on situations.

Business Dynamics

The dynamic character of an enterprise also affects the degree to which authority may be decentralized. If a business is growing fast and facing complex problems of expansion, its managers, particularly those responsible for top policy, may be forced to make a disproportionate share of the decisions. But, strangely enough, this very dynamic condition may force these managers to delegate authority and take a calculated risk on the costs of error. Generally this dilemma is resolved in the direction of delegation, and, in order to avoid delegation to untrained subordinates, close attention is given to rapid formation of policies and accelerated training in management. An alternative often adopted is to slow the rate of change, including the cause of fast change, expansion. Many top managers have found that the critical factor limiting their ability to meet change and expand a business or other enterprise is the lack of trained personnel to whom authority may be delegated. Often, also, authority is delegated to untrained and undirected hands in order to meet the requirements of change, with the recognized future task of taking in the reins and rectifying mistakes when the pace of change has slowed.

In old, well-established, or relatively static businesses, there is a natural tendency to centralize or recentralize authority. When few major decisions must be made, the advantages of uniform policy and the economies of having a few well-qualified persons make the decisions dictate that authority be centralized. This may explain why in many banks and insurance companies and in certain railroads, decentralization is not extensive. Nevertheless, in static businesses too much centralization may carry dangers. New discoveries, vigorous competition from an unexpected source, or political change are only a few of the factors that might introduce dynamic conditions, and if this occurs, the overcentralized firm may not be able to meet a situation requiring decentralized decision making.

Environmental Influences

The determinants of the extent of decentralization dealt with so far have been largely interior to the enterprise, although the economics of decentralization of performance and the character of dynamics include elements well beyond the control of an enterprise's managers. In addition, there are definite external forces affecting the extent of decentralization. Among the most important of these are governmental controls, national unionism, and tax policies.

Government regulation of many facets of business policy makes it difficult and sometimes impossible to decentralize authority. If prices are regulated, the sales manager cannot be given much real freedom in determining them. If materials are allocated and restricted, the purchasing and factory managers are not free to buy or use them. If labor may be worked only a limited number of hours at a given rate of pay, the local division manager cannot freely set hours and wages.

But the restriction goes further. Top management itself no longer has authority over many aspects of policy and cannot, therefore, delegate authority it does not have. Much authority in areas controlled by government action could still be decentralized. But managers often do not dare trust subordinates to interpret government regulations, especially since the penalties and the public opprobrium for breaking laws are so serious and since the interpretation of most laws is a matter for the specialist.

In the same way, the rise of national unions in the past five decades has had a centralizing influence on business. So long as departmental or divisional managers can negotiate the terms of the labor contract, by dealing either with local unions or with employees directly, authority to negotiate may be delegated by top management to these subordinates. But where, as is increasingly the case, a national union enters into a collective bargaining contract with headquarters management, with the terms of the contract applicable to all workers of a company wherever located, a company can no more chance decentralization of certain decision making than it can in the case of government controls.

The tax system of the national, state, and local governments has had a marked regulatory effect on business. The tax collector, especially the federal income tax collector, sits at the elbow of every executive who makes a decision involving funds. As a matter of fact, with high rates applicable to corporate income, the impact of taxation is often a policy-determining factor that overshadows such traditional business considerations as plant expansion, marketing policies, and economical operations. Uniformity of tax policy becomes a consideration of primary importance to company management. This spells centralization because managers without appropriate tax advice cannot be expected to make wise decisions. It may even require a central tax department acting not only in an advisory capacity and as a tax service agency but also with a degree of functional authority over matters with tax implications.

RECENTRALIZATION OF AUTHORITY

At times an enterprise can be said to recentralize authority—to centralize authority once decentralized. This process is normally not merely a reversal of decentralization, for the authority delegations are not wholly withdrawn by the managers who made them. What occurs is a centralization of authority over a certain type of activity or a certain kind of function, wherever in the organization it may be found.

Thus, the growing importance of taxes, the requirements of uniform labor policy, and the realities of government regulation may dictate that authority over these areas be recentralized or managed by a department with functional authority over them. This recentralization may also occur when, through growth and extensive decentralization, top managers feel that they have lost control over the business. Or if a business falls on difficult times, managers may wish to reinforce their authority over the expenditure of funds, the level of costs, or the character of sales effort. Such recentralization, sometimes intended to be temporary, often becomes permanent. Many top managers take pride in their cost control, budget, or internal auditing departments and in the authority of these departments not only to advise but also to supervise many previous prerogatives of lower managers.

OBTAINING THE DESIRED DEGREE OF DECENTRALIZATION

Underlying the discussion to this point has been the assumption that managers can obtain the degree of decentralization upon which they have decided. In other words, the emphasis has been upon how much decentralization, rather than on whether the desired degree can be realized and maintained.

Many managers who believe that authority should be pushed down in an organization as far as it will go are faced with the practical problem of how to push it down there. It is a rare top manager who does not find in the organization somewhere an authority hoarder who simply will not delegate. One of the authors had occasion once to observe a division controller whose office was piled high with major policy and contractual matters requiring attention, while he engaged in minute examination of employees' expense accounts, excusing himself with the statement that none of this work could be entrusted to his subordinates.

In obtaining the degree of decentralization desired, an understanding of decentralization is essential. This concept is based upon the knowledge that decentralization cannot mean autonomy, that it implies establishment of policies to guide decision making along desired courses, that it requires careful delegation of authority by managers who know how and want to delegate, and that, not being an abdication of responsibility, it must be accompanied by controls designed to ensure that delegated authority is used properly. Although the art of authority delegation lies at the base of proper decentralization, it is apparent that the mere act of delegation is not enough to ensure decentralization.

No manual can indicate how to ensure authority being properly decentralized or appropriately withheld, but several techniques may be used with some chance of success. One of the forceful of these is to assure that a system of verifiable objectives is established and that each person is held responsible for achieving certain goals and is given the necessary authority for doing so. Another is merely a technique of organization, the provision of a statement of each manager's duties and of the responsibility and the degree of authority delegated to that position. Besides being clear and, preferably, written, the statement should be issued in such a way that all employees may know what it contains. This can serve a vital purpose in settling jurisdictional squabbles and excursions beyond the authority area of a given manager.

Another important technique lies in the example and teaching of the superior, starting at the top of the organization. The character of top leadership in an enterprise permeates any organization. There are in every firm of any size those who will reach out for power, impinge upon activities assigned to others, and bully the timid. Rules and job descriptions are often subject to differences in interpretation, which can be conveniently stretched or circumscribed, depending upon the political environment. Their unreliability, despite their obvious usefulness, stands as a warning to executives that the most dependable foundation for achieving the desired degree of decentralization is the education of subordinate managers in the rights of others—teaching them restraint as well as aggressiveness.

One of the means of forcing delegation of authority, particularly in middle and lower levels of organization, is to require managers to have a large number of subordinates and, at the same time, hold them to a high standard of performance. When the span of management is stretched, there is no alternative but to delegate authority. At the same time, in order to protect their own performance, managers learn to select good subordinate managers, train them well, establish clear-cut policies, and find efficient means of control.

Another technique used to force decentralization has been the policy of promoting managers only when they have subordinates able to take their places. To accomplish this end, managers are forced to delegate authority. Moreover, this policy removes a major cause of hoarding authority, the desire of managers to gain indispensability by making sure that their duties cannot be handled by any of their subordinates.

Occasionally the problem concerns how to retain a predetermined degree of authority. Division and branch managers—because they are far away from the home office, often wish to build empires, or want to do a complete job—may assume too much authority and resent the outside auditor, sabotage centralized controls, and oppose central management. The answer, of course, to this problem is primarily one of leadership, clear policy determination and authority delegation, and proper training of subordinate managers. But perhaps the principal problem lies in the character of the top executives. If they temporize, do not support the authority delegations they have made, ignore the organization structure, condone serious deviations from policy, and neglect in other ways to do a thorough managerial job, little can be done to retain any predetermined degree of decentralization.

CLARIFYING DECENTRALIZATION

As in so many areas of managing, conflict, friction, and inefficiencies result from lack of clarification of individual roles. This is nowhere more true in practice than in clarifying the extent and nature of decentralization. This problem can be greatly simplified and clarified by means of a chart of executive approval authorizations. The chart is a technique by which, normally on a single sheet of paper or chart, the various authority delegations of a company are specified. Since most of these delegations have to do with the right to commit the company for money, most of the chart has to do with expenditure limits. However, there are other matters, such as policies and programs, which can be and are often shown on such a chart.

An example of a chart of approval authorizations for a small to medium-sized company is shown in Table 15.1. It will be noted that a list of major decision areas appears on the left-hand side of the chart. It was found useful in this company to group these decision areas under the classifications of personnel, operating expenses, capital expenditures and commitments, prices and sales commitments, and general. Across the top of the chart are listed those various managerial levels which have approval authority, along with certain staff personnel who have functional authority in a decision matter or whose consultation is required for advice or information.

In developing a chart, it is apparent that the authority and responsibility for doing so must rest at the top of a company. Because it even

Table 15.1 Chart of Approval Authorization*

Nature of transaction	Department manager	Staff manager	Division director	President (corporate and domestic), chairman of the board (international)	Board of directors
(a) Personnel					
Employment of new personnel:					
Hourly	All	Personnel manager to process and review for consistency with company policy	All exceptions to company policy		
Salaried	All	Personnel manager to process	All over $1,500 per month	All over $2,500 per month	All over $3,000 per month
Wage and salary increases:					
Hourly	All	Personnel manager to process and review for consistency with company policy	All exceptions to company policy		
Salaried	All	Personnel manager to process	All	All resulting in salary over $2500 per month	All resulting in salary over $3000 per month
Moving expenses	All	To be processed by controller	All	All over $2000 in cost	
Leaves of absence	All	To be processed by personnel manager	All	All over 30 days	All over 60 days
(b) Operating expenses					
Procurement of materials and services (approval of manufacturing and engineering schedule by vice president of manufacturing and engineering:					
In accordance with approved schedules	Manager of purchasing on all				
Not in accordance with approved schedules		Vice president of manufacturing and engineering on all. Controller on all exceeding $5000	All		
Consultation services			All	All corporate services	All contracts or retainers over $5000 per year

Table 15.1 Cont.

Nature of transaction	Department manager	Staff manager	Division director	President (corporate and domestic), chairman of the board (international)	Board of directors
(b)					
Supplies and maintenance materials and services	All		All over $40,000		
Travel and entertainment requests and reports	All those reporting to him		All those reporting to him	All those reporting to him and all over $4000	President and chairman of the board approved by board of directors
Advertising and public relations:					
In accordance with approved program	Manager of advertising and sales promotion on all				
Not in accordance with approved program			General sales manager on all	All outside total budget	
Contributions:					
Budgeted	Controller			Chairman of the board	
Nonbudgeted				Chairman of the board on all except technical magazines and books	
Memberships and subscriptions	All				
Research and development projects	All		Director of research and development on all	All involving new product lines	
Miscellaneous expenses	All		All over $1000	All over $10,000	
Tax payments and adjustments		Controller on all		President and corporate secretary where law requires	Tax adjustments over $15,000
Guarantees and replacements		General sales manager and controller on all		All over $5000	All over $100,000
Contract cancellations		General sales manager and controller on all		All involving more than $25,000	

Leases:

Item					
Temporary, not to exceed $1000 in total commitment	All	Controller on all	All		
Other		Controller and secretary treasurer on all	All	All	All
Summary: Operating expense budgets:					
Basic variable budget formula	All	Controller on all	All	All	All
(c) Capital expenditures and commitments					
Capital expenditures:					
In accordance with approved budget		Controller to check for budgetary accuracy	All	All individual items exceeding $10,000	All items exceeding $50,000
Not in accordance with approved budget		Secretary-treasurer on all	All	All items over $1000	All items exceeding $5000
Capital expenditure budgets	All	Secretary-treasurer on all	All	All	All
Disposal of capital assets		Secretary-treasurer and controller on all	All	All over $5000	All over $100,000
Patent applications, licensing and patent agreements		Secretary-treasurer on all	All	All	All basic policy
(d) Prices and sales commitments					
Sales price formulas		Secretary-treasurer on all	All	All	
Sales commitments:					
Catalog standard items	Manager of sales service on all	Controller on all acceptance of credit	General sales manager on all orders exceeding $100,000		
Nonstandard items	Manager of sales service on all	Controller on all acceptance of credit	General sales manager on all exceeding $10,000	All exceeding commitment of $50,000	All exceeding commitment of $200,000
Variations from standard prices	Manager of sales on all		General sales manager on all over $5000 / Vice president of manufacturing and engineering on all over $25,000	Inform president of variations in excess of 10% on orders exceeding $50,000	

Table 15.1 Cont.

Nature of transaction	Department manager	Staff manager	Division director	President (corporate and domestic), chairman of the board (international)	Board of directors
New product lines		General sales manager on all	All	All	All
Contracts with sales representatives		Form approved by legal counsel	General sales manager on all	All nonstandard contracts	Basic items of commitment in standard form
(e) General Bank loans for company operations:					
Line of credit		Secretary-treasurer on all		All	All
Loans within line		Secretary-treasurer on all			
Loans for buildings and land		Secretary-treasurer on all		All	All
Acquisition of financial interest in or loan to any company		Secretary-treasurer		All	All

*A person required to approve transactions as outlined in the above chart may authorize another person to sign in case of his or her absence. The person so authorized must affix the proper signature showing his or her initials under such signature. Source: H. Koontz, *The Board of Directors and Effective Management* (New York: McGraw-Hill Book Company, 1967), pp. 46–49. (Certain limits revised in 1979.)

distinguishes between decision matters that the board of directors reserves for itself and those delegated to operating management, the board must necessarily be called upon to approve at least this area of delegation. The effective board may wish to do more. If its organizational policy is really one of decentralization, with centralized decision making in only certain matters at the top, it may wish to approve the entire chart, at least enough so as to perceive that its policy is being followed in practice.

In addition to promoting clarity, the chart has other advantages. It acts as a system of communication of the entire structure of decision making in a company so that people down the line, or in departments whose coordination in a decision is necessary, can see what the decision-making relationships are. Also, in a multidivision company, by having separate divisional charts, as well as a corporate chart, authority may be delegated in varying degrees. Thus, in a large division, more authority may be delegated; or in a division staffed by less experienced managers a smaller degree of authority could be delegated. A further advantage is that authority delegations can be changed with greater ease than where they are included in a number of individual position descriptions.

Although the chart of approval authorizations is only a tool, it is regarded by the authors as an essential one. If it is to work, it should be made a way of life in an enterprise; it must be updated whenever there is any significant change in organization structure or authority delegation and must be communicated wherever decision-making relationships exist. It seldom, if ever, includes matters that should be held confidential. Along with position descriptions and the formulation of verifiable goals for each position in an enterprise, it helps define the roles which individuals must fill.

BALANCE: THE KEY TO DECENTRALIZATION

Any program for decentralizing authority must reflect the principles of delegation if practical pitfalls are to be avoided. There are, in addition, several other matters to be considered. The widespread practice of decentralization in recent years has taught important lessons.

Strong forces favor the practice of decentralization. The nature of organized effort requires coordination of people at every level, and most of the managers responsible for coordination are found at middle and lower organization levels; these cannot function without the authority to manage. The growing size of the average organized activity requires an increasing number of managers. And while enterprise does not decentralize in order to develop managers, it is nevertheless quite true that these will not be developed internally unless they have an opportunity to exercise authority. Moreover, the presence of large numbers of well-educated and ambitious young people in enterprise is a steady pressure on top managers to decentralize.

At the same time, extensive decentralization is not to be blindly applied. In many organizations the size and complexity of operations do not require it. Decentralization is not without costs, even in larger companies. In addition to the dangers from nonuniform policy and the problems of control, there are often real financial costs. As authority is decentralized, managers become more and more like independent operators of small businesses. They may acquire their own accounting force, statisticians, and engineering staff, and these may soon be duplicating specialized services of the top organization.

Perhaps the principal problem of decentralization is loss of control. No enterprise can decentralize to the extent that its existence is threatened and the achievement of its goals is frustrated. If organizational disintegration is to be avoided, decentralization must be tempered by selective centralization of certain areas of vital major policy. The company with well-balanced centralized decentralization will probably centralize decisions at the top on such things as financing, overall profit goals and budgeting, major facilities and other capital expenditures, important new product programs, major marketing policies, basic personnel policies, and the development and compensation of managerial personnel. The key to effective decentralization is the proper balance between what is to be centralized and what is to be decentralized.

But, judging from experience, a proper balance is not easy to achieve. Many prominent enterprises have had serious problems in this area. Even the large General Electric Company lived too long with a highly centralized functional organization structure; then, when it reorganized after 1954, it decentralized too much, giving far more discretion than later proved to be wise to some 120 integrated and highly autonomous departments. The classic example of excessive decentralization without adequate control was the General Dynamics Company in the late 1950s, when its Convair Division surprised its parent with an almost bankrupting loss of more than $430 million on its ill-fated jet airplane program. The history of many other companies shows cyclical trends in decentralization, at times dispersing too much authority and at other times overcentralizing.

The achievement of balance is perhaps one of the greatest accomplishments of Alfred Sloan in his managing of General Motors over the years. Although practicing and preaching decentralization, he and his top management team realized that no department or division could be given complete freedom. As a result, this company, long after Sloan's retirement and death, and as large as it has been, has always continued to hold at the very top major policy and program decisions on those matters necessary for maintaining the soundness and success of the entire company. Yet, once major program and policy decisions are made at the top, the countless decisions involving their execution have been decentralized in the operating divisions.

1 Why could it be that inept delegation of authority is often found to be the most important single cause of managerial failure?

2 If you had a subordinate who failed to delegate authority in his or her department, what would you do?

3 Why has there been so much written and said, in the last 30 years, in favor of decentralizing authority?

4 What is the distinction between decentralizing "some of all authority" and "all of some authority"? What is actually done?

5 In many foreign countries very little authority is decentralized. What do you think would explain this phenomenon? What effect does it have?

6 If you were a manager, would you decentralize authority? State several reasons for your answer. How would you make sure that you did not decentralize too much?

7 There is considerable justification for the position of some top managers that they do not have a free choice in deciding upon the extent of decentralization of authority. Comment.

8 Should authority be pushed down into an organization as far as it will go?

chapter 16 Committees and Group Decision Making

One of the most ubiquitous and controversial devices of organization is the committee. Whether it is referred to as a "board," "commission," "task force," or "team," its essential nature is the same, for the committee is a group of persons to whom, as a group, some matter is committed. It is this characteristic of group action that sets the committee apart from other organization devices, though, as we will see, not all committees involve group decision making.

Committees are a fact of organizational life. Although committees are widely criticized, properly conducted committee meetings used for the right purpose can result in greater motivation, improved problem solving, and increased output.[1] In a study of subscribers to the *Harvard Business Review*, only 8 percent of the respondents indicated that they would eliminate committees if it were within their power.[2] The problem, then, is not the concept of committees, but rather the way committees are conducted and where they are used.

THE NATURE OF COMMITTEES

Because of variation in authority assigned to committees, much confusion has resulted as to their nature.

Some committees undertake managerial functions, and others do not. Some make decisions; others merely deliberate on problems without authority to decide. Some have authority to make recommendations to a manager, who may or may not accept them, while others are formed purely to receive information, without making recommendations or decisions.

A committee may be either line or staff, depending upon its authority. If its authority involves decision making affecting subordinates responsible to it, it is a plural executive and a line committee; if its authority relationship to a superior is advisory, then it is a staff committee.

Committees may also be formal or informal. If established as part of the organization structure, with specifically delegated duties and authority, they are formal. Most committees with any permanence or standing fall into this class. Or they may be informal, that is, organized without specific delegation of authority and usually by some person desiring group thinking or group decision on a particular problem. Thus managers may have a problem on which they need advice from other managers or specialists outside their department and may call a special meeting for the purpose. Indeed, this kind of motivation, plus the occasional need for gathering together in one room all the authority available to deal with an

[1] J. Presley and S. Keen, "Better Meetings Lead to Higher Productivity: A Case Study," *Management Review*, vol. 64, no. 4, pp. 16–22 (April 1975).
[2] R. Tillman, Jr., "Committees on Trial," *Harvard Business Review*, vol. 38, no. 3, pp. 6–12, 162–173 (May–June 1960).

unusual problem, gives rise to many of the numerous conferences in organizational life.

Moreover, committees may be relatively permanent, or they may be temporary. One would expect the formal committees to be more permanent than the informal, although this is not necessarily so. A formal committee might be established by order of a company president, with appropriate provision in the organization structure, for the sole purpose of studying the advisability of building a new factory and be disbanded immediately upon completion of its task. And an informal committee set up by the factory manager to advise upon the improvement of product quality or to help coordinate delivery dates with sales commitments might continue indefinitely.

However, the executive who merely calls assistants into the office or confers with department heads is not creating a committee. It is sometimes difficult to draw a sharp distinction between committees and other group meetings. The essential characteristic of the committee is that it is a group charged with dealing with a specific problem.

The committee is in wide use in all types of organization. In government, one finds a large number of standing and special committees of every legislative body; indeed, state and national legislatures are committees, as are the cabinets of the chief executives of the federal and state governments. Committees manage many government agencies such as the Tennessee Valley Authority, the Federal Reserve Board, the Federal Deposit Insurance Corporation, and the Export-Import Bank. Even the courts make liberal use of the device.

In education, faculties of great universities, jealous of academic freedom and distrustful of administrative rights, traditionally circumscribe the authority of presidents and deans with a myriad of committees. In one large university more than 300 standing committees share in administration or advise on policy, ranging from the academic senate and the budget committees to committees on committees, coordinating committees, and committees on alumni records, university welfare, and maintenance of order during examinations.

Religious institutions likewise lean heavily on committees, partly to encourage active participation by members and partly to delimit the authority of leaders. Although their authority may vary widely, depending upon the traditions of the sect, committees—ranging from the church board to the committee in charge of a church supper—are ever present.

Committees are also prevalent in business. A board of directors is a committee, as are its various constituent groups, such as the executive committee, the finance committee, the audit committee, and the bonus committee. Occasionally, one finds a business managed by a management committee instead of a president. And almost invariably under the president there will be a variety of management or policy committees, planning committees, wage and salary review committees, grievance committees, task forces for particular projects, and numerous other standing and special committees. Moreover, at each level of the organization structure, one or more committees are likely to be found. A perhaps extreme example of the use of committees in a large bank is shown in Figure 16.1. Indeed, a survey by Robert H. Hayes & Associates, Inc., of the 500 largest industrial enterprises showed that group management increased from 39 to 70 percent in the early 1970s alone.[3]

The use of formal committees appears to be related to the size of the enterprise. In the study of *Harvard Business Review* subscribers it was found that of the organizations with over 10,000 employees, 94 percent had regular or standing committees. This compares with 64 percent of the enterprises with fewer than 250 employees reporting the use of such committees.[4]

REASONS FOR USING COMMITTEES

One need not look far for reasons for the widespread use of committees. Although the committee is sometimes regarded as having democratic origins and as being characteristic of democratic society, the reasons for its existence go beyond mere desire for group participation. Committees are widely used even in authoritarian organizations, such as Soviet Russia and Communist China.

Group Deliberation and Judgment

Perhaps the most important reason for the use of committees is the advantage of gaining group deliberation and judgment—a variation of the adage that "two heads are better than one." A group of people can bring to bear on a problem a wider range of experience than a single person, a greater variety of opinion, a more thorough probing of the facts, and a more diverse training in specialized aspects. Few indeed are important business problems that fall entirely into a single area such as production, engineering, finance, or sales. Most problems, on the contrary, require more knowledge, experience, and judgment than any individual possesses.

It should not be inferred that group judgment can be obtained only through use of committees. The staff specialist who confers individually with many persons in a given phase of a problem can obtain group judgment without the formation of a committee, as can the executive who asks key subordinates or other specialists for memorandums analyzing a problem and making recommendations thereon. At times group judgment can thus be obtained more efficiently, in terms of time, without the long deliberations of a committee. The keen manager can usually grasp ideas

[3]"The Frustrations of the Group Executive," *Business Week*, pp. 102–110 (September 25, 1978).
[4]Tillman, op. cit.

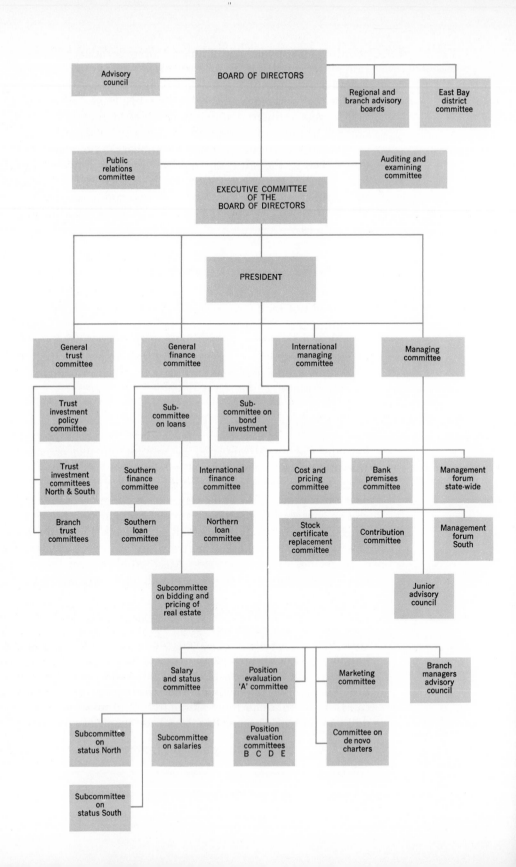

and the reasoning behind them more quickly from a concise written memorandum than from an oral presentation.

However, one of the advantages of group deliberation and judgment, not to be obtained without an actual meeting, is the stimulation resulting from discussion of ideas and the cross-examination techniques of the committee meeting. Leading, as it does, to clarification of problems and development of new ideas, this interchange has been found to be especially enlightening in policy matters. It is true that sometimes the results obtained by group judgment are superior to those obtained by individual judgment.

Fear of Too Much Authority in a Single Person

Another reason for the widespread use of the committee is the fear of delegating too much authority to a single person. This fear, especially pronounced in government, dictated to the framers of the American Constitution not only the establishment of a two-house legislature and a multimember Supreme Court but also the division of the powers of government among the Congress, the Supreme Court, and the President. However, despite this fear of centralized authority, the founders of the American republic placed the *administration* of laws in the hands of a single top executive, recognizing the advantages of this system. Yet, as former President Nixon discovered, the legislature has the power to remove or force the resignation of the chief executive.

Fear of delegating too much authority to an individual has been experienced in educational organizations and in charitable and religious enterprises. Although the willingness of people to be bound by the authoritarianism of faith has led to concentration of authority in the head of the Roman Catholic Church, in the various Protestant denominations one finds far less willingness to trust any single executive.

This fear has had less influence in business than in other types of organization. Business enterprises have, for one thing, developed primari-

Figure 16.1 Committee organization in a large bank. This bank has supplemented its management organization structure with a large number of committees and subcommittees. All these groups exert influence on management policy and decision, and certain committees, such as the position evaluation committee, actually make decisions. Others, such as the advisory council of the board of directors and the regional and branch advisory boards, operate only in an advisory capacity. Likewise, the general trust committees make actual decisions. Most of the committees have as their members senior or other key managers from all the important departments and divisions of the company. The junior advisory council, however, consists of lower-level managers or those about to be placed in a managerial capacity. While it carries on important analyses and projects and advises senior management groups, its primary purpose is training junior managers for future increased responsibilities in the bank.

ly from small beginnings within the institution of private property, with its implications of authority of the owner; workers, too, have been free to avoid abuse of power by moving from one company to another; and the overriding importance of efficiency, finally, has favored the single manager. At the same time, the traditional existence of a board of directors as the top managing group of the business corporation may be traced, to a great extent, to the fear of property owners of delegating too much authority to a managing director.

This motive has likewise influenced the formation of many internal business committees. A committee may be established to make recommendations on a problem largely because the president or department head does not wish to take full responsibility for making a decision or to trust the decision to a subordinate. Bonus committees often result from such motivation, and major financial and capital investment policies are developed by committees, partly because of unwillingness to trust a single individual with complete authority to make so important a decision.

Representation of Interested Groups

The desire to have various interested groups represented in policy matters makes itself felt in all branches of government where either law or tradition requires that the two major political parties, various sections of the country, or various pressure groups be represented.

Representation plays a part, too, in the establishment and staffing of committees in business. Boards of directors are often selected on the basis of groups interested in the company and, perhaps more often, on the basis of groups in which the company has an interest. When executives have a particularly difficult internal problem involving managers and specialists in various departments and activities, they may choose committee members in such a way as to give these interested parties representation. They may ostensibly do this in order to get a more balanced group judgment and a more diversified point of view, but they may actually be doing it to ensure that these groups will be represented and will thereby feel a sense of loyalty and commitment to the decision reached.

Coordination of Departments, Plans, and Policies

There is general agreement that committees are very useful for coordinating activities among various organizational units. For example, in one study 90 percent of the respondents agreed with the statement that "committees promote coordination among departments." There was similar agreement on this point among various levels, although lower-middle management agreed slightly less (a little over 80 percent) than upper-middle and top management (about 90 percent agreed with the statement).[5]

[5]Ibid.

Committees are also useful for coordinating planning and the execution of programs. The dynamics of modern enterprise place a heavy burden on its managers to integrate plans and activities. With complications, change, and numerous specialized departments, it is difficult to coordinate every activity, every subordinate plan, and every expenditure.

A committee permits the individuals concerned not only to obtain firsthand a picture of overall plans and of their place in them but also to contribute suggestions on the spot for improvement of plans. The committee also furnishes a place where agreement may be reached on the steps in coordination.

Transmission and Sharing of Information

The committee is useful for transmitting and sharing information. All group members affected by a mutual problem or project can learn of it simultaneously, and decisions and instructions can be received uniformly with opportunities for clarification. The time thus saved may be considerable; and the spoken word, with its possibilities for overtones and emphasis and the opportunities for clarification, may carry its point better than even carefully written memorandums.

Consolidation of Authority

A manager in a department, branch, or section often has only a portion of the authority necessary to accomplish a program. As noted earlier, this is known as splintered authority. Good organization practice normally provides managers with the power appropriate to their position. However, this is not possible in every instance, and some matters call for the exercise of authority that the manager at the level concerned does not possess.

One way to handle problems of this sort is to refer them upward in the organizational hierarchy until they reach a point at which the requisite authority exists. But this place is often in the office of the president, and the problem may not be of sufficient importance to be decided at that level. Suppose, for example, that a customer of a machine-tool manufacturer wished a slight but unusual change in design in a piece of equipment. He or she would approach the sales department, which, if there were no established procedure for handling this change, could not act without the authority of the engineering department, the production department, and the cost estimating department. In this case, the sales manager might establish a special purpose committee to study the problem, to agree on the nature and cost of the change, and to use the combined authority of its members to approve the request.

This informal use of the committee gives much flexibility to organization. However, consolidating splintered authority through a committee should be watched carefully to ascertain whether the organizational structure itself might not be changed to concentrate in one position the appropriate authority to make *recurring* decisions.

Motivation through Participation

Committees permit wide participation in decision making. Persons who take part in planning a program or making a decision usually feel more enthusiastic about accepting and executing it. Even limited participation can be helpful.

The use of committees to motivate subordinates to get behind a program or decision requires skillful handling. It is by no means certain that deliberations of this kind will kindle enthusiastic support, for they can also result in the deepening of existing divisions among participants. On the other hand, there are people who seem to be against every move unless they have been previously consulted. Thus, it requires a skillful chairperson to direct conflicting interests toward common objects.

Avoidance of Action

It cannot be denied that committees are sometimes appointed by managers when they do not want any action to ensue. One of the surest ways to delay the handling of a problem and even to postpone a decision indefinitely is to appoint a committee, and sometimes many subcommittees, to study the matter, particularly if the membership is carefully selected with delay in mind. In organizations of all kinds, skillful managers resort to this delaying action when they see fit.

DISADVANTAGES OF COMMITTEES

Certain dangers of committees have been so widely publicized that many managers make little use of committees. Disparaging attitudes are reflected in such definitions as "a committee is made up of the unfit selected by the unwilling to do the unnecessary" or "a place where the loneliness of thought is replaced by the togetherness of nothingness."

High Cost in Time and Money

The cost of committee action in time is likely to be considerable. A committee may require members to travel some distance to reach a meeting. During the meeting, all members have the right to be heard, to have their points of view discussed, to challenge and cross-examine the points of view of others, and to analyze the reasons for a considered group conclusion. The spoken word, though valuable for emphasis and clarification, is seldom concise, and the "thinking out loud" that takes place is sometimes a waste of time for those who must listen. If the committee is supposed to reach a unanimous or nearly unanimous decision, the discussion is likely to be lengthy. And if a decision can be reached quickly, the meeting may have been unnecessary in the first place.

The monetary cost of committee discussion can also be very high. One must consider not only the cost of executive time (which for even a $40,000-per-year executive runs to $20 an hour) but even more the cost to the company of loss of the executive time that would otherwise have been devoted to more important duties. However, it is quite possible that the cost of executive time in a group meeting might be less than when a superior meets individually with subordinates.

This cost in time and money becomes all the more disadvantageous when a committee is assigned a problem that could as well, or better, be solved by a single individual or by an individual with the help of a smaller and lesser-paid staff. Thus, the advantages of committee action must be considerable to offset the costs.

Compromise at the Least Common Denominator

Where committees are required to come to some conclusion or to reach some decision, there is danger that their action will be watered down or may even be meaningless. If the matter under consideration is so simple that differences of opinion do not exist, the use of committee time is wasteful. If differences of opinion exist, the point at which all or a majority of the committee members can agree will tend to be at the least common denominator of group agreement. Most often this is not as strong and positive a course of action as that undertaken by an individual, who has only to consider the facts as he or she sees them and then reach a conclusion. Because of the necessity for seeking out common ground, committees often take innocuous action or defer action entirely.

The danger of compromise at the level of the least common denominator of agreement grows as the percentage of agreement felt necessary for committee action increases. Even committees whose authority delegation requires only majority agreement sometimes develop traditions of unanimity. Small groups of people frequently seek—from feelings of politeness, mutual respect, and humility—to reach conclusions on which all can agree. Since committee members are ordinarily picked from organization equals, reluctance to force a conclusion on a recalcitrant minority is understandable, increasing thereby the probability of weak decisions.

Indecision

Another disadvantage of committees is that the time required for thorough deliberation, the discussion of peripheral or tangential subjects, and the difficulty of reaching agreement often result in adjournment without action.

Committee meetings are often characterized by an official and a hidden agenda. The hidden agenda pertains to the disguised individual motives of members. It is not unusual for these motives to prevent the committee from reaching agreement on the official topic of discussion since, if desires and feelings of members are not candidly discussed, members may not really know what the committee, as a group, concludes.

Tendency to Be Self-destructive

Indecisiveness may give the chairperson or a strong member an opportunity to force the committee into a decision, for it is a rare group of people who can participate in the exercise of authority on a team basis. Almost invariably, one person emerges as the leader. But when an individual becomes dominant, the nature of the committee as a decision-making group of equals changes, and there actually emerges an executive with a group of followers or advisers. Executives often delude themselves into believing that committees operate on group management principles with a group of equals, when, as a matter of fact, the "team" is composed of subordinate advisers or even yes-sayers following a superior's leadership.

A committee which does not make decisions often disintegrates into an assembly dominated by a leader or leaders of two or three opposing factions. When the committee ceases to operate as a group of equals, and especially when it becomes a battleground for warring camps, the politics of the situation may lead to decisions or recommendations even worse than those weak ones based on the least common denominator of agreement.

Splitting of Responsibility

When authority to study, make recommendations, or arrive at a decision is delegated to a group, the fact is that the authority is dispersed throughout the group. Thus, individual members hardly feel the same degree of responsibility that they would if they personally were charged with the same task. This splitting of responsibility is one of the chief disadvantages of a committee. Since no one can practically or logically feel personally accountable for the actions of a group, no individual feels personally responsible for any action within it.

Minority Tyranny

As was pointed out above, committees tend to seek unanimous or near-unanimous conclusions or decisions. Minority members are therefore in a strong position. By their insistence upon acceptance of their position or of a compromise position, they exercise an unwarranted tyranny over the majority. The minority members of a jury have such power. The authors recall an important committee of nine members in which a tradition for unanimous agreement developed. One member actually controlled the committee, not through force of leadership but through power to withhold his vote. The matters which he blocked or on which he forced a watered-down conclusion fell in the area of committee authority and responsibility; the committee, though having failed because of his tyranny, provided cover for him. Had he borne individual authority and responsibility for his actions, he could hardly have been the obstructionist he was.

THE PLURAL EXECUTIVE

Most committees are nonmanagerial in nature. However, some groups are given the power to make decisions and to undertake one or all of the managerial functions of planning, organizing, staffing, leading, and controlling. It is this latter type of committee that is referred to as the "plural executive."

Origin

The plural executive may be established by law, or it may result from a managerial decision. Examples of the former are the board of directors of a corporation and the plural executive (commission, board) established by various legislatures to operate one of their agencies. In the case of the corporation, legislatures have traditionally required that the board be elected to act for the stockholders. State and federal legislatures have, especially in recent years, provided for direction of most government agencies by a single manager, but in many instances a plural executive is still operating.

Authority

The extent of authority to manage and to make decisions held by a plural executive is not always easy to ascertain. Some, such as the board of directors, clearly have this power, although they may not exercise it. Some companies have been managed from the top, on a day-to-day or weekly basis, by a plural executive, but this is rare.

There are, however, many boards of directors and executive committees of organizations which potentially have the power to manage but actually do not, since decisions are made by a prominent stockholder or a strong leader in the group. Usually, the president is the dominant figure, with the other members often little more than advisers. In other words, the plural executive is not always what it seems, and a single executive often in reality makes the decisions. Then there are other committees established with advisory authority only. Sometimes these actually operate as plural executives if, through tradition, weakness of leadership, or insistence of the chairperson on agreement before a decision is made, they actually make decisions or undertake managerial functions as a group.

Role in Policy Making

The plural executive is often found in the field of policy making. Many companies have an executive or management committee to develop major plans and adopt basic policy. They go by various names: General Motors has its executive and finance committees, United States Rubber Company its operating policy committee, the Sun Chemical Company its management committee, Lockheed Aircraft Corporation its corporate policy committee, and the Koppers Company its policy committee.

The extent of authority of these committees varies considerably, although their influence on decision making is perhaps greater in policy making or planning than in any other area. These committees also engage in control, for their concern with policies and plans must be followed up to make sure that events conform to decisions.

Furthermore, these committees often are useful in settling differences of opinion or in the settlement of questions of organizational jurisdiction. The plural executive is an ideal arbitrator of disputes since the determination of a group will usually be accepted by contesting parties as being more impartial than that of a single arbiter. Besides, personality clashes in a given situation are more easily submerged in group action.

Where committees are successful in policy formulation, they are dependent upon accurate and adequate staff work. A committee can hardly develop a proposal, forecast probable profits and costs from alternative courses of action, or investigate the numerous tangible and intangible factors influencing a basic decision. These are matters for study, and the committee is a notoriously poor study or research device. Therefore, if group deliberation is to be productive, facts and estimates must be developed and presented so that the members have readily available the data upon which to base a decision.

Role in Policy Execution

Many companies and management experts distinguish between policy making and policy execution. It has been said that the former is concerned with "the establishment of broad principles by which administration is guided," while the latter is concerned with "the daily conduct of the company's affairs—setting standards and procedures to guide and govern execution of policies, establishing controls to ensure adherence to standards, solving interdivisional disputes, improving interdivisional coordination, and meeting various emergencies as they arise."[6]

---

[6]E. Dale, *Planning and Developing the Company Organization Structure*, Research Report No. 20 (New York: American Management Association, 1952), pp. 96–97.

In companies where this distinction is made, special committees are established in functional areas—such as engineering, distribution, manufacturing, public relations, and labor relations—to deal with the more specialized and technical aspects of planning; such committees may make recommendations to policy committees or may bolster basic policy with detailed enabling plans and programs.

In reality, there is little difference between policy-making committees and those which are thought of as executing policy. Both committees are engaged primarily in planning. The difference between them is one of degree, with the former usually engaged in major planning and the latter in less important planning. But because the latter are often facilitative and involve technical tasks requiring specialists, use of the committee in these areas is sometimes far less effective than the single administrator.

PLURAL VERSUS INDIVIDUAL EXECUTIVE

Committees without managerial authority are far more numerous than those which are true plural executives. While much experience exists in organization with committees and with plural executives, the benefits of group management, as compared to individual management, have not been widely studied.

AMA Survey

One attempt to measure the merits of group versus individual management was made some years ago by the American Management Associa-

Table 16.1 Relative Effectiveness of Individual and Committee Action in Functional Activities, Percent

Management function	Can be exercised by committee effectively	Can be exercised by committee but more effectively by individual	Individual initiative essential but may be supplemented by committee	Individual action essential; committee ineffective
Planning	20	20	25	35
Control	25	20	25	30
Formulating objectives	35	35	10	20
Organization	5	25	20	50
Jurisdictional questions	90	10		
Leadership			10	90
Administration	20	25	25	30
Execution	10	15	10	65
Innovation	30	20	20	30
Communication	20	15	35	30
Advice	15	25	35	25
Decision making	10	30	10	50

tion.[7] Through interviews with executives and analysis of records of some twenty representative companies, some interesting results were found. Breaking down management activity into twelve functions, the survey roughly estimated the proportion of each function that could (1) be exercised effectively by committee action; (2) be exercised effectively by committee action but more effectively by individual action; (3) be exercised by individual action, though helpfully supplemented by committee action; or (4) be effectively exercised only by individual action.

The results of this survey are summarized in Table 16.1. Although the sample is small, the breakdowns rough, and the percentages no more than approximate, the survey shows what the top executives in some well-managed companies thought of group, as compared to individual, executive action. The survey results indicate a strong preference for the plural executive only in the settling of jurisdictional questions. The emphasis on the superiority of individual action in practically every function of management is pronounced. Even where committee action was found effective (the first two classifications), though not in all cases as effective as individual action, the score in favor of committees, with one exception, was still not particularly high. While this survey was made some years ago, the authors' experience and study lead them to believe the results are still valid.

Evaluation

The foregoing discussion of the plural executive points to certain conclusions. The plural executive succeeds fairly well in helping to coordinate the activities of managers. It has a high potential for aiding in defining objectives, selecting alternative ways of achieving them, and measuring the success attained. In terms of managerial functions, the plural executive is thus especially useful in planning and in certain of the broader aspects of control. However, all the disadvantages of the committee form apply with special force to the true plural executive.

BOARD OF DIRECTORS: TOP PLURAL EXECUTIVE

One of the most interesting organizational devices established in the form of a plural executive is the board of directors. Its importance to American business management and to a variety of nonbusiness enterprises is sometimes underestimated, although a growing interest in boards is occurring, primarily because of the actions and attitudes of government agencies, particularly the Federal Securities and Exchange Commission.

State laws under which corporations are established almost invariably require that the corporation be "managed" by a board of directors

---

[7]Ibid., pp. 92–93.

composed of at least three members. The logic behind the requirement is that the corporation is an artificial entity, established by a sovereign power through contract with a group of owners (the stockholders), and therefore must have real persons responsible for managing.

Deficiencies of Corporate Boards

Observation of boards of directors, however, shows that most of them actually do not manage, and corporate boards have often been criticized for this. Instead, managing, in its usual sense, is given completely to the president and other chief officers. The separation of ownership and management sometimes makes the inside managerial group all-powerful and the board of directors a legal sham. Prominent stockholders, often controlling with a minority interest, occasionally make boards of directors approve their wishes. Yet boards of directors have an important managerial job to do. Under the corporation laws they are charged with the duty of managing the entire corporation on behalf of the stockholders, who are usually too numerous and unorganized to take part in policy determination. Moreover, directors of publicly owned companies are definitely liable for their conduct, particularly under the Securities Act of 1933 and the Securities Exchange Act of 1934. The criticism of American business in the decades after 1933, coupled with increasing legal liabilities and rising interest in the quality of managing and the need for the modern company to be responsive to its environment, as well as recent court decisions on director liabilities, have reawakened interest in the board and its proper functioning in the modern corporation.

There is evidence that boards heading all kinds of enterprises—business corporations, charitable foundations, universities, and others—are not doing a very effective job. When a financial or other crisis arises, as happened with Penn Central, LTV, Equity Funding, and others, the first question raised by the public, government officials, and financial analysts is: Where was the board?

Also, boards have been under heavy pressure in recent years, ostensibly to ensure that various total forces and interests be considered by boards, to place on their membership women, members of minority races, consumerists, and other special interest representatives. Many boards have done this. However, the best thinking, and even the thinking of intelligent leaders of special interests, is that every board member's concern and responsibility must be to the enterprise as a whole. If members have the qualifications for board membership, the fact that they are white or black, Chicano or Oriental, or male or female should be neither a special qualification nor a disqualification.[8]

---

[8]For a discussion of this matter, see H. Koontz, "The Corporate Board and Special Interests," *Business Horizons*, vol. 14, no. 5, pp. 75–82 (October 1971). See also "Firms Add More Independent Directors-But Find Doing So Can Mean Headaches," *The Wall Street Journal*, p. 36 (May 26, 1978).

What has become important to all kinds of enterprises and to those who bear responsibility for their management is a conscious attempt to ensure that the enterprise operates in an open system. In other words, in its operation a business or any other kind of enterprise must be responsive, in its own self-interest, to the entire external environment with which it must interact. This may mean that a variety of special interests and talents are useful to a board. But it should never mean that board members forget their obligation to *total* enterprise interests.

Major Board Functions

Many of the problems of all forms of boards stem from a failure to appreciate the major functions of these top plural executives. While the more important of these are discussed in this section as they apply to business boards,[9] most of these functions apply to boards of other kinds of enterprises as well.

Trusteeship   Probably the most important function of the board of directors may be summed up in the term "trusteeship," the husbanding of the corporation assets for the long-term benefit of the stockholders. Even the most ineffectual board cannot escape this obligation.

Especially in the large, publicly held corporation, the concept of trusteeship will extend beyond a narrow obligation to the stockholders to include obligation to the public, without whose support a corporation, as a social institution, could not endure; obligation to the employees of the corporation, whose efforts are necessary for its success; and obligation to the customers, who buy its products.[10] The position may be taken, on the other hand, that a director has the duty to operate exclusively for the benefit of the stockholders because it is their funds that the director manages. To manage them for the benefit of other groups might then be interpreted as misappropriation of private property. It is, however, likely to be in the interest of stockholders to administer also for the benefit of employees and the public generally. With the lessening of privacy of the large corporation, the very proper need to take into account all influential environmental factors, the importance of labor relations forced on management by unionism, and the recognition that all organizations operate in an open system, directors operating on behalf of their stockholders will find it wise to respond judiciously to various external obligations.

Determination of enterprise objectives   Another major function of the board of directors is the establishment of basic objectives of the business.

[9]For a more thorough discussion of the functions of the board of directors and its role in management, see H. Koontz, *The Board of Directors and Effective Management* (New York: McGraw-Hill Book Company, 1967).

[10]See chap. 4 for more detailed analysis of the social responsibilities of enterprise managers.

Although making a profit by furnishing economic goods and services demanded by buyers is a necessary requirement for survival and continued public service, this must be achieved by establishing verifiable enterprise goals and basic strategies and policies by which to achieve these goals.

Selection of top executives The board's function in selecting the chief executive of the corporation is a planning matter with long-run implications.

Basic policy making and the choice of an executive are both functions of the board of directors, and in fact they are closely related. Every action by a board regarding the choice of a chief executive involves basic policy examination. If the person chosen is expected to follow the course of a predecessor, that action is a reaffirmation of the predecessor's policies and a decision to proceed as before. When a board maps out a new course preliminary to the choice of an executive or when it accepts policy changes as conditions of acceptance stipulated by a candidate, the board of directors is making a long-run major planning decision.

In numerous ways, therefore, the effects of the decision reached by a board of directors in choosing a new executive will be apparent for a long time in the future.

While boards of directors actually elect other corporate officers, most directors regard it as the job of the chief executive officer to nominate them. This is as it should be. Chief executive officers are the heads responsible to the board, and if they cannot select their lieutenants, they can hardly be held responsible for the successful operation of the corporation as a whole. On the other hand, a responsible board must satisfy itself as to the quality of the company's entire management team, and certain powers of *approval* of nominations of top managers, rather than actual selection, should be reserved to the board.

Ensuring of adequate plans and checking on results Directors, by establishing corporate objectives and formulating major policies, are of course doing basic planning. But this is not enough. Being responsible for seeing that the company is well managed, the board should assure itself that the operating managers are making adequate plans. Thus a board should review and approve, or be informed of, management programs in such areas as new products, marketing approaches, personnel, organization, manager development, and finance. The very presentation of such programs is often assurance that adequate planning is being done.

A board should also see that results are being accomplished in accordance with plans. Such evaluation means more than a study of financial statements and the audit reports. In the financial area, it means a careful review of forecasts and expected performance. In the area of organizing, reports on actual organization practice, as dictated by board policy, should be submitted to the board. Similar reports should be made in the other areas of board interest. Too often, boards of directors approve planning programs and then forget them. Above all, boards should take steps to appraise the performance of the chief executive officer and members of senior management.

Approval of budgets   Final approval of budgets is usually a key function of boards of directors. Whether applying to cash, revenues, expenses, capital expenditures, or number of employees, budgets are planning instruments whereby anticipated results are reduced to numerical terms. After adoption, they become the standard against which performance is measured for a given future period. To the extent that they are focused on overall corporate affairs, as in the case of budget summaries, or matters of major corporate concern, such as cash and capital expenditures, they are properly subject to board approval.

Securing of long-range stability   An often-overlooked function of the board of directors is securing long-range business stability in a changing environment. Even though people have a natural propensity to organize—and many organizations exist at any one time—few survive for a long period, since most fail to adjust their objectives and plans to a changing environment. From the standpoint of business, these changes include new technology, markets, and tastes; varying political, ethical, and economic conditions; and the growth of new business enterprises.

There are those who feel that securing long-range stability is the fundamental function of a board of directors. Board and management have a similar interest in avoiding calamity, preserving the company, and ensuring its continuity. In other words, the duty of the board is to accept responsibility for survival of the enterprise.

Distribution of earnings   Another major function that must be exercised by directors—at least to meet the requirements of corporation law and the obligation to stockholders—is the distribution of earnings. Directors must decide whether earnings should be distributed as dividends, retained in the business for expansion, or used to eliminate outstanding indebtedness.

This decision is of exceptional importance. If directors decide that earnings should be distributed, they are taking the position that the owner would rather have immediate earnings in hand than invest in future earnings of the business or in capital gains. Should they decide to keep the earnings for expansion, they are to some extent forcing owners to reinvest funds in the corporation. If earnings are to be used to retire debt, directors are once more exercising their trusteeship of investors' funds. The distribution of earnings is, to stockholders, second in importance only to the actual utilization of their original capital investment.

Checking of plans and operations through discerning questions   A director should ask discerning questions, an activity that does not depend upon a detailed familiarity with the affairs of a business. Such questions force the proponents of a proposal, usually the corporation's executives, to defend it with facts and analysis or considered judgment. Questions seek to make sure that all facets of a problem have been explored, that all facts have been considered, and that alternative courses of action have been properly analyzed and rejected.

The ability to ask discerning questions comes from experience in decision making; consequently, some of the best corporation directors are not those who know every detail of a company's operation but those who have had experience in a variety of situations. Such persons often develop an intuitive feeling about problems and know what is likely to affect them.

Perhaps more important than the effect of discerning questions on a board's deliberations is their effect on the study and preparation of a proposal before it is submitted to the board. Although questions are not designed to represent cross-examination or to discredit management, they frequently embarrass the unprepared manager. Executives who know they will be questioned will naturally try to anticipate it, and their assistants will take far greater care analyzing reports and proposals and in briefing them.

Boards in Small Corporations

Boards in smaller businesses are often mere legal forms, with the owner or owners and members of their immediate families as directors. Indeed, it is not unusual for the necessary minutes of such boards to be prepared by legal counsel to cover matters required by state laws, while the actual operation of the board is practically nonexistent. On the other hand, many small businesses have found a board of directors useful for improving the quality of their management, and studies have indicated that the board has an important place in the small corporate business.[11]

A dominant reason why typical small-corporation owners do not attach much importance to the board of directors but make it a family board is their distrust of outsiders. Having built their own business from a garage machine shop or a basement office in their house, they often regard it as their offspring, their life, and their prized possession. Moreover, they may feel timid about asking a banker or lawyer or a management consultant to serve on the board. On the other hand, many public-spirited business and professional people see in the small business the heart of the private enterprise system, a challenge to professional experience and ingenuity, and a means of being of genuine service in building a well-managed business enterprise.

---

[11]An excellent study of this subject, even though made many years ago, is that of M. L. Mace in *The Board of Directors in Small Corporations* (Boston: Division of Research, Harvard Business School, 1948). This study should be read by every owner of a small corporate business.

A small corporation may not be able to afford specialized talent, managerial and technical, and yet its problems are the same, except in degree and scope, as those of the large corporation. The owner-manager of the typical small corporation frequently has several limitations, both in education and in experience. Outside directors can be extremely useful in at least partly eliminating them.

An outside director can assist materially in basic policy making in the small corporation. Such policy is often overlooked by the small-business manager, who becomes overburdened by recurring operating problems and details that could easily be handled by reference to an established policy.

Managers of small businesses often fail to plan. Sales and production dips come without warning. Income taxes may come due without having enough cash on hand. Inventories build up and working capital becomes frozen before the manager realizes what is happening. The temptation to accept orders without thought of the capital required to meet them sometimes causes the owner to become overextended in the midst of promise of profits. An outside director, whose approach to the business is uncluttered by day-to-day problems, can often bring the necessary foresight to this kind of situation.

Again, the review and reestablishment of company objectives in the light of new technical, political, or economic developments may be overlooked by the harassed owner-manager but will be natural subjects for consideration by the more detached outside directors. Problems of management succession become especially important to the small business, which normally has no trained understudies to take over active management. Misunderstandings or jealousies between owner-managers and their key subordinates may reach exaggerated proportions if left unsolved. The interests of minority stockholders may be overlooked by the ambitious owner of a majority of the stock in a small corporation. These and other problems, although not peculiar to the small corporation, are likely to be aggravated in it. Their solution requires skill, tact, and an objective point of view—qualities that can be found in the well-selected outside board member.

Revitalization of Boards

Although subject to the various inherent drawbacks of the plural executive, boards of directors stand at the apex of the pyramid of corporate organization. The character of leadership, the tone of managerial policy, and the basic direction of the enterprise are among their far-reaching concerns. There are signs that the authoritative position of boards is coming to be better recognized, and their independence encouraged. Special surveys of board effectiveness made in 1962, 1964, 1967, 1973, 1974, and 1977 disclosed that more outsiders were serving on boards, more boards were made up of specialists, more was being expected of directors, more and longer meetings were being held, and directors were being paid more.[12]

This evidence of some revitalization of corporate boards results from several factors. The rise in stockholder interest in corporate affairs and the instances of stockholders ousting company managements have led many top managers to seek the protection and help of an effective board. The larger holdings of institutional investors in corporate stocks and the fact that these investors have become a major source of capital funds have likewise contributed to the establishment of more effective boards with more outside members.[13] Also, the increased tempo of business competition has caused company officers and prominent stockholders to secure more outside specialists on the board and to seek their counsel in major policy matters.

In place of the former resentment of interference by outsiders on the board, there is a rising realization by top corporate managers that major decisions call for thorough analysis and deliberation on the part of the best available management brains, that some of this can come from outside the corporation, and that advantages may offset disadvantages in group decision making. With recent searching studies and the focus of attention upon corporate responsibilities, a continuing revitalization of boards as molders of business policy may be expected.

MISUSE OF COMMITTEES

The committee form has often fallen into disrepute through misuse. The five following abuses should be avoided when committees are set up and operated.

In Place of a Manager

The weakness of the committee as a managing device has already been noted. Leadership is essentially a quality of individuals. If decision making is to be sharp, clear, prompt, and subject to unquestioned

---

[12]See John R. Kinley, *Corporate Directorship Practices,* Studies in Business Policy No. 103 (New York: National Industrial Conference Board, Inc., 1962); J. Bacon, *Corporate Directorship Practices,* Studies in Business Policy No. 125 (New York: National Industrial Conference Board, Inc., 1967); J. Bacon, *Corporate Directorship Practices: Membership and Committees of the Board* (New York: The Conference Board, Inc., 1973); and J. Bacon, *Corporate Directorship Practices: Compensation* (New York: The Conference Board, Inc., 1973); J. Bacon and J. K. Brown, *Corporate Directorship Practices: Role, Selection and Legal Status of the Board* (New York: The Conference Board, Inc., 1975); J. Bacon, *Corporate Directorship Practices: Compensation* (New York: The Conference Board, Inc., 1975); and J. Bacon, *Corporate Directorship Practices: Compensation, 1977* (New York: The Conference Board, Inc., 1978).

[13]In 1964 the New York Stock Exchange required a minimum of two outside directors for all newly listed companies and recommended the same for companies then listed, a suggestion that has actually been followed.

responsibility, it is better exercised by an individual, as is the leading of subordinates.

There are times, it must be admitted, when managerial effectiveness is not an overriding consideration. In certain government agencies the danger of putting too much authority in the hands of an individual may be so great as to supersede questions of pure efficiency. As a matter of fact, before criticizing the waste, duplication, and inefficiency of governmental management, one should face the question of whether these costs are a fair price to pay for curtailing possible abuses of authority. Similarly, in business, a certain area of decision might be so important to the welfare of the company and the dangers of abuse of authority in that area so great that no individual should be entrusted with this power.

One can hardly say that a committee has no place in management, but the advantages of group thinking and participation in policy questions can be gained in most cases through advisory committees. Most business committees function this way, leaving the real decision making and managing to the line executives to whom they report. As Ralph Cordiner, former president of the General Electric Company, has said, "We have no committees to make decisions that individuals should make."

For Research or Study

A group meeting together can hardly engage in research or study, even though it may well weigh and criticize the results of these. When the solution to a problem requires data not available to a committee, no amount of discussion or consideration can turn up the missing information. This is essentially an individual function, even though, of course, individuals may be coordinated into a team with individual research assignments. Most committees, therefore, need a research staff, providing at least analyses of alternative courses of action, historical summaries, or well-considered forecasts.

For Unimportant Decisions

Even where the committee is clothed with advisory authority only, the disadvantages of this device should dictate that its use be limited to important matters. Moreover, no intelligent specialist or manager can help feeling uncomfortable when time is wasted by a group deliberating at length on trivial subjects. This impatience reaches its frustrating climax when a committee member insists on considering at length a question upon which a certain decision is a foregone conclusion.

For Decisions beyond Participants' Authority

Where committees are used for decision making, if committee members with authority attend the meetings or send duly empowered representatives, and if the agenda deals with matters within the competence of the members, no authority problem will be encountered. But, altogether too often, the executive with the requisite authority cannot or does not attend the meeting and sends a subordinate who has not been delegated the superior's authority or who hesitates to bind the superior. The result is that the committee cannot function as intended. Delay results as the substitute refers questions to the superior, and much advantage of group decision making and deliberation is lost.

This misuse is probably the most usual reason for failure of the well-constituted committee. In a sense, it is inherent in the system. The committee is most useful in major policy determination, which is ordinarily the province of relatively few upper-level executives. If the same executives belong to many committees, they cannot afford time to attend all meetings and must send subordinates. Yet they hesitate to delegate binding authority, a situation that causes many executives to be critical of committees. The way out of this dilemma is twofold: careful preparation of the agenda, so that executives know precisely what will come up and can give their subordinates the authority necessary for the meeting, and careful advance study of proposals, so that executives can offer their opinions intelligently even by proxy.

To Consolidate Divided Authority

A disadvantage of departmentation is that authority is so delegated that, in some cases, no executive except the chief officer has adequate authority to do what must be done. Even within departments or sections, authority may be so splintered that group meetings are necessary to consolidate authority for making decisions. If divided authority can be eliminated by changing the organization structure and the delegations of authority, recourse to a committee is certainly a misuse of the device.

SUCCESSFUL OPERATION OF COMMITTEES

There is evidence that the use of committees in all types of organizations continues to increase. The increase is linked not only to the democratic tradition in American social life but also to a growing emphasis on group management and group participation in enterprise affairs. To enable committees to function effectively and to try to overcome some of the disadvantages of the committee system, managers will need to develop fresh approaches and to sharpen their skills.

Need for Well-Defined Authority and Scope

Unless a committee's authority is carefully spelled out, the members may not know whether they are responsible for a decision, a recommendation, or merely inconclusive deliberation from which the chairperson may gain some insights. The members should also know the exact scope of subjects

Figure 16.2 Increased complexity of relationships through increase in group size.

the group is expected to consider. Inefficiency of committee action results when members wander from the subject or when the chairperson introduces subjects that are beyond the committee's scope.

Furthermore, with authority and scope clear, committee members are better able to gauge whether they are meeting their responsibilities to the organization. Some companies make extensive efforts to review committee work, dissolving or consolidating those whose work is no longer justified. Some companies have an evaluating committee that periodically analyzes committees in this way.

Determining Size

One of the important questions pertains to the optimal size of committees. As shown in Figure 16.2, the complexity of interrelationships greatly increases with the size of the group. If the group is too large, there may not be enough opportunities for adequate communication among its members. On the other hand, if the group consists of only three persons, there is the possibility that two may form a coalition against the third member. No precise conclusions can be drawn here. As a general rule, a committee should be large enough to promote deliberation and include the breadth of expertness required for its job but not so large as to waste time or foster indecision. This is thought by some to mean as large as five or six members but no larger than fifteen or sixteen.[14] An analysis of small-group research indicates that the ideal committee size is five, when the five members possess adequate skills and knowledge to deal with problems facing the committee.[15] It is obvious that the larger the group, the greater the difficulty in obtaining a "sense of the meeting," and the more time necessary to allow everyone to contribute.

If a committee is to have all interested parties participate in its deliberations, the number may be too large. If all interests are not

[14]E. Dale, op. cit., p. 90. W. H. Newman, in *Administrative Action* (Englewood Cliffs, N.J.: Prentice-Hall, 1950), p. 234, believes, however, that a committee should be held down to three or four members. C. J. Berwitz, in "The Work Committee: An Administrative Technique," *Harvard Business Review*, vol. 30, pp. 110–124 (January 1952), suggests a maximum of seven members. R. Tillman, in his study of subscribers to the *Harvard Business Review*, op. cit., found that the average size of committees reported was eight members, but his respondents believed the ideal size to be five.
[15]See A. C. Filley, "Committee Management: Guidelines from Social Science Research," *California Management Review*, vol. 13, no. 1, pp. 13–21 (Fall 1970).

represented, the committee's work may be subject to criticism. Where representation is important, the answer may be found in a structure of subcommittees, with the problems to be considered properly broken down for action. However, in many instances, the need for representation is overstressed. The true purposes of committees are often accomplished by complete staff preparation for scrutinizing the various facets of a problem and by limitation of the membership to individuals who can look at the problem as a whole rather than regard their membership as a means of protecting a narrow interest.

Selecting Members

For a successful committee, the members must be suitably representative of the interests they are intended to serve, must possess the requisite authority, and they must be able to perform well in a group. Not everyone has the temperament, verbal and analytical ability, and capacity for working with others to do these things.

Members should also have the capacity for reaching group decisions by integrating group thinking rather than by compromise or by conclusions forced by position or political strength. Committees are more likely to reach agreement without weak compromise or power politics if the members are friendly, known to one another, and mutually respectful of one another's positions and interests. This means that the participants should generally be on approximately the same organizational level and independent enough of one another not to fear reprisal. Where committees are used as the forum of the traditional dissenter or as the rostrum of the ambitious climber anxious to use his or her talents, waste of time may be the sole result. Again, some individuals feel a need to engage in hypothetical discussions achieving no concrete results. It is a rare and enjoyable committee that does not have the committee bore among its members.

Selecting Subject Matter

Committee work must be limited to subject matter that can be handled in group discussion. Certain kinds of subjects, therefore, lend themselves to committee action, while others do not. Other than jurisdictional questions, where the prestige and impersonal nature of group action are definitely superior, the best area for group action is policy formulation or major planning. Along with planning, subjects for committee action lie in the area of control, especially over managers responsible for implementing major plans.

The way subjects are presented is also important. Proposals made before the committee should be sharply presented. Ideally, an agenda should be circulated to members well in advance of the meeting so that they may know what will be discussed. Even the cleverest and best-informed committee member can hardly be expected to have a considered opinion on important matters without some notice of what to expect. Masses of carefully prepared recommendations available for cursory study at the member's place at the table seldom meet this need. Often the meeting time is consumed in laborious study of reports or in listening to various members think aloud; or else the reports are meekly accepted by the members and the results railroaded by the chairperson; or the meeting may be postponed to a later date after the members have had an opportunity to study the proposals.

Importance of the Chairperson

The success of a committee will seldom be greater than the skill of the chairperson.[16] A good chairperson can avoid many of the wastes and drawbacks of committees by planning the meeting, preparing the agenda, seeing that the results of research are available to the members ahead of time, arranging definite proposals for discussion or action, and conducting the meeting efficiently.

The chairperson sets the tone of the meeting—formal or informal, with the argument casual or pointed. By anticipating objections and playing the devil's advocate, chairpersons may completely overcome many objections before they are raised. When the subject matter is especially open to contention, they may lead the discussion so that members are not forced into a position, at least until the subject has been fully discussed. Human nature being what it is, individuals who take a premature position are likely to defend it to the end. Since a committee is after results of group deliberation, lines should not be too sharply drawn, at least not early in the discussion.

It usually falls to the chairperson to integrate committee deliberation. Integration of ideas, as contrasted with compromise, builds a point of view, often quite new, from the basic positions of the group. If the chairperson is weak or not fully familiar with the subject or the way individual members think, integration of ideas is unlikely to result. When leadership is assumed by a committee member, that member often becomes the de facto chairperson of the meeting.

The chairperson must also keep discussion from wandering. This often takes great skill, especially when a committee includes persons who enjoy the sound of their own voices or who lack ability to recognize essentials and to speak of them concisely. The chairperson must handle the meeting firmly without imposing personal opinions or thwarting freedom of discussion, and yet without yielding power.

Thus, chairpersons of committees must be chosen with great care. On

[16]For an analysis of the role and duties of a chairperson, see Koontz, *The Board of Directors and Effective Management,* chap. 8.

their shoulders falls most of the responsibility for assuring that the committee acts effectively. Obviously, it is a great help if the members and subject matter have been well selected. Even a skilled chairperson can hardly make up for the deficiencies of a poorly constituted committee.

Circulating Minutes and Checking Conclusions

The use of a committee allows a group of people to participate in the discussion or solution of a problem and to be informed simultaneously concerning it. Yet individuals may walk away from meetings with varying interpretations as to what was accomplished. To avoid this, it is good to take careful minutes of the meeting, circulate them in draft for correction or modification, and then have the final copy approved by the committee. This procedure has the advantage of forcing committee members to agree or disagree with the results of the discussion and the further advantage of supplementing oral discussion with the written word.

Checking conclusions also provides for follow-up. If a committee makes a recommendation to a superior manager, it should be informed as to the action, if any, which is taken; if the recommendation is not followed, explanations are required in order to preserve committee morale and to educate its membership on management policy. Even if a committee makes neither decision nor recommendation but merely explores ideas, some report to the membership is of value.

The Committee Must Be Worth Its Cost

In measuring the success of committee operation, one must continually question whether the committee's benefits are worth its cost. It may be difficult to count the benefits, especially in such intangible forms as morale, enhancement of status, teamwork, and training. But the committee can be justified only if the costs, often considerable, are definitely offset by tangible and intangible benefits.

FOR DISCUSSION

1 A prominent novelist-critic of the management scene has said: "I don't think we can go on very much longer with the luxurious practice of hiring ten men to make one man's decision. With all its advantages, professional management tends to encourage bureaucratic corpulence." Comment.

2 Distinguish between a "committee," a "team," and a "group."

3 Where in an organization would you suggest, if any place, that committees should be used? Why?

4   What are the reasons for using committees? If there are good reasons, why are committees criticized so much?

5   What is meant by the term "plural executive"?

6   What is the relative effectiveness of individual and committee action in functional activities? Identify the activities that can be undertaken most effectively by a committee.

7   What are the major functions of the board of directors?

8   What is the value of boards in small enterprises?

9   Describe and discuss the nature of misapplications of committees.

10 What would you recommend for making committees effective?

chapter 17

Making Organizing Effective

MAJOR CHAPTER OBJECTIVES

1 To summarize some common mistakes made in organizing.
2 To emphasize the importance of planning organization structures.
3 To show how organizing can be made more effective by maintaining flexibility, by clarifying relationships and structure, and by making sure that everyone understands the structure.
4 To summarize some major principles or guidelines to be kept in mind in designing organization structures.

Organizing is aimed essentially at developing an intentional structure of roles for effective performance, a network of *decision* communications centers from which to secure coordination of individual effort toward group goals. Yet to make an organization structure work, certain common mistakes—certain inflexibilities and conflicts which arise in practice—should be avoided, the organization structure should be understood, and principles should be put into practice. In organizing, as elsewhere in managing, there is no universal best way. What works will always depend on the contingencies of a situation.

SOME MISTAKES IN ORGANIZING

Despite their obviousness and their thwarting of personal and enterprise goals, certain mistakes of organizing persist, striking evidence of the difficulty of managing, the lack of sophistication of managers, or both.

Failure to Plan Properly

It is not unusual to find an enterprise continuing a traditional organization structure long after its objectives, plans, and external environment have changed. For example, a company may keep its product research department under manufacturing division control long after the business environment has changed from being production-oriented (as in a typical sellers' market) to being marketing-oriented (as in a typical buyers' market). Or a company may continue its functional organization structure when product groupings and the need for integrated, decentralized profit responsibility demand decentralized product divisions.

Also, a company may need managers of a kind not currently available, or, just as likely, may find that certain managers have not grown with the company or do not fit current needs. Small, growing businesses often make the mistake of assuming that employees can grow with the company, only to find that a good engineering designer, made a vice president of engineering, can no longer fill the larger role of the engineering chief or that a once-adequate production superintendent may not be qualified to head a larger manufacturing department.

Another failure in planning involves organizing around people. Organization structure must normally be modified to take people into account, and there is much to be said for trying to take full advantage of employee strengths and to overcome their weaknesses. But organizing *primarily* around people overlooks several facts. In the first place, there can never be assurance by so doing that all bases will be covered, that all the necessary tasks will be undertaken. In the second place, there is danger that different people will desire to do the same things, resulting in conflict or multiple command. In the third place, people have a way of coming and going in an enterprise—through retirement, resignation, promotion, or death—which makes organizing around people risky and their positions, when vacated, hard to determine accurately and to fill adequately.

Such mistakes occur when an enterprise fails to plan properly toward a future substantially different from the past or present. By looking forward, a manager should determine what kind of organization structure will best serve future needs and what kind of people will best serve an organization.

Failure to Clarify Relationships

The failure to clarify organization relationships, probably more than any other mistake, accounts for friction, politics, and inefficiencies. Since the authority and the responsibility for action are critical in organization, lack of clarity here means lack of knowledge of the part members are to play on an enterprise team. This implies neither that a detailed and minute job description is needed nor that people cannot operate as a team. Although some enterprise leaders have prided themselves on having a team of subordinates without specified tasks and authority lines, any sports coach could tell them that such a "team" is likely to be a group of jealous, insecure, buck-passing individuals jockeying for position and favor.

Failure to Delegate Authority

A common complaint in organization life is that managers are reluctant to push decision making down into the organization. In some businesses, where uniformity of policy is necessary and decision making can be handled by one or a few managers, there may be neither need nor desire to decentralize authority. But bottlenecks of decision making, excessive referral of small problems to upper echelons, overburdening of top executives with detail, continual "fighting fires" and "meeting crises," and underdevelopment of managerial experience in the lower levels of organization give evidence that failing to delegate authority to the proper extent is usually a decided mistake.

Failure to Balance Delegation

Another mistake made in organizing is failure to maintain balanced delegation. In other words, some managers—in their zeal for decentralization—may take literally the organizational bromide to "push decision making down in the organization as far as it will go." Obviously, to do this pushes it down to the very bottom of the structure and develops a system of independent organizational satellites. Even without going to this extreme, not maintaining authority suitable for the various levels of organization has caused many organizational failures.

As was pointed out in Chapter 15, on decentralization, top managers must retain some authority, particularly over decisions of company wide impact and at least enough to review the plans and performance of subordinates. Managers must not forget that there is some authority they should not delegate. Nor should they overlook the fact that they must maintain enough authority to make sure that when they do delegate authority to a subordinate, it is being used in the way and for the purposes intended.

Confusion of Lines of Authority and of Information

The problems and costs of levels of organization and departmentation can be reduced by opening wide the channels of information. Unless information is confidential (and businesses and governments, as well as other enterprises, overdo this classification) or is unavailable except at too great expense, there is no reason why lines of information should follow lines of authority. Information gathering should be separated from decision making, since only the latter requires managerial authority. Managers often force lines of information to follow authority lines, when the only valid reason for following a chain of command is to preserve the integrity of authority for decision making and the clarity of responsibility.

Granting of Authority without Responsibility

A significant cause of mismanagement is the granting of authority without exacting responsibility. Authority delegation is not responsibility delegation; the delegant remains responsible to his or her superior for the proper exercise of authority by a subordinate. And, of course, a subordinate is always responsible to the superior for proper use of delegated authority. Any other relationship would lead to organizational anarchy. Moreover, all those to whom authority is delegated must be willing to be held responsible for their actions.

Granting of Responsibility without Authority

A common complaint of subordinates is that superiors hold them responsible for results without giving them the authority to accomplish them. Some of these complaints are unjustified and based on misunderstanding the fact that subordinates can seldom have unlimited authority in any area because their actions must be coordinated with those in other areas and must remain within defined policies. Subordinates often see their jobs as all-encompassing and forget that their authority must be limited to their own departmental boundaries and within controlling policies.

Too often, however, the complaints are justified; managers, sometimes without realizing it, do hold subordinates responsible for results they have no power to accomplish. This does not happen as frequently where organization lines and duties have been clearly set forth, but where an organized structure of roles is unclear or confused, it does occur.

There are many valid reasons for using a staff assistant or staff specialist and even building entire advisory departments. However, there is danger that staff people will be used to undermine the authority of the very managers they are intended merely to advise.

The undermining of managerial authority may extend to subordinate line managers. There is an ever-present danger that top managers may surround themselves with staff specialists and become so preoccupied with the specialists' work as to exclude from their schedule the time and attention needed for their line subordinates; or they may assign problems to their staff that should be more appropriately assigned to line lieutenants.

In other instances, staff personnel exercise line authority which has not been delegated to them. It is easy to understand the impatience of staff specialists who see clearly how a situation should be handled, while the line officer in charge of it seems to be dilatory or clumsy. The very quality that makes staff specialists valuable—specialized knowledge—also makes them impatient to command. Yet if they were to exercise this authority without clear delegation, they would not only be undermining the authority of the responsible line official but also breaking down the unity of command.

Misuse of Functional Authority

Perhaps even more perilous to good managing are the dangers in undefined and unrestricted delegation of functional authority. This is true especially because the complexities of modern enterprise often create cases where it is desirable to give a predominantly staff or service department functional authority over activities in other parts of the organization.

In the quest for economies of specialization and for advantages of technically expert opinion, managers often unduly exalt staff and service departments at the expense of operating departments. Many line officers—from the vice president in charge of operations to a first-level supervisor—feel, with justice, that the business is being run by the staff and service departments through this exercise of functional authority.

Multiple Subordination

The principal danger of too great proliferation of functional authority delegations is the breakdown of unity of command. One has only to look at the various departments of a typical medium-sized or large business to see how such a breakdown occurs. The controller prescribes accounting procedures throughout the company. The purchasing director prescribes how and where purchases are to be made. The personnel manager dictates (often according to union contracts or government regulations) how employees shall be classified for pay purposes, how vacations shall be scheduled, and how many hours are to be worked. The traffic manager guides the routing of all freight. The general counsel insists that all contracts bear his approval and be made in prescribed form. The public relations director requires that all public utterances of managers and other employees be cleared or meet a prescribed policy line. And the tax director reviews all program decisions for clearance on their tax aspects.

Thus, with all these staff and service specialists having some degree of line authority over other parts of the organization, plus counterparts in divisions and regions, key operating managers find themselves subject to the direction of a number of people with functional authority in addition to their principal superiors, who usually have the final decision concerning their pay scale and chances for promotion. One frustrated general supervisor of a factory subdepartment informed the authors that he just did the best he could to satisfy everyone and that, when he did not have time and energy to satisfy all, he resorted to the "decibel" principle of management, paying attention to those who made the most noise.

Multiple subordination results also from faulty organization structure and from instances of plural executives. Wherever found, it tends to cause confusion, undermine the definiteness and effectiveness of authority, and threaten organizational stability.

Misuse of Service Departments

These departments are often looked upon as not much concerned with the accomplishment of major enterprise objectives, when they are in fact just as immediately concerned as any operating department. Sometimes people, particularly in so-called line departments, regard a service department as relatively unnecessary, unimportant, and therefore something to be ignored when possible.

On the other hand, many service departments mistakenly look upon their function as an end unto itself rather than a service to other departments. Thus, a purchasing department may not realize that its purpose is to purchase efficiently items ordered by authorized departments; or a statistics department may forget that it exists to furnish data desired by others rather than to produce reports of its own choosing.

Perhaps the greatest misuse of service departments is summed up in the words "efficient inefficiency." When managers establish service departments, looking more to their cost savings than to the efficiency of the entire enterprise, a highly "efficient" service may do an inefficient job of serving. For example, little is gained in putting out low-cost reports not useful to managers, nor is it sensible to set up a low-cost central recruiting section if the employees recruited do not meet enterprise needs.

Overorganization and Underorganization

Overorganization usually results from failure to put into practice the concept that the activity-authority structure of the enterprise is merely a system for efficient performance of people. Unduly complicating the structure through too many levels ignores the fact that efficiency demands that managers supervise as many subordinates as they can. Narrow spans may reflect misunderstanding of the span-of-management principle, managerial inability to minimize the time requirements of necessary human relationships, or lack of time to manage—a lack often caused by poor assignments and authority delegations. Likewise, the multiplication of staff and service activities or departments may be caused by inadequate delegation to line subordinates and the tendency to regard service specialization and efficiency so narrowly that larger enterprise efficiency is overlooked.

Managers also overorganize by having unnecessary line assistants (for example, assistant or deputy managers). Having a line assistant is justified when managers wish to devote their time to matters outside their department, during their long absences from the office, when they wish to delegate line authority in a given area such as engineering, or during a limited training period for a subordinate to whom full managerial status is soon to be given. Otherwise, the separation of managers from their other subordinates and the confusion as to who is really their superior lead the observer to conclude that this form of overorganization should be undertaken carefully.

Sometimes, excessive procedures are confused with overorganization. Overorganization—particularly if interlaced with functional authority—can lead to excessive procedures. But much of the "red tape" often blamed on overorganization really results from poor planning. The failure to regard procedures as plans—and to treat them with the respect given other areas of planning—often results in bewilderingly complex and even unnecessary procedures.

Similarly, too many committees, sapping the time and energies of managers and their staffs, are often blamed on overorganization rather than on *poor* organization (particularly when committees make decisions better made by individuals). Excessive committees often result from splintered authority or vague delegation. Such excess of committees may actually point to underorganization.

AVOIDING MISTAKES BY PLANNING

As with the other functions of management, establishment of objectives and orderly planning are necessary for good organization. As Urwick has said, "Lack of design [in organization] is illogical, cruel, wasteful, and inefficient."[1] It is illogical because good design, or planning, must come first, whether one speaks of engineering or social practice. It is cruel because "the main sufferers from a lack of design in organization are those

---

[1]L. Urwick, *The Elements of Administration* (New York: Harper & Brothers, 1944), p. 38

individuals who work in an undertaking."[2] It is wasteful because "unless jobs are clearly put together along lines of functional specialization it is impossible to train new men to succeed to positions as the incumbents are promoted, resign or retire."[3] And it is inefficient because, unless based on principles, managing becomes based on personalities, with the resultant rise of company politics, for "a machine will not run smoothly when fundamental engineering principles have been ignored in construction."[4]

Planning for the Ideal

Essential to organization planning is the search for an ideal form to reflect enterprise goals under given circumstances. This entails charting the main lines of organization, considering the organizational philosophy of the enterprise managers (for example, shall authority be as centralized as much as possible, or should the company divide its operations into semiautonomous product or territorial divisions?), and sketching out consequent authority relationships. The ultimate form established, like all plans, seldom remains unchanged, and continuous remolding of the ideal plan will normally be necessary. Nevertheless, an ideal organization plan constitutes a standard, and, by comparing present structure with it, enterprise leaders know what changes should be made when possible.

The organizer must always be careful not to be blinded by popular notions in organizing, because what may work in one company may not work in another. Principles of organizing have general application, but the factual background of each company's operations and needs must be considered in applying these principles. Organization structure needs to be tailor-made.

Modification for the Human Factor

If available personnel do not fit into the ideal structure and cannot or should not be sidetracked, there is no alternative but to modify the structure to fit individual capabilities, attitudes, or limitations. Although this smacks of organizing around people, the difference is that it is organizing *first* around the goals to be met and only *then* making modifications for the human factor. In this way, planning will be available to eliminate compromises with principle whenever changes in personnel occur.

Advantages of Planning

Good organization structure can go far to make up for deficiencies in leadership by furnishing a support for available abilities. Such a support

---

[2]Ibid. In this connection Urwick quotes the following lines from Browning:
    It's an awkward thing to play with souls
    And matter enough to save one's own.
[3]Ibid.
[4]Ibid.

increases managerial efficiency by cutting down on meetings to determine who has the authority to do what, or how this program or that policy
is to be implemented, and relieves the manager of constantly correcting subordinates on the nature of their functions, responsibilities, or
authority.

Planning the organization structure also helps determine future
personnel needs and attendant training programs. Without knowing what
managerial personnel will be needed and what experience to demand, an
enterprise cannot intelligently recruit people and train them.

Furthermore, organization planning can disclose weaknesses. Duplication of effort, unclear lines of authority, too long lines of communication, too much red tape, and obsolete practices show up best when
desirable and actual organization structures are compared.

AVOIDING ORGANIZATIONAL INFLEXIBILITY

One basic advantage of organization planning is avoidance of organizational inflexibility. Many enterprises, especially those which have been in
operation for many years, become too rigid to meet the first test of
effective organization structure—adaptation to changing environment and
meeting new situations.

Signs of Inflexibility

Some of the older companies provide ample evidence of these inflexibilities: an organization pattern no longer suited to the times; a district or
regional organization that could be either abolished or enlarged because
of improved communications; or a too highly centralized structure for an
enlarged enterprise requiring decentralization.

Reasons for Reorganization

Although reorganization is intended to meet changes in the enterprise
environment, there may be other compelling reasons. Those related to the
business environment include changes in operations caused by acquisition or sale of major properties, changes in product line or marketing
methods, business cycles, competitive influences, new production techniques, labor-union policy, government regulatory and fiscal policy, or
the state of current knowledge about organizing. New techniques and
principles may become applicable, such as that of developing managers
by allowing them to manage decentralized semiautonomous units of a
company; or new methods may come into use, such as that of gaining
adequate financial control with a high degree of decentralization.

Moreover, a new chief executive officer and new vice presidents and
department heads are likely to have some definite organizational ideas of
their own. Shifts may be due merely to the desire of new managers to

make changes from ideas formulated through their previous experience or to the fact that their methods of managing and their personalities require a modified organization structure.

Furthermore, reorganization may also be caused by demonstrated deficiencies in an existing structure. Some of these arise from organizational weaknesses themselves: excessive spans of management, too many levels, inadequate communication, poor interdepartmental coordination, excess committees, lack of uniform policy, slow decision making, failure to accomplish objectives, inability to meet delivery schedules, excessive costs, or breakdown of financial control. Other deficiencies may stem from inadequacies of managers. Lack of knowledge or skill on the part of a manager, who, for some reason cannot be replaced, may be avoided by organizing so as to move much of the authority for decision making to another position.

Personality clashes between managers also may be solved by reorganization. Staff-line conflicts may develop to such an extent that they can be resolved only by reorganization.

Need for Readjustment and Change

In addition to impelling reasons for reorganization, there is a certain need for moderate and continuing readjustment merely to keep the structure from developing inertia. "Empire building" is not so attractive when all those involved know that their positions are subject to change. As a company president told his subordinates: "Don't bother to build any empires, because I can assure you that you won't be in the same position 3 years from now." Some enterprise managers, realizing that an organization structure must be a living thing, make structural changes merely to accustom subordinates to change.

Much can be said for developing a tradition of change. People who are accustomed to change tend to accept it without the frustration and demoralization that result when need for reorganization is allowed to reach the stage at which change must be revolutionary. On the other hand, a company continually undertaking major reorganization may so damage morale as to harm the enterprise by losing key personnel or by causing people in all ranks to spend much of their time wondering what will happen to them.

AVOIDING CONFLICT BY CLARIFICATION

A major reason why conflict develops in organizations is that people do not understand their assignments and those of their coworkers. No matter how well conceived an organization structure, people must understand it to make it work. Understanding is aided materially by proper use of organization charts, accurate job descriptions, the spelling out of authority and informational relationships, and the introduction of specific goals to breathe life into positions.

Organization Charts

Every organization structure can be charted, even a poor one, for a chart merely indicates how departments are tied together along the principal lines of authority. It is therefore somewhat surprising occasionally to find top managers taking pride in not having an organization chart or feeling that the charts should be kept secret.

Advantages   A prominent manufacturer once informed the authors that although he could see some use for an organization chart for his factory, he had refused to chart the organization above the level of factory superintendent. His argument was that charts tended to make people overly conscious of being superiors or inferiors, tended to destroy team feeling, and gave persons occupying a box on the chart too great a feeling of "ownership." Another top executive informed the authors that if an organization is left uncharted, it can be changed more easily, and it also encourages a competitive drive for higher executive positions on the part of the uncharted middle-management group.

These reasons for not charting organization structures are clearly untenable. Subordinate-superior relationships exist not because of charting but rather because of essential reporting relationships. As for any too-comfortable feeling engendered and a lack of drive for those who have "arrived," these are matters of top leadership—of reorganizing whenever the enterprise environment demands, of developing a tradition of change, and of making subordinate managers continue to meet adequate and well-understood standards of performance. Managers who believe that team spirit can be engendered without clearly spelling out relationships are deluding themselves and preparing the way for politics, intrigue, frustration, buck passing, lack of coordination, duplicated effort, vague policy, uncertain decision making, and other evidences of organizational inefficiency.

Since a chart maps lines of decision-making authority, sometimes merely charting an organization shows inconsistencies and complexities and leads to their correction. A chart also reveals to managers and new personnel how they tie into the entire structure. It has been generally found that those firms which have comprehensive organization charts appear to have sound organization structures.

Limitations   Organization charts are subject to important limitations. In the first place, a chart shows only formal authority relationships and omits the many significant informal and informational relationships. It does not even picture how much authority exists at any point in the structure. While it would be interesting to chart an organization with lines of different widths to denote varying degrees of formal authority, authority is not subject to such measurement. And if the multiple lines of functional authority, informal relationships, and information dissemination were drawn, it would so complicate a chart that it would lose its value.

Many charts show structures as they are supposed to be or used to be, rather than as they really are. Managers hesitate or neglect to redraft charts, forgetting that organization is dynamic and that a chart should not be allowed to become obsolete.

Another difficulty with organization charts is that individuals may confuse authority relationships with status. The staff officer reporting to the corporation president may be depicted at the top of the organization chart, while a major line officer may be shown one or two levels lower. Although good charting attempts to make levels on the chart conform to levels of position importance, it cannot always do so. This problem can be handled by clearly spelling out authority relationships and by that best indicator of status—salary and bonus levels. No one is likely, for example, to hear that the general manager of Chevrolet in General Motors feels a sense of inferiority because his position on the chart is below that of the patent section director.

Position Descriptions

Every managerial position should be defined. A good position description informs the incumbent and others what he or she is supposed to do. A modern position description is not a detailed list of all the activities a manager is expected to undertake and it certainly does not specify *how* to undertake them. Rather, it states the basic function of the position, the major end-result areas for which the manager is responsible, the reporting relationships involved, and makes reference to the current chart of approval authorizations for clarifying the position's authority and the current set of verifiable objectives in effect.

In this way, position descriptions may be made far less detailed than they once were. Also, by merely referring to the current authority chart and set of objectives, the description can be made much more flexible as authority delegations and objectives change. For example, the basic function of one vice president in charge of marketing was described as being responsible to the president for effectively and efficiently planning, organizing, staffing, leading, and controlling company activities in market research, advertising and promotion, and sales. The vice president was given authority in accordance with a separately published chart of executive approval authorizations and was held responsible for setting and achieving approved objectives as they were developed from time to time in consultation with the president.

Such descriptions have many benefits. As jobs are analyzed, attendant duties and responsibilities are brought into focus and areas of overlapping or neglected duties come to light. The authors have found that forcing people to consider what should be done and who should do it is more than worth the effort. Further benefits of job descriptions include their guidance in training new managers, in drawing up candidate requirements, and in setting up salary levels. Finally, as a means of control over organization, the position guide furnishes a standard against which to judge whether a position is necessary and, if so, what its organization level and exact location in the structure should be.

Need to Define Relationships

Some statement of authority and information relationships is usually included, at least by reference to a chart of approval authorizations, in position descriptions. People often do not cooperate because they do not know with whom their cooperation is required. People often fail to communicate because they do not know to whom their message should be directed, not because they have nothing to say or do not know how to say it.

By showing up vague authority, inappropriate or misunderstood communication lines, and inefficiencies of organization levels or management spans, spelling out a position and its relationships is a major step toward removing conflict. As with organization charts, the very spelling out furnishes a standard against which effectiveness of organization can be measured. Perhaps the most powerful tool for defining and clarifying relationships is the chart of executive approval authorizations, discussed in Chapter 15. By spelling out clearly what organizational positions have the authority for approving actions involving commitments and where final approvals lie, as well as which managers are to exercise functional authority, the whole system of authority relationships may be made clear. This clarity extends not only to the manager who is given approval authority but also, if proper publicity is given to the chart, to other persons who are involved.

ENSURING UNDERSTANDING OF ORGANIZING

To be made to work, organization structures must be well understood by the members of the enterprise. This requires teaching. Also, it must be remembered, formal organization, as conceived in this book, does not cover all organizational relationships but is supplemented by informal organization, which plays a part in making formal organization work. Since this is so, members of an enterprise must understand the general working of informal as well as formal organization.

Many soundly conceived organization plans fail because organization members do not understand them. To be sure, a well-written organization manual—containing a statement of organization philosophy, programs, charts, and an outline of position descriptions—goes far toward making organizing understandable. Certainly, if an organization structure is put into written words and charts, it has a better chance of being clear than if it is not. However, because even the best-written words and charts do not always clearly convey the same meaning to every reader, effective managers cannot stop with written clarification. They must teach those in their operation the meaning of the organization structure, their position in it, and the relationships involved.

This may be done by individual coaching, through staff or special meetings, or by simply watching how the structure works. If subordinates pass decisions up the line when they should be making them, managers can take this opportunity to clarify authority. Likewise, if communication between members of a group seems to be inadequate, managers can look for causes in either a poorly conceived or a poorly understood organization structure. Too many group meetings or too much committee work is a signal for managers to do some investigating. Thus managers are obligated continually to teach the fundamentals of organizing, for if they do not, their enterprise or department is likely to fail.

Recognizing the Importance of Informal Organization

Another way of making the formal organization work effectively is to recognize and take full advantage of informal organization. Since formal organization is a social tool for the conscious coordination of activities toward a goal, informal organization, as Barnard has pointed out, necessarily precedes it.[5] Before coordination and structure can be given to group behavior, there must be communication, association, and a concrete goal. People seek associations and the satisfactions that arise from them. This gregarious impulse and association to accomplish goals that an individual alone cannot gain form the basis for formal organization. When a group is coordinated, with a conscious joint purpose and a structure to gain this purpose, it becomes a formal organization.

Formal organizations, according to Barnard, create additional informal organizations. Interrelationships of authority that cannot be charted, unwritten rules of organization conduct, the necessity for new employees' "learning the ropes," and other typical phenomena lead to informal organization.

---

[5]*The Functions of the Executive* (Cambridge, Mass.: Harvard University Press, 1938), chap. 9.

The grapevine One of the most interesting and significant informal relationships, almost always supplementing formal organization, is referred to as the "grapevine." This relationship is generally quite structureless but comes to life when members of the formal organization who know one another well enough pass on information in some way connected with the enterprise. In the typical enterprise—the members of which spend many hours a day deriving both material security and status from it—the desire for information concerning the organization and its people is strong enough so that such information is rapidly transmitted between persons who know and trust one another.

The grapevine, of course, thrives on information not openly available to the entire group, whether because it is regarded as confidential, because formal lines of communication are inadequate to disperse it, or because it is of the kind that would never be formally disclosed. Even a management that conscientiously informs employees through company bulletins or newspapers never so completely or quickly discloses all information of interest as to make the grapevine purposeless.

Since all informal organization serves essential human communication, the grapevine is inevitable and valuable. Indeed, the intelligent top manager would probably be wise to feed it with accurate information, since it is very effective for quick communication. There is much to be said for every manager's gaining a place—personally or, as is more likely, through a trusted staff member or secretary, on the company grapevine.[6]

Benefits Informal organization brings cohesiveness to formal organization. It brings to the members of a formal organization a feeling of belonging, of status, of self-respect, and of gregarious satisfaction. Barnard observes in this connection that informal organizations are an important "means of maintaining the personality of the individual against certain effects of formal organizations which tend to disintegrate personality."[7] Many managers, understanding this fact, consciously use informal organizations as channels of communications and molders of employee morale.

CONTINGENCIES IN ORGANIZING

Throughout this book it has been emphasized that to be effective, organizations must adapt to the specific requirements of the situation.

---

[6]For a detailed discussion of the grapevine and its role in informal organizations, see K. Davis, *Human Behavior at Work*, 5th ed. (New York: McGraw-Hill Book Company, 1979), chap. 16.
[7]Barnard, op. cit., p. 122.

Major contributions toward a contingency, or situational, theory of organizing have been made by researchers in the United States and in Britain. This discussion briefly examines some major contributions.

Studies by Burns and Stalker

Tom Burns and G. M. Stalker investigated the relationship between management practices and characteristics of the external environment. Specifically, they interviewed key persons in twenty English and Scottish companies and developed a conceptual scheme with two different systems of management practices. One system was called "mechanistic," the other "organic."[8]

The *mechanistic* management system appears to be appropriate for a relatively stable organization environment. This system is characterized by, among other things, specialized differentiation of tasks, by individuals viewing their tasks as being distinct from the whole, by precisely defined rights and obligations, by a hierarchical structure, by vertical interactions between the superior and the subordinates, and by having instructions and decisions come from the superior.

The *organic* management system, on the other hand, is characterized by individual performance based on knowledge of the task of the whole concern, continued redefinition of tasks through interaction with others, and a great deal of lateral interaction and consultation. This system, it is suggested, is more suitable for coping with unstable and changing conditions and unpredictable problems.

Studies by Woodward

The studies of 100 British firms conducted by Joan Woodward indicate that there is a relationship between organization design and different types of technology.[9] This researcher classified the enterprises into three groups according to increasing degrees of technological complexity: (1) small-batch and unit production making such items as special purpose equipment or custom-made products; (2) large-batch and mass production as, for example, in the manufacture of items produced in large quantities on the assembly line; and (3) process or continuous flow production, such as that found in chemical firms and oil refineries.

The findings suggest that the more successful firms in the large-batch and mass production category were organized in a manner similar to what Burns and Stalker described as mechanistic.

---

[8]T. Burns and G. M. Stalker, *The Management of Innovation* (London: Tavistock Publications, 1961).

[9]J. Woodward, *Industrial Organization: Theory and Practice* (London: Oxford University Press, 1965), especially chap. 5.

On the other hand, the small-batch and unit production firms as well as the process or continuous flow production firms were more effective with organic structures. In short, the Woodward research suggests that to be effective, organization design is contingent on production technology.

Studies by Lawrence and Lorsch

Building on the studies by Woodward and Burns and Stalker, the research by Paul R. Lawrence and Jay W. Lorsch focused on the relative stability of environments. Organizations with changing environments demand greater "differentiation," a term defined as ". . . the difference in cognitive and emotional orientation among managers in different functional departments."[10] A company in the plastics industry, for example, working in a dynamic environment, requires considerable differentiation. Such an organization also has a great need for "integration," a term defined as ". . . the quality of the state of collaboration that exists among departments that are required to achieve unity of effort by the demands of the environment."[11] Thus, more unstable environments call for more organic types of organization, using, for example, teams that cut across functions in order to integrate activities.

On the other hand, more stable environments demand less differentiation, and the means for integration may differ from those in dynamic environments. For example, Lawrence and Lorsch found that a company in the container industry with a relatively stable environment was effective in using more mechanistic organizational arrangements such as a managerial hierarchy.

FOR DISCUSSION

1 Many psychologists have pointed to the advantages of "job enlargement," whereby tasks are not so specialized that an individual loses a sense of doing things which are meaningful. Assuming that managers wish to limit specialization of tasks and "enlarge" jobs, can they do so and still apply the basic principles of organizing?

2 Taking an organized enterprise with which you have some familiarity, can you find any of the deficiencies commonly found in organization structures?

3 It is sometimes stated that the typical hierarchical organization chart is an undemocratic device that emphasizes the superiority and inferiority of positions. Comment.

[10]P. R. Lawrence and J. W. Lorsch, *Organization and Environment* (Homewood, Ill.: Richard D. Irwin, Inc., 1969), p. 11.
[11]Ibid.

4   What, in your judgment, makes an organization structure "good"? How does "good" organization structure support leadership?

5   What would you need to know to plan an organization structure? How far ahead would you plan it? How would you go about making such a plan?

6   A prominent scholar has forecast that a system of well-defined organizational hierarchy will give way to one of democracy in organization. What do you think?

SUMMARY OF MAJOR PRINCIPLES FOR PART THREE: ORGANIZING[12]

Although no one would claim that the science of organizing has developed to the point where principles are infallible laws, it is surprising how much unanimity there is among management scholars and practitioners as to the existence of a number of them. These principles are truths of general application, although the generality of their application is not so precise as to give them the exactness of the laws of pure science. They are more in the nature of criteria for good organizing. They are, as Urwick has pointed out, "a beginning, if only a beginning, of a comprehensive philosophy of the task of administration, whether in business or elsewhere."[13]

In order to summarize the major principles of organizing and to see them in a logical framework, the authors propose an outline in which they may be grouped under the following aspects of organizing: the purpose of organizing, its cause, the structure of organization, and the process of organizing. To define these aspects succinctly, it might be said that *the attainment of an objective* is the purpose of organizing, *span of management* the cause, *authority* the cement, *departmentized activities* the framework, and *effectiveness in supporting performance* the measure.

The Purpose of Organizing

The purpose of organizing might be summarized by the following general truths.

Principle of unity of objective An organization structure is effective if it facilitates the contribution of individuals in the attainment of enterprise objectives.

Principle of efficiency An organization is efficient if it is structured to aid in the accomplishment of enterprise objectives with the minimum of unsought consequences or costs.

Thus, a structure must be effective, as Barnard has emphasized, in furnishing individuals *as a group* the organizational means for gaining enterprise objectives. Every division, branch, department, or section should be judged in the light of how well it contributes to the attainment of enterprise objectives. But the fact that an organization may be effective in gaining enterprise objectives, with every part contributing to this end, does not imply that it does so efficiently. Certainly the concepts of effectiveness and efficiency must be considered together. Moreover, both principles imply the existence of formulated and understood enterprise objectives or goals.

---

[12]Included in this summary are a few principles applicable to organizing dealt with in part 1. An increasing number of companies are summarizing principles of organizing and incorporating them in their organization manuals. See, for example, *Preparing the Organization Manual*, Studies in Personnel Policy No. 157 (New York: National Industrial Conference Board, Inc., 1957), and J. J. Famularo, *Organization Planning Manual* (New York: American Management Association, 1971).

[13]L. Urwick, *The Need Is Urgent to Make Leadership a Reality* (Toronto: Manufacturing and Industrial Engineering, 1952), p. 34. This monograph is a series of six lectures given by Urwick at the University of Toronto in 1951.

The Cause of Organizing

One finds the basic cause of organization structure in the limitations of the span of management. Certainly, if there were no such limitation, one could have an unorganized enterprise with only one manager.

Span-of-management principle There is a limit in each managerial position to the number of persons an individual can effectively manage, but the exact number will vary in accordance with the effect of underlying variables and contingencies and their impact on the time requirements of effective managing.

Much confusion has arisen in the statement and application of this limitation because of the tendency to make a specific law of it through attaching some maximum number of subordinates. This is, of course, erroneous. The number of subordinates a manager can effectively manage may be few or many, depending upon one's ability, the job, and basic factors that influence time demands.

The Structure of Organization: Authority

Authority is the cement of organization structure, the thread that makes it possible, the means by which groups of activities can be placed under a manager and coordination of organizational units can be promoted. It is the tool by which a manager is able to exercise discretion to create an environment for individual performance. Authority furnishes the primary line of communication in an enterprise, since it deals with those communications which are composed of decisions. One finds, as might be expected, that some of the most useful principles of organizing are related to it.

The scalar principle The clearer the line of authority from the top manager in an enterprise to every subordinate position, the more effective will be the responsible decision making and organization communication system.

Principle of delegation Authority delegated to individual managers should be adequate to assure their ability to accomplish results expected of them.

Principle of absoluteness of responsibility The responsibility of subordinates to their superiors for performance is absolute, and superiors cannot escape responsibility for the organization activities of their subordinates.

Principle of parity of authority and responsibility The responsibility for actions cannot be greater than that implied by the authority delegated, nor should it be less.

Principle of unity of command The more completely an individual has a reporting relationship to a single superior, the less the problem of conflict in instructions and the greater the feeling of personal responsibility for results.

The authority level principle Maintenance of intended delegation requires that decisions within the authority competence of individual managers be made by them and not referred upward in the organization structure.

The Structure of Organization: Departmentized Activities

This aspect of organization involves both the departmental framework itself and the problems of assigning activities to these departmental units. Although a number of fundamental truths might be summarized in this area, three appear to be of major importance.

Principle of division of work   The more an organization structure reflects a classification of the tasks or activities necessary to attain goals and assists in their coordination, and the more that roles are designed to fit the capabilities and motivations of people available to fill them, the more effective and efficient an organization structure will be.

The principle of division of work has at times been incorrectly interpreted to mean that activities should be thoroughly specialized. In this instance, it has been confused with the economic principle of occupational specialization. Formal organization, rather than economic specialization, has consequently been blamed by some persons for the existence of highly specialized and limited tasks. It is true that Fayol's discussion of this principle perhaps implies this, but it is likewise true that Fayol wisely recognized that "division of work has its limits which experience and a sense of proportion teach us may not be exceeded."[14]

The principle of division of work should be distinguished from occupational specialization in its detailed and ultimate sense. Division of work does imply that an enterprise will gain from specialization of tasks. But this specialization can be in the broad areas of sales or accounting, or it can even be in a project form in which a variety of fairly specialized tasks are aimed at the accomplishment of a certain integrated project. The point of the principle is that the activities of an enterprise should be so defined and grouped as to contribute most effectively to objectives. In some cases, this might mean a department with the specialized task of doing nothing more than fuel accounting, or it can mean an engineering project section working to design a complicated piece of electronic gear.

Principle of functional definition   The more a position or a department has a clear definition of results expected, activities to be undertaken, organization authority delegated, and authority and informational relationships with other positions, the more adequately individuals responsible can contribute toward accomplishing enterprise objectives.

Principle of separation   If some activities are designed to be a check on others,

---

[14]*General and Industrial Administration* (New York: Pitman Publishing Corporation, 1949). Fayol says (p. 20), "Division of work permits of reduction in the number of objects to which attention and effort must be directed and has been recognized as the best means of making use of individuals and of groups of people."

individuals charged with the former cannot adequately discharge their responsibility if they report to the department whose activity they are expected to evaluate.

The Process of Organizing

In a real sense, the various principles of authority delegation and of departmentation are fundamental truths dealing with the process of organizing. But they deal with phases of the two primary aspects of organizing—authority and activity groupings. There are other principles that appear to deal with the process of organizing as a whole. It is through their application that one gains a sense of proportion or a measure of the total organizing process.

Principle of balance The application of principles or techniques must be balanced in the light of the overall effectiveness of the structure in meeting enterprise objectives.

The principle of balance is common to all areas of science and to all functions of the manager. Perhaps, however, its application is more dramatic in the case of organizing then with the other functions.[15] In every structure there is need for balance. The inefficiencies of broad spans of management must be balanced against the inefficiencies of long lines of communications. The losses of multiple command must be balanced against the gains from expertness and uniformity in delegating functional authority to staff and service departments. The savings of occupational specialization in departmentizing in accordance with the enterprise function must be balanced against the advantages of establishing profit-responsible, semiautonomous product or territorial departments. This again proves that management theory must be contingency or situational theory.

Principle of flexibility The more provisions are made for building flexibility in organizational structures, the more adequately an organization structure can fulfill its purpose.

This principle has to do with building into every structure devices, techniques, and other environmental factors in anticipating and reacting to change. Every enterprise moves toward its goal in a changing environment, both external and internal. The enterprise that develops inflexibilities, whether these are resistance to change, too complicated procedures, or too firm departmental lines, is risking inability to meet the challenges of economic, technical, biological, political, and social change. It should not be forgotten that one of the obligations of the manager, and one of the tasks role structures are designed to perform, is the perpetuation of the enterprise.

---

[15]To expect all principles to pull in exactly the same direction in every environmental situation is to overlook the facts of life. Although a principle is a fundamental truth of general applicability and of predictive value in given situations, there are often varying sets of circumstances in a single complex social (or physical or biological) system. Certainly a physicist would not argue that the principle of gravitation is void merely because it might be offset by principles of centrifugal force, as is the case with satellites. Yet there are those who argue that a principle of management may be invalid because another principle, or a group of forces, tends to offset it in individual instances.

Principle of leadership facilitation   The more an organization structure and its authority delegations make it possible for managers to design and maintain an environment for performance, the more it will facilitate their leadership abilities.

Since managership depends materially upon the quality of leadership of those in managerial positions, it is important for the organization structure to do its part in creating a situation in which the manager can most effectively lead. In this sense, organizing is a technique of promoting leadership. If the authority allocation and the structural arrangements create a situation in which heads of departments tend to be looked upon as leaders and in which their task of leadership is facilitated, structuring has accomplished an essential task. But if department heads are buried in detail or if the actual authority for planning, organizing, staffing, leading, or controlling their departments is out of their hands, the organization structure has overshadowed and thwarted its managers.

CASES FOR PART 3

1 Baskin-Robbins Ice Cream Company

According to a report in a business magazine recently, the famous Baskin-Robbins Ice Cream Company was having troubles. As Americans in droves went to the familiar pink-and-brown ice cream parlors to buy the fancy concoctions served in them, the company's sales and earnings nearly tripled in just 4 years. From a few stores it had grown to having over 1600 stores all over the United States and abroad.

But, inside the company, Baskin-Robbins was having problems. The company was suffering from severe growing pains. As Irvine Baskins, founder and president, pointed out, "The problem was that the conventional system of delegating authority and responsibility just wasn't working. Various departments were each going their own way, with little or no regard for each other, so that almost literally the right hand did not know what the left hand was doing."

When Irv Baskins discussed the problem with a friend in a university, the management professor pointed out that his predicament was not at all unusual, that the mess in management accountability was a widespread problem in many fast-growing companies, and that "many companies are finding they really aren't sure who is responsible to whom for what."

1   Why do you believe that Baskin-Robbins had this problem?
2   What more will you want to know to diagnose this problem?
3   How would you suggest to Mr. Baskins that this problem be solved?

2 Measurement Instruments Corporation

William B. Richman, president of the Measurement Instruments Corporation, was explaining his organizational arrangements to the board of directors. His organization chart is shown below (on p. 502).

When asked by a board member whether he thought he had too many people reporting to him, Mr. Richman replied: "I do not believe in the traditional principle of span of control, or management, that managers should have only four or five persons reporting to them. This is what makes waste and bureaucracy. All my subordinates are good people and know what they are doing. All can reach me readily with their problems when they have them. All feel close to the top because they are close to the top. Moreover, I want to know firsthand how every person is doing and to detect any weaknesses or errors as soon as possible. Furthermore, if a store manager at Sears, Roebuck can have twenty-five to thirty persons reporting to him, I ought to be able to handle nineteen. In addition, too few reporting to a manager doesn't give him enough to do, and I assume that you hired me to give the company my full time."

1 How would you respond to Mr. Richman's arguments?
2 If you were a member of the board of directors, what would you suggest that Mr. Richman do?

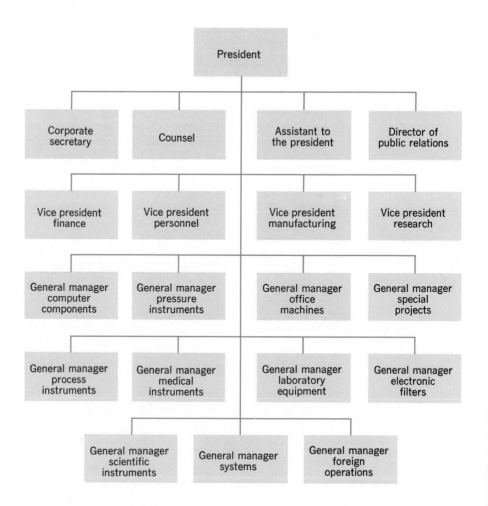

3 Ready-Fit Clothing Company

"I will have no organization charts or position descriptions of any kind in this company," declared Henry Shoup, president and founder of the Ready-Fit Clothing Company, manufacturer of men's ready-to-wear suits and sport jackets. "We are a successful and fast-growing company where I want all our managers and employees to feel that they are members of a team. Organization charts and job descriptions have a way of making people feel that they own a position—a box on a chart—and want to keep it to themselves. I will have none of that! We grew from a small company doing $100,000 per year in sales to a company now selling more than $5 million because we all pulled together and came up with good designs and low costs. We are no General Motors with its complicated organization chart, and I never want us to be."

In discussing his boss's opinion of organization charts and position descriptions at lunch one day, John Hoffman, company controller, strongly defended the president, making the point that true teamwork is essential to success. Anne Luden, head of manufacturing, declared that the president's attitude was the "silliest thing" she had ever heard of. "As a matter of fact," Ms. Luden said, "I could not run my shop without an organization chart and position descriptions and I do have them hidden in my desk where Henry Shoup never sees them."

1 What do you think of Henry Shoup's position?
2 Why do you feel that Anne Luden believed that she must have a chart and position descriptions? Do you agree with her?
3 Assuming that most of the company did not have organization charts or position descriptions, what would you expect might be happening with the relationships of people working in the company?

4 Universal Food Products Company

Sylvia Owen, president of the Universal Food Products Company, was tired of being the only one in the company actually responsible for profits. While she had good vice presidents in charge of finance, sales, advertising, manufacturing, purchasing, and product research, she realized she could not hold any of them responsible for company profits, as much as she would like to. She often found it difficult even to hold them responsible for the contribution of their various areas to company profits. The sales vice president, for example, had rather reasonably complained that he could not be fully responsible for sales when the advertising was ineffective, when the products customer stores wanted were not readily available from manufacturing, or when he did not have the new products he needed to meet competition. Likewise, the manufacturing vice president had some justification when he made the point that he could not hold costs down and still be able to produce short runs so as to fill orders on short notice; moreover, financial controls would not allow the company to carry a large inventory of everything.

Ms. Owen had considered breaking the company down into six or seven segments by setting up product divisions with a manager over each with profit responsibility. But she found that this would not be feasible or economical since many of the company's branded food products were produced on the same factory equipment and used the same raw materials, and a salesperson calling on a store or supermarket could far more economically handle a number of related products than one or a few.

Consequently, Ms. Owen came to the conclusion that the best thing to do was to set up six product managers reporting to a product marketing manager. Each product manager would be given responsibility for one or a few products and would oversee, for each product, all aspects of product research, manufacturing, advertising, and sales, thereby becoming the person responsible for the performance and profits of the products.

Ms. Owen realized that she could not give these product managers actual line authority over the various operating departments of the company since that would cause each vice president and his or her department to report to six product managers and the product marketing manager, as well as the president. She was concerned with this problem, but knew that some of the most successful larger companies in the world had used the product manager system. Moreover, one of her friends on a university faculty had told her that she must expect some lack of clearness and some confusion in any organization and that this might not be bad since it forced people to work together as teams.

Ms. Owen resolved to put in the product manager system as outlined and hoped for the best. But she wondered how she could avoid the problem of confusion in reporting relationships.

1   Do you agree with Ms. Owen's program? Would you have done it differently?
2   Exactly what would you do to avoid any confusion in this organization?

5 Decentralization at American Business Computers and Equipment Company

Because of its excellent new products, imaginative marketing, and fine service to company customers, the American Business Computers and Equipment Company grew to be a leader in its field, with sales over $1 billion annually, high profit margins, and continually rising stock prices. It became one of the favorites of investors, who enjoyed its fast growth rate and high profits. But it soon became apparent to the president that the organization structure, which had served the company so well, no longer fitted the company's needs.

For years the company had been organized along functional lines, with vice presidents in charge of finance, marketing, production, personnel, purchasing, engineering, and research and development. In its growth, the company had expanded its product lines beyond business computers to include electric typewriters, photocopying machines, moving picture cameras and projectors, computer controls for machine tools, and electronic accounting machines. As time went on, concern had arisen that its organization structure did not provide for profit responsibility below the office of the president, did not appear to fit the far-flung nature of the business now being conducted in many foreign countries, and seemed to accentuate the "walls" impeding effective coordination between the functional departments of marketing, production, and engineering; there seemed to be too many decisions that could not be made at any level lower than the president's office.

As a result, the president decentralized the company into fifteen independent domestic and foreign divisions, each with complete profit responsibility. However, after this reorganization was in effect, he began to feel that the divisions were not adequately controlled. There developed considerable duplication in purchasing and personnel functions, each division manager ran his or her operations without regard to company policies and strategies, and it became apparent to the president that the company was disintegrating into a number of independent parts.

Having seen several large companies get into trouble when a division manager made mistakes and the division suffered large losses, the president concluded that he had gone too far with decentralization. As a result, he withdrew some of the authority delegations to the division managers and required them to get top corporate management approval on such important matters as (1) any capital expenditures over $10,000, (2) the introduction of any new products, (3) marketing and pricing strategies and policies, (4) plant expansion, and (5) changes in personnel policies.

The division general managers were understandably unhappy when they saw some of their independence taken away from them. They openly complained that the company was on a "yo-yo" course, first decentralizing and then centralizing. The president, worried about this problem, calls you in as a consultant to advise him what to do.

1 In your opinion, what did the president do wrong when he set up the fifteen independent divisions?
2 Do you agree that what the president did to regain control was correct?
3 What would you have done under the circumstances?

6 ABC Airlines

The president of ABC Airlines, seeing that costs were getting out of control as the company grew, brought in as an assistant a brilliant young man who was a certified public accountant. He was told the nature of the company's problem of rising costs and asked for his help in solving the problem.

The new assistant gathered a staff of high-quality industrial engineers, financial analysts, and recent top graduates from one of the nation's best-known graduate schools of business administration. After laying out the company's problem, he assigned them to investigate cost problems and management methods in the airline's operations, maintenance, engineering, and sales departments. After a number of studies, the president's assistant found many sources of inefficiency in the various departments and initiated a number of changes in operating practices. In addition, he made many reports to the president outlining in detail the inefficiencies his staff had found and the measures being taken to correct them. These reports also showed, with ample supporting detail, the millions of dollars which his actions were saving the company.

In the midst of these cost-savings programs, the vice presidents in charge of operations, maintenance, engineering, and sales descended on the president and insisted that the assistant be discharged.

1 Why should the assistant who was doing so well be so much resented by the vice presidents? What went wrong?
2 Assuming that the findings of the assistant and his staff were accurate, what should have been done by the president, the assistant, the vice presidents, and others to make these findings useful?

7 The Miracle Products Company

Adam Stonebridge inherited from his father a small regional household cleansing products company. Through seeing that the three large companies in the field could not compete for quality products on a price basis because of their high advertising and promotional costs and by his extraordinary talent in setting up an imaginative sales program, Mr. Stonebridge succeeded in profitably developing the company's sales from $2 million to $20 million per year from 1957 to 1965. Because of the attractiveness of his shares to investors and their high market price, he was then able to acquire a number of smaller companies throughout the country so that by 1973, his company grew to $80 million of sales with six plants, a national sales organization, and approximately 2500 employees.

Throughout the company's growth, Mr. Stonebridge found it difficult to delegate authority. Following the pattern adopted when the company was much smaller, Mr. Stonebridge continued to make all final decisions on new products, advertising, pricing, sales plans and organization, hiring of people, operating budgets, production plans, capital expenditures, purchase orders above $1000, credits given to stores, union agreements, production plans, and many other matters. As the controller, who had been with the company for many years, said to a new executive who asked what the company's policy was in a given area: "We don't need any policies here; whenever we want to know what to decide, we ask Adam."

Long before the company grew to its present size, the key executives—vice presidents, plant managers, sales managers—became frustrated by bottlenecks in the president's office. They finally approached one of the outside directors whom they trusted and knew to be a close friend of the president and asked his aid in solving the problem.

When the director investigated their complaints, he found them to be justified. He also found the president to be receptive to the idea of delegation, knowledgeable in the principles of delegation, and aware of the importance of delegating. He finally came to the conclusion that the president's unwillingness to delegate was due to a justifiable fear of losing control over the company's operations.

1 What would you do in order to get Mr. Stonebridge to delegate authority?
2 Exactly what kinds of authority would you suggest be delegated?

8 Agricultural Fertilizer Division of the Northern Chemical Corporation

At the end of a busy day, a group of middle-level managers of the Agricultural Fertilizer Division of the Northern Chemical Corporation gathered together to reflect on their problems. The headquarters of Northern Chemical had recently set up a central data processing department in Houston where all the corporation's data processing would be done for its various divisions located over the entire United States. At that time, the data processing equipment of every division had been taken away from it, each division headquarters office was given a terminal connected to Houston, and each division was required to get any report processing it needed from the Houston facility.

The headquarters of the Agricultural Fertilizer Division was located in Sacramento, California. This division had long concentrated on developing and selling fertilizers to the large agricultural growers in the West and on distributing its garden and plant fertilizers to stores throughout the country. In doing so, it had been very successful, with sales growing rapidly and profits even faster. But the line managers of the division were quite unhappy about not being able to have their own computer facilities to give them the analyses and reports they needed.

Barbara Jacobs, production planning and control supervisor, was particularly disturbed about this move to centralize data processing. "There is no way," said Ms. Jacobs, "that I can plan our production, especially with our many products and customers and the demands of our large growers for good service, if Houston runs our programs. They do not always have the data needed in their data bank, and, by the time I get it worked out with them, I have lost much valuable time."

Barry Hill, district sales manager for northern California, was even unhappier. He pointed out that he often needed to run productivity and profitability studies for large growers and he could not do that unless the division had a computer operation in its own offices in Sacramento. "These large growers will never understand why I cannot make these analyses for them quickly and will never understand why they must be made in Houston; they will soon tell me that there are other companies that can serve their needs," moaned Mr. Hill.

"You do have a problem," said Mona Fredericks, head of statistical analyses and reports in the division controller's office, "but yours is a small one compared with mine. I have to get many special and regular reports to headquarters, to the division manager, and to all you people in sales, market research, product development, and production. You always want them right now and in the form you can use most easily. How can I do that for you now?"

The frustration reached its peak when Joe Morey, cost control supervisor, startled the group by saying: "Did you know that all our departments in the division are being charged fees each month for Houston's services and that these are higher than when we each had our own little computer system?"

1 Do you agree that these people had a serious problem?
2 If you were one of them, what would you do about it?
3 If you were to look at this as a purely organization problem, what does it indicate?

The management consultant was lunching with Allen Murray, the president of American Aircraft Corporation. She did this quite often, largely in order to facilitate communication between them.

"This just isn't my day," she told the president. "For instance, I was out in the factory an hour ago. I happened to run into the plant manager, so I asked him, 'Why do you have that conference room filled with people every morning?' 'Well,' the plant manager replied, 'the people in there, some twenty-two of them, represent assembly, production control, purchasing, personnel, quality control, shipping, and accounting. They meet each day for 3 hours. They iron out the problems we have in coordinating effort around here. It is effective as a means of maintaining our shipping schedule.

"Then," she continued, "just as I reached the administration building, I met the sales manager. He really looked wrung out like a rag. He told me that the weekly Tuesday meeting of department managers had just concluded. It appears that it was my friend's turn to be at the center of the stage explaining the performance reports of his department. Every week his division manager spends a staff meeting given over to reviewing the performance of one of the departments. My friend did say with a spark of revenge that next week it will be the turn of engineering."

"I don't see why you are depressed by these events," Mr. Murray remarked.

"Well, it is just this way. I think that these techniques of communication are all wrong. They are expensive, they tend to expose individual managers to criticism before their associates, and they create the wrong circumstances for corrective action. There are other and better means of control. It seems managers agree with theory but never let it influence their practices."

1   Was the consultant right in being depressed about what he had found?
2   What do you believe was wrong with the methods of communication being used?
3   What would you have done to solve the communications matter without having so many long staff meetings?

10 Staff and Service Domination of Line Operations

Several members of an American Management Association conference were discussing informally the tendency of staff and service departments to dominate line operations.

"I remember one case," said Henry Lorenz, a chief of audit in one of the Internal Revenue districts, "where many complaints from line managers were registered concerning the autocratic way the facilities and financial management people handled requests. In our business we had to make the annual fiscal budget some 2 years before it became operable. I'm afraid we did not anticipate our needs for equipment very well, perhaps because we thought no one could see that far ahead. Anyway, some of us would become distraught when the facilities department turned down our requests with the remark, 'Why didn't you put that in your budget request?' At first it seemed to be rather high-handed that a service group could deny a request by a line manager. Then we finally figured out that we could get most of the things we really needed if we got them approved in the budget."

"We had a different problem in our company," said George Marshall, engineering director for an aerospace company. "We really try to make plans in a democratic fashion for the following year's operation. We start early, have several reviews at group level, and eventually acquire a quite firm grasp on next year's expense, capital, and work-force budgets. I notice that in allocating indirect labor and G&A (general and administration) money to the divisions, our group executive uses ratios provided by the controller or the vice president for administration. This never sits well with us line managers, and we have often chided the group chief about using rules of thumb rather than business sense. I never get very far in my protests, however, because the group executive always says, 'Give me a better guide and I'll use it.' I have never been able to devise a substitute."

"In our business we are concerned about the arbitrary decisions of service departments," said Helen Lester, marketing director, Argon Manufacturing Corp. "For instance, their charges to our department are outrageous. I can get outside service for half the price. When these people submit a budget they seem to look at last year's figures, the profit projection for next year, and add 10 percent. Then they palm off a lot of services we don't want. Personnel is particularly effective in this game. Maintenance has a monopoly on service, so we get it when it suits them, not us."

Other participants added their experiences to the general topic. Finally someone remarked, "These examples do make the picture quite bleak. But I would suggest that we still have need of service and staff departments. The salient issue would appear to be how we can use them efficiently. Lorenz appears to have solved his problem. The rest of us have not. Can we generalize an effective approach?"

1 What is the basic problem being discussed? What is the issue that needs solution?

2 How do you suggest that this problem be solved?

4 Staffing

Every enterprise should be vitally concerned about the quality of its people, especially its managers. The function of staffing has to do with filling the roles within an organization structure in such a way as to ensure that an enterprise can be competently operated both for the present and the future. Staffing must be regarded as a system, a subsystem of the whole system of managing, which includes the interrelated processes of managerial appraisal, inventorying, selection, and development.

Primary attention is given in this book to the staffing of managerial personnel. This is not meant to overlook the staffing problems of the first-level supervisors who are responsible for nonmanagerial personnel; but this subject, well treated in many personnel management books, is not specifically dealt with here.

Chapter 18 examines the nature and logic of the staffing task, emphasizing the importance of a systems approach. To furnish a background for the major aspects of staffing, attention is paid to what it means to be a manager, to the rewards of being a manager, to the external and internal situational factors affecting staffing, and to the policies of promotion from within versus open competition.

In Chapter 19, the major problems of selection of managers are treated and the important aspects of a systems approach to selection are discussed. Special attention is given to the analysis of skills and personal characteristics desired of managers and to approaches to evaluating managerial positions. Because of the great importance attached to accurate selection, the authors discuss the problem of matching job requirements with needed qualifications and analyze various techniques and approaches for accomplishing this. They point out that even with great effort and attention given to ensure accurate selection of managers, there are important, almost unavoidable, limitations. They also discuss the importance and nature of orienting new managers to their positions, an activity which they regard as a vital part of the selection process.

In Chapter 20, appraisal of managers is analyzed. After explaining the deficiencies of traditional appraisal methods, the authors suggest what they regard to be the most promising means of appraising, keeping in mind what they consider the specific qualities that should be measured when evaluating managers. Their program has two major parts. One is the evaluation of performance of managers against their ability to set and achieve verifiable objectives. In the second part of the program, managers are appraised *as managers* by utilizing as standards the major principles of management. It is the authors' view that managers must know not only how to achieve goals but also how to manage effectively. The element of chance, or even a favorable situation, may produce successful perform- ance for a time, but effective managing is the best assurance of continuing success.

In Chapter 21, the important area of manager development and training, as well as the broader subject of organization development, is explained, and the various techniques used in organization and manager development are described. This is followed by discussion of the major behavioral approaches to manager training, the various types of forma- lized training programs, and an operational-management approach to training. Finally, special attention is given to the techniques and ap- proaches of organization development.

chapter 18

Nature and Purpose of Staffing

MAJOR CHAPTER OBJECTIVES

1. To recognize the importance of staffing.
2. To summarize what it means to be a manager.
3. To point out the rewards of managing.
4. To describe the logic and importance of the systems approach to staffing.
5. To identify external and internal situational factors affecting staffing.
6. To analyze the policies of promotion from within and open competition.
7. To explain the nature and use of the management inventory as a staffing tool.

The managerial function of staffing involves effective recruitment, selection, placement, appraisal, and development of people to occupy the roles in the organization structure. Staffing is closely related, therefore, to organizing, that is, to the setting up of intentional structures of roles and positions. Many writers on management theory do in fact discuss staffing as a phase of organizing.

The authors of this text, however, have separated staffing as a managerial function, for several reasons. First, the staffing of organizational roles includes knowledge and approaches not usually recognized by practicing managers, who often think of organizing as just setting up a structure of roles and give little attention to filling these roles. Second, making staffing a separate function allows even greater emphasis to be given to the human element in selection, appraisal, and manager development. After all, people are essential to the effectiveness of an enterprise. Third, an important body of knowledge and experience has been developed in the area of staffing. The fourth reason for separating staffing from organizing is that managers often overlook the fact that staffing is their responsibility—not that of the personnel department. To be sure, this department provides valuable assistance, but in the final analysis it is the job of managers to fill the positions and keep them filled with qualified people.

This chapter provides an overview of the staffing function. The importance of, and the need for, good managers are highlighted; then, different views about the nature of the managerial role are introduced. Most important, the systems approach to staffing is suggested. Specifically, a model is shown which not only identifies the important aspects of staffing (discussed in the various chapters of this part), but also indicates the relationship of staffing to the other managerial functions of planning, organizing, leading, and controlling. Furthermore, since staffing is not carried out in a vacuum, the authors show how it is related to the enterprise environment and to various external factors. Finally, the authors emphasize that while managing is not an easy task, it may provide gratifying rewards for those who do it well.

THE IMPORTANCE OF STAFFING

Staffing involves people. The manager's functions of planning, organizing, and controlling can be viewed as essentially objective tasks which may even have some important mechanistic features. On the other hand, the functions of staffing and leading are concerned almost exclusively with people. Naturally this introduces complexities that do not yield so well to the efficacy of logic. Thus uncertainties in the selection and direction of people may lead to frustration of managers who know the importance of staffing and, at the same time, recognize the limitations of the tools available for carrying out this function effectively.

Few executives would argue with the fact that people are vital for the effective operation of a company. Yet the "human assets" are virtually never shown on the balance sheet as a distinct category, although a great deal of money is invested in the recruitment, selection, and training of people. It is for this reason that Rensis Likert and his colleagues have suggested that we maintain accounts of the value of human assets. They refer to this process as "human resource accounting."[1] There are problems, however, with their approach.[2] In fact, there is conflict among managerial experts, between the proponents of human resource accounting and the financial people who have to develop the system for measuring the human assets.[3] What is important here is the recognition that staffing, which involves people, is a crucial function of managers and one that may well determine the success or failure of the enterprise. It is not surprising, then, that executives of companies become concerned and begin to face up to one of their toughest challenges: human resource planning.[4]

THE FUTURE SUPPLY OF GOOD MANAGERS

There are conflicting views about the future supply of managers. Some writers suggest that there is and will continue to be a shortage of managers, while others foresee a coming oversupply of executives. If the latter view is correct, it suggests that individuals aspiring to management positions need to be even better prepared in order to compete for the available jobs. Moreover, the rapid rate of change places great pressure on managers and calls for establishing a support system that will help them adapt to the fast-changing environment.[5]

Why a Shortage of Managers

A number of factors suggest a future shortage of managers. First, there has been a great expansion of enterprises since World War II. This has been true for business, government, and service companies. Second, the increasing complexity of the task of managing requires managers who are better educated than those of the past. Third, some people who have the

---

[1] R. Likert, *The Human Organization: Its Management and Value* (New York: McGraw-Hill Book Company, 1967), chap. 9.

[2] For a detailed discussion of the problems see P. H. Mirvis and B. A. Macy, "Human Resource Accounting: A Measurement Perspective," *The Academy of Management Review*, vol. 1, no. 2, pp. 74–83 (April 1976).

[3] J. D. Powell, H. A. Sciullo, and G. Mattson, "Human Resource Accounting: Why the Delay?" *Journal of Management*, vol. 2, no. 2, pp. 25–31 (Fall 1976).

[4] "Big Push in Manpower Planning," *Dun's Review*, vol. 104, no. 5, pp. 103, 106–107 (November 1974).

[5] F. J. Staszak and N. J. Mathys, "Organization Gap: Implications for Manpower Planning," *California Management Review*, vol. 17, no. 3, pp. 32–38 (Spring 1975).

intellectual ability and training may not have the motivation to become managers. John B. Miner found in his studies (1) a more negative attitude toward authority, (2) a decrease in the desire to compete, (3) less-assertive behavioral patterns, and (4) a declining sense of responsibility.[6] Whether these findings will continue to be valid over a period of time remains to be seen. At any rate, Miner recommended that special educational efforts must be undertaken if what he calls "the will to manage" is to be increased.

Why There Could Be an Oversupply of Managers

Those who predict an oversupply of young managers cite the baby boom in the United States in the late 1940s and 1950s as the cause.[7] Thus, John W. Buckley of the Graduate School of Management at the University of California at Los Angeles foresees a surplus of potential managers, especially among those with undergraduate degrees. The situation of those with graduate degrees is also noteworthy. In 1977, an estimated 32,000 Master of Business Administration degrees were granted; this number is expected to go above 60,000 in 1985. On the other hand, due to the increased number of business graduates, in the immediate future companies may find themselves with many young managers who have insufficient managerial experience to fill responsible positions. This situation certainly would call for greater emphasis on the development of managerial skills within the firms.

It is, of course, risky to predict the future. For example, an expansion of programs in research and development could create new technologies that would increase the demand for managers. But whichever forecast about the supply of managers will be correct, there almost certainly will be greater demands on individual managers. They will need to be equipped with new knowledge, new skills, and probably even new value systems to cope with the turbulent, ever-changing environment.

WHAT DOES IT MEAN TO BE A MANAGER?

There is no complete agreement about what exactly the job of manager consists of. In fact, the nature of managerial tasks has been studied from several different perspectives.[8] One group of writers, known as the *great man school*, studied successful managers and described their behaviors

[6]J. B. Miner, "The Real Crunch in Managerial Manpower," *Harvard Business Review*, vol. 51, no. 6, pp. 146–158 (November–December 1973); J. B. Miner, "Implications of Managerial Talent Projections for Management Education," *The Academy of Management Review*, vol. 2, no. 3, pp. 412–420 (July 1977).

[7]T. J. Murray, "The Coming Glut in Executives," *Dun's Review*, vol. 109, no. 5, pp. 64–65, 69 (May 1977).

[8]For a comprehensive review see H. Mintzberg, *The Nature of Managerial Work* (New York: Harper & Row, Publishers, Incorporated, 1973), chap. 2.

and habits. Although the stories about these people are interesting, the authors usually do not provide an underlying theory to explain the success of their subjects. Another group of writers—primarily economists—focus on the *entrepreneurial* aspects of managing. Their main concern is profit maximization, innovation, risk taking, and similar activities. Yet another group of writers emphasize *decision making*, especially the kinds of decisions that cannot be easily programmed. An additional view of the managerial job draws attention to *leadership*, with an emphasis on particular traits and managerial styles. Closely related to this approach is the discussion about *power and influence*, that is, the leader's control of the environment and subordinates. Other writers focus their attention on the *behavior of leaders* by examining the content of the manager's job. Finally, the approach favored by Mintzberg is based on observing the *work activities* of managers. It is interesting that the extensive research of the literature by Mintzberg resulted in a grouping of management "schools" which is not altogether different from the approaches to management discussed in Chapter 3 of this book.[9]

Managing is not an easy job, nor do managers carry out their activities in a systematic sequence. Mintzberg found through observation of five executives that their work is characterized by brevity, variety, discontinuity, and action orientation. He also found that executives favor oral communication and that they engage in many activities that link the enterprise with its environment.[10]

One fact is unassailable: The nature of managerial work is complex, even more so today than in the past. To bring order into this complexity, the authors have found it useful to organize the key tasks of managers into the five functions of planning, organizing, staffing, leading, and controlling, and these constitute the framework of this book.[11]

REWARDS OF MANAGING

Managing is demanding; it is hard work which seldom is confined to a 40-hour week; it involves stress; it means dealing with conflicts of competing groups and individuals; it requires tough decisions; it also demands coping with uncertainties. So why does any person want to be a manager?

The answer to this question is as complex as the job of managing. Managers are different; they have different needs, desires, and motives.

---

[9]H. Mintzberg, "The Manager's Job: Folklore and Fact," *Harvard Business Review*, vol. 53, no. 4, pp. 49–61 (July–August 1975).
[10]Ibid.
[11]It is also interesting to note that Dow Jones & Company, Inc., in preparing an index for management articles published in *The Wall Street Journal*, adopted a similar framework of planning, organizing, staffing, directing, and controlling for classifying their material on management topics; an environmental section was also included.

The topic of motivation will be discussed in detail in Chapter 23. The concern here is with some of the general rewards of managing. Since managerial candidates differ widely in age, economic position, and level of maturity, they want many things, but these usually include opportunity, income, and power.

First, a main concern of managerial candidates is often an opportunity for a progressive career that provides depth and breadth of managerial experience. Related to this is the challenge found in meaningful work. Managers want to feel that they make a contribution to the aims of an enterprise.

Second, managers find the financial rewards associated with the position attractive. They want to, and should, be rewarded for their contributions. Money is not the only inducement for managers, but one cannot overlook the fact that money represents many things, including recognition.

The third reward for managing is power. There are different kinds of power, including coercive power (the power to force or punish), reward power (the power to hand out rewards), expert power (the power that comes from being regarded as an expert), referent power (follower identifies with the leader), and the legitimate power that comes from the authority associated with the position in the organizational hierarchy.

Managing offers many rewards, but also frustration and stress. An individual aspiring to a managerial position should evaluate the pros and cons of managing before pursuing this career. A proper fit between individual needs and demands of the task will benefit both—the individual and the enterprise. Managers will gain by getting satisfaction and a feeling of competence from their work, and enterprises will have a well-motivated work force.

THE SYSTEMS APPROACH TO STAFFING—AN OVERVIEW OF THE STAFFING FUNCTION

How the managerial function of staffing relates to the total management system is shown in Figure 18.1.[12] Specifically, "enterprise plans" (discussed in Part 2) become the basis for "organization plans" (Part 3), which are necessary to achieve enterprise objectives. The present and projected organization structure determines the "number and kinds of managers required." These demands for managers are compared with available talent through the "management inventory." Based on this analysis, "external and internal sources" are utilized in the processes of "recruitment, selection, placement, and promotion." Other essential aspects of staffing are "appraisal" and "training and development" of managers.

---

[12]Figure 18.1 is an overview of the staffing function. The variables not discussed in this chapter, but which also focus on staffing, are enclosed with broken lines.

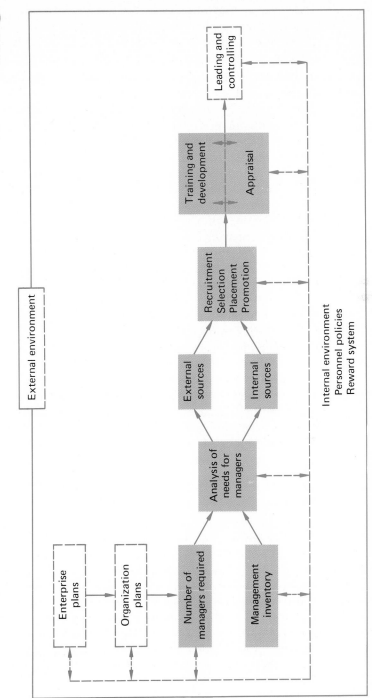

Figure 18.1 Systems approach to staffing.

Staffing, as seen in the model, affects "leading and controlling." For instance, well-trained managers create an environment in which people, working together in groups, can achieve enterprise objectives and at the same time accomplish personal goals. In other words, proper staffing facilitates the function of leading (Part 5). Similarly, selecting quality managers affects controlling by, for example, preventing many undesirable deviations from becoming major problems (Part 6).

The model presents only a static overview of staffing, and many dynamic factors must also be taken into account. Among these are the ages of people in the different managerial positions, the increase or decrease in the number of managerial positions, and the rate at which managers leave the enterprise through retirement or for other reasons.[13]

Staffing requires an open-system approach. It is carried out within the enterprise, which, in turn, is linked to the external environment. Therefore, *internal* factors of the firm—such as personnel policies, the organizational climate, and the reward system—must be taken into account. Clearly, without adequate rewards it is impossible to attract and keep quality managers. The *external* environment cannot be ignored either; high technology demands well-trained, well-educated, and highly skilled managers. Inability to meet the demand for such managers may well prevent an enterprise from growing at a desired rate.

It is evident from all this that staffing is a complex process. But this does not mean that it cannot be systematic. On the contrary, the authors view staffing as a systematic way of managing human resources.

The model shown in Figure 18.1 presents the macroview of staffing.[14] Some of the elements in the model have been discussed in earlier chapters. Here we will discuss them as they relate specifically to the staffing function. At the same time, we will take a closer look at several key staffing activities.

Enterprise Plans as the Basis of Staffing

At the basis of staffing are enterprise plans which are formulated in the planning process. In planning, opportunities for an enterprise are identified and objectives are set based on forecasts and strategy. Alternative courses of action are developed, evaluated, and selected. For example, a favorable market for product line X may be identified. Consequently, a specific market share objective—let us say 5 percent by the end of the year—for the new product line may be considered reasonable. This may be based on the premise that gross national product will grow at 6 percent annually. Alternative product lines are also considered, but based on the data, product line X is selected as having the best prospects for success.

[13]K. Ray, "Managerial Manpower Planning—A Systematic Approach," *Long Range Planning*, vol. 10, no. 2, pp. 21–30 (April 1977).
[14]A more specific discussion of staffing activities—the microview—will be presented in succeeding chapters in this part.

Because the enterprise operates in an uncertain environment, however, contingency plans are also developed. In short, enterprise plans become important considerations for the staffing function; after all, people will have to implement the plans.

Organization Plans Give Key to Staffing Needs

In order to carry out the plans, organizational arrangements must be made. For example, to develop product line X, necessary activities are identified, classified, and grouped. Furthermore, the plan involves delegating necessary authority to managers to perform the activities of developing, producing, distributing, and marketing product line X. Finally, provisions are planned for vertical and horizontal integration of authority and information relationships. To carry out every phase of this program successfully, the organization structure must be filled and maintained with competent managers, and this is the purpose of staffing.

In this connection the question arises of how much time in the future an organization and staffing plan should encompass. Basically, this depends on the degree of flexibility an enterprise has, and the commitment principle. This principle, as will be recalled, covers the time in the future necessary to foresee the fulfillment of commitments involved in a decision made today. If, for instance, an enterprise develops its own managers, as many firms do, fairly long-range plans are required. On the other hand, firms that adhere to a policy of open competition will be more flexible, because they may also fill positions with managers from outside as needs become apparent. Flexibility also varies with the size of the enterprise. In a big company that has many positions, managers can be transferred to departments that have the greatest needs. But even that kind of flexibility, while desirable, does not eliminate the need for long-range human resource planning.

Number of Managers Required Depends on Various Factors

The number of managers needed in an enterprise depends not only upon its size but also upon the complexity of the organization structure, its plans for expansion, and the rate of turnover in managerial personnel. The ratio between the number of managers and the number of employees does not follow any law of proportion. It is possible, by enlarging or contracting the delegation of authority, to modify structures so that the number of managers in a given enterprise will increase or decrease regardless of the size of its operations.

The rate of annual appointments to managerial positions can be determined by a review of past experience and future expectations. Analysis will also reveal the relative importance of age for retirement, vacancies created by ill health, demotions, and separations, and the steady demand of other enterprises for able young subordinates whom the firm has trained but is unable to hold.

Although the need for determining the number of managers required has been stressed here, clearly "number" is only part of the picture. Specifically, the qualifications for individual positions must be identified so that the best-suited managers can be chosen. This kind of detailed analysis of position requirements will be discussed in the next chapter on selection of managers.

Determination of Available Managerial Resources: The Management Inventory

It is common for any business, as well as for most nonbusiness enterprises, to keep an inventory of raw materials and goods on hand to enable it to carry on its operations. It is far less common for enterprises to keep an inventory of available human material, particularly managers, despite the fact that the required number of competent managers is a vital requirement to ensure success. Keeping abreast of the management potential within a firm can be done by the use of an inventory chart, which is simply an organization chart of a unit with all managerial positions indicated and keyed as to the promotability of each incumbent.

Figure 18.2 is a typical inventory chart. At a glance the controller can see where he or she stands with respect to the staffing function. The controller's successor is probably the manager of general accounting, and this person in turn has a successor ready for promotion. Supporting that person in turn is a subordinate who will be ready for promotion in one year, but below that position is one person who does not have potential and two newly hired employees.

The cost accounting manager represents the all-too-frequent case of a person who is acceptable but not promotable. This individual stands in the way of one subordinate who is promotable now. The remaining people in this department represent extremes of nonpromotability and good potential. Overall, the staffing pattern in this department is not satisfactory.

The manager of budget and analysis has considerable development to accomplish before being ready for promotion. There is no immediately promotable successor. And to complicate matters, no further potential exists among the remaining two subordinates.

Contract pricing portends some problems. Its manager is not promotable but there is good potential in the subordinates.

Actions to Be Taken from Inventory Charts

On the basis of an inventory chart, a plan of action can be developed, geared to both the short term and the long run. For the short term, action may be taken to replace an unsatisfactory manager, to begin the training of

Figure 18.2   Manager inventory chart.

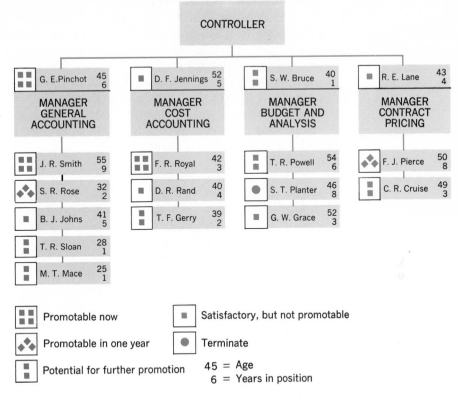

a successor for the next higher level, to transfer managers in order to broaden their experience specifically for their next promotion, or to transfer surplus people, now ready for promotion, to other departments where managerial vacancies exist.

For the long run, age may play as important a part as efficiency. If it is true, as is sometimes asserted, that a manager's most productive period is between the ages of 40 and 60, then it is important to the future welfare of a firm that its managers—especially its top managers—be at varying ages above 40. If they are not scattered along the productive age range, it might happen that in 10 years' time all top managers would be over 60. Such a situation may be avoided by judicious promotion of persons in the right age group. The long-run plan of action for qualified managers needs to be integrated with short-run action. For instance, it is clearly inadvisable in the short run to identify a backup person (successor) who is the same age as his or her immediate superior, for they will both grow old together. It may be clearly advantageous to name as immediate successor a person even older than the incumbent and to begin to train as ultimate successor a third person a number of years younger. This arrangement will satisfy the short-run requirements for a trained successor in the person of the older employee, and the long-run needs in the person of the trainee.

One question that the manager inventory chart does not answer is, Promotable to what? It is not enough to become aware that a person is promotable. Provision needs to be made for actualization of promotion. One may take the position that, with respect to area of specialization, the promotable simply remains there until an opening occurs. Is one really promotable if he or she happens to be listed in this way by the production control manager and an opening occurs for a manager of industrial engineering or general superintendent? In the case of Figure 18.2, is J. R. Smith in general accounting promotable to manager of budget and analysis?

This common difficulty of the promotion process can scarcely ever be solved in the short run. It is essential for the top managers of every enterprise to insist that young people with managerial potential be identified in the very early years of their employment and be given real opportunities to broaden their experience through lateral assignments. Breadth of experience is essential during the years *prior to* succession to upper managerial positions. From a practical point of view, at lower levels of management such experience might be provided on an intradivisional, but not interdivisional, basis. This practice will maintain the integrity of the divisional staffing plan and permit the promotable manager to be an active candidate for interdepartmental openings. Interdivisional training for promotable candidates for upper-level management positions is considered in the following chapter.

Another difficulty encountered in large enterprises is the hoarding of promotable people by their immediate superiors. Quite naturally, these managers dislike depriving themselves of able subordinates. But the interests of the enterprise must be controlling. Therefore, upper-level managers must carefully and constantly watch over the manager inventory.

Charts Force Attention to Staffing

By systematically examining their staffing needs, managers can give this often-neglected function adequate attention. They will be alert to the requirements for potential managers to be at specific levels of preparation at a given time, and they will funnel off to other departments excess subordinates before these become disenchanted with their prospects and leave the organization.

By doing this, managers will be serving the interests of their subordinates, who want to know their prospects and their development needs so that they can determine whether their best interests lie in staying with the organization or whether they should look for opportunities elsewhere. They can now be answered honestly by their superiors, who have a moral responsibility to deal candidly with subordinates. Superiors should recognize that while the highest good for the enterprise arises from recognition of the career interests and abilities of subordinates, what is good for the enterprise may not necessarily be desired by the individual.

Analysis of Needs for Managers: External and Internal Sources

As shown in Figure 18.1, the need for managers is determined by enterprise and organization plans and, more specifically, by an analysis of the number of managers required and the number of managers available, as identified through the management inventory. These data give rise to four demand and supply situations, each requiring a different emphasis in personnel actions. This is illustrated in the matrix shown as Figure 18.3.

With a "high supply" of managers and a "high demand," the focus will be on selection, placement, and promotion. Consequently, particular efforts are made to most effectively match the available managers with enterprise needs.

A "low supply" of managers and a "high demand" requires a different emphasis. If the company favors internal promotions—and most alertly managed firms do—special emphasis would be placed on training and development to enlarge and improve the pool of managers. But this takes time, and planning far in advance of actual needs is essential. Staffing should be based on open competition for available jobs, and managers from outside the firm should also be considered. Thus recruitment would be another option. In a situation with a high demand for managers within the enterprise, chances are that there is also a general demand for managers in the external environment. It is therefore crucial

		Supply of managers	
		High	Low
Demand for managers	High	Selection Placement Promotion	INTERNAL Training and development Compensation EXTERNAL Recruitment
	Low	Change in company plans Outplacement Layoffs Demotions Early retirement	Training and development if change in demand is expected in the future

Figure 18.3 Personnel actions based on manager supply and demand within the enterprise.

that compensation be competitive. This is important for managers already employed by the enterprise so that they do not leave the firm, and it is also essential for attracting managers through the recruitment process.

A company with a "high supply" of managers and a "low demand" has several alternatives available. Either the firm can change plans to take advantage of the managerial assets, or it may resort to replacement or "outplacement" (a conscious attempt to help managers find and select other suitable employment),[15] layoffs, demotions, or early retirements.

An enterprise with a "low supply" of managers and a "low demand" should be giving special attention to enterprise plans because this indicates a degree of stagnation in growth of the firm. Since developing managers is a long process, if there are prospects of growth and changes in demand for managers in the future, the company should start developing managers early.

Recruitment, Selection, Placement, and Promotion

After the need for managerial personnel has been determined, a number of candidates may have to be recruited. This involves attracting qualified managerial candidates to fill organizational roles. From these, managers or potential managers are selected; this is the process of choosing from among the candidates the most suitable ones. The aim is to place people in positions where they can utilize their personal strengths and, perhaps, overcome their weaknesses by getting experience or training in those skills in which they need improvement. Finally, placing a manager into a new position within the enterprise often results in a promotion, which normally involves more responsibility. Since recruitment, selection, placement, and promotion are complex processes, they will be discussed in greater detail in the next chapter.

Appraising Managers

Managerial appraisal is closely related to selection, placement, and promotion. One could even argue that appraisal should logically be placed before these other activities. It is true that appraisal serves as a basis for identifying persons within the enterprise who are ready for promotion. On the other hand, the candidates from outside the firm have first to be recruited, selected, and placed before their performance can be appraised. For this reason, managerial selection precedes appraisal in the model. But there is no doubt that appraisal is closely linked to selection,

---

[15]This fairly recent concept has been discussed by J. L. Mendleson, "Does Your Company Need Outplacement?" *Society for Advancement of Management Advanced Management Journal*, vol. 40, no. 1, pp. 4–12 (Winter 1975); J. L. Mendleson, "What's 'Fair' Treatment for Terminated Employees?" *Supervisory Management*, vol. 19, no. 11, pp. 25–34 (November 1974).

placement, and promotion and is so indicated by the feedback arrows in Figure 18.1.

Appraisal is a necessity in organizational life. Superiors need to know about the quality of performance of their subordinates. Subordinates also want to know where they stand. Yet some of the traditional performance appraisals which focus on personality traits do not give a clear answer to the question, How well am I doing? For this reason, a new approach is suggested in Chapter 20. The focus is on two sets of criteria: (1) performance as managers—how well they carry out the managerial functions and activities, and (2) performance in accomplishing goals and plans.

Training and Development

Managerial appraisal should also be used as the basis for identifying training and development needs. In the chapter on managers and organization development, a systematic approach will be introduced which provides for self-development and the utilization of managers' strengths and potentials, with emphasis on the integration of managerial needs and enterprise demands.

Leading and Controlling

Throughout the book, the systems approach to managing has been advocated. Consequently, the last part in the model in Figure 18.1 shows that the activities in the staffing function must not be viewed in isolation; rather, they are related to leading (discussed in Part 5) and controlling (Part 6 in this book). For example, well-selected and well-trained managers provide good leadership and create an environment in which people are motivated and communicate effectively. Likewise, controlling is enhanced by effective staffing. Specifically, what better control is there than direct control? This means that the higher the quality of selected managers and their subordinates, the lower the need for correcting undesirable deviations from performance standards.

SITUATIONAL FACTORS AFFECTING STAFFING

The actual process of staffing shown in Figure 18.1 is affected by many environmental factors. Specifically, external factors include the level of education, the prevailing attitudes in society (such as the attitude toward work), the many laws and regulations that directly affect staffing, economic conditions, and the supply of and the demand for managers outside the enterprise.

But there are also many internal factors that affect staffing. They include, for example, organizational goals, tasks, technology, organization structure, the kinds of people employed by the enterprise, the demand for and the supply of managers within the enterprise, the reward system, and various kinds of policies. Some organizations are highly structured; others are not. For some positions—such as the position of a sales manager—skill in human relations may be of vital importance, while the same skill may be less critical for a research scientist working fairly independently in the research laboratory. Effective staffing, then, requires recognition of many external and internal situational factors, but the focus will be on those that have a particular relevance for staffing.

The External Environment Affects Staffing

The factors in the external environment, discussed particularly in Chapter 5 on comparative management, do affect staffing to varying degrees. As will be recalled, these influences were grouped into educational, sociocultural, legal-political, and economic constraints, or opportunities. For example, the high technology used in many industries requires extensive and intensive education. Similarly, managers in our particular sociocultural environment generally do not accept orders blindly; they want to become active participants in the decision-making process. Furthermore, now and in the future, managers will have to be more oriented toward the public, responding to their legitimate needs and adhering to high ethical standards. Legal and political constraints require firms to follow laws and guidelines issued by various levels of government. The economic environment—including the competitive situation—determines the external supply of, and demand for, managers.

Finally, one must look beyond the immediate external environment and recognize the worldwide influences brought about primarily by advanced communication technology and by the existence of multinational corporations. In the future, it will not be unusual for large international firms to have top management teams composed of managers of many different nationalities. Thus the concept of the external environment that influences staffing is becoming broader and for many firms already has a worldwide scope.

The Internal Environment Affects Staffing

The internal factors selected for this discussion concern the staffing of managerial positions with personnel from within the firm as well as from the outside, determining the responsibility for staffing, and the need for top management support to overcome resistance to change.

Promotion from within   Originally, promotion from within implied that workers proceeded into front-line supervisory positions and then upward through the organizational structure. Thus, a firm was pictured as receiving a flow of nonmanagerial employees from which future managers emerged. As used to be said in the railroad industry, "When a president retires or dies, we hire a new office boy."

So long as the matter is considered in general terms, there is little question that employees overwhelmingly favor a policy of promotion from within. The banning of outsiders places limits on competition for positions and gives employees of a firm an established monopoly on managerial openings. Employees come to doubt the wisdom of the policy, however, when they are confronted with a specific case of selection of one of their own for promotion. This feeling is present at all levels of the organization, largely because of rivalry for promotion or jealousy. The difficulty becomes most evident when selecting a general officer from among the sales, production, finance, or engineering managers. Managers are often inclined to choose the easy way and select an outsider.

Many companies advocate promotion from within. For example, William P. Given, when president of the American Brake Shoe Company, wrote, "It is our policy to give our own people the benefit of advancement as openings occur. We believe that unless we have no one who can possibly qualify it is not fair to our people to hire an outsider." Even more emphatic is the position taken by Sears, Roebuck and Company. In a booklet given to prospective employees is the statement, "At Sears the policy of 'promotion from within' is not just a phrase or slogan. It is a fact, insured by specific administrative measures to make sure that it happens." Similarly, Mobil Oil Company states that its policy is to fill all jobs, whenever possible, from within; and Procter & Gamble asserts that it adheres strictly to its policy of promotion from within.

Such statements on the internal source of managerial candidates probably represent the general and official attitude of most corporate executives. There can be little question that they place heavy emphasis on the policy for the purpose of encouraging prospective managerial candidates to accept employment, with the view of long-run commitment and of bolstering employee morale. It is not always clear whether these same firms give similar assurance to their middle and top functional executives. The saving phrase "whenever possible" is quite sufficient to provide an escape.

Making promotions from the personnel within the enterprise not only has positive values relating to its morale and reputation but also permits taking advantage of the presence of potentially fine managers among its employees. However, even though these positive but unmeasurable values are important, their pursuit should not blind executives to the dangers of either overemphasizing this source or relying upon it exclusively.

The assumption underlying the policy of promotion from within is either that new employees are hired with a view to their managerial potential or that, from among the new and old employees, there will emerge a sufficient number of qualified candidates for promotion. The latter assumption is unsafe for modern enterprise. It is increasingly dangerous as our population becomes differentiated in the degree to which its members seek education, since well-educated persons are more likely than the less well-educated to be the successful candidates for managerial positions.

The assumption that all employees are hired with a view to their managerial potential is contrary to fact. Indeed, most employees are hired for their skills as machinists, electricians, typists, accountants, engineers, or statisticians. Those who are wanted because of such skills are not turned down because they may have low managerial potential.

Another danger presented by an exclusive policy of promoting from within is that it may lead to the selection of persons for promotion who have, perhaps, only imitated their superiors. This is not necessarily a fault, especially if only the best methods, routines, and viewpoints are cultivated; but this is likely to be an unapproachable ideal. The fact is that enterprises often need people from the outside to introduce new ideas and practices. Consequently, there is good reason to avoid a policy of exclusive promotion from within.

On the other hand, a policy of promotion from within may be quite suitable for a very large company such as Sears, Roebuck, Du Pont, or General Motors. Companies like these and large nonbusiness organizations may have so many qualified people for positions that promotion from within actually approaches a condition similar to an open-competition policy. Even in these large companies, however, it may be necessary to go outside, as General Motors did when it hired a vice president to head up its environmental control staff.

The policy of open competition Managers must decide whether the benefits of a policy of promotion from within outweigh its shortcomings. There are clear-cut reasons for implementing the principle of open competition in which vacant positions are open to the best-qualified persons available, whether inside or outside the enterprise. It gives the firm, in the final analysis, the opportunity to secure the services of the best-suited candidates. It counters the shortcomings of an exclusive policy of promotion from within, permits a firm to adopt the best techniques in the recruiting of managers, and motivates the complacent heir apparent. To exchange these advantages for a part-time morale factor allegedly attributed to internal promotion would appear questionable.

Large, diversified firms, even though they follow a policy of promotion from within, can provide a high degree of competition for positions because of their enormous and varied operations. Unfortunately, many of these diversified firms in practice tend to confine selection for promotions to candidates in their own division or department. Consequently, they encounter the same problems associated with promotion from within as do much smaller firms.

A policy of open competition is a much better and more honest means of assuring managerial competence. However, it does put the managers who use it under a special obligation. If morale is to be protected in applying an open-competition policy, the enterprise must have fair and objective methods of appraising and selecting its people. It should do everything possible to help them develop so that they can qualify for promotions.

With these requirements, it would be expected that every manager, in considering an appointment to a vacancy or a new position, would have available a roster of qualified candidates within the entire enterprise. If people know that their qualifications are being considered, if they have been fairly appraised and have been given opportunities for development, they are far less likely to feel a sense of injustice if an opening goes to an outsider. Other things being equal, present employees should be able to compete with outsiders. If a person has the ability for a position, he or she has the considerable advantage of knowing the enterprise, its personnel, history, problems, policies, and objectives. For the superior candidate, the policy of open competition should be a challenge and not a hindrance to advancement.

Selection of key managers from outside   Key managers are the ones who spark a program and carry it to completion. Although these executives may be found at all organizational levels, key managers will most probably be found at or near the top of the organization structure. They provide the tone, imagination, and judgment with which an enterprise attains its objectives. Since subordinate managers tend to reflect the attitudes of their superior, their contribution to a program may often be ascribed to the inspiration of the outstanding personality.

The negative reasons for recruiting managers from the outside have already been suggested; that is, the morale problem of dealing with frustrated, uncooperative managers who have not been selected for promotion. Rather than create such unfavorable conditions, it is not uncommon for an enterprise to recruit a key person from outside, though he or she may not be superior to the internal candidates for the position.

Often there are positive reasons for selecting key executives from outside the enterprise. Outside candidates may be considered superior to the internal contenders. For example, when firms reach a position in their development where the outstanding need is for their energies to be directed vigorously toward the solution of marketing problems, they are likely to turn to the outside. Promotion of insiders may not be advisable, since they have brought the enterprise to its stagnant position. Indeed, this is the situation that faced many firms during the 1960s when key marketing executives were brought in to guide firms through a highly competitive period. For similar reasons, production managers were imported during the early decades of the twentieth century, and engineers have more recently been brought into conspicuous positions with firms in the aerodynamics, electronics, and plastics industries. Here the factor being sought was vision, new ideas, and new applications. And in some time periods, financial executives seemed to be preferred because of their experience with money and controls and with looking at an organization as a total enterprise.

Responsibility for staffing   While responsibility for staffing should rest with every manager at all levels, the ultimate responsibility is with the chief executive officer and the policy-making group of executives. They have the duty of developing policy, assigning its execution to subordinates, and making certain it is being properly carried out. Policy considerations, for example, include decisions about the development of a staffing program, whether to promote from within or to secure managers from the outside, where to seek candidates, which selection procedure to follow, the kind of appraisal program to use, the nature of manager and organization development, and what promotion and retirement policies to follow.

Line managers should certainly request the services of staff members—usually from the personnel department—to assist in recruiting, selecting, placing, promoting, appraising, and training of people. In the final analysis, however, it is the manager's responsibility to fill the positions with the best-qualified persons.

Top management support is crucial to overcoming resistance to effective staffing   The prestige and power of top management are necessary for staffing to be effective. Some managers within the organization will resent losing promising subordinates, even though they can make a greater contribution to the enterprise in a different department. Others will resist changes required by managerial and organizational development efforts. There are also those who may be threatened by imaginative and achievement-oriented subordinates. Still others may not see staffing as a pressing matter and neglect it altogether. To overcome these human tendencies, top management involvement in staffing is necessary.

FOR DISCUSSION

1   What differences do you see between staffing for managers and nonmanagers?
2   What are the different perspectives regarding the nature of the managerial tasks? Which perspective do you find most useful? Explain.
3   What rewards would you expect from becoming a manager? What are some of the negative aspects of managing?
4   Why is the function of staffing so seldom approached logically? Briefly describe the systems approach to staffing. How is staffing related to other managerial functions and activities?

5 List and evaluate external factors affecting staffing. Which ones are most critical today? Explain.

6 What are the key characteristics of a manager inventory chart? Discuss the advantages and limitations of such a chart.

7 What are the dangers and difficulties in applying a policy of "promotion from within"?

8 What is meant by a policy of open competition? Do you favor such a policy? Why? Why not?

9 Do you believe that a manager inventory should be kept confidential? Why, or why not?

chapter 19 Selection of Managers

The quality of managers is one of the most important single determining factors for the continuing success of any organization. It necessarily follows, therefore, that the selection of managers is one of the most critical steps in the entire process of managing. Few would deny that plant, equipment, materials, and people do not make a business any more than airplanes, tanks, ships, and people make an effective military force. One other element is indispensable: effective managers.

Because selection of managers is so important, it is an extremely difficult task. While it may appear to be easier to make proper selections for upper-level positions than for first-level supervisors, since those who have already managed have some kind of track record on which their competence can be assessed, that is not ordinarily the case. The wrong selection at the top levels can be a far more serious mistake. It is likely to take a year before anyone can be certain that upper- or top-level managers are performing well; then more time will probably be needed to decide whether or how to replace them, if necessary. In the meantime, not only are expenses incurred through salaries paid but valuable time is lost in making progress that would have been achieved if a good selection had been made initially.

SYSTEMS APPROACH TO SELECTION OF MANAGERS

Since qualified managers are critical to the success of an enterprise, a systematic approach to selection is essential for determining present and future needs for managerial personnel.

An overview of the systems approach to selection is illustrated in Figure 19.1. The variables that are closely related to selection, but are discussed in other chapters, are marked with broken lines in the model. The "human resource plan," discussed in the previous chapter, or the managerial requirements plan as we may call it, is based on the firm's objectives, forecasts, plans, and strategies. This plan is translated into "position requirements," which are matched with such "individual characteristics" as intelligence, knowledge, skills, attitudes, and experience. To meet organizational requirements, managers "recruit, select, place, and promote" people. This, of course, must be done with due consideration for the "internal environment" (for example, company policies, supply and demand of managers, and the organizational climate), and the "external environment" (laws, regulations, availability of managers). After people have been selected and placed into positions, they must be introduced to the new job. This "orientation" involves learning about the company, its operation, and its social aspects.

The newly placed managers then carry out their managerial and nonmanagerial functions (such as marketing), resulting in "managerial performance," which eventually determines "enterprise performance." Subsequently, managerial performance is "appraised," and managers are

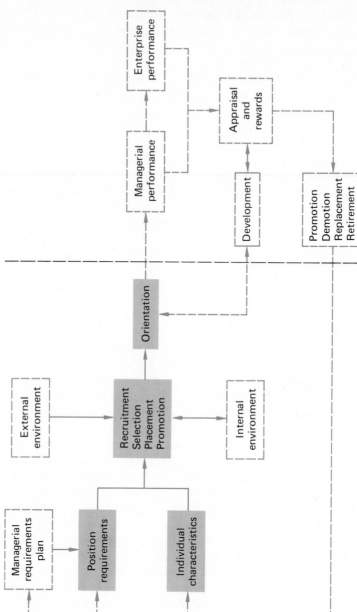

Figure 19.1 Systems approach to selection. Variables marked with broken lines are staffing activities that are discussed in other chapters.

"rewarded" (Chapter 20). Based on this evaluation, manager and organization "development" are initiated (Chapter 21). Finally, appraisal may also become the basis for "promotion, demotion, replacement, and retirement" decisions.

That is the selection model in brief; now each variable in the model will receive closer attention.

POSITION REQUIREMENTS

Effective selection of managers requires having a clear understanding of the nature and purpose of the position which is to be filled. This calls for an objective analysis of position requirements. Among the factors to be considered are the skills required—technical, human, conceptual and design—since these vary with the level in the organizational hierarchy. In addition, positions must be evaluated and compared so the incumbents can be treated fairly and equitably.

Identifying Job Requirements

In identifying job requirements, it is necessary to answer questions such as What has to be done in this job? How is it done? What background knowledge, attitudes, and skills are required? Since positions are not static, additional questions may have to be considered: Can it be done differently? If this is the case, what are the new requirements? To find answers to these and similar questions, the job must be analyzed. This can be done through observation, interviews, questionnaires, or even a systems analysis. Thus, a job description, based on job analysis, usually lists important duties, authority-responsibility relationships (although these are better handled by reference to a chart of approval authorization, discussed in Chapter 15), and the relationship to other positions. More recently, some firms have also included objectives and expected results in job descriptions. To keep the job description from being too bulky, however, the current set of objectives is usually only referred to in the description, although it is regarded as a key part of a person's job. After all, what counts is the manager's contribution to the aims of the enterprise.

There is, of course, no foolproof rule for designing managerial jobs. Nevertheless, one can avoid mistakes by following some guidelines.

The scope of the job should be appropriate   A job too narrowly defined provides no challenge, no opportunity for growth, and no sense of accomplishment. Consequently, good managers will be bored and dissatisfied. On the other hand, a job must not be so broad that it cannot be effectively handled by a manager. The result will be stress, frustration, and loss of control.

The position should involve a full-time, challenging job Sometimes managers are given a job that does not require their full-time and effort. They are not challenged by their task and feel underutilized. Consequently, they meddle in the work of their subordinates, who then also feel that they do not have sufficient authority and discretion to do their jobs. Some time ago, one of the authors was approached by a utility company for help in solving organizational conflicts. It was found that people did not have full-time jobs; they were quarreling about jobs, duties, and tasks; they were in each other's way. Thus, they channeled their energy against each other instead of toward the aims of the company. The need to redesign full-time jobs with challenging objectives, duties, and responsibilities should be obvious.

The job should reflect required managerial skills Generally the design of the job should start with the tasks to be accomplished. The design is usually broad enough to accommodate people's needs and desires. But Fred E. Fiedler suggests that one may have to learn to engineer the job to fit the leadership style of people.[1] This may be especially appropriate for exceptional persons, in order to utilize their potential. The problem, of course, is that the position would probably have to be restructured every time a new manager occupied it. The job description, then, must provide a clear idea of the performance requirements for a person in a particular position, but must also allow some flexibility to take advantage of individual characteristics.

These guidelines, although useful, must of course be adapted to fit specific situations. The position description is contingent on the particular job and the organization. For example, in a bureaucratic and fairly stable organizational environment, the position may be described in relatively specific terms. In contrast, in a dynamic organization with an unstable, fast-changing environment, a job description may have to be more general and most likely will have to be reviewed more frequently. A situational approach to job descriptions and job designs is called for.

MANAGERIAL SKILLS IN THE ORGANIZATIONAL HIERARCHY

Effective managers need different skills, and the relative importance of skills may vary with the level in the organization. Robert L. Katz identified three kinds of skills for administrators.[2] The authors of this book are suggesting a fourth—the ability to design solutions.

[1] F. E. Fiedler, "Engineer the Job to Fit the Manager," *Harvard Business Review*, vol. 43, no. 5, pp. 115–122 (September–October 1965).
[2] R. L. Katz, "Skills of an Effective Administrator," *Harvard Business Review*, vol. 33, no. 1, pp. 33–42 (January–February 1955); and R. L. Katz, "Retrospective Commentary," *Harvard Business Review*, vol. 52, no. 5, pp. 101–102 (September–October 1974).

1 *Technical skill* pertains to knowledge and proficiency in activities involving methods, processes, and procedures. Thus it involves working with tools and specific techniques. For example, mechanics work with tools, and their supervisors should have the ability to teach these skills to their subordinates. Similarly, accountants apply specific techniques in doing their job.

2 *Human Skill* is the ability to work with people; it is cooperative effort; it is teamwork; it is the creation of an environment in which people feel secure and free to express their opinions.

3 *Conceptual skill* refers to the ability to see the "big picture"; to recognize significant elements in a situation; to understand the relationships among the elements.

4 *Design skill.* To be effective, particularly at upper organizational levels, managers must be able to do more than see a problem. They must have, in addition, the skill of a good design engineer in working out a practical solution to a problem. If managers merely "see" the problem and become "problem watchers," they will fail. Managers must also have that valuable skill of being able to design a workable solution to the problem in the light of the realities they face.

The relative importance of these skills may differ for various levels in the organization hierarchy. As shown in Figure 19.2, technical skills are of greatest importance at the "supervisory level." Human skills are also important in the frequent interactions with subordinates. Conceptual skills, on the other hand, are usually not critical for lower-level supervisors. At the "middle-management level," the need for technical skills decreases; human skills are still essential; the conceptual skills gain in importance. At the "top management level," conceptual and design abilities and human skills are especially important, but there is relatively

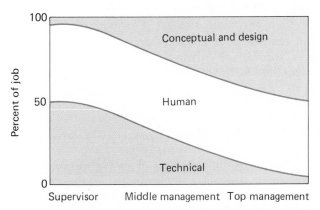

Figure 19.2 There is a variation in skills important at different management levels. [*Adapted from K. Davis*, Human Behavior at Work *(New York: McGraw-Hill Book Company, 1977), p. 110.* Used by permission of the publisher.]

little need for technical abilities. It is assumed, especially in large companies, that chief executives can utilize the technical abilities of their subordinates. In smaller firms, however, technical experience may still be quite important.

The differences in skill requirements have important implications for the selection of managers; namely, the special requirements for a position in the organizational hierarchy should be evaluated and matched with the skills of the candidate.

Analytical and Problem-Solving Abilities

Of all skills thought to be desirable for managers, perhaps the most generally appreciated and emphasized are analytical and problem-solving abilities. But as Alan Stoneman, former president of the Purex Corporation used to say, "We have no problems here; all are opportunities; all a problem should be is an opportunity." This means that managers must be able to identify problems, analyze complex situations, and by solving the problems encountered, exploit the opportunities presented. They must scan the environment and identify, through a rational process, those factors that stand in the way of opportunities. But problem identification and analysis are not enough. Also needed is the will to implement the solution; this requires recognition of the emotions, needs, and motivations of the people involved in initiating the required change as well as of those who resist change.

Placing too much emphasis on problems can blind a manager to opportunities. After all, solving problems results only in bringing the operation to normal. Extraordinary results are obtained by focusing on opportunities, not by merely solving problems. Thus, analytical skills should be used to find opportunities and needs of present customers—or potential ones—and then to satisfy these needs with a product or service. It has been amply demonstrated that this opportunity-seeking approach can mean corporate success. For example, Edwin H. Land of Polaroid filled the needs of people who wanted instant photographs. Similarly, Heinz Nordhoff of Volkswagen satisfied those customers in the late 1940s, 1950s, and 1960s who wanted a low-cost, reliable, and efficient automobile.

EVALUATING MANAGERIAL POSITIONS

One of the most difficult tasks of managing is the evaluation of managerial *positions*, a task which should be distinguished from evaluating the performance of a person in it. Should a company controller's position be rated higher than that of assistant to the president? Is a personnel manager's position less or more valuable than that of an engineering manager or a plant manager? Should the vice president for marketing outrank the vice president for manufacturing? Should the position of sales manager over one product line be more or less highly placed than the position of a sales manager over another product line? Should controllers of companies of similar size be rated equally?

Obviously the evaluation of positions within an enterprise has great importance for such matters as compensation, prestige, office allocations and furnishings, and the many other things that are meaningful to those who occupy managerial, as well as other, positions. One would think, therefore, that this would be one of the most highly developed areas of management; unfortunately, it is not.

Comparison Method

The most common method of evaluating managerial positions in practice is through comparing, or "slotting," them. Given a few key positions on which some standard of pay and status exists, such as president, manager of accounting, or plant superintendent, others are compared with them, and a largely subjective judgment is made as to whether, in a given company, one rates higher than another in the hierarchy of organization. The extent of the difference is usually expressed in various salary levels. These, in turn, tend to be established, at least for selected key positions, by statistics on salaries paid by similar companies, as disclosed in surveys made by the American Management Associations or other agencies.[3] The process is thus a kind of recognition that market competition sets the salaries for similar positions.

Job Factor Method

Some companies evaluate managerial positions by using variations of the point-rating system, a common practice used in evaluating lower-level jobs, such as those of factory or clerical employees. This is done by selecting job factors, assigning them weights and points, and then giving a numerical expression to each factor. Such factors include education required, experience, mental or physical effort, responsibility, and work conditions. On the basis of these point evaluations, a series of grades is developed, and by reference to those grades where competitive salaries or wages are known, compensation levels and ranges are set for each grade. These point-rating systems have been used for many professional posi-

---

[3]William F. Glueck lists the following enterprises as examples of conducting pay surveys: American Management Associations, Administrative Management Society, American Society for Personnel Administration, and International Personnel Management Associations. Among the many journals reporting pay surveys are: *Compensation Review*, Business Week, *Dun's, Forbes, Fortune, Hospital Administration, Nation's Business,* and *Monthly Labor Review*. In addition, the U.S. government conducts a variety of pay surveys. For a detailed discussion see W. F. Glueck, *Personnel—A Diagnostic Approach* (Dallas: Business Publications, Inc., 1978), pp. 415–419.

tions and, in some cases, even for managerial positions, understandably with different job factors and weightings; however, traditional point ratings have not been widely used for middle- and upper-level managerial jobs.

In managerial job evaluations, one of the more popular adaptations of the point system is the *guide-chart profile method*, developed over the years by Edward N. Hay and Associates.[4] In this approach, positions are evaluated in three areas: (1) know-how required; (2) problem solving involved; and (3) degree and extent of accountability, or responsibility. Within each area, factors are analyzed and weighted, and the score profile is used as a basis of comparing positions.

Time-Span of Discretion Method

One of the most original and interesting, but not yet proven, approaches to evaluating any kind of position, but with particular interest for manageri-al positions, is the *time-span of discretion* technique developed by Elliott Jaques, distinguished British management scholar, psychiatrist, and consultant.[5] Jaques believes, and has considerable research to make his point persuasive, that the worth of any job can be measured by the time-span of discretion in the position. This he defines as follows:

> The longest period which can elapse in a role before the manager can be sure that his subordinate has not been exercising marginally substandard discretion continuously in balancing the pace and the quality of his work.[6]

In other words, the time-span of discretion is that longest period of time that must elapse before it is known whether a person is exercising discretion accurately. For example, with a supervisor in an assembly operation, mistakes due to low skill or poor judgment might show up rather quickly, but for a company president it might take years to ascertain the correctness of discretion used in certain tasks, such as a marketing or new product strategy. This criterion serves to emphasize the importance of choosing top executives especially carefully.

Jaques' technique involves measuring the length of time-span of discretion by analyzing tasks in a position. His research shows that the longer the time-span, the more a position should be, and is, paid. Although greater practical application of the technique is necessary to

---

[4]J. Doulton and D. Hay, *Managerial and Professional Staff Grading* (London: George Allen & Unwin, Ltd., 1962), especially chap. 2.

[5]See his *Equitable Payment* (New York: John Wiley & Sons, Inc., 1961) and *Time-Span Handbook* (London: William Heinemann, Ltd., 1962). For a description of the system see E. F. Beal, "In Praise of Job Evaluation," *California Management Review*, vol. 5, no. 3, pp. 9–16 (Summer 1963).

[6]Jaques, op. cit., p. 23.

show its value, his approach is original and offers one of the better hopes for obtaining objectivity in managerial job evaluation.

Deficiencies in Managerial Job Evaluation

All methods of evaluating managerial positions suffer from deficiencies. Titles vary so much in terms of what is included in a job that slotting may be extremely imprecise, and even point systems or time-span approaches may not adequately detect what a job really involves. Even though the latter two systems reduce greatly the element of subjectivity so prevalent in the position-comparison method, they still suffer from a significant degree of subjectivity.

Perhaps the greatest reason for concern in position evaluation is that not everyone who fills a given position does the same thing in the same way. Managerial positions, like many other professional jobs, have a high degree of elasticity, and much depends upon what incumbents make of their jobs. This is particularly true with higher-level positions, but it is implicit even in middle- and lower-level managerial jobs. To be sure, differences in performance should normally be weighed by evaluation of the person in the position, but the fact is that many positions depend to a greater or lesser degree on the persons who have them. The spectrum of important tasks and expected results is not easy to define completely in managerial roles.

PERSONAL CHARACTERISTICS NEEDED BY MANAGERS

In addition to the various skills that effective managers are thought to need, several personal characteristics are also important. These are (1) a desire to manage; (2) ability to communicate with empathy; and (3) integrity and honesty. The person's experience, his or her past performance as a manager, is another characteristic, perhaps the most significant one, that should also be considered.

Desire to Manage

One of the basic requirements for successful managers is a strong desire to manage, to influence others, and to get results through team efforts of subordinates. To be sure, many people want the niceties of the managerial positions, which include high status and salary, but they lack the basic motivation to achieve results by creating an environment in which people work together toward common aims. What is needed is the "will to manage," which requires effort, time, energy, usually long hours, and separation from family life.[7]

[7]M. Bower, *The Will to Manage* (New York: McGraw-Hill Book Company, 1966).

Another important characteristic of managers is the ability to communicate. This is done through written reports, letters, and discussions. Communication demands clarity, but even more, it demands empathy. This is the ability to understand the feelings of another person and to deal with the emotional aspects of communication. Communication skills are important for effective *intragroup* communication, that is, communication with people in the same organizational unit. As one goes up in the organization, however, *intergroup* communication becomes increasingly important. This kind of communication is not only with other departments but also with groups outside the enterprise: customers, suppliers, governments, the community, and, of course, the stockholders in business enterprises.

Integrity and Honesty

Managers must be morally sound and worthy of trust. Integrity in managers includes the following:

Honesty in money and material matters, and in dealing with others

Effective and efficient use of time

Keeping superiors informed

Adhering to the full truth

Strength of character

Behaving in accordance with ethical standards

Many of these qualities, and others, have been cited by top executives of major companies. Henry Ford II, chairperson of Ford Motor Company, mentioned as appealing qualities honesty, candor, and openness. Similarly, Donald M. Kendall, chairperson of Pepsico, Inc., listed work ethics and integrity as essential characteristics of executives.

To be sure, many of these characteristics do not lend themselves to easy measurement, but this does not make them less important. In fact, integrity may be the crucial characteristic of both a great person and a great manager.

Performance as a Manager

Perhaps the most important characteristic to evaluate is past performance as a manager. It is probably the most reliable forecast of a manager's future performance. Of course, an assessment of this is not possible in selecting first-line supervisors from the ranks, since they have not had previous managerial experience. But past accomplishments are important considerations in the selection of middle- and upper-level managers.

The selection process, then, should be results-oriented and should make use of highly objective appraisal systems. Such a system is discussed in Chapter 20.

MATCHING REQUIREMENTS WITH MANAGER QUALIFICATIONS

After the organizational positions are identified, managers are obtained through recruitment, selection, placement, and promotion (see variables in Figure 19.1). There are basically two sources of managerial personnel: People from within the enterprise may be promoted or transferred, and managers may be hired from the outside. For internal promotions, a computerized information system may facilitate the identification of qualified candidates. Such a system can be used in conjunction with a comprehensive human resource plan. Specifically, it can be utilized to anticipate staff requirements, new openings, attritions, development needs, and career planning.

There are also several external sources available, and the enterprise may use different methods in finding qualified managers. Many employment agencies—public and private—provide the service of locating suitable candidates for positions. Other sources for managers are professional associations, educational institutions, referrals from people within the enterprise, and of course, unsolicited applications from persons interested in the firm.

Recruitment of Managers

Recruiting involves attracting candidates to meet enterprise objectives. Before recruiting begins, the position's requirements—which should relate directly to the task—must be clearly identified. This facilitates the recruitment of suitable candidates from the outside. Enterprises with a favorable public image find it easier to attract qualified candidates. A company such as IBM (International Business Machines) has a well-recognized image, while small firms—which frequently offer excellent growth and development opportunities—may have to make great efforts to communicate to the applicant the kinds of products, services, and opportunities the firm offers.

Recruitment in the public sector has many similarities to recruitment in the private sector. However, government regulations or policies may demand adherence to special hiring guidelines. For example, legislation may require that potential employees live within the municipality's boundaries. Another difference is that applicants for public sector positions often have to take competitive tests, such as civil service examinations.

In summary, effective recruitment requires a clear idea of the position to be filled, collection of data on the applicant, the projection of a favorable—yet realistic—image of the enterprise, and attracting the best qualified recruits for the position. This calls for effective communication between the firm and the potential manager.

Information Exchange Contributes to Successful Selection

The information exchange works two ways in recruitment and selection: the enterprise provides applicants with an objective description of the company and the position, while the applicants provide information about their capabilities.

Business and other organizations attempt to portray a favorable image, stress opportunities for personal growth and development, highlight potential challenges, indicate promotion possibilities, and convey information about pay, fringe benefits, and perhaps job security. This can, of course, be overdone, raising unrealistic expectations in the applicant. In the long run, this may have undesirable side effects resulting in low job satisfaction, turnover, and unfulfilled dreams. Certainly the enterprise should indicate its attractiveness for the candidate, yet the opportunities should be discussed in a factual and realistic manner which also includes mentioning limitations and even unfavorable aspects of the job.

On the other hand, management should elicit from the applicants an objective demonstration of their knowledge, skills, abilities, aptitudes, and even their motivation. To obtain this information, a number of techniques and instruments are used that are further discussed below. To be sure, the collection of data about an applicant can go too far and can become an invasion of privacy. The managerial candidate will only tolerate a reasonable amount of interviewing, testing, and disclosure of personal information. Clearly, restraint must be exercised, and the requested information should be essential and relevant to the job.

Selection, Placement, and Promotion

Managerial selection is logically choosing from among the candidates the one that best meets the position requirements. The selection may be for a specific job opening, or it may be for future managerial requirements. Thus, some experts distinguish between the selection and placement approaches in filling organizational positions. In the "selection" approach, applicants are sought to fill a position with rather specific requirements, while in the "placement" approach, the strengths and weaknesses of the individual are evaluated and a suitable position is found or even designed.[8]

"Promotion" is a change within the organization to a higher position with greater responsibilities and need for more advanced skills than in the previous position. It usually involves greater status and an increase in

---

[8]S. J. Carroll and H. L. Tosi, *Organizational Behavior* (Chicago: St. Clair Press, 1977), pp. 278–279.

pay. The various facets discussed in selection generally apply also to promotion, which may be a reward for outstanding performance or for greater utilization of the individual's skills and abilities.

Approaches to Selection

Different approaches are used in selecting people for positions. George S. Odiorne and Edwin L. Miller described and evaluated four approaches and then suggested their own system, "selection by objectives."[9] The first method, *personal preference*, may be based on hunches, likes, and dislikes in the selection of managers. The second, the *occupational characteristic* approach, focuses on aptitudes. The third, the *behavioral* approach, takes behavior patterns as predictors for managerial success. The fourth, the *background* approach to selection, presumes that by studying the careers of successful managers and other professionals, one gains insights helpful in selecting managers who fit these patterns. While these approaches do have some merits, they have even more limitations. Consequently, a new approach—the fifth one—is suggested, *selection by objectives*. It does not replace the others, but focuses on the more reliable selection criteria of results and past performance.

Selection by objectives starts with a statement of job objectives. Specifically, the objectives are categorized into (1) regular and routine objectives, (2) problem-solving objectives, and (3) innovative or change objectives. The candidate's past performance is then evaluated against these objectives. The following example of an objective for a general supervisor and the related questions illustrate the selection-by-objectives method.

Objective or Key Task	*Results Achieved*
Production output	What were the normal output requirements for this job?
	What results were achieved (quantity, quality, cost)?
	What was the reject rate as compared to when the manager assumed the position?
	What innovation was undertaken to improve production quantity and quality?

Other questions may be raised for cost control, employee relations, and training of supervisors. The answers to these questions give an indication of a person's achievements. This approach focuses on results rather than on more subjective evaluations such as personal appearance, aptitudes, behavior, and the background of individuals.

[9]This discussion is based on G. S. Odiorne and E. L. Miller, "Selection by Objectives: A New Approach to Managerial Selection." *Management of Personnel Quarterly*, vol. 5, no. 3, pp. 2–10 (Fall 1966).

The selection-by-objectives approach is a step in the right direction. Yet it too has limitations. It assumes that past accomplishments are predictors for future performance. This, unfortunately, is not always true. New tasks may be substantially different from previous tasks, and people may be promoted beyond their potential. Another limitation is the difficulty in collecting results-oriented information on candidates from outside the enterprise. Their previous superiors may be reluctant to discuss the performance of former subordinates.

Still another limitation of this approach is that managers may overachieve or underachieve objectives as a result of external factors unrelated to their own managerial competence. For example, the bankruptcy of a competitor may lead to an unexpected increase in demand and overachievement of sales objectives. On the other hand, poor performance due to an unforeseen economic depression may place the manager in an unfavorable light. Finally, short-run performance alone may be misleading. Consequently, a longer period of sustained results should be considered when selecting managers by objectives. However, despite these limitations, the results-oriented selection process appears to be an improvement over the more subjective selection methods that are commonly used today.

Balancing Skills and the Age Factor

There are other important considerations for selection. Managerial positions demand a variety of skills: technical, human, conceptual, and problem-solving. Since one person may not have all the required abilities, others may have to be selected to compensate for these deficiencies. For example, a top manager with excellent conceptual and design skills may need assistance from persons with technical skills. Similarly, a manager with a strong marketing and financial background may have to be complemented by an operations expert.

The age factor must also be taken into account when selecting managers. It is not uncommon to find that all vice presidents and middle managers in a company are in the same age bracket. Problems will thus occur when several managers on a similar organization level retire at the same time, a situation that can be avoided by considering the age factor at the time appointments are made. Care must be taken, however, to avoid illegal discrimination based on age. Systematic work-force planning can provide for fair distribution of managers in different age groups within the organizational structure.

The Peter Principle

Errors in selection are possible, perhaps even common. This leads to the rather cynical notion of the "Peter Principle."[10] According to Laurence J.

---

[10]L. J. Peter and R. Hall, *The Peter Principle* (New York: Bantam Books, Inc., 1969).

Peter and Raymond Hall, managers tend to be promoted to the level of their incompetence. Specifically, if a manager succeeds in a position, this very success may lead to promotion to a higher position, often one requiring skills that the person does not possess. Such a promotion may place a manager "over his or her head." To be sure, this is a rather pessimistic view, one which does not recognize the possibility of individual growth. On the other hand, the Peter Principle may serve as a caveat for those who take selection and promotion lightly.

Who Should Select?

The final decision in the selection of a person for a new position should rest with the candidate's prospective superior; only then can the selector be held accountable for the performance of the selected candidate. It is also advisable to get the opinions of others, especially those with whom the candidate will have working relationships. In addition, the superior of the selector should be involved by approving, rather than actually making, the selection decision. This gives additional assurance that qualifications rather than friendships are the basic reasons for the choice. It also is a way of making more certain that the selecting manager is selecting people with adequate qualifications and potential for growth.

SELECTION TECHNIQUES, INSTRUMENTS, AND PROCESSES

To assist a manager in choosing from among the candidates, a number of instruments, techniques, and resources are available, including interviews, tests, and the assessment center. For good selections, the information about the applicant should be both valid and reliable. "Validity" concerns the question: "Are we measuring what we think we measure?" In selection, validity pertains to the degree to which the data predict the candidate's success as a manager. The information should also have a high degree of "reliability," which refers to accuracy and consistency of the measurement. This means, for example, that if a test were repeated under the same conditions, it would give essentially the same results.

Interviews

Virtually every manager hired or promoted by a company is interviewed by one or more people. Despite its general use, there is considerable distrust of the interview as a reliable and valid means for selecting managers. Various interviewers may weigh or interpret the obtained information differently. Interviewers often do not ask the right questions. They may be influenced by the interviewee's general appearance, which may have little bearing on job performance. It has also been found that interviewers frequently make up their minds early in the interview, before they have all the information necessary to make a fair judgment.

To overcome some of these weaknesses, several techniques can improve the interviewing process. First, the interviewers should be trained so that they know what to look for. For example, in interviewing people from within the enterprise, past records should be analyzed and discussed. The results achieved should be studied as well as the quality of carrying out key managerial activities. The next chapter on appraisal shows in greater detail how this can be done. When selecting managers from outside the firm, these data are more difficult to obtain, and it is usually done by checking with the listed references.

Second, the interviewer should be prepared to ask the right questions. There are structured, semistructured, and unstructured interviews. In an unstructured interview, one may say something like "Tell me about your last job." In the semistructured interview, the manager follows an interview guide but may also ask other questions. In a structured interview, a set of prepared questions is asked, such as

What were your specific duties and responsibilities in your last job?

What did you achieve in this job?

Who could be asked to verify these achievements?

To what extent were these achievements due to your efforts?

What were the contributions of other people?

Who are they?

What did you like and dislike about your job?

Why do you want to change your job?

A third way to improve selection is through multiple interviews utilizing several different interviewers. This facilitates a comparison of evaluations and preceptions. It does not mean, however, that all the interviewers should vote in selecting the candidate; rather, it provides additional information to the manager who will be responsible for the final selection decision.

Fourth, the interview is just one aspect of the selection process. It should be supplemented by data from the application form, the results of various tests, and the information obtained from persons listed as references. These reference checks and letters of recommendation may be necessary to verify the information given by the applicant. To be useful, the person giving the reference must know the applicant well and give a truthful and complete assessment of the applicant. Many people are reluctant to provide complete information, so an applicant's strong points are often overemphasized while his or her shortcomings may be glossed over. The Privacy Act of 1974 and related legislation and judicial rulings have made it even more difficult to obtain objective references. Under this act, the applicant has a legal right to inspect letters of reference unless this right is waived. This is also one of the reasons that teachers are sometimes reluctant to make objective and accurate job referrals. [11]

Tests

The primary aim of testing is to obtain data about the applicants that help to predict their probable success as managers. Some of the expected benefits from testing include finding the best person for the job, obtaining a high degree of job satisfaction for the applicant, and reducing turnover. The most commonly used tests can be classified in four groups:

1 *Intelligence* tests are designed to measure mental capacity and to test memory, speed of thought, and ability to see relationships in complex problem situations.
2 *Proficiency and aptitude* tests are constructed to discover interests, existing skills, and potential for acquiring skills.
3 *Vocational* tests are designed to show a candidate's most suitable occupation.
4 *Personality* tests are designed to reveal candidates' personal characteristics and the way they may affect others, thereby giving a measure of potentiality for leadership.

A few observations may be made concerning tests. In the first place, competent industrial psychologists agree that tests are not accurate enough to be used as the sole way of measuring candidates and must be interpreted in the light of each individual's entire history. Second, any test user must know what tests do and what their limitations are; one of the major limitations is uncertainty about whether the tests are really applicable. There has not yet been a high degree of confidence, even among psychologists, that tests developed thus far are effectively aimed at measuring managerial abilities and potentials. Third, before any test is broadly used it should be tried out, if possible on existing personnel in an enterprise, to see whether it is valid as applied to employees whose managerial abilities are already known. Fourth, it is also important that tests be administered and interpreted by experts in the field. Finally, tests should not discriminate unfairly and should be congruent with laws and government guidelines. [12]

[11]L. R. Gallese, "Campus Concern: Student Job Referrals by Teachers Hit Snag Due to Privacy Law," *The Wall Street Journal*, pp. 1, 16 (January 14, 1977); and "References Dry Up," *The Wall Street Journal*, p. 1 (January 6, 1976).
[12]J. B. Miner, "Psychological Testing and Fair Employment Practices: A Testing Program That Does Not Discriminate," *Personnel Psychology*, vol. 27, no. 1, pp. 49–62 (Spring 1974); W. H. Mobley, "Meeting Government Guidelines on Testing and Selection," *The Personnel Administrator*, vol. 19, no. 8, pp. 42–48 (November–December 1974); and M. T. Matteson. "Employment Testing: Where Do We Stand?" *The Personnel Administrator*; vol. 20, no. 3, pp. 27–29 (May 1975).

In recent years, an increasing number of companies have used assessment centers as aids in the selection of managers.[13] They are used primarily for selection of first-level managers, although some companies also use them for promotion of managers to higher levels. The assessment center technique was used by the Germans, the British, and the Americans in World War II for selection of candidates for the Office of Strategic Services, but the first industrial use is generally attributed to the American Telephone and Telegraph Company over two decades ago.

Intended to measure how a potential manager will act in typical managerial situations, the usual center approach is to have candidates take part in a series of exercises. During this period they are observed and assessed by psychologists or experienced managers. A typical assessment center will have the candidates do some of the following: (1) take various psychological tests; (2) engage in small groups in management games; (3) engage in "in-basket" exercises, in which they are asked to handle a variety of matters that they might face in a managerial job; (4) participate in a leaderless group discussion in solving some problem; (5) give an individual, brief oral presentation on a particular topic or theme, usually one recommending a course of desirable action to a mythical superior; and (6) engage in various other exercises, such as preparing a written report.

During these exercises, the candidates are observed by their evaluators, who also interview them from time to time. At the end of the assessment center period, the assessors summarize their appraisals of each candidate's performance, compare their evaluations with those of other assessors, come to conclusions with them concerning a candidate's managerial potential, and write a summary report on the candidate. These reports are made available to appointing managers for their guidance. They are also often used as guides for management development. In many cases candidates are given feedback on their evaluation; in other cases feedback is given only when candidates request it. Sometimes the summary evaluation as to promotability remains confidential, even though candidates may be informed by assessors about their performance in the various exercises.

The usefulness of the assessment centers approach—although not conclusive—is encouraging. Specifically, its reliability seems high enough to suggest that further use is warranted. Similarly, high predictive validity of this approach for managerial jobs was found in two studies at the American Telephone and Telegraph Company.[14]

Assessment centers do present some problems however. First, they

---

[13]For an excellent analysis of assessment centers and their use, see Ann Howard, "An Assessment of Assessment Centers," *Academy of Management Journal*, vol. 17, no. 1, pp. 115–134 (March 1974).
[14]Ibid., p. 122.

are costly in terms of time, especially since the most effective programs extend over at least a 5-day period. Second, there is the problem of training assessors, particularly in those companies which believe, with some justification, that the best assessors are likely to be experienced line managers rather than trained psychologists. Third, although a number of different exercises are used to cover the kinds of things a manager does, questions have been raised as to whether these are the best criteria for evaluation. An even greater problem exists in determining what evaluation measures should be applied to each exercise. Most assessment centers, being highly oriented to individual and interpersonal behavior under various circumstances, may be overlooking the most important element in selecting managers, especially those about to enter the managerial ranks for the first time. That element is motivation, whether or not a person truly wants to be a manager. This requires that candidates know what managing is, what it involves, and what is required to be a successful manager. Obviously, this is a difficult quality to evaluate. However, by making clear to a candidate what managing involves and requires and then asking the candidate to think this over and respond, some progress can be made.

Limitations in the Selection Process

The diversity of selection approaches and tests indicates that there is no one perfect way to select managers. Experience has shown that even carefully chosen selection criteria are still imperfect in predicting performance. Furthermore, there is a distinction between what persons "can do," that is, their ability to perform, and what people "will do," which relates to motivation. The latter is a function of the individual and the environment. For example, a person's needs may be different at various times. Similarly, the organizational environment also changes. The climate of an enterprise may change from one which encourages initiative to a restrictive one because of a different managerial philosophy of new top management. Therefore, the selection techniques and instruments are not a sure way to predict what people "will do," even though they may have the ability.

Testing itself, especially psychological testing, has limitations. Specifically, some of the information sought may be considered an invasion of privacy. In addition, it has been charged that some tests may unfairly discriminate against members of minority groups or women. These complex issues are not easily resolved, yet they cannot be ignored when selecting managers.

Still another concern in selection and hiring is the time and cost involved in making personnel decisions. It is important to identify such factors as advertising expenses, agency fees, test material, time spent for interviewing candidates, costs for reference checks, medical exams, start-up time required to get acquainted with the new job, relocation, and orientation of the new employee. In one case it was found that hiring a $60,000-a-year executive cost $47,200.[15] When these high costs are realized, it becomes evident that turnover can be very expensive to an enterprise.

One way to reduce turnover and to shorten the start-up time is through effective orientation. Some authors discuss this topic together with training and development. However, since orientation follows immediately the selection and hiring of employees, it is included in this chapter.

ORIENTING AND SOCIALIZING THE NEW MANAGER

The selection of the best person for the job is only the first step in building an effective management team. Even companies that make great efforts in the recruitment and selection process often ignore the needs of new managers after they have been hired. Yet the first few days and weeks can be crucial for integrating the new person into the organization. Failure to socialize new managers—and nonmanagers as well, of course—can result in costly labor turnover, not to mention the loss of a good person for the enterprise.

Orientation involves the introduction of new employees to the enterprise, its functions, tasks, and people. Large firms usually have a formal orientation program which explains these features of the company:

History

Products and services

General policies and practices

Organization (divisions, departments, and geographic locations)

Benefits (insurance, retirement, vacations)

Requirements for confidentiality and secrecy in defense contracts

Safety and other regulations

These items may be further described in detail in a company booklet, but the orientation meeting provides new employees with an opportunity to ask questions. It is important to stress that although these formal programs are usually conducted by persons from the personnel department, the primary responsibility for orienting the new manager still rests with the superior.

[15]R. E. Sibson, "The High Cost of Hiring," *Nation's Business*, vol. 63, no. 2, pp. 85–88 (February 1975).

There is another and perhaps even more important aspect of orientation: the socialization of new managers. In addition to meeting the specific requirements of the job, new managers will usually encounter new values, new personal relationships, and new modes of behavior. They do not know people they can ask for advice, they do not know how the organization works, and they have a fear of being unsuccessful in the new job. All this uncertainty can cause a great deal of anxiety in the new employee, especially among management trainees. Because the initial experiences in an enterprise can be very important for future management behavior, it has been suggested that the first contact of trainees should be with the best superiors in the enterprise, people who can serve as models for future behavior.

To cope with some of these problems, Texas Instruments, for example, held a one-day anxiety-reducing session. The group participating in this session was compared with a control group that did not have the benefit of such a program. It was found that the session saved the company a great deal of money in training, absenteeism, tardiness, and rejects. Improvement in job performance resulted in an additional savings.[16]

Although the participants in this study were not managers, it appears that all new employees have to cope with similar anxieties and that effective orientation and socialization can be beneficial for the enterprise. At any rate, selection of managers is just the beginning of building an effective organization; orientation is an important, but often neglected, next step.

FOR DISCUSSION

1 What is the systems approach to selection of managers? Why is it called a systems approach? How does it differ from other approaches?

2 What are the important managerial skills? In what ways do you think these skills differ for various levels in the organizational hierarchy?

3 What are some methods used for evaluating and comparing managerial positions? Which method do you favor? Explain your position.

4 What kinds of individual characteristics are important for managerial success?

5 What are the various approaches in the selection of managers? Which approach do you prefer? Why?

6 The Peter Principle has been widely quoted in management circles. What do you think of it? Do you think that it could ever apply to you? Does it mean that all chief executives are incompetent? Explain.

[16]E. R. Gomersall and M. S. Myers, "Breakthrough in On-the-Job-Training," *Harvard Business Review*, vol. 44, no. 4, pp. 62–72 (July–August 1966).

7 What kinds of tests may be used in selecting managers? What are the benefits and limitations of these tests?

8 What is an assessment center? How does it work? Would you like to participate in such a center? Why or why not?

9 Why are orientation and socialization important?

chapter 20 Appraisal of Managers

MAJOR CHAPTER OBJECTIVES

1 To emphasize the importance of effectively appraising managers.
2 To suggest what should be measured in appraising managers.
3 To show why traditional trait appraisals have not been effective.
4 To suggest and analyze a system of managerial appraisal based on evaluating performance against verifiable objectives and performance as a manager.

[1]Much of this chapter has been drawn from H. Koontz, *Appraising Managers as Managers* (New York: McGraw-Hill Book Company, 1971).

Managerial appraisal has sometimes been referred to as the "Achilles' heel" of management development. But one could say more. It is probably a major key to managing itself. It is, of course, important to management development because if a manager's strengths and weaknesses are not known, it is only accidental if development efforts were aimed in the right direction. Appraisal is, or should be, an integral part of a system of managing. Knowing how well a manager plans, organizes, staffs, leads, and controls is really the only way to ensure that those occupying managerial positions are actually managing effectively. If a business, a government agency, charitable organization, or even a university is to reach its goals effectively and efficiently, ways of accurately measuring management performance must be found and implemented.

There are, then, a number of reasons for effective appraisal of managers. Appraisal must be looked upon as an essential element in the whole system of managing and in the subsystem of managerial staffing. Among the urgent needs for appraisal are the need to know the quality of managers in an enterprise, the requirements for a management development and selection program, the appropriate structuring of organization and managerial roles, and the establishment of a rational basis for rewarding success. When appraisals are truly effective, they should be tied into the reward system, since prompt recompense and recognition for demonstrated achievement are the most powerful motivating forces known.

THE PROBLEM OF MANAGEMENT APPRAISAL

There has long been a reluctance on the part of managers to appraise subordinates.[2] However, in an activity as important as managing, there should be no reluctance in measuring performance as accurately as we can. No one should get excited about the concern of those who fear that measuring the performance of others tends to put a manager in the untenable position of measuring the worth of subordinates and of acting on these judgments. It is sometimes difficult to comprehend the fear of "playing God" in a culture where individual performance has been rated at least from the time a person enters kindergarten and throughout school and university life. In almost all kinds of group enterprise, whether in work or play, performance has long been rated in some way. Moreover, most people, and particularly people of ability, *want to know* how well they are doing.

It is difficult to believe that the controversy, the misgivings, and even the disillusionment, still so widespread, with respect to managerial

[2]See, for example, B. F. White and L. B. Barnes, "Power Networks in the Appraisal Process," *Harvard Business Review*, vol. 49, no. 3, pp. 101–109 (May–June 1971).

performance appraisal have come from the *fact* of measuring and evaluating. It rather appears that they have arisen from the things measured, the standards used, and the way measurement is done. Managers can understandably take exception, feel unhappy, or resist when they believe that they are evaluating, or being evaluated, inaccurately or against standards that are inapplicable, inadequate, or subjective.

Some light and hope have emerged in the past 20 years and offer promise of making evaluation effective. The interest in evaluating managers by comparing actual performance against preset verifiable objectives or goals is a development of considerable potential. However, examination of actual programs in operation raises questions as to how many of these are truly effective. Indeed, a fair question may be raised as to whether there is still more talk than action. In addition, one might question whether this outbreak of attention, even though based on sound principles, may fade from the scene. People have a way of becoming disenchanted and resistant when new ideas or programs do not work as intended.

But appraisal against verifiable objectives is not enough. As will be noted presently, this needs to be supplemented by appraisal of managers as managers. Moreover, neither system is without difficulties and pitfalls, and neither can be operated by simply adopting the technique and doing the paperwork. One needs to do more. In the first place, it is essential that managing by verifiable objectives, as explained in Chapter 7, be a way of life in an enterprise. In the second place, there is needed a clear concept of the managerial job, the fundamentals underlying it, and the ability to apply these in practice.

WHAT SHOULD BE MEASURED?

It hardly seems necessary to say that managerial appraisal should measure *performance* as a *manager* in meeting goals for which the manager is responsible. Yet, obvious as this is, or at least should be, examination of a large number of appraisal systems used by business, government, and other enterprises shows a lack of understanding of this truism, or at least an unwillingness or inability to translate understanding into practice.

Note then that appraisal should measure both *performance* in accomplishing goals and plans and *performance as a manager*. No one would want a person in a managerial role who appeared to do everything right as a manager, but who could not turn in a good record of profit making, marketing, controllership, or whatever the area of responsibility might be. Nor should one be satisfied to have a performer in a managerial position who cannot operate effectively as a manager. Performers tend to be "flashes in the pan," and many are the performers who have succeeded through no fault of their own.

In assessing performance, systems of appraising against verifiable prese-lected goals have extraordinary value. Given consistent, integrated, and understood planning designed to reach specific objectives, probably the best criteria of managerial performance relate to the selected goals, including the intelligence with which they are chosen, the planning programs devised to accomplish them, and the person's success in achieving them. Those who have operated under some variation of this system have often claimed that this is adequate and that elements of luck or other factors beyond the manager's control are taken into account in arriving at any appraisal. To some extent this may be true. But there are too many cases in which sparkling performers are promoted despite these factors and performing failures are inaccurately blamed.

Performance as Managers

Although an impressive record of setting and accomplishing goals is persuasive evidence of any group leader's ability, it should be supple-mented by an appraisal of a manager *as a manager*. One must grant that managers at any level undertake nonmanagerial duties and that these cannot be overlooked. The primary purpose for which managers are hired, and against which they should be measured, however, is their perform-ance as managers. This indicates that they should be appraised on the basis of how well they understand and undertake the managerial functions of planning, organizing, staffing, leading, and controlling. For standards in this area we must turn to the fundamentals of management.

TRADITIONAL TRAIT APPRAISALS

For many years, and even commonly today, managers have been evaluat-ed against standards of personal traits and work characteristics. These typical trait-rating evaluation systems might list ten to fifteen personal characteristics, such as ability to get along with people, leadership, analytical competence, industry, judgment, and initiative. The list might also include such work-oriented characteristics as job knowledge, ability to carry through on assignments, production or cost results, or seeing that plans and instructions are carried out. However, at least until recent years, personal traits have far outnumbered work-oriented characteristics. Given these standards, the rater was then asked to evaluate subordinates on the basis of one of five or six ratings ranging from unacceptable to outstanding.

Typical of trait-oriented appraisal is that used by the U.S. Navy for many years in appraising officers. While the total "Report on the Fitness of Officers" required additional information on duties, study courses carried out, whether the reviewing officer would desire to have the subordinate in his or her command, and any open-ended comments, the major portion of the evaluation was involved in the kind of trait analysis shown in Table 20.1.

Weaknesses of Trait Appraisals

Managers resist doing trait rating or tend to go through the paperwork without knowing exactly how to rate. Even where earnest attempts have been made to "sell" such programs, to indoctrinate managers, and to train them in the meaning of traits so that they can improve their appraisal ability, few managers can or will do them well.

One practical problem of the trait approach to appraisal is that because trait evaluation cannot be objective, serious and fair-minded managers do not wish to utilize their obviously subjective judgment on a matter so important as performance. And employees who receive less than the top rating almost invariably feel that they have been unfairly dealt with. Most regard this "playing with people's souls" as possibly being the province of the professional psychiatrist, but hardly that of a manager.

Another problem is that the basic assumption of trait appraisals is open to question. The connection between performance and possession of specific traits is doubtful. It also tends to be outside of, separated from, a manager's actual operations. It substitutes what someone *thinks* of an individual for what the person actually *does*. This is made even more constraining when we find in trait-appraisal forms too few references to the actual job being done.

The results of resistance by managers are several. Many look upon it as only a paperwork exercise that must be done because someone has ordered it. When this happens, people go through the paperwork and tend to make ratings as painless (on the subordinate and the manager) as possible. Consequently, they tend not to be very discriminating. It is interesting, but hardly surprising, that a study of ratings of Navy officers a few years ago came up with an arithmetic paradox: that of all officers of the U.S. Navy rated over a period of time, some 98.5 percent were outstanding or excellent, and only 1 percent were average.

Trait criteria are at best nebulous. Raters are dealing with a blunt tool, and subordinates are likely to be vague about what it is they are being rated on. In the hands of most practitioners it is a crude device, and since raters are painfully aware of this, they are reluctant to use it in a manner which would damage the careers of their subordinates. One of the principal purposes of appraisal is to provide a basis upon which to discuss performance and plan for improvement. But trait evaluations provide little tangible to discuss, little on which participants can agree as fact, and therefore little mutual understanding of what would be required to obtain improvement.

Table 20.1 Qualities and Rating Form of U.S. Navy Report on Fitness of Officers

	Not observed	Outstanding	Excellent	Average	Unsatisfactory
(a) Intelligence (With reference to the faculty of comprehension; mental acuteness)		Exceptionally quick-witted; keen in understanding	Grasps essentials of a situation quickly	Understands normal situations and conditions	
(b) Judgment (With reference to a discriminating perception by which the values and relations of things are mentally asserted)		Unusually keen in estimating situations and reaching sound decisions	Can generally be depended on to make proper decisions	Fair judgment in normal and routine things	
(c) Initiative (With reference to constructive thinking and resourcefulness; ability and intelligence to act on own responsibility)		Exceptional in ability to think, plan, and do things without waiting to be told and instructed	Able to plan and execute missions on his own responsibility	Capable of performing routine duties on own responsibility	
(d) Force (With reference to moral power possessed and exerted in producing results)		Strong, dynamic	Strong	Effectual under normal and routine circumstances	
(e) Leadership (With reference to the faculty of directing, controlling, and influencing others in definite lines of action and of maintaining discipline)		Inspires others to a high degree by precept and example. Requires a high standard of discipline	A very good leader	Leads fairly well	
(f) Moral courage (With reference to that mental quality which impels one to carry out the dictates of his conscience and convictions fearlessly)		Exceptionally courageous	Courageous to a high degree	Fairly courageous	

A MARK TO THE RIGHT OF THIS LINE

Trait				CONSTITUTES AN ADVERSE REPORT	
(g) Cooperation (With reference to the faculty of working harmoniously with others toward the accomplishment of common duties)	Exceptionally successful in working with others to a common end	Works in harmony with others	Cooperates fairly well		
(h) Loyalty (Fidelity, faithfulness, allegiance, constancy—all with reference to a cause and to higher authority)	Unswerving in allegiance; frank and honest in aiding and advising	A high sense of loyalty	Reasonably faithful in the execution of his duty		
(i) Perseverance (With reference to maintenance of purpose or undertaking in spite of obstacles or discouragement)	Determined, resolute	Constant in purpose	Fairly steady		
(j) Reaction in emergencies (With reference to the faculty of acting instinctively in a logical manner in difficult and unforeseen situations)	Exceptionally cool-headed and logical in his actions under all conditions	Composed and logical in his actions in difficult situations	Fairly logical in his actions in general		
(k) Endurance (With reference to ability for carrying on under any and all conditions)	Capable of standing an exceptional amount of physical hardship and strain	Can perform well his duties under trying conditions	Of normal endurance		

Table 20.1 Cont.

	Not observed	Outstanding	Excellent	Average	Unsatisfactory
(l) Industry (With reference to performance of duties in an energetic manner)		Extremely energetic and industrious	Thorough and energetic	Reasonably energetic and industrious	
(m) Military bearing and neatness of person and dress (With reference to dignity of demeanor, correctness of uniform, and smartness of appearance)		Exceptional	Very good	Fair	

14. A report containing adverse matter must be referred to the officer reported on for statement pursuant to article 1701 (8) USNR. His statement should be attached to this report. Statements of minor deficiencies either in character or performance of duties must be brought to the attention of the officer reported on either orally or in writing.

Has this been done? ———— What improvement, if any, has been noted? ————

————

————

(Signature of reporting senior)

As the deficiencies of trait rating have come to be recognized, a number of changes and additions have been introduced. Some are aimed at making the traits more comprehensible to raters. As will be noted with reference to the U.S. Navy form, instead of saying merely "judgment," the report defines this quality as "discriminating perception by which values and relations to things are mentally asserted." In a form of a well-known business corporation, "judgment" means "how capable is he in recognizing the significant from the less significant in arriving at sound conclusions?" Likewise, attempts are made, as was done on the Navy form, to give meanings to various grades under each category.

Often, too, trait and work-quality forms are supplemented by open-ended evaluations in which, without specific guidance, appraisers are asked to supply whatever evidence on performance they feel is pertinent. Sometimes, also, this approach is used for the entire appraisal. Appraisers may be given a broad outline to guide them, such as asking for comments under such items as "operations," "organization," "personnel," and "financial," and they may be asked specifically to consider such things as quality, quantity, time element of work, customer relations, and subordinate employee morale. While these are helpful, experience has shown that they do not greatly improve the quality of ratings.

Attempts have also been made to improve the effectiveness of the rating process. In some systems, subordinates are required to rate themselves, and superiors must compare their ratings with those made by subordinates. In other instances, the superior's superior is asked to rate the former's subordinate or at least carefully review the evaluation made by the immediate superior. Sometimes, discrimination in rating is forced by a system of requiring a rater to rank subordinates from the best to the least able. In still other cases, rating has been done through the use of critical incidents that are assumed to give meaning to grades given.

There have been other methods designed to improve the rating process. One is to have subordinates rate their superiors. Another is to have a manager's colleagues on the same level, individually or as a group, do the rating.

Some of the various techniques to improve the rating process do make for better rating; others do not. Self-rating and having the superior's superior rate have proved to be effective. Systems requiring that all subordinates be rated from best to poorest are subject to severe weaknesses. It would not be at all unlikely that the number 1 person in a given group is no better than number 10 in another group, yet, in the records, one is rated number 1 and the other is rated number 10.

The rating of superiors by their subordinates has also not been effective. Despite assurances of confidentiality of their ratings, subordinates are not likely to believe this and therefore fail to rate bosses objectively. Also, subordinates find it very difficult to be objective about their superiors. In most cases superiors are held in awe by subordinates, and in some cases a frustrated "sorehead" is likely to be unreasonably and unfairly critical of a superior.

Likewise, experience with peer rating has not been very encouraging. Word is likely to leak out about the ratings peers make on their associates. The person doing the rating is consequently likely to feel some justifiable reluctance to be anything but highly favorable, knowing that the person being rated will probably be his or her rater at a later time.

While these and other devices that have been used to offset the disadvantages of trait rating have helped, they cannot overcome the fact that traits and work qualities are subjective and are not correlated with what a manager's job really is.

APPRAISING MANAGERS AGAINST VERIFIABLE OBJECTIVES

One of the most promising tools of managerial appraisal to have developed is the system of evaluating managerial performance against the setting and accomplishing of verifiable objectives. As noted in Chapter 7, setting a network of meaningful and actionable objectives lies at the base of all managing. This is simple logic since people cannot be expected to accomplish a task with effectiveness or efficiency unless they know what the end points of their efforts should be. Nor can any organized enterprise in business or elsewhere be expected to do so.

The Appraisal Process

Once a program of managing by verifiable objectives is operating, a major phase of appraisal is a fairly easy step. What is involved is seeing how competently managers set objectives and how well they performed against them. In those cases where appraisal by results has failed or been disillusioning, the cause can usually be traced to the fact that it was seen *only* as an *appraisal* tool. Even though search for a better appraisal method probably did give managing by objectives its initial and strongest impetus, the system is not likely to work if used only for this purpose. Management by objectives must be a way of managing, a way of planning, as well as the key to organizing, staffing, leading, and controlling. When it is this, appraisal boils down to whether or not managers establish adequate but reasonably attainable objectives and how they performed against them in a certain period.

This can be done by looking at the system of managing and appraising by objectives, as was done in Figure 7.3 (on page 202). As can be seen, appraising is only a last step in the entire process.

But there are problems. Were the goals adequate? Did they call for "stretched" performance? These questions can be answered only by the judgment and experience of the person's superior, although this judgment can become sharper with time and trial and can take on a high degree of objectivity in those instances where goals of other managers in a similar position can be used for comparison.

In assessing goal accomplishment, the evaluator must take into account such considerations as whether the goals were reasonably attainable in the first place, whether intervening factors beyond one's control unduly helped or hindered in accomplishing goals, and what the reasons for the results were. Another matter which the reviewer should watch is whether an individual continued to operate against obsolete goals when situations changed and revised goals were called for.

As in any case of control, progress toward goals should be regularly reviewed. It may be dangerous to limit appraisal to looking at performance once a year. For a top manager, such as a president or a division general manager, progress should probably be reviewed and appraised quarterly in fair detail and more broadly, in the light of probable accomplishment, for three or four additional quarters in the future. Alert and intelligent managers hardly wish to risk having obsolete objectives, naturally prefer to have both goal setting and evaluation be a regular activity, and certainly, in most instances, would not wish to wait too long to know how they and their subordinates were doing.

For individuals below the top level, quarterly reviews may be enough. And they may not. The real factor is the time-span necessary to determine whether a goal is still valid and whether satisfactory progress is being made. It is probable that for certain positions, such as those of first-level supervision, reviews could be usefully made each month. Note that this does not necessarily involve much additional work by a superior. It is merely carrying on the function of managing, and actual appraising becomes a relatively easy by-product of the process.

Strengths of Appraisal Against Verifiable Objectives

The strengths of appraising against accomplishment of objectives are almost the same as those of managing by objectives. Both are part of the same process, both are basic to effective managing, and both are means of improving the quality of managing.

In the area of appraising there are special and important strengths, especially when compared with the traditional methods of evaluating people against personal traits or work characteristics. Appraising on the basis of performance against verifiable objectives has the great advantage of being operational. Appraisals are not apart from the job managers do, but are a review of what they actually did as managers. There are, however, always questions of how well a person did; of whether goals were missed or accomplished, and for what reasons; and of how much in the way of goal attainment should be expected.

But information on what a person has done, measured against what that individual agreed was a reasonable target, is available. It thus furnishes strong presumptions of objectivity and reduces the element of pure judgment in appraisal. Moreover, the appraisal can be carried on in an atmosphere of superiors working with subordinates and not sitting in Olympian judgment on them.

Weaknesses of Appraisal Against Verifiable Objectives

As noted in Chapter 7, there are certain weaknesses in the system and practice of managing by objectives. These, of course, apply with equal force to appraisal. One of them is that it is entirely possible for persons to meet or miss goals through no fault of their own. Luck often does play a part in performance. It is possible, for example, that a new product will be accepted far beyond expectations and make the marketing manager look exceptionally good, even though the quality of the marketing program and its implementation might actually be poor. Or an unpredictable cancellation of a major defense contract might make the record of a division manager look deficient.

Most evaluators will say that they always take uncontrollable or unexpected factors into account in assessing goal performance, and to a very great extent they do. But it is extremely difficult. In an outstanding sales record, for example, how can anyone be sure how much was due to luck and how much to competence? Outstanding performers are rated highly, at least as long as they perform. Nonperformers can hardly escape having a cloud cast over them.

With its emphasis on accomplishing operating objectives, the system of appraising against these may overlook needs for individual development. Goal attainment tends to be short-run in practice. Even where longer-range considerations are put into the system, seldom would they be so long as to contemplate adequate long-term development of managers. Managers concerned primarily with results might be driven by the system to take too little time to plan, implement, and follow through with programs required for their development and that of their subordinates.

On the other hand, it can be argued that since management by objectives gives better and more accurate visibility to managerial needs, development programs can be better pinpointed. As possible as this is, if development is to be ensured, goals in this area should be specifically set.

From an appraisal as well as an operating management point of view, perhaps the greatest deficiency of management by objectives is that it appraises operating performance only. Not only is there the question of luck, mentioned previously, but there are also other factors to appraise, notably an individual's *managerial* abilities. This is why the authors of this book feel that an adequate appraisal system must appraise performance as a manager as well as performance in setting and meeting goals.

A number of companies have recognized the importance of evaluating the quality of a manager, although these have been relatively few. Some have been satisfied to ask for appraisal in such broad areas as planning, organizing, coordinating, leading, motivating, and controlling. Others have broken down these areas into broad categories such as "organizing," "job assignments," "clarity of staff responsibilities and authorities," and "delegation." One company, at least, the St. Regis Paper Company, aided managers in their appraisals by preparing and distributing a booklet entitled *Guidelines for Managing*, which was really a brief summary of basic principles of management.[3] However, the standards thus far used for appraising managers as managers have seemed to be too broad and too susceptible to general and subjective judgment.

A Suggested Program

It has been the authors' position for many years that the most appropriate standards to be used for appraising managers as managers are the fundamentals of management. It is not enough to appraise a manager on such broad areas as the basic functions of the manager. While important, these are too broad to be used as standards of appraisal. To do as the St. Regis Paper Company has done and give these terms some concrete meaning is a help. But for appraisal we should go further.

The best approach the authors have found is to utilize the basic concepts and principles of management as standards. If they are basic, as they have been found to be in a wide variety of managerial situations and cultures, they should serve as reasonably good standards. As crude as they may be and even though some judgment may be necessary in applying them to practice, they do give the evaluator some benchmarks to weigh whether subordinates understand and are following out the functions of managing. They are definitely more specific and applicable than evaluations based on such general standards as work habits, integrity, cooperation, intelligence, judgment, or loyalty. They at least focus attention on what may be expected of a manager *as a manager*. And, when taken in conjunction with the performance of plans and goals, they can help remove much of the weakness in many management appraisal systems.

In brief, the program involves classifying the functions of the manager as done in this book and then dealing with each function by a series of questions designed to reflect the most important fundamentals of managing in each area. While the total list of key questions, the form used,

[3]As reported in W. S. Wikstrom, *Managing by and with Objectives* (New York: National Industrial Conference Board, Inc., 1968), pp. 38–56.

the system of ratings, and the instructions for operating the program are too extensive to be treated in this book,[4] some sample checkpoints may be given.

For example, in the area of planning, a manager would be rated by such check questions as the following:

Does the manager—

set for the departmental unit both short-term and long-term goals in verifiable terms that are related in a positive way to those of superiors and of the company?

understand the role of company policies in decision making and ensure that subordinates do likewise?

check plans periodically to see whether they are consistent with current expectations?

recognize in choosing from among alternatives, and give primary attention to, those factors which are limiting or critical to the solution of a problem?

Also, in the area of organizing, such questions are asked as the following:

Does the manager—

delegate authority to subordinates on the basis of results expected of them?

refrain from making decisions in that area once authority has been delegated to subordinates?

regularly teach subordinates, or otherwise make sure that subordinates understand, the nature of line and staff relationships?

distinguish in all operations between lines of authority and lines of information?

The other areas of managing are dealt with similarly for a total of seventy-three checkpoints over the five areas of planning, organizing, staffing, leading, and controlling. Also, in order to solve the problem of semantics so prevalent among managers, practitioners are advised to use as a guide a standard book on management with reference to where every check question is treated in the book.

In developing this system, it was hoped to make the ratings completely objective by designing the checkpoints and questions to be "go-no-go";

[4]All these may be found in H. Koontz, *Appraising Managers as Managers* (New York: McGraw-Hill Book Company, 1971), chaps. 5–6 and apps 2–5.

that is, the manager being rated either did or did not. This was not found to be possible, and degrees of "how well" had to be inserted in each question, with rankings from 0 ("inadequate") to 5 ("superior"). In order to give the numerical ratings some rigor, however, each is defined; "superior," for example, is defined as "a standard of performance which could not be improved upon under any circumstances or conditions known to the rater." Other attempts to reduce subjectivity and lack of discrimination in rating include (1) the requirement in the final annual appraisal that incident examples be given to support certain ratings, (2) review of ratings by the superior's superior, and (3) raters' being informed that their own evaluation would depend in part on discrimination shown in the ratings they make. A degree of objectivity is also introduced by the number and specific nature of the checkpoint questions.

Advantages of the New Program

Clinical experience with the program in a multinational company showed certain advantages. By focusing on the essentials of management, this method of evaluation gave operational meaning to what management really is. Also, the use of a standard reference text for interpretation of concepts and terms removes many of the semantic and communication difficulties so commonly encountered. Such things as "variable budgets," "verifiable objectives," "staff," "functional authority," "delegation" take on consistent meaning. Likewise, many management techniques become uniformly understood.

The system, furthermore, has proved to be a tool for management development by calling to managers' attention certain basics that they may have long disregarded or not understood. In addition, the approach has been found useful in pinpointing areas where weaknesses exist and to which development should be pointed. Finally, as intended, the program acts as a supplement and a check on appraising managers with respect to their effectiveness in setting and achieving goals. If a manager has an outstanding performance in goal accomplishment but is found to be a less than average manager, those in charge would look for the reason. Normally, one would expect a truly effective manager to be also effective in meeting goals.

Weaknesses of the New Program

There are, however, a number of weaknesses or shortcomings in the approach. It applies only to managerial aspects of a given position and not to such technical qualifications as marketing or engineering abilities that might also be important. These, however, can be weighed on the basis of goals selected and achieved. There is also the problem of the apparent complexity of the total of seventy-three checkpoints; to rate on all these does take time, but it is believed that the time is well spent.

Perhaps the major shortcoming of the proposed approach to appraising managers as managers is the question of subjectivity. As was mentioned earlier, it was found that some subjectivity in rating each checkpoint was unavoidable. However, the program still has a high degree of objectivity and is far more objective than having managers appraised on the broader areas of the managerial functions, as has been common in the few cases where attempts have been made to appraise managers as managers. At least the checkpoints are specific and go to the essentials of managing.

TOWARD MORE EFFECTIVE APPRAISALS

After many years of frustration with traditional approaches to managerial appraisal, based primarily on evaluating traits, there is real hope that this key aspect of managing is becoming meaningful. Appraisal of managerial ability based on performance against preselected, verifiable objectives is a tremendous step in the right direction. It concentrates, as it should, on what managers *do* rather than on what someone subjectively thinks of them. When utilized as a standard for evaluation along with appraisal of a manager as a manager, there is hope that we are, at long last, beginning to approach the area of evaluating managers with logic and effectiveness.

But devices and approaches will not solve the problem. There is always the danger that people will adopt techniques without accompanying them with an understanding of the philosophy back of them, without the tools and assistance subordinates need, or without the hard work, time, commitment, and leadership to make them work. No management technique is self-actuating. They all require patient leadership, intelligent application, and willingness to take the time required.

In the area of managerial appraisal, the results should be worth the effort required. As has been said before, there is little dispute that the quality and vigor of managers make the difference, at least for the long-term success of any kind of enterprise. There should likewise be no doubt that if we are to have competent managers in an enterprise, this cannot happen without effective selection, appraisal, development, and motivation. These are all links in a system, and appraisal has historically been the weakest one.

FOR DISCUSSION

1 Do you think managers should be appraised regularly? If so, how?
2 What problems may arise from the fact that different managers on the same level appraise differently, some generally rating higher than others?
3 Many organizations still evaluate middle and top managers on such

personality factors as aggressiveness, cooperation, leadership, and attitude. Do you think this makes any sense?

4 The argument has been made in this book for appraising managers on their ability to manage effectively. Should anything more be expected of them?

5 How do you feel about an appraisal system based upon results expected and realized? Would you prefer to be appraised on this basis? If not, why?

6 What is your assessment of the degree of objectivity or subjectivity involved in the appraisal approaches suggested in this chapter? Can you suggest any further means for making appraisal more objective?

chapter 21

Manager and Organization Development

Good executives look to the future and prepare for it. One important way is to develop and train managers so that they are able to cope with new demands, new problems, and new challenges. Indeed, executives have the responsibility to provide training and development opportunities for their employees so that they can reach their full potential.

Before World War II, the view prevailed that through practical experience alone people would rise to managerial positions. During the war the need for training at the first-line supervisory level became evident, and concentrated efforts were made to satisfy this need. But no systematic training was conducted for middle- and upper-level managers. They simply were assigned to responsible jobs with little or no formal training in management theory. However, during the 1950s, firms became aware that managers do indeed require special knowledge and skills that can be taught. Strangely enough, although the need was recognized many years ago, the outlook for the future is not encouraging. According to John Miner, the United States faces a shortage of managerial talent that could threaten the growth and effectiveness of major enterprises.[1] This has created a need for manager development even more urgent than that of the past.

Educational institutions offer a great variety of management programs geared to the needs of practicing managers. Furthermore, the American Management Associations (AMA) conduct about 2000 meetings a year for over 47,000 participants. Both the Conference Board, a highly respected institution, and the American Management Associations have expanded their activities by offering courses in Europe as well as in the United States. Besides the availability of external programs, many firms are also conducting their own management training, which allows them to tailor the instruction to their specific needs.[2]

The costs of training represent major investments, and executives are justifiably concerned about effectiveness. The authors share this concern and therefore emphasize in this chapter the need for a systematic approach to manager and organization development.

MANAGER DEVELOPMENT, MANAGERIAL TRAINING, AND ORGANIZATION DEVELOPMENT

The authors use the term "manager development" to refer to progress a manager makes in learning how to manage. "Managerial training," on the other hand, pertains to the programs that facilitate the learning process. There is less agreement on what should be considered "organization

---

[1] J. B. Miner, "Implications of Managerial Talent Projections for Management Education," *The Academy of Management Review*, vol. 2, no. 3, pp. 412–420 (July 1977).
[2] See "The Big Business of Teaching Managers," *Business Week*, pp. 106, 108 (July 25, 1977).

development" (OD).[3] Perhaps the most popular definition is by Beckhard, who states: "Organization development is an effort (1) planned, (2) organizationwide, and (3) managed from the top, to (4) increase organization effectiveness and health through (5) planned interventions in the organization's 'processes,' using behavioral-science knowledge."[4] This comprehensive definition includes many processes that will be elaborated on later in the chapter. OD focuses on the total organization, while manager development concentrates on the progress individuals make. These approaches are supportive of each other and should be integrated for improved management and enterprise effectiveness.

THE NEED FOR EFFECTIVE MANAGER DEVELOPMENT

Many companies have substantial training budgets and large training staffs which design, develop, and market different programs. Nevertheless, some companies do not get the results they seek.

Management Development Failures

Many of the failures in management development programs can be attributed to an unsystematic approach to training. To avoid costly mistakes, some typical problems are highlighted below.

Development efforts do not support enterprise objectives   The purpose of training is to achieve enterprise objectives and develop professional managers. Unfortunately, there often is little relationship between the training activities and the aims of the firm.

In an effective and efficient training program managers determine enterprise objectives and integrate them with developmental needs of employees. An enterprise with a need for long-range planning, for example, should match these demands with talents and aspirations of managers in the company. Such a situation is shown in Figure 21.1, with the shaded area indicating a high degree of integration between enterprise and manager development objectives.

Emphasis on programs instead of results   Some executives take pride in the large number of employees enrolled in management development courses. Unfortunately, benefits derived from attending these meetings are negligible unless they satisfy a clearly defined training need; too often there is an emphasis on training activities, with little concern about

---

[3]For a review of OD literature see S. E. White and T. R. Mitchell, "Organization Development: A Review of Research Content and Research Design," *The Academy of Management Review*, vol. 1, no. 2, pp. 57–73 (April 1976).

[4]R. Beckhard, *Organization Development: Strategies and Models* (Reading, Mass.: Addison-Wesley Publishing Company, Inc., 1969), p. 9.

Figure 21.1   Integration of enterprise and manager development objectives.

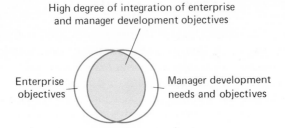

High degree of integration of enterprise
and manager development objectives

Enterprise
objectives

Manager development
needs and objectives

training results. One company which had a generous training and development budget, with many employees participating in a great variety of programs, made no effort to evaluate the effects, if any, on the performance of the employees. Clearly, there is a need for greater concern about the benefits derived from management development.

Manager development for a selected few   There is a mistaken notion that manager development requires placing a few people with high potential in a training program, while ignoring the rest of the employees. It is, of course, difficult to identify the potential of prospective managers, but to rely on a few trainees is also risky. It is even more risky if the trainees are selected on the basis of friendship or kinship with executives, without regard for capabilities. Manager development programs should be available for all qualified employees who aspire to a career in management.

Premises of the Operational-Management Theory Approach to Training and Development

The operational-management theory approach to training and development is a situational one that integrates principles, concepts, theory, and behavioral knowledge with management practices to achieve optimum results. This approach rests on the following assumptions:

Top managers must actively support the program   The support of top executives is essential for training and development. But it is particularly important for programs that involve people from different levels of the enterprise, as, for example, in many organization development efforts. The support of top managers must go beyond a policy statement regarding training. It must include their active involvement and participation in development.

Training and development must involve managers at all levels   Training is not just for a selected few "crown princes and princesses," nor is training only for those at lower levels. Top management may recognize the training needs of first-line supervisors, but not of themselves. Yet top managers should be trained first to provide an example of their commitment to the continuing development of all people in the enterprise.

Learning is voluntary   Since there is no generally accepted theory of learning, this premise must be qualified. Some psychologists feel that learning occurs through emotional experience, as on the level of fear. For instance, many of us can remember our refusal to learn to swim, but, on being thrown into the water, we learned—involuntarily, as it were—because of our fear of drowning. Similarly, we may learn through unstudied observation, or chance.

However, these basic motivations have little to do with the learning processes of a manager. Even clarity and brilliance in teaching will not make a person learn; you can lead a person to class, but you cannot make an individual think.

Training and development needs vary   Needs vary not only for positions at different levels in the organization hierarchy but also for individuals, since their backgrounds, requirements, aspirations, and potential are peculiar to each of them. Consequently, training and development activities should be tailored to these specific and individual needs.

Training and development needs determine methods   No program or method fits all needs. Instead, programs and methods should be selected on the basis of how effectively and efficiently they satisfy personal needs and accomplish the developmental objectives of managers and the enterprise.

Theory and practice must go hand in hand   It has been said that nothing is as practical as good theory. There is little doubt that theory provides an excellent framework for learning; but theory and practice must be integrated. Training is one side of the coin, which is the teaching of theory and the demonstration of techniques; the other is the actual practice of management. The need for situational management experience is obvious when applying training to practice.

THE SYSTEM OF MANAGER DEVELOPMENT

In Chapter 18 the systems approach to staffing was introduced. Manager development, an important part of the staffing function, needs to be further systematized; it must be integrated with the managerial process.

An Application of the Manager Development System

The processes related to the development of managers have to be integrated into a model that shows important variables and their relationships. Rather than discussing management development in abstraction, consider how an automobile company might apply the model in Figure 21.2.

In identifying "planning premises" (discussed in Chapter 8), forecasts are discussed that show the demand for a small, economic car in the United States market. Fortunately, these market needs are consistent with the "enterprise objectives" (see Chapter 7) that include the mass production of low-cost and high-quality cars.

The "strategy," then, is to make a thorough analysis of the market, the needs of potential customers, the characteristics of domestic and foreign car companies, and the feasibility of setting up a dealer network. Then more detailed "plans" and "policies" are drawn up for engineering, production, service, marketing, finance, and personnel (see Chapters 10 and 11). Also, the enterprise plan calls for setting up a new division to produce the new model to be marketed in the United States. The division objective (named "unit objectives" in the model) is to have the new plant operating at its full capacity within 2 years. An organization plan is developed that shows the "organization structure" (see Chapters 12 and 13). The "manager objectives" (see Chapter 7) are derived from the division objectives. For our illustration, the production manager selected has an objective of having the production line in operation at 80 percent capacity within 18 months.

Based on the manager's objective and the organization structure of the division, a broad "staffing plan" is drawn up (Chapter 18). Then, in a more detailed plan, individual "managerial positions" within the new division are defined (Chapter 19). Consequently, qualified employees who are ready for "promotion"—identified through the "management inventory" (Chapter 18)—are selected for the new positions. Also persons who are not now qualified, but may become qualified through a suitable development program, are identified. In addition, if it is found that needs cannot be met from the inside, managers from the outside may be "recruited" (Chapter 19).

After the production line has operated for some time, the production manager and his or her subordinates are "reviewed" at regular intervals and progress is noted. Furthermore, once a year a "comprehensive appraisal" is conducted (Chapter 20). Managers are evaluated on the degree to which verifiable objectives were achieved and in respect to the individual's performance as a manager in carrying out the functions. At this time, "individual development needs" are also identified.

The production manager and certain subordinates may be found deficient in setting objectives and in leadership. Therefore, "individual and group training" is initiated to satisfy these needs. In the potential review (called "identification of management potential" in the model), it is determined that the relatively good performance of the production manager makes that person a candidate for a division manager position with broader responsibilities. Consequently, additional training needs in marketing and finance are identified.

During the appraisal, an additional need is recognized. It is not so

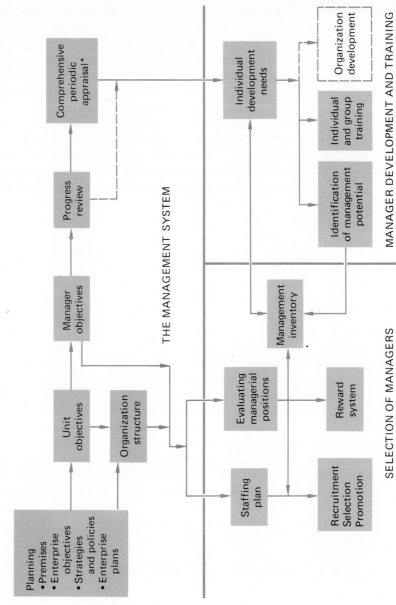

THE MANAGEMENT SYSTEM

MANAGER DEVELOPMENT AND TRAINING

SELECTION OF MANAGERS

*Appraisal against verifiable objectives and appraisal of managers as managers (Chapter 20).

Figure 21.2   The system of manager development.

much related to any deficiency in the performance of the production manager, but rather pertains to the organization structure. The problem concerns conflicts between organizational units. This leads to the initiation of a comprehensive "organization development" program.

The above illustration shows that manager and organization development are an integral part of the total management process, which starts with comprehensive planning, continues with the development of an organization structure, a staffing system, a method of setting individual manager objectives, and the appraisal of managers. The comprehensive appraisal becomes the basis for development and training. This discussion demonstrates that, through a systematic approach, the enterprise demands and individual needs for professional development can be integrated.

Manager Development Process and Training

To become operational, the manager development process has to be broken down into more detailed steps. These are depicted in Figure 21.3. A good training program is not static; it considers the training needs of managers in the present job and in the next job. It also takes into account broad enterprise needs and plans in the distant future.

Present job Manager development and training must be based on a needs analysis derived from a comparison of "actual performance" and behavior with "required performance" and behavior. Such an analysis is shown in Figure 21.4. If a district sales manager has decided that the selling of 1000 units is a reasonable expectation, but the actual sales are only 800, a "gap" results that is 200 units short of the sales target. Analysis of the deviation from the standard might indicate that the manager lacks the knowledge and skills for making a "forecast," and that "conflicts among subordinate managers" hinder effective teamwork. Based on this analysis, the "training needs and methods" to overcome the deficiencies are identified. Consequently, the district sales manager enrolls in "courses in forecasting and conflict resolution." Furthermore, "organization development" efforts are undertaken to facilitate cooperation among organization units.

Next job As shown in Figure 21.3, a similar process is applied in the identification of the training needs for the next job. Specifically, the "present competency" is compared with the "required competency" demanded by the next job. For instance, a person who has worked mainly in production may be under consideration for a job as a project manager. This requires training in the functional areas such as engineering, marketing, and even finance. Thus, the systematic preparation for a new assignment certainly is a more professional approach than simply thrusting a person into a new work situation without training.

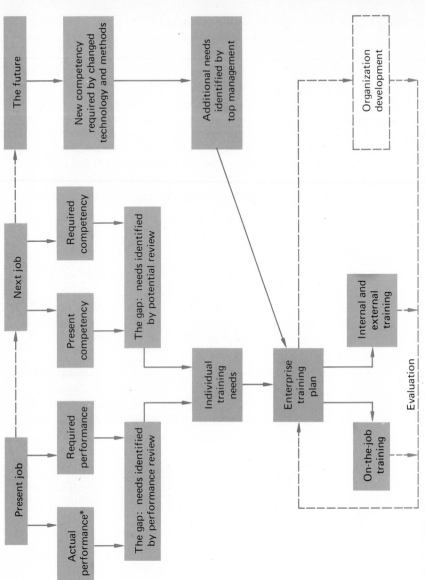

Figure 21.3 Manager development process and training*[*Adapted from John W. Humble,* Improving Business Results *(Maidenhead, England: McGraw-Hill Book Company (UK) Ltd., 1968.) Copyright © 1968 Management Centre Europe. Used by permission of the publisher.*]

*This includes performance measured against verifiable objectives and performance in carrying out managerial functions.

Figure 21.4 Training needs analysis.

Future   Progressive organizations go even one step further in their training and development approach; they prepare for the more distant future. This requires a forecast of new competency that will be demanded by changing technology and methods. For example, the expected energy shortages may require that managers be trained not only in the technical aspects of energy conservation but also in energy-related long-range planning and creative problem solving. These new demands—created by the external environment—have to be integrated into enterprise training plans which focus on the present and the future.[5] These plans are contingent, on the one hand, on the training needs and, on the other, on the various approaches to manager development that are available.

APPROACHES TO MANAGER DEVELOPMENT: ON-THE-JOB TRAINING

Many opportunities for development are to be found on the job. The trainees learn and at the same time contribute to the aims of the enterprise. However, because this approach requires competent managers who can teach and coach trainees, there are limitations to on-the-job training.

Planned Progression

This on-the-job technique gives managers a clear idea of their path of development. Managers know where they stand and where they are going. For example, a lower-level manager may have available an outline of the path from superintendent, to works manager, and eventually to production manager. The manager then knows the requirements for advancement and the means to achieve it. Unfortunately, there may be an overemphasis on the next job instead of good performance of present

[5]An interesting discussion on training for the future is by R. M. Fulmer, *The New Management*, 2d ed. (New York: The Macmillan Company, 1978), chap. 15.

tasks. Planned progression may be perceived by trainees as a smooth path to the top, but it really is a step-by-step approach which requires that tasks be well done at each level.

Job Rotation

The basic purpose of job rotation is to broaden the knowledge of managers or potential managers. The trainees learn about the different enterprise functions by rotating into different positions. This includes rotations (1) to nonsupervisory work, (2) to observation assignments, (3) among managerial training positions, and (4) to middle-level "assistant" positions; and (5) there is even unspecified rotation to different managerial positions.

The theory behind job rotation would appear to be good, but there are difficulties. As the term indicates, in some job rotation programs participants do not actually have managerial authority. Instead, they observe or assist line managers, which does not give them the responsibility they would have if they were actually managing. Even in rotations to managerial positions, the participants in the training program may not remain long enough in the position to prove their future effectiveness as managers. Furthermore, when the rotation program is completed, there may be no suitable positions available. Despite these drawbacks, if the inherent difficulties are understood by both managers and trainees, the positive aspects of job rotation should benefit trainees.

Creation of "Assistant-to" Positions

The creation of "assistant-to" positions is frequently used to broaden the viewpoints of trainees by allowing them to work closely with experienced managers who can give special attention to the developmental needs of trainees. Managers can, among other things, give selected assignments to test the judgment of trainees. As in job rotation, this approach can be very effective when superiors are also qualified teachers who can guide and develop trainees until they are ready to assume full responsibilities as managers.

Temporary Promotions

Individuals are frequently appointed "acting" managers when, for example, the permanent manager is on vacation, is ill, is making an extended business trip, or even when a position is vacant. Thus, temporary promotions are a developmental device as well as a convenience to the enterprise.

When the acting manager makes decisions and assumes full responsibility, the experience can be valuable. On the other hand, if such a manager is merely a figurehead, makes no decisions, and really does not manage, the developmental benefit may be minimal.

Committees and Junior Boards

Committees and "junior boards," also known as multiple management, are sometimes used as developmental techniques. These give trainees the opportunity to interact with experienced managers. Furthermore, trainees become acquainted with a variety of issues that concern the whole organization. Thus they learn about the relationships between different departments and the problems created by the interface of these organizational units. Trainees may be given the opportunity to submit reports and proposals to the committee or the board and to demonstrate their analytical and conceptual abilities. On the other hand, trainees may be treated in a paternalistic way by senior executives; although trainees are appointed to committees or junior boards, they may not be given opportunities to participate, which would frustrate and discourage them. The program would then be detrimental to their development.

Coaching

On-the-job training is a never-ending process. This is evident in athletic coaching. To be effective, coaching, which is the responsibility of every line manager, must arise from a climate of confidence and trust between superior and trainees. Patience and wisdom are required of superiors, who must be able to delegate authority and give recognition and praise for jobs well done. Effective coaches will develop the strengths and potentials of subordinates and help them to overcome their weaknesses. To be sure, coaching requires time; but, if done well, it will save time, money, and costly mistakes by subordinates, which in the long run will benefit all—the superior, the subordinates, and the enterprise.

APPROACHES TO MANAGER DEVELOPMENT: INTERNAL AND EXTERNAL TRAINING

Besides on-the-job training, there are many other approaches to developing managers. These programs may be conducted within the company or they may be offered externally by educational institutions, as indicated in Figure 21.3.

Sensitivity Training, T-Groups, and Encounter Groups

Sensitivity training, also called "T-group" ("T" stands for training), "encounter group," or "leadership training," is a controversial approach to manager development. The objectives of sensitivity training generally include (1) better insight into one's own behavior and how one "appears" to others; (2) better understanding of group processes; and (3) development of skills in diagnosing and intervening in group processes.

Although the sensitivity training process has many variations, one characteristic is that it usually lacks an agenda and directive guidance. People simply interact and receive feedback on their behavior from the trainer and other group members who are expected to express their opinions freely and openly. The feedback may be candid and direct: "Jim, I think you are a phony." Jim may accept this comment and resolve to change his behavior. But he also may feel hurt and withdraw from the group. The T-group process may lead to personal anxieties and frustrations, but if properly administered, it should result in collaborative and supportive behavior.

The benefits of sensitivity training must be balanced against the criticisms of it.[6] For example, some people may be psychologically harmed because they simply cannot cope with the frustrations. Sensitivity training also can be an invasion of privacy. Due to the group pressure and group dynamics, participants may reveal more about themselves than they actually intended to do. There also is concern that some trainers may not be qualified to conduct any sessions that become highly emotional. Finally, the relevancy of the outcomes of sensitivity training to the work situation has been questioned.

Despite these concerns mentioned by researchers and observers, many enterprises do use T-groups in their development efforts. The following guidelines can help to reduce potential harm and increase effectiveness:

Participation in T-groups should be voluntary.

Participants should be screened, and those who could be harmed, such as highly defensive people, should be excluded from this experience.

Trainers should be carefully evaluated and their competence clearly established.

Potential participants should be informed about the goals and process before they commit themselves to sensitivity training.

Before deciding on sensitivity training, development and training needs and objectives should be clearly identified. Based on these, more conventional methods should also be considered.

Organizational Behavior Modification

Another approach to development is behavior modification, which is based to a great extent on the work of B. F. Skinner.[7] When it is applied in

---

[6]For an evaluation of sensitivity training, see A. C. Filley, R. J. House, and S. Kerr, *Managerial Process and Organizational Behavior* (Glenview, Ill.: Scott, Foresman and Company, 1976), pp. 498–503.

[7]B. F. Skinner, *Science and Human Behavior* (New York: The Macmillan Company, 1953); and B. F. Skinner, *Contingencies of Reinforcement* (New York: Appleton-Century-Crofts, Inc., 1969).

enterprises, it is called "organizational behavior modification;" in short, "O.B. Mod."[8] This approach, which applies learning theory, suggests that *behavior is a function of its consequences.* Behavior with favorable consequences tends to be repeated more often, while behavior with unfavorable consequences tends to disappear. For example, workers will do a good job (behavior) because they are praised by their superiors (consequence).

Behavior modification uses the concepts of reinforcements, punishment, and extinction. *Positive reinforcement,* which is emphasized in O.B. Mod., is rewarding a productive behavior with incentives such as money, social approval, and responsibility. Positive reinforcement strengthens the relationship between the response and the stimulus. In other words, a positive reinforcer strengthens behavior. For example, if a manager praises the employee for doing a task well, the worker is likely to develop a habit of repeating this behavior. For greatest effectiveness, reinforcement should follow the response as soon as possible; the manager should not wait for the next performance appraisal to recognize a good job of the subordinate.

Negative reinforcement occurs when an employee works harder (increases desired behavior) to avoid complaints of the superior (avoid an unfavorable consequence). *Punishment* imposes a penalty for undesirable behavior. Employees may be given dirty jobs (penalty) because they were late (undesirable behavior). *Extinction* is another way of changing behavior. It occurs when nothing happens after a specific kind of behavior. For example, an employee who greets a supervisor will soon stop this practice if the supervisor does not respond.

As can be seen, the basic concepts of positive reinforcement are primarily matters of motivation and will be dealt with more fully in Chapter 23.

Transactional Analysis

Transactional analysis (TA) originated with Eric Berne[9] and was further popularized by Thomas Harris.[10] At the beginning it was a method of psychotherapy, but later TA became a useful tool to improve human relations and communication in business. More recently, TA also has been linked directly to the managerial process.[11]

Although TA considers both the emotional and intellectual aspects, the emphasis is on the rational process of understanding human behavior. The common components of TA are: (1) the ego states, with the focus on

[8]F. Luthans and R. Kreitner, *Organizational Behavior Modification* (Glenview, Ill.: Scott, Foresman and Company, 1975).
[9]E. Berne, *Games People Play* (New York: Grove Press, Inc., 1964).
[10]T. A. Harris, *I'm OK—You're OK* (New York: Harper & Row, Publishers, Incorporated, 1969).
[11]H. Weihrich, "MBO: Appraisal with Transactional Analysis," *Personnel Journal,* vol. 55, no. 4, pp. 173–175 (April 1976); and H. Weihrich, "MBO in the 'OK' Organization," *Management World,* vol. 6, no. 5, pp. 10–14 (May 1977).

the individual, (2) the analysis of transactions between people, (3) the way time is used, and (4) the life positions in respect to the "OKness or Not-OKness" of people. The first two TA concepts, the ego states and transactions, are the foundations of TA and deserve elaboration.

Ego States   Every person, according to TA theory, has three ego states: the Parent, the Adult, and the Child. The Parent ego state pertains to experiences and related behavior patterns influenced by the external environment, especially during early life. Words and phrases that may indicate the Parent ego state include "do, don't, always, everyone knows." The Adult ego state, on the other hand, refers to the rational part of the personality and is characterized by objectivity, problem solving, and rational decision making. Words and phrases indicating the Adult are "what, why, when, how, where, who, what is the probability of success," and so on. The Child ego state pertains to the part of the personality that is the source of fear, anger, rebellion, and hurt; but it also includes happiness, laughter, and creativity. Verbal clues may include "I want, I can't, help me, great!"

All three ego states are important for a well-rounded personality. Parent behavior may be appropriate in an emergency, as in leading employees to safety. Similarly, the Child ego state can be useful as a source of creative behavior. But problems usually occur when an ego state unsuitable for a particular situation determines behavior. It is, therefore, the Adult that must decide which ego state is effective for a specific situation.

Transactions   Ego states do not exist in isolation; rather, they exist in interaction with the ego states of other people. There are many different kinds of transactions, but the following examples will illustrate a typical work situation. The superior may say, "John, fix the engine right away and do not ask any questions." The subordinate may respond, "You mind your own business. I will do it when I have time." This crossed transaction, shown in Figure 21.5, usually stops further communication.

The superior could say, "John, how long will it take to fix the engine?" The subordinate then might answer, "It appears that the carburetor needs to be cleaned and this will take 2 hours." This parallel transaction, Adult to Adult, can be diagramed as in Figure 21.6.

There are many other kinds of transactions with different degrees of effectiveness. In general, transactions on the Adult-Adult level are not used often enough, even though they can facilitate the delicate process of dealing with people in the enterprise.

TA has several benefits. It is easy to learn, yet it is a powerful tool for analyzing and improving complex human interactions at work. Furthermore, TA improves communication; it increases personal effectiveness; and it can facilitate solving organizational and personal problems.

Figure 21.5 Crossed transaction.

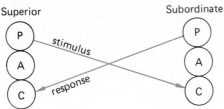

But TA has limitations. It is only one of many tools a manager can use. It is not a substitute for management theory, nor is it a panacea for all enterprise problems. To be effective, training must show how TA can be applied to the managerial processes, such as goal setting, appraising, and leadership. This requires trainers who are familiar with management concepts, principles, and practice.

Applications of TA to training Several companies have used TA in their developmental efforts. For example, the Bank of America trained supervisors in applying TA concepts to improve relationships with subordinates, peers, and superiors.[12] American Airlines, which calls its program "TACT," an acronym for "Transactional Analysis in Customer Treatment," uses TA for training supervisors, ground service personnel, and flight service employees to improve relations with customers. This program has been evaluated and has received a favorable review. It has been reported, for example, that customers got better treatment after employees completed the TACT program.[13]

It can be concluded that while the recognition of one's predominant ego state in transactions is an important step toward better self-knowledge and greater effectiveness as a manager, evidence is insufficient at this time to make a final judgment about TA's usefulness for improving managers' interpersonal competence.

[12]W. C. Bessey and R. M. Wendlinger, "TA Applied to Supervision," in D. Jongeward, *Everybody Wins: Transactional Analysis Applied to Organizations* (Reading, Mass.: Addison-Wesley Publishing Company, Inc., 1973), pp. 245–265.
[13]L. K. Randall, "Red, White, and Blue TA at 600 MPH," in D. Jongeward, ibid., pp. 123–150.

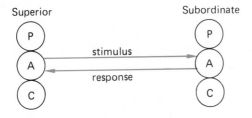

Figure 21.6 Parallel transaction.

Conference Programs

Conference programs may be used for internal or external training. In this approach managers or potential managers are exposed to ideas of speakers who are experts in their field. Within the company, people may be instructed in the history of the firm, its purposes, policies, and relationships with customers, consumers, and other groups. External conferences may vary greatly, ranging from programs on specific managerial techniques to programs on broad topics such as the relationship between business and society.

These programs can be valuable if they satisfy a training need and are thoughtfully planned. A careful selection of topics and speakers will increase the effectiveness of this training device. Furthermore, conferences can be made more successful when they include discussions; two-way communication allows participants to ask for clarification of specific topics that are of particular relevance to them.

University Management Programs

Many universities now conduct courses, workshops, conferences, institutes, and formal programs for training managers. These offerings include evening courses, short seminars, live-in programs, a full graduate curriculum, and even custom-designed programs for the needs of individual companies. Some of the executive development centers even provide career development assistance with programs designed to fit typical training and development needs of first-line supervisors, middle managers, and top executives.

These programs expose managers to theories, principles, and new developments in management. In addition, there is usually a valuable interchange of experience among managers who, in similar positions, face similar challenges.

Many university programs have little management theory and policy in them. They are likely to concentrate on such tool or functional areas as accounting, statistics, operations research, economics, finance, production, and marketing. This is understandable in view of the expertise of the faculty of many universities which tends to be in these subjects rather than in pure management theory and practice.

American Management Associations Programs

The American Management Associations, headquartered in New York, offer a great variety of programs throughout the United States and in various parts of the world. International programs are conducted through their management centers in Belgium, Mexico, Argentina, and Brazil. The offerings include seminars and workshops in accounting, communication, financial management, women managers in a changing environment, planning, and zero-based budgeting, just to mention a few. The leaders of the seminars and workshops are often business executives with considerable practical experience.

The advantages of such training are knowledgeable leadership, cooperative learning through the exchange of ideas, and concentration upon a limited subject. One disadvantage is that most sessions are held in a few large cities. Also, problems may be approached from a "how to do it" viewpoint, without providing sufficient background information on management theory, concepts, and principles.

Readings

Another approach to development is planned reading of relevant and current management literature. This is essentially self-development. A manager may be aided by the training department, which often develops a reading list of valuable books. This learning experience can be enhanced through discussions of articles and books with other managers and the superior.

Special Training Programs

Management development is an open-system approach that responds to the needs and demands of the external environment. Recently, government and industry have become aware of the need for training programs specifically designed for women, members belonging to minority groups, and individuals who are physically handicapped. Many firms have made special efforts to train these people so that they may utilize their full potential while contributing to the aims of the enterprise.

Evaluation and Transfer

The effectiveness of training programs can only be determined through measurements against standards. For this reason, emphasis is placed on a systematic identification of training needs and objectives.

In general, developmental objectives include (1) an increase in knowledge, (2) development of attitudes conducive to good managing, (3) acquisition of skills, (4) improvement of management performance, and (5) achievement of enterprise objectives.

In training, it is extremely important that the criteria used in the classroom situation resemble as closely as possible the criteria relevant in the working environment. One of the authors observed a T-group which had as its goals openness, leveling, and feedback about each person's conduct in the group. The behavioral change of one of the participants would have had to be rated "excellent" when measured against the T-group criteria. However, when this person attempted to transfer his new values and behavior to the job, he met resistance and outright hostility.

Arguments occurred and the result was that this person had to leave the company. Although the person changed, his boss did not; nor did the fellow workers and the total work environment. This illustration shows that manager development requires a situational approach in which training objectives, techniques, and methods should be sufficiently congruent with the values, norms, and characteristics of the environment.

ORGANIZATION DEVELOPMENT

Organization development, typically shortened to "OD," is a systematic, integrated, and planned approach to improve the effectiveness of an enterprise. It is designed to solve problems that adversely affect operating efficiency at all levels. These efforts may include the "vertical or diagonal slice," which involves managers (or representatives of managers) from all levels working together to solve specific management problems facing the division or firm. Such problems may include lack of cooperation, excessive decentralization, and poor communication.

The techniques involve laboratory training, managerial grid training, and survey feedback. Some OD practitioners also use team building, process consultation, job enrichment,[14] organizational behavior modification, and management by objectives as part of their approach.

General Motors (GM) uses OD to improve the effectiveness of its management system. OD is a long-range, situational effort that is based on action research and problem-solving techniques. Scientific analysis is used to identify factors that bear on a particular problem. Based on the findings, improvements are made through interventions such as changes in the job content, the organization structure, and the enterprise environment.

At GM's Oldsmobile division the OD program reduced absenteeism and turnover; the Chevrolet group improved employee job satisfaction; and the Buick division, using a job enrichment program, increased productivity, reduced petty grievances, improved departmental morale, and facilitated better interpersonal relationships.[15]

The Need for Organization Development

Organization development evolved in response to changes in the external and internal environment. For enterprises to remain viable and survive in the world of change, they have to respond quickly. Products rapidly become obsolete and are replaced by new ones. For example, only a few people predicted the application of space age technology to consumer

---

[14]For a more thorough discussion of job enrichment, see chap. 23.
[15]S. P. Robbins, *The Administrative Process* (Englewood Cliffs, N.J.: Prentice-Hall, Inc., 1976), pp. 340–345, 347–349.

products, including hand-held electronic calculators and electronic watches. Flexible firms such as Texas Instruments and Hughes Aircraft Company seized on opportunities created by the new technologies and produced these electronic components for the consumer market.

Another reason for the rise of OD is the knowledge explosion and the change of the labor force. Not only scientists but also other "knowledge" workers who are not directly involved in manual activities make up a greater proportion of the labor force than ever before. In general, people today are better educated and have a greater need for a degree of independence.

To respond to demands of employees, many enterprises have used OD to provide an environment for experiential learning in which people become involved in solving job-related problems.

A final reason for the evolvement of OD was the recognition that traditional training methods that focused on the individual rather than on the total organization were insufficient. Often difficulties were encountered in the transfer of knowledge and skills from the classroom to the job and the work environment. All these considerations led to the recognition of the need for the more comprehensive approach of organization development that considers people, structure, technology, and social aspects as an interrelated system.[16]

Organization Development Process

Organization development is a situational or contingency approach to improving enterprise effectiveness. Although different techniques are utilized, the process often involves the steps shown in Figure 21.7. An example can illustrate the application of the model.

Consider a firm that experiences problems of conflicts between organizational units, low morale, customer complaints, and increasing costs ("problem recognition" in the model). The chief executive contacts an OD expert to discuss the situation. Both agree on the necessity of an "organizational diagnosis." The consultant then collects information from several organizational units through questionnaires, interviews, and observations. The data are analyzed and prepared for feedback.

The executive confers with other managers and gathers support for an off-site workshop. After some introductory comments, the consultant presents the findings grouped under the headings "relations between departments," "enterprise goals," and "customer relations" ("feedback"). The group then ranks the problems in order of their importance. With the guidance of the consultant, the group discusses the difficulties, identifies the underlying causes, and explores possible solutions.

The role of the consultant is that of a coach facilitating the group

[16]A. P. Raia, "Organizational Development—Some Issues and Challenges," *California Management Review*, vol. 14, no. 4, pp. 13–20 (Summer 1972).

Figure 21.7 A model of the organization development process. [*Adapted from H. M. F. Rush,* Organization Development: A Reconnaissance *(New York: National Industrial Conference Board, Inc., 1973), p. 6. Used by permission.*]

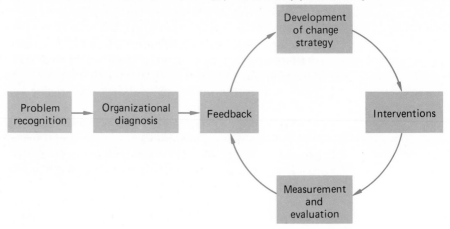

process. Short lectures and exercises on decision making, team building, and problem solving are integrated into this group process. At times subgroups are established to deal with specific issues. The emphasis is on openness and objectivity. The meeting ends with an agreement on a "change strategy."

The specific "interventions" may include a change in the organization structure, a more effective procedure for handling customer complaints, and the establishment of a team charged with the responsibility of implementing a cost reduction program. Furthermore, it is agreed to meet again in 3 months to "measure and evaluate" the effectiveness of the OD efforts.

Although these phases complete the OD cycle, the effort does not end. Instead, OD becomes a continuous process—planned, systematic, and focused on change—that aims at making the enterprise more effective.

Grid Organization Development and Other Methods

One systematic program in organization development is the grid approach.[17] Because the grid itself is discussed in Chapter 24, the emphasis here is on the six phases of the grid organization development.

Phase 1   is an introduction to the basic concept of the grid. Robert Blake and Jane Mouton state that the concern for people and the concern for production are not mutually exclusive; they are complementary. The aim of the grid is to develop a high concern for both.

---

[17]R. B. Blake and J. S. Mouton, *Building a Dynamic Corporation Through Grid Organization Development* (Reading, Mass.: Addison-Wesley Publishing Company, Inc., 1969).

Phase 2 is a continuation of Phase 1, but the focus is on the *team* instead of the individual. In this phase group members set standards, develop ways to achieve objectives, and identify barriers that hinder the enterprise from achieving its full potential.

Phase 3 concerns *intergroup development*. It is in this phase that OD really begins. The focus is now on the organization, rather than on individuals. The aim is to reduce conflicts between groups that work together.

Phase 4 involves *organizational goal setting*. In this phase top management identifies the aims of the enterprise and designs an *ideal strategic corporate model*. Managers from all enterprise functions, such as production, engineering, sales, finance, and personnel, are usually members of this policy-setting team.

Phase 5 concerns the *implementation of the strategic model*. This phase may extend over several years. Managers from all levels of the organization hierarchy have responsibilities in carrying out the activities necessary to achieve the goals set in the previous phase.

Phase 6 is a *systematic critique*. Managers evaluate achievements as well as mistakes made in the previous phases; they also discuss new challenges.

The managerial grid is but one of several approaches to OD. Another one is the *survey feedback* method; it emphasizes the collection, organization, analysis, and feedback of data to participants. Still another technique of OD is *process consultation*, which is concerned with the role of the consultant in facilitating processes within and between groups. In *team building*, people who work together meet to identify barriers that hinder the functioning of the group. Then the team members develop change objectives and action plans to make the group more effective in achieving enterprise goals.

As these illustrations demonstrate, the parameters of OD are not clearly defined. Instead, OD is eclectic, in the sense that it chooses from a variety of tools, methods, and techniques that are suitable to facilitate the solving of particular enterprise problems.

An Example of an OD Program

Donnelly Mirror, Inc., of Holland, Michigan, used OD to make the enterprise more effective. This moderate-sized firm employs about 350 people to produce 70 percent of the "day-night" rearview mirrors for automobiles.

Interest in OD began when the employees attended managerial grid seminars. Later, the company also sought the services of the Institute of

Social Research at the University of Michigan to collect data on the organization, to feed back this information, and to act as a general change agent. The OD approach focused on participative management, with emphasis on problem solving and decision making at the organizational level where problems actually occurred. Furthermore, the company also utilized the "linking pin" concept with overlapping work teams. Basically, the "linking pin" is the person who is a subordinate in one group and a superior in another, thus linking the two groups.

The results of these and a number of other OD changes at Donnelly Mirror are impressive: considerable cost reductions, improved quality levels, and a noticeable increase in employee satisfaction.[18]

These achievements are certainly encouraging, but more research needs to be done in other companies under different conditions to make a definitive evaluation of OD. Today there is still a major gap in research on the cost and effectiveness of OD efforts. No doubt this is a complex task because it is not easy to isolate cause and effect relationships. For instance, improved enterprise performance may be attributable to favorable market conditions and not to OD efforts. However, the great interest in measuring productivity—indicated by recent writings in management journals—will eventually provide more sophisticated tools to assess the effects of OD and other managerial approaches.

FOR DISCUSSION

1 It has been argued that firms have an obligation to train and develop all employees with managerial potential. Would you agree?
2 What are some typical failures in manager development and training? Can you explain these failures? What would you recommend to overcome the shortcomings?
3 Explain the current status, and project the future, of the contingency approach to staffing.
4 To be truly effective, management development and training have to be viewed as a system. What does this really mean? Can you give an example of such a system?
5 Evaluate the advantages and limitations of different approaches to on-the-job training.
6 Evaluate sensitivity training, organizational behavior modification, and transactional analysis as techniques for training managers. Which technique would be most valuable to you?
7 What are the main characteristics of organization development? How does OD differ from manager development?

[18]H. M. F. Rush, *Organization Development: A Reconnaissance* (New York: National Industrial Conference Board, Inc., 1973), pp. 42–50.

SUMMARY OF MAJOR PRINCIPLES
FOR PART 4: STAFFING

There are no completely accepted staffing principles. Consequently, those listed have a degree of tentativeness. Yet, they are useful as guidelines for understanding the staffing function. These principles are grouped into the "purpose" and "process" of staffing.

The Purpose of Staffing

The purpose of staffing is summarized by the following principles:

Principle of staffing objective   The objective of managerial staffing is to ensure that organization roles are filled by those qualified personnel who are able and willing to occupy them.

Principle of staffing   The clearer the definition of organization roles, their human requirements, and techniques of manager appraisal and training, the more assurance there will be of managerial quality.

The first principle stresses the importance of desire and ability to undertake the responsibilities of management. There is considerable evidence of failure to achieve results when these qualities are lacking. The second principle rests upon an important body of knowledge concerning management practices. Those organizations that have no established job definitions, no effective appraisals, and no system for training and development will have to rely upon coincidence or outside sources to fill positions with able managers. On the other hand, enterprises applying the systems approach to staffing will utilize the potentials of individuals in the enterprise more effectively and efficiently.

The Process of Staffing

The following principles indicate the means for effective staffing:

Principle of job definition   The more precisely the results expected of managers are identified, the more the dimensions of their positions can be defined.

This principle is similar to the principle of functional definition discussed in Part 3 on organizing. Since organizational roles are occupied by people with different needs, these roles must have many dimensions—such as pay, status, power, discretion, and possibility of accomplishment—that induce managers to perform.

Principle of managerial appraisal   The more clearly verifiable objectives and required managerial activities are identified, the more precise is the appraisal of managers against these criteria.

This principle suggests that performance should be measured both against verifiable objectives—such as in an appraisal approach based on management by objectives—and against appraisal of performance as managers. The appraisal of managers as managers considers how well the functions of planning, organizing, staffing, leading, and controlling are carried out.

Principle of open competition
The more an enterprise is committed to the assurance of quality management, the more it will encourage open competition among all candidates for management positions.

Violation of this principle has led many firms to appoint managers with inferior abilities. Although social pressures strongly favor promoting people from within the firm, these forces should be resisted whenever better candidates can be brought in from the outside. At the same time, the application of this principle obligates an organization to appraise its people accurately and to provide them with opportunities for development.

Principle of management training and development
The more management training and development are integrated with the management process and enterprise objectives, the more effective developmental programs and activities will be.

This principle suggests that in the systems approach, training and development efforts are related to the managerial functions, the aims of the enterprise, and the professional needs of managers.

Principle of training objectives
The more precisely the training objectives are stated, the more likely are the chances of achieving them.

The analysis of training needs is the basis for training objectives which give direction to development and facilitate the measurement of the effectiveness of training efforts. This principle brings into focus the contribution training makes to the purpose of the enterprise and the development of individuals.

Principle of continuing development
The more an enterprise is committed to managerial competence, the more it requires managers to practice continuing self-development.

This principle suggests that in a fast-changing and competitive environment, managers cannot stop learning. Instead, they have to update their managerial knowledge continuously, reevaluate their attitudes, and improve their managerial skills and performance to achieve enterprise results.

CASES FOR PART 4

1 Aerospace Inc.

Jim Smith was the manager of the systems development department of Aerospace Inc. During his 15 years with the company, he trained many managers and encouraged their development, only to see many of them leave the firm after they got their advanced degrees. The company had a liberal policy of educational reimbursement (75 percent of tuition costs and books), and many engineers (about 50 percent of them have a master's degree in a technical field) took advantage of the educational opportunities.

Joan Harris, an electrical engineer, came to see her boss, Jim Smith, who congratulated Ms. Harris for obtaining her master's degree in business administration, which she received through the assistance of the educational program of the firm.

Ms. Harris, to the surprise of Mr. Smith, said that she was leaving the company to go to a competitor, because she did not see any opportunities for advancement in the firm.

Mr. Smith was furious because this had happened several times before. He immediately went to see the vice president of operations and complained about the educational reimbursement policy and the lack of a systems approach to staffing.

1 What might be the reason that employees left after receiving their degrees through educational reimbursements?
2 If you were the vice president, what would you do?
3 How can the labor turnover be prevented?

2 Identifying First-Level Supervisors

A few years ago the executives of one of the best-managed agencies of the federal government decided that they should establish an early identification program for first-level supervisors. This agency had long been in the forefront of management education and was quite ready to heed the advice of management specialists concerning this subject. They surveyed their own experience only to find that many young people, professionally trained, were leaving the agency for private employment, where the rewards were thought to be greater. This left the agency with something less than the best-qualified candidates for supervision; it also left it with a notably older group of supervisors.

A career development program was carefully worked out. Its chief feature included thorough indoctrination concerning its nature and method of operation, an annual invitation to every nonmanager to apply for the career program, and an understanding that all future supervisors would be selected from within the membership of the program. The development of the candidates comprised (1) a week of formal supervisory training; (2) assignment to an established supervisor who would act as a teacher and guide, advising the candidate on a course of reading and enrollment in college courses wherever available, discussing the theory and practice of management with the candidate, and evaluating his or her progress; and (3) work on task-force assignments as available and appropriate. Frequently, candidates were appointed to supervisory positions before they finished their programs; if not, they would either stay within the program until assigned or resign from it to resume a technical career.

Several advantages emerged from this program. The candidates were pleased that their careers were a matter of interest and concern to the agency executives; candidates could more easily bring themselves to the attention of their superiors; the agency was provided with a group of youthful candidates for supervision; the brain drain from the agency almost stopped; gradually more vigor in management levels became evident; and young men and women could establish a broader base of experience from which to decide whether they really wanted to be managers.

Certain disadvantages also became apparent. Many good candidates failed to apply for the program because they were not sure of their own career objectives, they did not want to move away from the localities in which they were domiciled, or they felt too busy to undergo the training described (it was in addition to their full-time positions). Some complained of inadequate counsel, and many who failed to apply were later disgruntled when they found themselves no longer among the candidates for supervisory appointments.

The agency is now in a mood to reassess its experience with the program.

1   Is this a good program? Are there any defects or missing elements?
2   If you were asked to suggest improvements, what would you say?

3 The Denied Promotion

Jerry Nolan worked at the headquarters of the Worldwide Motorbike Company. His task was to process warranty claims and advise service engineers working in the field with distributors throughout the world. Then Mr. Nolan heard of an opening for a field engineer.

As a first step, Jerry Nolan approached his immediate superior, Donald Brown, and asked to be considered as a field engineer in Ms. Smith's department. The idea was rejected with the comment: "Let's talk about it later." When Mr. Brown left for a business trip, Jerry approached Jane Smith, the service manager for international operations, who was not only the superior of Brown but was also responsible for the field engineers. During the discussion, Ms. Smith, who favored promoting young talent from within the company, recognized that Jerry Nolan was well qualified for the position of field engineer. Ms. Smith promised to talk to Mr. Brown after his return from the trip.

One week later Mr. Brown called Jerry Nolan into his office and opened the conversation as follows: "I heard that you talked to Ms. Smith while I was out of town, about the position of field engineer. I cannot let you take this position. We just switched to a computerized claim-processing system and I need you because you have the broadest experience of any of my seven subordinates." Jerry was shocked. Should he be denied the promotion because he was the best person in the group? Two weeks later, a field engineer was hired from outside the firm. Jerry Nolan was wondering what he should do next.

1   If you were Jerry Nolan, what would you do?
2   What do you think about the staffing practices of the company? What policies, if any, would you recommend?
3   What do you think about the managerial behavior of Mr. Brown?

4 Selecting Supervisors

The department manager was holding a regular staff meeting with her four section heads. Her practice was to confine each meeting to one chief problem, and on this day the subject was the indifferent quality of the twenty supervisors reporting to the section heads.

"We have a rather poor record in selecting good supervisors in this department," she began. "We do have five or six who are outstanding, but there are too many who are unsuccessful. What do you people look for when you recommend candidates to me?"

"I think my best technical people make the best supervisors," said one. "They have the respect of their associates and their subordinates, who all rate technical competence highly. I find that they can train new staff members very effectively, and can also pitch in and do the most demanding jobs themselves."

"Maybe that is just the trouble," said the department manager. "People like that may never learn to manage because they spend their time on technical work."

"When I think about it," said another section head, "I have made my recommendations on the basis of seniority. It is the popular thing to do because everyone seems to expect succession on this basis."

"You think, then," said the manager, "that age is the only, or at least the most important, qualification for supervision? Such a practice conveniently ignores everything that has been learned about managing, or else it assumes that the candidate has the capability and the will to become proficient in management knowledge after getting the job. Is this realistic?"

In the general conversation that followed, other elements, such as getting along with people, making a good impression, having the capability for further promotion, and being able to exact responsibility, were championed.

The department manager became clearly frustrated, and as she closed the meeting, she remarked, "No wonder we have a 40 percent failure rate in selecting supervisors!"

1 What, if anything, was wrong in this department?
2 What would you advise the department manager do?

5 Hardstone Corporation

William Hardstone, president of the Hardstone Corporation, was interested in putting in a bonus plan for his top managers and their immediate subordinates. The management consultant whom he engaged to help him with the plan strongly recommended that the bonus plan be based on (1) establishing a bonus pool of 8 percent of profits after retaining 12 percent on stockholders' equity plus long-term borrowing, and (2) allocating bonus shares to each person on the basis of position, salary level, and performance on the job.

Mr. Hardstone readily agreed to having the plan based on these principles. The consultant then pointed out that if such a plan were to be instituted, an objective as possible appraisal of individual performance would be a necessary part.

Mr. Hardstone agreed, but told the consultant: "I don't want any formal plan of appraisal. I had one once, and all that paperwork was meaningless since everyone was marked 'outstanding' or 'excellent.' I will do my own evaluation and allocate the bonuses to each person. I know how they are all doing and how well they are performing."

1   Do you believe that bonuses should be based, in part at least, on every individual's performance?
2   How would you answer Mr. Hardstone? Is he right, or could he be? What would you suggest?

6 The XYZ Electronics Company

The XYZ Electronics Company, a fairly large defense and space electronics manufacturer with sales exceeding $500 million per year, has been using the manager evaluation form on pages 603–604. Many of the top managers have expressed dissatisfaction with it as an adequate means of appraising managers. However, the president of the company strongly believes that no form should be longer than a single page.

1   What is your opinion of the effectiveness of this form for evaluating managers?
2   How would you suggest the appraisal system be improved?

7 Apex Machine Products Company

John Willis, a prominent department manager of the Apex Machine Products Company, was being considered for promotion to division manager. He was a strong personality; he ran a tight shop; he clearly discharged his responsibility; he was known as a "good" manager. Upon close inquiry, it became clear that this candidate was "carrying" all his section heads; they were weak yes-sayers, and none was remotely able to succeed the department manager. The candidate was not appointed, and Dale Thompson, the group executive, was explaining to him why he was passed.

"John," he said, "you should know that we all wanted nothing but success for you. You are well thought of among all the people I talked to, and everyone wanted to see you get the chance at division management.

"This did not make the decision any easier for me, but I had other considerations to ponder. Basically, I was worried about the big risk of failure that you would run. In your present position you have carried the total load. I think this means that if you headed a division you would try to do the same thing, and you would surely fail and perhaps have a breakdown in health. Since you did not develop subordinate managers to carry the departmental load, I don't think you would or could use divisional department managers properly.

"Then there is the problem of manager succession. We don't have anybody to take your old job, and you have not prepared any of your subordinates to do so. I'm just afraid that the same thing would happen at the division level, and we just cannot afford to take that kind of a risk.

"I really don't know what the future holds for you. You are now 40 years of age. I don't think it is really possible for you to change your managing style. Maybe you can, but I feel that at the first sign of pressure you would revert to doing all the managing yourself."

"Well, Mr. Thompson," replied John, "I can certainly see the problem from your

NAME _____ POSITION _____ DEPARTMENT _____

APPRAISAL OF MANAGER PERFORMANCE

A. LEADERSHIP:
Consider ability to communicate objectives, inspire motivation and teamwork, and build and maintain morale.

☐ Respected, inspiring leader. Generates unusually high degree of cooperation and productivity.	☐ Motivates employees to perform effectively. Capable and consistent leader.	☐ Unable to effectively direct work or command respect of subordinates. Has difficulty communicating objectives.
		☐ Tends to be inconsistent in instructions. Has difficulty exercising authority and control over subordinates.
		☐ Generally motivates employees to satisfactory performance with minimum friction.

B. PLANNING AND ORGANIZATION:
Consider ability to anticipate conditions, plan ahead, establish priorities, and meet schedules.

☐ Effectively plans flow of routine work and generally adjusts to new requirements. Meets routine schedules.	☐ Versatile in approach to establishing priorities, dealing with changes and coordinating activities. Generally meets schedules.	☐ Unable to plan effectively. Tends to be inflexible. Not able to respond to deadlines.
	☐ Displays unusual flexibility in planning and coordinating work. Can be relied upon to meet schedules.	☐ Has some difficulty planning ahead and establishing routine priorities. Usually behind schedule.

C. DEVELOPMENT OF SUBORDINATES:
Consider ability to give instruction and guidance, delegate effectively, and give attention to evaluation and training.

☐ Has difficulty delegating responsibility effectively. Gives little attention to development of subordinates.	☐ Plans assignments to maximize employee performance and potential. Delegates effectively and increases capability of subordinates.	☐ Effectively utilizes employee capabilities and ordinarily provides guidance necessary to develop subordinates.
	☐ Generally knows the capabilities of subordinates and makes assignments and delegates accordingly.	☐ Unable to delegate responsibility or utilize subordinates effectively.

D. EMPLOYEE RELATIONS: Consider attention and support given to implementation of Company personnel policies, including Equal Employment Opportunity, attainment of affirmative action goals, adherence to labor agreements, and laws such as Equal Pay Act and Fair Labor Standards Act.

Tends to resist implementation of Company policies or achievement of established goals.	Aware of Company policies. Conscientious in efforts to attain goals.	Fully understands and is receptive to Company policies. Aggressively strives to achieve goals.	Often unaware of Company policies. Has difficulty establishing or implementing goals.	Understands and accepts Company policies. Makes consistent effort to achieve goals.
☐	☐	☐	☐	☐

COMMENTS: (Document any important aspect of employee's job performance which should be highlighted. Use additional paper if necessary.)

RATING SUPERVISOR: _____ _____ _____
                        SIGNATURE   TITLE   DATE

ORGANIZATION REVIEW: _____ _____ _____
                          SIGNATURE   TITLE   DATE

point of view. What I don't see is why I have not been counseled on this point in the years past. I would have changed."

"Would you really?" mused Mr. Thompson.

1   Do you believe anything could have been done for John Willis? If so, what?
2   Is there anything that could be done now? If so, what?

8 Developing Managers

The executive vice presidents of two corporations were exchanging ideas concerning the efficiency of management education and development within their companies. Both had had considerable experience with various types of formal training. They had experimented over a 10-year period with sending selected people to universities for both individual courses and degree work. They had extensive and costly internal programs under their personal guidance, directed by their chief training officers. At one time or another, representatives of the various approaches to management theory were employed to present a series of conferences and seminars in a program and make individual speeches on the subject.

"I must say," said Michael, "that our experience may be summed up as very expensive in time and fees and no improvement in management skills has appeared beyond those that one would see in any able manager who is ambitious. It is not that the 'trainers' were incompetent, or uninteresting. It is not that they didn't have something to say. In fact, our people had a good time and the reports they turned in were highly complimentary. But I really don't think we made a nickel."

"A year ago I would have said the same thing," observed Jim. "We had the same results, though we tried everything. And the funny thing about it was that our people thought every program was great. They were unable to discern quality and productivity. I guess this was because they could see little relevance of anything to their jobs. But we changed that."

"What did you do?" inquired Michael.

"One thing we did was to stop these programs that wander all over human experience, on the one hand, and on the other we dropped those interminable lectures. We decided to identify a particular aspect of managing that was rather poorly practiced. For instance, we thought our coaching of subordinates was being neglected, or at least poorly done. We called together a group of department heads, explained why we wanted a better coaching job done, explained how to go about it, and asked them all to confer with their managers concerning the need for coaching individual supervisors, the techniques to be used, and a later review of results. This way, we thought we had a direct line on a management need, and we insisted that the line managers do the training. On the whole, we feel we have got something that will work."

"I see," said Michael, who was now in a thoughtful mood. "It is not enough for top managers to show an interest in the development program. They actually have to train their own subordinates."

"That is right," concluded Jim. "If there is to be training, we have to do it. The manager is the great teacher in organized enterprise."

1   Can any manager be "trained" to manage better?
2   What should be done to get the most out of university programs?
3   Briefly describe your learning philosophy. If you were the director of training and development in a large company, what kind of an approach would you take?

9 Management Development at the Pendleton Department Stores Corporation

During a discussion by a consultant with a group of executives at the Pendleton Department Stores Corporation headquartered in Chicago, concerning the problems of improving the quality of management, the executive vice president asked whether there were any broad guidelines in the field of management development. Addressing the consultant, he said, "We know you have had many and varied experiences in the development of managers at all levels in many types of enterprise. Have you reached any conclusions that might approach the quality of general truths or, perhaps, principles?"

"While I would not want to assert that there are principles in this field," the consultant replied, "there are certain convictions that I have about programs for manager development. In the first place, the top manager—whether head of a large division, a region, or the whole enterprise—must know specifically what the proposed program is expected to accomplish, must be convinced that this is the way to go, and must have the patience and willpower to insist that every manager will put the theory into practice.

"In the second place," he continued, "the program must be implemented by operating managers and not by a consultant or the personnel department. Third, every program should be evaluated on the basis of its contribution to company results. And finally, I am certain that when the key top manager loses direct interest in, and contact with, the program, the quality and effectiveness of the program will deteriorate."

"But," said the executive vice president, "how can we take so direct a part in such programs? We have so many things to do. Anyway, that is the reason we have a trianing section of the personnel department."

1   Do you agree with the consultant? If so, just how would you accomplish what he suggests be done?
2   What of the executive vice president's position—how can a top executive do all these things to ensure manager training and still have time to do the rest of his job?

5 Leading

Leading is concerned with the interpersonal relations of managers and nonmanagers. Planning, organizing, staffing, and controlling, as effectively done as they might be, must be supplemented by giving people guidance, by good communication, and by an ability to lead. Managing, as leadership, must be based on an understanding of what motivates people and on an ability to build into roles and interpersonal relationships systems of inducements so that people will obtain satisfaction from contributing to the achievement of enterprise and department goals.

The first chapter of this part, Chapter 22, deals with managing and the human factor. Because leading is so much an interpersonal area of practice and effective leadership is vitally important to effective managing, special attention is given in this chapter to an analysis of the human factor in enterprises. Certain general characteristics of people are noted, and a variety of human behavior models, as they have been perceived by such specialists as Schein, McGregor, Likert, Argyris, Davis, and others are explained and analyzed. The importance of perceptual awareness by managers of these behavior patterns is emphasized. In addition, the human factor, as it is displayed in groups, is discussed and analyzed. The chapter concludes by emphasizing how the key to leading by managers is to harmonize individual and organizational objectives.

Chapter 23 treats the area of motivation as it applies to managing. Because managing involves the creation and maintenance of an environment in which individuals working together in groups are led to accomplish objectives, a consideration of what motivates people is central to effective managing. A considerable amount of theory and research has been undertaken in this area, and the purpose of this chapter is to summarize some of the most important knowledge of motivation that is loosely related to managing. Various kinds of theories of human behavior and motivation are discussed, as are certain of the programs using motivation theory in actual managing, such as job enrichment, and their practical meaning for managers.

Chapter 24 deals with leadership. Clearly, one of the keys to being an effective manager is to become an effective leader. Leadership is simply influence—the art or process of influencing people so that they will strive willingly toward the accomplishment of group goals. But the authors of this book like to think of effective leadership as being that quality which induces people to strive not only willingly but also with enthusiasm. As will be seen in this chapter, understanding leadership depends heavily on motivation theory. However, the major approaches to, and theories of, leadership are discussed, and their practical meaning for effective managing is dealt with. It is also pointed out that managers who manage well are likely to become good leaders.

Communication is the means by which leading is primarily accomplished. This is discussed in Chapter 25. Communication in management is a major problem and most top managers say that it is their most important problem. Sometimes this is a matter of understanding communication difficulties and techniques. But often it is not a communication problem, in the usual meaning of communication, at all, but a problem of knowing whom to communicate with on what—which is really a matter of clear delegation and organization structure. In other cases, it may be a problem of not having the right things to communicate; since people usually want to know what is expected of them, where the enterprise is heading and why, and how they are doing, communication deficiencies can be due to lack of planning and control. However, there is much to be appreciated about the nature of communication itself, the barriers that often exist, the principles to follow, and the fact that communication represents a restricted network in a social system. Chapter 25 develops these and other aspects of communication.

chapter 22

Managing and the Human Factor

MAJOR CHAPTER OBJECTIVES

1 To introduce the managerial function of leading by looking at its nature.
2 To explore the different views about the nature of people.
3 To point out tendencies in perception and their implications for managers.
4 To describe the characteristics and functions of groups.
5 To emphasize that the key to leading is to harmonize personal and enterprise objectives.

Management and leadership are often thought of as the same thing. Although it is true that the most effective manager will almost certainly be an effective leader and that leading is an essential function of managers, there is more to managing than just leading. As indicated in previous chapters, managing involves doing careful planning, setting up an organization structure that will aid people in achieving plans, and staffing the organization structure with people who are as competent as possible. The reader will see in Part 6 that the measurement and correction of activities of people through controlling is also an important function of management. However, all these managerial functions accomplish little if managers do not know how to lead people, and to understand the human factor in their operations in such a way as to produce desired results.

In a very basic sense, leadership relates to followership and one must discover why people follow. Basically, people tend to follow those in whom they see a means of satisfying their own needs. The task of managers is to encourage people to contribute effectively and willingly toward the accomplishment of enterprise goals, and to satisfy their own needs in the process.

Thus the broad function of leading has to do with the interpersonal aspect of managing. This is where the behavioral sciences can make their major contribution to managing. In attempting to analyze the pertinent knowledge in this area, it is useful to consider managing as it relates to the human factor, motivation, leadership, and communication.

THE HUMAN FACTOR IN ENTERPRISES

All organized effort is undertaken to achieve enterprise objectives; in general, the objective is to produce and make available some kind of goods or services. This effort is by no means restricted to business activity; it also applies to universities, hospitals, charitable associations, and governments. It is obvious that while the enterprise objectives may be primary in these various organizations, the individuals involved also have needs and objectives that are especially important to them. It is, then, through the function of leading that managers help people see that they can satisfy their own needs, and utilize their potential, while at the same time they are contributing to the aims of the enterprise. This requires an understanding of the roles assumed by people, their individuality, their dignity, and their holistic nature.

People Assume Different Roles

It is important to recognize that individuals are much more than a productive factor; they are members of social systems of many organizations; they are consumers of the produced goods and services, and thus they vitally influence demand; they are members of families, schools, and churches; and they are citizens. In these different roles, the influence they exercise establishes laws that govern managers, ethics that guide behavior, and a tradition of human dignity that is a major characteristic of our society. In short, managers and the people they lead are interacting members of a broad social system.

There Is No Average Person

It is important to recognize not only that people act in different roles but also that people are different. There is no average person. Yet, in organized enterprises, this assumption is often made. Firms develop rules, procedures, work schedules, safety standards, and position descriptions—all with the implicit assumption that people are alike. Of course, this uniformity is necessary to a great extent in organized efforts, but it is equally important to acknowledge that people are unique—they have different needs, different ambitions, different attitudes, different desires for responsibility, different levels of knowledge and skills, and different potentials.

Unless the complexity and individuality of people are clearly understood, the generalizations about motivation, leadership, and communication may be misapplied by managers. This means that principles and concepts—although generally true—have to be adjusted to fit the specific situation. In an enterprise, not all the needs of individuals can be completely satisfied, but managers do have considerable latitude in making individual arrangements. Although it is true that position requirements are usually derived from enterprise and organization plans, this does not necessarily exclude the possibility of "engineering" the job to fit the person in a specific situation. This is one of the alternatives suggested by Fred E. Fiedler for making better use of management talent already existing in the enterprise.[1]

Personal Dignity Is Important

Managing involves achieving enterprise objectives. Certainly results are important, but in achieving them the means must never violate the dignity of people. The concept of individual dignity, derived from ethical philosophy, means that people must be treated with respect, no matter what their position in the organization. The president, vice president, manager, first-line supervisor, and worker all contribute to the aims of the enterprise. Each is unique, with different abilities and aspirations, to be sure, but all are human beings and all deserve to be treated as such.

[1]"Engineer the Job to Fit the Manager," *Harvard Business Review*, vol. 43, no. 5, pp. 115–122 (September–October 1965).

One cannot talk about the nature of people unless one considers the whole person, not just separate and distinct characteristics such as knowledge, attitudes, skills, or personality traits. A person has all these to different degrees. Moreover, these characteristics interact with each other, and their predominance in a specific situation changes quickly and unpredictably. The human being is a total person influenced by inputs received from external factors such as family, neighbors, schools, churches, union or trade associations, political associations, and fraternal groups. People cannot divest themselves of the impact of these forces when they come to work. Managers must recognize these facts and be prepared to deal with them.

MODELS OF PEOPLE

In order to understand the complexity of people, several models have been developed. A model is an abstraction of reality. It includes variables that are considered important, but it also leaves out those factors less critical for explaining phenomena. Managers, whether they consciously know it or not, have in their mind a model of individual and organizational behavior that is based on assumptions about people. These assumptions and their related theories influence managerial behavior.

Over the years, various views about the basic nature of people have been suggested. To deal with all of them would not be practicable here. Thus, we focus on selected models by Schein, Porter and his colleagues, and on McGregor's classic assumptions about people. In addition, organization behavior models on a macrolevel by Davis and Miles are examined.

From the Rational-Economic View to Complex Person

Edgar H. Schein developed four conceptions about people. First, he noted the concept of *rational-economic man*, based on the assumption that people are primarily motivated by economic incentives.[2] Since these incentives are controlled by the enterprise, this assumption is based on a belief that people are essentially passive and are manipulated, motivated, and controlled by the organization. This assumption is essentially similar to that listed as Theory X by McGregor, discussed later in this chapter.

Schein's second model, *social man*, is based on Elton Mayo's assumptions that, basically, people are motivated by social needs. Thus, social forces of the peer group are more important than controls by

---

[2]*Organizational Psychology*, 2d ed. (Englewood Cliffs, N.J.: Prentice-Hall, Inc., 1970), pp. 55–76. Because of space limitations, only a few assumptions are mentioned.

management. Eric Trist's coal mining studies showed that the installation of new mechanical equipment impacted on social relations due to the change in group size.

The third model, *self-actualizing man*, is based on assumptions which suggest that motives fall into five classes in a hierarchy ranging from simple needs for survival, such as safety and security, to the highest needs of self-actualization with maximum use of a person's potential. According to this conception, people are self-motivated—they want to be and can be mature.

The fourth model, *complex man*, presents Schein's own view of people. The underlying assumptions he makes are that people are complex and variable and have many motives which combine into a complex motive pattern. In addition, people are able to learn new motives and to respond to different managerial strategies.

Contrasting Views and Models of People

Because the understanding of the behavior of people is so dependent on their nature, it is no surprise that many attempts have been made to categorize the basic views about the underlying nature of people. Lyman W. Porter, Edward E. Lawler, III, and J. Richard Hackman identified six such models.[3] In addition, they discussed the assumptions of McGregor's Theory X and Theory Y.

Rational or emotional? According to the *rational* view, people are seen as behaving rationally: they collect and evaluate information systematically and make decisions based on an objective analysis of the different alternatives available. A manager with this view probably would try to interact with people on a rational basis, but would tend to ignore their feelings, their emotions, and the human side of their personalities. The *emotional* view holds that people are ruled primarily by their emotions, some of which are uncontrollable. A manager with this view might, for example, play the role of amateur psychiatrist by trying to unearth the underlying psychological causes of employees' behavior.

Behavioristic or phenomenological? The *behavioristic* view is that people's behavior is controlled by their environment. Managerial strategies based on this theory would suggest changing the environment to get the desired behavior from subordinates. Directly opposed is the *phenomenological* view, which holds that people are unpredictable, unique, subjective, and relative, but with potential. A manager adopting this model would probably have to understand the complex functioning of the brain of the subordinates, because it is there that behavior originates.

[3]*Behavior in Organizations* (New York: McGraw-Hill Book Company, 1975), chap. 2.

Since this is not possible, people cannot be understood through scientific and behavioral observation.

Economic or self-actualizing?   According to the *economic* view, people are motivated by economic factors. Thus it is assumed that people act rationally to get satisfaction from monetary rewards. Managers with this view probably would see money as the prime (if not the only) way to elicit contributions from subordinates. Furthermore, these managers would create a competitive environment in which people's primary concern is self-interest. In contrast, the *self-actualizing* view holds that people want to increase their competence, they want to develop, and they strive to use their potential. A manager adhering to this model would establish an environment in which people could exercise self-direction and reach their full capabilities.

McGregor's Theory X and Theory Y

Another view about the nature of people has been expressed in two sets of assumptions developed by McGregor and commonly known as Theory X and Theory Y. Because these assumptions generated great interest in managerial circles, they are discussed in detail.

Douglas McGregor explicitly dramatized the question of the human factor through his use of the two sets of assumptions: Theory X and Theory Y.[4] Managing, he suggested, must start with the basic question of how managers see themselves in relation to others. This requires some thought on the perception of human nature. McGregor identified two sets of assumptions—two theoretical constructs—about the nature of people. He called one "Theory X" and the other "Theory Y." Why did he choose these terms? Apparently, he wanted a neutral terminology without any connotation of being "good" or "bad."

Theory X assumptions   The traditional assumptions, according to McGregor, about the nature of people are included in Theory X as follows:

1   Average human beings have an inherent dislike of work and will avoid it if they can.
2   Because of this human characteristic of dislike of work, most people must be coerced, controlled, directed, and threatened with punishment to get them to put forth adequate effort toward the achievement of organizational objectives.
3   Average human beings prefer to be directed, wish to avoid responsibility, have relatively little ambition, and want security above all.

Theory Y assumptions   The assumptions under Theory Y are seen by McGregor as follows:

[4]*The Human Side of Enterprise* (New York: McGraw-Hill Book Company, 1960).

1 The expenditure of physical effort and mental effort in work is as natural as play or rest.

2 External control and the threat of punishment are not the only means for bringing about effort toward organizational objectives. People will exercise self-direction and self-control in the service of objectives to which they are committed.

3 Commitment to objectives is a function of the rewards associated with their achievement.

4 Average human beings learn, under proper conditions, not only to accept but also to seek responsibility.

5 The capacity to exercise a relatively high degree of imagination, ingenuity, and creativity in the solution of organizational problems is widely, not narrowly, distributed in the population.

6 Under the conditions of modern industrial life, the intellectual potentialities of the average human being are only partially utilized.[5]

That these two sets of assumptions are fundamentally different is evident. Clearly, Theory X is pessimistic, static, and rigid. Control is primarily external, that is, imposed on the subordinate by the superior. In contrast, Theory Y is optimistic, dynamic, and flexible, with an emphasis on self-direction and the integration of individual needs with organizational demands. There is little doubt that each set of assumptions will affect the way managers carry out their managerial functions and activities. Before further examination of the implications of the theories, however, a few misconceptions should be clarified.

Misunderstanding of the theories   McGregor was apparently concerned that Theory X and Theory Y might be misinterpreted.[6] The following points will clarify some of the areas of misunderstanding and serve to keep the discussion in proper perspective. First, Theory X and Theory Y assumptions are just that: they are assumptions only. They are *not* prescriptions or suggestions for managerial strategies. Rather, these assumptions must be tested against reality. Furthermore, these assumptions are intuitive deductions and are not based on research.[7] Second, Theories X and Y do not imply hard or soft management. The hard approach may produce resistance and antagonism. The soft approach may result in laissez faire management and is not congruent with Theory Y. Instead, the effective manager recognizes the dignity and capabilities, as well as the limitations, of people and adjusts behavior as demanded by the situation. Third, Theories X and Y are not to be viewed as being on a continuous scale, with X and Y on opposite extremes. They are not a matter of degree; rather they are completely different views of people.

[5]Ibid., chaps. 3, 4.
[6]H. M. F. Rush, *Behavioral Science—Concepts and Management Application* (New York: National Industrial Conference Board, Inc., 1969), pp. 13–16.
[7]McGregor, op. cit., preface, p. vi.

The fourth area of potential misunderstanding is that the discussion of Theory Y is not a case for consensus management, nor is it an argument against the use of authority. Instead, under Theory Y, authority is seen as only *one* of the many ways a manager exerts leadership. Fifth, different tasks and situations require a variety of approaches to management. At times, authority and structure may be effective for certain tasks, as found in the research by John J. Morse and Jay W. Lorsch.[8] They suggest that different approaches are effective in different situations. Thus, the productive enterprise is one that fits the task requirements to the people and the particular situation.

Managerial implications of Theories X and Y   Stated in a simplified manner, the managerial process involves:

1   Setting objectives and developing plans to achieve them
2   Implementing the plans through leadership
3   Controlling and appraising performance against previously set standards

These key managerial activities are selected to illustrate the possible effects of Theory X and Theory Y on managerial actions. These effects, summarized in Table 22.1, present a conjectural view that awaits validation by data-based research.

In "Theory X," the superior assumes that people dislike work and must be forced to put forth effort. Consequently, the superior tends to take a directive, authoritarian role in the goal-setting process. Such a manager sets objectives for subordinates with little opportunity for their participation. Similarly, plans originate on the upper levels of the organization and are transmitted downward. The enterprise atmosphere, then, is not conducive to exploring alternative objectives or plans. Because of limited opportunities for subordinates to participate in goal setting and action planning, there is low commitment to objectives and plans.

Leadership, because of the limited view of employees, tends to be autocratic in Theory X. In leading subordinates, authority is seen as the *only* means to get things done. Although people may follow orders, hidden resistance and suspicion are frequent. Superiors issue orders, but may neglect coaching subordinates. The communication flow is one-way; from the top down with little feedback. Moreover, subordinates have only limited information regarding factors bearing on their jobs.

The control and appraisal functions are carried out rigidly, with standards imposed externally that allow little opportunity for individual self-direction. The superior assumes a domineering role in the appraisal, acting as a judge rather than as a coach. The appraisal meeting may be marked by low trust between the superior and subordinate, with the

[8]"Beyond Theory Y," *Harvard Business Review*, vol. 48, no. 3, pp. 61–68 (May–June 1970).

Table 22.1   An Illustration of the Management Process with Theory X and Theory Y Assumptions

Selected key managerial activities	Theory X and Theory Y	
	Theory X: People dislike work; people must be forced to work; people do not willingly assume responsibility	Theory Y: People like work; people work best under self-direction; people like to assume responsibility
(a) Planning (including setting objectives)	Superior sets objectives for subordinates There is little participation by subordinates in setting objectives and developing plans Few alternatives are explored There is low commitment to objectives and plans	Superior and subordinate set objectives jointly There is a great deal of participation by subordinates in setting objectives and developing plans Many alternatives are explored There is high commitment to objectives and plans
(b) Leading	Leadership is autocratic, based on authority only People follow orders, but hidden resistance and mistrust exists Communication is one-way, top-down, with little feedback Information flow is limited	Leadership is participative and teamwork is based on competence People seek responsibility, feel accountable, and are committed to performance Communication is two-way with a great deal of feedback Necessary information flows freely
(c) Controlling and appraising	Control is external and rigid Superior acts as a judge There is low trust in appraisal Focus is on the past, with emphasis on fault finding	Control is internal and based on on self-control Superior acts as a coach There is high trust in appraisal People learn from the past, but focus on the future; feedforward control emphasizes problem-solving

focus on faultfinding rather than on finding ways to prevent undesirable deviations in the future. With Theory X assumptions actuating the appraisal meeting, there is little opportunity for self-control and self-development.

"Theory Y" is based on assumptions that people want to work, are capable of exercising self-direction, and like to assume responsibility. These assumptions affect the setting of objectives and development of plans. For example, subordinates, after thinking about their jobs, set their own objectives and reach agreement about them with their superiors. In fact, there is a great deal of subordinate participation in setting goals and developing plans for their achievement. Moreover, alternative plans are also explored and evaluated. Because of their active involvement in the managerial process, people are committed to challenging, yet realistic, goals.

Leadership with Theory Y assumptions is participative, flexible, and adaptive to the needs of the particular enterprise. The emphasis is on teamwork, utilizing the talents of group members. People seek responsibility and feel accountable for results. Because of their involvement, people are committed to high performance. Communication flows several ways: from the top of the organization down to individual members, from the bottom toward the top of the organization hierarchy, and even crosswise from department to department whenever necessary. Moreover, frequent feedback provides for accuracy of the transmitted information. People in such an environment have the data necessary to make effective decisions.

Control, according to Theory Y, is internal and primarily self-control. Subordinates, setting their standards jointly with superiors, are committed to working toward their goals. Although standards are not changed lightly, they are adjusted if environmental changes demand it; it would be absurd to pursue standards that are obsolete or inappropriate in light of changed realities. The superior assumes the role of a coach who assists subordinates to achieve their goals, which, of course, are congruent with the team's objectives. The appraisal meeting is characterized by trust. Both superiors and subordinates learn from past mistakes, but the focus is on future improvement. The accent is on feedforward control that prevents deviations before they even occur (see below in Chapter 26). Consequently, the environment in which Theory Y assumptions prevail is conducive to self-development, with an emphasis on problem solving rather than on faultfinding.

Behavioral Models in a Historical Perspective

While many models focus on the general nature of people, Keith Davis identifies three behavioral models that deal with people within the enterprise context. Specifically, he shows how assumptions and related theories influence managerial behavior. Moreover, he suggests that each of these models was emphasized in certain periods in our history.[9]

The autocratic model   The autocratic model prevailed for a long time, especially during the industrial revolution. The dominant force was power: managers saw authority as the only means to get things done, and employees were expected to follow orders. The result was high dependency of subordinates on their boss. This dependent relationship was possible because employees at that time lived on the subsistence level. Performance under the autocratic model was, as one might expect, minimal.

[9]K. Davis, *Human Behavior at Work—Organizational Behavior* (New York: McGraw-Hill Book Company, 1977), pp. 95–101.

The custodial model   The custodial model became popular in the 1920s and 1930s in the United States. The managerial orientation was toward the use of money to pay for employee benefits. This model depended on the availability of economic resources of the firm and the ability to pay for those benefits. While employees hoped to obtain security, at the same time they became highly dependent on the enterprise. Rather than producing up to their capacity, however, employees' contributions may be described as passively cooperative.

The supportive model   The supportive model of organizational behavior depends on managerial leadership rather than on the use of power or money. The aim of managers is to support employees in their achievement of results. The focus is on participation and involvement of individuals in the managerial process. This model is similar to Theory Y, as discussed by McGregor, and to Rensis Likert's "principle of supportive relationships," which states:

> The leadership and other processes of the organization must be such as to ensure a maximum probability that in all interactions and all relationships with the organization, each member will, in the light of his background, values, and expectations, view the experience as supportive and one which builds and maintains his sense of personal worth and importance.[10]

The supportive model is found in affluent societies with complex technologies. This model, for example, is widely accepted in theory by managers in the United States, but not necessarily widely practiced. In fact, the discussion that follows indicates that managers subscribe to one model in their relationship with their bosses, but prefer another model for their relations with subordinates.

A Dual-Model Theory

According to Raymond E. Miles, the managerial task is to integrate organizational variables (goals, technology, and structure) with human variables (capabilities, attitudes, values, needs, and demographic characteristics) into an effective and efficient sociotechnical system.[11] This integration, shown in Figure 22.1, is achieved through activities such as directing, selecting, training, appraising, communicating, and controlling. It also includes designing the organization and jobs, developing people,

---

[10]R. Likert and J. G. Likert, *New Ways of Managing Conflict* (New York: McGraw-Hill Book Company, 1976), p. 108.

[11]*Theories of Management: Implications for Organizational Behavior and Development* (New York: McGraw-Hill Book Company, 1975), especially chap. 2.

Figure 22.1 Managerial integration of variables. [*R. E. Miles*, Theories of Management: Implications for Organizational Behavior and Development *(New York: McGraw-Hill Book Company, 1975), p. 22. Reprinted by permission of the publisher.*]

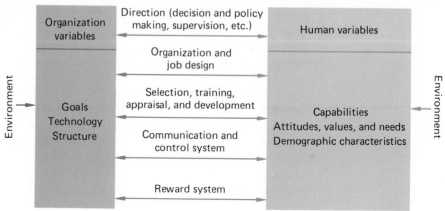

and rewarding individuals for their contributions. This framework, as the reader will readily recognize, is similar to the managerial activities discussed in this book.

Miles suggests that the manager's own concepts about managing partially determine the way the key managerial activities are carried out. Consequently, he identifies three "theories" of management known as the traditional, the human relations, and the human resources models.[12] The models, shown in Table 22.2, begin with assumptions about people; then policies related to these assumptions are described; finally, the expected results are stated. The important point is that managers apparently subscribe not only to one but to two models. One concerns the way they manage subordinates, and the other concerns the way they believe they should be managed by their superiors.

Three managerial models In the "traditional model," emphasis is on control and directing. The underlying assumption is that members of the enterprise will comply if tasks and procedures are specified and members are properly selected, trained, and paid. The "human relations model" is modified so that attention is given to social and egoistic needs. Thus, it is recognized that fair treatment and pay are not enough. Nevertheless, the emphasis by managers is still on controlling, although preventive steps are also taken to obtain the contributions of enterprise members. The

[12]A theory is defined by Miles in this context as "... simply a more or less complete explanation of how and why someone or something behaves, occurs, or responds as he or it does under a given set of circumstances." In Miles, op. cit., p. 32.

Table 22.2 Alternative Theories of Management

Traditional model	Human relations model	Human resources model
Assumptions		
1. Work is inherently distasteful to most people	1. People want to feel useful and important	1. Work is not inherently distasteful. People want to contribute to meaningful goals which they have helped establish
2. What workers do is less important than what they earn for doing it	2. People desire to belong and to be recognized as individuals	
3. Few want or can handle work which requires creativity, self-direction, or self-control	3. These needs are more important than money in motivating people to work	2. Most people can exercise far more creative, responsible self-direction and self-control than their present jobs demand
Policies		
1. The manager's basic task is to closely supervise and control his subordinates	1. The manager's basic task is to make each worker feel useful and important	1. The manager's basic task is to make use of his "untapped" human resources
2. He must break tasks down into simple, repetitive, easily learned operations	2. He should keep his subordinates informed and listen to their objections to his plans	2. He must create an environment in which all members may contribute to the limits of their ability
3. He must establish detailed work routines and procedures and enforce these firmly but fairly	3. The manager should allow his subordinates to exercise some self-direction and self-control on routine matters	3. He must encourage full participation on important matters, continually broadening subordinate self-direction and control
Expectations		
1. People can tolerate work if the pay is decent and the boss is fair	1. Sharing information with subordinates and involving them in routine decisions will satisfy their basic needs to belong and to feel important	1. Expanding subordinate influence, self-direction, and self-control will lead to direct improvements in operating efficiency
2. If tasks are simple enough and people are closely controlled, they will produce up to standard	2. Satisfying these needs will improve morale and reduce resistance to formal authority—subordinates will "willingly cooperate"	2. Work satisfaction may improve as a "by-product" of subordinates making full use of their resources

Source: R. E. Miles, *Theories of Management: Implications for Organizational Behavior and Development* (New York: McGraw-Hill Book Company, 1975), p. 35. Reprinted by permission of the publisher.

"human resources model" is different. The manager is seen as a developer and facilitator to help subordinates achieve performance aims. There is a great deal of participation in goal setting. Furthermore, if problems occur, several factors—rather than a single cause—are evaluated as potential reasons for the difficulties. Although self-direction and self-control are important to this model, the need for other controls is also recognized.

Separate theories for subordinates and for managers themselves   Based on extensive research evidence, Miles concluded that managers actually believe in *two* models: one for subordinates and the other for themselves. Studies conducted at Stanford University and at the University of California at Berkeley showed a basic agreement about the desirability of the concept concerning participation in decision making by subordinates, sharing of information, and increasing self-control. However, managers did not indicate strong belief in the capabilities of their subordinates, and in fact, exhibited a lack of confidence in them. Nor did these managers think that the capacity for leadership was widely distributed among subordinates. Thus, these managers seemed to reject the human resources model when it came to their own relationships with their subordinates.

The picture was quite different, however, for managers viewing their relationships with their own superiors. There was a tendency for these managers to rate themselves as equal or higher than their superiors on factors such as creativity, ingenuity, flexibility, and willingness to change. In addition, these managers felt that their superiors should use participation which, in turn, would result in better enterprise performance at their level. In summary, then, these managers appeared to suggest that their superiors should follow practices which would allow them to operate consistently with the human resources model. On the other hand, these same managers, in their relationships with subordinates, seemed to subscribe to the human relations model.

These findings have repeatedly been noted in a variety of our consulting and management development experiences. For example, in seminars on management by objectives, there is little disagreement among participants about the desirability of participation in goal setting; they favor placing responsibility for planning at the level where actions are carried out and providing an environment in which people can use their potential, self-control, self-direction, and accountability for results. Frequently heard from seminar participants are phrases such as "Great idea, but my boss should really attend this session," and "If only top management would practice this participative philosophy." Then, if the same people are observed interacting with their subordinates in the organizational setting, it is not unusual to find that they do not practice what they supposedly believe to be effective. In other words, their position is that the human resources model is effective at their level, but not in their relationships with subordinates.

Which of these many views of individuals is valid? Earlier in this chapter it was noted that Schein suggested four conceptions of people, ranging from the rational-economic view to a view that stresses complex motivations. Porter and his colleagues presented six different views about the nature of individuals. McGregor grouped assumptions into Theory X and Theory Y. Davis's organizational behavior approach identified autocratic, custodial, and supportive models. And Miles suggested three different models. Which model, then, is valid?

It appears that no single model is sufficient to explain the full range of individual and organizational behavior. People are different—there is no average person. Moreover, people also behave differently in diverse situations; and, to complicate matters, they even behave differently in similar situations at different times. In some situations people act rationally, in other situations they are guided by emotions. It is the manager's responsibility to create an environment in which people are induced to contribute to the aims of the enterprise. Yet to assume that people can be manipulated ignores their individuality and underestimates their intelligence. Economic rewards certainly are important in an enterprise, but people often want more than money from a job. They usually want to develop their capabilities, their competence, and their potential as well.

The effective manager will take an eclectic approach by drawing from different models that describe the nature of people. At the very least, one must recognize that people are different and do not fit neatly into one conceptual model. They must be treated with respect and dignity, must be considered as whole persons, and they must be seen in the context of their total environment in which they assume different roles. It is important to realize that different situations require a variety of managerial approaches for utilizing most effectively and efficiently the most valuable resource of the enterprise, namely, people.

PERCEPTION IN THE ENTERPRISE ENVIRONMENT

People's perceptions of reality are influenced by many factors, such as background, past experiences, values, expectations, interests, attitudes, and rigid views about the nature of people. It is important for a manager to understand some common perceptual fallacies in order to achieve increased personal awareness which, in turn, should result in better managing.

Perception pertains to information received from the environment. It includes, for example, *seeing* the factory, *hearing* the noise of the machines, *feeling* the heat from the furnace, *tasting* the food in the cafeteria, and *smelling* the fumes of the engine exhaust. The concern here is not with all of our senses; rather, the focus will be on those particularly relevant for managing.

Tendencies in Perception

What one perceives is not necessarily the real world. People see things from their own perspectives. Perception may be distorted by various factors. First, there is the object or event being perceived. Thus, objects or events with outstanding characteristics are more easily noticed than unobtrusive ones. Then there are the characteristics and tendencies of perceivers, who may be unduly influenced by first impressions or who may project their own faults onto others. Finally, perception is also affected by the physical and social environment.[18] A reprimand in front of the group, for example, will be perceived differently from one made in the privacy of the office.

The characteristics of the perceiver—the focus in our discussion—do influence the process of perception. In "selective perception," some information is processed, while other data are ignored. Frequently, outstanding characteristics are noted while less obvious factors are overlooked. There is also a tendency to disregard the unpleasant and to be more receptive to the positive and pleasant. Thus, some managers seem to be unable to face up to problems, unpleasant decisions, and realities of organizational life. At times, however, selective perception can serve as a useful "defense," when, for example, a manager tunes out disturbing conversation next door in order to concentrate on the task at hand.

Selective perception is influenced to a large extent by a person's background. For instance, students in a college-level business policy course may take different views when analyzing a complex case. Students majoring in accounting and finance often identify finance-related problems as critical issues. At the same time, marketing students frequently identify marketing issues, while management majors note deficiencies related to planning, organizing, or other managerial functions. All are looking at the same situation, but from different perspectives, influenced by their special training.

The term "stereotyping" usually refers to judgments about people who belong to certain ethnic or other groups. Personality traits are then ascribed to members of these groups. Thus, people develop stereotypes about union members, scientists, salespeople, and people with long hair, without regard for their individuality.

The term "halo effect" is used to describe the process in which a general impression—favorable or unfavorable—influences the judgment of specific factors. This can, of course, result in invalid or at least inaccurate appraisal of managers. Thus, a punctual employee may receive

---

[18]H. J. Reitz, *Behavior in Organizations* (Homewood, Ill.: Richard D. Irwin, Inc., 1977), pp. 142–143.

a high overall rating in the appraisal, even though the quantity and quality of his or her performance may be low.

Another problem in perception is "projection." This means ascribing one's own characteristics to other people. This often involves attributing one's own faults to others. An indecisive manager, for instance, may accuse others of being unable to make decisions.

Sheldon S. Zalkind and Timothy W. Costello, after examining several research studies, suggest that (1) a better self-knowledge helps one to see others more accurately; (2) there is a likelihood that one sees one's own characteristics in others; if one accepts one's self, one is probably more able to see favorable characteristics in others; and (3) accuracy of perception depends on sensitivity to the differences between people and the norms used for judging them.[14]

The Importance of Perceptual Awareness for Managers

Accurate perception is important in assessing situations in daily life. For managers, awareness of perceptual fallacies is critical in carrying out all managerial functions. In selecting subordinates, managers should be aware that they might favor a candidate simply because they have something in common, such as a degree from the same university. In appraisal, especially if not carried out professionally as suggested in Chapter 20, managers may rate employees on just a few traits while ignoring actual job performance. In training and development, managers may selectively see only interpersonal problems and choose behavioral training, although the important need may be for training in more accurate forecasting methods.

Similarly, in motivating employees, some managers may assume that money is the only way to elicit organizational contributions because they project their own need for monetary rewards onto subordinates. In assessing leadership qualities, a person may receive a high rating for making a valuable contribution in a task force where that person was the only member with sufficient knowledge to solve the problem. This is no assurance, however, that similar leadership can be expected in daily operations as a manager. Finally, communication may fail because people hear what they want to hear—they seldom like to hear bad news—and thus do not perceive the impending problems and their consequences.

CHARACTERISTICS AND FUNCTIONS OF GROUPS

In addition to understanding how perception affects behavior, people must also be seen and understood in their interactions with others in

[14]S. S. Zalkind and T. W. Costello, "Perception: Some Recent Research and Implications for Administration," *Administrative Science Quarterly*, vol. 7, no. 2, pp. 218–235 (September 1962).

group situations. A group is more than a collection of individuals; rather, through their interactions, new forces and new properties are created that can be identified and studied in themselves.

A group may be defined as "two or more people acting interdependently in a unified manner toward the achievement of common goals." The goal may pertain to a specific task, but it may also mean that the people share some common concerns, values, or ideology. Thus, group members are usually attracted to each other and have some social bonds.

The focus of this book is not on group theory, yet because a great deal of managerial action involves group activities, to ignore it would be an omission. For instance, committees, teams, conferences, task forces, and negotiation sessions all involve group activities. Fremont A. Shull and Andre L. Delbecq describe the value of small-group concepts for management as follows:

> The theoretical relevance of this body of knowledge is evident from a number of standpoints, since the small group: (1) is an ubiquitous and inevitable element of complex social systems; (2) plays an important part in the development and elaboration of personality; (3) is a major factor in processes of socialization and control; (4) bears many resemblances—as a social system—to large-scale social systems; and (5) can be mobilized as a powerful motivational force.[15]

Characteristics of Groups

Groups—and the focus is on groups in the organization—have a number of characteristics. First, group members share one or more common goals, such as the goals of a product group to develop, manufacture, and market a new product. A second characteristic of groups is that they normally require interaction and communication among members. It is impossible to coordinate the efforts of group members without communication. Third, members within the group assume roles. In a product group, for example, individuals are responsible for designing, producing, selling, or distributing the product. Naturally, the roles are in some kind of relationship to each other in order to achieve the group task. Fourth, groups usually are a part of a larger group. The product group may belong to a product division which produces many products of a similar nature. Large groups may also consist of subgroups. Thus, within the product group may be a subgroup specializing exclusively in the selling of the product. Also, groups interface with other groups. Thus, product group A may cooperate with product group B in the distribution of their products. It is evident, then, that the systems point of view, which focuses on the

[15]F. A. Shull, Jr., and A. L. Delbecq, *Selected Readings in Management* (Homewood, Ill.: Richard D. Irwin, Inc., 1962), p. 313.

interrelatedness of parts, is appropriate in understanding the functioning of groups.

There are a number of other sociological characteristics of groups that must be recognized. Groups develop "norms," which refer to expected behavior of members belonging to the group. If individuals deviate from the norm, pressure is exerted to make them comply. This can be functional when, for example, a person who frequently shows up late for work is admonished by other group members; but there also are situations in which groups may be dysfunctional. Ambitious, highly motivated employees may be pressed to produce in congruence with generally accepted norms rather than according to their abilities.

In a widely publicized experiment, S. E. Asch showed the impact of pressure of the group toward conformity.[16] Members of a small group were asked to match a standard line (8 inches long) with three comparison lines (6¼, 8, and 6¾ inches long). The experimental group members were not aware that some people (confederates of the experimenter) were instructed to give occasionally wrong answers, such as saying that the 6¾-inch line was as long as the 8-inch standard line. It was found that "innocent" members made wrong choices when the confederates did so unanimously. In later interviews, subjects reported that they wanted to agree with the majority. This illustrates that even in a rather uncomplicated task, people may decide against their better judgment due to group pressure. These findings explain to some extent the influence of group pressure toward conformity and how it may result in managerial decisions which are less than optimal.

Functions and Advantages of Groups

Groups have many functions. They are powerful in changing behavior, attitudes, and values, and in disciplining members. As noted, deviant members may be pressured to adhere to group norms. In addition, groups are used for decision making, negotiating, and bargaining. Thus, group members with diverse backgrounds may bring different perspectives to the decision-making process. This does not mean, however, that group decisions are always better than individual decisions.

Group concepts are very important for the topics covered in the next three chapters. Specifically, different group structures influence *communication* patterns. Thus, communication will differ when it is channeled through one key member or when communication flows freely among all the group members. One can hardly consider a number of people a team when each member communicates only with the boss; teamwork requires open communication among all members. Effective group interactions may also affect *motivation*. For example, group members participating in

---

[16]See D. Krech, R. S. Crutchfield, and E. L. Ballachey, *Individual in Society* (New York: McGraw-Hill Book Company, 1962), pp. 507–508.

setting objectives may become committed to the achievement of group goals. Finally, *leadership* must be seen in the context of group processes. A grasp of group concepts helps in understanding the interactions between the leader and followers as well as the interactions among all the group members. In short, an understanding of groups is important for carrying out all managerial functions, particularly the function of leading. Groups are a fact of organized and unorganized life. It is important to know how they work and to use them in an effective and efficient manner in situations that favor group actions.

Groups are not only essential and beneficial for the enterprise, they also have advantages for individuals. Groups do provide social satisfaction for their members, a feeling of belonging, and support for the needs of individuals. Another benefit of groups is that they promote communication. It may be the give-and-take in a formal meeting, or it can take the form of the grapevine, which is the informal communication through which group members become aware of "what is really going on in the firm." Groups also provide security. Labor unions are sometimes formed precisely for this reason—to give job security to their members. Finally, groups provide opportunities for promoting self-esteem through recognition from, and acceptance by, peers.

Disadvantages of Groups

Group activities also may present problems. Certainly the disadvantages of committees mentioned before are relevant here. As pointed out in our discussion of committees, when a compromise can be reached only at the lowest common denominator or when decisions must be postponed, the use of groups may be costly in time and money. A chairperson or a strong member may use the group for selfish purposes rather than for the well-being of the enterprise. Responsibility may be divided so that no one feels accountable for a decision. Finally, a few members may tyrannize the group and inhibit its proper functioning.

HARMONIZING OBJECTIVES: THE KEY TO LEADING

Understanding the human factor in enterprises is important for the managerial function of leading. How a manager views human nature influences the selection of motivational and leadership approaches. A number of models presenting various conceptions of the nature of people have been proposed; however, no single view is sufficient to understand the whole person. Therefore, an eclectic view of the nature of people is suggested.

People do not work in isolation; rather they work to a great extent in groups toward the achievement of personal and enterprise objectives. Unfortunately, these objectives are not always harmonious. Nor should one take for granted that the goals of subordinates are the same as those of the superior. Therefore, one of the most important single activities of managers is to harmonize the needs of individuals with the demands of the enterprise.

Leading is that priceless additional element of influence in an organization that bridges the gap between, on the one hand, logical and well-considered plans, carefully designed organization structures, good programs of staffing, and efficient control techniques, and, on the other hand, the need for people to understand, to be motivated, and to contribute all they are capable of to enterprise and department goals. There is no way that the desires and objectives of individuals can be made to help achieve enterprise objectives unless it is known what individuals want. Even then, managers must be able to design an environment that will take advantage of these individual drives. Managers must know how to communicate with and guide their subordinates so that they will see how their interests are served by working efficiently for an organization.

FOR DISCUSSION

1   What are Theory X and Theory Y assumptions? State your agreements or disagreements with these assumptions. What are some misunderstandings of Theories X and Y?

2   What are some possible implications of Theories X and Y for carrying out the managerial functions of planning, organizing, staffing, leading, and controlling?

3   According to Miles, managers may subscribe to *two* managerial models. What does this actually mean? What has been your experience?

4   According to Davis, different behavioral models within the enterprise have been emphasized at various times in the history of the United States. How can you explain this?

5   Identify some typical tendencies in perception. Does any one apply to you? What are the implications for your everyday life? How can you guard against perceptual fallacies?

6   Do you as a student, an employee, or as a manager work at your capacity? Why, or why not?

7   Why is harmonizing of personal and enterprise objectives seen as a key to leading?

chapter 23 Motivation

Because managing involves the creation and maintenance of an environment for the performance of individuals working together in groups toward the accomplishment of a common objective, it is obvious that a manager cannot do this job without knowing what motivates people. The necessity of building motivating factors into organizational roles, the staffing of these roles, and the entire process of directing and leading people must be built on a knowledge of motivation. To emphasize the importance of knowing and taking advantage of motivating factors is not to cast managers in the role of amateur psychiatrists. Their job is not to attempt to manipulate people but rather to recognize motivating factors in designing an environment for performance.

The basic element of all human behavior is some kind of activity, whether physical or mental. We can look at human behavior as a series of activities. The question arises as to what activities human beings will undertake at any point of time, and why. We know that activities are goal-oriented; that is, people do things that lead them to accomplish something. But individual goals can be elusive. Sometimes people know exactly why they do things; often, however, individual drives lie buried in the subconscious. For example, do you know why you did what you did today and what all your various activities were designed to achieve?

The primary task of managers is to get people to contribute activities which help to achieve the mission and goals of an enterprise or of any department or other organized unit within it. Clearly, to guide people's activities in desired directions requires knowing, to the best of any manager's ability, what leads people to do things, what motivates them.

THE NEED FOR RECOGNIZING MOTIVATING FACTORS

It is true that people participate in an organized enterprise—and, indeed, in all kinds of groups—in order to achieve some goal that they cannot attain as individuals. But this does not mean that they will necessarily work and contribute all they can to be sure that these goals are accomplished. As Barnard saw so perceptively many years ago:

> If all those who may be considered potential contributors to an organization are arranged in order of willingness to serve it, the scale gradually descends from possibly intense willingness through neutral or zero willingness to intense unwillingness or opposition or hatred. The *preponderance of persons in a modern society always lies on the negative side* with reference to any existing or potential organization.[1]

This startling observation contains more truth than most of us are

[1]C. I. Barnard, *The Functions of the Executive* (Cambridge, Mass.: Harvard University Press, 1938), p. 84..

willing to admit. But a moment's reflection will show how true it is. All we need to do is to think of the various organizations we belong to—church, club, company, professional society, or other—and ask ourselves how intensely we are willing to serve them without some inducement other than the fact of our membership.

This means, of course, that all those who are responsible for the management of any organization must build into the entire system factors that will induce people to contribute as effectively and efficiently as possible. A manager does this by building into every possible aspect of the organizational climate those things which will cause people to act in desired ways.

MOTIVATION AND MOTIVATORS

Human motives are based on needs, whether consciously or subconsciously felt. Some are primary needs, such as the physiological requirements for water, air, food, sex, sleep, and shelter. Other needs may be regarded as secondary, such as self-esteem, status, affiliation with others, affection, giving, accomplishment, and self-assertion. As can be readily seen, these needs vary in intensity and over time with various individuals.

Motivation

As Berelson and Steiner have defined the term, a motive "is an inner state that energizes, activates, or moves (hence 'motivation'), and that directs or channels behavior toward goals."[2] In other words, "motivation" is a general term applying to the entire class of drives, desires, needs, wishes, and similar forces. Likewise, to say that managers motivate their subordinates is to say that they do those things which they hope will satisfy these drives and desires and induce the subordinates to act in a desired manner.

The Need-Want-Satisfaction Chain

We can, then, look at motivation as involving a chain reaction, starting out with felt needs, resulting in wants or goals sought, which give rise to tensions (that is unfulfilled desires), then causing action toward achieving goals, and finally satisfying wants. This chain is shown in Figure 23.1.

The chain explanation is not simple   However, in reality this chain is more complex than it looks. In the first place, needs are not simple. Except for physiological needs, such as hunger, needs are not independent of a

---

[2]B. Berelson and G. A. Steiner, *Human Behavior: An Inventory of Scientific Findings* (New York: Harcourt, Brace & World, Inc., 1964), p. 240.

Figure 23.1 Need-want-satisfaction chain.

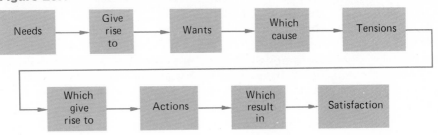

person's environment. We can easily see also that many physiological needs are stimulated by environmental factors: The smell of food may make us feel hungry, a high thermometer reading may make us suddenly feel hot, or the sight of a cold drink may cause an overwhelming thirst. Who, for example, has not had certain physiological needs accentuated by an attractive advertisement?

Environment has a major influence on our perception of secondary needs. The promotion of a colleague may kindle our desire for higher status. A challenging problem may whet our desire to accomplish something by solving it. A congenial social group may increase our need for affiliation, and, of course, being alone more than we want to be can give us strong motivation for affiliation.

In the second place, the need-want-satisfaction chain does not always operate as simply as portrayed. Needs do cause behavior. But needs also may result from behavior. Satisfying one need may lead to a desire to satisfy more needs. For example, a person's need for accomplishment may be made keener by the satisfaction gained from achieving a desired goal; or it might be dulled by failure. The one-way nature of the chain has also been challenged by the work of some of the biological scientists, especially in recent years, who have found that needs are not always the cause of human behavior, but a result of it.[3] In other words, behavior is often *what* we do and not *why* we do it.

Also, the chain does not take into account what happens to "satisfaction" if there is a goal failure, that is, if a person's actions do not satisfy in any way. In this event a person might either change his or her goal or may be involved in developing alibis or other defenses for having missed the goal.

Motives May Be Complex and Conflicting

It takes only a moment's thought to realize that at any given time, an individual's motives may be quite complex and often conflicting. A

[3]See summary of findings referred to in Robert Ardrey, *The Territorial Imperative* (New York: Dell Publishing Co., Inc., 1966).

person may be motivated by desires for economic goods and services (groceries, a better house, a new car, or a trip), and even these desires may be complex and conflicting (should one buy a new house or a new car?). In addition, an individual may want self-esteem, status, a feeling of accomplishment, or relaxation (who has not felt a conflict between the time demands of a job and the desire to play golf or go to a movie?).

Motivators   Motivators are those things which induce an individual to perform. They may include higher pay, a prestigious title, a name on the office door, the acclaim of colleagues, and a host of other things that give people a reason to perform. To be sure, while motivations reflect wants, they are the perceived rewards, or incentives, that sharpen the drive to satisfy these wants. They are also the means by which conflicting needs may be reconciled or one need may be accentuated so that it will be given priority over another.

A manager can do much to sharpen motives by establishing an environment conducive to certain drives. For example, people in a business which has developed a reputation for excellence and high quality tend to be motivated to contribute to this reputation. Similarly, the environment of a business in which managerial performance is intelligent and effective tends to breed a desire for high-quality management in the entire system.

A motivator, then, is something that influences an individual's behavior. It makes a difference in what a person will do. Obviously, in any organized enterprise, managers must be concerned about motivators and also inventive in their use. People can often satisfy their wants in a variety of ways. A person can, for example, satisfy a desire for affiliation by being active in a social club rather than in a business, meet economic needs by performing a job just well enough to get by, or satisfy status needs by spending time working for a political party. What a manager must do, of course, is to use those motivators which will lead people to perform effectively for the enterprise that employs them. No manager can expect to hire the whole person since people always have desires and drives outside the enterprise. But if a company or any other kind of enterprise is to be efficient and successful, enough of every person's drives must be stimulated and satisfied to assure this.

Motivation and satisfaction are different   Motivation refers to the drive and effort to satisfy a want or goal. Satisfaction refers to the contentment experienced when a want is satisfied. In other words, motivation implies a drive toward an outcome, while satisfaction involves outcomes already experienced.

From a management point of view, this means that a person might have high job satisfaction but a low level of motivation for the job, or the reverse might be true. There is understandably the probability that highly motivated persons with low job satisfaction will look for another position. Likewise, those people who find their position rewarding but are being paid considerably less than they desire or think they deserve will probably search for another job.

MOTIVATION: THE CARROT AND THE STICK

In examining the various leading theories of motivation and motivators, one seldom hears recently any reference to "the carrot and the stick." This is, of course, the use of rewards and penalties in order to induce desired behavior and comes from the old story that the best way to make a donkey move is to put a carrot out in front of him or jab him with a stick from behind.

Despite all the researches and theories of motivation that have come to the fore in recent years, it should not be forgotten that reward and punishment are still strong motivators. For centuries, however, they were too often thought of as the only forces that could motivate people. As we shall see in the succeeding sections, there are many other motivators.

In all theories of motivation, the inducements brought by some kind of "carrot" are recognized. Often this is money in the form of pay or bonuses, even though it is somewhat fashionable for writers to say that money is no longer a strong motivator. To be sure, it is not the only motivating force, but it has been and will continue to be an important one. The trouble with the money "carrot" approach is that too often everyone gets a carrot regardless of performance, through such practices as salary increases and promotion by seniority, automatic "merit" increases, and executive bonuses not based on individual manager performance. It is as simple as this: If a person put a donkey in a pen full of carrots and then stood outside with a carrot in his hand, would the donkey be induced to come out of the pen?

The "stick" in the form of fear—fear of loss of job, loss of income, reduction of bonus, demotion, or some other penalty—has been and continues to be a strong motivator. Yet it is admittedly not the best kind. It often gives rise to defensive or retaliatory behavior, such as union organization, poor-quality workmanship, executive indifference, failure of a manager to take any risks in decision making, or even dishonesty. But fear of penalty cannot be overlooked. And most managers never fully comprehend the power of their position. Whether they are first-level supervisors or chief executives, the power of their position to give or withhold rewards or impose penalties of various kinds gives them an ability to control, to a very great extent, the economic and social well being of their subordinates. It is hardly a wonder that a substantial number of managers have "yes-sayers" reporting to them and seldom realize it.

One of the most widely referred-to theories of motivation is the "hierarchy of needs" theory put forth by psychologist Abraham Maslow.[4] He saw human needs in the form of a hierarchy, starting in an ascending order from the lowest to the highest needs, and concluded that when one set of needs was satisfied, this kind of need ceased to be a motivator. Although the hierarchical aspects of Maslow's theory are subject to question and often not accepted, his identification of basic needs has been fairly popular.

The Need Hierarchy

The basic human needs identified by Maslow in an ascending order of importance are the following:

1 Physiological needs. These are the basic needs for sustaining human life itself—food, water, clothing, shelter, sleep, and sexual satisfaction. Maslow took the position that until these needs are satisfied to the degree necessary to maintain life, other needs will not motivate people.
2 Security, or safety, needs. These are the needs to be free from physical danger and the fear of loss of a job, property, food, clothing, or shelter.
3 Affiliation, or acceptance, needs. Since people are social beings, they need to belong, to be accepted by others.
4 Esteem needs. According to Maslow, once people begin to satisfy their need to belong, they tend to want to be held in esteem both by themselves and by others. This kind of need produces such satisfactions as power, prestige, status, and self-confidence.
5 Need for self-actualization. Maslow regards this as the highest need in his hierarchy. It is the desire to become what one is capable of becoming—to maximize one's potential and to accomplish something.

Do Needs Follow a Hierarchy?

Maslow's concept of a hierarchy of needs has been subjected to considerable research. Lawler and Suttle collected data on 187 managers in two different organizations over a period of 6 months to 1 year.[5] They found little evidence to support Maslow's theory that human needs conform to a hierarchy. They did, however, find that there were two levels of needs—biological and other needs—and that the other needs would

---

[4]*Motivation and Personality* (New York: Harper & Brothers, 1954). See also his *Eupsychian Management* (Homewood, Ill.: Richard D. Irwin, Inc., 1965).
[5]E. E. Lawler and J. L. Suttle, "A Causal Correlation Test of the Need-Hierarchy Concept," *Organizational Behavior and Human Performance*, vol. 7, no. 2, pp. 265–287 (April 1972).

emerge only when biological needs were reasonably satisfied. They found, further, that at the higher level, the strength of needs varied with individuals, some individuals social needs predominated, and in others self-actualization needs were strongest.

In another study of Maslow's need hierarchy involving a group of managers over a period of 5 years, Hall and Nougaim did not find strong evidence of a hierarchy.[6] They found that as managers advance in an organization, their physiological and safety needs tend to decrease in importance, and their needs for affiliation, esteem, and self-actualization tend to increase. They insisted, however, that the upward movement of need prominence resulted from upward career changes and not from the satisfaction of lower-order needs.

Porter likewise found that needs do not follow a hierarchy, especially after lower-level needs are satisfied.[7] He discovered that managers at all levels had similar security and social needs and that the three higher needs on the Maslow hierarchy varied greatly with managerial ranks, with lower-level managers being less satisfied than higher-level managers. Yet, in all ranks, except possibly that of the top management group, satisfaction of these needs was definitely more or less deficient.

How Can Managers Use Maslow's Hierarchy?

Research on the realities of Maslow's hierarchy of needs does raise questions about the accuracy of the hierarchical aspects of these needs. However, the identification of the kinds of needs appears to be useful. It is unquestionably true that if basic needs—physiological and security—are clearly unsatisfied, this can have a material effect on motivation. But even these needs are fairly elastic. How much is enough? Take clothing and shelter, for example. One person might be reasonably well satisfied with a level that to another person would be inadequate. Likewise, research indicates that even the lowliest employee has needs for esteem and self-actualization, although what might represent status or pride of accomplishment to one person would not be at all satisfying to another. One has only to look at the esteem attached to such things as office space. A first-level supervisor might be very happy with a small, simple office, while a top executive would be satisfied only with a large and well-furnished office.

In practice, this means that perceptive managers must take a situational, or contingency, approach to the application of Maslow's theory. What needs they must appeal to will depend on the personality,

---

[6]D. T. Hall and K. Nougaim, "An Examination of Maslow's Need Hierarchy in an Organizational Setting," *Organizational Behavior and Human Performance*, vol. 3, no. 1, pp. 12–35 (February 1968).
[7]L. W. Porter, "Job Attitudes in Management. I. Perceived Deficiencies in Need Fulfillment as a Function of Job Level," *Journal of Applied Psychology*, vol. 46, no. 6, pp. 375–387 (December 1962).

wants, and desires of individuals. In any case, managers should not forget that most people, especially in a developed society, have needs that spread over the entire spectrum of Maslow's hierarchy.

THE MOTIVATOR-HYGIENE APPROACH TO MOTIVATION

Sparked by research of Brayfield and Crockett[8] and of Herzberg and associates,[9] but closely related to Maslow's theory, the need approach has been considerably modified. Herzberg's research purports to find a two-factor explanation of motivation. In one group of needs are such things as company policy and administration, supervision, working conditions, interpersonal relations, salary, status, job security, and personal life. These were found by Herzberg and his associates to be only "dissatisfiers" and not motivators. In other words, if they exist in a work environment in high quantity and quality, they yield no dissatisfaction. Their existence does not motivate in the sense of yielding satisfaction; their lack of existence would, however, result in dissatisfaction.

In the second group Herzberg listed certain "satisfiers"—and therefore motivators—all related to job content. These included the factors of achievement, recognition, challenging work, advancement, and growth in the job. Their existence will yield feelings of satisfaction or no satisfaction (not dissatisfaction). A comparison of Maslow's and Herzberg's theories is shown in Figure 23.2.

The first group of factors Herzberg called "maintenance" or "hygiene" factors. Their presence will not motivate people in an organization; yet they must be present, or dissatisfaction will arise. Also, as Herzberg has made clear, motivation will not be very effective if hygiene factors are missing. The second group, or the "job content" factors, are found to be the real motivators because they have the potential of yielding a sense of satisfaction. Clearly, if this theory of motivation is sound, it does mean that managers must give considerable attention to upgrading job content.

The Herzberg research has not gone unchallenged. Some question Herzberg's methods.[10] It is charged that his questioning methods tended to prejudice his results. For example, the well-known tendency of people to attribute good results to their own efforts and to blame others for poor results is thought to have prejudiced Herzberg's findings. Other research-

[8]A. Brayfield and W. Crockett, "Employee Attitudes and Employee Performance," *Psychological Bulletin*, vol. 52, no. 5, pp. 396–424 (1955).

[9]F. Herzberg, B. Mausner, R. Peterson, and D. Capwell, *Job Attitudes: Review of Research and Opinion* (Pittsburgh: Psychological Services of Pittsburgh, 1957), and F. Herzberg, B. Mausner, and B. Synderman, *The Motivation to Work* (New York: John Wiley & Sons, Inc., 1959).

[10]See, for example, B. L. Hinton, "An Empirical Investigation of the Herzberg Methodology and Two-Factor Theory," *Organizational Behavior and Human Performance*, vol. 3, no. 3, pp. 286–309 (August 1968).

Figure 23.2 Comparison of Maslow's and Herzberg's theories of motivation. (*Note*: Supervision can be a matter of satisfying both affiliation and security needs.)

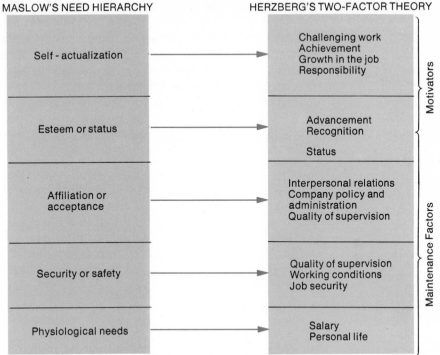

ers not following Herzberg's methods have found that the so-called hygiene factors were actually potent in yielding satisfaction or dissatisfaction.[11]

An interesting application of Herzberg's methods was made in the research at Texas Instruments by Myers.[12] In a study of 282 employees of this firm, including scientists, engineers, supervisors, technicians, and assembly workers, his findings only partially supported Herzberg's theory. He found that those persons who sought opportunities for achievement and responsibility, whom he characterized as "growth seekers," did indeed fit Herzberg's model in that they were concerned with satisfiers and relatively little concerned with environmental factors, that is, "maintenance" or "hygiene" factors. By contrast, other people, whom he called "maintenance seekers," were greatly concerned with maintenance conditions. In other words, what motivates individuals was found to be largely a matter of personality.

[11]See, for example, H. R. Bobbitt and O. Behling, "Defense Mechanisms as an Alternate Explanation of Herzberg's Motivator-Hygiene Results," *Journal of Applied Psychology*, vol. 56, no. 1, pp. 24–27 (January 1972).
[12]M. S. Myers, "Who Are Your Motivated Workers?" *Harvard Business Review*, vol. 42, no. 1, pp. 73–86 (January–February 1964).

Moreover, Myers found that if growth seekers were treated like maintenance seekers, they soon developed the characteristics and concerns of this latter group. In other words, if opportunities for advancement and achievement were not given to growth seekers, they soon became maintenance seekers. Thus, according to Myers, the effectiveness of a motivation system depends on the ability of supervisors to (1) provide conditions of motivation (mainly through careful planning and organizing of work) and (2) satisfy maintenance needs (especially through such actions as being fair and friendly and dispensing adequate information).

EXPECTANCY THEORY OF MOTIVATION

Another approach to explaining motivation and one that many believe has great potential for understanding and practice may be referred to as the "expectancy theory." The essential element of this theory is that people will be motivated to do things to achieve some goal to the extent that they expect that certain actions on their part will help them achieve the goal. In a sense this is a modern expression of what Martin Luther observed centuries ago when he said that "everything that is done in the world is done in hope."

Vroom's Valence-Expectancy Theory

Attacking Herzberg's two-factor theory and research as being too dependent on the content and context of the work roles of the people being questioned, Vroom offered an expectancy approach to the understanding of motivation.[13] He suggested that a person's motivation toward an action at any time would be determined by his or her anticipated values of all the outcomes (both negative and positive) of the action multiplied by the strength of that person's expectancy that the outcome would yield the desired goal. In other words, he argued that motivation was a product of the anticipated worth to a person of an action and the perceived probability that that person's goals would be achieved.

Using his own terms, Vroom's theory may therefore be stated as follows:

Force = valence × expectancy

where force is the strength of a person's motivation, valence is the strength of an individual's preference for an outcome, and expectancy is the probability that a particular action will lead to a desired outcome.

As can be seen from this model, a valence of zero occurs when an individual is indifferent about achieving a certain goal, and there is a

[13]Victor H. Vroom, *Work and Motivation* (New York: John Wiley & Sons, Inc., 1964).

negative valence when the person would rather not achieve the goal. The result would be, of course, no motivation. Likewise, a person would have no motivation to achieve a goal if the expectancy were zero or negative. The force exerted to do something will depend on *both* valence and expectancy. Moreover, a motive to accomplish some action might be determined by a desire to accomplish something else. For example, a person might be willing to work hard to get out a product for a valence in the form of pay. Or a manager might be willing to work hard to achieve company goals in marketing or production for a promotion in position or pay "valence."

The Vroom Theory and Practice

One of the great attractions of the Vroom theory is that it recognizes the importance of various individual needs and motivations. It thus avoids some of the simplistic features of the Maslow and Herzberg approaches. It does seem more realistic. It fits the concept of harmony of objectives advanced in this book—that individuals have personal goals different from organization goals but that these can be harmonized. Furthermore, Vroom's theory is completely consistent with the entire system of managing by objectives.

The strength of Vroom's theory is also its weakness. His assumption that senses of value vary between individuals at different times and in various places appears more accurately to fit real life. It is consistent also with the idea that a manager's job is to *design* an environment for performance, necessarily taking into account the differences in various situations. On the other hand, Vroom's theory is difficult to research and apply in practice. But this weakness, which is really not a weakness except in practice, simply recognizes that motivation is a much more complex thing than the approaches of Maslow and Herzberg seem to imply.

The Porter and Lawler Model

Built in large part on expectancy theory, Porter and Lawler have derived a substantially more complete model of motivation and have applied it in their study primarily to managers.[14] The model may be summarized as in Figure 23.3.

As this model indicates, "effort" (the strength of motivation and energy exerted) depends on the "value of a reward" plus the perceived energy a person believes is required and the probability of actually receiving the reward. The "perceived effort and probability of reward" are, in turn, also influenced by the record of actual "performance."

---

[14]L. W. Porter and E. E. Lawler, *Managerial Attitudes and Performance* (Homewood, Ill.: Richard D. Irwin, Inc., 1968).

Figure 23.3 The Porter and Lawler motivation model. [*Adapted from L. W. Porter and E. E. Lawler,* Managerial Attitudes and Performance *(Homewood, Ill.: Richard D. Irwin, Inc., 1968), p. 165.*]

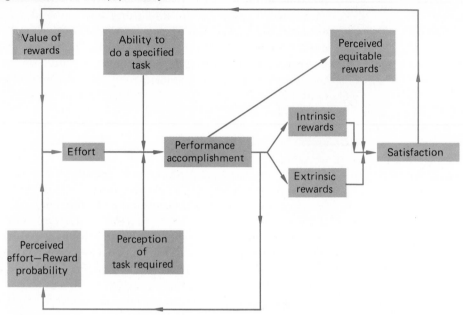

Clearly, if people know they can do a job or have done it, they have a better appreciation of the effort required and know better the probability of rewards.

Actual performance in a job (the doing of tasks or the meeting of goals) is determined principally by effort expended. But it is also greatly influenced by an individual's "ability" (knowledge and skills) to do it and his or her "perception" of what the required task is (the extent to which goals, required activities, and other elements of a task are understood). Performance, in turn, is seen as leading to "intrinsic rewards" (such as a sense of accomplishment or self-actualization) and "extrinsic rewards" (such as working conditions and status). These, as tempered by what the individual perceives as "equitable rewards," lead to "satisfaction." But performance also influences perceived equitable rewards. As can be readily understood, what the individual perceives as a fair reward for effort will necessarily affect the satisfaction derived. Likewise, the actual value of rewards will be influenced by satisfaction.

Implications for Practice

The Porter and Lawler model of motivation, while more complex than other theories of motivation, is almost certainly a more adequate portrayal of the system of motivation. To the practicing manager, this means that motivation is not a simple cause and effect matter. It means, too, that managers should carefully assess their reward structures and that through careful planning, managing by objectives, and clear definition of duties and responsibilities by good organization structuring, the effort-performance-reward-satisfaction system should be integrated into an entire system of managing.

McCLELLAND'S NEEDS THEORY OF MOTIVATION

David C. McClelland of Harvard University has contributed to the understanding of motivation by identifying three types of basic motivating needs.[15] He classified these as need for power (n/PWR), need for affiliation (n/AFF), and need for achievement (n/ACH). Considerable research has been done on methods of testing people with respect to these three types of needs, and McClelland and his associates have done substantial research especially on the need-for-achievement drive. Research on achievement need has been noteworthy and is often used by psychologists as a prototype of how knowledge should be researched and discovered in the behavioral sciences.[16]

All three drives—power, affiliation, and achievement—are of special relevance to management since all must be recognized to make an organized enterprise work well. Because any organized enterprise and every department of it represent groups of individuals working together to achieve goals, the need for achievement is of paramount importance.

Need for Power

McClelland and other researchers have found that people with a high need for power have a great concern for exercising influence and control. Such individuals generally are seeking positions of leadership; they are forceful, outspoken, hardheaded, and demanding; and they enjoy teaching and public speaking.

Need for Affiliation

People with a high need for affiliation usually derive pleasure from being loved and tend to avoid the pain of being rejected by a social group. As

[15]*The Achievement Motive* (New York: Appleton-Century-Crofts, 1953), *Studies in Motivation* (New York: Appleton-Century-Crofts, 1955), and *The Achieving Society* (Princeton, N.J.: D. Van Nostrand Company, Inc., 1961). See also his "Achievement Motivation Can Be Developed," *Harvard Business Review*, vol. 43, no. 1, pp. 6–24, 178 (January–February 1965), and (with David G. Winter) *Motivating Economic Achievement* (New York: The Free Press, 1969).
[16]Luthans, *Organizational Behavior* (New York: McGraw-Hill Book Company, 1973), p. 400.

individuals, they are likely to be concerned with maintaining pleasant social relationships, to enjoy a sense of intimacy and understanding, to be ready to console and help others in trouble, and to enjoy friendly interaction with others.

Need for Achievement

People with a high need for achievement have an intense desire for success and an equally intense fear of failure. They want to be challenged, set moderately difficult (but not impossible) goals for themselves, take a realistic approach to risk (they are not likely to be coin tossers but rather to analyze and assess problems), prefer to assume personal responsibility to get a job done, like specific and prompt feedback on how they are doing, tend to be restless, like to work long hours, do not worry unduly about failure if it does occur, and tend to like to run their own shows.

How McClelland's Approach Applies to Managers

In researches made by McClelland and others, entrepreneurs showed a very high need-for-achievement and a fairly high need-for-power drive, but were quite low in need for affiliation. Managers generally showed high on achievement and power and low on affiliation, but not as high or low as entrepreneurs.

McClelland found the patterns of achievement motivation clearest in small companies, with the president normally having very high achievement motivation. In large companies, interestingly enough, he found chief executives only to be average in achievement motivation and often stronger in drives for power and affiliation. Managers in the upper middle level of management in such companies rated higher than their presidents in achievement motivation. Perhaps, as McClelland indicated, these scores are understandable. The chief executive has "arrived," and those below him are striving to advance.

The question is often raised as to whether all managers should rate quite high on achievement motivation. It has been found true that people who do rate high tend to advance faster than those who do not. But, because so much of managing requires other characteristics besides achievement drive, it is probable that every company should have many managers who, while possessing fairly strong achievement motivation, also have a high need for affiliation. This latter need is important for working with people and for coordinating the efforts of individuals working in groups.

Achievement Motivation Can Be Taught

One of McClelland's interesting findings is that the achievement drive can even be taught to people in varying cultures. Experimenting with people from the United States, Italy, Poland, and India, McClelland found that in all cases, training programs were successful in increasing individual need for achievement. These programs emphasized prestige, the practicability of effecting change, teaching the language and thinking patterns of high need achievers, emotional support of class members (especially through sharing of experience), and transmitting research evidence on the achievement drive.[17]

PATTON'S IDENTIFICATION OF MANAGERIAL MOTIVATORS

Most of the research into motivation has been done with people who are in the nonmanagerial ranks, although some, like that of Porter and Lawler and McClelland, has included professionals and managers. While there is little doubt that motivators apply to all kinds of people at all levels, newer researchers have made it clear that the problem of motivation is complicated by the fact that what motivates people varies with people, with individuals, and with situations.

One of the nation's top experts in the area of executive motivation and compensation, Arch Patton, has identified those motivators which he has found to be especially important in the case of executives. They are the following:[18]

1 The challenge found in work. If this is to be maximized, people must know the purpose and scope of their job responsibilities, what their authority is, and what is expected of them, and they must have a belief in the value of what they are doing.
2 Status. Although recognized for centuries by churches, the military, and government, industry has come to see status as a motivator only in recent years; it includes titles, promotions, and such symbols as office size and appointments, an "executive" secretary, a company car, and club memberships.
3 The urge to achieve leadership. While difficult at times to distinguish from the desire for power, it is really the wish to be a leader among one's peers.
4 The lash of competition. This important motivating factor is present in many aspects of life.
5 Fear. This takes many forms, including fear of errors, of loss of a job, or of reduction of a bonus.
6 Money. While placed last, money is by no means the least effective motivator; most often it is more than mere money, being generally a reflection of other motivators.

[17] A report on these experiments can be found in McClelland and Winter, op. cit.
[18] See his *Men, Money, and Motivation* (New York: McGraw-Hill Book Company, 1961), chap. 2.

As can be seen, these basic motivators, while simple and practical, do not differ substantially from most of those which could be derived from the above discussion of motivation theory and research. They do put money in a proper perspective as being far more than a "maintenance" factor, as Herzberg suggests.

SPECIAL MOTIVATIONAL TECHNIQUES

After looking at all the theories of motivation, we may well ask what they mean to managers. What are some of the major motivational techniques and means managers can use? While, as has been made clear, motivation is so complex and individualized that there can be no single best answer, some of the major motivational techniques can be identified.

Money

As mentioned earlier in the discussion of the carrot and the stick and as emphasized by Patton, money can never be overlooked as a motivator. Whether in the form of wages, piecework or any other incentive pay, bonuses, stock options, company-paid insurance, or any of the other things that may be given to people for performance, money is important. And, as Patton pointed out, money is often more than money, in that it can be a reflection of other motivators.

Economists and most managers have tended to place money high on the scale of motivators, while behavioral scientists tend to place it low. Neither view is probably right. But if money is to be the kind of motivator that it can and should be, managers should remember several things.

In the first place, money, as money, is likely to be most important to people who are younger and are raising a family than to people who have "arrived" in the sense that their money needs are not as urgent. Money is an urgent means of achieving a "minimum" standard of living, although this minimum has a way of expanding upward as people become more affluent. For example, an individual who was once satisfied with a small house and a low-priced car may now be able to derive the same satisfaction only from a large and comfortable house and a fairly luxurious automobile. And yet we cannot generalize in even these terms. For some people money will always be of the utmost importance, while to others it may never be.

In the second place, it is probably fairly generally true, as Gellerman has pointed out, that in most kinds of businesses and other enterprises, money is actually used as a means of keeping an organization adequately staffed and not primarily as a motivator.[19] This can be seen in the practice of making wages and salaries competitive between various enterprises so as to attract and hold people.

[19]S. W. Gellerman, *Management by Motivation* (New York: American Management Association, 1968), p. 173.

A third factor to bear in mind is that money as a motivator tends to be dulled somewhat by the practice of making sure in a company that salaries of various managers are equitable. In other words, we often take great care to be sure that people on comparable levels are given the same, or nearly the same, compensation. This is understandable since people usually evaluate their compensation in the light of what their peers are receiving. As can be readily seen, this practice serves to make money, to use Herzberg's terms, a hygiene, or maintenance, factor and not a source of motivation.

From the equity theory of pay arises a fourth consideration. If money is to be an effective motivator, people in various positions, even though at a similar level, must be given salaries and bonuses that reflect their individual performance. Perhaps we are committed to the practice of comparable wages and salaries. But a well-managed company need never be committed to the same practice with respect to bonuses. In fact, it would appear that, unless bonuses to managers are based to a major extent on every individual's performance, an enterprise is not buying much motivation with them. This is certainly the way to assure that money has meaning as a reward for accomplishment and as a way of giving people prestige gratification.

Also, it is almost certainly true, as Gellerman says, that money can motivate only when the prospective payment is large relative to a person's income.[20] The trouble with most wage and salary increases, and even bonus payments, is that they are not large enough to motivate the receiver. They may keep the individual from being dissatisfied and from looking for another job, but unless they are large enough to be "felt" and unless they are tied to performance, they are not likely to be a strong motivator.

Positive Reinforcement

An interesting special application of motivation, which has been introduced as a technique of training in Chapter 21, is the technique apparently successfully applied by Harvard psychologist B. F. Skinner. Called either "positive reinforcement" or "behavior modification," this approach holds that individuals can be motivated by properly designing their work environment and praising their performance and that punishment for poor performance produces negative results.

Skinner and his followers do far more than praise good performance. They analyze the work situation to determine what causes workers to act the way they do and then initiate changes to eliminate troublesome areas and obstructions to performance. Specific goals are then set with workers' participation and assistance, prompt and regular feedback of results is made available, and performance improvements are rewarded with recognition and praise. Even when performance does not equal goals,

---

[20]Ibid., p. 189.

ways are found to help people and praise them for the good things they do. It has also been found highly useful and motivating to give people full information on a company's problems, especially those in which they are involved.

This technique sounds almost too simple to work, and many behavioral scientists and managers are skeptical about its effectiveness. However, a number of prominent companies have found the approach beneficial. Emery Air Freight Corporation, for example, found that this approach saved the company over $500,000 per year by merely inducing employees to take great pains to be sure that containers were properly filled with small packages before shipment.

Perhaps the strength of the Skinner approach is that it is so akin to the requirements of good managing. It will be noted that the approach emphasizes removal of obstructions to performance, careful planning and organizing, control through feedback, and the expansion of communication. It also has an element of participation by people responsible for performance.

Participation

One technique that has been given strong support as the result of motivation theory and research is the increased awareness and use of participation. There can be no doubt that only rarely are people not motivated by being consulted on action affecting them—by being "in on the act." There is also no doubt that most people in the center of an operation have knowledge both of problems and of solutions to them. As a consequence, the right kind of participation yields both motivation and knowledge valuable for enterprise success.

Participation does respond to a number of basic motivators. It is a means of recognition. It appeals to the need for affiliation and acceptance. And, above all, it gives people a sense of accomplishment. As will be recalled, these are major advantages of a well-conceived and well-operated system of managing by objectives.

But encouraging participation does not mean that managers abdicate their positions. While they encourage participation of subordinates on matters where they can help and while they listen carefully, on matters requiring their decisions they must make these decisions themselves. The best subordinates would not have it any other way, and few subordinates can ever have respect for a wishy-washy superior.

JOB ENRICHMENT

Research and analysis of motivation appear to emphasize the importance of making jobs challenging and meaningful. This applies to managers as well as nonmanagers and is consistent with Herzberg's theory of motivation, where job content factors such as challenge, achievement, recognition, and responsibility are seen as the real motivators. Even though Herzberg's theory, as was discussed earlier, has not gone unchallenged, it has led to a widespread interest both in the United States and overseas in developing ways for enriching job content, particularly for nonmanagerial employees.

Job enrichment should be distinguished from job enlargement. The latter technique attempts to make a job more varied by removing the dullness associated with performing repetitive operations. In job enrichment, the attempt is to build into jobs a higher sense of challenge, importance, and achievement. A job may be enriched by giving it variety. But it also may be enriched by (1) giving workers more latitude in deciding about such things as work methods, sequence, and pace or by letting them make decisions about accepting or rejecting materials; (2) encouraging participation of subordinates and interaction between workers; (3) giving workers a feeling of personal responsibility for their tasks; (4) taking steps to make sure that people can see how their tasks contribute to a finished product and the welfare of the enterprise; (5) giving people feedback on their job performance, preferably before their supervisors get it; and (6) involving workers in analysis and change of physical aspects of the work environment such as layout of office or plant, temperature, lighting, and cleanliness.[21]

The Claims of Job Enrichment

A number of companies have introduced programs of job enrichment. The first company to do so on a fairly large scale was Texas Instruments, and other companies, such as AT&T, Procter & Gamble, and General Foods, have had considerable experience with it. In all these companies claims have been made that productivity was increased, that absenteeism and turnover were reduced, and that morale improved.

Perhaps the most glowing claims for job enrichment are contained in the report of a study made by the U.S. Department of Health, Education, and Welfare published in 1973.[22] As the result of an analysis of worker attitudes and the quality of working life, this study concluded that (1) the primary cause of dissatisfaction of workers is the nature of their work—the quality of their working life—and (2) blue-collar workers will work harder if their jobs are enriched and expanded so as to give them greater control over their work and more freedom from their supervisor.

[21]For a more thorough analysis of job enrichment, see A. N. Turner and P. R. Lawrence, *Industrial Jobs and the Worker* (Boston: Harvard Graduate School of Business Administration, 1965). See also E. E. Lawler and J. R. Hackman, "Corporate Profits and Employee Satisfaction: Must They Be in Conflict?" *California Management Review*, vol. 14, no. 1, pp. 46–55 (Fall 1971), and R. N. Ford, "Job Enrichment Lessons from AT&T," *Harvard Business Review*, vol. 51, no. 1, pp. 96–106 (January–February 1973).
[22]*Work in America* (Washington: Government Printing Office, 1973).

There are differences of opinion as to how effective job enrichment for nonmanagerial employees has been. As noted, personnel managers and consultants in certain companies have claimed great success. However, one analyst finds the record not nearly so bright. After going over a number of programs and many studies of experiences, Fein disclosed the following.[23]

1   A large-scale study of the University of Michigan Survey Research Center found that people ranked interesting work first in importance, pay fifth, and security of employment seventh. However, when Fein removed managers and professional people from the sample, he discovered that blue-collar workers ranked pay and job security higher than interesting work.

2   In Texas Instruments, a company regarded as a leader in job enrichment, Fein found that only 10.5 percent of employees were actually involved; in the case of janitorial and cleaning employees, where excellent results were reported, Fein noted that these were probably due to the fact that the employees had been taken over from a contracting firm and had become company employees with much higher wages and benefits.

3   In the case of AT&T, Fein claims that the benefits that occurred were due not to job enrichment but to simple redesign of jobs that were poorly designed in the first place.

4   Fein claims not to be impressed with the apparently good results at the Topeka plant of General Foods because this was a small and new plant in which the 63 employees were carefully selected from among 700 applicants highly desirous of a job in the new plant.

5   Likewise, Fein believes that the apparent success of programs at Procter & Gamble took place in a company long known for its concern for employees "matched by few other firms in this country."

6   Fein also found no evidence to support the presumption that there is a strong demand on the part of blue-collar workers for job enrichment. He quotes labor leaders who declare that they have never been asked by their members to negotiate for this and that all the programs, both in the United States and in Europe, have been initiated by managers and not by workers. He quotes Leonard Woodcock, then president of the United Automobile Workers, as saying with respect to job enlargement that "a lot of academic writers . . . are writing a lot of nonsense."

Despite Fein's analysis and criticisms, it is difficult to believe that

[23]Mitchell Fein, "Job Enrichment: A Reevaluation," *Sloan Management Review*, vol. 15, no. 2, pp. 69–88 (Winter 1974).

people do not want more meaningful work. This must be true of managers and professionals, and there must be some demand from blue-collar workers. But as will be noted presently, it could be true that proponents of job enrichment attribute their own scale of values to people who are not strongly motivated by the same values.

Limitations of Job Enrichment

Even the strongest supporters of job enrichment readily admit that there are limitations in its application. One of these is a matter of technology. With specialized machinery and assembly line techniques, it may not be possible to make jobs very meaningful. Another is cost. General Motors tried six-person and three-person teams in the assembly of motor homes, but found that this was too difficult, slow, and costly. Two Swedish auto manufacturers, Saab and Volvo, have used the team approach and have found costs to be somewhat higher, but they believe that this was more than offset by reductions in absenteeism and turnover. Another problem has been the difficulty of enriching any job that requires low levels of skill.

One of the major limitations is the question of whether workers really want job enrichment, especially of the kind that changes the basic content of their jobs. Various surveys of worker attitudes, even the attitudes of assembly line workers, have shown that a high percentage of workers are not dissatisfied with their jobs and that few want "more interesting" jobs.[24] What these workers seem to want above all is job security and pay. Moreover, there has been considerable feeling that when managers begin changing the nature of jobs, the increased productivity sought may even mean loss of jobs.

It should be pointed out that the limitations of job enrichment apply mainly to jobs requiring low skill levels. The jobs of highly skilled workers, professionals, and managers already contain varying degrees of challenge and accomplishment. Perhaps these could be enriched considerably more than they are. But this can probably be done best by modern management techniques such as managing by objectives, utilizing more policy guidance with delegation of authority, introducing more status symbols in the form of titles and office facilities, and tying bonus and other rewards more closely to performance.

What Are the Problems?

On the surface, job enrichment as a response to motivating factors is an attractive idea. But it apparently has not worked as well as anticipated. There do seem to be a number of problems in the way it has been approached.

[24]Fein reports this from a number of surveys. See ibid., pp. 82–86.

One of the major problems appears to be the tendency for top managers and personnel specialists to apply their own scale of values of challenge and accomplishment to other people's personalities. As pointed out above, some people are challenged by jobs that would appear unconscionably dull to many of us. In one company, an employee who had spent his life doing no more than keeping daily records of orders received honestly felt he had one of the most important jobs in the company. In another business, a girl who had had a job-enriched position with a variety of tasks told her supervisor that she was greatly relieved to be freed of this responsibility when she was given a repetitive assembly line job. Similarly, a woman who was found to have considerable leadership ability in her outside activities with the Girl Scouts and PTA turned down a supervisory position because she felt that her present job allowed her to think about the problems and programs she was interested in outside the company.

Another difficulty is that job enrichment is usually imposed on people; they are told about it, rather than asked whether they would like it. This appeared to be, at least in part, the problem General Motors encountered in enlarging the jobs of assembly line workers at the Vega plant in Lordstown. We can never overlook the importance of consultation, of getting people involved before making any significant changes.

Also, there has been little or no support of job enrichment by union leaders. If job enrichment were so important to workers, one would think that this would be translated into union demands, a move that apparently has not occurred.

What Is Needed to Make Job Enrichment Effective?

Several approaches can be used to make job enrichment appeal to higher-level motivations. In the first place, we need a better understanding of what people want. As certain motivation researchers have pointed out, this varies with people and situations. Research has shown that workers with few skills want such extrinsic factors as job security, pay, benefits, less restrictive plant rules, and more sympathetic and understanding supervisors. As we move up the ladder in an enterprise, we find that intrinsic factors do become increasingly important. But professionals and managers have not been the primary targets of the job enrichers.

Second, if productivity increases are the main goal of enrichment, the program must show how workers will benefit. For example, in one company with fleets of unsupervised two-person service trucks, a program of giving these employees 25 percent of the cost savings from increased productivity, while still making it clear that the company would profit from their efforts, resulted in a startling increase of output and a much greater interest in these jobs.

In the third place, it should not be overlooked that people like to be involved, to be consulted, and to be given an opportunity to offer suggestions. They like to be considered as people. In one aerospace missile plant, increased morale and productivity, as well as greatly reduced turnover and absenteeism, resulted from the simple technique of having all employees' names on placards at their work stations and of having each program group—from parts production and assembly to inspection—work in an area in which their machines and equipment were painted the same color as one another but a different color from those of other groups.

A fourth factor is that people like to be able to feel that their managers are truly concerned with their welfare. Workers like to know what they are doing and why. They like feedback on their performance. They like to be appreciated and recognized for their work.

A SYSTEMS AND CONTINGENCY APPROACH TO MOTIVATION

The above analysis of theory, research, and application demonstrates that motivation must be looked upon from a systems and contingency point of view. Given the complexity of motivation in the light of varying personalities and situations, it is clear that risks of failure exist when any single motivator or group of motivators is applied without taking into account these variables. Human behavior is not a simple matter, but must be looked upon as a system of variables and interactions of which certain motivating factors are an important element.

Elton Mayo and His Pioneering Work

One of the earliest recognitions that motivation is a part of a complex system of human behavior was contained in the pioneering work in industrial behavioral research of Elton Mayo and his associates at Harvard.[25] They were originally interested in the relation between fatigue and monotony in the work situation at the Western Electric Hawthorne plant. They were unable to prove a direct relationship between environmental factors and output, but they discovered something theretofore unexpected: Workers were not merely a collection of individuals; they perceived themselves as members of a group. Interpersonal and group values were superior to managerial or individual values, and this made members vulnerable to group attitudes and pressures. In practice, this means that managers who do not have the enthusiastic support of the groups they supervise will be unable to motivate individual members to a significant degree.

[25]See F. Roethlisberger and W. J. Dickson, *Management and the Worker* (Cambridge, Mass.: Harvard University Press, 1939).

Kurt Lewin's field theory is perhaps the clearest explanation of how motivations depend on organizational climate and must be looked upon as an element in a larger system.[26] This theory starts from his celebrated formula for human behavior:

$$B = (P,E)$$

Translated, this formula means that human behavior (B) is a function of a person (P) and his or her environment (E). In other words, to understand someone's behavior at a given point of time, we need to know something about the individual as well as about his or her environment at that time. Put in the context of motivation, this means that people have differing motivations at various times and that the power with which something motivates an individual depends on the climate in which he or she operates.

Lewin's field theory is derived from the physicists' concept of the magnetic field. Human beings are seen as operating in a "field" of various forces, and human behavior can be thought of as a product of forces in this field.

Relating this to production, people are viewed as operating in a field of restraining forces and driving forces. This is shown in Figure 23.4. As can be seen, the actual behavior will depend on the strength of these counteracting forces. Thus there are forces that tend to limit productivity and forces that tend to motivate individuals to be more productive. From a managerial point of view, productive effort can be improved either by reducing restraining forces or by strengthening driving forces. By applying the techniques, principles, and concepts of management outlined in this book, the effective manager can do both.

Effective Motivation Depends on Organizational Climate

Motivating factors definitely do not exist in a vacuum. Even individual desires and drives are conditioned by physiological needs or by culturally induced needs. But what people are willing to strive for is also dulled or sharpened by the organizational climate in which they operate. At times a climate may repress motives; at other times it may arouse them.

This is illustrated by the research of Litwin and Stringer.[27] Using McClelland's need for achievement, need for affiliation, and need for power as major types of motivation, they found that the strength of these motives was affected by organizational climate. For example, they found that in a sample of 460 managers in a bureaucratically structured

[26]*The Conceptual Representation and the Measure of Psychological Forces* (Durham, N.C.: The Duke University Press, 1938).
[27]G. H. Litwin and R. A. Stringer, Jr., *Motivation and Organizational Climate* (Boston: Harvard Graduate School of Business Administration, 1968).

Figure 23.4 Lewin's force field theory.

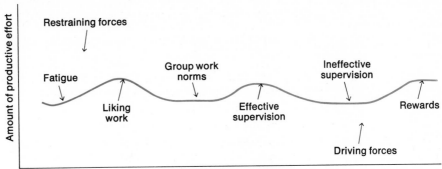

organization, there existed a strong correlation between such structure and power motivation and a negative correlation with achievement and affiliation motivation. In a climate with high responsibility and clear standards, they found a strong relationship of this climate to the achievement motivation, a moderate correlation to power motivation, and an unrelated to negatively related relationship with affiliation motivation.

Litwin and Stringer found that their researches gave considerable support to the theory that there is a relationship between climate and the arousal or reduction of motivating forces. A summary of their research results is given in Table 23.1.

Motivation, Leadership, and Managership

The interaction of motivation and organizational climate not only underscores the systems aspects of motivation but also emphasizes how motivation both depends on and influences leadership styles and management practice. Both leaders and managers (who, if effective, will almost certainly be leaders) must respond to the motivations of individuals if they are to design an environment in which people will perform willingly. Likewise, they can design a climate that will arouse or reduce motivation.

Styles of leadership will be discussed in Chapter 24. As for the ways and means by which managers design an environment for performance, that is really the subject of this entire book. In short, managers do this when they see that verifiable goals are set, strategies are developed and communicated, and plans to achieve objectives are made. They do it also in designing a system of organizational roles in which people can be effective (it should be pointed out in this connection that "organization structure" is not used in the restrictive bureaucratic sense that Litwin and Stringer use the term "organization"). Managers do it also when they

Table 23.1 Relationship of Climate to Motivation

Climate dimension	Effect on power motivation	Effect on achievement motivation	Effect on affiliation motivation
Structure (rigid structure with rules, regulations, and procedures)	Arousal	Reduction	Reduction
Responsibility (the feeling of being one's own boss)	Arousal	Arousal	No effect
Reward (emphasis on positive rewards rather than punishment)	No effect	Arousal	Arousal
Risk (emphasis on taking risks and assuming challenges)	Reduction	Arousal	Reduction
Warmth (friendly, informal group atmosphere)	No effect	No effect	Arousal
Support (mutual support; perceived helpfulness of managers and associates)	No effect	Arousal	Arousal
Standards (perceived importance of implicit and explicit goals and performance standards; emphasis on doing a good job; challenge in goals)	Arousal	Arousal*	Reduction
Conflict (emphasis on hearing different opinions; getting problems out in the open)	Arousal	Arousal*	Reduction
Identity (feeling that a person belongs to a company and is a valuable team member)	No effect	Arousal	Arousal

Source: Adapted from G. H. Litwin and R. A. Stringer, Jr., *Motivation and Organizational Climate* (Boston: Harvard Graduate School of Business Administration, 1968), pp. 81–82, 90–91.
*Proof of this effect on motivation was weak.

make sure that the structure is well staffed. Their styles of leadership and their ability to solve communication problems are also central to managing. And managers do much to create an effective environment when they make sure that control tools, information, and approaches furnish people with the feedback knowledge they must have for effective motivation.

Motivation Must Be Based on Situations

Even the brief analysis of motivation in this chapter certainly makes clear that it must be based on situations. What a manager does to induce individual effort toward the accomplishment of enterprise objectives must clearly take into account the differences between individuals, groups, times, and organizational climates. There can be no other way to approach the problem, as complex as it is. To realize that motivation requires a situational approach is at least to be aware that there are few pat answers or panaceas. We do know a great deal more about motivation now than we did a few decades ago. We know better what to look for and a little more about how to look. But we still know too little. We do know, however, that fitting motivation into a system of management is an exceptionally complex task.

Perhaps this is but another way of saying that the problem of understanding human behavior, and especially human motivation, is indeed formidable and is not yet completely solved. Some scholars think that the issues are so complex and that the technical problems of research in this area are so difficult that it may be many years before a total breakthrough is achieved. In the meantime, managers have before them theories which purport to explain motivation. What is even more important, these newer theories tend to establish a sound basis for the commonsense approach of intelligent managers. This is encouraging for the prosecution of research activities in this field. Although the managers of enterprise cannot await the discovery of complete knowledge, they should be fully aware of the current state of understanding and apply it as best they can in the operations for which they are responsible. This is the issue of ultimate leadership, a subject considered in the next chapter.

FOR DISCUSSION

1 What is motivation? How does effective managing take advantage of, and contribute to, motivation?

2 Why is the need-want-satisfaction chain too simplified an explanation of motivation?

3 Why has the Maslow theory of needs been critized? To what extent, if any, is it valid?

4 Compare and contrast the Maslow and Herzberg theories of motivation. On what grounds has the Herzberg theory been criticized? Why would you suspect that Herzberg's approach has been so popular with managers?

5 Explain Vroom's expectancy theory of motivation. How does it vary from the Porter and Lawler approach? Which appeals to you as being more accurate? Which is more useful in practice?

6 Explain McClelland's theory of motivation. How does it fit into a

systems approach? What does the impact of organizational climate show?

7 "You cannot motivate managers. They are self-propelled. You just get out of their way if you really want performance." Comment.

8 To what extent, and how, is money an effective motivator?

9 What contributions to motivation theory and practice does the Porter and Lawler model of motivation make?

10 Is a contingency, or situational, approach to motivation necessary for the practicing manager?

chapter 24 Leadership

MAJOR CHAPTER OBJECTIVES

1 To define the nature, functions, and ingredients of leadership.
2 To present the leading theories of, and approaches to, leadership, with special emphasis on situational or contingency theories.
3 To analyze various major approaches to leadership behavior and styles.
4 To present some things that people can do to cultivate leadership ability.
5 To summarize the analysis of leadership by showing the close relationship between leading and managing.

Although some people treat the terms "managership" and "leadership" as synonyms, the authors of this book believe they should be distinguished. As a matter of fact, there can be leaders of completely unorganized groups, but there can be managers, as conceived here, only where organized structures create roles. There are also important analytical advantages in separating leadership from managership. It permits leadership to be singled out for study without the encumbrance of qualifications relating to the more general issues of managership.

Leadership is an important aspect of managing. Indeed, as will be made clear in this chapter, the ability to lead effectively is one of the keys to being an effective manager; also it should become clear that undertaking the other essentials of managing—doing the entire managerial job—has an important bearing on assuring that a manager will be an effective leader. Managers must exercise all the elements of their role in order to combine human and material resources to achieve desired group objectives. The key to doing this is the existence of a clear role and a degree of discretion or authority to support managers' actions. As one writer remarked:

> Having a common position with reference to the source of originations or direction, subordinates develop cooperative patterns toward one another that facilitate the work process. These would be much more difficult to develop were there not a common source of authority acting on them; witness the difficulties inherent in cooperative endeavors among individuals who have not had this experience.[1]

By carrying on their functions of planning, organizing, staffing, and controlling, managers will get some results, as is illustrated in Figure 24.1. But these results are likely to be far inferior to what could be achieved if managers added to their operations the extra ingredient of effective leadership.

The essence of leadership is followership. In other words, it is the willingness of people to follow that makes a person a leader. Moreover, people tend to follow those whom they perceive as providing a means of achieving their own desires, wants, and needs. As a consequence, we can see that leadership and motivation are closely interconnected. By understanding motivation, we can appreciate better what people want and why they act as they do. Also, as noted in the previous chapter, leaders may not only respond to these motivators but also arouse or dampen them by means of the organizational climate they develop. Both of these factors are as important to leadership as they are to managership.

[1]Leonard Sayles, *Managerial Behavior* (New York: McGraw-Hill Book Company, 1964), p. 145.

Figure 24.1 Impact of leadership on employee utilization of capability. Leadership is the ability of a manager to influence subordinates (followers) to work with confidence and zeal. If subordinates are guided only by rules and requirements enforced by managerial authority, they may work at about 60 or 65 percent of capacity—just enough to satisfy the requirements for holding their jobs. (*Note* : These numbers are illustrative and not based on research.) To raise effort toward total capability, the manager must induce devoted response on the part of subordinates by exercising leadership. This is done through numerous means, all solidly based on the needs of subordinates.

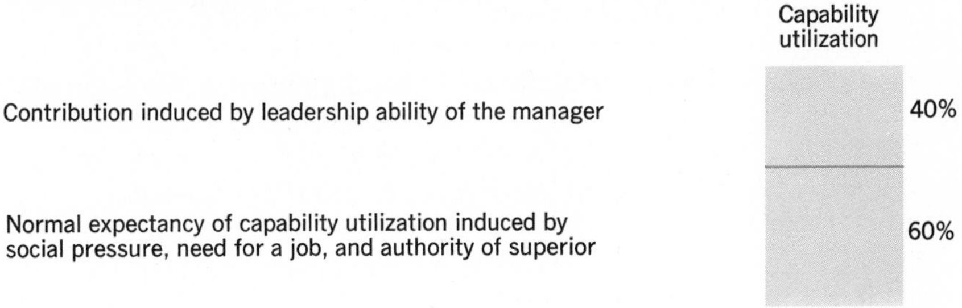

Capability
utilization

Contribution induced by leadership ability of the manager — 40%

Normal expectancy of capability utilization induced by
social pressure, need for a job, and authority of superior — 60%

LEADERSHIP DEFINED

Leadership is generally defined simply as influence, the art or process of influencing people so that they will strive willingly toward the achievement of group goals. This concept can be enlarged to imply not only willingness to work but also willingness to work with zeal and confidence. Zeal reflects ardor, earnestness, and intensity in the execution of work; confidence reflects experience and technical ability. To lead is to guide, conduct, direct, and precede. Leaders act to help a group achieve objectives with the maximum application of its capabilities. They do not stand behind a group to push and to prod; they place themselves before the group as they facilitate progress and inspire the group to accomplish organizational goals. A pertinent example is that of the orchestra leader, whose function is to produce coordinated sound and correct tempo through the integrated effort of the instrumentalists. Depending upon the quality of the director's leadership, the orchestra will respond in desultory fashion or with accuracy and enthusiasm.

A slightly different, but interesting, concept of leadership is that proposed by Katz and Kahn.[2] They see it, at least as applied to formally organized enterprises, as "the influential increment over and above mechanical compliance with the routine directives of the organization." In other words, an organizational role may encompass definite objectives and plans to achieve them, clear position duties, and all the many

[2]D. Katz and R. L. Kahn, *The Social Psychology of Organizations*, 2d ed. (New York: John Wiley & Sons, Inc., 1978), chap. 16.

nonpersonal things an individual must do to carry out a job. But there is much to add to these if an individual is to perform effectively. According to Katz and Kahn, these include supplementing the organizational design with information necessary for persons to perform their roles, clarifying roles in view of the changing environment, and recognizing the fact that every role is a part of an open social system that responds to change by being aware of the dynamics of an organized enterprise and interpreting them to those working in it and by making adjustments for human beings and their various behavior patterns.

The idea of leadership as an influential increment made especially necessary by the fact that all enterprises are open systems and that people have varying drives, attitudes, and desires fits in very well with the approach of this book. The authors, by recognizing leading as a major function of managers, support the idea that we need an incremental influence beyond those portions of people's roles that can be defined through effective planning, organizing, staffing, and controlling.

FUNCTIONS OF LEADERSHIP

If enterprise managers could rely upon all subordinates to contribute toward group goal accomplishment with zeal and confidence, there would be no need to develop the art of leadership. Morale would always be high, and all would produce to their maximum capability. Whether as a result of lack of motivation or opportunity, adverse environmental circumstances, or mediocre managers, few subordinates work with continuing zeal and confidence. Perhaps it is not within the gifts of human beings to do so, at least over considerable periods of time.

It is not known what proportion of a group of subordinates or followers are "self-starters" in the sense that they *naturally* work enthusiastically and with confidence. Undoubtedly, many factors contribute to their numbers. Even among them there are those who would benefit from the manager's leadership as his or her effort is directed toward organizational goals. But for most people leadership is required to elicit desired contributions to goals.

History is replete with instances of mediocre performance in the absence of leadership, and of superb performance with it. It is clearly in the interest of every enterprise, if it has other than "make-work" goals, that its employees work with zeal and confidence. Only then can their morale be said to be high; only then will they achieve greater efficiency. Indeed, in competitive situations this condition is the way to preserve organizational existence if it is true, as is often said, that morale is three-quarters of victory. The function of leadership, therefore, is to induce or persuade all subordinates or followers to contribute willingly to organizational goals in accordance with their maximum capability.

Every group of people that performs near its total capability has some person as its head who is skilled in the art of leadership. This skill seems to be a compound of at least three major ingredients—the ability to comprehend that human beings have differing motivating forces at varying times and in different situations, the ability to inspire, and the ability to act in a way that will develop a climate for responding to and arousing motivations.

As in all practices, it is one thing to know motivation theory, categories of motivating forces, and the nature of a system of motivation and another thing to be able to apply this knowledge to people and situations. All managing is situational and dependent on contingencies. But a manager or other leader who at least knows the present state of motivation theory and who sees the elements in a system of motivation is better aware of the nature and strength of human needs and is more able to define and design ways of satisfying them and to administer a system that will get the desired responses.

The second ingredient of leadership seems to be a rare ability to inspire, that is, to animate or to enliven followers to apply their full capabilities to a project. While the use of motivators seems to center about subordinates and their needs, inspiration emanates from group leaders. They may have charismatic qualities that induce loyalty, devotion, and a zeal on the part of followers. This is not a matter of need-satisfaction; it is, rather, a matter of people giving altruistic support to a chosen champion. The best evidences of inspirational leadership come from hopeless and fearful situations such as a nation on the eve of battle, a prison camp with exceptional morale, or a defeated leader undeserted by faithful followers. Some may argue that such devotion is not entirely altruistic—that it can also explain why those who face catastrophe will follow one whom they trust. But few would deny the value of charisma in either case.

A third ingredient of leadership has to do with the style of the leader and the climate he or she develops as a result. We have seen in the previous chapter how much the strength of motivation depends on expectancies, perceived rewards, the amount of effort required, the task to be done, and other factors which are a part of the environment of performance. We have seen also how an organizational climate influences motivation. This awareness has led to considerable research on, and theories of, leadership behavior. Those who have long approached leadership as a psychological study of interpersonal relationships have tended to merge their thinking with that of the authors of this book, who see the primary task of managers as the design and maintenance of an environment for performance.

It should be clear that, since almost every possible role in organized enterprise is made more satisfying to participants and more productive for the enterprise by those who can help others fulfill their desire for such things as money, status, power, or pride of accomplishment, leaders must always exist in social life. As a matter of fact, perhaps the fundamental principle of leadership is: *Since people tend to follow those whom they see as a means of satisfying their own personal goals, the more managers understand what motivates their subordinates and how these motivations operate, and the more they reflect this understanding in carrying out their managerial actions, the more effective leaders they are likely to be.*

As can be readily seen, the principle of leadership is closely related to the principle of harmony of objectives discussed in Chapter 22. If managers can induce subordinates to believe that their personal objectives are in harmony with those of an organization, this very accomplishment tends to make managers effective leaders.

LEADERSHIP THEORY AND RESEARCH

Because of its importance to all kinds of group action, we are not surprised to find a considerable volume of theory and research concerning leadership, although most of it has come into being in the period beginning with World War II. Analyses have disclosed an average of twenty-one studies per year from 1930 to 1939, thirty-one studies per year between 1940 and 1944, fifty-five studies per year in the period 1945 to 1949, and 152 studies per year from 1950 to 1953.[3] It is no wonder that when Stogdill completed his survey of leadership theory and research in 1974, he found it necessary to abstract and analyze over 3000 books and articles in the field.[4]

It is difficult to summarize such a large volume of research in a form relevant to management. However, in the succeeding pages we shall identify several major types of leadership theory and research and outline some basic kinds of leadership styles.

THE TRAIT APPROACH TO LEADERSHIP

The earliest studies of leadership were based largely on an attempt to identify the traits that leaders actually possessed. Starting with the "great man" theory that leaders are born and not made, a belief dating back to the ancient Greeks and Romans, inquiries were made to identify the physical, mental, and personality traits of various leaders. The "great man" theory

---

[3]As reported in F. E. Fiedler, *A Theory of Leadership Effectiveness* (New York: McGraw-Hill Book Company, 1967), p. 6.
[4]R. M. Stogdill, *Handbook of Leadership* (New York: The Free Press, 1974). As noted on the jacket of the book.

lost much of its acceptability with the rise in influence of the behaviorist school of psychology, which emphasized that people are not born with traits, other than inherited physical characteristics and perhaps tendencies toward good health.

Prior to 1949, most studies of leaders did tend to concentrate on identifying traits. Even in more recent years, such studies have been made. Stogdill found that various researches identified five physical traits related to leadership ability (such as energy, appearance, and height), four intelligence and ability traits, sixteen personality traits (such as adaptability, aggressiveness, enthusiasm, and self-confidence), six task-related characteristics (such as achievement drive, persistence, and initiative), and nine social characteristics (such as cooperativeness, interpersonal skills, and administrative ability).[5]

In general, the study of leader traits has not been a very fruitful approach to explaining leadership. Not all leaders possess all the traits, and many nonleaders may possess most or all of them. Also, the trait approach gives no guide as to how *much* of any trait a person should have. Furthermore, out of dozens of studies, there is no uniformity of identified traits or any significant correlations of traits with actual instances of leadership. As psychologist Eugene E. Jennings has said: "Research has produced such a variegated list of traits presumably to describe leadership that, for all practical purposes, it describes nothing. Fifty years of study have failed to produce one personality trait or set of qualities that can be used to discriminate between leaders and nonleaders."[6]

Nevertheless, some studies have indicated a significant correlation between certain traits and leadership effectiveness. Stogdill found from a review of the literature that there was a definite correlation between the traits of intelligence, scholarship, dependability, responsibility, social participation, and socioeconomic status of leaders compared with nonleaders.[7] Ghiselli found significant correlation between leadership effectiveness and the traits of intelligence, supervisory ability, initiative, self-assurance, and individuality in the way work was done.[8] Keith Davis, likewise, found that leaders do have high intelligence, broad social interests and maturity, strong motivation to accomplish, and great respect for, and interest in, people.[9]

But even these correlations between traits and leadership are not

[5]Ibid., pp. 74–75.

[6]"The Anatomy of Leadership," *Management of Personnel Quarterly*, vol. 1, no. 1, p. 2 (Autumn 1961).

[7]R. M. Stogdill, "Personal Factors Associated with Leadership: A Survey of the Literature," *Journal of Psychology*, vol. 25, pp. 35–71 (1948).

[8]E. E. Ghiselli, "Managerial Talent," *American Psychologist*, vol. 16, no. 10, pp. 631–641 (October 1963).

[9]*Human Behavior at Work*, 4th ed. (New York: McGraw-Hill Book Company, 1972), pp. 102–104.

persuasive. Most of these so-called traits are really patterns of behavior that one would expect from a leader and particularly from a leader in a managerial position.

THE SITUATIONAL APPROACH TO LEADERSHIP

After increasing disillusionment with the "great man" and trait approaches to understanding leadership, attention turned to the study of situations and the belief that leaders are the product of given situations. A large number of studies have been made on the premise that leadership is strongly affected by the situation from which the leader emerges and in which he or she operates. That this is a persuasive approach is indicated by the situation that gave rise to a Hitler in Germany in the 1930s, the earlier rise of Mussolini in Italy, the emergence of F. D. Roosevelt in the Great Depression of the 1930s in the United States, and the rise of Mao Tse-tung in China in the period after World War II. This approach to leadership recognizes that there exists an interaction between the group and the leader. It supports the follower theory that people tend to follow those in whom they perceive (accurately or inaccurately) a means of accomplishing their own personal desires. The leader, then, is the person who recognizes these desires and does those things, or undertakes those programs, designed to meet them.

This multidimensional approach to leadership was detected early in the studies of Stogdill and his associates when it was discovered that, in analyzing 470 Navy officers occupying forty-five different positions, their leadership ability was heavily affected by such situational factors as their jobs, the organizational environment in which they operated, and the characteristics of people they were assigned to lead.[10] Other studies made over the years have shown that effective leadership depends upon response to such environmental factors as the history of the enterprise, the community in which the organization operates, the psychological climate of the group being led, group member personalities and cultural influences, and the time required for making decisions.[11]

This approach obviously has much meaning for managerial theory and practice. It also ties into the system of motivation discussed in the previous chapter. It has meaning for practicing managers who must take into account the situation in its entirety when they design an environment for performance.

[10]R. M. Stogdill, C. L. Shartle, and Associates, *Patterns of Administrative Performance* (Columbus, Ohio: Bureau of Business Research, The Ohio State University, 1956), sec. IV.
[11]For a summary of these researches, see A. C. Filley, R. J. House, and S. Kerr, *Managerial Process and Organizational Behavior* 2d ed. (Glenview, Ill.: Scott, Foresman and Company, 1976), chap. 12.

Although their approach to leadership theory is primarily one of analyzing leadership style, Fiedler and his associates at the University of Illinois have combined, to some extent, the trait and situational approach and have suggested a contingency theory of leadership.[12] Fiedler's theory implies that leadership is any process in which the ability of a leader to exercise influence depends upon the group task situation and the degree to which the leader's style, personality, and approach fit the group. In other words, according to Fiedler, people become leaders not only because of the attributes of their personality but also because of various situational factors and the interaction between the leaders and the situation.

Fiedler's findings and theory are based on a considerable volume of research. The groups he has studied and with whom he has tested his hypotheses include B-29 bomber crews, army tank crews, antiaircraft artillery crews, infantry squads, open-hearth steel supervisors and crews, upper-level company managers, managers of gas stations, student groups, and church leaders. If one applies statistical methods carefully to the findings of Fiedler and his associates, their results are fairly impressive.

Critical Dimensions of the Leadership Situation

On the basis of his studies, Fiedler found three "critical dimensions" of the situation that affect a leader's most effective style.[13]

1 Position power. This is the degree to which the power of a position, as distinguished from other sources of power such as charismatic or expertise power, enables a leader to get group members to comply with directions; as can be seen in the case of managers, this is the power arising from organizational authority. As Fiedler points out, a leader with clear and considerable position power can more easily obtain better followership than one without such power.
2 Task structure. With this dimension, Fiedler had in mind the extent to which tasks can be clearly spelled out and people held responsible for them, in contrast to situations where tasks are vague and unstructured. Where tasks are clear, the quality of performance can be more easily controlled, and group members can be more definitely held responsible for performance than where tasks are ambiguous.
3 Leader-member relations. This dimension, which Fiedler regards as most important from a leader's point of view, since position power and task structure may be largely under the control of an enterprise,

[12]Fiedler, op. cit.
[13]Ibid., pp. 22–32. See also F. E. Fiedler, "Engineer the Job to Fit the Manager," *Harvard Business Review*, vol. 43, no. 5, pp. 115–122 (September–October 1965).

has to do with the extent to which group members like and trust a leader and are willing to follow him or her.

Leadership Styles

To approach his study, Fiedler postulated two major styles of leadership. One of these is primarily task-oriented, in which a leader gains satisfaction from seeing tasks performed. Another is oriented primarily toward achieving good interpersonal relations and toward attaining a position of personal prominence.

Favorableness of the situation was defined as the degree to which a given situation enables the leader to exert influence over a group. To measure leadership styles and determine whether a leader was more task-oriented or people-oriented, Fiedler used an unusual testing technique. He based his findings on two types of scores: (1) scores on the least preferred coworker (LPC), ratings made by people in a group as to those with whom they would least like to work, and (2) scores on assumed similarity between opposites (AS_0), ratings based on the degree to which leaders perceive group members to be like themselves, on the assumption that people will like best and work best with those who are perceived as most like themselves.

In his studies using this method, supported also by studies of others, Fiedler found that people who rated their coworkers high (that is, in favorable terms) were those who derived major satisfaction from successful interpersonal relationships. People who rated their least preferred coworker low (that is, in unfavorable terms) were seen as deriving their major satisfaction from task performance. Likewise, he found that people who rated their coworkers with high assumed similarity between opposites also rated them fairly high on the scale of least preferred coworkers, and vice versa. Thus there was a high correlation between AS_0 and LPC scores.

Fiedler's Contingency Model

From his studies of least preferred coworkers and assumed similarity between opposites and his findings that a match between a leader's perceptions will result in effective leadership in a group situation, Fiedler developed a contingency theory of leadership. Put in its simplest terms, this model "states that the group's performance will be contingent upon the appropriate matching of leadership styles and the degree of favorableness of the group situation for the leader, that is, the degree to which the situation provides the leader with influence over his group members."[14]

From his research and the application of this model, Fiedler comes to

[14]Ibid., p. 151.

some interesting conclusions. Recognizing that personal perceptions may be ambiguous and even quite inaccurate, Fiedler nonetheless found that:

> Leadership performance depends then as much on the organization as it depends on the leader's own attributes. Except perhaps for the unusual case, it is simply not meaningful to speak of an effective leader or an ineffective leader; we can only speak of a leader who tends to be effective in one situation and ineffective in another. If we wish to increase organizational and group effectiveness we must learn not only how to train leaders more effectively but also how to build an organizational environment in which the leader can perform well.[15]

Fiedler's contingency model of leadership can be summarized by reference to Figure 24.2. As presented, this figure is really a summary of Fiedler's research. As the figure indicates, Fiedler found that in "very unfavorable" or "very favorable" situations the highly task-oriented leader would be the most effective. In other words, when position power and task structure are very unclear and leader-member relations are poor, the situation is highly unfavorable and the most effective leader will be one who is task-oriented. Likewise, at the other extreme, where position power is very high, task structure very clear, and leader-member relations very good—a highly favorable situation—Fiedler found that the task-oriented leader was most effective. However, where the situation was only

[15]Ibid., p. 261.

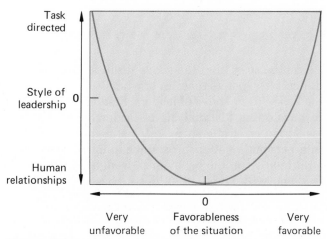

Figure 24.2 Fiedler's Model of Leadership. [*Adapted from F. E. Fiedler*, A Theory of Leadership Effectiveness (*New York: McGraw-Hill Book Company, 1967*), chap. 9.

moderately unfavorable or favorable, the human relations-oriented leader was found to be most effective.

Fiedler's Model and Management

In reviewing Fiedler's research, one finds that there is nothing automatic or "good" in either the task-oriented or the people-satisfaction-oriented style. Leadership effectiveness depends upon the various elements in the group environment. This might be expected. Cast in the desired role of leader, managers who apply knowledge to the realities of the group reporting to them will do well to recognize that they are practicing an art. But in doing so, they will necessarily take into account the motivations to which people will respond and their ability to satisfy them in the interest of attaining enterprise goals.

Several scholars have put Fiedler's theory of leadership to tests in various situations. One of the recent studies indicates that where there is a good relationship between managers and group members, the latter will put forth greater effort to achieve results. Most significantly, it has been found that, irrespective of manager-group relationships, the task-oriented manager is clearly associated with a higher-quality product.[16]

Thus we can say, as every experienced manager has recognized for many years, that the nature and style of the most effective leadership depend upon the situation. In leadership, the major situational variables are likely to be the leader's personality, the nature of leader-member relations (which certainly implies the importance of people being led), the task, and organizational climate of the enterprise. But what is true of leadership is also true of managing. All managers, applying any theory or technique, must design their approaches to suit the situation.[17]

LEADERSHIP BEHAVIOR AND STYLES

As can be seen from the above discussion of theories of leadership, it is difficult to separate theories of what leadership is and depends upon from the behavior or styles of leaders. Fiedler, for example, found it important in developing his analysis of leadership to postulate two basic styles: task-oriented leadership and leadership oriented toward people and interpersonal relationships. But a number of researchers have concentrated primarily on the behavior of leaders on the assumption that ability to lead and willingness to follow are based on leadership styles.

[16]D. E. Hovey, "The Low-powered Leader Confronts a Messy Problem: A Test of Fiedler's Theory," *Academy of Management Journal*, vol. 27, no. 2, p. 362 (June 1974).
[17]Even Mary Parker Follett recognized this "new" management in 1920 when she wrote of the "law of the situation." H. C. Metcalf and L. Urwick (eds.), *Dynamic Administration: The Collected Papers of Mary Parker Follett* (New York: Harper & Brothers, 1941), pp. 58–66.

Some earlier explanations of leadership styles classified them on the basis of how leaders use their authority. Leaders were seen as applying three basic styles. The autocratic leader was seen as one who commands and expects compliance, who is dogmatic and positive, and who leads by the ability to withhold or give rewards and punishment. The democratic, or participative, leader consults with subordinates on proposed actions and decisions and encourages participation from them. This type of leader was perceived to be on a spectrum ranging from the person who does not take action without subordinates' concurrence to the one who makes decisions but consults with subordinates before doing so.

The third type of leader uses his or her power very little, if at all, giving subordinates a high degree of independence, or "free rein," in their operations. Such leaders depend largely on subordinates to set their own goals and the means of achieving them, and they perceive their role as one of facilitating the operations of followers by furnishing them information and acting primarily as a contact with the group's external environment.

There are variations from this simple classification of leadership styles. Some autocratic leaders are seen as "benevolent autocrats." Although they listen considerately to their followers' opinions before making a decision, the decision is their own. They may be willing to hear and consider subordinates' ideas and concerns, but when a decision is to be made, they may be more autocratic than benevolent.

A variation of the participative leader is the person who is supportive. Leaders in this category may look upon their task as not only consulting with followers and considering carefully their opinions but also doing all they can to support subordinates in accomplishing their duties. As will be seen below, this is the cornerstone of Likert's approach to leadership and managing.

Those who subscribe to these three styles of leadership are likely to recognize that the use of any style will depend on the situation. A manager may be highly autocratic in an emergency; one can hardly imagine a fire chief meeting with his crew to consider the best way of fighting a fire. Managers may also be autocratic when they alone have the answers to certain questions, such as the daily volume of shipments a plant should make to customers.

A leader may gain considerable knowledge and a better commitment on the part of persons involved by consulting with subordinates. We saw how this was true in developing verifiable objectives under systems of managing by objectives. Furthermore, a manager dealing with a group of research scientists may give them considerable free rein in developing their experiments. But the same manager might be quite autocratic in enforcing compliance concerning protective covering to be worn when handling certain dangerous chemicals.

Rensis Likert and his associates at the University of Michigan have seriously studied the patterns and styles of leaders and managers for three decades.[18] In the course of these researches, Likert has developed certain concepts and approaches important to understanding leadership behavior. He is a proponent of participative management. He sees the effective manager as strongly oriented to subordinates, relying on communication to keep all parties working as a unit. All members of the group, including the manager or leader, adopt a supportive relationship in which they feel a genuine common interest in terms of needs, values, aspirations, goals, and expectations. Since it appeals to human motivations, Likert sees this approach as the most effective way to lead a group.

As guidelines for research and for the clarification of his concepts, Likert has postulated four systems of management. System 1 management is described as "exploitive-authoritative"; these managers are highly autocratic, have little trust in subordinates, motivate people through fear and punishment with occasional rewards, engage only in downward communication, limit decision making to the top, and display similar characteristics. System 2 management is called "benevolent-authoritative"; these managers have a condescending confidence and trust in subordinates, motivate with rewards and some fear and punishment, permit some upward communication, solicit some ideas and opinions from subordinates, and allow some delegation of decision making but with close policy control.

System 3 management is referred to as "consultative"; these managers have substantial but not complete confidence and trust in subordinates, usually try to make constructive use of subordinates' ideas and opinions, use for motivation rewards with occasional punishment and some participation, engage in communication flow both down and up, make broad policy and general decisions at the top with specific decisions at lower levels, and act consultatively in other ways.

Likert sees system 4 management as the most participative of all and referred to it as "participative-group"; system 4 managers have complete trust and confidence in subordinates in all matters, always get ideas and opinions from subordinates and constructively use them, give economic rewards on the basis of group participation and involvement in such areas as setting goals and appraising progress toward goals, engage in much communication down and up and with peers, encourage decision making throughout the organization, and otherwise operate with themselves and their subordinates as a group.

In general, Likert has found that those managers who applied the

---

[18]See especially his *New Patterns of Management* (New York: McGraw-Hill Book Company, 1961) and *The Human Organization* (New York: McGraw-Hill Book Company, 1967), from which material in this section has been obtained.

system 4 approach to their operations had greatest success as leaders. Moreover, he found that departments and companies managed by the system 4 approach were most effective in setting goals and achieving them and were generally more productive. He ascribed this mainly to the extent of participativeness in management and the extent to which the practice of supportive relationships is maintained.

Argyris's Immaturity-Maturity Continuum

Similar in some respects to Likert's systems of management is the immaturity-maturity continuum model of Chris Argyris, of Yale and Harvard.[19] His research has been focused primarily on the problem of coexistence of individual and organizational needs. He agrees with other behavioral scientists that people have strong self-actualization needs, and he makes the point that organizational controls leave the employee feeling submissive and dependent. Argyris asserts that the operational techniques employed in large-scale enterprises often ignore the social and egoistic needs of the employee. Paired with this assumption is a second that maintains the inability of one person to motivate another. Having what Argyris calls "psychological energy," subordinates will attach top priority to the satisfaction of their own needs. The greater the disparity between individual needs and company needs, the more an employee is likely to reflect dissatisfaction, apathy, conflict, tension, or subversion. In this conception, the technique of achieving motivation would involve offering job challenge and opportunity to employees who may need training to take advantage of the changed environment.

From this position, Argyris argues that the effective leader or manager will help people move from a state of immaturity, or dependence, toward a state of maturity. His position is that if an organization does not provide people with opportunities for maturing and for being treated like mature individuals, they will become frustrated and anxious and will act inconsistently with organization goals. The seven elements of Argyris's immaturity-maturity continuum may be depicted as shown in Table 24.1.

The Managerial Grid

One of the most widely known approaches to dramatizing leadership styles is the managerial grid, developed some years ago by Robert Blake and Jane Mouton.[20] Building on previous research that showed the importance of a manager's having concern both for production and for people, Blake and Mouton devised a clever device to dramatize this

---

[19]See his *Personality and Organization* (New York: Harper & Brothers, 1957), especially chap. 2, and *Integrating the Individual and the Organization* (New York: John Wiley & Sons, Inc., 1964).

[20]*The Managerial Grid* (Houston: Gulf Publishing Company, 1964).

Table 24.1 Argyris's Immaturity-Maturity Continuum

Immaturity characteristics	Maturity characteristics
Passivity	Activity
Dependence	Independence
Capable of behaving in few ways	Capable of behaving in many ways
Shallow interests	Deep interests
Short-term perspective	Long-term perspective
Subordinate position	Superordinate position
Lack of self-awareness	Self-awareness and control

Source: Adapted from C. Argyris, *Personality and Organization* (New York: Harper & Brothers, 1957), pp. 50–51.

concern. This grid, shown in Figure 24.3, has been used widely throughout the world as a means of managerial training and of identifying various combinations of leadership styles.

The grid dimensions   As can be seen, the grid has two dimensions. As Blake and Mouton have emphasized, their use of the term "concern for" is meant to convey "how" managers are concerned about production or "how" they are concerned about people, and not such things as "how much" production they are concerned about getting out of a group.

"Concern for production" is conceived as the attitudes of a supervisor toward a wide variety of things, such as the quality of policy decisions, procedures and processes, creativeness of research, quality of staff services, work efficiency, and volume of output. "Concern for people" is likewise interpreted in a broad way. It includes such elements as degree of personal commitment toward goal achievement, maintaining the self-esteem of workers, responsibility based on trust rather than obedience, maintaining good working conditions, and having satisfying interpersonal relations.

The four extreme styles   Blake and Mouton recognize four extremes of basic styles. Under the 1.1 style (referred to by some authors as "impoverished management"), managers concern themselves very little with either people or production and have minimum involvement in their job; to all intents and purposes, they have abdicated their job and only mark time or act as messengers communicating information from superiors to subordinates. At the other extreme are the 9.9 managers who display in their actions the highest possible dedication both to people and to production. They are the real "team managers" who are able to mesh the production needs of the enterprise with the needs of individuals.

Another style is identified as 1.9 management (called by some "country club management") in which managers have little or no concern for production but are concerned only for people. They promote an

Figure 24.3 The managerial grid. [*Adapted from R. R. Blake and J. S. Mouton, The Managerial Grid (Houston: Gulf Publishing Company, 1964), p. 10.*]

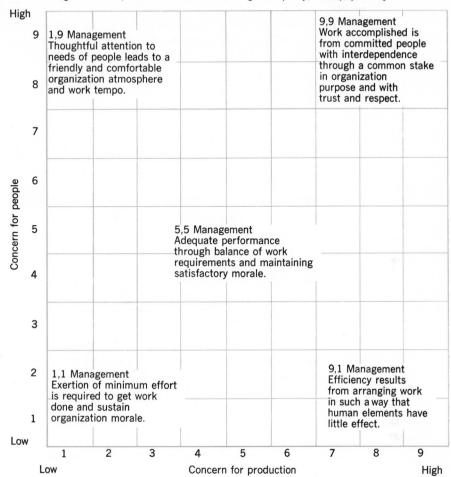

environment where everyone is relaxed, friendly, and happy and no one is concerned about putting forth coordinated effort to accomplish enterprise goals. At another extreme are the 9.1 managers (sometimes referred to as "autocratic task managers"), who are concerned only with developing an efficient operation, who have little or no concern for people, and who are quite autocratic in their style of leadership.

Using these four extremes, every managerial technique, approach, or style can be placed somewhere on the grid. Clearly 5.5 managers have medium concern for production and for people. They obtain adequate, but not outstanding, morale and production. They do not set goals too high, and they are likely to have a rather benevolently autocratic attitude toward people.

As is clear, the managerial grid is a useful device for identifying and classifying managerial styles. But it does not tell us why a manager falls in one part or another of the grid. To find this out, as Blake and Mouton readily admit, one has to look to underlying causes. These may be found in such things as the personality of the leader or of followers, the ability and training of managers, the enterprise environment, and other situational factors that influence how both leaders and followers act.

Leadership as a Continuum

The situational and contingent nature of leadership styles has been well characterized by Tannenbaum and Schmidt in their concept of a leadership continuum.[21] As is shown in Figure 24.4, they see leadership as involving a variety of styles, ranging from one that is highly boss-centered to one that is highly subordinate-centered. These vary with the degree of authority a leader or manager grants to subordinates. Thus, instead of suggesting a choice between the two styles of leadership—authoritarian or democratic—this approach offers a range of styles, with no suggestion that one is always right and another is wrong.

The concept of the continuum recognizes that an appropriate style of leadership depends on situations and personalities. Tannenbaum and Schmidt saw the most important elements that might influence a manager's style along this continuum as (1) the forces operating in the manager's personality, including his or her value system, confidence in subordinates, inclination toward leadership styles, and feelings of security in uncertain situations; (2) forces in subordinates that will affect the manager's behavior; and (3) forces in the situation, such as organization values and traditions, how effectively subordinates work as a unit, the nature of a problem and whether authority to handle it can be safely delegated, and the pressure of time.

In reviewing their continuum model in 1973, Tannenbaum and Schmidt placed circles around it, as is shown in Figure 24.4, to represent the influences on style imposed both by the "organizational environment" and by the "societal environment."[22] This was done to emphasize the open-system nature of leadership styles and the various impacts both of the enterprise organizational environment and of the social environment outside the enterprise. In this later revision, they put increased stress on the interdependency of leadership style and environmental forces, such as labor unions, greater pressures for social responsibility, the civil rights movement, and the ecology and consumer movements, that challenge the rights of managers to make decisions

---

[21]R. Tannenbaum and W. H. Schmidt, "How to Choose a Leadership Pattern," *Harvard Business Review*, vol. 36, no. 2, pp. 95–101 (March–April 1958).

[22]See reprint of their "How to Choose a Leadership Pattern" and their "Retrospective Commentary" on their earlier article in *Harvard Business Review*, vol. 51, no. 3, pp. 162–180 (May–June 1973).

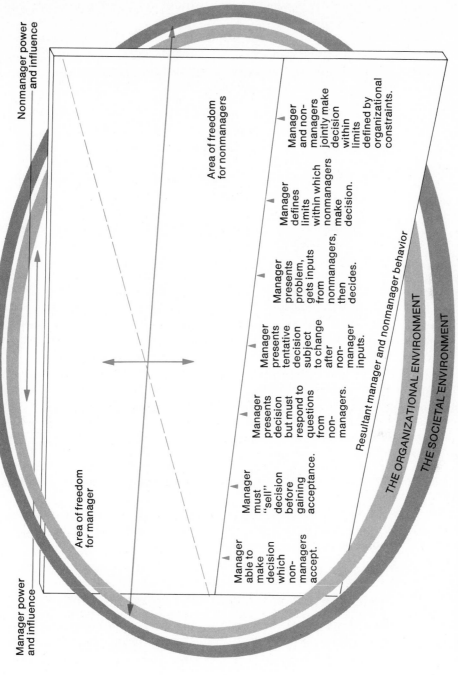

Figure 24.4 Continuum of manager-nonmanager behavior. *[Reprinted with permission from R. Tannenbaum and W. H. Schmidt, "Retrospective Commentary" on "How to Choose a Leadership Pattern," Harvard Business Review, vol. 51, no. 3, p. 167 (May-June, 1973)].*

or handle their subordinates without considering interests outside the organization.

The Path Goal Approach to Leadership Effectiveness

The path goal theory or approach to leadership effectiveness is of particular interest to managers. As perceived by Robert House, who builds on various motivational and leadership theories of others, this theory sees the most effective leadership style as one where leaders, or managers, take various steps to design a situation where the latent and aroused motivations of group members are responded to effectively.[23] House has supported this theory by his own research and finds considerable support for it from the research of such motivation scholars as Vroom and Porter and Lawler and such leadership researchers as Fiedler.

In essence, the path goal approach finds that the most effective leaders are those who help subordinates achieve both enterprise goals and their personal goals, particularly achievement and reward goals such as money, promotion, interesting tasks, and opportunities for growth and development. Leaders do this by defining position and task roles clearly, by removing obstacles to performance, by enlisting the assistance of group members in setting goals, by promoting group cohesiveness and team effort, by increasing opportunities for personal satisfaction in work performance, by reducing unnecessary stresses and external controls, by making reward expectations clear, and by doing other things that meet people's expectations.

Research indicates that the path goal approach is especially valid for upper-level positions and professional tasks, where the behavior of leaders can have considerable influence on designing an environment for performance. Its application to routine production jobs is not nearly as clear, probably because what managers can do for these tasks is seen as redundant and because they cannot do much to make such tasks more satisfying.

As can be seen from this simplified description of the path goal theory, what the effective leader does in a structured role situation is no more than be a good manager.

CULTIVATED BEHAVIOR OF LEADERS

The interpersonal relationships of leaders and followers can be improved considerably as a leader cultivates certain behavior. This is an area where the contributions of psychologists aid us. It becomes even more important

---

[23]For an elaborate discussion of this theory, see R. J. House, "A Path Goal Theory of Leadership Effectiveness," *Administrative Science Quarterly*, vol. 16, no. 3, pp. 321–338 (September 1971).

than mere knowledge because certain behavioral patterns can be learned and used with skill.

Awareness

One of the most striking observations about some managers is that they seem to be concerned only with the routine of their jobs and execute them unimaginatively and with a lack of appreciation of what they can do to be better managers and leaders. Being aware of the factors that make for leadership effectiveness and of the way in which styles are contingent on a range of situational considerations should help any manager learn to be a more effective leader.

To be sure, the body of leadership theories and research is so large that no manager can be expected to be familiar with it all. However, there is no reason why any manager cannot learn and appreciate the essentials of motivation and leadership outlined in this chapter and the preceding one. These chapters represent a very limited impression of all that has been conjectured and what has been found to be true. But it is enough for a considerable start.

Furthermore, as is true in every area of management, knowing and being knowledgeable are not enough. A manager must also have the ability to apply this knowledge to practice.

Empathy

Webster defines empathy as "the imaginative projection of one's own consciousness into another being." As commonly used, it is the ability to place one's self in the position of another, simulating that person's feelings, prejudices, and values.

Managers without empathy have objectives, ambitions, values, and biases like other people, and they often assume that their subordinates have the same ones. It is not likely they would have. People widely differ in every respect but one: They all are guided less by reason than by emotion, and the causes of emotion are deeply personal. Therefore, leaders could not be more wrong than to assume that their followers feel as they do. This wrong assumption underlies paternalism. Many managers provide subordinates with benefits they like themselves. The big difference is that they have freedom to choose, while their followers may value the freedom to choose more than they value any "given benefits." Then they are charged with a lack of appreciation.

As managers contemplate their subordinates with a view to understanding their feelings and attitudes, they are severely handicapped. Outside of their work, they know very little about subordinates—their personal relationships, economic and health conditions, ambitions, spiritual values, and loyalties. We hardly know ourselves that well, let alone our subordinates!

Placing ourselves in the position of subordinates is but half the problem; even then, would we know what their reactions to issues would be? Yet a forthright and conscientious effort to understand subordinates is much better than none. The mere practice of asking "How would I react in their position?" is an attempt to learn, and with practice may come a skill.

Objectivity

Managers should strive to observe and trace the causes of events unemotionally. Even though they must depend heavily on subordinates and often become emotional about them, it is important to evaluate from a distance, determine the actual causes of results, and take intelligent steps to correct poor ones and encourage good ones.

This is a tightrope to walk, particularly if empathy is overemphasized, because empathy requires an attitude opposite to remoteness and unemotional analysis. A neat balance between empathy and objectivity is difficult to achieve, but each has its place in effective leadership.

To cultivate objectivity by schooling one's self to analyze before taking action, a leader needs strong willpower. With determination one can overcome a natural tendency toward snap judgment, anger, vituperation, or undue exuberance, even though the folk rule of counting to ten must be followed. Restraint and the habit of analysis are learned behavior.

Self-Knowledge

The injunction to "know thyself" is used in the context of making people aware of why they behave as they do and also what they do to draw forth certain response, lack of response, or even hostility from others. It is impossible to empathize or to be objective without self-knowledge. The plain fact is that some people irritate others unwittingly by their habitual attitude, words, or actions. Of course, in other cases, this may be their intention! In some situations this may be the correct technique to obtain a desired response. More usually, friendliness, cooperation, and approval get better results. It is well to know what one is doing.

Managers—like everyone else—should therefore learn the effects on others of their attitudes and habits so that they can correct those which elicit negative responses; that is, they should cultivate self-knowledge and put it to work intelligently by watching for favorable and unfavorable reactions to their behavior and by identifying causes. They can make discreet inquiries, either direct or indirect, to learn the cause of an observed response. This is a matter in which T groups can help.

One major point should be remembered here: People do not all respond in the same way to anything. People are different; not all are irritated by the same thing. Furthermore, people respond differently at different times to the same stimulus depending on their immediate interior climate. Some personalities clash with few but please the many; some, conversely, seem bad-tempered but are amenable to certain personalities they find congenial. These variations in people explain, in part, why the much-publicized sensitivity training often demonstrates essentially that people respond differently to the same stimulus.

ENVIRONMENTAL AND SYSTEMS PROBLEMS IN LEADERSHIP

Pleased as one must be with the apparent progress that has been made in understanding leadership, it is nonetheless important to realize that there is still much that is not known about this activity. Not only must old ground be still cultivated but there are also many areas that have not yet been adequately researched. Some of these will be stressed in this section. As will be seen, all of them dramatize the importance of a contingency, situational, and open-system approach to leadership.

Societal Change through Time

One of the weaknesses of leadership research is that most of it neglects longitudinal studies. This is entirely understandable, but the fact remains that solutions to immediate problems may become quite useless tomorrow. It is not accurate to assume that the nature of people remains the same through time. It must be realized that only certain facets of one's nature surface within a given moment in time. Central to the concern of any manager is the attitude of people toward work.

Political change brings fundamental modifications in the reasons for the application of effort to work. Autocracies can and do select what work is to be done by individuals irrespective of talent or desire. Socialization of work may remove much of the positive motivations favoring higher productivity and may deny the potential for individual economic independence through the tax system. And the complexities of regulation restrict freedom and innovation. Can leaders be prepared for political changes through time, or must they always operate in the present?

Long-run changes in the economic order may call for change in leadership style. Beyond the economic factors mentioned in the preceding paragraph, there are others of fundamental importance. Changes in technology and human tastes, as well as the drive to protect the environment, are considerably modifying the economic picture. The increased size of government and its expenditures is having a strong impact on the economic order. These factors, and others, are modifying the situations leaders must face.

There is another problem of leadership when the members of society become economically affluent. Work attitudes of younger employees in an affluent society who inherit the bounty made possible by preceding generations sometimes reflect the lower priority placed on productivity. With family and state support available and sufficient to maintain good living standards without work, how is a leader to cope with those employees who do not have to work, who can always find work, who have little or no enterprise loyalty, and who feel quite free to offer advice on how the establishment should be run? This situation clearly calls for a special kind of leadership.

Finally, there are social changes through time that are of special significance to the leadership role. In newly independent countries the attitude of sharing the wealth without work, and of instant enjoyment of living standards as they exist in advanced nations, leads to a most difficult environment for leaders of organized activities. Even in advanced nations the emphasis on affirmative action in the treatment of minorities, and the reverse discrimination which this may lead to if time-proven qualifications for work or study or promotions are ignored, gives rise to leadership issues of immense proportions.

Employee Unions and Leadership

In countries which encourage unionism, the growth of trade, industrial, professional, and civic unions has been rapid. The causes of this development lie deep within our social structure. Some see economic affluence as a key element—the corporation and the state can afford to share high profits or huge tax accumulations. Others see the cause deep within the democratic political structure—we know how to organize and control large bodies of voters who can threaten and thus force politicians to do their will. Still others see the cause in the breakdown in law enforcement wherein old laws prohibiting strikes against schools and other government agencies and new laws requiring a return to work are simply ignored by union personnel and unenforced by the legal system. And then there is the possibility that great wealth in the hands of union officers sometimes tempts them to act in ways that the holders of great wealth have often acted, namely, for selfish ends.

Whatever the cause of effective unionism may be, these organizations often create difficult leadership problems for the affected enterprise managers. In the presence of some unions—with work restrictions relating to quantity, quality, and technique; with membership raids and counterraids tying up operations; with constant interference with management prerogatives; and with the harassment of work grievances—real or imaginary or political—individual managers may find themselves at sea without a compass on a cloudy night. What leadership style will achieve organizational objectives when there are contending forces for its exercise?

Giving rise to much less spectacular issues but nonetheless very serious problems of leadership is the ubiquitous informal organization. "Informal organization" refers to groups of two or more people who communicate more or less regularly for purposes of exchanging information, for pleasure, or for the development of a consensus with respect to future action. As we saw in Chapter 12, informal organizations have a close relationship to formal organizations. They also have a distinct bearing on motivation and leadership. People obtain satisfaction from them and leaders must be keenly aware of them as they strive to influence persons in a formal organization.

Types   There are several types of informal organizations, depending, in large part, upon their purposes.[24] Sociologists have classified them as kinship-friendship groups, cliques, and subcliques. The first, readily identified by its descriptive title, is most often confined to persons between whom compatibility is of prime importance. Sociablity is the chief objective, both at and away from work, but collateral purposes include the communication of information, whether fact or gossip, and mutual aid in achieving improved status through such means as promotion or transfer.

Cliques are composed of persons commonly in close working association: selected members of the payroll, personnel, engineering, or machine-shop "crowd" or persons representing different functional activities who feel the need for cooperation. Sometimes the group has certain standards to maintain or practices to retain, and members drift together for purposes of protection. Acceptance into such a group may require the approval of all the members. There is unlikely to be any democracy here.

Subcliques include one or a few persons identified with a clique. Other members of the subclique may be employed by another firm. Often, such a subclique can control the destinies of a clique or even a professional or trade association by its insistence that standards or customs be adhered to by prospective members. The subclique may control a clique, which in turn may control a whole formal group. In this way, a large number of people in an organized group may be controlled by a very few who have no formal authority.

[24]C. I. Barnard in *The Function of the Executive* (Cambridge, Mass.: Harvard University Press, 1938), states on p. 114, in his pioneer chapter on informal organizations, that such groups have no ". . . specific conscious *joint* purpose. The contact may be accidental, or incidental to organized activities, or arise from personal desire or gregarious instinct; it may be friendly or hostile." Whatever the incident which originally throws people together, it appears that the continuing informal organization implies some kind of purpose, even though members may not be consciously aware of it.

Genesis The existence, variety, and virility of informal organizations lead to the conclusion that they satisfy human needs in a way that formal organizations do not. What are these needs? One of them is to perpetuate the culture of a group. For instance, a group may be unified in its desire to maintain a certain standard of education, discipline, or training. If a given department employs engineers exclusively, an informal group of them might oppose the use of technicians for some of the jobs. Or the insistence of an informal group upon the continuance of hazing new members of a department or of trade apprenticeship reflects the desire to perpetuate a highly prized cultural figment.

Need for information is a second reason for the existence of informal organizations—both the need for news and the need for *prompt* news. If organizational information were communicated as soon as it was available, there would be no need for an informal organization to perform this function. In practice, enterprises often circulate news slowly, transmit it poorly, or even withhold it. Informal organizations provide the channels, or grapevine, for speedy communication with their members. Management, however, cannot fully rely upon this method because persons who are not members of informal organizations cannot tap this grapevine.

Since informal organizations can either aid or interfere with enterprise interests, their activities should be directed into constructive channels. Once leaders of informal groups are identified and their cooperation gained, organizing and directing become markedly easier. The good will, energy, and initiative of informal organizations supplement the purposes of the formal organization, and each stands to gain from the satisfaction of the other's needs. Just how this is to be done is left to the ingenuity of the leader.

Crises and the Emergence of Leadership

The relationship of leadership to the management of crises is intriguing as a case of the situational approach to leadership. There are many facets to consider. In times of prosperity well-developed hygiene factors—supervision, interpersonal relations, working conditions, wages, policies, and job security—may, to a variable degree, be used by the leader as reinforcing agents to provide a "set" that will produce good results. But if adverse conditions develop, such as a long, drawn-out depression or defeat by an enemy in war, there will be an inevitable erosion of these factors. There may be no jobs and inadequate pensions; there may be wage cuts and negative changes in working conditions. What, then, is the perferred leadership style?

Another hygiene factor, not included in the usual enumeration, is the relationship of managerial success or failure to leadership potential. It would appear that in our society success is assumed and therefore is not a positive factor as a leadership role. On the other hand, can a manager with a succession of failures effectively lead?

The emergence of spontaneous leaders in times of crises used to be a favorite theme for developing an understanding of leadership itself. The group at play selects its leader and follows orders; at the scene of an accident the doctor emerges as the leader. Are we saying that the best leadership emerges during crises? Often there is no time for a leader to come to the fore. Revolutions have been successful when engineered by a small power group that gave its potential opposition no time to respond effectively, and many are the times when hundreds have cowered before the show of force of a single criminal. Clearly, followership may be forced by a strong minority.

LEADERSHIP AND MANAGING

The above sections underscore the importance of effective managing in making managers effective leaders. Implied by most research and theory on leadership is the clear message that an effective leader designs a system that takes into account the expectancies of subordinates, the variability of motives between individuals and from time to time, situational factors, interpersonal relations, and types of rewards. As was pointed out in summarizing the discussion of motivation in the previous chapter, knowledgeable and effective managers do these things when they design a climate for performance, when goals and means of achieving them are planned, when organizational roles are defined and well structured, when roles are competently and intelligently staffed, and, so we shall see in the following section, when control techniques and information are designed to make possible control by self-control.

The importance of managing for leadership was perceptively noted by the distinguished management consultant Marvin Bower.[25] He believed that the requirements for business leadership, in terms of both personal qualifications and leadership abilities, are far less than those necessary for political leadership. His position is based on two reasons. One is the fact that, in what he calls a "system-managed" business, the components of the system provide people with guidelines for action; therefore, highly inspirational leadership may not be necessary. In the second place, he believes that political leadership often requires inspiring people to do the unusual, while business leadership need only stimulate them toward achieving their understandable goal of making a living and of doing this well and with personal satisfaction.

But notice that Bower is thinking only of system-managed businesses through which leadership is facilitated and where exceptional inspirational and other personal qualities are not so necessary. By "system-managed" enterprises, Bower means those businesses where strategic and

---

[25]See his book entitled *The Will to Manage* (New York: McGraw-Hill Book Company, 1966), especially chap. 8.

operational planning are well developed; where action guidelines, such as policies, planned organization structure, and information, are available to people; where people are well selected and trained as well as rewarded; and where the other essentials of an effective management system are practiced.

FOR DISCUSSION

1 To what extent, and how, may we regard managing and leading as different activities or the same?

2 What do you see as the essence of leadership?

3 Why has the trait approach as a means of explaining leadership been so open to question?

4 What is Fiedler's theory of leadership? Applying it to cases of leaders you have known, does it seem to be accurate?

5 How are leadership theory and styles related to motivation?

6 What explanation of leadership style appeals to you as being most accurate and useful? Why?

7 Can you see why the managerial grid has been so popular as a training device?

8 Why does Bower believe that to become an effective leader in business is less demanding than to become a political leader? Do you agree? Would his observation apply also to such nonbusiness enterprises as government agencies and universities?

chapter 25 Communication

Although communication applies to all phases of managing, it is particularly important in the function of leading. There is general agreement about the necessity of effective communication, yet there is less agreement on an exact definition. Daniel Katz and Robert L. Kahn suggest that ". . . communication—the exchange of information and the transmission of meaning—is the very essence of a social system or an organization."[1] In this book the authors define communication as "the transfer of information from the sender to the receiver with the information being understood by the receiver." This definition, then, becomes the basis for the communication process model—discussed in greater detail below—which focuses on the sender of the communication, the transmission of the message, and the receiver of the message. The model also draws attention to noise, which interferes with good communication, and feedback, which facilitates communication.

This chapter begins with a discussion of the communication function. Then, an overview of the communication process is given through the introduction of a model. Next, those enterprise characteristics that affect the information exchange are identified and analyzed, and specific barriers to communication are highlighted. Finally, recommendations are made to improve communication, which should result in more effective managing.

THE COMMUNICATION FUNCTION IN AN ORGANIZATION

It is no exaggeration to say that the communication function is the means by which organized activity is unified. It may be looked upon as the means by which social inputs are fed into social systems. It is also the means by which behavior is modified, change is effected, information is made productive, and goals are achieved. Whether we are considering a church, a family, a scout troop, or a business enterprise, the transfer of information from one individual to another is absolutely essential.

The Importance of Communication

Over the years, the importance of communication in organized effort has been recognized by many authors. Chester I. Barnard, for example, viewed communication as the means by which people are linked together in an organization to achieve a common purpose.[2] This is still the fundamental function of communication. Indeed, group activity is impossible without communication because coordination and change cannot be effected.

Psychologists have also been interested in communication. They

---

[1]D. Katz and R. L. Kahn, *The Social Psychology of Organizations*, 2d ed. (New York: John Wiley and Sons, Inc., 1978), p. 428
[2]*The Functions of the Executive* (Cambridge, Mass.: Harvard University Press, 1938).

emphasize human problems that occur in the communication process of initiating, transmitting, and receiving information. They have focused on the identification of barriers to good communication, especially those that involve the interpersonal relationships of people. Sociologists and information theorists, as well as psychologists, have concentrated on the study of communication. For example, Katz and Kahn, who studied communication from a sociological perspective, saw social systems as "restricted communication networks."[3]

The Purpose of Communication

In its broadest sense, the purpose of communication in enterprise is to effect change—to influence action toward the welfare of the enterprise. Business, for example, requires information about prices, competition, technology, and finance, as well as information about the business cycle and government activity. This knowledge is the basis for decisions affecting product lines, production ratios, quality, marketing strategy, the mix of productive factors, and internal information flow. The immediate digestion of information and action in response to it, however, become extremely difficult in a large enterprise where several thousand or more people are involved.

Communication is essential for the *internal* functioning of enterprises because it integrates the managerial functions. Specifically, communication is needed

to establish and disseminate goals of an enterprise

to develop plans for their achievement

to organize human and other resources in the most effective and efficient way

to select, develop, and appraise members of the organization

to lead, direct, motivate, and create a climate in which people want to contribute

to control performance

Communication also relates the enterprise to its *external* environment. It is through information exchange that managers become aware of the needs of customers, the availability of suppliers, the claims of stockholders, the regulations of governments, and the concerns of a community. It is through communication that any organization becomes an open system interacting with its environment, a fact whose importance is emphasized throughout this book.

[3]Op. cit., pp. 430–431.

It is generally known that managers determine the organizational climate and influence the attitudes of enterprise members. This is done mainly through communication initiated by top management. Although organizational leaders have a major responsibility to set the right tone for effective communication, every person in an organization also shares this responsibility.

Superiors must communicate with subordinates and vice versa. Communication is a two-way process in which everyone is both an originator and a receiver of communication. Information flows vertically along the chain of command and crosswise. Crosswise communication, as used here, involves the horizontal flow of information among persons on the same or similar organizational levels and diagonal flow of information among people at various levels, without superior-subordinate relationships. The best way to approach the analysis of the various facets of communication is through the introduction of a communication model.

THE COMMUNICATION PROCESS

Simply stated, the communication process, diagramed in Figure 25.1, involves the "sender," who "transmits a message" over a selected channel to the "receiver." However, to gain better insight into communication, it is necessary to examine closely the specific steps in the process.

The Sender of the Message

Communication begins with the sender who has a "thought" or an idea, which is then "encoded" in a way that can be understood by the receiver. One usually thinks of encoding a message into the English language, but there are many other ways of encoding, such as translating the thought into computer language. The sender also communicates nonverbally through facial expressions or gestures.

The Transmission of the Message

The information is transmitted over a channel that links the sender with the receiver. The media used may be in oral or written form, and may be transmitted through a written memorandum, a computer, telephone, telegraph, or television. The latter, of course, also facilitates the transmission of gestures and visual cues. At times, two or more channels are used. In a telephone conversation, for instance, a basic agreement may be reached that is later confirmed by a letter to provide documentation. Since there are many channel choices available, each with advantages and disadvantages, the proper selection of the media is of vital importance for effective communication.

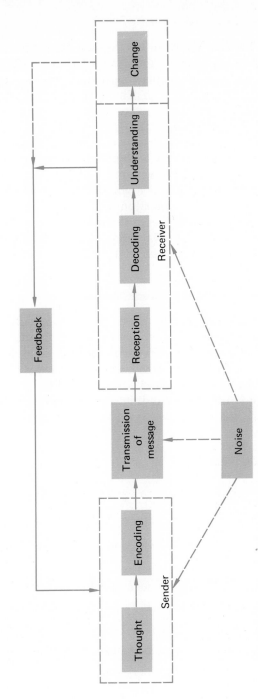

Figure 25.1 A communication process model.

The receiver has to be ready for the message so that it can be decoded into thought. A person thinking about an exciting football game may pay insufficient attention to what is being said, thus increasing the probability of a communication breakdown. The next step in the process is "decoding," which involves the conversion of the message into thoughts. Accurate communication can only occur when both the sender and the receiver attach the same or at least similar meanings to the symbols. A message encoded into French requires a receiver who understands French. This is obvious; less obvious, and frequently overlooked, is the use of technical or professional jargon that may be foreign to the recipient of the message. So communication is not complete unless it is understood. This "understanding" is in the mind of the receiver. Persons with closed minds will not normally completely understand messages, especially if the information is contrary to their value system.

Change as the Result of Communication

The variable "change" in the model above is actually beyond the basic communication process. Yet, in a broad sense, the purpose of communication in an enterprise is to effect change. For example, a directive from top management has to go through the various steps shown in the model before a behavioral change can be expected. Naturally, this change does not depend only on understanding the message, but also on motivation and leadership, the topics discussed in the two previous chapters.

Noise and Feedback in Communication

Unfortunately, communication is affected by what has been called "noise." It is anything—whether in the sender, the transmission, or the receiver—that hinders communication. For example:

A noisy or confined environment may hinder the development of a clear thought.

Encoding may be faulty because of the use of ambiguous symbols.

Transmission may be interrupted by static in the channel, such as may be experienced in a poor telephone connection.

Inaccurate reception may be caused by inattention.

Decoding may be faulty because the wrong meaning may be attached to words and other symbols.

Understanding can be obstructed by prejudices.

Desired change may not occur because of fear of possible consequences of the change.

To check the effectiveness of communication, "feedback" is essential. One can never be sure whether or not a message has been effectively encoded, transmitted, decoded, and understood unless it is confirmed by feedback. Similarly, feedback indicates whether individual or organizational change has taken place as a result of communication.

Situational and Organizational Factors in Communication

Many situational and organizational factors affect the communication process. Such factors in the external environment may be educational, sociological, legal-political, and economic factors. For example, a repressive political environment will inhibit the free flow of communication. Another situational factor is geographical distance. A direct face-to-face communication is different from a telephone conversation with another person on the other side of the globe, and this from an exchange of cables or letters. Time must also be considered in communication. The busy executive may not have sufficient time to accurately receive and send information. Other situational factors that affect communication within the enterprise include the organization structure, managerial and non-managerial processes, and technology. An example of the latter is the pervasive impact of computer technology on handling very large amounts of data.

In summary, the communication model provides an overview of the communication process, identifies the critical variables, and shows their relationships. This, in turn, helps managers to pinpoint communication problems and to take steps to solve them, or even better, to prevent the difficulties from occurring in the first place.

COMMUNICATION IN THE ENTERPRISE

In today's enterprises, information must flow faster than ever before. Even a short downtime on a fast-moving production line can be very costly in lost output. It is, therefore, essential that production problems be communicated quickly for corrective action. Another important element is the amount of information, which has greatly increased over the years, frequently causing an information overload. What is often needed, however, is not more information, but relevant information. It is necessary to determine what kind of information the manager needs to have for effective decision making. To obtain this information frequently requires the vertical information flow to be supplemented by crosswise communication.

The Manager's Need to Know

A manager, to be effective, needs information necessary to carry out managerial functions and activities. Yet, even a casual glance at communication systems shows that managers often lack vital information for decision making or may get too much information, resulting in overload. When one of the authors made a system analysis, it was found that many documents were distributed to people who had no apparent use for the information. When the person responsible for the flow of paperwork was asked why certain people received the documents, the answer was, "We have always done it this way." The amount of time, money, and effort wasted over the years can only be imagined.

The need for discrimination in the selection of information for a particular job is evident. A simple way for a manager to start is to ask: "What do I really need to know for my job?" Or, "What would happen if I did not get this information on a regular basis?" It is not maximum information a manager needs, but pertinent information. Clearly, there is no universally applicable communication system; rather, it must be tailored to the individual manager's needs.

The Communication Flow in the Enterprise

In an effective enterprise, communication flows in various directions: downward, upward, and crosswise. Traditionally, downward communication was emphasized, but there is ample evidence that if this is the only direction of communication, problems will develop. Peter F. Drucker is even more emphatic when he states that downward communication does not work because it ignores the receiver of the communication. In fact, he suggests that communication has to start with the recipient, the subordinate, and this means primarily upward communication.[4] Communication also flows horizontally, that is, between people on the same or similar organizational levels, and diagonally, involving persons from different levels who are not in direct reporting relationships with each other. Since there are many similarities between these two kinds of communication flows, they will be discussed together in crosswise communication.

Downward communication   Downward communication flows from people at higher levels to those at lower levels in the organizational hierarchy. This kind of communication can be found especially in organizations with an authoritarian atmosphere. The types of downward *oral* communication include instructions, speeches, meetings, the use of telephones, loudspeakers, and even the grapevine. Examples of *written* downward communication are memorandums, letters, handbooks, pamphlets, company newspapers and periodicals, bulletin boards, policy statements, and procedures.

Katz and Kahn identified five basic types of communication from the superior to the subordinate:

[4]*An Introductory View of Management* (New York: Harper's College Press, 1977), pp. 414–416.

Directives for handling tasks

Information for understanding the relationships of the tasks

Procedures and enterprise-practice information

Feedback about the performance of subordinates

Information about enterprise goals[5]

Unfortunately, information is often lost or distorted as it comes down the chain of command. Top management's issuance of policies and procedures does not assure communication. In fact, many of these directives are not understood or even read. Consequently, a feedback system is essential for finding out whether information was perceived as intended by the sender.

Downward flow of information through the different levels of the organization is time-consuming. Indeed, delays may be so frustrating that some top managers insist that information be sent directly to where it is required.

One chief executive, for example, adopted the rule that no superior was to receive information concerning a subordinate's areas of operation *before* the subordinate received it. In other words, he emphasized a lateral flow of information. Thus, he encouraged the flow of information so that employees would be informed as soon as possible about events affecting their operation.

Upward communication   Upward communication travels from subordinates to superiors, and continues up the organizational hierarchy. Unfortunately, this flow is often hindered by managers in the communications link who filter the messages and do not transmit all the information—especially unfavorable news—to their bosses. Yet objective transmission of information is essential for control purposes. Upper management needs to know specifically about production performance, marketing information, financial data, what lower-level employees are thinking, and so on.

There is also a human perspective to upward communication, which is primarily nondirective and is usually found in participative and democratic environments. Typical means for upward communication—besides the chain of command—are suggestion systems, appeal and grievance procedures, complaint systems, counseling sessions, the grapevine, group meetings, the practice of open door policy, morale questionnaires, the exit interview, and the ombudsman. The concept of the ombudsman was used relatively little in the United States until recently, and seems to be gaining wider acceptance. The Xerox Corporation, which established such a position in 1972, found through experience that the

[5]Op. cit., pp. 440–443.

resulting decisions favored employees in 40 percent of the cases and opposed employees in 30 percent of the cases. The remaining 30 percent of the decisions resulted in compromise.[6]

Effective upward communication requires an environment in which subordinates feel free to communicate. Since the organizational climate is greatly influenced by upper management, it means that the responsibility for creating a free flow of upward communication rests to a great extent—although not exclusively—with superiors.

Crosswise communication   Crosswise communication, as stated before, includes horizontal flow of information, with people on the same or similar organizational levels, and diagonal flow, with persons at different levels who have no direct reporting relationships. This kind of communication is used to speed information flow, to improve understanding, and to coordinate efforts for the achievement of organizational objectives.

A great deal of communication does not follow the organizational hierarchy, but cuts across the chain of command. In fact, one study indicated that only one-third of communication by managers was vertical, while two-thirds was crosswise, that is, horizontal or diagonal.[7]

The enterprise environment provides many occasions for *oral* cross-communication. They range from the informal meeting of the company bowling team and lunch hours spent together, to the more formal conferences, and committee and board meetings. This kind of communication also occurs when individual members of different departments are grouped into task teams or project organizations. Finally, communication cuts across organizational boundaries when staff—which has an advisory function—interacts with line managers.

There are, in addition, many *written* forms of communication that keep people informed about the enterprise, such as the company newspaper or magazine, published policies and procedures, and bulletin boards. It is evident, then, that modern enterprises use many kinds of oral and written crosswise communication patterns to supplement the vertical flow of information.

Because information does not follow the chain of command, proper safeguards need to be taken to prevent potential problems. Specifically, crosswise communication should rest on the understanding that (1) crosswise relationships will be encouraged wherever they are appropriate, (2) subordinates will refrain from making commitments beyond their authority, and (3) subordinates will keep superiors informed of important interdepartmental activities. In short, crosswise communication may create potential difficulties, but it is a necessity in many enterprises in order to respond to the needs of the complex and dynamic organizational environment.

[6]"Where Ombudsmen Work Out," *Business Week*, pp. 114–116 (May 3, 1976).
[7]A. K. Wickesberg, "Communications Networks in the Business Organization Structure," *Academy of Management Journal*, vol. 11, no. 3, pp. 253–262, (September 1968).

In the previous section on information flow, written and oral communication media were mentioned. Both have favorable and unfavorable characteristics; consequently, both types are often used to complement each other. In addition, visual aids may be used to supplement both oral and written communications. For example, the lecture in the management training session may be made more effective by using written handouts, transparencies, and films. Evidence has shown that when a message is repeated through several media it will be more accurately received, comprehended, and recalled.[8]

In selecting the media, the communicator, the audience, and the situation must be considered. An executive who feels uncomfortable in front of a large audience may choose written communication rather than a speech. On the other hand, certain audiences who may not read a memo may be reached and become motivated by direct oral communication. Situations may also demand a specific medium. For example, President Kennedy would probably not have been able to handle the Cuban Missile Crisis effectively through lengthy written communication. Face-to-face interaction, give-and-take with his advisers, was called for in this crisis situation.

Written communication   Written communication has the advantage of providing records, references, and legal defenses. The message can be carefully prepared, can be read by a large audience through distribution of mass mailings, can promote uniformity in policy and procedures, and can reduce costs in some cases.

The disadvantages are that written messages create mountains of paper, may be poorly expressed by ineffective writers, and provide no immediate feedback. Consequently, it may take a long time to know whether a message has been received and properly understood.

Effective writing may be the exception rather than the rule; education and intelligence do not guarantee good writing, either. There are many scientists who have fallen into the habit of using technical jargon that can only be understood by experts in the same field. Common complaints are that writers omit the conclusion or bury it in the report, are too "wordy," and use poor grammar, ineffective sentence structure, and incorrect spelling. The failures of communication have led to establishment of a mini-industry that teaches managers how to write.[9] Yet a few guidelines suggested by Keith Davis may do much to improve written communication:

Use simple words and phrases.

[8]H. J. Hsia, "Redundancy: Is It the Lost Key to Better Communication?" *AV Communication Review*, vol. 25, no. 1., pp. 63–85 (Spring 1977).
[9]"Teaching the Boss to Write," *Business Week*, pp. 56, 58 (October 25, 1976).

Use short and familiar words.

Use personal pronouns (such as "you") whenever appropriate.

Give illustrations and examples; use charts.

Use short sentences and paragraphs.

Use active verbs such as "the manager plans . . ."

Economize on adjectives.

Express thoughts logically and in a direct way.

Avoid unnecessary words.[10]

Oral communication   A great deal of information is communicated orally. One study found that 70 percent of the respondents stated that superiors gave 75 percent of the assignments orally.[11] Henry Mintzberg found in his observation that managers favored the oral media of the telephone and meetings.[12] Oral communication can be a face-to-face meeting of two people, or a manager addressing a large audience; it can be formal or informal, and it can be planned or accidental.

The advantages of oral communication are that it can provide for speedy interchange with immediate feedback. Questions can be asked and points can be clarified. In a face-to-face interaction the affect can be noted. Furthermore, a meeting with the superior may give the subordinate a feeling of importance. Clearly, informal or planned meetings can greatly contribute to the understanding of the issues.

However, oral communication also has disadvantages. It does not always save time, as any manager knows who has attended meetings in which no results or agreements were achieved. It will be recalled from Chapter 16 that committees may be costly in terms of time and money. Furthermore, committees may suffer from the tyranny of individual members, or members of the group may fail to raise the proper questions, or may deviate from the issues at hand.

Nonverbal communication   One communicates in many different ways. What is said can be reinforced (or contradicted) by nonverbal communication such as gestures, facial expressions, and body gestures. For instance, the three ego states in transactional analysis—the Parent, the Adult, and the Child—discussed in Chapter 21 on Manager and Organization Development, can be expressed in different nonverbal ways. The Parent ego state may be indicated by gestures of supercorrectness, by facial

[10]K. Davis, *Human Behavior at Work, Organizational Behavior,* 5th ed. (New York: McGraw-Hill Book Company, 1977), pp. 384–385.
[11]M. H. Brenner and N. B. Sigband, "Organizational Communication—An Analysis Based on Empirical Data," *Academy of Management Journal,* vol. 16, no. 2, pp. 323–325 (June 1973).
[12]H. Mintzberg, "The Manager's Job: Folklore and Fact," *Harvard Business Review,* vol. 53, no. 5, pp. 49–61 (July–August 1975).

expressions such as frowns and disappointed looks, by placing the hands on the hips, and pointing the finger in accusation. The Adult ego state may be shown by attentive eye contact, active listening, a show of confidence, or leaning forward to better understand the other person. Finally, the Child ego state may be indicated by slouching, self-consciousness, excitement, laughter, helplessness, moist eyes, wringing hands, or raising of the hand to ask for permission to speak in a meeting.[13]

Nonverbal communication is expected to support the verbal. But this is not always so. For example, an autocratic manager who pounds his fist on the table, while announcing that from now on participative management will be practiced, certainly creates a credibility gap. Similarly, managers who state that they have an open door policy, but then have a secretary carefully screen people who want to see the boss, create an incongruency between what managers say and how they behave. Clearly, nonverbal communication may support or contradict verbal communication, giving rise to the saying that actions often speak louder than words.

Organization as a Communication Technique

As was made clear in Chapters 12 and 17, both formal organization structuring and informal organizational relationships make assertive contributions to communication among members of groups working together. In the formal organization structure, the clarification of roles and role relationships, of activity groupings and authority delegation, is essential to the understanding by people of whom to communicate with on what. In fact, the formal organization structure can be regarded as a decision-communication network.

But the informal organization, of which the grapevine is a popularly understood form, also has a significant role to play in communication. People working together develop interpersonal relationships which thrive on communicating information not available from formal organizational sources. Some of this is not available because it is simply not communicated over formal systems. Some is not widely available because it is gossip not ordinarily handled through formal channels. But it is essential that people develop and become involved in what is referred to as informal organization.

Moreover, if we follow the meaning given to informal organization by Chester Barnard, the great management pioneer and theorist, we find that a dominant purpose of informal organization is communication. If we accept Barnard's definition of informal organization as "the social interactions of people without a conscious, deliberate, joint purpose,"[14] it

---

[13]Transactional analysis has been widely recognized as a way to improve communication. Since this topic has already been discussed previously, it will not be repeated here. However, attention is drawn to two sources: E. Berne, *Games People Play* (New York: Grove Press, Inc., 1964), and T. A. Harris, *I'm OK—You're OK* (New York: Harper & Row, Publishers, Incorporated, 1969).

[14]*The Functions of the Executive*, op. cit., chap. 9.

becomes clear, as Barnard has pointed out, that language itself is an important form of informal organization.

As a practical matter, managers must have respect for the informal organization and the grapevine particularly. Studies and experience show that the grapevine is fast and exceptionally accurate. It is therefore of great importance that managers use it both to receive information and to disseminate information.

Social Systems as Communication Networks

As indicated earlier, communication must not only be seen as interaction between the sender and the recipient of messages, it must also be considered in the context of the social system in which communication occurs. Indeed, as mentioned before, social psychologists suggest that all social systems are communication networks.

As a loosely knit group moves toward an organized state, a number of constraints must be recognized. To be sure, the communication network becomes more complex as the enterprise grows, but unrestricted information flow does not result in better communication, it results in chaos. Although there are many advocates of more information, what is really needed is the right kind of needed information and an improvement in the nature of communication between individuals, groups, and organizational units.

Information overload is a common phenomenon of our times; it is due, to a great extent, to technology. J. G. Miller reports that over 1,200,000 articles appear in 60,000 books and 100,000 reports every year. Moreover, the number of scientific and technical publications in the United States has doubled about every 20 years since 1800.[15] But information overload can also be experienced within an enterprise, especially when the computer is used indiscriminately. When one of the authors analyzed a control system, it was found that the controller was overloaded with information he neither used nor understood. Computer output sheets were piled up from the floor to the top of his desk—output he never digested. The control system was designed for maximum output rather than tailored to the specific needs of the user; the result was information overload.

In the enterprise, people respond in various ways to information overload.[16] First, people may *omit* certain information. A person under great pressure may simply ignore letters that should be answered. Second, people react to information overload by *making errors*. They may leave out the word "not" in a message, which, of course, reverses the intended

[15]J. G. Miller, "Information Input, Overload, and Psychopathology," *American Journal of Psychiatry*, vol. 116, pp. 695–704 (1960), reported in Katz and Kahn, op. cit., p. 451.
[16]For a detailed discussion of this topic, see Miller's analysis of information overload in Katz and Kahn, op. cit., pp. 451–455.

meaning. Third, people may *delay* processing information either permanently or with the intention of catching up in the future. Fourth, a person may *filter* information. Filtering may be helpful when the most pressing and most important information is processed first and the less-important messages receive lower priority. However, chances are that attention will be given first to matters that are easy to handle, while more difficult but perhaps critical messages are ignored. Finally, people respond to information overload by simply *escaping* from the task of communication. In other words, they do not pay attention to incoming information, nor are they concerned about informing others.

Some responses to information overload may be adaptive tactics that can, at times, be functional. For example, delaying the processing of information until the amount is reduced can be effective. On the other hand, withdrawing from the task of communicating is usually dysfunctional. Another way to approach the overload problem is to reduce the demands for information. Within the enterprise this may be accomplished by insisting that only essential data be processed, such as information showing critical deviations from plans. Reducing the external demand for information is usually more difficult because these demands are less controllable by managers. An example may be the government's demand for detailed documentation on governmental contracts. Companies that do business with the government simply have to comply with these requests.

BARRIERS AND BREAKDOWNS IN COMMUNICATION

It is probably no surprise that managers frequently cite communication breakdowns as one of their most important problems. In one study, 80 percent of managers cited communication as the cause for difficulties on their jobs.[17] It should be noted, however, that communication problems are often symptoms of more deeply rooted problems. For example, poor planning may be the cause for uncertainty about the direction of the firm. Similarly, a poorly designed organization structure may not clearly communicate organizational relationships. Vague performance standards may leave managers uncertain about what is expected of them. Thus, the perceptive manager will first look for the causes of communication problems instead of just dealing with the symptoms.

Besides the problems mentioned in the discussion of information overload within the social system, additional communication barriers must be considered. Some have been mentioned already in this chapter, others need to be singled out for further discussion. The first set of communication barriers focuses on the sender, the second on the transmission of the message, and the third on the receiver.

[17]H. L. Cox, "Opinions of Selected Business Managers about Some Aspects of Communication in the Job," *The Journal of Business Communication*, vol. 6, no. 1, p. 7 (Fall 1968).

Good communication seldom happens by chance. Too often people start talking and writing without prior thinking, planning, and stating the purpose of the message. Yet, giving the reasons for a directive, selecting the most appropriate channel, and choosing proper timing can greatly improve understanding and reduce resistance to change.

Unclarified Assumptions

Often overlooked, yet very important, are the uncommunicated assumptions that underlie messages. A customer may send a note that she will visit a vendor's plant. Then she assumes that the vender will meet her at the airport, reserve a room, make transportation available, and set up a full-scale review of the program at the plant. But the vendor may assume that the customer is coming to town mainly to attend a wedding and will make a routine call at the plant. These unclarified assumptions in both instances may result in confusion and the loss of good will.

Semantic Distortion

Another barrier to effective communication can be attributed to semantic distortion, which can be deliberate or accidental. An advertisement saying "We sell for less" is deliberately ambiguous; it raises the question: Less than what? Words may evoke different responses. To some people the word "government," may mean interference, or deficit spending; to others the same word may mean help, equalization, and justice.

Badly Expressed Messages

No matter how clear the idea in the mind of the sender of communication, it may still be marked by poorly chosen words, omissions, lack of coherence, poor organization of ideas, awkward sentence structure, platitudes, unnecessary jargon, and a failure to clarify the implications of the message. This lack of clarity and precision, which can be costly, can be avoided through greater care in encoding the message.

Loss by Transmission and Poor Retention

In successive transmissions from one person to the next, the message becomes less and less accurate. Consequently, companies often use multiple channels to communicate the same message. Poor retention of information is another serious problem. One study found, for example, that employees retain but 50 percent of the information they receive and supervisors only 60 percent.[18] This makes the necessity for repetition of the message and the use of several channels rather obvious.

[18]R. Bellows, T. Q. Gilson, and G. S. Odiorne, *Executive Skills* (Englewood Cliffs, N.J.: Prentice Hall, Inc., 1962), pp. 60–61.

There are many talkers but few listeners. Everyone probably has observed people entering a discussion with comments that have no relation to the topic. One reason is that these persons are pondering their own problems—such as preserving their own egos, or making a good impression on other group members—instead of listening to the conversation.

Listening demands full attention and self-discipline. It also means avoiding premature evaluation of what the other person has to say. A common tendency is to judge, to approve or disapprove what is being said, rather than trying to understand the speaker's frame of reference. Yet, nonevaluative listening can sometimes enhance the effectiveness and efficiency of enterprise operation. For example, sympathetic listening can result in better labor-management relations and greater understanding among functionally oriented managers; specifically, sales personnel may better understand the problems of the production people, and the credit manager may realize that an overrestrictive credit policy may lead to a disproportionate loss in sales. In short, listening with empathy can reduce some of the daily frustrations in organized life and result in better communication.

Distrust, Threat, and Fear

Distrust, threat, and fear undermine communication. In such a climate any message will be viewed with skepticism. Distrust can be the result of inconsistent behavior by the superior, or it can be due to past experiences in which the subordinate was punished for honestly reporting unfavorable, but true, information to the boss. Similarly, in the light of threats—whether real or imagined—people tend to tighten up, become defensive, and distort information. What is needed is a climate of trust, which facilitates open and honest communication.

Insufficient Adjustment Period to Change

As shown in the communication model, the purpose of communication often is to effect change which may seriously concern employees: shifts in the time, place, type, and order of work or shifts in group arrangements or skills to be used. Some communications point to the need for further training, career adjustment, or status arrangements. Changes affect people in different ways, and it may take time to think through the full meaning of a message. Consequently, it is important to efficiency not to force change before people can adjust to its implications.

TOWARD EFFECTIVE COMMUNICATION

There are several approaches that can be used to improve communication. The first one is to make a communication audit. The findings then become the basis for organization and systems changes. The second approach is to apply communication techniques, with the focus on interpersonal relations and listening.

The Communication Audit

One way to improve communication in the enterprise, the macro approach, is the communication audit.[19] It is a tool for auditing communication policies, networks, and activities. Organizational communication is viewed as a group of communication factors related to organizational goals, as shown in Figure 25.2.

What is interesting in this model is that communication is not considered for its own sake, but rather as a means to achieve organizational goals, a fact sometimes forgotten by those concerned only with interpersonal relations. This model is consistent with our systems model of the operational approach to managing (see Chapter 1). In our model, as will be recalled, the communication system integrates the managerial functions of planning, organizing, staffing, leading, and controlling. In addition, it is important to remember that the communication system has another function, namely, to link the enterprise with its environment.

[19]H. H. Greenbaum, "The Audit of Organizational Communication," *Academy of Management Journal*, vol. 17, no. 4, pp. 739–754 (December 1974).

Figure 25.2 Relationship of communication factors to organization goals. *[H. H. Greenbaum, "The Audit of Organizational Communication,"* Academy of Management Journal, *vol. 17, no. 4, p. 743 (December 1974). Used by permission of the author.]*

The four major communication networks that need to be audited are as follows:

1 The regulative or task-related network pertaining to policies, procedures, rules, and superior-subordinate relationships
2 The innovative network, which includes problem solving, meetings, and suggestions for change
3 The integrative network, which consists of praise, rewards, promotions, and those items that link enterprise goals with personal needs
4 The informative-instructive network, which includes company publications, bulletin boards, and the grapevine[20]

The communication audit, then, is a tool for analyzing communication related to many key managerial activities. It is used not only when problems occur but to prevent them in the first place. The format of the audit can take many shapes and may include observations, questionnaires, interviews, and analyses of written documents. Although the initial audit of the communication system is highly desirable, it needs to be followed by periodic reports.

Communication Techniques and Guides

A basic understanding of the communication process model introduced at the beginning of this chapter (Figure 25.1) helps to identify the critical elements in the communication process. At each stage, breakdowns can occur—in the encoding of the message by the sender, in the transmission of the message, and in the decoding and understanding of the message by the receiver. Certainly noise can interfere with effective communication at each part of the process.

As noted in the communication process model, effective communication requires that encoding and decoding be done with symbols that are familiar to the sender and the receiver of the message. Thus, the manager (and especially the staff specialist) should avoid technical jargon, which is intelligible only to the experts in their particular field.

Another important aspect of good communication, noted earlier, is listening. The rushed, never-listening manager will seldom get an objective view of the functioning of his organization. Time, empathy, and concentration on the communicator's message are prerequisites to understanding. People want to be heard, want to be taken seriously, want to be understood. Thus, the manager must avoid interrupting subordinates and putting them on the defensive. It is also wise to give and ask for feedback, for without it one can never be sure if the message is understood. To elicit

---

[20]H. H. Greenbaum and N. D. White, "Biofeedback at the Organizational Level: The Communication Audit," *The Journal of Business Communication*, vol. 13, no. 4, pp. 3–15 (Summer 1976).

honest feedback, an atmosphere of trust and confidence, and a supportive leadership style, are desirable, with a deemphasis on status symbols (such as barricading one's self behind an extrawide executive desk).

The following is a useful set of brief suggestions made by the American Management Association[21]

Clarify ideas before attempting to communicate.

Examine the purpose of communication.

Understand the physical and human environment when communicating.

In planning communication, consult with others to obtain their support as well as the facts.

Consider the content and the overtones of the message.

Whenever possible, communicate something that helps or is valued by the receiver.

Communication, to be effective, requires follow-up.

Communicate messages that are of short-run and long-run importance.

Actions must be congruent with communication.

Be a good listener.

The last point in this list needs additional comment. Listening is a skill that can be developed. Carl R. Rogers and F. J. Roethlisberger suggest a simple experiment. It goes like this. The next time you have an argument try to use the following simple rule: A person may only speak after the ideas and feelings of the previous speaker are repeated accurately to the speaker's satisfaction.[22] This rule sounds simple, yet is difficult to practice. It requires listening, understanding, and empathy. But managers who have used this technique have reported to the authors a considerable number of cases in which they were not communicating accurately.

Perhaps less demanding, and thus more practical, are ten guides proposed by Keith Davis to improve effective listening: stop talking, put the talker at ease, show the talker that you want to listen, remove distractions, empathize with the talker, be patient, hold your temper, go easy on arguments and criticism, ask questions, stop talking! The first and last guides are the most important because one has to stop talking before one can listen.[23]

[21]"Ten Commandments of Good Communication," Copyright © 1955 by American Management Associations, Inc. All rights reserved. Reprinted by permission.
[22]"Barriers and Gateways to Communication," *Harvard Business Review*, vol. 30, no. 4, pp. 46–52 (July–August 1952).
[23]Davis, op. cit., p. 387.

1 Briefly describe the communication process model. Select a communication problem and determine the cause(s) by applying the model in your analysis.

2 List different channels for transmitting a message. Discuss the advantages and disadvantages of the various channels.

3 What are some types of downward communication? Discuss the ones that are used most frequently in an enterprise you are familiar with. How effective are the various types?

4 What are some problems in upward communication? What would you suggest to overcome the difficulties?

5 What are the advantages and disadvantages of written and oral communication? Which one do you prefer? Under what circumstances?

6 What is information overload? Do you ever experience it? How do you deal with it?

7 What is a communication audit? How would you conduct such an audit in a large enterprise? Be specific.

8 How well do you listen? How could you improve your listening skills?

SUMMARY OF MAJOR PRINCIPLES
FOR PART 5: LEADING

For the managerial function of leading, several principles or guides can be identified.

Integration of Goals of Claimants

The better the legitimate goals of the claimants to the enterprise are integrated and balanced, the more effective will be the enterprise.

In the systems model, several groups of people with divergent goals were identified as possible claimants to the enterprise. Examples of claimants would be employees, consumers, suppliers, stockholders, governments, and the community. This guide suggests that the task of managers is to integrate these claims in a way that satisfies their legitimate demands as well as the long-term interests of the enterprise.

Harmony of Objectives

The more managers can harmonize the personal goals of individuals with the goals of the enterprise, the more effective and efficient the enterprise will be.

This guide suggests that it is one of the major tasks of managers to create an environment in which individuals can utilize their knowledge, their skills, and their drives while at the same time making contributions to the achievement of enterprise goals.

Principle of Unity of Command

The more completely an individual has a reporting relationship to a single superior, the less the problem of conflict in instructions and the greater the feeling of personal responsibility for results.

Unity of command is a principle of both organizing and leading. People respond best when they are directed by a single superior. Of course, it is true that sometimes the net efficiency of an enterprise is improved by the introduction of multiple command, such as functional authority, but this should be done only when the gains clearly outweigh the costs.

Principle of Motivation

The more managers carefully assess a reward structure, look upon it from a situational point of view, and integrate it into the entire system of managing, the more effective a motivational program will be.

Since what people will respond to depends on their personalities, their perceptions and expectancies of rewards and tasks, and the organizational climate, simply identifying needs in general and building a system for motivating people on the basis of these needs often does not work. Because motivation is a highly personal thing and is contingent on many factors in a situation at a given time, it is an area of great complexity. Programs trying to deal with this complexity must try to build motivators into the entire system of managing. They cannot be looked on as a separate and independent phenomenon.

Principle of Leadership

The more managers understand what motivates their particular subordinates and how these motivators operate, and the more they reflect this understanding in carrying out their managerial actions, the more effective leaders they are likely to be.

In a very real sense, this principle combines motivational considerations with managerial actions. Even though we may not understand exactly what motivates people in all circumstance and why, maybe the basic reactions of individuals are well enough known to be used for practical guidance. Moreover, there is much that managers can do to enhance opportunities for money, status, power, sense of accomplishment, and other motivation factors in the way they structure roles and plans, in the way they staff, in their leading abilities and techniques, and even through effective systems of control, since most people want to know how well they are doing. This is not to manipulate people; this is rather a recognition that people are people and that they are most likely to follow superiors in whom they see a means of fulfilling their desires and their goals.

Communication Clarity

Communication is clear when it is expressed in a language and transmitted in a way that can be understood by the receiver.

This guide emphasizes the responsibility of the sender to formulate the message so that it is understandable to the receiver. It pertains primarily to written and oral communication and points to the necessity for planning the message, stating the underlying assumptions, and applying the generally accepted rules for effective writing and speaking.

Communication Integrity

The greater the integrity and consistency of written, oral, and nonverbal messages, as well as of the moral behavior of the sender, the greater the acceptance of the message by the receiver.

This guide suggests that phony communication and the psychological games some people play are ineffective in organizational communication. Rather, communication must be genuine, honest, and consistent. A manager who advocates participative management must also practice this approach. In other words, actions (and nonverbal behavior) often speak louder than words.

Supplemental Use of Informal Organization

Communication tends to be more effective when managers utilize the informal organization to supplement the communication channels of the formal organization.

Informal organization is a phenomenon managers must accept. Information, true or not, flows quickly through the informal organization. Consequently, managers should take advantage of this device to correct misinformation and to provide information that would not fit appropriately into the formal communication pattern.

CASES FOR PART 5

1 What Do We Know for Sure?

The class in management was nearing the conclusion of its study of human behavior. Several members had reported on the research and conclusions of prominent writers in the field. All were quite familiar with the work of Mayo, Lewin, Maslow, McGregor, and the more recent scholars such as Herzberg, Argyris, Likert, Filley, Vroom, and House.

Hoping to focus attention to the conclusions that might be reached, the professor asked, "Do you feel that the research conducted by these scholars has enabled us to move from hypothesis to truth about the motivations of people?"

One thoughtful student, almost talking to herself, commented: "When I read the work of these investigators, I was convinced that each had a most telling case. I thought that here indeed was truth. Then I recalled that in each instance, these writers were inferring understanding based upon observed behavior. While I was convinced that what people *did* was accurately reported, I could not help but feel that other observers, looking at the same behavior, would have different explanations. Perhaps we will never *know* why people behave as they do. Indeed, I don't understand myself; does the professor understand himself?"

The pragmatist in the class had little use for this line of thought. "What difference does it make," he said, "why people behave in a particular way? Isn't it enough to know that they do so behave? Using this, why can't we establish a motivation system within any enterprise that will work?"

A voice in the back of the room was heard to say, "I'm afraid of generalizations."

1 In your opinion, which of the many theories explains best why people behave as they do? Why?
2 Select two theories by authors mentioned in the case and discuss the similarities and differences in their views about the nature of people.

2 Motivation at the Bradley Clothing Company

Alice Johnson, personnel manager of the Bradley Clothing Company, manufacturers of women's clothing and accessories, had just returned from a management development seminar where considerable attention had been given to motivation and especially the theories of Maslow and Herzberg. Impressed by Maslow's clear hierarchy of needs and Herzberg's motivator-hygiene theory, she felt that the company could immediately make practical use of them. She liked the simplicity of these two approaches to motivation and, feeling that the company's wage and salary levels were among the best in the industry, she was convinced that the company should concentrate on Herzberg's motivators.

As a result, she was able to convince the executive committee of the company to embark on various programs of emphasizing recognition, advancement, greater personal responsibility, achievement, and making work more challenging. After the various programs emphasizing these factors had been in operation for a number of months, she was puzzled to find that the results were not as she had expected.

Clothing designers did seem to react enthusiastically to the programs, although some felt that they were a poor substitute for higher pay. Salespeople took the position that they already had a challenging job, that their sense of achievement was fulfilled by exceeding their sales quotas, that their recognition was in their commission checks, and that all these new programs were a waste of time with them. Cutters, seamsters, pressers, and packagers had mixed feelings. Some responded favorably to the recognition they got from the new programs, but others regarded them as a managerial scheme to get them to work harder without any increase in pay. Their union business agent, agreeing with the latter group, openly criticized the programs.

With reactions so variable, Ms. Johnson came under considerable criticism by the company's top officers, who believed they had been taken in by an overzealous personnel manager. On discussing the problem with the company's management consultant, Ms. Johnson was advised that she had taken too simple a view of human motivations.

1   Why do you believe this program caused so much difficulty?
2   Why did the management consultant say that Ms. Johnson had taken too simple a view of human motivation?
3   If you were Ms. Johnson, what would you have done?

3   Consolidated Motors Corporation

One of the problems that had long concerned the top managers of the Consolidated Motors Corporation was the lack of workers' interest in doing their jobs on both the components and the final car assembly lines, with the result that quality had to be assured by the inspection department. For those cars that could not meet final inspection, the company found its only answer to be the setting up of a group of highly skilled mechanics in a special shop where quality problems were fixed at the end of the line. Not only was this costly but it also caused considerable concern since most of the problems were the result of lack of care in assembling components and the automobile itself.

At the urging of the company president, the division general manager called a meeting of his key department heads to see what could be done about the problem.

Bill Burroughs, production manager, claimed that some of the problems were a matter of engineering. He held that if only engineering would design components and the automobile carefully enough, many quality problems would disappear. He also blamed the personnel department for not making sure that workers were more carefully selected and for not getting the union business agent involved in the problem. He pointed out especially that there was a high turnover of better than 5 percent per month among assembly workers and that absenteeism on Mondays often reached 20 percent. His position was that no production department could operate effectively with this kind of labor force.

Charles Wilson, chief engineer, held that the components and cars were engineered well enough and that if engineering tolerances were any more strict, the fitting of parts would be so difficult and time-consuming that the company's automobiles would be too costly to make.

Alice Turner, the personnel manager, defended the personnel problems in several ways. First, she pointed out that her department had little or no control over whom the company hired or kept, in view of the strong labor union the company had. Second, she observed that assembly work was dull, deadening drudgery and that the company should not expect people to have much interest in this work beyond their paychecks.

But Ms.Turner did say she was persuaded that the company could develop more worker interest and consequently higher-quality work and less absenteeism and turnover if assembly jobs could be enlarged. When asked what she would suggest, Ms. Turner recommended that the company do two things. One was to have workers handle several operations on the assembly line and work as a team, instead of doing only one simple task. A second was to rotate workers each week from one location on the line to a completely different one in order to give them new and more challenging work.

These suggestions were adopted and put into effect. To everyone's surprise, workers expressed great dissatisfaction with the new program. After a week, the assembly lines were closed down by a strike, the workers claiming that the new program was only a management scheme to get them to do more work than they had done before and to train them to replace other workers without any increase in pay.

The division manager and the personnel manager were surprised. When asked by the division manager what had happened, Ms. Turner could only say: "This is a mystery to me. We make their jobs more interesting, and they strike!"

1 What do you believe went wrong with the program?
2 What would you have done if you had been the personnel manager? Would you have used this program, a different one, or none at all? Why?

4 Columbian Life Insurance Company

Frank Houston, president of Columbian Life Insurance Company was a mild-mannered executive who had worked for the company for 35 years, going to work out of college as an actuary and rising to vice president in charge of the company's investment operations before being elected president 10 years ago. When Mr. Houston was promoted to the presidency, Columbian was the third-largest life insurance company in the nation. During subsequent years, however, while its business increased, it did not grow as fast as major competitors, and Columbian dropped from third to sixth place.

This naturally worried Frank Houston, as it did the company's board of directors.

Finally, after a long board meeting, it was concluded that the company's major problem was the lack of leadership in sales of both ordinary life policies and group life insurance. Although it was generally concluded that the two vice presidents in charge of sales in these two major business areas were competent executives and leaders, it was believed that the regional and district sales managers were not.

As a result of this turn of events and pressure put on the president by the board to get better sales leadership, Mr. Houston lost his normal composure and summarily called his two vice presidents into his office. At the start of this meeting, he thundered in rage:

"Let's get some strong leaders in this company. I want us either to make our regional and district managers strong leaders or to replace them with strong leaders. Surely you men know how to do this, and if you don't, we will have to get vice presidents who do!"

As the vice presidents left the meeting, one turned to the other and said, "Now, just how do we make people leaders? How can we be sure a person is a leader? You know, this is a tough one."

1 If you were one of the vice presidents, how would you have answered the questions that the other raised?
2 What would you do about developing or finding strong leaders?

5 Leaders in Government Departments and Agencies

"The trouble with government departments and agencies today," said Senator Paul Murphy, chairman of the Special Committee to Improve Government Management, "is that we have many managers, or administrators, who get high salaries, but too few leaders. I tell you that leaders are born and not made by any management development program you people have. We put people in positions of responsibility and expect them to be leaders. What we should do is to select people for government administrative positions who have demonstrated such personality traits as intelligence, energy, drive, initiative, enthusiasm, honesty, self-assurance, ability to get along with people, and ability to inspire confidence in their subordinates."

"But," responded Helen Baxter, Civil Service Commission management recruitment administrator, "you do not understand, Senator. We need people who are managers to head up our departments, divisions, and sections. Personal traits and qualities may be essential to political leaders. However, in government management we need persons who are concerned with getting tasks done as well as concerned with people. Well-known and respected psychologists, such as Dr. Fred Fiedler, Dr. Rensis Likert, Dr. Robert Blake, Dr. Jane Mouton, Dr. Robert Tannenbaum, and Dr. Warren Schmidt have made all this clear in their theories and researches."

At that point, Senator Murphy declared: "I don't care what these psychologists say. What do they know about leaders? Our government departments and agencies have long suffered from lack of leadership at all levels and I want the Civil Service Commission to do something to assure that we have leaders in administrative positions."

1 To what extent do you agree with Senator Murphy?

2 If you were Helen Baxter, how would you respond to the senator?

3 Combine the research and theories of Fiedler, Likert, Blake and Mouton, Tannenbaum and Schmidt, and others, and come up with an answer on how the government can be assured that government administrators will become effective leaders.

6 Haynes Fashion Stores, Incorporated

Joyce Haynes, just graduated from college, joined her father, Dudley Haynes, president of Haynes Fashion Stores, Incorporated, a chain of thirty women's apparel stores in the New England area. The company had been founded by Ms. Haynes' grandfather over 50 years ago. With her grandfather's and, for the past 20 years, her father's drive and knowledge of women's fashions and of how to buy and sell them, the company had developed from a single store in Hartford, Connecticut, to a fairly large and highly profitable chain of stores. Dudley Haynes was much like his father had been. He knew what he was doing and how to do it and he prided himself on being able to keep his hands on details in buying, advertising, and store management. Every one of his store managers, as well as his top vice presidents and headquarters staff people, met with the president each 2 weeks in Hartford. Between these meetings, Mr. Haynes spent 2 or 3 days each week visiting the stores and working with store managers.

But his major worries were communication and motivation. He felt that at the conferences he held, all his managers and staff people listened carefully. But judging from what they did, he began to wonder whether they heard him or whether they had listened carefully. The results were that many of his policies were not being strictly followed in the stores; he often had to rewrite advertising copy; in some of the stores the employees had joined the clerks union; and he increasingly heard of things he did not like. Among them were reports that many of his employees and even some of his managers felt that they did not know what the Haynes company was trying to do and believed they could do better if they had a chance to communicate with Mr. Haynes and his headquarters vice presidents. He also had a strong feeling that many of his managers in headquarters and in the stores, as well as most of the store clerks, were merely doing their jobs without showing any real imagination or drive. He was also concerned that some of his best people had quit and taken positions with a competitor.

When his daughter walked into his office to take a position as his special assistant, he said, "Joyce, I am worried about how things are going. Apparently, my two problems are communication and motivation. Now, I know that you took some courses in management in school. I have heard you talk of the problems, barriers, and techniques of communication. I have heard from you about some fellows—Maslow, Herzberg, Vroom, McClelland, and others—who you thought knew a great deal about motivation. While I doubt that these psychology types knew much about business and I feel that I know what motivates people—primarily money, good bosses, and a good place to work—I wonder if you have learned anything that will help me. I hope so, for that college education of yours has cost me a lot of money. What do you suggest?"

1 If you were Ms. Haynes, what would you say to your father?
2 How would you go about analyzing the communication problem, and what problems do you see already from the case?
3 How would you suggest that the motivation theories of the various people you have studied might be applied to the Haynes Fashion Stores? Is there anything else you would want to know?

7 Home Radio and Television Company

Robert Gates founded a small radio manufacturing plant in Detroit in the 1930s. From this small start came one of the nation's largest radio, television, and allied products companies. By 1965 its sales approached $300 million annually, with 15,000 employees and ten manufacturing locations. Throughout its growth the founder remained the active, imaginative, and driving force of the company. In earlier days every manager and worker knew him, and he was able to call most of them by their first names, so even after the company grew fairly large, people felt that they knew the founder and chief executive, and this strong feeling of personal loyalty had much to do with the fact that the company was never unionized.

However, as the company prospered and grew, Mr. Gates worried that it was losing its "small-company" spirit. He also worried that communications were suffering, that his objectives and philosophy were not being understood in the company, that much wasteful duplication was occurring through poor knowledge of what others in the company were doing, and that new product development and marketing were suffering as a result. Likewise, he was concerned that he had lost touch with the people.

To solve the communication problem, he hired and had report to him a director of communication. Between the two, they put into effect every communication device they found other companies using: bulletin boards in every office and plant throughout the country; a revitalized company newspaper carrying much company and personal news affecting all locations; "Company Facts Books" for every employee, giving significant information about the company; regular profit sharing letters; company-sponsored courses to teach communication; monthly 1-day meetings at headquarters for the top 100 executives; annual 3-day meetings of 1,200 managers of all levels at a resort area; and a large number of special committees to discuss company matters.

After much time, effort, and expense, Mr. Gates was disappointed to find that his problems of communication and of the small-company feeling still existed and that the results of his programs did not seem to be significant.

1 Why do you believe that Mr. Gates was disappointed? Should he have been?
2 What do you see as the company's real communication problem?
3 What would you suggest to improve communication in the company?
4 Was Mr. Gates right in believing that communication would solve his desire to maintain the "small-company" spirit?

6 Controlling

Controlling implies measurement of accomplishment of events against the standard of plans and the correction of deviations to ensure attainment of objectives according to plans. Once a plan becomes operational, control is necessary to measure progress, to uncover deviations from plans, and to indicate corrective action. The latter may involve simple measures such as minor changes in leadership. In other cases, adequate control may result in setting new goals, formulating new plans, changing the organization structure, improving staffing, and making major changes in techniques of leading. In reading the chapters on the control function, it is important to bear in mind that it involves much more than mere measurement of deviations from plans. True control implies that corrective action can and will be taken to get wayward operations back on course. It is thus, to a great extent, the function that closes the loop in the system of managing.

The nature and process of controlling are discussed in Chapter 26. Simple definition of the control function makes it apparent that it remains essentially the same no matter what activity is under consideration. The essence of most control is some sort of feedback; for example, the operating principle of a thermostat or a steam engine governor. When temperature or speed becomes too great, a thermostat or a governor corrects the condition through feedback. Although the cycle in management is more complex and has many longer delays, managerial control operates in much the same manner. However, because of the time lags in a managerial system and the deficiencies of usual feedback, Chapter 26 emphasizes the importance of developing forward-looking controls. In this chapter, special attention is given to the point that good control involves the tailoring of control devices and information to suit the individual plan, the organization structure, the specific needs of an enterprise, and the ability and willingness of people to understand.

In Chapter 27, major techniques of control are discussed. Some of them may be classified as traditional in the sense that they have been long used by managers. Of these, the most widely used is the budget, or "profit plan." Even budgeting, which is more or less traditional, has been sharpened and improved by the use of program budgeting and the more recent technique referred to as "zero-based budgeting." This chapter also deals with some of the newer control tools in common use. These are almost all based on systems techniques brought over from the physical sciences. This chapter also explains time-event network analyses, usually referred to as "PERT" or "CPM."

Most controls are partial; they concentrate on one aspect of operation—quality of product, cash flow, costs, or some other rather narrow area. In many enterprises, a difficult problem is the development of overall control so that managers may have a check on the progress of the entire organization or of an integrated product or territorial division. Chapter 28 discusses the most widely used solutions. As one might expect, these overall controls tend to be expressed in financial terms. The reader should recognize that financial or money measurement is a natural basis for control since inputs and outputs of many enterprises are most easily expressed in terms of money. Overall financial controls are very useful in business and even in some nonbusiness organizations. Expenditures for personnel, material, and facilities are always an important factor against which to weigh results, and these are usually reflected in expenditures of money. The most valuable overall control devices are budget summaries, profit and loss statements, rate of return on investment, and the enterprise self-audit.

In spite of traditional emphasis on various control techniques, Chapter 29 demonstrates that the most direct form of control is ensuring the quality of managers. The chapter of course does not advocate scrapping other controls, but it does make the point that many deviations from plans will not occur if an enterprise is well managed. A major point made in this book is that almost all the devices usually thought of as control tools are indirect. They are based on the fact that human beings make mistakes. Controlling performance through control of the quality of managers is direct in that it is based on the belief that qualified managers make the fewest mistakes and therefore do not require as much "indirect" control. The authors believe that this direct control is more satisfactory to all the groups interested in the fate of the enterprise—investors, employees, customers, vendors, managers, and society as a whole.

This concluding chapter of the book attempts to summarize what needs to be done to ensure effective management. Even this brief analysis indicates that because the problems and opportunities are great, solving problems and making progress requires continuing effort on the part of everyone who is responsible for the performance of others. Managing is far from realizing its potential. But in an area so important to social development in all its aspects, and where the task is so complex, even small improvements can have a remarkable effect on the quality of society.

chapter 26 The System and Process of Controlling

MAJOR CHAPTER OBJECTIVES

1 To describe the nature and requirements of effective management control systems.

2 Because of time lags in feedback control systems, to show how even real-time information will not solve the problems of management control and to demonstrate how a feedforward system has the potential of making management control most effective.

3 To emphasize that controls should be tailored to plans and positions in the organization structure, to individual personalities, and to specified needs for effectiveness.

The managerial function of controlling is the measurement and correction of the performance of activities of subordinates in order to make sure that enterprise objectives and the plans devised to attain them are being accomplished. It is thus the function of every manager, from president to supervisor. Some managers, particularly at lower levels, forget that *the primary responsibility for the exercise of control rests in every manager charged with the execution of plans.* As Henri Fayol so clearly recognized decades ago, "In an undertaking, control consists in verifying whether everything occurs in conformity with the plan adopted, the instructions issued and principles established. It has for object to point out weaknesses and errors in order to rectify them and prevent recurrence. It operates on everything, things, people, actions."[1] Or, as Billy E. Goetz put it in his pioneering analysis, "Managerial planning seeks consistent, integrated and articulated programs," while "management control seeks to compel events to conform to plans."[2]

Occasionally, in view of the authority of upper-level managers and their resultant responsibility, top- and upper-level control is so emphasized that the impression is gained that little controlling is needed at lower levels. Although the scope of control varies among managers, those at all levels have the responsibility for the execution of plans, and control is therefore an essential managerial function at every level.

TWO PREREQUISITES OF CONTROL SYSTEMS

Two major prerequisites must exist before any manager can devise or maintain a system of controls. Yet we occasionally find people concentrating on control techniques and systems without having made sure that the prerequisites have been met.

Controls Require Plans

It is obvious that before a control technique can be used or a system devised, controls must be based on plans, and that the clearer, more complete, and more integrated plans are, the more effective controls can be. It is as simple as this: There is no way that managers can determine whether their organizational unit is accomplishing what is desired and expected unless they first know what is expected.

[1]Henri Fayol, *General and Industrial Management* (New York: Pitman Publishing Corporation, 1949), p. 107.
[2]Billy E. Goetz, *Management Planning and Control* (New York: McGraw-Hill Book Company, 1949), p. 229. For an interesting summary of other pioneer writers on control, most of whom perceived control as used here, see G. B. Giglioni and A. G. Bedeian, "A Conspectus of Management Control Theory: 1900–1972," *Academy of Management Journal*, vol. 17, no. 2, pp. 292–305 (June 1974).

Controls are the reverse side of the coin of planning. First, managers plan; then plans become the standards by which desired actions are measured. This simple truth means several things in practice. One is that all meaningful control techniques are, in the first instance, planning techniques. Another is that it is fruitless to try to design control without first taking into account plans and how well they are made. This simple truth is nowhere better illustrated than in the case of budgeting. As will be recalled from the earlier discussion of planning (in Chapter 6), budgets were identified as a type of plan, that is, numberized plans. To look on budgeting only as a form of control tends to make it meaningless and ineffective. Yet, even today, some businesses and many government agencies and other kinds of organizations appear to view budgeting thus.

Controls Require Organization Structure

Since the purpose of control is to measure activities and take action to ensure that plans are being accomplished, we must also know where in an enterprise the responsibility for deviating from plans and taking action to make corrections lies. Control of activities operates through people. But we cannot know where the responsibility for deviations and needed action is unless organizational responsibility is clear and definite. Therefore, a major prerequisite of control is the existence of organization structure, and, as in the case of plans, the clearer, more complete, and more integrated this structure is, the more effective control action can be.

One of the most frustrating situations managers can find themselves in is knowing that something is going wrong in their company, agency, or department and not knowing exactly where the responsibility for the trouble lies. If costs are too high, a promised contract is late, or inventory is beyond desired limits, but managers do not know where the responsibility for the deviation lies, those in charge of an operation are powerless to do anything about the situation. In one company, for example, reports showed that inventory was millions of dollars above the level deemed necessary. When inquiry was made about who was responsible for inventory planning and control, it was disclosed that no one below the president of the company had this responsibility, and that, because of his other demanding duties, he could not personally control inventories.

THE BASIC CONTROL PROCESS

Control techniques and systems are essentially the same for cash, office procedures, morale, product quality, or anything else. The basic control process, wherever it is found and whatever it controls, involves three steps: (1) establishing standards, (2) measuring performance against these standards, and (3) correcting deviations from standards and plans.

Because plans are the yardsticks against which controls must be devised, it follows logically that the first step in the control process would be to establish plans. However, since plans vary in detail and complexity and since managers cannot usually watch everything, special standards are established. Standards are by definition simply criteria of performance. They are the selected points in an entire planning program where measures of performance are made so as to give managers signals as to how things are going without their having to watch every step in the execution of plans.

Standards may be of many kinds. Among the best are verifiable goals or objectives, whether stated in quantitative or qualitative terms, regularly set in well-operated systems of managing by objectives. These were discussed earlier in this book (Chapter 7). Because end results for which people are responsible are the best measures of plan achievement, they furnish excellent standards of control. These goal standards, as well as others, may be stated in physical terms, such as quantities of products, units of service, labor-hours, speed, or volume of rejections, or they may be expressed in monetary terms, such as volume of sales, costs, capital expenditures, or profits. They may also be expressed in verifiable qualitative terms or in any other way that can give a clear indication of performance.

Measurement of Performance

As we shall soon see, and although it is not always practicable to do so, the measurement of performance against standards should ideally be on a forward-looking basis so that deviations may be detected in advance of their actual occurrence and avoided by appropriate actions. The alert, forward-looking manager can sometimes predict probable departures from standards. In the absence of such ability, deviations should be disclosed as early as possible.

If standards are appropriately drawn and if means are available for determining exactly what subordinates are doing, appraisal of actual or expected performance is fairly easy. But there are many activities in which it is difficult to develop accurate standards, and there are many that are hard to measure. It may be quite simple, especially with techniques of time and motion study, to establish labor-hour standards for the production of a mass-produced item, and it may be equally simple to measure performance against these standards, but if the item is custom-made, the appraisal of performance may be a formidable task.

Moreover, in the less technical kinds of work, not only may standards be difficult to develop but appraisal may also be formidable. For example, to control the performance of the finance vice president or the industrial relations director is not easy because definite standards are not easily developed. The superior of these managers often relies on vague standards, such as the financial health of the business, the attitude of labor unions, the absence of strikes, the enthusiasm and loyalty of subordinates, the expressed admiration of business associates, and the overall success of the department (often measured in a negative way by lack of evidence of failure). The superior's measurements are often equally vague. At the same time, if the department seems to be making the contribution expected of it at a reasonable cost, without too many serious errors, and if the measurable accomplishments give evidence of sound management, a general appraisal may be adequate. The point is that, as jobs move away from the assembly line, the shop, or the accounting machine, controlling them becomes more complex and often more important.

Nevertheless, as already noted, as managers at all levels develop verifiable objectives, stated in either quantitative or qualitative terms (see Chapter 7), these become standards against which all position performance in the organization hierarchy can be measured. Also, as new techniques are developed to measure, with a reasonable degree of objectivity, the quality of managing itself in upper as well as lower positions, useful standards of performance will emerge. As we saw in the discussion of managerial appraisal (in Chapter 20), promising progress has been made in this area.

Correction of Deviations

If standards are drawn to reflect organization structure and if performance is measured in these terms, the correction of negative deviations is expedited, since the manager then knows exactly where in the assignment of individual or group duties the corrective measures must be applied.

We are, of course, most likely to think of control as a matter of detecting and correcting for negative deviations, that is, correcting deficient performance. It is possible, and it does happen fairly often, that deviations from standards are positive, that performance is better than standard. While this kind of performance is a happy matter, it may be worthwhile in this event to look at the accuracy and adequacy of standards and to determine whether the positive deviation was the result of luck or superior performance. Correction of negative deviations in performance is the point at which control is seen as a part of the whole system of management and where it coalesces with the other managerial functions: Managers may correct deviations by redrawing their plans or by modifying their goals. (This is an exercise of the principle of navigational change referred to in Chapter 6.) Or they may correct deviations by exercising their organizing function, through reassignment or clarification of duties. They may correct, also, by additional staffing, by better selection and training of subordinates, or by that ultimate of restaffing—firing. Or, again, they may correct through better directing and leading—fuller explanation of the job or more effective leadership.

It has been argued by some that correcting deviations is not a step in the process of control at all but merely the point where the other managerial functions come into play. Surely control is not confined to measuring performance against standards without doing anything when performance falls short. This overlap of the control function with the others merely demonstrates the systems unity of the manager's job. It shows the managing process to be an integrated system. As has been previously emphasized in this book, controlling has been separated from the other managerial functions, particularly planning, only because (1) it is a useful, operational way to organize knowledge and (2) practicing managers have long understood their functions this way.[3]

CONTROL AS A CYBERNETIC SYSTEM

Managerial control is essentially the same basic process as is found in physical, biological, and social systems. As pointed out by Norbert Wiener,[4] communication, or information transfer, and control occur in the functioning of many systems. Wiener used "information" in the general sense to include a mechanical transfer of energy, an electric impulse, a chemical reaction, a written or oral message, or any other means by which a "message" might be transmitted. In the science he called "cybernetics," Wiener showed that all types of systems control themselves by information feedback which discloses error in accomplishing goals and initiates corrective action. In other words, systems use some of their energy to feed back information that compares performance with a standard. Simple feedback is charted in Figure 26.1.

The steam engine governor is a simple mechanical cybernetic system. In order to control an engine's speed under different load conditions, weights (balls) are whirled. As the speed increases, centrifugal force makes these weights exercise an outward thrust, which in turn transmits a force (a message) to cut down the input of steam and thereby reduce the speed. As speed is reduced, the reverse occurs. Likewise, in the human body, a number of cybernetic systems control temperature, blood pressure, motor reactions, and others. In electrical systems such as a voltage regulator, the operation of feedback is used. And in social systems, even

[3]But there are those who believe that most of the function of planning and control should be combined in one—control. See, for example, R. N. Anthony, *Planning and Control Systems: A Framework for Analysis* (Boston: Division of Research, Harvard Business School, 1965), pp. 10–15.
[4]*Cybernetics: Control and Communication in the Animal and the Machine* (New York: John Wiley & Sons, Inc., 1948).

Figure 26.1   Simple feedback.

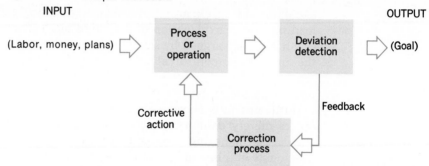

other than managed formal organizations, one also finds feedback. For example, in the social system of baseball, there are such standards as three strikes cause an out.

CONTROL AS A FEEDBACK SYSTEM

Management control is usually perceived as a feedback system similar to that which operates in the usual household thermostat. This can be seen more clearly by looking at the feedback process involved in management control shown in Figure 26.2. As will be noted, this places control in a more complex and realistic light than simply regarding it as a matter of establishing standards, measuring performance, and correcting for deviations. To be sure, managers "measure actual performance," "compare this against standards," and "identify and analyze deviations." But then, to make the necessary corrections, they must develop a "program for corrective action" and "implement" this program in order to arrive at the "performance desired."

REAL-TIME INFORMATION AND CONTROL

One of the interesting advancements arising from the use of the computer and electronic gathering, transmission, and storage of data is the development of systems of real-time information. This is information on what is happening as events are occurring. It is technically possible through various means to obtain real-time data on many operations. For years, airlines have obtained information about vacant seats by simply putting a flight number, trip segment, and date into a memory system that immediately responds with information as to whether seats are available. Supermarkets and department stores have electronic cash registers in operation that transmit data on every sale immediately to a central data

Figure 26.2 Feedback loop of management control.

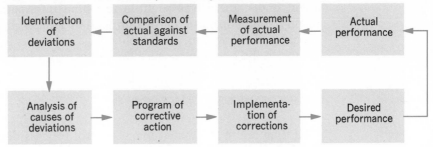

storage facility, where inventory, sales, gross profit, and other data can be obtained as they occur. A factory manager can have a system that reports at any time the status of production programs in terms of such things as the production point they have reached, labor-hours accumulated, and whether a product is late or on time in the manufacturing process.

Some information enthusiasts have seen real-time information as a means of getting real-time control in areas of importance to managers. But reference to the nature of the management control feedback loop in Figure 26.2 will show that real-time information does not, except possibly in the simplest and most unusual cases, make possible real-time control. It is possible in many areas to collect real-time data measuring performance. It may also be possible in most of these cases to compare these data with standards and even to identify deviations. But as can be seen, the analysis of causes of deviations, the development of a program of correction, and the implementation of this program are likely to be time-consuming tasks.

That undertaking the latter steps in the control loop is likely to be time-consuming is illustrated by several examples. In the simple case of quality control, it may take considerable time to discover what is causing factory rejects and more time to put corrective measures into effect. In the more complex case of inventory control, particularly in a manufacturing company where there are many items—raw materials, component parts, goods in process, and finished goods—the time for correction may be very long. Once it is found that an inventory is too high, the steps to get it back to the desired level may take a number of months. And so it goes with most instances of management control problems.

This does not mean that prompt measurement of performance is unimportant. The sooner managers know that activities for which they are responsible are not proceeding in accordance with plans, the faster they can take action to make corrections. But there is always the question of whether the cost of gathering real-time data is worth the few days saved. Often it is, as in the case of the airline business, where ready information on availability of seats is likely to be crucial to serving customers and filling airplanes. But one of the authors expressed surprise that in a major defense company producing one of the highest-priority defense equipment items, there was so little real-time information in an otherwise highly sophisticated control information system; he was informed that even for this program, the benefits of gathering real-time data would not be worth the expense because the correction process took so long.

FEEDFORWARD CONTROL[5]

The time lag in the management control process demonstrates the need for future-directed control if control is to be effective. It illustrates the problem of using only simple feedback from the output of a system and measuring this output as a means of control. It shows the deficiency of historical data such as those received from accounting reports. One of the difficulties with such historical data is that they tell business managers in November that they lost money in October (or even September) because of something that was done in July. At this time, such information is only a distressingly interesting fact.

What managers need for effective management control is a system of control that will tell them, in time to take corrective action, that problems will occur if they do not do something about them now. Simple feedback of output of a system, of the results of a program, is not good enough for control. This kind of feedback is not much more than a postmortem, and no one has found a way to change the past.

Need for Future-Directed Control

Intelligent and alert managers have recognized that the only problems they can solve are those they can see and that, in the case of management control, as has been noted above, they can exercise it effectively only if they can see deviations coming in time to do something about them.[6] It is fallacious to regard planning as looking forward and control as looking back, as some managers and writers do.

The simple matter of future-directed control is largely disregarded in practice, mainly because managers have been so dependent for purposes of control on accounting and statistical data. To be sure, in the absence of any means of looking forward, reference to history, on the questionable assumption that what is past is prologue, is admittedly better than not looking at all.

[5]For a discussion of feedforward control techniques, see H. Koontz and R. W. Bradspies, "Managing through Feedforward Control," *Business Horizons*, vol. 15, no. 3, pp. 25–36 (June 1972). Much of the material for this section is drawn from that paper.
[6]The idea of future-directed control was emphasized by one of the authors many years ago. See Harold Koontz, "A Preliminary Statement of Principles of Planning and Control," *Academy of Management Journal*, vol. 1, no. 1, pp. 45–61 (April 1958). As one of his major principles, he stated: "Since the past cannot be changed, effective control should be aimed at preventing present and future deviations from plans."

Even Norbert Wiener, the father of cybernetics, recognized the deficiency of common feedback. He noted that where there are time lags in a system, corrections must predict, or anticipate, errors. However, neither he nor the many scholars of feedback systems have appeared to develop this aspect of cybernetics.

Techniques of Future-Directed Control

This does not mean that nothing has been done to engage in future-directed control. One common way many managers have done this is through careful and repeated forecasts using the latest available information, comparing what is desired with the forecasts, and taking action to introduce program changes so that forecasts can become something desired. For example, a company may have a sales forecast made which indicates that sales will be at a lower level than desirable. At this time, managers may develop new plans for advertising, sales promotion, or introduction of new products so as to improve the sales forecast.

Likewise, most businesses and other enterprises engage in future-directed control when they carefully plan the availability of cash to meet requirements. Businesses, for example, would hardly find it wise to wait for a report at the middle or end of May to find out whether they had enough cash in the banks to cover checks issued in April.

One of the better techniques of future-directed control in use today is the technique of network planning, exemplified by PERT networks, to be discussed in the following chapter. As will be seen, this technique of planning and control does enable managers to see that they will have problems in such areas as costs or on-time delivery unless they take action now.

Feedforward in Engineering

In recent years, particularly in chemical and electrical process systems, engineers have designed systems of feedforward control. For example, it was found that because of surges in water usage, thermostatic control of water temperature with measurements at the outlet was not good enough for holding constant temperatures required for water being mixed into certain chemical compounds. As a result, process engineers designed systems whereby the needs for various quantities of water could be anticipated so that temperature could be controlled in advance of the outlet of water flow.

In engineering, then, feedforward is accomplished by analyzing the inputs to a process, seeing how they interact, and monitoring the inputs so that adjustments can be made in them or in the process *before* output from the system occurs. For example, in the problem of making sure that varying needs for water of a given temperature were met, engineers designed into the system a control device that would send steam, or withhold it, into a heat exchanger to warm water, a move triggered by a device signaling, in advance, the need for warm water.

Feedforward in Human Systems

Interestingly enough, we find many examples of feedforward in human systems. A motorist, for example, who wished to maintain a constant speed would not usually wait for the speedometer to signal a drop in speed before depressing the accelerator in going up a hill. Instead, knowing that the hill represents a disturbing variable in the system, the driver would likely correct for this by pressing the accelerator before speed falls. Likewise, a hunter will always aim ahead of a duck's flight to compensate for the time lag between a shot and a hoped-for hit.

Feedforward versus Feedback Systems

As can be understood, simple feedback systems measure outputs of a process and feed into the system or the inputs of a system corrective actions to obtain desired outputs. As has been made clear, in most management problems, because of time lags in the correction process, this is not good enough. Feedforward systems monitor inputs into a process to ascertain whether the inputs are as planned; if they are not, the inputs, or perhaps the process, are changed in order to ensure the desired results.

The nature of a feedforward as compared with a feedback system is depicted in Figure 26.3.

In a sense, we could say that a feedforward control system is really one of feedback. This is true, but the information feedback is at the input side of the system so that corrections can be made before the system output is affected. Also, no one would deny that, even with a feedforward system, a manager would still want to measure final system output, since nothing can guarantee that the final output will always be exactly what is desired.

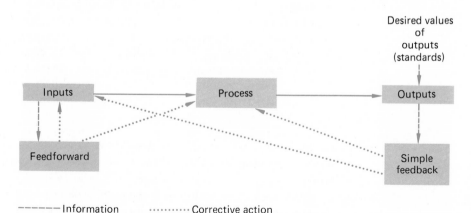

Figure 26.3 Comparison of simple feedback and feedforward systems.

Figure 26.4 System of inputs for feedforward cash control.

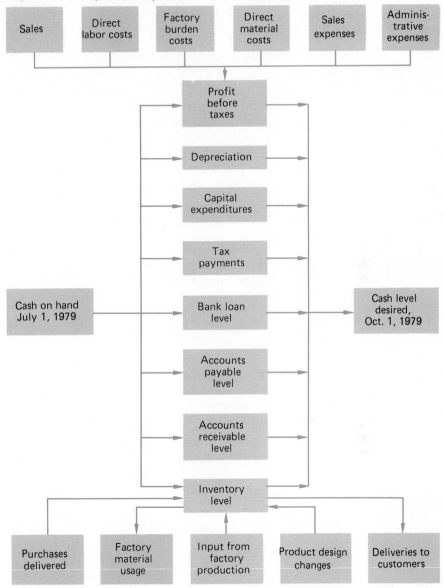

Feedforward in Management

To give the reader an idea of what feedforward means in management
control, examples of cash and inventory planning systems might be used.
Figures 26.4 and 26.5 illustrate what is involved.

The somewhat simplified schematic drawings of input variables
involved in the charts for cash and for inventory planning and control
indicate that if managers are to exercise effective control over either cash

Figure 26.5   System of inputs for feedforward inventory control.

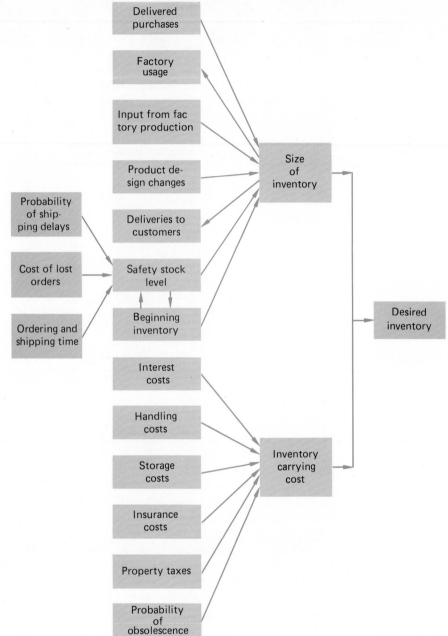

or inventories, they must identify them as an interacting system. As can be seen in each instance, some of the variables interact, and some have either a negative or a positive effect on either cash or inventory.

Also, it can be seen that if the system of variables and their impact on a process to obtain a desired output is accurately portrayed—and users should design their own system appropriate to the realities of their situation—and if the inputs are carefully monitored, a deviation from any planned input can result in an unplanned output unless something is done about it in time. For example, in the case of the inventory model, if purchase deliveries are greater than planned or if factory usage turns out to be less than planned, the result will be a higher inventory unless corrective action is taken before the inventory increases.

It should be noted, furthermore, that in the best kind of feedforward control program, the model of input variables should be extended to include in the system model inputs that influence the inputs. For example, purchase deliveries tend to increase inventories. But these deliveries are, of course, dependent on orders placed, and the placing of orders is in turn dependent on other factors.

The system of feedforward may appear to be rather complex. But for major problem areas at least, it should not be difficult to identify system input variables, to see them as an interacting system, and to computerize the model. From that point it should be an easy matter to gather information on the inputs and to ascertain periodically their effect on the desired end result. Certainly in view of its importance to management control, this would not appear to be too much trouble to take to assure meaningful control.

One of the problems in all feedforward control systems is the necessity to watch for what engineers call "disturbances." These are factors which have not been taken into account in the input model but which may have an impact on the system and desired end results. Obviously, it would be impracticable to take into account in a model all inputs that might possibly affect the operation of a program. For example, for a company with a long history of adequate flow of bank loans for financing needs, the possibility that the company's bank may suddenly find itself in a position of having to restrict credit might not have been a variable put into the input system. Or the bankruptcy of a large customer or supplier might be an unanticipated, and unprogrammed, input variable. Since the unprogrammed events do sometimes occur and may upset a desired output, monitoring of regular inputs must be supplemented by watching for, and taking into account, unusual and unexpected "disturbances."

Requirements for Feedforward Control

The requirements for a workable feedforward control system may be summarized as follows:

1 Thorough and careful analysis of the planning and control system must be made, and the more important input variables identified.
2 A model of the system should be developed.
3 Care should be taken to keep the model dynamic; in other words, the model should be reviewed regularly to see whether the input variables identified and their interrelationships still represent realities.
4 Data on input variables must be regularly collected and put into the system.
5 The variations of actual input data from planned-for inputs must be regularly assessed, and their impact on expected end results evaluated.
6 Action must be taken; like any other technique of planning and control, all that can be done is to show people problems, and action is obviously required to solve them.

REQUIREMENTS FOR ADEQUATE CONTROLS

It is understandable that all alert managers would want to have an adequate and effective system of controls to assist them in making sure that events conform to plans. It is sometimes not realized that the controls used by managers must be designed for the specific task and person they are intended to serve. While the basic process and the fundamentals of control are universal, the actual system requires special design.

Indeed, we can say that if controls are to work, they must be specially tailored. In short, they must be tailored (1) to plans and positions, (2) to the individual managers and their personalities, and (3) to the needs for efficiency and effectiveness.

Controls Should Be Tailored to Plans and Positions

All control techniques and systems should reflect the plans they are designed to follow. Every plan and every kind and phase of an operation have unique characteristics. What managers need to know and should know is information that will tell them how the plans for which they are responsible are progressing. Certainly the information for following the progress of a marketing program will be quite different from that needed to check on a production plan.

In the same way, controls should be tailored to positions. What will do for a vice president in charge of manufacturing will certainly not be appropriate for a shop supervisor. Controls for the sales department will differ from those for finance department, and these from controls for the purchasing department. And a small business will need some controls different from those for a large business. The very nature of control emphasizes the fact that the more controls are designed to deal with and reflect the specific nature and structure of plans, the more effectively they will serve managerial needs.

Certain techniques, such as budgets, standard hours and costs, and various financial ratios, have general application in various situations. However, it should never be assumed that any of these widely used techniques is completely applicable in any given situation. Managers must always be aware of the critical factors in their plans and operations requiring control, and they must use techniques and information suited to them.

Also, as has been made clear in the previous discussion of future-directed control, because controls have as their purpose making sure that plans are accomplished, they must relate to plans. This means in practice not only that deviations from plans should be reported quickly but also that a manager should have a system that will give an indication of possible deviations before they occur so that there is time to do something about them.

Controls should also reflect the organization pattern. Organization structure, being the principal vehicle for clarifying the roles of people in an enterprise, furnishes the key to where responsibility for the execution of plans, and any deviation from them, lies. It is therefore imperative that controls reflect the organization structure, and it can hardly be denied that the more controls are designed to reflect the place in the organization where responsibility for action lies, the more they will facilitate correction from deviation of plans. For example, unless product costs are accumulated so as to fit the organization structure of the manufacturing department, and unless each factory superintendent and supervisor knows the costs incurred by the department toward the production of an item, actual costs may be out of line without any of these managers knowing whether he or she is responsible. Fortunately, cost accountants have recognized the importance of relating cost data to organization structure, and the cost centers now typically used in industry provide data appropriate for each manager and his or her responsibility.

Controls Should Be Tailored to Individual Managers and Their Personalities

Controls must also be tailored to the personalities of individual managers. Control systems and information are of course intended to help individual managers carry out their function of control. If they are not of a type that a manager can or will understand, they will not be useful. It really does not matter whether people cannot understand a control technique or information or whether they are just unwilling to understand it. In either case, it is not understood. And what individuals cannot understand they will not trust. And what they will not trust they will not use.

It is especially important that controls be tailored to individual personalities. Some people, such as certain statisticians and accountants, like their information in forms of complex tables of data or voluminous computer printouts. In such cases, let them have it that way. Other people like their information in chart form; if so, it should be furnished this way. And a few people known to the authors, such as scientists and mathematicians, even like their information in mathematical model form; in this event it should be given to them that way. And it is sometimes said that if people will not understand the information they need in any other way, we might consider giving it to them in comic-book form. The important thing is that people get and understand the information they need.

Many experts in statistical methods, computer technology, or exhaustive analyses fail to communicate the meaning of their control data to managers who must use them. "Control" staffs and departments often develop information that will not be used by managers because it is not simple enough or adapted to the manager's understanding. This is, of course, one of the problems of data processing systems. Too often the output consists of thousands of sheets of printouts that many people cannot or will not understand and use.

What is said about tailoring information for understanding can be said also of control techniques. Even quite intelligent people may be "turned off" by some of the sophisticated techniques of the expert. The authors have seen highly sophisticated techniques of planning and control, like variable budgeting or network planning, fail in practice simply because the systems either were not comprehensible to the people who had to use them or appeared to be too complex for them. Intelligent experts in these matters will not try to show others how expert they are, but will rather design a system at the level of ready comprehension so that people will use it. Such experts will realize that if they can get 80 percent of the benefit with a fairly crude system, this is far better than obtaining no benefit from a more perfect, but unworkable, system.

Controls Should Point up Exceptions at Critical Points

One of the most important ways of tailoring controls to needs for efficiency and effectiveness is to make sure that they are designed to point up exceptions. In other words, by concentrating on exceptions from planned performance, controls based on the time-honored exception principle allow managers to detect those places where their attention is required and should be given.[7]

But it is not enough merely to look at exceptions. Some deviations from standards have rather little meaning, and others have a great deal. Small deviations in certain areas may have greater significance than larger

---

[7]For a complete and thoughtful analysis of the exception principle, see L. R. Bittel, *Management by Exception* (New York: McGraw-Hill Book Company, 1964).

exceptions in other areas. A manager, for example, might be concerned if the cost of office labor deviated from budget by 5 percent, but be unworried if the cost of postage stamps deviated from budget by 20 percent.

Consequently, the exception principle must be accompanied in practice by the principle of critical-point control. It is not enough just to look for exceptions; we must also look for them at critical points. While it is true that the more managers concentrate their control efforts on exceptions, the more efficient their control will be, this principle had best be considered in the light of the fact that effective control requires primary attention to those points which are critical to appraising performance.

Controls Should Be Objective

Management necessarily contains many subjective elements, but whether a subordinate is doing a good job should ideally not be a matter for subjective determination. Where controls are subjective, a manager's or a subordinate's personality may influence judgments of performance inaccurately; but people have difficulty in explaining away objective control of their performance, particularly if the standards and measurements are kept up to date through periodic review. This may be summarized by saying that effective control requires objective, accurate, and suitable standards.

Objective standards can be quantitative, such as costs or labor-hours per unit or date of job completion; they can also be qualitative, as in the case of a training program that has specific characteristics or is designed to accomplish a specific kind of upgrading of the quality of personnel. The point is that, in either case, the standard is determinable and verifiable.

Controls Should Be Flexible

Controls should remain workable in the face of changed plans, unforeseen circumstances, or outright failures. As Goetz has remarked: "A complex program of managerial plans may fail in some particulars. The control system should report such failures, and should contain sufficient elements of flexibility to maintain managerial control of operations despite such failures."[8] In other words, if controls are to remain effective, despite failure or unforeseen changes of plans, flexibility is required in their design.

The need for flexible control can readily be illustrated. A budget system may project a certain level of expenses and grant authority to managers to hire labor and purchase materials and services at this level. If, as is usually the case, this budget is based on a forecast of a certain level of sales, it may become meaningless as a system of control if the actual sales

---

[8]Goetz, loc. cit.

volume is considerably above or below the forecast. Budget systems have been brought into ill repute among some companies because of inflexibility in such circumstances. What is needed, of course, is a system that will reflect sales variations as well as other deviations from plans. This has been provided, as will be noted presently, by the flexible, or variable, budget.

In production scheduling, the production manager must be prepared for failures occasioned by the breakdown of a machine or the illness of a key worker. If the control system is too inflexible to account for such hitches, the slowdown, even though temporary, may impair control. Much flexibility in control can be provided by having alternative plans for various probable situations. In fact, flexible control is normally best achieved through flexible plans.

The Control System Should Fit the Organizational Climate

To be most effective, any control system or technique must fit the organizational climate.[9] For example, a tight control system applied in an organization where people have been given considerable freedom and participation may go so "against the grain" that it would be doomed to failure. On the other hand, if subordinates have been managed by a superior who allows little participation in decision making, to have a generalized and permissive control system would hardly succeed. People with a low desire to participate, or who have not been accustomed to participating, are likely to want to have clear standards and measurement and be told what to do.

Controls Should Be Economical

Controls must be worth their cost. Although this requirement is simple, its practice is often complex, for a manager may find it difficult to know what a particular control system is worth, or to know what it costs. Economy is relative, since the benefits vary with the importance of the activity, the size of the operation, the expense that might be incurred in the absence of control, and the contribution the system can make.

A small company cannot afford the extensive control system of a large company. The elaborate charts and detailed analyses used by the top management of the Monsanto Chemical Company or the Du Pont Company doubtless represent hundreds of thousands of dollars in investment of time and many more thousands each year for their maintenance. Expensive preparation, approval, and administration of complex budgetary control programs may be well worth their cost to the

---

[9]C. Camman and D. A. Nadler, "Fit Control Systems to Your Managerial Style," *Harvard Business Review*, vol. 54, no. 1, pp. 65–72 (January–February 1976).

large enterprise, but only a simple system would be economical for the small one. Likewise, a finance vice president may feel that many thousands of dollars have been well spent for historical and forecast data on cash flow or capital investment, but in the same company a much smaller expenditure for tracing the handling of scrap inventories might be too costly.

Since a limiting factor of control systems is relative economy, this, in turn, will depend a great deal on managers' selecting for control only critical factors in areas important to them. If tailored to the job and to the size of the enterprise, control will probably be economical. On the other hand, one of the economies of large-scale enterprise results from being able to afford expensive and elaborate control systems. Often, however, the magnitude of the problems, the wider area of planning, the difficulty of coordinating plans, and poor management communication in a large business require such expensive controls that their overall efficiency suffers in comparision to controls in a small business. This leads to the principle of efficiency of controls: *Control techniques and approaches are efficient when they detect and illuminate the causes of actual or potential deviations from plans with the minimum of costs or other unsought consequences.*

Controls Should Lead to Corrective Action

A control system will be little more than an interesting exercise if it does not lead to corrective action. An adequate system will disclose where failures are occurring and who is responsible for them, and it will assure that some corrective action is taken. It cannot be forgotten that control is justified only if indicated or experienced deviations from plans are corrected through appropriate planning, organizing, staffing, and leading.

CRITICAL CONTROL POINTS AND STANDARDS

As indicated above, the establishment of standards furnishes the yardstick against which actual or expected performance is measured. In a simple operation, a manager might control through careful personal observation of the work being done. However, in most operations this is not possible because of the complexity of the operations and the fact that a manager has far more to do than personally observe performance. A manager must then choose points for special attention and then watch them to be sure that the whole operation is proceeding as planned.

The points selected for control should be critical, in the sense either of being limiting factors in the operation or of showing better than other factors whether plans are working out. With such standards managers can handle a larger group of subordinates and thereby increase their span of management, with resulting cost savings and improvement of communication. In other words, the principle of critical-point control is one of the more important of all control principles. It can be stated as follows: *Effective control requires attention to those factors critical to performance as measured against individual plans.*

There are no specific catalogs of controls available to all managers because of the peculiarities of various enterprises and departments, the variety of products and services to be measured, and the innumerable planning programs to be followed. At the same time, as will be noted presently, a number of types of critical-point standards have been used. Nonetheless, as was emphasized above in the discussion of requirements for adequate controls, all managers must tailor their own controls and control standards to fit their individual needs.

The ability to select critical points of control is one of the arts of management, since sound control depends on them. In this connection, managers must ask themselves such questions as, What will best reflect the goals of my department? What will best show *me* when these goals are not being met? What will best measure critical deviations? What will inform *me* as to who is responsible for any failure? What standards will cost the least? For what standards is information economically available?

Types of Critical-Point Standards

Every objective, every goal of the many planning programs, every activity of these programs, every policy, every procedure, and every budget become standards against which actual or expected performance might be measured. In practice, however, standards tend to be of the following types: (1) physical standards, (2) cost standards, (3) capital standards, (4) revenue standards, (5) program standards, (6) intangible standards, and (7) verifiable goals.

Physical standards These deal with nonmonetary measurements and are common at the operating level where materials are used, labor employed, services rendered, and goods produced. They may reflect quantitative performance, such as labor-hours per unit of output, pounds of fuel per horsepower produced, ton-miles of freight traffic carried, units of production per machine-hour, or feet of wire per ton of copper. Physical standards may also reflect quality, such as hardness of bearings, closeness of tolerance, rate of climb of an airplane, durability of a fabric, or fastness of a color. As Goetz has said,[10] these standards are the "building blocks of planning," since "whether management must choose between alternate policies, organizational configuration, procedures, or resources, it must always analyze the rival programs in terms of their physical elements, determine the financial implications of these elements, integrate or synthesize the elements into programs, and select the

---

[10]Op. cit., p. 93.

best program it can devise." To the extent that physical standards can be the building blocks of planning, they are also the fundamental standards for control.

Cost standards These deal with monetary measurement and, like physical standards, are common at the operating level. They attach monetary values to the costs of operations. Illustrative of cost standards are such widely used measures as direct and indirect cost per unit produced, labor cost per unit or per hour, material cost per unit, machine-hour costs, costs per plane reservation, selling costs per dollar or unit of sales, and costs per foot of well drilled.

Capital standards These are a variety of cost standards, arising from the application of monetary measurements to physical items. But they have to do with the capital invested in the firm rather than with operating costs and are therefore related to the balance sheet rather than the income statement. Perhaps the most widely used standard for new investment, as well as for overall control, is return on investment. The typical balance sheet will disclose other capital standards, such as ratios of current assets to current liabilities, debt to net worth, fixed investment to total investment, cash and receivables to payables, notes or bonds to stock, and the size and turnover of inventories.

Revenue standards These arise from attaching monetary values to sales. They may vary from such standards as revenue per bus passenger-mile and dollars per ton of steel shapes sold, to average sale per customer and sales per capita in a given market area.

Program standards A manager may be assigned to install a variable budget program, a program for formally following the development of new products, or a program for improving the quality of a sales force. While some subjective judgment may have to be applied in appraising program performance, timing and other factors can be used as objective standards.

Intangible standards More difficult to set are standards not expressed in either physical or monetary measurements. What standard can managers use for determining the competence of the divisional purchasing agent or personnel director? What can they use for determining whether the advertising program meets both short- and long-term objectives, whether the public relations program is successful, or whether supervisors are loyal to the company's objectives? Such questions show how difficult it is to establish goals that have not been given clear and verfiable quantitative or qualitative measurement.

Many intangible standards exist in business because thorough research into what constitutes desired performance for all kinds of operations has not generally been done.

Perhaps a more important reason is that where human relationships count in performance, as they do especially above the basic operating levels, it is very hard to measure what is "good," "effective," or "efficient." Tests, surveys, and sampling techniques developed by psychologists and sociometrists have made it possible to probe human attitudes and drives, but many managerial controls over interpersonal relationships must continue to be based upon intangible standards, considered judgment, trial and error, and even, on occasion, sheer hunch.

Goals as standards   However, with the present tendency for better-managed enterprises to establish an entire network of verifiable qualitative or quantitative goals at every level of management, the use of intangible standards, while still important, is diminishing. In complex program operations as well as in the performance of managers themselves, modern managers are finding that through research and thinking it is possible to define goals that can be used as performance standards. While the quantitative goals are likely to take the form of the standards outlined above, definition of qualitative goals represents a new development in the area of standards. For example, if the program of a district sales office is spelled out to include such elements as training salespeople in accordance with a plan with specific characteristics, the very fact of the plan and its characteristics furnish standards which tend to become objective and, therefore, "tangible."

FOR DISCUSSION

1   Planning and control together are often thought of as a system; control alone is also often referred to as a system. What is meant by these assumptions? Can both statements be true?
2   Why is real-time information not good enough for effective control?
3   What is feedforward control? Why is it important to managers? Besides the examples of cash and inventory control mentioned in this chapter, can you think of any other areas where feedforward would be used? Selecting one of these, how would you proceed?
4   If you were asked to develop a system of "tailored" controls in a company, how would you do it? What would you need to know?
5   If you were going to institute a program of special control reports and analyses for a certain top manager, how would you go about it?
6   Develop a set of standards for any area of interest to you where you might wish to exercise effective control.

chapter 27 Control Techniques

MAJOR CHAPTER OBJECTIVES

1 To describe traditional control techniques, with special emphasis on the nature and types of budgets, on problems encountered in budgeting, and on making budgeting work in practice.

2 To present newer techniques of flexible budgeting in the form of variable and zero-based budgets.

3 To explain the nature and difficulties of program budgeting.

4 To present the nature and problems of the new information technology and how electronic data processing equipment can be most effectively used for information.

5 To discuss the special need for procedures planning and control.

6 To point out the possibilities of using operations research and logistic systems as control techniques.

7 To discuss and analyze the use of time-event networks as a major technique of control.

Although the basic nature and purpose of management control do not change, a variety of tools and techniques have been used over the years to help managers in this task. As will be seen in all these techniques, they are in the first instance tools for planning. They illustrate the fundamental truth that the task of control is to make plans succeed, and naturally, in doing so, must reflect plans.

Some of these tools may be classed as traditional, in the sense that they have long been used by managers. Others, like Program Evaluation and Review Technique (PERT), represent a new generation of planning and control tools. While there are many more of these than discussed here, the newer tools generally reflect the systems techniques long used in the physical sciences. Operations research, discussed earlier in connection with decision making, is such a technique. It uses mathematical and computing techniques through the formulation of a model that simulates a problem situation with its goal, variables, and their relationships. As can be seen, if managers have such a model to guide them in their planning, they can use the same model for control purposes. They know what their goals are and what the variables are that influence performance. In this way, detecting variations and making corrections becomes clearer and somewhat easier.

Even with all the new techniques of planning and control, the traditional tools are still extremely important. As a matter of fact, most managerial control as actually practiced uses them.

TRADITIONAL CONTROL TECHNIQUE: THE BUDGET

A widely used device for managerial control is the budget. Indeed, it has sometimes been assumed that budgeting is the primary device for accomplishing control. As will be noted, however, many nonbudgetary devices are also essential. Primarily because of the negative implications of budgeting in the past, the more positive-sounding phrase, "profit planning" is often used, and the budget is then known as the profit plan.

Concept of Budgeting

Budgeting is the formulation of plans for a given future period in numerical terms. As such, budgets are statements of anticipated results, in financial terms—as in revenue and expense and capital budgets, or in nonfinancial terms—as in budgets of direct-labor-hours, materials, physical sales volume, or units of production. It has sometimes been said that financial budgets represent the "dollarizing" of plans.

Sometimes people do not understand how and why budgets must be based on plans. In fact, some enterprises, especially nonbusiness enterprises, do attempt to develop budgets without knowing plans. But when they do so, money allocated to pay for people and their salaries, for office space and equipment, and for other expenses becomes a matter of negotiation between a top authority and the managers in an enterprise. The usual result is that funds are not intelligently allocated on the basis of what is really needed to accomplish desired goals. Many of us have seen this kind of uncertainty and consequent "jockeying for position" in government and university budgeting. Only by having clear goals and action plans to accomplish them can anyone in a top position of authority know how much money is necessary to do what is desired.

Purpose of Budgeting

Through numerical statement of plans and breaking of these plans into components consistent with the organization structure, budgets correlate planning and allow authority to be delegated without loss of control. In other words, reducing plans to definite numbers forces a kind of orderliness that permits managers to see clearly what capital will be spent by whom and where, and what expense, revenue, or units of physical input or output plans will involve. Having ascertained this, managers can more freely delegate authority to carry out the plan within the limits of the budget. Moreover, a budget, to be useful to a manager at any level, must reflect the organizational pattern. Only when plans are complete, coordinated, and developed enough to be fitted into departmental operations can a useful departmental budget be prepared as an instrument of control.

Types of Budgets

Since budgets express plans and since the typical enterprise has a large variety of plans, there are many types of budgets. These may be classified into five basic types, with a budget summary portraying the total planning picture of all the budgets: (1) revenue and expense budgets; (2) time, space, material, and product budgets; (3) capital expenditures budgets; (4) cash budgets; and (5) balance sheet budgets.

Revenue and expense budgets By far the most common business budgets spell out plans for revenues and operating expenses in dollar terms. The most basic of these in a business is the sales budget, the formal and detailed expression of the sales forecast. As the sales forecast is the cornerstone of planning, the sales budget is the foundation of budgetary control. Although a company may budget other revenues, such as expected income from rentals, royalties, or miscellaneous sources, the revenue from sales of products or services furnishes the principal income to support operating expenses and yield profits.

Operating expense budgets can be as numerous as the expense classifications in an enterprise chart of accounts and the units of organization in its structure. These budgets may deal with individual items of expense, such as direct labor, materials, supervision, clerical, rent, heat, power, travel, entertainment, office supplies, shop supplies, and many others. Sometimes the department head will budget only major items and lump together other items in one control summary. For example, if the manager of a small department is expected to take one business trip a year at a cost of $240, budgeting this cost each month at $20 would mean little for monthly planning or control.

Time, space, material, and product budgets Many budgets are better expressed in physical than in monetary terms. Although such budgets are usually translated into monetary quantities, they are much more significant at a certain stage in planning and control if dealt with in physical quantities. Among the more common of these are the budgets for direct-labor-hours, machine-hours, units of materials, square feet allocated, and units produced. Most firms budget product output, and most production departments budget their share of the output of components of the final product. In addition, it is common to budget either in labor-hours or labor-days, by types of work force workers required.

Capital expenditure budgets The capital expenditure budget outlines specifically capital expenditures for plant, machinery, equipment, inventories, and other items. Whether for a short or a long term, these budgets require care in giving definite form to plans for spending the funds of an enterprise. Since capital resources are generally one of the most limiting factors of any enterprise, and since investment in plant and equipment usually requires a long period for recovery, capital expenditure budgets should be diligently tied in with long-range planning.

Cash budgets The cash budget is simply a forecast of cash receipts and disbursements against which actual cash experience is measured. Whether called a budget or not, this is perhaps the most important single control of a business. The availability of cash to meet obligations as they fall due is the first requirement of business existence, and handsome profits do little good when tied up in inventory, machinery, or other noncash assets. Cash budgeting also shows availability of excess cash, thereby making possible planning for investment of surpluses.

Balance sheet budgets The balance sheet budget forecasts the status of assets, liabilities, the capital account as of particular times in the future. Since the sources of change in balance sheet items are the various other budgets, it proves the accuracy of all other budgets. In addition to the balance sheet budget, many of its items may be budgeted in various degrees of detail. The more common, in addition to cash and capital investments, are special budgets of accounts receivable, inventories, and accounts payable.

Budget summaries   Complete balance sheet budgets are a form of budget summary. In addition, a master operating budget gathers together all the budgets for the several departments and summarizes them, first in a forecast income statement, and then in a forecast balance sheet. The former may be in detail, or it may be in a summary form showing only the principal items of revenue, expense, loss, and profit (for example, net sales, cost of sales, gross profit, administrative and selling expenses, net operating profit, other income and charges, income taxes, and net profit). The latter reflects the principal items of the balance sheet.

Dangers in Budgeting

Budgets should be used only as a tool of planning and control. Some budgetary control programs are so complete and detailed that they become cumbersome, meaningless, and unduly expensive. There is danger in overbudgeting, through spelling out minor expenses in detail and depriving managers of needed freedom in managing their departments. For example, a department head was thwarted in important sales promotion because expenditures for office supplies exceeded budgeted estimates; new expenditures had to be limited, even though his total departmental expenses were well within the budget and he had funds to pay personnel for writing sales promotion letters. In another department, expenses were budgeted in such useless detail that the cost of budgeting of many items exceeded the expenses controlled.

Another danger lies in allowing budgetary goals to supersede enterprise goals. In their zest to keep within budget limits, managers may forget that they owe primary allegiance to enterprise objectives. The authors recall a company with a thorough budgetary control program in which the sales department could not obtain information needed from the engineering department on the grounds that the latter's budget would not stand such expense! This conflict between partial and overall control objectives, the excessive departmental independence sometimes engendered, and the consequent lack of coordination are symptoms of inadequate management, since plans should represent a supporting and interlocking network and every plan should be reflected in a budget in a systems way.

A latent danger sometimes found in budgeting is that of hiding inefficiencies. Budgets have a way of growing from precedent, and the fact that a certain expenditure was made in the past becomes evidence of its reasonableness in the present; if a department once spent a given amount for supplies, this becomes a floor for future budgets. Also, managers sometimes learn that budget requests are likely to be pared down in the course of final approval and therefore ask for much more than they need. Unless budget making is accomplished by constant reexamination of standards and conversion factors by which planning is translated into numerical terms, the budget may become an umbrella under which slovenly and inefficient managers can hide.

Perhaps inflexibility is the greatest danger in budgets. Even if budgeting is not used to supplant management, the reduction of plans to numerical terms gives them a kind of illusive definiteness. It is entirely possible that events will prove that a larger amount should be spent for this kind of labor or that kind of material and a smaller amount for another, or that sales will exceed or fall materially below the amount forecast. Such differences may make a budget obsolete almost as soon as it is made; and if managers must stay within the straightjacket of their budgets in the face of such events, the usefulness of the budgets is reduced or negated. This is especially true where budgets are made for long periods in advance.

Variable Budgets

Because of the dangers arising from inflexibility in budgets and because maximum flexibility consistent with efficiency underlies good planning, attention has been increasingly given to variable or flexible budgets. These are designed to vary usually as the volume of sales or some other measure of output varies and so are limited largely in application to expense budgets. The variable budget is based upon an analysis of expense items to determine how individual costs *should* vary with volume of output. Some costs do not vary with volume, particularly in so short a period as a month, 6 months, or a year. Among these are depreciation, property taxes and insurance, maintenance of plant and equipment, and the costs of keeping a minimum staff of supervisory and other key personnel on a readiness-to-serve basis. Some of these standby, or period, costs—such as for maintaining a minimum number of key or trained personnel for advertising or sales promotion and for research— depend upon managerial policy.

Costs that vary with volume of output range from those which are perfectly variable to those which are only slightly variable. The task of variable budgeting is to select some unit of measure that reflects volume, to inspect the various categories of costs (usually by reference to the chart of accounts), and, by statistical studies, methods-engineering analyses, and other means, to determine how these costs should vary with volume. At this stage, each category of cost is related to volume, sometimes with recognition of "steps" as volume increases and sometimes with a factor allowing increases in expenses with rising volume. Each department is given these variable items of cost, along with definite dollar amounts for its fixed, or standby, costs. Periodically—usually each month—depart- ment heads are then given the volume forecast for the immediate future, from which is calculated the dollar amounts of variable costs that make up the budget. In this way, a basic budget can be established for 6 months

Figure 27.1 Variable budget chart. As volume increases, certain costs remain fixed; others vary according to volume, based on the assumption that period costs are constant for a volume range from 0 to 6000 units.

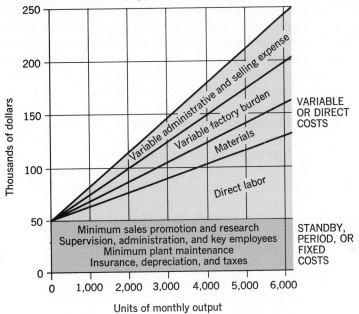

or a year in advance, but be made variable with shorter-term changes in sales and output.

This type of budget may be illustrated by Figure 27.1, which depicts the fixed and variable portions of business cost. A chart of a departmental budget would have essentially the same appearance, with suitable cost components. Although this chart uses units of monthly output as the base for volume and although direct labor and materials are included, many variable budgets assume that volume will automatically control direct labor and materials and are consequently used to control only indirect and general expense.

As can be seen, Figure 27.1 is based on the assumption that period costs will remain the same for a volume output of 0 to 6000 units. In most cases, a variable budget will represent a range of output where plant, managerial, organizational, and other components of period cost will be the same. But in practice this may be over a range of 3000 to 10,000 units. If it were less than 3000 units, a different variable budget would be required with the level of period costs more suitable for the smaller volume; if it were more than 10,000 units, another variable budget would be necessary to reflect the level of period costs necessitated by a larger operation.

A typical variable budget resulting from such an analysis is shown in

Table 27.1. This shows an expense budget for an entire company based on a range of volume of $575,000 per month of sales to $875,000 per month. The assumption is that if sales were thought to be below $575,000, the company would probably have to reorganize its operations to profitably sustain this smaller volume. On the other hand, if sales rose above $875,000, an expansion of company plant and organization would require a completely new variable budget.

A difficulty in all kinds of variable budgets is that a department manager must still make future plans. It may be easy to tell a supervisor that during the month of May twelve trained electronic assemblers can be used, then, several weeks later, that fifteen can be used in June, and a month later that the budget for July will permit having only ten. But the problems of hiring and training competent personnel make accomplishing these variations more costly than they are worth. In other words, efficiency may demand that department managers not vary certain of their expenses with short-term variations in volume. In the quest for flexibility in budgets, as with other tools of management, the intelligent manager will not lose sight of basic objectives and efficiencies by blindly following any system.

Observation of many variable budgets in practice leads to the conclusion that these work best when sales or other measures of volume can be reasonably well forecast and reasonably long-range plans made, so that the level of expenses will not have to be changed so often and on such short notice as to make the job of supervisors intolerable. Under these circumstances, one might well ask what are the advantages of variable budgeting. Although a fixed budget will work as well with good plans and accurate sales forecasts, a variable budget *forces* study of, and preoccupation with, factors which translate work load into labor or expense needs.

Table 27.1 A Typical Variable Budget for an Entire Company

Item of expense	Monthly sales volume (000's)						
	$575	$625	$675	$725	$775	$825	$875
Material	$184	$200	$216	$232	$248	$264	$280
Direct labor	70	76	82	88	94	100	106
Overhead costs	150	155	161	168	170	171	174
Cost of production	$404	$431	$459	$488	$512	$535	$560
Engineering	$ 35	$ 36	$ 38	$ 38	$ 38	$ 38	$ 40
Research and development	10	10	10	10	12	12	12
Sales and advertising	64	66	69	72	73	74	75
Administrative costs	60	62	63	63	64	65	66
Total costs	$573	$605	$639	$671	$699	$724	$753
Profit from operations	$ 2	$ 20	$ 36	$ 54	$ 76	$101	$122
Profit to sales	0.3%	3.2%	5.4%	7.5%	9.8%	12.3%	14%

Carefully worked out conversion factors—worked out and applied in advance—are necessary for any good budgeting. This, rather than flexibility itself, appears to be the principal advantage of variable budgeting.

Zero-Based Budgeting

Another type of budgeting, which has much in common with the purpose of a well-operated system of variable budgeting, is zero-based budgeting.[1] The idea behind this technique is to divide enterprise programs into "packages" comprising goals, activities, and needed resources and then to calculate costs for each package from the ground up. By starting each program budget from base zero, costs are calculated afresh, thus avoiding the common tendency in budgeting to look only at changes from a previous period.

This technique has generally been applied to so-called support areas, rather than to actual production areas, on the assumption that there is some discretion on amounts of expenditures for most programs in such areas as marketing, research and development, personnel, planning, and finance. The various programs thought to be desirable are costed and reviewed in terms of their benefits to the enterprise and are then ranked in accordance with benefits and selected against cost-benefit criteria.

The principal advantage of this technique is, of course, the fact that it forces managers to plan each program package afresh. In doing so, established programs and their costs are reviewed in their entirety, along with newer programs and their costs.

Alternative and Supplementary Budgets

Another method of obtaining variable budgeting is to establish alternative budgets for alternative eventualities. Sometimes a company will establish budgets for a high level of operation, a medium level, and a low level, and the three budgets will be approved for the company as a whole and for each organizational segment for 6 months or a year in advance. Then, at stated times, managers will be informed as to which budget to use in their planning and control. Alternative budgets are a modification of variable budgets, the latter being virtually infinitely variable instead of limited to a few alternatives.

Budget flexibility is also obtained via a plan referred to as the supplemental monthly budget. Under this plan, a 6-month or 1-year budget is prepared for the primary purpose of outlining the framework of the company's plans, coordinating them among departments, and establishing department objectives. This is a basic or minimum budget. Then a supplementary budget is prepared each month on the basis of the volume

---

[1]For a description of this kind of budgeting as it has been used in Texas Instruments, see P. A. Pyhrr, "Zero-Base Budgeting," *Harvard Business Review*, vol. 48, no. 6, pp. 111–121 (November–December 1970).

of business forecast for that month. This budget gives each manager authority for scheduling output and spending funds above the basic budget, if and to the extent that the shorter-term plans so justify. It avoids some of the detailed calculations necessary under the typical variable budget. But these budget approaches do not usually have the advantage of forcing complete analysis of all costs and relating them to volume.

PROGRAM BUDGETING

One of the more widely publicized tools of planning and control, used primarily in government operation but applicable to any kind of enterprise, is program planning and budgeting (PPB), or, more simply, program budgeting. Although really not more, at least in its fundamentals, than what budgeting should always be, its emphasis and approach, as well as its initial, but now disappointing, popularity, make it deserving of analysis as a special tool of managing.

What Program Budgeting Is

Program budgeting is basically a means for providing a systematic method for allocating the resources of an enterprise in ways most effective to meet its goals. By emphasing goals and programs to meet them, it overcomes the common weakness of all kinds of budgets, even in business, of being too tied to the time-frames of accounting periods of months, quarters, or years. By concentrating on goals and programs in the light of available resources, it puts stress on the desirability of assessing costs against benefits in selecting the best course toward accomplishing a program goal.

Special Application in Government

Program budgeting has particularly great actual and potential benefit in government, where budgeting has too often been regarded as a mere control technique, used to control the allocation and expenditure of funds, rather than as a planning and control tool. For too many years, government budgeting—at federal, state, and local levels—has been handled largely on a "line" basis, with allocation of funds to such functions as personnel, training, office supplies, transportation, and printing, rather than for programs designed to accomplish identifiable goals. Also, since program responsibility is often fragmented among various agencies, bureaus, or divisions, and most objectives are expressed in such generalities as "providing adequate police protection," budgeting has tended to be an exercise by various government departments of competing and negotiating for funds, rather than of getting necessary support to accomplish specific desired program goals.

In the Defense Department, at least, program budgeting has worked fairly well, primarily because it has been easier to make defense objectives and strategies clear and definite. It has likewise appeared to work well in such essentially program-oriented agencies as those dealing with water resources and housing programs. However, for most government agencies, one cannot say that program budgeting has been the great tool in practice that its logic would imply. There is even evidence that the once-great enthusiasm for program budgeting has faded and that it is now not very widely used. There are a number of reasons for this.

In the first place, many federal, state, and local executives, particularly at the middle and lower levels of management, do not understand the philosophy and theory of the technique; they have tended to be given directives and forms without really knowing what the system entails. A second major hurdle has been the lack of clearly defined goals; obviously no one can program, plan, and budget for an unknown or vague goal. Another difficulty is the lack of attention to planning premises; even with clear program goals, the program budgeter is in the dark without knowledge of critical planning premises. Another problem arises from the long tradition in government of doing line budgeting, and most legislators, accustomed to this kind, often will not tolerate program budgets unless they are recast in a line-item form. Also, many government budgetary divisions or staffs have been reluctant to make the change from their practice and procedures of annual budgets to longer-range program budgets. Other roadblocks include the fact that accounting data are seldom consistent with program budgeting, the lack of information in many areas to make meaningful cost effectiveness analyses, and the political problems of reorganizing government departments to improve concentration for program responsibility.

The problems in government have been such that there is some question whether program budgeting will ever be made to work as it should. But a tool that makes so much sense in an area where effective management is so important and so difficult should not be allowed to fall into disuse. Unfortunately, those who introduced it in most government agencies, or ordered its introduction, apparently failed to realize that much is required to make this technique successful. Attention must be given to teaching the system to managers and staffs at all levels who are expected to operate under it; even the nature of the system should be taught to those legislators who ultimately control taxpayers' purse strings. Also, emphasis should be placed first on developing verifiable program objectives and consistent planning premises; accounting systems need modification to fit programs, rather than line activities; and means should be developed for making possible better cost benefit analyses. Additionally, enthusiastic experts must realize that mathematical analyses often leave out critical intangibles; and administrators and legislators must have the perception and will to modify organization structures to fit programs.

All this might seem like a large order. And it is. But as a strategic start to develop sound government budgeting, it is worth it. Moreover, such features as the time-span of program budgeting and the use of cost benefit analysis are features that even business and other enterprises would do well to adopt.

MAKING TRADITIONAL BUDGETARY CONTROL WORK

If budgetary controls are to work well, managers must remember that they are designed only as tools and not to replace management, that they have limitations, and that they must be tailored to each job. Moreover, they are the tools of all managers and not alone of the budget administrator or the controller. The only persons who can administer budgets, since they are plans, are the managers responsible for budgeted programs. No successful budget program can be truly "directed" or "administered" by a budget director. This staff officer can assist in the preparation and use of budgets by the responsible managers, but, unless the entire company management is to be turned over to the budget officer, this person should not be given the job of making budget-commitment or expenditure decisions.

To be most effective, budget making and administration must receive the wholehearted support of top management. To establish an office of budget administrator by decree and then forget about it leads to haphazard budget making and to saddling subordinate managers with another procedure or set of papers to prepare. On the other hand, if top management actively supports budget making and grounds the company budget firmly in company plans, encourages divisions and departments to make and defend their budgets, and participates in this review, budgets encourage alert management throughout the organization.

Related to the participation of top management, another means of making budgets work is to make sure that all managers expected to administer and live under budgets have a part in their preparation. Real participation in budget making, rather than pseudoparticipation, is necessary. As one student of the subject found, most budget administrators and controllers recognize that participation is crucial to budget success, but too often in practice this amounts to pressured "acceptance."[2]

Although budgets do furnish a means of delegating authority without loss of control, there is danger that they will be so detailed and inflexible that little real authority is, in fact, delegated. Some executives even believe that the best budget to give managers is one that lumps all their allowable expenditures for a period of time into a single amount and then provide them complete freedom as to how these funds are to be spent in

[2]Chris Argyris, "Human Problems with Budgets," *Harvard Business Review*, vol. 31, no. 1, p. 108 (January 1953).

pursuance of the company's goals. This kind of decentralization has much to commend it, although better planning and control might be forthcoming, without centralizing authority unduly, by allowing the department manager real participation in budget making. It may also be well to allow department managers a reasonable degree of latitude in changing their budgets and in shifting funds, as long as they meet their *total* budgets.

One of the keys to making budgeting work is to develop and make available standards by which the manager's work can be translated into needs for work force, operating expenses, capital expenditures, space, and other resources. Many budgets fail for lack of such standards, and many upper-level managers hesitate to allow subordinates to submit budget plans for fear that there may be no logical basis for reviewing budget requests. With conversion factors available, superior managers can review such requests and justify their approval or disapproval of them. Moreover, by concentrating on the resources required to do a planned job, managers can base their request on what they need to have for meeting output goals and improving performance. They no longer must cope with arbitrary across-the-board budget cuts—a technique more frustrating to the superior than to the subordinate who, on the occasion of the next request, has the foresight to pad for the inevitable slice. In fact, it can be said that across-the-board cuts are the surest evidence of poor planning and loss of control.

Lastly, if budgetary control is to work, managers need ready information as to actual and forecast performance under budgets by *their* departments. This must be designed to show them how well *they* are doing, preferably before the fact; unfortunately, however, such information is usually not available until it is too late for the manager to avoid budget deviations.

TRADITIONAL NONBUDGETARY CONTROL DEVICES

There are, of course, many traditional control devices not connected with budgets, although some may be related to, and used with, budgetary controls. Among the more important of these are statistical data, special reports and analyses, analysis of break-even points, the operational audit, and personal observation.

Statistical Data

Statistical analyses of the innumerable aspects of a business operation and the clear presentation of statistical data, whether of a historical or forecast nature, are, of course, important to control. Some managers can readily interpret tabular statistical data, but most managers prefer presentation of the data on charts. Comprehensible presentation of statistical data, whether in tabular or chart form, is an art that requires imagination.

It is probably safe to say that most managers understand statistical data best when they are presented in chart form since trends and relationships are not easily seen, except by those accountants and statisticians accustomed to them, in the tabular sheets of computer printouts. Moreover, if data are to be meaningful, even when presented on charts, they should be presented in such a way that comparisons to some standards can be made. What is the significance of a 3 or 10 percent rise or fall in sales or costs? What was expected? What was the standard? How serious is the deviation? Who is responsible?

Moreover, since no manager can do anything about history, it is essential that statistical reports show trends so that the viewer can extrapolate where things are going. This means that most data, when presented on charts, should be made available in time averages to rule out variations due to accounting periods, seasonal factors, accounting adjustments, and other variations associated with given times. One of the simplest and best devices for giving perspective is the moving average. In the 12-month moving average, for example, 12 consecutive months, divided by 12, are used. The difference in clarity may be shown by the comparative data presented graphically in Figure 27.2.

Special Reports and Analyses

For control purposes, special reports and analyses help in particular problem areas. While routine accounting and statistical reports furnish a

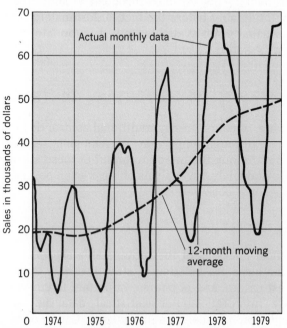

Figure 27.2 Actual monthly data versus 12-month moving average. Sales of company X, 1974–1979.

good share of necessary information, there are often areas in which they are inadequate. One successful manager of a complicated operation hired a small staff of trained analysts and gave them no assignment other than investigating and analyzing operations under his control. This group developed a surprising sense for detecting situations where things did not seem just right. Almost invariably, their investigation disclosed opportunities for cost improvement or better utilization of capital that no statistical chart would have disclosed.

It may be that some of the funds being spent for elaborate information programs could be more profitably spent for special analyses. Their very nonroutine nature can highlight the unusual and, in so doing, reveal places for significant improvement in efficiency. In routine search for pennies and accounting for them, opportunities for saving dollars may be overlooked.

Break-Even Point Analysis

An interesting control device is the break-even chart. This chart depicts the relationship of sales and expenses in such a way as to show at what volume revenues exactly cover expenses. At any lesser volume the company would suffer a loss, and at a greater volume it would enjoy a profit.

Figure 27.3, a simple form of such a chart, shows the level of revenues and expenses for each volume of sales and indicates that at $17 million of sales the company would break even. (The break-even point can be expressed as well in units of goods sold, percent of plant utilized, or

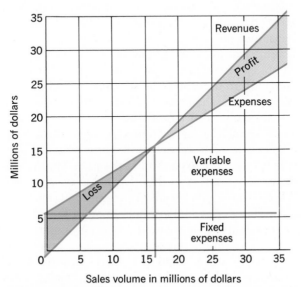

Figure 27.3 Break-even chart. The break-even point is reached when revenues equal expenditures.

similar terms.) It will be noted that the chart is similar to the variable budget chart (Figure 27.1), and break-even analysis is often confused with variable budgets. Although both use much the same kind of basic input data, the variable budget has as its purpose the control of cost, while the break-even chart has as its purpose the prediction of profit, which means that it must incorporate revenue data. Moreover, utilized for budgetary control, the variable budget must reflect organizational units, while the break-even chart is ordinarily used to determine profitability of a given course of action as compared with alternatives.

Break-even analysis is especially useful in planning and control because it emphasizes the marginal concept. Ratios, such as percentage of profits to sales, tend to overlook the impact of fixed costs, while the use of break-even points emphasizes the effects of additional sales or costs on profits. Likewise, in dramatizing the effect of additional expenses or incremental changes in volume, it brings to managers' attention the marginal results of their decisions.

Operational Audit

Another effective tool of managerial control is the internal audit, or, as it is now coming to be called, the operational audit. Operational auditing, in its broadest sense, is the regular and independent appraisal, by a staff of internal auditors, of the accounting, financial, and other operations of a business. Although often limited to the auditing of accounts, in its most useful aspect operational auditing involves appraisal of operations generally, weighing actual results in the light of planned results. Thus operational auditors, in addition to assuring themselves that accounts properly reflect the facts, also appraise policies, procedures, use of authority, quality of management, effectiveness of methods, special problems, and other phases of operations.

There is no persuasive reason why the concept of internal auditing should not be broadened in practice. Perhaps the only limiting factors are the ability of an enterprise to afford so broad an audit, the difficulty of obtaining people who can do a broad type of audit, and the very practical consideration that individuals may not like to be reported upon. While persons responsible for accounts and for the safeguarding of company assets have learned to accept audit, those who are responsible for far more valuable things—the execution of the plans, policies, and procedures of a company—have not so readily learned to accept the idea.

Where the broad form of operational audit has been employed constructively and where auditors operate as a group of internal management consultants with a view to helping operating managers, its acceptance has understandably been very high. In one large company, in which the emphasis of operational auditing is less on "snooping" and more on the "outside" look of the consultant, and where the auditors are conversant with management essentials and company policies and plans, line managers welcome the auditors and use them to improve operations. As one manufacturing manager informed the authors, the audit staff had immeasurably assisted him and his superintendents by advising on company policies and plans; raising questions about operations which had never been raised because of preoccupation with the work; and suggesting solutions for vexing managerial problems. Thus, the success of this program depended largely upon the concept of the task, the leadership given by the head auditor, and the quality of the auditors.

It is interesting that a recent survey of internal auditing practice in a total of 169 manufacturing companies and 115 nonmanufacturing companies found that the internal auditing function has been considerably broadened and professionally upgraded, and in many companies auditors have been given regular contacts with senior levels of management and even with audit committees of boards of directors.[3] It has also been disclosed that that the United States General Accounting Office, the congressional "watchdog" responsible for auditing government activities, has been in the forefront in defining and performing audits of broader scope.

As currently being practiced by the more managerially advanced business and nonbusiness enterprises, the core of the internal auditing group's responsibilities are the following:

1 Appraising financial and operational controls and promoting effective control at reasonable cost
2 Checking compliance with company policies and procedures
3 Safeguarding assets; preventing or detecting fraud and theft
4 Evaluating accuracy, reliability, and completeness of management data developed within the organization
5 Appraising the quality of management performance, including management's economy and efficiency in utilizing resources and effectiveness in achieving objectives
6 Recommending operating improvements

In almost every case where a broad form of internal auditing exists, it is made clear that the auditors do not have authority over activities being audited. These auditors are authorized only to function in information gathering and advisory capacities. Most also are directed to take up any deficiencies discovered in their audits with the immediate line manager involved before making any reports to top management.

Personal Observation

In any preoccupation with the devices of managerial control, one should never overlook the importance of control through personal observation.

---

[3]P. Macchlaverna, *Internal Auditing* (New York: The Conference Board, Inc., 1978).

Budgets, charts, reports, ratios, auditors' recommendations, and other devices are essential to control. But the manager who relies wholly on these devices and sits, so to speak, in a soundproof control room reading dials and manipulating levers can hardly expect to do a thorough job of control. Managers, after all, have the task of seeing that enterprise objectives are accomplished by *people*, and although many scientific devices aid in making sure that people are doing that which has been planned, the problem of control is still one of measuring activities of human beings. It is amazing how much information an experienced manager can get from personal observation, even from an occasional walk through a plant or an office.

IMPROVED INFORMATION TECHNOLOGY[4]

Electronic equipment permits fast and economical processing of huge amounts of data. While the machine cannot design relationships of data or originate basic information, it can, with proper programming, process data toward logical conclusions, classify them, and make them readily available for a manager's use. In fact, data do not become information until they are processed into a usable form that informs.

As an astute former business manager observed, "The reach of an executive is determined by the information system at his command."[5] Note that the information must be at a manager's command; he or she must be able to use it. A good information system must furnish knowledge that is material to the manager's job, that can be weighed against goals; it must be designed to determine how and where goals are being missed. It must furnish intelligible data. Above all, its success depends on managers who will listen and act intelligently.

Expanding Basic Data

The focus of attention on management information, coupled with its improved processing, has led to the reduction of long-known limitations. Managers for years have recognized that traditional accounting information, aimed at the calculation of profits, has been of limited value for control. Yet in many companies this has been virtually the only regularly collected and analyzed type of data. Managers have known that they need all kinds of nonaccounting information, including information on the social, economic, political, and technical climate in which plans must

---

[4]Although many writers use this term to apply to the entire field of information handling, including operations research and simulation techniques, it is used here in the sense of providing information most suitable to the manager for planning and control.
[5]Stahrl Edmunds, "The Reach of an Executive," *Harvard Business Review*, vol. 37, no. 1, pp. 87–96 (January–February 1959).

operate, as well as information on internal operations. And such information should include both qualitative and quantitative data.

While not nearly enough progress has been made in meeting these requirements, the computer, plus operations research, has led to enormous expansion of available managerial information. Problems in developing information inputs to fill existing gaps still exist, but now the gaps are apparent, and company after company is beginning to undertake research to make basic data available. One sees this especially in relation to data on marketing, competition, production and distribution, product costs, technological change and development, labor productivity, and goal accomplishment. The expansion of such information—required primarily for planning but also for control—is indicated for the marketing department of an oil company in Figure 27.4.

Sharpening Accounting Data by Direct Costing

The expansion of basic data is occurring not only in nonaccounting areas. Accountants themselves have made great strides in developing more useful data. The increasingly used technique of direct costing gives a means for revolutionizing managerial accounting.

Direct costing is simply recognition by accountants of certain basic economic principles. It is based on the fact that many costs, whether formerly classified as direct or indirect, vary in whole or in part with volume of output, while other costs (such as depreciation, advertising, general management salaries and expenses, and building rentals) are related to time. Thus, some costs are "direct" in the sense that they are based on producing as compared with not producing or on selling as compared with not selling. Other costs are "period" costs in that they are committed to provide capacity which expires with time.

In traditional, or absorption, accounting, direct costs include only the direct material used in a product and the factory or engineering labor directly working on the manufacture or engineering of a product. All indirect costs are then allocated to the product in accordance with some formula, utilizing as a base direct-labor-hours or costs, sales dollars, or some other measure. Also, in accounting for inventory, it has been customary to accumulate in inventory a pro rata allocation of factory burden, thus inventorying many costs really related to time rather than to volume of production. This practice can distort product costs and profits when inventories are rising or falling. When inventories of goods in process or finished goods are rising, for example, burden costs are absorbed—that is, carried into inventory—and cost performance and profits tend to be better than when those burden costs not related to volume are charged off in the period incurred.

Direct costing gives managers better information visibility in two major respects. From the standpoint of inventory and profit calculation, they know that period costs have been written off as incurred, that an

	Defects	Environment	Competition	Internal
Division and district expenses	No information on the total market for gasoline and other automotive products—its size, its location, its rate of growth, etc.	10-year industry sales by product, by marketing division, and where possible by trading area	10-year share-of-market reports by product, by division, and where possible, by trading area	5-year sales and realizations by product, by division, by class of trade
	No information on competitors—what they are doing, where, and how well	10-year car registration records by state and trading area (where possible)	Special price reports intended to show (a) competitor's price strategy and (b) areas of the country classified by the nature of price conditions—stable, volatile, strong, weak, etc.	Division and district expenses per gallon (without allocations of headquarters expenses)
Sales volume by product for divisions and districts	Marketing "profit and loss" concept encouraged faulty planning because of arbitrary transfer prices	10-year population records by trading area		Marketing "net back" statements by product, by division, by district, and by bulk plant (realizations less expenses)
	No information that discloses the company's marketing strengths and weaknesses by class of trade, for example, company-owned stations, independent dealers, distributors, etc.	10-year record of new road-mile construction by state and trading area (where possible)	5-year record of new station construction, by division and trading area	"Laid-down" costs by product, by terminal and bulk plant
		5-year projection of 100 fastest growing trading areas in country—by percentage and absolute numbers	5-year summary of new refinery, terminal, and bulk plant construction by competition	Frequency distribution studies of gasoline sales by size or retail station, by division and district
Marketing department profit and loss	Marketing expense information misleading because of allocations of headquarters overhead	5-year projection of car registration by state and trading area (where possible)	Analysis of 100 largest and 100 fastest growing markets (trading areas) showing leading competitors in terms of volume, market share, laid-down costs, facilities, construction, acquisitions activity, etc.	Share of company's total sales by product for each state
	Inadequate data on size "mix" of stations, for example, number and percentage of stations selling different volumes of gasoline	Report on federal road-building program		5-year report of number of stations by type (owned, leased, etc.) by division and district
Capital budgets by division for 5 years	Inadequate data on the sales performance of newly built or acquired stations	5-year report (and 5-year projection) on composition of country's automobile population by size, weight, horsepower, etc. for each division	Special reports on key market developments, for example, rebrander activity, additional qualities of gasoline, multiple octane pumps, etc.	5-year report of capital budgets by division and district (amounts authorized and spent)

Purpose (Environment): to provide an overall picture of the market, its composition, its size, its location, significant trends affecting any of these factors, etc.

Purpose (Competition): to identify who competitors are, how well they've been doing, and the likely direction of their future efforts

Purpose (Internal): to assess the company strengths and weaknesses, thus permitting a correlation between the company's capabilities and the opportunities of the market place

Figure 27.4 Comparative analysis of marketing planning information needed by an oil company. [D. R. Daniel, "Management Information Crisis," Harvard Business Review, *vol. 39, no. 5, p. 118 (September–October, 1961). Reproduced by permission.*]

inventory does not include the "air" of costs not related to product volume, and that profits are more real when they reflect the write-off of costs related to time. From the standpoint of cost analysis of individual products or projects, a manager can now look at cost in more nearly marginal terms. If direct costing is thoroughly done, the manager can see whether the product is covering the costs ascribable to volume and how much remains as a contribution to period costs and profits. Thus, a product might show a loss by the customary formula of taking direct labor and material and allocating burden plus selling and administrative costs; but the same product may very well show a handsome contribution to period costs and profits by the direct-costing method.

Even though direct costing is difficult to put into effect and faces some resistance, particularly from traditional accountants and tax authorities, it offers managers a number of advantages.[6] Direct costing was first suggested in 1936.[7] It was not until 1947 that a major company, the Pittsburgh Plate Glass Company, started using it. Even as late as 1953 only seventeen companies using it could be found by the National Association of Accountants, but by 1962, *Business Week* estimated, some 250 companies had adopted direct costing and more were converting to it. Experience with companies using direct costing has convinced the authors that this trend has continued and may accelerate in the future. In fact, there is logic in believing that direct costing should become the standard managerial accounting in the future.

In view of the great potential of direct costing for managerial planning and control purposes, since it gives managers better visibility of their operations, it is disquieting to find accounting audit firms reluctant to allow its use for stockholder reporting and to find the tax authorities opposed to its use for tax purposes. Although the federal Internal Revenue Service has permitted use of direct costing by many companies, it took the position late in 1974 that it would no longer do so. This unfortunate attitude was apparently dictated by the fear of loss of tax revenue if most companies switched to direct costing and wrote off a portion of their inventories, thus reducing earnings and taxes in the changeover year as a result. However, intelligent managers will realize that tax authority rulings are made for the purpose of collecting taxes and not for running a business. As a result, such managers will probably continue to follow direct-costing principles for their internal managerial control purposes.

[6]For an excellent analysis of the advantages and disadvantages of direct costing, see Willmar Wright and Felix T. Kollaritsch, "Direct Costing, Pro and Con," *The Controller*, vol. 30, no. 7, pp. 322ff. (July 1962). See also W. Wright, *Direct Standard Costs for Decision Making and Control* (New York: McGraw-Hill Book Company, 1962).

[7]These and the following data are from "Direct Costing to the Rescue," *Business Week*, pp. 45–48 (March 24, 1962).

Managers who have experienced the impact of better and faster data processing are justly concerned with the danger of information indigestion. Their appetite for figures whetted, the data originators and processors are turning out material at an almost frightening rate. Managers are complaining of being buried under printouts, reports, projections, and forecasts which they do not have time to read or cannot understand or which do not fill their particular needs.

Control techniques or information which are not properly aimed at the person and his or her job, or which are of a kind managers cannot or will not understand, will not work. As one experienced executive declared:

> If a little learning is a dangerous thing, too much—that is, knowledge not put to good use—can be a costly waste. Too many undigested facts can turn a man of action into a Hamlet, paralyzed by indecision. Like the raw materials of industry, information must be converted into something. What is required is a discriminating selection which can deliver relevant data in a form usable at the echelon of decision. The research study that collects dust on shelves may well have merit; the fault is failure to relate its data to the problem it was designed to solve.
>
> Information may involve anything from the most minute and finite to the universal. Processing information today calls not only for distinguishing the forest from the trees, but distinguishing leaves and chlorophyll—while still not losing sight of the forest.[8]

To combat information indigestion, it is necessary to design information suited for special use at all levels and in all functions of management. Special design of information may seem to be in opposition to the mass-production techniques and economies of the electronic computer, but computer experts claim this is not so. They insist that it is up to managers to ask for what they need to carry on their tasks of planning and control. Within limits of basic data input availability, desired information can almost invariably be designed for individual managers by proper programming. All the more modern machines permit tailoring this information by merely inserting appropriate cards or tape. So far as the machine is concerned, even changes in desired information outputs may be easily made. However, it should not be forgotten that small changes in information desired can mean considerable changes in a program, and programmers understandably complain that "small changes" can amount to a considerable cost in time and money. The important point to bear in

[8]Marion Harper, Jr., "A New Profession to Aid Management," Charles Coolidge Parlin Memorial Lecture, p. 13 (Philadelphia: Philadelphia Chapter, American Marketing Association, 1960).

mind is that it is not the computer that causes a deluge of data and a dearth of information, nor is it the computer specialists; the basic problem is that information users—operating managers—often do not know what they want.

Intelligence Services

Attempts are being made to solve the dilemma posed by managers who need special digested and digestible information and by information processors who do not know what managers require. One such attempt consists of establishing in a company an intelligence service and developing a new profession of intelligence experts. The service would be manned by experts who would know (or find out) what information managers need and who would know how to digest and interpret such information for managerial use.

This approach to making the new mass of information more usable has much to commend it, and a number of companies have already adopted it. However, few have gone so far as to design information for individual managers down the line of organization as well as at the top. Under such names as "administrative services" or "management analyses and services," many companies are recognizing that some sort of information design service is necessary if expansion of basic data is to result in useful information.

Some companies feel that this service should be centralized, and in many cases it can be. However, despite the efficiencies of a central department, doubt exists as to whether in medium-large and large companies centralization can satisfactorily cater to *all* managers or whether a number of such departments might understandably serve best those to whom they immediately report. It appears that the future will see multiple intelligence services located throughout an organization so that they can be more responsive to various information needs. However, the dispersal of such services need not mean that they cannot be served by a central data bank and processing facility.

Information Systems

With the increasing use of the computer, a great deal of attention has been given to the development of information systems. This is a recognition of the fact that many items of input data may be useful for a number of different outputs. Thus, input data on inventory are useful for different kinds of reports, including those to accounting for asset recording, to purchasing for reorder action, to production for planning assembly operations, and to sales for availability of product. Payroll data, likewise, are useful for accounting, labor cost control and production, labor turnover, and other concerns of managers.

It is consequently obvious that data should not be independently

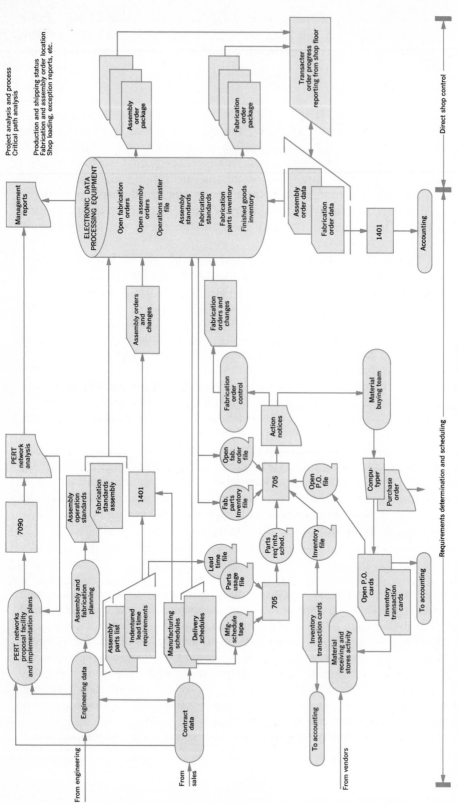

Figure 27.5 Integrated data processing and manufacturing control information flow. This chart shows how basic information from engineering, customers (sales), and vendors is combined with internal manufacturing standards and operational requirements to develop a complete and integrated system of manufacturing control information. This not only furnishes information required for buying, fabricating, assembling, inventorying, and accounting but also provides needed management reports from the same source. [*J. B. Friauf, Advanced Techniques for Manufacturing Control (Instrument Society of America, Conference Reprint 187-LA61 (1961).*].

gathered for special purposes, but rather the same basic input data should be made available for multiple end uses. Some data are developed in large part as a kind of by-product from the operation of procedures designed to get something done, such as material flow in production or computation of the labor payroll. Likewise, many procedures that are designed primarily to furnish data to guide managers in their decisions, such as inventory procedures, can be useful to accurate accounting and financial planning and for procurement decisions.

As a consequence of these multiple uses of data and the demands of economy in data development and processing, specialists in this area, as well as managers, should seek to view and utilize data processing and information flow as a complete system. This becomes particularly urgent if the almost incredible conclusion of one information specialist is even somewhat true; that "at least 50 percent of the cost of running our economy is information cost."[9]

Anyone who looks at the tremendous information requirements of managerial and nonmanagerial personnel in a typical enterprise and at the tremendous mass of input data necessary to produce this information is appalled at the possibility of tying all this into a single system. Perhaps the best approach is that recommended by Dearden: to recognize that we are dealing, in the typical company, with three major information systems and many minor systems.[10]

Dearden points out that the three major information systems typically found are financial, personnel, and logistics. The basis of the financial system is the flow of money through a company. The personnel information system has to do with the flow of data concerning people. The logistics system applies to those data reflecting the physical flow of goods through an enterprise. Other information systems identified by Dearden are those dealing with marketing, research and development, strategic planning, and executive compensation. While there are definitely interrelationships between all these, the interfaces are particularly noteworthy between financial, personnel, and logistics information systems.

While it is understandable that alert managers are eager to perfect information and utilize the computer for the improvement of managing, no one should overlook the fundamental problem of information as the authors of this book see it. Unless managers actively embrace the approach of tailored controls by deciding what end product they need for effective management, no information system can be successful. In the computer, systems analysis, and programming of data conversion, we have what has been referred to as an automated factory. And what has been often done is to pick up such raw materials as may be left lying around in the form of available data, put them in this automated factory,

---

[9]A. M. McDonough, *Information Economics and Management Systems* (New York: McGraw-Hill Book Company, 1963), p. 5. While the authors believe the cost is great, their own estimate would more nearly be 20 percent.

[10]J. Dearden, "How to Organize Information Systems," *Harvard Business Review*, vol. 43, no. 2, pp. 65–73 (March–April 1965).

and then wonder why the end product is unsatisfactory. Managers would never follow this process in manufacturing a product for sale. Instead, they would design the end product and work back through the production system to determine what raw materials were required. Unless this approach to management information is more thoroughly and rigorously followed, all the systems and hardware that experts can design will never solve the problem.

PROCEDURES PLANNING AND CONTROL

Procedures present a rewarding area of planning and control to which a systems approach can be applied. The extraordinary complexity of procedures and their inflexible channeling of action were discussed in relation to types of plans in Chapter 6. They are desirable tools for efficiently getting things done in a given way or for control when it is necessary not to deviate from this way, but procedures can also make for departmental rigidity that thwarts innovation and response to change. Although they *should* be designed to implement plans and to respond to change, they too often are not.

Effective planning and control of procedures depend on recognizing that they are inherently systems. Procedures normally extend into various departments, and it is a rare procedure which does not concern itself with more than two. This increases the importance of their control. Accounting departments, for example, tend to regard their procedures as concerned purely with their function, and yet a simple payroll or expense account procedure reaches into every nook and cranny of the company and affects many nonaccounting activities. Personnel, purchasing, and other functional departmental procedures do likewise.

How Procedures Get out of Control

Procedures often get out of control because of the specialized approach of each organization function in setting them up for its particular operation. Accounting procedures may conflict with or overlap purchasing procedures, differ slightly from personnel procedures, and somewhat duplicate sales department procedures. Duplication, overlapping, and conflict are usually elusive and partial; there is rarely either complete duplication or clear disagreement. Commonly, different forms and records are called for, though they use the same subject matter.

In addition, procedures can be expensive. Modern enterprise has created a sensational increase in the number of people doing paperwork. As was pointed out by Neuschel,[11] since 1870 the number of clerical personnel in the nation has increased 100 times, while the total number of

[11]R. F. Neuschel, *Management by System* (New York: McGraw-Hill Book Company, 1960), p. 3. It should be pointed out, of course, that not all this increase in clerical work force can be ascribed to procedures, but unquestionably most has.

gainfully employed increased 5 times; and it was estimated that in 1960, when the nation's employed work force numbered 67 million, nearly 10 million were clerical workers. Data for more recent years show that clerical workers have continued to expand faster than total people employed. In 1976 nearly 15.6 million out of 87 million civilian employees were clerical workers and by 1985 are forecast to be 20 million out of 101 million.[12]

Procedures also get out of control when managers try to use them to solve problems instead of solving the problems through better policies, clearer delegations, or improved direction. Then again, many procedures are instituted to correct a mistake which might never be made again. In one case, a division head ordered development of a complete system of procedures to prevent duplicating one serious customer complaint. This had happened only once. A clear policy statement, simple routing of complaints, and assigning the handling of complaints to the service manager would have taken care of the situation and avoided any recurrence.

Procedures also evade control by becoming obsolete, either because they are not kept up to date or because failure to police them permits deviations in practice. Moreover, procedures have a way of becoming customs, ingrained in departments and in individuals who have a stubborn resistance to change. And managers find it expedient to impose new procedures on the old, a haphazard practice.

Finally, a major reason why procedures get out of control is that the manager is not clear as to what procedures should do, how much they cost, when they are duplicated, how to overhaul them, and how to control them. And to top all this, managers often fail to obtain the interest and support of top managers in the tedious and unromantic planning and control of procedures.

Guidelines

In planning and control of procedures, managers may find it advantageous to follow these guidlines.

Minimize procedures   The first and perhaps most important guideline for the manager is to limit procedures to those which are clearly called for. The costs of procedures in paper handling, stifled thinking, delay, and lack of responsiveness to change are such as to make a concerned manager think twice before initiating them. In other words, managers must weigh the potential gain in money or necessary control against the disadvantages and costs.

Make sure they are plans   Since procedures are plans, they must be designed to reflect and help accomplish enterprise (not just departmental)

[12]H. Axel (ed.), *A Guide to Consumer Markets* (New York: The Conference Board, Inc., 1977), pp. 94–95.

objectives and policies. Have they been planned? If they are necessary, are they designed effectively and efficiently to accomplish plans? For example, a procedure to handle orders for spare parts or repair defective parts should expedite a job so as to meet customer service standards without undue delay.

Analyze them Procedures should be carefully analyzed to assure a minimum of duplication, overlapping, and conflict. To do this, the procedures must be visualized. This, in turn, necessitates mapping them with their various steps identified and interrelated. That this is not always easy is exemplifed by a defense material procurement procedure which, when charted, took a piece of paper 27 feet long and involved over 250 related required actions!

Recognize procedures as systems One of the failures of procedure design is to neglect to regard them as systems. Any given procedure, whether it specifies the handling of payroll, procurement, inventory planning and control, or other of many uses, is in itself a system of interrelated activities normally in a network rather than a pure linear form. Likewise, various procedures with special purposes are usually interrelated. Accounting procedures, for example, tend to be intertwined with personnel, purchasing, and other procedures. Therefore, groups of procedures are usually interrelated systems.

   The problem of procedures planning and control is not likely to be solved unless their complex systemic structure is recognized. The design and improvement of procedures calls for the same kind of analytical talent so readily applied to the design of a complex instrument or machine. But seldom do companies or any other kind of organization give procedures planning and control this kind of treatment or bring to bear on them the same high level of engineering and design talent they give to products. It is obvious that this should be done, particularly when one considers the cost in money, time, and organization friction that they are responsible for.

Estimate their cost The analysis of a procedure should include an estimate of what its operation will cost. While some costs cannot be ascertained, such as the cost of possible frustration to those involved, an estimate may bring into sharper focus the answer to the question, Is this procedure worthwhile?

Police their operation To be sure that procedures are needed and are doing the job intended, they must be policed. This requires three steps: First, knowledge of procedures must be made available in manual or other form to those who must follow them. Second, employees must be taught how to operate under them and, ideally, why the procedures are necessary and what purpose they are designed to serve. Third, there must be machinery to assure that people do understand and are employing up-to-date procedures and that the procedures are doing the job intended. This step involves constructive auditing.

Procedures Analysis and Electronic Data Processing

An encouraging consequence of present systems and procedures planning and the analysis of procedures as systems is that they are often programmed on electronic data processing (EDP) equipment. However, there remains the danger that the systems and procedures expert will become so enamored of programming as to forget that electronic automation of procedures can reflect the system of procedures only as it exists.

Despite this danger, EDP has stimulated broad analysis and improvement of procedures. Because the process of putting a personnel, accounting, or purchasing procedure on a machine is so expensive as well as awe-inspiring, a strong effort is normally made to assure that the procedure is workable and clear before it is automated. Moreover, the systems approach of the programmer forces an orderly approach to procedure analysis. Since, at the very least, a procedure cannot be put on a machine without having been mapped, the very process of mapping often shows up the existence of overlapping and the need for simplification, as well as the means of achieving it.

So far, analyzing and rationalizing procedures for EDP have mainly brought the subject to the surface and have unearthed the need for experts in this kind of planning and control. The universities are not doing much about training such experts. One wonders whether, if some of the intelligence and effort now applied to designing sophisticated instruments were applied to the more mundane problems of procedures analysis, the improvement of enterprise efficiency would not be vastly accelerated. The need is great for experts who understand the nature of procedures as a management tool and their importance in accomplishing enterprise objectives. Systems and procedures analysis—like improved information technology—is high-level, difficult, and challenging work. It should be treated as such.

OPERATIONS RESEARCH FOR CONTROL

As was made clear from the discussion of operations research in Chapter 9, this involves an analysis of logical relationships. It is thus a study of systems so conceptualized as to show the way to manipulating variables in order to optimize some desired goal. It was also pointed out that the best use of operations research occurs when inputs are quantifiable, but that the method can be useful even when variables are little more than broad approximations. Operations research, therefore, has shown its greatest promise in logistics systems, because in areas involving labor input and the flow of materials, the variables can be credibly quantified. Consequently, operations research has proceeded ·from subsystem areas, such as production and inventory, and by linking these subsytems has gone on to planning and control of the broader field of production and distribution combined.

Operations Research for Inventory Control

Although space does not permit a discussion of the application of operations research to all types of production or distribution subsystems, and considerable attention was given to operations research in Chapter 9, its early application to inventory control is selected as an example here. Perhaps in the history of operations research more attention has been directed to inventory control than to any other practical area in business.

If we wished to see the essential systems relationships as a little "black box" without going into detailed mathematics, we would depict them as is done in Figure 27.6.

Or, if these conceptual relationships were placed into one of the simpler mathematical forms covering approximately the system in Figure 27.6 it might look something like this:

$$Q = \sqrt{\frac{2R[S + E(s)]}{I}}$$

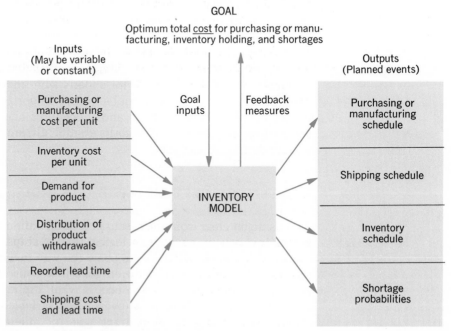

GOAL

Optimum total <u>cost</u> for purchasing or manufacturing, inventory holding, and shortages

Inputs
(May be variable or constant)

Outputs
(Planned events)

Purchasing or manufacturing cost per unit

Goal inputs

Feedback measures

Purchasing or manufacturing schedule

Inventory cost per unit

Demand for product

INVENTORY MODEL

Shipping schedule

Distribution of product withdrawals

Inventory schedule

Reorder lead time

Shipping cost and lead time

Shortage probabilities

Figure 27.6 Inventory control model.

where Q = reorder quantity
          R = sales requirement per year
          S = setup cost (per order)
          I = interest and carrying cost, including storage, all ex-
                pressed per piece, per year
       $E(s)$ = expected cost of stockouts per order cycle

and where $E(s)$ is defined by this equation:

$$E(s) = \pi \sum_{u = r + 1}^{u_{max}} (u - r)p(u)$$

where u = usage during any lead time
       $p(u)$ = probability of usage greater than u
          r = reorder point in units
          u = expected usage during lead time
          π = stockout cost per unit demanded but not available

As can be seen, even the simple "black box" representation of a subsystem of control can be very complex. Each of the inputs can be variable or constant. Each can be discrete or continuous, and the rate of distribution over time can be variable or constant. Moreover, as this is a planning model, feedback of information—to make sure the model attains the goals desired—should be added to make it a planning *and* control system.

With all its complexities, the model illustrates several things. It forces consideration of the goals desired and of the need for placing definite values on outputs and inputs. It also furnishes a manager with the basis for plans and with standards by which to measure performance. However, with all its advantages, this is a subsystem and does not incorporate other subsystems, such as production planning, distribution planning, and sales planning.

Distribution Logistics

One of the most exciting and profit-promising ways of using systems logistics in planning and control is in the expansion of inventory control to include other factors, referred to here as "distribution logistics." This was noted as a planning model above in Chapter 9. In its most advanced form, currently in operation in a few companies, this treats the entire logistics of a business—from sales forecast through purchase and process-ing of material and inventorying to shipping finished goods—as a single system. The goal is usually to optimize the total costs of the system in operation, while furnishing a desired level of customer service and meeting certain constraints, such as financially limited inventory levels. This gathers into one system a large mass of relationships and informa-tion, so as to optimize the whole. In doing so, it is entirely possible that transportation, manufacturing, or any other single area of cost will not be optimized, but the total cost of materials management will be.

Schematically, a distribution logistics system might appear as shown in Chapter 9 in Figure 9.3. This model, represented by a black box, would be expressed mathematically as an operating system.

This figure shows the relationships between the goal desired, the input variables and limits, and the expected outputs. The company represented by this model is a consumer goods company with a fairly broad line of products, a number of plants (some producing the whole line, others producing only part of the line), a number of finished-goods warehouses, and national distribution to grocery chains and wholesalers. It will be noted that customer service standards (that is, maximum time permitted between receipt and shipment of an order) are here inserted as a constraining input.

A fully developed distribution logistics system is a fine instrument of planning and control. By optimizing *total* costs in a broad area of operation, the system might show it would be cheaper to use more expensive transportation on occasion rather than to carry high inventories. Or it might show that production at less than economic order quantities would be justified in order to get better transportation or warehousing utilization or to meet customer service standards with limited inventories.

To be sure, even such a broad distribution logistics system is not a total system of a business enterprise, but it does apply to a considerable part of the total business operation. And it applies to those parts where the inputs can be quantified with a reasonable degree of accuracy.

Operations Control Systems

Another interesting type of planning and control system is one designed to integrate information on virtually an instantaneous basis, thereby cutting down considerably the delays usually impeding effective control. With development of the necessary hardware and software, it is now possible for virtually any measurable data to be reported as events occur. Systems are available to provide for fast and systematic collection of data bearing on a total operation, for keeping these data readily available, and for reporting without delay the status of any of thousands of projects at any instant. They are thus primarily information systems designed to improve planning and control.

Applied widely now only to the complex of purchasing, storing, manufacturing, and shipping, those systems operate through dispatch stations, widely dispersed in a plant, and input centers, also located throughout the plant. At the dispatch centers, events are recorded as they occur and the information is dispatched immediately to a computer. For example, when a supervisor finishes an assigned task on the assembly of a product, the work-order timecard is put into a transactor which electrically transmits to a computer the information that item x has passed through a certain process, has accumulated y hours of labor, and other pertinent data. The input centers are equipped automatically to originate, from programmed instructions, purchase orders, shop orders, and other authorizations. These data are likewise fed into the computer to be used as standards against which the actual operations, transmitted from the dispatch stations, may be compared.

In addition to fast entry, comparison, and retrieval of information, such an integrated operations control system furnishes needed information for planning programs in such areas as purchasing, production, and inventory control. Moreover, it permits almost instantaneous comparison of results with plans, pinpointing where they differ, and provides a regular (daily or more often, if needed) system of reports on items behind schedule or costs running above budget.

Other planning, control, and information systems have been developed to reflect quickly the interaction between production and distribution operations and such key financial measures as costs, profit, and cash flow. For example, Boulden and Buffa have described the development in a few companies of real-time corporate models that give operating managers virtually instant analysis of such "what-if" questions as the effects of reducing or increasing output, reduction in demand, the sensitivity of the system to labor cost increases, price changes, and new equipment additions.[13] To be sure, system models, simulating actual operations and their impact on financial factors, are primarily planning tools. But so are most control techniques. However, by making possible exceptionally quick responses to the many "what-if" questions of operating managers, the time elapsed in correcting for deviations from plans can be greatly reduced, and control materially improved.

These and the other systems sketched here—as well as many more which use the technology of science and fast computation—clearly promise to hasten the day when planning can be more precise and control more effective. The drawback is not the cost but, rather, the failure of managers to appreciate the potential. They are often unwilling to put in the mental effort to conceptualize the system and its relationships or to see that someone in the organization does so. But the principal deficiency of even real-time information, as pointed out in Chapter 26, can never make for adequate controls because of the time deficiencies in any feedback system.

TIME-EVENT NETWORK ANALYSES

One of the interesting planning and control techniques is a time-event network analysis called Program Evaluation and Review Tech-

---

[13]See J. B. Boulden and E. S. Buffa, "Corporate Models: On-Line Real-Time Systems," *Harvard Business Review*, vol. 48, no. 4, pp. 65–83 (July–August 1970). The detailed applications of such a system to a plywood and a steel operation are shown in this article.

nique (PERT). There have also been other techniques designed to watch how the parts of a program fit together during the passage of time and events.

The first of these were the chart systems developed by Henry L. Gantt early in the twentieth century and culminating in the bar chart bearing his name. Although simple in concept, this chart, showing time relationships between "events" of a production program, has been regarded as revolutionary in management. What Gantt recognized was that total program goals should be regarded as a series of interrelated derivative plans (or events) that people can comprehend and follow. The most important developments of such control reflect this simple principle and also such basic principles of control as picking out the more critical or strategic elements of a plan to watch carefully.

As the result of developing further techniques from the principles of the Gantt chart, and with better appreciation of the network nature of programs, "milepost" or "milestone" budgeting and PERT have been devised in recent years, contributing much to better control, particularly of research and development.

Milestone Budgeting

Used by many companies in recent years in controlling engineering and development, milepost or milestone budgeting breaks a project down into controllable pieces and then carefully follows them. As was pointed out in the discussion of planning, even relatively simple projects contain a network of subsidiary plans or projects. In this approach to control, milestones are defined as identifiable segments. When accomplishment of a given segment occurs, cost or other results can be determined.

Engineering control was long hampered because few people knew how much progress was being made on a project. The common device of estimating completion time, with planned inputs of labor and materials, runs into the difficulty that, although accurate records of personnel and material costs can be kept, estimates of percentage of completion tend to reach 85 or 90 percent and stay there, while time and costs continue.

The best way to plan and control an engineering project is to break it down into a number of determinable events, for example, completion of preliminary drawings, a "breadboard" model, a package design, a packaged prototype, and production design. Or a project might be broken down vertically into subprojects—for example, the design of a circuit, a motor, a driving mechanism, a sensing device, a signal feedback device, and similar components—that can be designed, individually, in a time sequence, to be ready when needed. Milestone budgeting allows managers to see a complex program in its simpler parts, thereby giving them some control through knowing whether it is succeeding or failing. The transition from the Gantt chart to PERT is shown in Figure 27.7.

Developed by the Special Projects Office of the U.S. Navy,[14] PERT was first formally applied to the planning and control of the Polaris Weapon

[14]But also separately developed as the Critical Path Method by engineers at the Du Pont Company at virtually the same time. Only PERT is discussed here because the Critical Path Method, although different in some respects, utilizes the same basic principles.

I. GANTT CHART

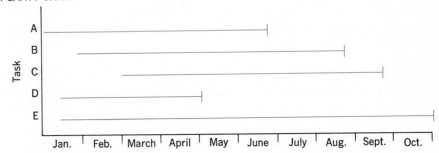

II. GANTT WITH MILESTONES

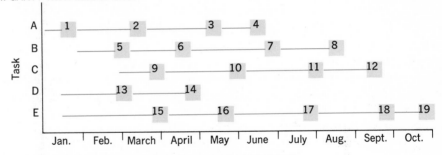

III. GANTT WITH MILESTONES AND NETWORK OF MILESTONES

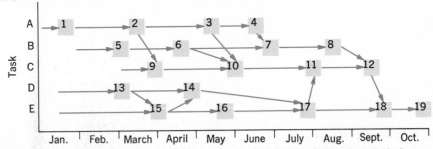

Figure 27.7 Transition from a Gantt chart to PERT. The Gantt chart in *I* above shows the scheduled time of accomplishing a task, such as procurement (Task A), and the related schedules of doing other tasks, such as manufacture of parts (Task B). When each of these tasks is broken down into milestones, such as the preparation of purchase specifications (Task A-1), and then network relationships between the milestones of each task to those of other tasks are worked out, the result is the basic elements of a PERT chart.

System in 1958 and worked well in expediting the successful completion of that program. For a number of years it was so enthusiastically received by the armed services that it became virtually a required tool for major contractors and subcontractors in the armament and space industry. Although PERT is no longer much heard of in defense and space contracts, for reasons that will be noted presently, its network fundamentals are still essential tools of planning and control. Moreover, in a host of nongovernmental applications, including construction, engineering and tooling projects, and even the scheduling of activities to get out monthly financial reports, PERT or its companion network technique, CPM (Critical Path Method), is widely and profitably used.

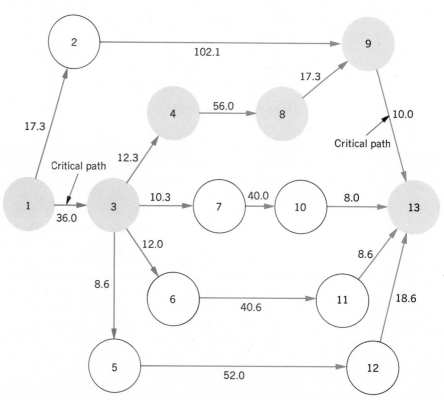

Figure 27.8 PERT flow chart: major production of an airplane. Events (each major milestone of progress) are: 1—program go-ahead; 2—initiate engine procurement; 3—complete plans and specifications; 4—complete fuselage drawings; 5—submit GFAE requirements; 6—award tail assembly subcontract; 7—award wings subcontract; 8—complete manufacture of fuselage; 9—complete assembly of fuselage-engine; 10—receive wings from subcontractor; 11—receive tail assembly from subcontractor; 12—receive GFAE; 13—complete aircraft. (*Note:* GFAE is government-furnished airplane equipment.)

Major features   In a sense, PERT is a variation of milestone budgeting. It uses a time-event network analysis, as shown in Figure 27.8. This very simple example illustrates the basic nature of PERT. Each circle represents an event—a subsidiary plan whose completion can be measured at a given time. Each arrow represents an activity—the time-consuming element of a program, the effort that must be made between events; "activity time" is the elapsed time required to accomplish an event.

In this example only a single time is shown, but in the original PERT program there were three time estimates: "optimistic" time, an estimate of time required if everything goes exceptionally well; "most likely" time, an estimate of what the project engineer really believes necessary to do the job; and "pessimistic" time, an estimate based on the assumption that any logically conceivable bad luck—other than a major disaster—will be encountered. These estimates are often included in PERT because it is very difficult, in many engineering and development projects, to estimate time accurately. Also, it is believed that engineers will be willing to make a variety of estimates and will do their level best to beat the pessimistic estimate. When several estimates are made, they are usually averaged, with special weight given to the most likely estimate, and a single estimate then used.

The next step is to compute the "critical path," that sequence of events which takes the longest time and which involves, therefore, the least slack time. In Figure 27.8, the critical path is indicated as from events 1-3-4-8-9-13. Over this path, the activity time for the entire sequence of events is 131.6 weeks; if promised delivery is in 135 weeks, even this critical path would have a slack of 3.4 weeks. Some of the other paths are almost as long as the critical path. For example, the path 1-2-9-13 is 129.4 weeks. This is not unusual in PERT charts, and it is customary to identify several critical paths in order of importance. Although the critical path has a way of changing, as key events are delayed on other parts of the program, identifying it at all times makes possible close watching of this particular sequence of events to ensure that the total program will be on schedule.

Typical PERT analyses run into hundreds or thousands of events. Even though smaller PERT analyses—including the input of event accomplishment and the frequent calculation of critical path—can be done manually, it is estimated that when upward of approximately 700 events are involved, it is virtually impossible to handle the calculations without an electronic computer.[15]

It is customary to summarize very large and complex time-event networks by subnetworks and to prepare the summarized network for top

---

[15]As estimated by Ivars Avots, "The Management Side of PERT," *California Management Review*, vol. 4, no. 2, pp. 16–27 (Winter 1962). Most experts would estimate far fewer than 700 events.

management consideration. Thus, the top management network might include some forty or fifty major events, each a summary of a number of subsidiary events. In fact, it is possible to group, or to break down, events so as to have a PERT network appropriate to every level of management.

Strengths and weaknesses There are five strong advantages of PERT. First, it forces managers to plan, because it is impossible to make a time-event analysis without planning and seeing how the pieces fit together. Second, it forces planning all down the line, because each subordinate manager must plan the event for which he or she is responsible. Third, it concentrates attention on critical elements that may need correction. Fourth, it makes possible a kind of feedforward control; a delay will affect succeeding events, and possibly the whole project, unless the manager can somehow make up the time by shortening that of some action in the future. Fifth, the network system with its subsystems makes possible aiming of reports and pressure for action at the right spot and level in the organization structure at the right time.

PERT also has certain limitations. Because of the importance of activity time to its operation, it cannot be useful when a program is nebulous and no reasonable "guesstimates" of schedule can be made; even here, however, insurance can be "bought" by such devices as putting two or more teams to work on an event when costs permit. PERT is also not practicable for routine planning of recurring events, such as mass production; while it could be used here, once a repetitive sequence of events is clearly worked out, so elaborate a continuing control is not required. A major disadvantage of PERT has been its emphasis on time only, not costs. While this is suitable for programs where time is of the essence or where, as so often is the case, time and costs have a close direct relationship, the tool is more useful when considerations other than time are introduced.

PERT/COST The above description of PERT is called PERT/TIME and has led logically to the development of PERT/COST, with the application of costs to activities in the PERT network. While this would appear to be an easy transition, a number of complications exist. In the first place, the PERT network must be complete enough to reflect any activity which incurs cost. In the second place, in any complex project, the number of events is so great that it becomes difficult and expensive to establish job center accounts for each activity. As a result, in practice, the events are grouped in what are known as work packages for purposes of accumulating costs. A third complication is one of working into the cost structure a number of overhead costs not directly related to an activity or even a work package. For example, the cost of overall project management would be one extending over the entire network, while the cost of project direction for a portion of the network would be spread over that series of events. Likewise, the progress of a program against the time budget is not likely to be the same as against a cost budget.

There is no question that PERT/COST has added considerably to the managerial effectiveness of the PERT approach to planning and control. But it is also true, particularly in many large programs such as those contracted for by the Department of Defense, that the complexity of the PERT system has been greatly increased by introducing costs.

In recent years, little has been heard in military and aerospace contracts or companies about PERT, although PERT or CPM are widely used in many operations, particularly in construction projects. In a survey made a few years ago by one of the authors, he was surprised to find out that many companies were keeping network plans and information but that they were not being used for actual control of operations. What had apparently happened to PERT and CPM, in these industries at least, is what happens to so many good management techniques. The specialists in the field promise too much, and users become disillusioned. But, even worse, specialists, particularly those in the Pentagon, made the programs so complex that people responsible for operations, not being able to understand them, simply could not or would not use them. However, the fundamentals of network planning and control still exist in many defense and aerospace programs, even though the acronym of PERT has been replaced by a succession of others.

PERT is not a cure-all. It will not *do* the planning, although it *forces* planning. It will not make control automatic, although it establishes an environment where sound control principles may be appreciated and used. And it apparently involves rather less expense than might be thought. Setting up the network, analyzing it, interpreting it, and reporting from it probably requires little, if any, more expense than most other planning and control techniques, unless, of course, PERT is made unduly complicated.

FOR DISCUSSION

1 The techniques of control appear to be as much techniques of planning as they are of control. In what ways is this true? Why should we expect it to be so?

2 "Variable budgets are flexible budgets." Discuss critically.

3 To what extent, and how, can budgets be approached on a "grass roots" basis, that is, having people build their budgets from the bottom of the organization structure up?

4 Why has program budgeting been regarded as so important in government and other nonbusiness enterprises? If you were to introduce it in a government department, how would you proceed?

5 How does zero-based budgeting differ from ordinary traditional budgeting? From variable budgeting? From program budgeting?

6 How would you set out to solve the problem of "information indigestion" in a company? A government department? A university?

7 PERT is a management invention that takes basic principles and knowledge and, through design to get a desired result, comes up with a useful technique of planning and control. Analyze PERT with this in mind. Why has PERT not been used more broadly in managerial planning and control practice?

8 It has often been claimed that an operating expense budget must be set at levels lower than expenses are really expected to be in order to ensure the attainment of real budgetary expense goals. Do you agree? Why? Why not?

chapter 28 Control of Overall Performance

MAJOR CHAPTER OBJECTIVES

1 To present the concept of overall control.

2 To analyze the most widely used techniques of overall control of an enterprise, or an integrated division or project within it, including budget summaries, profit and loss control, and control through rate of return on investment.

3 To define the new attempts to measure and control the human organization and human resources.

4 To present and discuss the enterprise self-audit.

Most controls are designed for specific things: policies, wages and salaries, employee selection and training, research and development, product quality, costs, pricing, capital expenditures, cash, and other areas where performance should conform to plans. Such controls are partial in the sense that they apply to a part of an enterprise and do not measure total accomplishments against total goals. Moreover, it is not possible to be precise about practical details of partial control without, at the very least, reference to a given plan, to the position and personality of the manager involved, and to specific enterprise goals.

Planning and control are being increasingly treated as an interrelated system. Along with these special techniques, and preceding many of them, control devices have been developed to measure the overall performance of an enterprise—or an integrated[1] division or project within it—against total goals.

There are many reasons for control of overall performance. In the first place, as overall *planning* must apply to enterprise or major division goals, so must overall *controls* be applied. In the second place, decentralization of authority—especially in product or territorial divisions—creates semiautonomous units, and these must be subjected to overall controls to avoid the chaos of complete autonomy. In the third place, overall controls permit measuring the total effort of an integrated area, rather than parts of it.

To a great extent, overall controls in business are, as one might expect, financial. Business owes its continued existence to profit making; its capital resources are a scarce, life-giving element; and, in the environment in which it operates, the best gauge of effectiveness is money. Since finance is the binding force of business, financial controls are the most important single objective gauge of the success of plans. Even in nonbusiness enterprises overall controls are likely to be financial but related, of course, to the goals of the organization.

Financial measurements also summarize, through a common denominator, the operation of a number of plans. Further, they accurately indicate total expenditures of resources in reaching goals. This is true in all forms of enterprise. Although the purpose of an educational or government enterprise is not to make monetary profits, all responsible managers must have some way of knowing what their goal achievement has cost in terms of resources. Therefore, in all forms of enterprise, control of overall performance is likely to be financial. Moreover, financial analyses furnish an excellent "window" through which accomplishment

---

[1]"Integrated" here is used as meaning that an operation includes the functions necessary to gain an overall objective. Thus, a product division of a company would normally include engineering, manufacturing, and marketing, and this represents enough of a total operation for the division manager—even though subject to some direction and control from headquarters—to be held basically responsible for a profit. To a lesser degree, but nonetheless important, an engineering design operation might be regarded as integrated; if its head has under him all the engineering functions and specialties necessary for complete product design, he can then be held responsible for the efficient accomplishment of the project.

in nonfinancial areas can be seen. A deviation from planned costs, for example, may lead a manager to find the causes in nonfinancial factors.

In recent years, however, we have come increasingly to realize that one of the key areas of control, both for individual segments and for an entire enterprise, is the measurement of the quality of the human organization. While this area of overall control is only in its embryonic stage, there is hope that measurement and correction for unwanted deviations can be developed so as to give warning to those responsible for an enterprise when human resources lag.

BUDGET SUMMARIES AND REPORTS

A widely used control of overall performance takes the form of a summary of budgets. A budget summary, being a résumé of all the individual budgets, reflects company plans so that sales volume, costs, profits, utilization of capital, and return on investment may be seen in their proper relationship. In these terms, it shows top management how the company as a whole is succeeding in its objectives.

The comprehensive nature of this final budget may be readily grasped if consideration is given to the preliminary steps required. These involve the sales forecast and its translation into expenditure budgets with statements of costs, output, and attendant requirements. As these are summarized, the budget maker is in a position to develop a pro forma balance sheet and statement of profit and loss to accompany the final budget. These three documents permit top management to weigh the effect of departmental activities on the enterprise as a whole or on an integrated division.

Uses

For the best control through a budget summary, a manager must first be satisfied that total budgets are an accurate and reasonably complete portrayal of enterprise plans. The budget reports and any material accompanying them should be scrutinized to determine whether the comparison of budget and actual costs shows the real nature of any deviations.

Minor discrepancies should receive appropriately little attention. The purpose of a control system is to draw attention to important deviations, and both the budget reports and the attention paid to them should reflect this. Above all, a manager should never forget that a budget summary is no substitute for successful operation. Moreover, budgeting is never more perfect than the planning behind it, and plans—especially long-range plans—are subject to the imperfections wrought by change and uncertainty. There may even be times when managers must forget their budgets and take special action to meet unexpected events. We cannot forget that budgets are meant to be tools, and not masters, of managers.

On the other hand, the value of budget summaries, in providing an effective means for overall control in the face of decentralization of authority, should not be underestimated. They furnish a means whereby enterprise objectives can be clearly and specifically defined, and departmental plans can be made to contribute toward such objectives. Should the budget summary and the reports of actual events indicate that the enterprise as a whole is not tending toward its objectives, top managers have a convenient and positive means of finding out where the deviations are occurring. The summaries thus furnish a useful guide for corrective action.

PROFIT AND LOSS CONTROL

The profit and loss statement for a business enterprise as a whole serves important control purposes, largely because it shows the constituent parts of a profit or a loss for a given period and, therefore, is useful for determining the immediate revenue or cost factors that have accounted for success or failure. Obviously, in the form of a pro forma forecast, it is even a better control device, in that it gives a manager a chance, before the event, to influence revenues, expenses, and consequently, profits.

Since business survival usually depends on profits and they are a definite standard against which to measure success, many companies use the profit and loss statement for divisional or departmental control. Because this is a statement of all revenues and expenses for a given time, it is a true summary of the results of business operations. Profit and loss control is usually applied to divisions or departments, based on the premise that if it is the objective of the entire business to make a profit, each part of the enterprise should contribute to this goal. Thus, the ability of a part to make an expected profit becomes a standard for measuring its performance.

In profit and loss control, each major department or division details its revenues and expenses—normally with a pro rata share of the company overhead—and calculates periodically a statement of its profit or loss. Some units have their own accounting group, while in others the statement is prepared by the central accounting department. In either case, the organizational unit, in being expected to turn in a separate record of profitable operation, is considered by the enterprise in much the same way a holding company considers its subsidiary companies.

Profit and loss control usually is practicable only to major segments of the company, since the paperwork in building up profit and loss statements for smaller departments tends to be too heavy. Also, profit and loss control implies that managers of a division or department have a fairly wide authority to run their part of the business as they see fit, with profit the primary standard of success. However, many companies that do not so decentralize authority have nonetheless found profit and loss control valuable. The focus on profit and the sensitiveness of the organizational unit to it are worthwhile even when managers have limited independence to seek profit as they wish.

The more integrated and complete the organization unit, the more accurate a measuring stick profit and loss control can be. For this reason, it works best in product or territorial divisions, where both sales and production functions for a product or service are under one jurisdiction. For example, it is much easier to use the standard of profit for measuring the operations of the general manager of the Buick division of General Motors than it would be to use it in the motor-block boring section of the manufacturing department of this division.

At the same time, companies organized on a functional basis do occasionally employ profit and loss control. The heat-treating department may produce and "sell" its service to the machining department, which in turn "sells" its product to the assembly department, which in turn "sells" a complete product to the sales department. This can be done, although the paperwork required is often not worth the effort, and the problem of determining the right transfer price may occasion much negotiation or difficult executive decisions. If the transfer is made at cost, clearly only the sales department would show a profit. If it is made at a figure above cost, the question becomes one of what price to charge.

In most instances, profit and loss control is not applied to central staff and service departments. Although these departments could "sell" their services, the most satisfactory practice is to place them under some other form of control, such as a variable budget.

Limitations

Profit and loss control suffers its greatest limitations from the accounting expense and paper transactions involving intracompany transfers. The duplication of accounting records, the efforts involved in allocating the many burden and overhead costs, and the time and effort required to calculate intracompany sales can make this control too costly when its application is carried too far.

Profit and loss control also may be inadequate to measure overall performance completely. Top managers may not wish to yield so much authority to division managers and may at least desire the additional assurances of good budgetary control. In addition, profit and loss control in and of itself does not provide a standard of desired profits or policy controls in the areas of product lines, development, or other matters of long-term overall company concern.

Another limitation of profit and loss control, especially if carried very far in the organization, is that departments may come to compete, with an aggressive detachment not conducive to enterprise coordination. On the other hand, in many companies there is not enough feeling of departmental responsibility for company profit, and departments may develop the smugness of a monopolist with an assured market. The fabrication department that knows its products must be "bought" by the assembly department, the manufacturing or service department that can force its output on the sales department, and the engineering group that has a monopolistic hold on both production and sales are dangerous monopolists indeed. Profit and loss control can break down these islands of monopoly. So, in spite of limitations—and especially if accompanied by an intracompany pricing policy requiring departments to meet outside competitive prices rather than being based on cost—profit and loss control can give top managers an extraordinary measure of overall control.

CONTROL THROUGH RETURN ON INVESTMENT

One of the most successfully used control techniques is that of measuring both the absolute and relative success of a company or a company unit by the ratio of earnings to investment of capital. This approach has been an important part of the control system of the Du Pont Company since 1919[2] and has received much attention in recent years. A large number of companies have adopted it as their key measure of overall performance.

This yardstick is the rate of return that a company or a division can earn on the capital allocated to it. This tool, therefore, does not look at profit as an absolute, but as a return on capital employed in the business. The goal of a business is, accordingly, not necessarily to optimize profits but to optimize returns from capital devoted to business purposes. This standard recognizes the fundamental fact that capital is a critical factor in almost any enterprise and through its scarcity limits progress.

Some Examples

As the system has been used by the Du Pont Company, return on investment involves consideration of several factors. Return is computed on the basis of capital turnover multiplied by earnings as a percentage of sales. This calculation recognizes that one division, with a high capital turnover and a low percentage of earnings to sales, may be more profitable in terms of return on investment than another with a high percentage of profits to sales but with low capital turnover. Turnover is computed on the basis of total sales divided by total investment, and investment includes not only the permanent plant facilities but also the working capital of the unit. In the Du Pont system, investment and working capital represent amounts invested without reduction for liabilities or reserves,

---

[2]Although it was actually devised by Donaldson Brown in 1914. See his *Some Reminiscences of an Industrialist* (privately printed, 1957), chap. 3.

on the grounds that such a reduction would result in a fluctuation in operating investments, as reserves or liabilities change, which would distort the rate of return and render it meaningless. Earnings are, however, calculated after normal depreciation charges, on the basis that true profits are not earned until allowance is made for the write-off of depreciable assets.

Return-on-investment control is perhaps the best summarized in the traditional Du Pont chart form as in Figure 28.1. Here, an analysis of variations in rate of return leads into every financial facet of the business. Rate of return is the common denominator used in comparing divisions, and differences can easily be traced to their causes.

However, other companies have taken the position that the return on investment should be calculated on fixed assets less depreciation. Such companies hold that the depreciation reserve represents a write-off of the

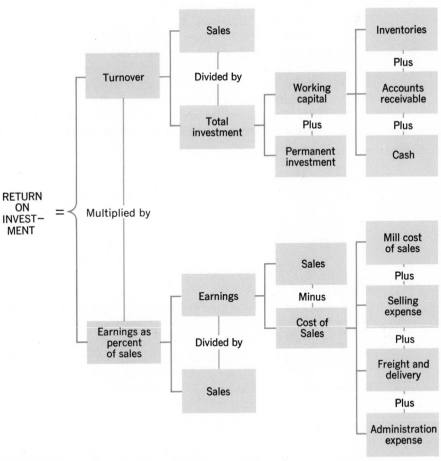

Figure 28.1 The relationship of factors affecting return on investment.

initial investment and that funds made available through such charges are reinvested in other fixed assets or used as working capital. Such a treatment appears more realistic to operating people, partly because it places a heavier rate-of-return burden on new fixed assets than on worn or obsolete ones.

In any control through return on investment, the number of ratios and comparisons behind the final yardstick figure cannot be overlooked. Although improvement in rate of return can come from a higher percentage of profit to sales, improvement could likewise come from increasing the rate of turnover by reducing return on sales. Moreover, the ratio of return on investment might be improved by getting more product (and sales) out of a given plant investment or by reducing the cost of sales for a given product.

Application to Product Lines

A typical functional-line organization without integrated product or territorial divisions has applied return-on-investment control to its various product lines. By grouping its many products into a number of major classifications, this company follows through with the allocation of sales, costs, and investment in fixed assets and working capital to arrive at the same kind of rate-of-return analysis used by multidivision companies. A simplified example of these results is shown in Table 28.1.

To operate the rate-of-return yardstick for product lines, the company has allocated certain expenses and assets, but these allocations apparently

Table 28.1 Comparative Rates of Return: Multiproduct Company (in thousands of dollars)

	Total sales		Assets employed		Operating income*		
	Amount	Percent of total	Amount	Per dollar of sales	Amount	Percent return on sales	Percent return on assets
Base year:							
Product A	$ 39,300	40	$ 20,700	52.9%	$ 4,800	12.2	23.1
Product B	29,500	30	16,900	57.3	2,800	9.4	16.4
Product C	19,600	20	8,900	45.1	2,100	10.8	23.9
Product D	9,800	10	2,700	27.5	500	5.1	18.5
Total	$ 98,200	100	$ 49,200	50.1%	$10,200	10.4	20.8
Current year:							
Product A	$ 48,100	25	$ 28,400	59.0	$ 5,600	11.6	19.7
Product B	96,200	50	75,300	78.3	8,500	8.8	11.2
Product C	38,500	20	19,500	50.7	3,900	10.2	20.1
Product D	9,600	5	2,900	29.9	500	5.2	17.2
Total	$192,400	100	$126,100	65.5%	$18,500	9.6	14.6

*Before interest on borrowed money and federal income taxes.

have not caused much difficulty. Most production costs are maintained by product, and common costs, such as sales branch expenses, are allocated by volume of sales. More difficulty is incurred in determining asset usage by product lines, but cash, accounts receivable, and administrative and sales facilities are allocated in accordance with sales: inventories and factory and plant equipment are prorated to the various products on the basis of special analyses.

In addition to comparative rates of return as between products, as indicated in Table 28.1, the company compares actual experience with trends for the various products (identified for purposes of simplicity as the "base year" in the table). An advantage of these comparisons is that the company is able to maintain a sharp look at its product lines, with a view to determining where capital is being most efficently employed and as a guide toward obtaining a balanced use of capital for maximum overall profit. Thus, the company has been able to identify products that are either strong and established, new and improved, or past their peak in growth and profitability.

Advantages and Limitations

One of the principal advantages of using return on investment to control overall performance is that it, like profit and loss control, focuses managerial attention on a central measure of business success—to make the best profit possible on the capital available. It measures the efficiency of the company as a whole, its major divisions or departments, its products, and its planning. It takes attention away from mere increase in sales volume or asset size, or even from the level of costs, and draws attention to the combination of factors making for successful operation.

Another advantage of control by return on investment is that it is helpful where authority is decentralized. Not only is it an absolute guide to capital efficiency but it also offers the possibility of comparing efficiency in capital employment, both within the company and with other enterprises. By holding departmental managers responsible for performance in terms of the dollars invested in their segments of the business, it forces them to look at their operations from the point of view of top management. Managers often insist on heavy capital for new equipment or drive for lower prices to increase sales without taking into account the possible effect of their requests on the company as a whole. They also often feel isolated, particularly in large businesses, with respect to their performance. If they are furnished a guide to efficiency that reaches into many facets of the business, managers develop a keener sense of responsibility for their department or division, and top managers can more easily hold subordinate managers responsible.

A further advantage of return-on-investment control, if it is complete and shows all the factors bearing upon the return, is that it enables managers to locate weaknesses. If inventories are rising, the effect will be shown on the rate of return, or if other factors camouflage inventory variations and leave the rate looking good, tracing back influences will disclose any weakness of the inventory situation and open the way for consideration of a remedy.

With all its advantages and with its increasing use by well-managed and successful companies, this method of control is not foolproof. Difficulties involve availability of information on sales, costs, and assets and proper allocation of investment and return for commonly sold or produced items. Does the present accounting system give the needed information? If not, how much will it cost to get it, through either changes in the system or special analyses? Where assets are jointly used or costs are common, what method of allocation between divisions or departments shall be used? Should the manager be charged with assets at their original costs, their replacement costs, or their depreciated values? Setting up a return-on-investment control system is no simple task.

Another question is, What constitutes a reasonable return? Comparisons of rates of return are hardly enough because they do not tell the top manager what the optimum rate of return *should* be. Perhaps as good a standard as any is one that meets or surpasses the level of competition of other firms, since, in a practical sense, the optimum tends to be measured not by an absolute level but rather by competition for capital.

One of the dangers of overemphasis on the rate of return is that it may lead to undesirable inflexibility in investing capital for new ventures. Many companies using this important measuring tool have set minimum rates which a division, new product program, or investment must meet before the allocation of capital would be approved. It is said that even Du Pont, for many years, would not approve a new product program which would not promise a yield of a minimum of 20 percent return on investment. According to one executive of the company, this rigid minimum caused it to pass up such great product opportunities as xerography and the Land (Polaroid) camera.[3] More recently, the company has used a more flexible minimum rate of return, requiring a higher rate when risks are greater and a lower rate when results are very promising, more certain, or when an investment supplements an established business.

Conflict between Return on Investment and Earnings per Share

In many, if not most, American business coporations, growth goals have tended to surface from return on investment to earnings per share of common stock. Although a focus on return on investment may, in the long run, be consistent with and even supportive of growth in earnings per share, this is often not the case.[4] It is possible that increasing sales through

---

[3]See "Lighting a Fire under the Sleeping Giants," *Business Week,* pp. 40–41 (September 12, 1970).
[4]For a clear discussion of this problem, see F. W. Searby, "Return to Return on Investment," *Harvard Business Review,* vol. 53, no. 2, pp. 113–119 (March–April 1975).

heavy asset investment can improve earnings per share while penalizing return on investment. Conversely, a company might improve its return on investment by selling low-return facilities or businesses at a loss, but this would harm earnings per share. A company oriented to earnings per share might favor the use of financing growth through debt, but a company working to improve return on investment would likely prefer financing with common stock with a resulting dilution of earnings per share.

This conflict between two widely used standards of profitable growth must naturally be recognized. Perhaps return on investment is the best standard to use; but then again, it may not be as attractive to many top managers and investors as an earnings per share standard.

Perhaps the greatest danger in return-on-investment control, as with any system of control based on financial data, is that it can lead to excessive preoccupation with financial factors, either within a firm or within an industry. Undue attention to ratios and financial data can cause a firm to overlook environmental factors such as social and technical developments. It might also lead the company to overlook the fact that capital is not the only scarce resource from which a business can grow, prosper, and endure. Every bit as scarce are competent managers, good employee morale, and good customer and public relations. A well-managed company would never regard any financially based control as the sole gauge of overall performance.

MEASURING AND CONTROLLING THE HUMAN ORGANIZATION

An important special area of control is measuring critical human variables, based on the valid and widely recognized fact that the human organization of any enterprise makes the most difference in end results. To a very great extent, this is what managing is about, and throughout this book, by emphasizing the manager's task of creating and maintaining an environment for performance, the authors have recognized this fact. However, it is true that, except in the area of appraising managers as managers, control subjects and techniques have been devoted largely to measuring *activities* and *results* in such areas as profits, costs, sales, production output, and program performance.

Likert's System 4 Management

One of the pioneers in developing means of measuring human variables is Rensis Likert, who has for many years directed the nation's largest academic social science center, the Institute for Social Research at the University of Michigan. His research over the years has indicated to him that the best managerial producers (1) are supportive in that they lend support to those reporting to them; (2) facilitate people's work with the necessary tools, training, inside or outside help, and other things necessary to ensure that assigned tasks will be accomplished; (3) encourage interaction, talk, and mutual help among all members of the work group; and (4) expect high performance standards.[5] As noted in Chapter 24, Likert has referred to this type of management as "system 4," or participative-group, management, as contrasted to three other types: exploitive-authoritative, benevolent-authoritative, and consultative. Since his research indicates that shifts toward system 4 management bring, at least over time, an improvement in goal performance, as well as in satisfaction of subordinates, he has sought out the underlying variables that indicate the type of managing an individual is undertaking and has developed a means of measuring them. While the ability of subordinates or even specialists to measure these objectively is open to some question, there are a fairly large number of checkpoints and, within limits, the measurement does appear to be worthwhile.

Measuring Causal and Intervening Variables

Likert's main thesis is that the causal variables of managerial behavior and organization structure affect and are affected by certain intervening variables (such as motivating factors, goal performance, extent and nature of communication, and the character of the interaction-influence factors) to cause end-result variables in the areas of profits, sales, costs, and other enterprise goals, plus the end result of human satisfaction. A view of the interaction of these variables is given in Table 28.2, where a comparison is made between exploitive-authoritative (system 1) or benevolent-authoritative (system 2) and participative-group (system 4) managing.

The control aspect of Likert's approach is twofold. One is the measurement of individual managers and their groups. Another is primarily a matter of human-asset accounting and overall control of the human organization of an enterprise. In other words, through measuring the causal and intervening variables periodically, it is Likert's conviction that any enterprise can see what is happening to the ability of a group to perform. In this connection, however, he makes it clear that there may be a time lag before end results may be apparent. His research has indicated a number of cases where costs were reduced and profits increased by highly authoritative managing, as in the instance of a rapid and arbitrary budget-cutting program; however, in some cases, while performance immediately improved, later performance suffered through the negative influence of the underlying human variables he has identified.

[5]See, for example, his *New Patterns of Management* (New York: McGraw-Hill Book Company, 1961) and *The Human Organization* (New York: McGraw-Hill Book Company, 1967). See also M. R. Weisbord, "Management in Crisis," *The Conference Board Record*, vol. 7, no. 2, pp. 10–16 (February 1970). Ideas similar to Likert's have long been advocated by other behavioral scientists. See, for example, C. Argyris, "The Organization: What Makes It Healthy?" *Harvard Business Review*, vol. 36, no. 6, pp. 107–116 (November–December 1958).

Table 28.2 Sequence of Developments in a Well-Organized Enterprise, as Affected by Use of System 2 or System 4

If a manager has:

Well-organized plan of operation

High performance goals

High technical competence
(manager or staff assistants)

Causal variables

and if the manager manages via:

system 1 or 2	system 4
e.g., uses direct hierarchical pressure for results, including the usual contests and other practices of the traditional systems	e.g., uses principle of supportive relationships, group methods of supervision, and other principles of system 4

the organization will display:

Intervening variables

Less group loyalty	Greater group loyalty
Lower performance goals	Higher performance goals
Greater conflict and less cooperation	Greater cooperation
Less technical assistance to peers	More technical assistance to peers
Greater feeling of unreasonable pressure	Less feeling of unreasonable pressure
Less favorable attitudes toward manager	More favorable attitudes toward manager
Lower motivation to produce	Higher motivation to produce

and the organization will attain:

End-result variables

Lower sales volume	Higher sales volume
Higher sales costs	Lower sales costs
Lower quality of business sold	Higher quality of business sold
Lower earnings by salespeople	Higher earnings by salespeople

Source: R. Likert, *The Human Organization* (New York: McGraw-Hill Book Company, 1967), p. 76. After Rensis Likert, "New Patterns in Sales Management," in Martin R. Warshaw (ed.), *Changing Perspectives in Marketing Management* (Ann Arbor, Mich.: University of Michigan Bureau of Business Research, 1962). By permission of the publishers. See also R. Likert and J. G. Likert, *New Ways of Managing Conflict* (New York: McGraw-Hill Book Company, 1976).

While this system of measurement is still rather crude and much more empirical research is needed to verify its utility, the measurement and control of human variables are important and techniques for doing so can surely improve the quality of management. While Likert has, perhaps, made too much of his system 4 type of managing and appears to be overly biased toward a highly participative managing style, the underlying facts of his approach belie this. For example, few managers could disagree with the following characteristics he identifies with system 4 managing: (1) communication initiated at all levels; (2) full use of economic, ego, and other motives; (3) high performance goals; (4) personnel feeling responsibility for the organization's goals; (5) decision makers being well aware of problems; and (6) widespread responsibility for review and control. Nor would most managers disagree with Likert's conclusion that "a manager who has high performance goals and excellent job organization but who relies solely on economic needs and direct pressure to motivate his men is very likely to be disappointed by their achievements."[6] These and many other behavioral variables are those regularly associated with good managing.

Individual and Overall Control

As indicated earlier, control of the human organization may be looked upon both as control of individual managers and as the overall control of the human side of enterprise. In other words, by measuring the causal and the intervening variables identified by Likert, one can look at and predict probable results in end-result variables. Likewise, the same thing can be done for an entire enterprise. This becomes especially significant in view of the well-known fact that all enterprises tend to reflect the managerial styles of the top managers. Therefore, attempts to measure the quality of the causal variables of managerial behavior and organization structure, as well as of the intervening variables, is likely to be an essential and helpful approach to the overall control of performance.

Human Asset Accounting

This approach has led Likert and his associates to attempt methods for measuring the value of the human assets of an enterprise. It is, indeed, common to read in shareholders' reports the statement that "our human resources are the company's greatest asset." Also, many top managers, when asked to estimate how much it would cost to replace the human organization, come up with very high estimates exceeding three times annual payroll, or about 24 to 25 times annual earnings.[7] Yet, in

---

[6]*The Human Organization*, p. 64.
[7]According to Likert, who claims to have asked "thousands" of managers this question. See Weisbord, op. cit., p. 13.

commonly accepted accounting, the value of this asset is not shown in balance sheets or accounted for in earnings statements, and no rate of return is calculated on it.

To offset this deficiency, Likert and his associates have undertaken experiments in "human asset accounting."[8] To cover the entire spectrum of human resources, the originators of this kind of accounting would have it include not only the asset represented by people within the enterprise but also values represented by customer good will. They point out two deficiencies of ordinary accounting. When an enterprise is investing in human capabilities and values, conventional accounting practice involves writing off these costs through operating expenses, thus actually understating profits; likewise balance sheet values are understated. On the other hand, a company might be using up its human assets and showing high current earnings at the expense of almost certain lower future earnings.

In moving toward this kind of accounting, two approaches have been suggested. One is the cost approach through measuring dollar investments (recruiting, transfer, training, and investments in customer good will) offset by reductions (through obsolescence, retirement, transfers, separations, and loss of customer franchise). In one company, where human resource accounting supplementary to traditional financial accounting has been undertaken, the balance sheet and income statements were reported as shown in Table 28.3.

The second approach is to obtain a regular evaluation of the current worth of human resources through assessing the present value of individual members of the organization. It is believed by the originators that this can be done by applying the Likert measurements of causal and intervening variables—obtaining the individual's performance and potential value as modified by expected remaining tenure, and by assessing the value of the productive capabilities of various organizational groupings.

To date, only a few experiments have been undertaken to measure the investment costs and losses in human resources. While it is believed that present "value" of human resources, at least for those internal to the enterprise, can be reasonably well approached through the use of the Likert measurements, there is little evidence that this has been done with an acceptable degree of creditability. At the same time, there is much to be said for continuing efforts in this direction. No one interested in effective control of enterprise can afford to disregard the importance of maintaining the value of human assets. These, after all, are the best assurance of the future. But, again, perhaps the best way of ensuring this is through

[8]See, for example, R. Likert, *The Human Organization*, chap. 9; R. L. Brummet, W. C. Pyle, and E. G. Flamholtz, "Accounting for Human Resources," *Michigan Business Review*, vol. 20, no. 2, pp. 20–25 (March 1968); E. G. Flamholtz, "Human Resource Accounting: A Review of Theory and Research," *Journal of Management Studies*, vol. 11, no. 1, pp. 44–61 (February 1974); and E. G. Flamholtz, *Human Resource Accounting* (Encino, Calif.: Dickenson Publishing Company, Inc., 1974).

Table 28.3 Financial Statements Reflecting Human Resources at the R. G. Barry Corporation

"The Total Concept"—R. G. Barry Corporation and Subsidiaries Pro Forma (Financial and Human Resource Accounting)

Balance sheet	1969 Financial and human resource	1969 Financial only
Assets		
Total current assets	$10,003,628	$10,003,628
Net property, plant and equipment	1,770,717	1,770,717
Excess of purchase price of subsidiaries over net assets acquired	1,188,704	1,188,704
Net investments in human resources	986,094	
Other assets	106,783	106,783
	$14,055,926	$13,069,832
Liabilities and stockholders' equity		
Total current liabilities	$ 5,715,708	$ 5,715,708
Long-term debt, excluding current installments	1,935,500	1,935,500
Deferred compensation	62,380	62,380
Deferred federal income taxes as a result of appropriation for human resources	493,047	
Stockholders' equity		
Capital stock	879,116	879,116
Additional capital in excess of par value	1,736,253	1,736,253
Retained earnings:		
Financial	2,740,875	2,740,875
Appropriation for human resources	493,047	
Total stockholders' equity	5,849,291	5,356,244
	$14,055,926	$13,069,832

Statement of income	1969 Financial and human resource	1969 Financial only
Net sales	$25,310,588	$25,310,588
Cost of sales	16,275,876	16,275,876
Gross profit	9,034,712	9,034,712
Selling, general and administrative expenses	6,737,313	6,737,313
Operating income	2,297,399	2,297,399
Other deductions, net	953,177	953,177
Income before federal income taxes	1,344,222	1,344,222
Human resource expenses applicable to future periods	173,569	
Adjusted income before federal income taxes	1,517,791	1,344,222
Federal income taxes	730,785	644,000
Net income	$ 787,006	$ 700,222

Source: *1969 R. G. Barry Corporation Annual Report,* p. 14. From W. C. Pyle, "Monitoring Human Resources— 'On Line'," *Michigan Business Review,* vol. 22, no. 4, pp. 19–32, at p. 28 (July 1970).

applying the fundamentals of effective managing. Even Likert and his associates seem to recognize this.

THE ENTERPRISE SELF-AUDIT

J. O. McKinsey, who achieved an outstanding position in the realm of management nearly five decades ago, came to the conclusion that a business enterprise should periodically make a "management audit," an appraisal of the enterprise in all its aspects, in the light of its present and probable future environment. This type of audit has been referred to by Billy E. Goetz as "much the most comprehensive and powerful to these problem-seeking techniques" because it seeks in an overall way "to discover and correct errors of management."[9] Although McKinsey called this a management audit, it is actually an audit of the entire enterprise.

The enterprise self-audit appraises the company's position to determine where it is, where it is heading under present programs, what its objectives should be, and whether revised plans are needed to meet those objectives. In most enterprises of all kinds, objectives and policies become obsolete. If the enterprise does not change course to suit the changing social, technical, and political environment, it loses markets, personnel, and other requirements for continued existence. The enterprise self-audit is designed to force managers to meet this situation.

Procedure

The self-audit may be made annually or, more likely, once every 3 or 5 years. The first step is to study the outlook of the firm's industry. What are recent trends and prospects? What is the outlook for the product? Where are the markets? What technical developments are affecting the industry? How may demand be changed? What political or social factors may affect the industry?

A second step in the self-audit is to appraise the position of the firm in the industry, both currently and in prospect. Has the company maintained its position? Has it expanded its influence and markets? Or has competition reduced its position? What is the competitive outlook? To answer such questions, the company may undertake studies on competitor standing, development of competition, customer reactions, and other factors bearing on its position within the industry.

On the basis of such studies, the next logical step for the company would be to reexamine its basic objectives and major policies to decide where the company wishes to be in, say, 5 or 10 years. After this reexamination, the company may audit its organization, policies, proce-

---

[9]B. E. Goetz, *Management Planning and Control* (New York: McGraw-Hill Book Company, 1949), p. 167. For a discussion of the management audit, see below, pp. 809–813.

dures, programs, facilities, financial position, personnel, and management. This examination should identify any deviations from objectives and facilitate the revision of many major and minor plans.

Contribution

Most top managers do not think in terms of an enterprise's future or evaluate overall performance in relation to long-range objectives. The enterprise self-audit has the distinct advantage of forcing them to appraise overall performance in terms not only of current goals but also of future ones. Top managers who expend mental effort for this kind of audit will almost certainly be well repaid and will be surprised at how many day-to-day decisions will be simplified by a clear picture of where the business is attempting to go.

To a very considerable extent, this is often done when a company evaluates a firm it wishes to acquire. Without in any way detracting from the major importance of financial performance, it is realized that a firm's value depends upon its future rather than its past. To make this evaluation, financial factors need to be supplemented by such considerations as product lines and basic competition, marketing strengths, research and development record, personnel and public relations, and the quality of management.[10] If this is of importance to a buyer of a company one cannot help but wonder why it should not be significant on a regular and continuing basis to a firm.

FOR DISCUSSION

1 Why do most controls of overall performance tend to be financial in nature? Should they be? What else do you suggest?

2 "Profit and loss control is defective in that it does not emphasize return on investment; the latter is defective in that it places too great an emphasis on present results with possible endangering of future results." Discuss.

3 In applying rate of return on investment as a control tool, would you favor using an undepreciated or a depreciated asset base?

4 Selecting any federal, state, or local government agency you wish, how would you suggest that overall performance could best be measured?

5 If steps are taken to ensure effective managing throughout an enterprise, do you believe that it would be necessary or helpful to undertake an evaluation of the human organization?

6 A start has been made in human asset accounting including mainly

---

[10]For such a summary, see, for example, R. B. Buchele, "How to Evaluate a Firm," *California Management Review*, vol. 5, no. 1, pp. 5–16 (Fall, 1962), and, by the same author, *Business Policy in Growing Firms* (San Francisco: Chandler Publishing Company, 1967).

costs incurred and values used for the internal human organization. But there are important human values external to the firm, such as customer good will. How do you believe we could account for this and measure its current value?

7   J. O. McKinsey's enterprise self-audit has seldom been used in industry. Why do you feel this has happened? Do you believe this device would be worth its cost?

chapter 29

Direct Control: Ensuring Effective Managing

MAJOR CHAPTER OBJECTIVES

1 To present the principle of direct control and distinguish its nature and application from those of the many indirect controls.

2 To explain the nature and potential of management audits and to advance the idea of a certified management audit.

3 To present some major challenges facing managers, note some major unsolved problems, and suggest what needs to be done to ensure development of more effective managers.

4 To present, as a summary of the chapters on controlling, some major principles, or guidelines, in this area.

The preceding analysis of controls stresses the variety of approaches that managers follow to make results conform to plans. At the base of control is the fact that the outcome of plans is dependent on the people who carry them out. For instance, a poor educational system cannot be controlled by criticizing its product, the unfortunate graduate; a factory turning out inferior products cannot be controlled by their consignment to the scrap heap; and a firm plagued with customer complaints cannot be controlled by ignoring the complainers. Responsibility for controllable deviations lies with whoever has made unfortunate decisions. Any hope of abolishing unsatisfactory results lies in changing the future actions of the responsible person, through additional training, modification of procedures, or new policy. This is the crux of controlling the quality of management.

There are two ways of seeing to it that the responsible people modify future action. The normal procedure is to trace the cause of an unsatisfactory result back to the persons responsible for it and get them to correct their practices. This may be called "indirect control." The alternative in the area of management is to develop better managers who will skillfully apply concepts, techniques, and principles and who will look at managing and managerial problems from a systems point of view, thus eliminating undesirable results caused by poor management. This may be referred to as "direct control."

INDIRECT CONTROL

In every enterprise, hundreds, and even thousands, of standards are developed to compare the actual output of goods or services—in terms of quantity, quality, time, and cost—with plans. A negative deviation indicates—in terms of goal achievement, cost, price, personnel, labor-hours, or machine-hours—that performance is less than good or normal or standard and that results are not conforming to plans.

Causes of Negative Deviations from Standards

The causes of negative deviations will often determine whether control measures are possible. Although an incorrect standard may cause deviations, if the standard is correct, plans may fail because of (1) uncertainty and (2) lack of knowledge, experience, or judgment.

Uncertainty   Elements affecting a given plan may be grouped into facts, risks, and uncertainty. Facts are known, such as number of employees, costs, or machine capacity. Considerably less is known about the element of risk. Insurable risks are readily converted to factual status through the payment of a known premium, and costs of certain noninsurable risks may be included in a business decision on the basis of probability. But most risks arise from uncertainty. The total of facts and risks is small, compared with the element of uncertainty, which includes everything about which nothing is certain. For instance, the success of a plan to manufacture aluminum pistons will depend not only on known facts and risks but also on such uncertainties as future world conditions, competition of known and yet unknown metals, and power technology that may eliminate all piston prime movers. Not even probability can be estimated for all the uncertain factors, and yet they can wreck a plan.

Managerial errors caused by unforseeable events cannot be avoided. The fixing of personal responsibility by indirect control techniques is of little avail in such situations.

Lack of knowledge, experience, or judgement Plans may misfire and negative deviations occur when people appointed to managerial posts lack the necessary background. The higher in the organizational structure managers are placed, the broader the knowledge and experience they need. Long years as an engineer, a sales manager, a production executive, or a controller may be inadequate in qualifying a person to be a top manager.

Good judgment marks the mature person who intelligently applies educational and enterprise experience and is known for common sense. Unfortunately, some top managers who have gone through the motions of formal education, training of various kinds, and practical experience seem incapable of sound decisions and display poor judgment about such matters as product lines, expansion policy, innovation, and decentralization. At the top level, the chance of correction through separation from the firm tends to be fairly small. On the other hand, continuing errors of judgment at middle and lower levels are often followed by demotion, transfer, or separation.

If the cause of error is poor judgement, whether due to inadequate training or experience or to failure to use appropriate information in decision making, correction can be made. The manager may improve his or her education, be transferred to acquire broader experience, or be cautioned to take better stock of the situation before making decisions.

From this discussion, an interesting question arises: How often can negative deviations from standard be corrected? At present, little is known about this. But it is vital. If, for instance, only 40 percent of errors in decision making are subject to correction, then the effort made to place responsibility is of no avail 60 percent of the time. Such a ratio is likely to place on indirect controls an insuperable burden.

Questionable Assumptions

In addition to its cost, the shortcomings of indirect control may also sometimes rest on questionable assumptions: (1) that performance can be measured, (2) that personal responsibility for performance exists, (3) that the time expenditure is warranted, (4) that mistakes can be anticipated or discovered in time, and (5) that the person responsible will take corrective steps.

That performance can be measured At first glance, almost any enterprise appears to be a maze of controls. Input, output, cost, price, time, complaints, and quality are subject to numerous standards; and the standards may be expressed in terms of goal achievement, time, weight, tolerances, averages, ratios, dollars, and indexes. In terms of usefulness, the standards may be correct, acceptable, or merely better than nothing. Close analysis will often reveal shortcomings of two types. In the first place, the ability of a manager to develop potential managers, the effectiveness of research, the amount of creativity, foresight, and judgment in decision making can seldom be measured accurately.

The second shortcoming concerns the location of the control. Managers know that critical stages exist in acquiring input factors, manipulating them to produce a finished product, and selling and delivering the product. In a factory operation, for example, critical stages would include receiving inspection, inspection for each assembly process, shipping, and billing. These are critical because effective control here will minimize costs. No amounts of control at other points can make up for lack of control at these stages.

That personal responsibility exists Sometimes no manager is responsible for poor results. Government action to increase interest rates or inflation may cause the costs of many activities to rise precipitously. Scarcity of a particular fuel may necessitate use of less economical sources of power. And markets may shrink for reasons unconnected with the firm.

That the time expenditure is warranted Whether managers undertake the inquiry themselves or assign it to others, executive time must be spent in ferreting out causes of poor results. Large scrap losses, for example, may call for meetings attended by persons representing quality control, production planning, engineering, purchasing, and manufacturing. Passage of time may make the recall of facts quite difficult. These drawbacks may convince managers that the cost of investigation exceeds any benefit they may derive. This often precludes investigation of clear violations of standards.

That mistakes can be discovered in time Discovery of deviations from plans often comes too late for effective action. Although true control can be applied only to future action, most controls depend on historical data—all that most managers have available. Managers should, of course, interpret such data in terms of their implications for the future.

The costs of errors in major areas—such as cash or inventories—have led to the use of forecasts as the basis for control. Since forecasts are difficult to make and subject to error, the natural tendency to rely on historical reports seriously blocks adequate controls. As we have seen, feedforward control techniques offer hope, but as yet they have not been widely developed or utilized. No manager really has control unless he or she can correct mistakes. And the best way to correct mistakes is to avoid them.

That the person responsible will take corrective steps Fixing the responsibility may not lead to correction. High production costs, for example, might be traced back to a marketing manager who insists that "slight" product modification will make selling easier and that this involves "really" no change in a production run. If the marketing manager is a member of top management, a subordinate investigator may be intimidated; the president may attempt to mediate between marketing and production executives; and the marketing manager will remain unreconstructed. Although great effort may be made to correct subordinate managers, it is sometimes very difficult to correct superior executives.

THE PRINCIPLE OF DIRECT CONTROL

The principle of direct control embraces the idea that much of the responsibility for negative deviations from standards can be fixed by applying fundamentals of management. It draws a sharp distinction between performance reports, essential in any case, and determining whether managers act in accordance with established principles in carrying out their functions. The principle of direct control, then may be stated as follows: *The higher the quality of managers and their subordinates, the less will be the need for indirect controls.*

It is possible that the principle of direct control was vaguely perceived by Fayol, who possessed a mature and practical understanding of management. In a 1925 interview with the editors of *Chronique sociale de France*, Fayol said that the best method of looking at an organization and determining the necessary improvements was "to study the administrative apparatus. . . . One can ascertain immediately that forecasting and planning, organization, command, co-ordination, and control are properly provided for, that is to say, that the undertaking is well administered."[1]

The extensive adoption of direct control must await a wider understanding of managerial principles, functions, and techniques as well as

[1]Quoted by L. Urwick in his foreword to Henri Fayol, *General and Industrial Management* (New York: Pitman Publishing Corporation, 1949), p. x.

management philosophy. While such an understanding is not achieved easily, it can be gained in universities, through on-the-job experience, through coaching by the knowledgeable superior, and by means of constant self-education. Moreover, as progress is made in appraising managers as managers, we can expect direct control to have more practical meaning and effectiveness.

Assumptions of the Principle of Direct Control

The desirability of direct control rests upon four valid assumptions: (1) that qualified managers make a minimum of errors; (2) that managerial performance can be measured; (3) that management concepts, principles, and techniques are useful diagnostic standards in measuring managerial performance; and (4) that the application of management fundamentals can be evaluated.

That qualified managers make a minimum of errors   J. P. Morgan has often been quoted as saying that the decisions of good managers are right two-thirds of the time. However, an accurate analysis of the quality of decision making should not rely upon quantity of errors but be concerned with the nature of the error. As J. Paul Getty once told one of the authors, his concern in his worldwide empire was not the percentage of decisions in which an executive was right or wrong; he could be wrong on only 2 percent of them and seriously endanger a company by these errors if they were critical. Managers can logically be held strictly accountable for the performance of their functions because these functions should be undertaken in conformance with the fundamentals of management. However, accountability cannot be exacted for errors attributable to factors beyond managers' authority or ability reasonably to forecast the future.

That management fundamentals may be used to measure performance   The chief purpose of this book has been to draw together concepts, principles, theory, and basic techniques or approaches of management and relate them to a system of managerial functions. As was stated in previous chapters, the completeness and certitude of these vary considerably, depending largely upon the state of knowledge concerning managing. There is, for instance, greater general acceptance of some of the principles of organizing than there is of the principles relating to other functions. Nevertheless, the authors are convinced that the fundamentals set forth here are useful in measuring managerial performance even though their statement will undoubtedly be refined and better verified by future specialists.

That the application of management fundamentals can be evaluated   Evaluation can provide for periodic measurement of the skill with which managers apply management fundamentals to their five functions. This can be done not only by judging performance against these but also by casting them into a series of fairly objective questions. An approach to the proper evaluation of managers as managers was set forth in Chapter 20. The ability to set and achieve verifiable objectives reveals some measure of a manager's performance. But much depends on being able to evaluate the performance of a manager as a manager. As crude as these standards of measurement may be at the present state of the art of managing, they can still highlight the extent to which an individual has the knowledge and ability required to fill the managerial role.

Advantages

Directly controlling the quality of managers and thus minimizing errors has several advantages. In the first place, greater accuracy is achieved in assigning personal responsibility. The ongoing evaluation of managers is practically certain to uncover deficiencies and should provide a basis for specific training to eliminate them.

In the second place, direct control should hasten corrective action and make it more effective. It encourages control by self-control. Knowing that errors will be uncovered in an evaluation, managers will themselves try to determine their responsibility and make voluntary corrections. For example, a report of excessive scrap will probably cause the department supervisor to determine quickly whether the excess was due to poor direction of subordinates or to other factors. The same report will cause the chief inspector to look into whether inspection employees acted properly, the purchasing agent to check the material purchased with engineering specifications, and the engineers to determine whether appropriate material was specified. All this action can be immediate and voluntary. Managers who conclude privately that they were in error are likely to do their best to prevent recurrence, for they realize their responsibility.

The third advantage of direct control is the potential for lightening the burden now caused by indirect control. This is a net gain, since the evaluation of managers is already part of staffing. The amount of potential savings is as yet unknown, although it must be considerable.

Last, the psychological advantage of direct control is impressive. The feeling of subordinates that superiors do not rate fairly, rely on hunch and personality, and use improper measuring standards is almost universal, but direct control of the kind suggested in Chapter 20 can go far in removing this feeling. Subordinate managers know what is expected of them, understand the nature of managing, and feel a close relationship between performance and measurement. Intelligent superior managers will reciprocate this feeling because they will know what they are expected to evaluate in subordinates and will have a technique for doing so.

Application of the principle of direct control has led to action in several directions. One of the most promising and active has been the improvement of programs in recent years to appraise individual managers. Primarily, this has taken the form of appraising performance against the standard of setting and achieving verifiable goals. However, even in this widely accepted approach much must still be done to make it effective. A second essential aspect of this process, yet to be done except on a limited and experimental basis, is the appraisal of managers in their role as *managers*. Both these approaches have been discussed in Chapter 20.

Another direction in which the principle of direct control has led is in a developing interest in management audits. Compared with the practice of other forms of management evaluation, these do not aim at evaluating managers as individuals but rather at looking at the entire system of managing an enterprise. While little progress has been made in such management audits, some pioneering programs have been undertaken. Certain specialists are working in this direction, and some major buyers—the Department of Defense in particular—have used elements of the concept in appraising companies for the award of major contracts.

Management Audits and Operational Audits

A distinction should be made between auditing the quality of managing as a system and auditing the quality of operations. To some extent, this is similar to appraising managers in their ability to manage and in their ability to set and accomplish objectives. Both are important, but even where so-called management audits have been undertaken, this distinction has not always been made. It clearly should be since any enterprise may succeed as a marketing or engineering organization, while being ineptly managed; it may even succeed because of a favorable environment, such as a sellers' market, as often happens in wartime, despite inadequate management. If, as believed to be the case, the quality of managing will ultimately make the difference in success or failure, certainly this quality should be given an assessment separate from the ability to do well in marketing, engineering, producing, or financing.

At the same time, as long as operational auditing is clearly separated from management auditing, there may be distinct advantages in auditing both. In the case of the auditing approach suggested by Greenwood,[2] for example, the audit is divided into two parts. One is a management function audit covering evaluation in the fields of planning, organizing,

---

[2]See W. T. Greenwood, *A Management Audit System*, rev. ed. (Carbondale: School of Business, Southern Illinois University, 1967). See also his *Management and Organizational Behavior Theories: An Interdisciplinary Approach* (Cincinnati: South-Western Publishing Company, Incorporated, 1965), pp. 813–816, 868–880.

staffing, directing, and controlling. The other is a management decision audit, dealing with the quality of decisions in the areas of long-range and companywide planning, marketing, operations (production and material), personnel, accounting, and finance.

The Management Audit and the Enterprise Self-Audit

It will be recalled that in the previous chapter the enterprise self-audit was noted, and a question might be raised as to how a management audit may be distinguished from the enterprise self-audit. The latter form of audit emphasizes where a company is and is probably going in the face of present and future economic, political, and social developments. The enterprise self-audit, then, is really an audit of an organization's operations and only indirectly an audit of its managerial system.

The management audit is not nearly as broad as the enterprise self-audit in that it aims only at evaluating the quality of managing. The management audit thus focuses on the quality of managers and the quality of managing *as a system* in an enterprise.

American Institute of Management Program

One of the earliest programs attempting a management audit was developed by the American Institute of Management. This institute, founded and operated by Jackson Martindell, developed some years ago a procedure for direct control.[3] Using an extensive list of 301 questions, Martindell undertook to rate companies in the areas of economic function, corporate structure, health of earnings, fairness to stockholders, research and development, directors, fiscal policies, production efficiency, sales vigor, and executive ability. Each of these ten areas was, in turn, assigned point weightings, ranging, out of a total of 10,000 points, from 400 points assigned to economic function and 600 to health of earnings to 1400 for sales vigor and 2400 for executive quality. Out of the total of 10,000 possible points, only some 3500 points were assigned to managerial elements, the rest applying to other areas. In order for a company to obtain an "excellent" rating, the institute arbitrarily picked the requirement of 7500 points.

In view of Martindell's long experience and interest as an investment counselor, his appraisal system was understandably heavily oriented to the considerations of an investor. Moreover, examination of the many questions used for rating indicates that they involved a high degree of subjectivity. While Martindell's American Institute of Management program leaves much to be desired, its pioneering nature deserves praise. It

[3]See *The Scientific Appraisal of Management* (New York: Harper & Brothers, 1950); *Manual of Excellent Managements* (New York: American Institute of Management, 1957); and *The Appraisal of Management* (New York: Harper & Brothers, 1962).

did focus attention on controls of overall management and on the results that can be expected from "excellent management."

Other Approaches

A number of other approaches to this interesting and important area of direct control have been made. That of William Greenwood has been mentioned. It has 203 checkpoints for use in auditing decisions and 170 for use in auditing management functions. While not all the 373 questions asked give or imply any standard of what is good or poor and while many of the operational and managerial questions tend to overlap, there can be no doubt that any enterprise following Greenwood's approach would get a comprehensive and searching analysis of itself and its system of managing.

A comprehensive study of the management audit was also made by William P. Leonard in 1962.[4] Although this study deals more with methods of organizing, initiating, interpreting, and presenting a management audit than with the content of the audit itself, and it is valuable from this point of view, it does indicate what a management audit should cover.[5] Leonard's checklist deals with a number of searching questions on the subjects of (1) plans and objectives (for example, "Have definite plans and objectives been established?"); (2) organization structure (for example, "Is there any overlapping or duplication of functions?"); (3) policies, systems, and procedures (for example, "Are the policies positive, clear, and understandable?"); (4) department personnel (for example, "What is the rate of turnover?"); (5) layout and physical equipment (for example, "Is the office laid out in a manner to get maximum utilization of space and efficient work areas?"); and (6) operations and methods of control (for example, "What consideration has been given to the adequacy, clarity, and promptness of management reports?"). While the suggested checklist and audit approach made by Leonard does not distinguish carefully between operating-performance factors and management factors, and while many significant management factors are overlooked or are not gone into in any depth, it is an interesting starting point for anyone wishing to study the possibilities of a management audit.

Another approach to a management audit has been the activity of the Department of Defense, which has undertaken from time to time to evaluate companies bidding on major defense contracts. Not only has the Department been interested in engineering concepts and capabilities, probable price, and delivery promises, but it also has delved deeply into the kind of organization and management the company had and, particularly, the company's plans to manage the defense contract should it be the successful bidder. The authors have seen cases where this investigation

---

[4]*The Management Audit* (Englewood Cliffs, N.J.: Prentice-Hall, Inc., 1962).
[5]Ibid., pp. 120–126.

was very penetrating and information was required from the bidder and audited by the buyer, in virtually every function of managing. Among other things, bidders were required to submit their proposed organization structure, their precise staffing in key positions, and their approach to, and methods of, planning and control.

That this makes sense from the standpoint of the Department of Defense is clear. After all, in a major program there is almost certainly no single factor more important to economical and dependable performance than the quality of the company's management. Also, an interesting and beneficial result of this evaluation, particularly after word was circulated that a certain company lost a contract because of management deficiencies, was that a number of defense contractors have overhauled their management systems to remove identified weaknesses.

Management Audits and Accounting Firms

Although many management consulting firms have undertaken various kinds of appraisal of enterprise management systems, usually as a part of an organization study, the greatest interest in pursuing management audits has been demonstrated by accounting audit firms. One of the significant developments of recent years has been their entry into the field of management services of a broad consultancy nature. While this has been an attractive field of expansion for these auditing companies since they are already inside an organization and financial information furnishes a ready window to problems of managing, it does open some question of conflict of interest. In other words, the question is often raised whether the same firm can be in the position of a management consultant furnishing both advice and services and still be completely objective as an accounting auditor. To be sure, accounting firms have attempted to avoid this problem by organizationally separating these two activities.

Regardless of whether auditing firms should be in management services, the fact is that they are. Since many are experienced in both auditing and management services, it is only a short step to management auditing. If it is possible for these firms to set up a completely detached and objective management auditing operation and if this can be staffed by individuals with truly professional knowledge and ability in management, it is very possible that this may result in acceleration in the practice of management auditing. At least, as long as the various professional and academic associations with a specific interest in management seem to be doing little in this field, perhaps accounting firms will show the way.

The Certified Management Audit

Another possibility for the future is the development of a certified management audit, an independent appraisal of a company's management by an outside firm. For years investors and others have relied on an independent certified accounting audit designed to make certain that the company's records and reports reflect sound accounting principles. From the standpoint of investors and even from that of managers and those desiring to work for a company, an independent audit of management quality would be extremely important. It is probably not too much to say that an investor would get more value from a certified management audit than from a certified accounting audit, since the future of a company is likely to depend more on the quality of its management than on any other single factor.

To ensure objectivity, the certified management audit should be the responsibility of a recognized outside firm, staffed with individuals qualified to appraise a company's managerial system and the quality of its managers. Although this would require considerable study from the inside and a set of reasonably objective standards, it probably would take little more time than that necessary for a thorough accounting audit. Moreover, except for the audit of top-level managers, and the preparation of a final analysis of the company's entire management as a total system, much work on the management audit could be done, as in the case of accounting audits, with the help of suitable inside managerial and staff personnel. Furthermore, as with the accounting audit, when a group of special auditors once becomes familiar with a company, subsequent audits take less time than the first. In order to ensure real objectivity, a management audit should be made by a recognized and qualified group of management appraisers with a reporting responsibility, like that of most accounting auditors, to the board of directors.

It is quite obvious that any management audit report must go far beyond the typical accounting auditor's statements. It must do more than say that a management group has followed "generally accepted standards of management." To be meaningful it would require that the quality of managers and the system within which they manage be assessed objectively in fairly specific terms. This, as one can see, gives rise to problems. How many accounting or management consulting firms can really be expected to be objective where, as so often occurs, managerial deficiencies exist at the top and when they are retained by, and report to, these same top managers? This is not an easy hurdle to overcome, at least until almost completely objective standards can be agreed upon, learned by true professionals, and applied impartially. One cannot help but wonder whether this might not necessitate a specially licensed group independent of present accounting auditing and management consulting firms.

As standards for appraising, fundamentals of management as outlined in this book, it is believed, would be appropriate.

THE CHALLENGING TASK OF THE MANAGER

Despite recognized deficiencies and crudities in the state of organized knowledge underlying the task of managing, the fact is that a science of management is developing. As the behavioral sciences give us better understanding of people, groups, cultural factors, leadership, and motivation, we are becoming better able to design environments for performance. Likewise, managerial techniques and tools are evolving, borrowing, as so many other fields have, from the systems approach long applied with benefit in the physical sciences. Moreover, as practicing managers have more thoroughly understood the importance and nature of their task, they have been able to contribute considerably to the growing body of knowledge. As the science has improved, so has the art of managing, for organized knowledge furnishes the working basis of any art.

Management and Reality

Yet, there is always the danger that management knowledge will not be used to obtain results in practice. It has been one of the major purposes of this book to present fundamental knowledge regarding managing in a way that can be useful. Such knowledge should be operational. It must be intended for reality since managing, as an art, requires the use of knowledge to solve real problems, to develop operating systems and environments in which people can perform.

This means several things. In the first place, knowledge of management is not enough. There is always the danger in any field of developing a science aimed at elegance or polish rather than results. Every science has its "educated derelicts" who know a field but cannot apply it to reality to gain useful results. Moreover, it must always be remembered that the reality with which a manager must deal is always tomorrow. Reality is always a moving target.

Major Unsolved Problems

While it is not possible to summarize all the problems modern managers face, a few major continuing ones might be noted. One is the problem of maintaining flexibility to meet change in the face of the number of inflexibilities built into the operation and environment of any enterprise. Effective management is flexible management. Not only must effective managers be able to recognize the need for change but, in order to have time to meet it, they also should forecast and anticipate it. They need to design methods of obtaining organizational change in such areas as unproductive procedures and policies, obsolete organization patterns, and the normal human tendency to resist change. Their task must also be to design around inflexibilities, such as government regulations or labor rules, that they may be unable to modify.

Another major problem area challenging the modern manager is how to design and maintain a balanced environment for creativity and conformity. Perhaps there are in many enterprises too much conformity, too much togetherness, and too little individual responsibility and opportunity. However, it can never be forgotten that all group activity of any kind requires some conformity—speaking the same language, working certain hours, fitting into an organization structure, or contributing in a definite way toward the accomplishment of group goals. But this does not mean that the perceptive and intelligent manager cannot design roles for innovation and imagination where they are desired, while still maintaining needed conformity to make group cooperation effective. This is not usually easy, but it is possible, particularly for managers who keep mindful of their basic task of designing an environment for performance.

There is also the major problem of building into any system of effective group cooperation the necessary inducements to take advantage of individual motivations. In societies where the passion for equality has sometimes tended to reduce the motivating force of the carrot by giving almost everyone the same carrots despite individual performance, and where the force of the stick is often dulled by various security programs, a manager has a difficult problem of building necessary inducements into organizational systems. While difficult, to be sure, there are still many ways of doing so. With improved knowledge of motivation and better management science and techniques, a manager with understanding and imagination can do much.

Still another major problem facing most managers is that of coping with and using effectively increased sophistication in all aspects of managing. Of particular importance has been the introduction of newer systems techniques in the areas of planning and controlling. But evidence indicates that practice has been slow to adopt many of these and other new findings. In most cases, it is believed that practicing managers have not adopted them because they do not understand them; not understanding, they are likely even to mistrust them. Much of the cause is attributable to experts who thrive on mysticism and jargon and are satisfied with elegance rather than practical application. What is needed are experts who can and will communicate and managers who can appreciate applications of such things as operations research, without necessarily understanding the mathematical models and programs, and recognize how these can contribute to better practice.

At the same time, there are still many relatively unsophisticated techniques that are too little used or too ineptly applied. When one looks at such "cloud one" techniques as managing by objectives, authority delegation, variable budgeting, market-oriented organization, and appraisal of managers, one can see that these are not based on highly sophisticated techniques. Admittedly, however, even though these and many other tools and approaches are simple in concept, they may be difficult to apply in practice. But those managers who have earnestly and intelligently tried to apply them have reaped tremendous results.

Another urgent problem is that of taking advantage of the great potential of electronic data processing, direct costing, environmental forecasting, and similar advances to improve the quality and efficiency of information. Data are rather useless raw material until designed and produced to make useful information. People cannot expect a useful end product unless they know what they wish and put into motion the steps to get it. The long-promised information revolution has been slow in coming. But come it should and will with resourceful and intelligent managing.

Perhaps one of the most urgent of all problems is to continue ensuring the quality of managers. Despite widespread attention to training and appraisal in the past quarter century, the needs appear to be greater than ever before. The growth of management knowledge, the pace of change of all kinds, and the competitive urgencies for utilizing resources well in all kinds of enterprises have tended to outdistance action. One of the most promising developments has been improvements in evaluation of managers. If these can continue and be made better in practice, if they can be tied to programs of development and reward, and if they can become an integral part of the total managing process, great progress in this area can be expected. But we still have far to go.

Managerial Obsolescence

There can be no question that the manager's role—in every kind of enterprise and at every level—is expanding and changing materially. As new knowledge and techniques become better known and applied, and as these lead to the creation of environments in which it is possible for people to perform more effectively and efficiently, the varied demands of society will force managers to take increasing advantage of this science and its tools. Virtually every manager will increasingly be faced with requirements and opportunities for improvement and for a far more intellectual approach to managing.

This means for those who manage that the danger of becoming obsolete for the task will continually be greater. As long as managing was a task learned only from experience, obsolescence was fairly unimportant. But now experience and new knowledge have been distilled into meaningful principles, theory, concepts, and basic techniques which can be made useful to the manager who does not wish to risk the danger of becoming relatively more ignorant. There is no longer time for individuals to reach the state of required managerial excellence through trial and error. Absorption of new knowledge on a continuing basis *plus* the ability to use it for practical purposes are surely the only insurance against obsolescence.

DEVELOPING MORE EFFECTIVE MANAGERS

Although the introductory analyses of the task of the manager are presented in this book as a start toward understanding the science underlying managerial practice, more is required. Among the more important considerations in ensuring effective managers, the authors would like to offer the following. Surely effective future managerial practice will depend at least on these.

A Willingness to Learn

If managers are to avoid the stultifying effect of basing too much of their learning on experience, they must be aware of the dangers of experience. As was indicated earlier in this book, undistilled experience can lead an individual toward assuming that events or programs of the past will or will not work in a different future. But managers need more than this. They need to be *willing* to learn and to take advantage of new knowledge and new techniques. This necessitates a humble approach to their successes and limitations. It demands a recognition that there is no finishing school or terminal degree for management education.

Acceleration of Management Development

The above discussion underlines the urgent importance of accelerated programs of management development. This implies not only more pertinent management seminars and conferences but also other means of transmitting to practicing managers in as simple and useful a way as possible the new knowledge and tools in the field of management.

One of the major challenges in this connection is that of compressing and transmitting that knowledge which is available. Every field of art based on a burgeoning science has the same problem. No field has completely solved it, although certain areas, such as specialized aspects of medicine and dentistry, have made considerable progress.

The authors have no adequate answer for this problem. It does appear that those on the management faculties of our universities have an obligation to practicing managers to do much of the task of compressing and transmitting this knowledge as easily and quickly as possible. There is still inadequate evidence that many university professors see the social importance of this role. Also, one might expect a greater contribution from various management associations, as well as from management consultants, who can certainly greatly improve their value to clients by doing this. Perhaps more can be done through intelligent digesting of articles and books. Also, it is entirely possible that there might be regularly established a series of special management clinics in which managers at all levels in alert companies would spend a day every few weeks being brought up to date on a specific area of new knowledge and technique. But more and better techniques must be found if the widening gap between knowledge and practice is to be narrowed.

Importance of Planning for Innovation

As competition becomes sharper, as problem solving grows in complexity, and as knowledge expands, one expects that the manager of the future will have to place greater importance on planning for innovation. Even now it is widely recognized that a business enterprise, at least, must "innovate or die," that new products just do not happen, and that new marketing ideas do not often occur by luck. The manager of the future must place more emphasis than ever before on developing an environment for effective planning. This means, even more than at present, planning goals which call for stretch, creating policy guidelines to channel thinking toward them without stifling imagination, designing roles where people can be creative, keeping abreast of the entire external environment which affects every kind of organization, and recognizing the urgency of channeling research toward desired ends.

To develop these and other environmental elements for effective planning requires the highest order of intelligence and skill. Reference to those principles, techniques, and systems requirements for effective planning outlined in this book underlines the difficulties the manager of the future might expect. Moreover, as the future unfolds, the manager concerned may be certain that new and improved techniques and approaches will be discovered.

Measuring and Rewarding Management

One of the significant areas of proper concern to the manager of the future is the importance both of objectively measuring managerial performance and of rewarding good performance, imposing sanctions on a poor operation, and providing corrective action where it is indicated. Managers must be willing to work toward establishing objective measures of performance through both a verifiable results approach and the measurement of abilities of individuals as managers.

Tailoring Information

Another important area for the manager of the future is to obtain the right information in the right form and at the right time. Tailoring information, as outlined in this book, requires a high order of intelligence and design. Until managers increasingly realize that very little of their operation can be planned and controlled through "handbook" approaches, and until more managers recognize that they themselves must become involved in tailoring the information they require, progress will continue to be slow in this area. As long as information design is confused with the clerical work of information gathering and summarizing, managers will understandably continue to fret about the inadequacy of the data on which they are forced to act.

Need for Management Research and Development

In addition to the above areas which should command greater managerial attention, a great need exists to obtain more real research and development in management tools and techniques themselves. The level of research effort and support in the field of management is woefully low. It is also not particularly great in the disciplines underlying management or, for that matter, in the entire area of social science. Nevertheless, it is probable that research in underlying disciplines far outpaces that in the central area of management.

There are many reasons for this. General management research is a difficult, exceedingly complex, and dynamic field. It is one where facts and proved relationships are hard to come by and where the controlled experiment of the laboratory is difficult to use without dangerous oversimplification. Likewise, management research is expensive, and the funds that have gone into it are abysmally inadequate. It has been estimated that not more than 1½ percent of the total being spent annually for all research in this country, or less than one-twentieth of 1 percent of gross national product, goes into research in *all* social sciences. In turn, if funds spent on management and management-related research are more than one-twentieth of this, or two-thousandths of 1 percent of gross national product, the authors would be surprised.

Still another reason for the low state of management research is that there are few clinical analyses, despite a considerable volume of clinical experience. Consulting efforts of both professional consultants and individual academics, extensive management case collections, and studies and analyses made internally in business, government, and other enterprise almost certainly encompass a huge mass of undigested, largely unsummarized, and relatively useless information. If this clinical experience could be given the analytical and summarizing work so common in the health sciences, there might be now considerable evidence of what is workable in practice and where deficiencies exist.

In undertaking this research, patience and understanding are needed. Perfection of analysis to include all kinds of variables is a laudable goal for a researcher. But, particularly in the field of management, a little light can be a massive beam in a hitherto dark area of knowledge. We must often settle for small advances so that cumulatively, and over time, we may gain larger ones.

But research without development is insufficient. One of the major challenges for the manager of the future is the need for developing more managerial inventions. It is interesting how so much creative talent has been channeled into the invention of physical designs and chemical compositions and how little into social inventions. The Gantt chart has sometimes been regarded as the most important social invention of the first half of the twentieth century. Other management inventions include the variable budget, rate-of-return-on-investment analysis, linear organizational charts, and PERT (Program Evaluation and Review Technique). Mere reference to these inventions underscores the fact that they are inventive tools developed from a base of principles on the one hand and needs on the other. Reference to them indicates also that they are useful devices in improving the art of management.

Inventions tend to reflect the cultural level of an art. There are few of them in management. Surely even the present inadequate cultural level can be coupled with urgent needs to give rise to many more management innovations, particularly if those concerned are willing to spend some time and money to direct their energies toward these inventions. It is very easy to see that one significant management invention, such as those mentioned in the previous paragraph, can make important contributions to management effectiveness and economy of operation. Applied research and development in this field surely justifies a considerable expenditure of time and money.

NEED FOR INTELLECTUAL LEADERSHIP

That intellectual leadership in management is urgently needed can hardly be denied. Managing can no longer be only a practical art requiring merely native intelligence and experience. The rapid growth of underlying knowledge and the obvious need for even more, particularly that knowledge which is organized and useful for improvement of practice, are requirements which have tremendous social significance. It is not difficult to anticipate a 5 percent rise in productivity in the American economy due to improved management, or an effort, in sheer economic terms, worth to the United States alone approximately $100 billion per year. Even these dramatic data give no direct recognition to the potential rise in human satisfactions involved in such improvements.

This means that key elements in any society would do well to give the area of managerial scientific research and development a high priority. Our college and university administrators and scholars—people in what former President Clark Kerr of the University of California has called the "knowledge industry"—should take the lead by giving management research and teaching the support their social importance deserves. Private foundations have an obligation as instruments of social betterment to support meaningful research in this field. Likewise, there can hardly be a more important area of research for a government to support. Every part of society would do well to seize the opportunity to support management research and development with the same vigor with which it has pursued such goals as new products, improved physical health, defense, and public welfare. In short, what is needed is an awareness that the intellectual and practical requirements of management are urgent, manifold, and socially important.

For people in every type of enterprise and for those who provide intellectual leadership in the field, the challenge to create a better society through improved management is an impressive one. History teaches us that when needs exist and are recognized and when the cultural level reaches the point of ability to meet these needs, leadership usually arises to inspire solutions. The challenging needs are here. The cultural level appears to be rising to the point where many answers are feasible. The question is simply where and how this leadership can be developed.

FOR DISCUSSION

1 If direct control were completely effective, would a company need any indirect controls?

2 What distinction would you draw between management appraisal, as dealt with in Chapter 20, and the management audit discussed in this chapter?

3 How would you proceed to make a management audit? Are there any similarities between it and an accounting audit?

4 Taking any major area of management theory and principles, how can it be applied to reality?

5 By reference to specific management problem areas, such as new product development, organization structure, or budgets, what are the ways managers can introduce flexibility, and what are the inflexibilities usually encountered in each?

6 How may a manager design an environment to encourage imaginativeness and creativity?

7 How would you anticipate that the computer will affect the manager's role at the top management level? The middle-management level? First-level supervision?

8 If you were asked to organize and operate an effective management research and development staff, how would you proceed?

From the discussions reflected in the previous chapters on management control, there have emerged certain essentials, or basic truths. These, which are referred to as "principles," are designed to highlight aspects of control that are regarded as especially important. In view of the fact that control, even though representing a system itself, is a subsystem of the larger area of management, certain of these principles are understandably similar to those identified in the other managerial functions. Principles of control, like those in other managerial functions, can be grouped into three categories, reflecting their purpose and nature, structure, and process.

The Purpose and Nature of Control

The purpose and nature of control may be summarized by the following principles:

Principle of assurance of objective   The task of control is to ensure that plans succeed by detecting deviations from plans and furnishing a basis for taking action to correct potential or actual deviations.

Principle of future-directed controls   Because of time lags in the total system of control, the more a control system is based on feedforward rather than simple feedback of information, the more managers have the opportunity to perceive undesirable deviations from plans before they occur and to take action in time to prevent them.

These two principles emphasize the purpose of control in any system of managerial action as one of ensuring that objectives are achieved through detecting deviations and taking corrective action designed to attain them. Moreover, control, like planning, should ideally be forward-looking. This principle is often disregarded in practice, largely because the present state of the art in managing has not provided for systems of feedforward control. Managers have generally been dependent on historical data, which may be adequate for tax collection and determination of stockholders' earnings, but are not good enough for the most effective control. Lacking means of looking forward, reference to history, on the questionable assumption that "what is past is prologue," is better than not looking at all. But time lags in the system of management control make it imperative that greater efforts be undertaken to make future-directed control a reality.

Principle of control responsibility   The primary responsibility for the exercise of control rests in the manager charged with the performance of the particular plans involved.

Since delegation of authority, assignment of tasks, and responsibility for certain objectives rest in individual managers, it follows that control over this work should be exercised by each of these managers. An individual manager's responsibility cannot be waived or rescinded without changes in the organization structure.

Principle of efficiency of controls   Control techniques and approaches are efficient if they detect and illuminate the nature and causes of deviations from plans with a minimum of costs or other unsought consequences.

Control techniques have a way of becoming costly, complex, and burdensome. Managers may become so engrossed in control that they spend more than it is worth to detect a deviation. Also, should a control technique be employed by managers with such vigor and thoroughness as to negate authority delegations to their subordinates, or should it seriously interfere with the morale of those who must execute plans, it can easily result in costs beyond any possible value. Detailed budget controls that hamstring a subordinate, complex mathematical controls that thwart innovation, and purchasing controls that delay deliveries and cost more than the item purchased are instances of inefficient controls.

Principle of direct control   The higher the quality of every manager in a managerial system, the less will be the need for indirect controls.

Most controls are based in large part on the fact that human beings make mistakes and often do not react to problems by undertaking their correction adequately and promptly. The more qualified managers are, the more they will perceive deviations from plans and take timely action to prevent them. This means that the most direct form of all control is to take steps to ensure the highest possible quality of managers.

The Structure of Control

The principles that follow are aimed at pointing out how control systems and techniques can be designed to improve the quality of managerial control.

Principle of reflection of plans   The more that plans are clear, complete, and integrated, and the more that controls are designed to reflect such plans, the more effectively controls will serve the needs of managers.

It is not possible for a system of controls to be devised without plans since the task of control is to ensure that plans work out as intended. There cannot be doubt that the more clear, complete, and integrated these plans are and the more that control techniques are designed to follow the progress of these plans, the more effective they will be.

Principle of organizational suitability   The more that an organizational structure is clear, complete, and integrated, and the more that controls are designed to reflect the place in the organization structure where responsibility for action lies, the more they will facilitate correction of deviations from plans.

Plans are performed by people. Deviations from plans must be the responsibility primarily of managers who are entrusted with the task of executing planning programs. Since it is the function of an organization structure to define a system of roles, it follows that controls must be designed to suit the role where responsibility for performance of plan lies.

Principle of individuality of controls   The more that control techniques and information are understandable to individual managers, who must utilize them for results, the more they will be actually used and the more they will result in effective control.

Although some control techniques and information can be utilized in the same form by various kinds of enterprises and managers, as a general rule controls should be tailored to meet the individual needs of managers. Some of this individuality is related to position in the organization structure, as noted in the previous principle. Another aspect of individuality calls for tailoring controls to the kind and level of understanding of managers. The authors have seen both company presidents and supervisors throw up their hands in dismay (often for quite different reasons) at the unintelligibility and inappropriate form of control information that was a delight to the figure- and table-minded controller. Control information which a manager cannot or will not use has little practical value.

The Process of Control

Control, often being so much a matter of technique, rests heavily on the art of management, on know-how in given instances. However, there are certain propositions or principles which experience has shown have wide applicability.

Principle of standards   Effective control requires objective, accurate, and suitable standards.

There should be a simple, specific, and verifiable way to measure whether a planning program is being accomplished. Control is accomplished through people. Even the best manager cannot help being influenced by personal factors, and actual performance is sometimes camouflaged by a dull or a sparkling personality or by a subordinate's ability to "sell" a deficient performance. By the same token, good standards of performance, objectively applied, will more likely be accepted by subordinates as fair and reasonable.

Principle of critical-point control   Effective control requires attention to those factors critical to appraising performance against an individual plan.

It would ordinarily be wasteful and unnecessary for managers to follow every detail of planning execution. What they must know is that plans are being executed. Therefore, they concentrate attention on salient factors of performance that will indicate, without watching everything, any important deviations from plans. There are no easy guidelines to determine the critical points they should watch, since their selection is predominantly a matter of managerial art. Perhaps all managers can ask themselves what things in *their* operations will best show *them* whether the plans for which they are responsible are being accomplished.

The exception principle   The more managers concentrate control efforts on exceptions, the more efficient will be the results of their control.

This principle holds that managers should concern themselves only with significant deviations, the especially good or the especially bad situations. It is often confused with the principle of critical-point control, and they do have some kinship. However, critical-point control has to do with recognizing the points to be watched, while the exception principle has to do with watching the size of deviations, logically at these points.

Principle of flexibility of controls   If controls are to remain effective despite failure or unforeseen changes of plans, flexibility is required in their design.

According to this principle, controls must not be so inflexibly tied in with a plan as to be useless if the entire plan fails or is suddenly changed. Note that this principle applies to failures of plans, not failures of people operating under plans.

Principle of action   Control is justified only if indicated or experienced deviations from plans are corrected through appropriate planning, organizing, staffing, and leading.

There are instances in practice where this simple truth is forgotten. Control is a wasteful use of managerial and staff time unless it is followed by action. If deviations are found in experienced or projected performance, action is indicated, in the form of either redrawing plans or making additional plans to get back on course. It may call for reorganization. It may require replacement of subordinates or training them to do the task desired. Or there may be no other fault than a lack of direction and leadership in getting a subordinate to understand the plans or to be motivated to accomplish them. But, in any case, action is implied. This principle affirms the essential unity of management—the fact that no one can effectively manage who cannot appropriately undertake the functions of planning, organizing, staffing, leading, and controlling and who cannot, in doing so, recognize that these functions are a system, that they all must operate in an open social system, and that their application depends upon the contingencies of a situation.

CASES FOR PART 6

1   The Putnam Corporation

The Putnam Corporation was one of the country's leaders in the design and production of industrial and commercial air-conditioning equipment. While most of the products were standard items, a considerable number involving large sales volume were specially designed for installation in big office buildings and factories. Besides being an innovator in product design and having an exceptionally good customer service department, the company was well known for its high-quality products and its ability to satisfy customer demands for equipment promptly.

Because the company had grown rapidly, it had to be careful with its cash requirements, especially for accounts receivable and for inventories. For a number of years the company had kept inventories under close control at a level equal to 1.8 times the monthly sales, or a turnover of nearly seven times per year. Suddenly, and it seemed almost without warning, inventories soared to triple monthly sales, and the company found itself with $12 million worth of inventories above a normal level. Calculating a cost of carrying inventory at 30 percent of the value of inventories (including the cost of money, storage and handling, and obsolescence), it was easy to estimate that this excess inventory was costing the company some $3.6 million per year in profits before taxes. In addition, it forced the company to call on its bank for more loans than had been expected.

Richard Simpson, president of Putnam, was understandably worried and incensed when this matter came to his attention. He was told that the primary reasons for this rise in inventory were excessive buying of raw materials in advance because of anticipated shortages and the failure of a new computer program to work as expected, with the result that production and purchasing people did not have complete information on what was happening to inventory for several months.

Mr. Simpson, taking the position that no company should let something like this surplus inventory occur without advance notice and that no manager can be expected to control a business on the basis of history, instructed his vice president for finance to come up with a program to get better control of inventories in the future.

1 What do you find wrong with Putnam's controls?
2 Would a feedforward system of control help? How would you try to apply it to Putnam?
3 Are there any other techniques or approaches to control that you would suggest?

2 Western Petroleum Corporation

Western Petroleum Corporation was founded in 1957 with an investment of $250,000 by multimillionaire Victor Eastman and the same amount by several of his friends. With a few young geologists, recruited from several major oil companies, who saw a real chance for action in the company and with the daring of Mr. Eastman, the company embarked on a vigorous exploration program in northern California. Their approach was quickly rewarded by discovering a large gas field and several good oil-producing wells. With large profits from these fields and Mr. Eastman's ability to get a concession from a country in northern Africa, the brilliance of the young team of geologists paid off when the company discovered a large oil field in the African country.

As profits accumulated, as banks rushed to lend Western money, and as investors eagerly bought its stock, Western acquired a number of fairly large companies. They included (1) the Master Chemical Company, one of the largest producers of industrial chemicals and agricultural fertilizers in the United States, with annual sales of $500 million; (2) the Beverly Coal Company, third largest miner of coal in the country, with sales of more than $300 million per year; (3) the Pennant Gas and Oil Company, with refineries and retail oil products outlets in Europe and annual sales of $350 million per year; and (4) several other companies in such fields as oil marketing, real estate development, and plastics materials. In addition, Western continued its program of searching for oil both in the United States and overseas.

The company had an extraordinary history of growth. From sales of less than $500,000 in 1957, it grew to the remarkable size of $2.7 billion in sales by 1974.

Profits kept pace with growth and, although Western had heavy loans from banks and others and had sold more than 40 million new shares of stocks to the public, stock prices rose by more than twenty times in the period.

Although profits leveled off in 1974, sales still rose by 15 percent over 1973. This was not regarded as a problem by Western's top management since the company was investing heavily in new oil exploration, and its industrial chemical profits had almost disappeared because of the overbuilding and severe price competition of all companies in this field. But, obviously, the stock market had some misgivings about Western. The company's shares, which had risen to $105 in 1972, fell to $25 in 1974. But the top management of Western was not too concerned since all oil and industrial chemicals stocks had suffered a drop in price.

However, toward the end of 1974, a number of adverse events occurred which did shock and surprise Western's top management. Among the most important of these were the following:

1   Profits in industrial chemicals continued their decline as the new and larger competitors fought for business to keep their chemicals plants operating at capacity or as near to it as possible.

2   An industrywide coal strike closed down the coal mines for almost two months in October and November of 1974, with an impact on profits of more than $11 million.

3   In addition, a new national coal Mine and Safety Act required stringent changes in mining procedures, reducing productivity and requiring the employment of many new miners in an industry where there were few experienced miners to be hired, so that inexperienced miners had to be employed.

4   With a new labor union contract, mine labor wages went up considerably. The Beverly Coal Company found it could not pass on these increased costs, along with the higher costs from lower productivity, to most of its large public utility customers with whom it had entered long-term contracts at fixed prices per ton. The coal company management had defended these fixed-price contracts on the ground that past history had shown that cost increases had always been offset by productivity increases.

5   The plastic film, sheeting, and fabrics division suffered losses in 1974 exceeding $10 million primarily because (a) the new plant was poorly designed and more expensive to operate than had been anticipated; (b) the new and promising plastic coating material failed to meet specifications, with the result that buyers shipped it back to the company by the carload; and (c) large losses were incurred in raw material costs because of inadequate weighing, inspection, and storage procedures and facilities.

6   The largest loss charged against 1974's earnings was $88 million to charge off potential losses from some $200 million of 3-to5-year oil tanker charters. The general manager of the European operation had embarked on an ambitious program of chartering tankers so that the company could be assured of bringing oil to Europe from Saudi Arabia and other Persian Gulf sources, in the event that problems in the Mideast would result in loss of supply from the northern Africa fields. When the size of

these commitments was learned in 1974 and it became evident that the tanker charters would not be needed, and when tanker charter rates dropped considerably, the company was forced to take this large write-down. When the huge loss exposure was questioned, it was found that the European general manager had proceeded on his own to get these tanker charters. When he was called upon to resign as the result of his costly decision, he defended himself on the ground that he had suggested this idea to Mr. Eastman on one of his overseas trips and that the chairperson had commented that he "thought it was a good idea" to get some tanker charters.

7 Other disappointments came as the result of write-downs of a number of other unsuccessful investments. The general manager of a small division approved the construction of a new office building in the headquarters city of his division at a cost of $6 million, only to find, as the building neared completion, that his division was being combined with another division and the headquarters moved to another city. An executive in charge of drilling a well in a foreign oil field ran into unexpected difficulties and went over his budget by more than $5 million before anyone at Western's headquarters even knew that the money had been spent and the well abandoned.

Mr. Eastman was a strong believer in a lean and streamlined headquarters organization. He felt that he could keep his eye on Western's operations in his position as chairman and chief executive officer and that the job of the president was to keep in close touch with operations of the various divisions and subsidiaries. Mr. Eastman would make the company's major decisions and would especially negotiate new acquisitions and new oil-exploration leases and concessions. It was his firm conviction that each subsidiary and division top manager should run his own operation and be judged primarily on the earnings statement and balance sheet of the operation.

The principal control tool at headquarters was the budget for capital expenditures. Each year, the vice president in charge of finance would sit down with division and subsidiary top managers, hear their needs for capital expenditures, and then use his own judgment in allocating funds for these expenditures. In addition, all divisions and subsidiaries submitted balance sheets and earnings statements to headquarters each 3 months; these statements were reviewed by the financial department and then used to produce consolidated statements of the company for bankers and investors.

1 What is your evaluation of Western's management control approach and techniques?
2 To what extent and in which ways were Western's problems in 1974 due to lack of effective management control?
3 Precisely what program of controls would you recommend for Western?

3 Anchor Consolidated Industries, Inc.

"I heard it said in a management conference I attended last week," remarked Carol Sims, president of Anchor Consolidated Industries, Inc., a small company whose clever new pleasure-boat products had given rise to growth since its founding 5 years ago to a level of $5 million in annual sales, "that the sound way to run a company is to let all the department and section heads develop their own budgets. But I can't imagine doing this in this company. If I did, these people would spend so much money that we would soon be bankrupt. No! As long as I am in charge of this company, I will tell my people what they can spend. There will be no blank checks here. And I will hold my controller responsible for making sure this company makes the profits I want. I have heard of too many companies with the fast growth we have had that have gone broke because optimism and uncontrolled spending went through the ceiling. And this idea of variable budgets is even worse. Imagine what would happen if I let everyone vary their budgets each month, quarter, or year!"

1 To what extent do you agree or disagree with Carol Sims?
2 Do you believe that her way of budget making will work? Why?
3 If you were going to suggest to Ms. Sims how she could have her department and section heads involved in budgeting, how would you avoid the problem now worrying her?
4 How would you ensure effective control with variable budgets?

4 The Kappa Corporation

As George House, vice president of finance, and Helen Robbins, controller, walked into the office of Adrian Barnes, chairperson and chief executive officer of Kappa Corporation, they were met with the following outburst from the company's top officer:

"Why doesn't someone tell me things? Why can't I know what is going on around here? Why am I kept in the dark? No one informs me on how the company is going, and I never seem to hear of our problems until they become crises. Now, I want you both to work out a system where I can be kept informed, and I want to know by next Monday how you will do it. I am tired of being isolated from the things I must know if I am to take responsibility for this company."

After George House had left Mr. Barnes's office, he turned to his controller and muttered: "That silly jerk! Everything he wants to know or could possibly want to know is in that shelf of reports on the table back of his desk."

1 Who was right—Adrian Barnes or George House? Was Barnes getting information?
2 What would you do to make sure that the chairperson did get the information he needed for control?

5 The Wholesale Drug Company

Established in the 1940s, the Wholesale Drug Company grew from a twelve-person operation at the end of World War II to one of the largest firms of its kind in 1979. The success was due primarily to the leadership of the president, Ms. Johnson. Since many similar, but smaller, enterprises used the computer for recordkeeping and data processing, Ms. Johnson was under great pressure to install a computerized control system to keep track of twenty distribution centers scattered throughout the nation.

Up to that time, expenses and income were recorded by a relatively simple ledger sheet and a journal showing the data for the twenty centers. This kind of record-keeping, which was done by hand, allowed for easy comparison of the centers. Payrolls were done in a similar manner, and checks were usually processed within 24 hours. At that time five people and two supervisors were employed in the accounting department.

Several computer companies looked at the system but their analysis showed that cost savings were hardly possible. However, one company made a rather convincing case for a new data processing system. The consulting firm predicted the following benefits: (1) faster processing of information, (2) more detailed information on the operation, and (3) a reduction in costs.

After 2 years of using the new system, Ms. Johnson, who reluctantly agreed to computerize the system, related the following story: "Before the use of the computer, we had seven people in the accounting department. Now we have nine plus seven people in the data processing center. It is true that it takes only a few minutes to get the output from the computer, but we cannot run the program until the last distribution center provides the data. Unfortunately, this means delays, because we depend on the slowest operational unit for their input. It is true that we get more detailed information, but I do not know if anybody ever looks at it. It is just too time-consuming to find the relevant information in the stacks of computer output and to interpret the data. I just wish we could go back to the old ledger system. But, we invested so much money and have reached a point of no return."

1 Why did the computerized system not live up to its expectations?
2 What should Ms. Johnson do now?
3 How would you design a computerized system? What factors would you consider?

6 Hanover Space and Electronics Corporation

Warren Hanover, president of Hanover Space and Electronics Corporation, and the presidents of other large defense contractors had just met with the Secretary of Defense in Washington. The Secretary had impressed on the group of presidents the fact that the government must insist on better management and tighter control by defense contractors in order to get more product from increasingly scarce defense dollars, especially in view of the sharp inflation of recent years. The Secretary had strongly emphasized that, from now on, the Defense Department would carefully examine management practices of contractors and, at the very least, would not give any major contract to a company that did not have a strong, effective control system.

Warren Hanover, as well as the other presidents, got the message. On his return to his headquarters in Kansas City, he immediately called in his administrative vice president, told him of the Secretary's position, and ordered him to install an effective control system. The administrative vice president, in turn, called in the corporation controller and passed the order on to him. The controller then assigned the task to his staff assistant, asking her to scour the literature on control to find a system the company would adopt and to present a proposal to him within a week.

At the end of the week, the staff assistant had to report to the controller that she had not found a control system suitable for the company, despite the fact that she had reviewed dozens of books and journal articles.

1. Could the staff assistant have found a suitable control system if she had looked far enough?
2. If you were the staff assistant, what would you suggest be done to develop an effective control system?

7 Hospital Services, Inc.

In the decade of the 1960s considerable interest was generated in hospital care. The aged and the poor were heavily subsidized by government programs aimed, among other things, at helping those in need to get adequate hospital care. During the same time, the cost of hospital services doubled, and still there were not enough beds for patients. Federal and state governments saw the need to distinguish between the types of care that were most suitable. It was clear that not everyone needed the full-service care of general hospitals. The law contemplated that once discharged from such a facility, patients would be sent to a convalescent hospital for a limited time, where the service level and costs were much lower. And, theoretically, having completed the allowed time, or as much of it as was needed, in this institution, patients would be returned to their homes, where they could receive needed services.

Jane McDonald was among several people who had the idea of building or buying a chain of convalescent hospitals to serve the growing need for beds. She thought that a chain could probably achieve some economies of operation that a single hospital would not find possible. She intended to broaden her business by purchasing land, securing a mortgage to take care of the hospitals and selling the whole package to investors. She would place her own optical stores and drugstores within each hospital, have her own wholesalers in drugs and hospital equipment, and create her own construction companies.

Ms. McDonald needed money to do these things. She knew that the stocks of convalescent hospital chains were being traded in multiples from 60 to 200 times earnings, and so she determined to tap the investment market for capital. She got together a few scattered assets, packaged them attractively, and took her business public. It could not be said that she could show any earnings, but she stressed her prospective earnings per share. Amazingly, the idea sold, and she raised about $15 million.

With cash in the bank and an attractive vision in her head, Ms. McDonald was ready to go with her Hospital Services, Inc. Plush offices came first. Then a group of lawyers and tax accountants was added. A salesman sold her a computer. Convalescent hospitals were purchased at high prices; land was bought across the country and construction was begun; and acqusitions were eagerly sought. Ms. McDonald did not do this all by herself. She was especially gifted in her public relations, government relations, and negotiations skills and tended to specialize in them. Managers were hired to take care of construction, hospital management, and finance.

As the months passed, the cash raised from the public issue was fast used. On paper the cash flow from operations should have been adequate, but it did not actually materialize. No one, it seemed, was able to get a reading on hospital finances. In some cases, there were no profits; in other cases, the individual institution kept its own cash balance; and in others, there was a heavy drain of funds to cover expenses. The government did not help, either. Its agencies were new at this activity; interpretations were being made in the law so frequently that no one knew what practice to follow.

Throughout this period of operation there was no slowdown in activity. Ms. McDonald was in her element, but her controller failed to warn her of imminent bankruptcy. There did come a day when she ran out of money. This occurred at a time when bankers were tightening up credit and the stock market was falling fast.

As she looked over her wreck, she inquired, "What control system should I have had?"

1 How did Hospital Services, Inc., get out of control?
2 Exactly what controls should have been used and how?
3 To assess the success of the company, what other things should have been done?

Glossary of Management Terms and Concepts

A

Absolutness of responsibility *See* responsiblity, absoluteness of.

Administrators *See* managers.

Approach to management, communications-center An analysis of management in which the manager is looked upon as a communications center, receiving information, storing and processing it, and disseminating it.

Approach to management, contingency or situational An analysis of management that emphasizes the fact that what managers do in practice depends upon a given set of circumstances or the "situation" and that there is no single "best way" to manage.

Approach to management, cooperative social systems An analysis of management as a study of human relationships in a cooperative social system.

Approach to management, decision theory An analysis of management that concentrates on rational decision making as the core of the managerial task.

Approach to management, empirical, or case An analysis of management as a study of experience from instances of managing.

Approach to management, group behavior An analysis of management as a study in group behavior patterns.

Approach to management, interpersonal behavior An analysis of management as a study of interpersonal relations.

Approach to management, managerial roles A means of analyzing management by observing what managers actually do and from such observations come to conclusions as to what managerial activities (in roles) are.

Approach to management, mathematical, or "management science" An analysis of management primarily as a matter of developing mathematical models of managerial decision areas.

Approach to management, operational An analysis of management which draws together knowledge, both that unique to managing and that from other fields pertinent to managing, and relates it to the task of managing in a way most useful to the managerial practitioner; it is thus in part eclectic and in part a summary of the central core of knowledge which exists only in management situations.

Approach to management, systems approach An analysis of management which emphasizes looking at managerial knowledge from the point of view of systems.

Approaches to management, sociotechnical systems An analysis of management viewing managerial situations as involving a combination of interacting social and technical systems.

Art Practice.

Assessment center A technique to aid in the selection and evaluation of potential managers whereby candidates are subjected to various tests and exercises and their performance is observed and evaluated by assessors.

Authority, organizational See organizational authority.

Authority, parity with responsibility The principle that since authority is the discretionary power to carry out assignments and responsibilitity is the obligation owed a delegant to accomplish these activities, it logically follows that responsibility for action cannot be greater than authority delegated, nor should it be less.

B

Board of directors A plural executive, that is, a committee with power to exercise authority and make decisions, which normally stands at the top of a corporation and is charged by law with the responsibility of "managing" the corporation.

Boundaries See systems, boundaries.

Bounded rationality Rational action limited because of lack of information, lack of time or ability to analyze alternatives in the light of a goal sought, unclear goals, or the human tendency not to take risks in making a decision, to "play it safe."

Break-even point analysis Charting and analyzing relationships, usually between sales and expenses, to determine at what size or volume point an operation breaks even between a loss or a profit; it can be used in any problem area where marginal effects can be pinpointed.

Budget A statement of plans and expected results expressed in numerical terms; a "numberized" program.

Budget summary A master summary of operating and capital budgets with a forecast income statement and balance sheet.

Budgets, program *See* program budgeting.

Budgets, variable or flexible *See* variable budgets.

Budgets, zero-based *See* zero-based budgeting.

C

Centralization of authority The tendency to restrict delegation of decision making in an organization structure, usually by holding it at or near the top of the organization structure.

Chart of approved authorizations A technique by which the various authority delegations of an enterprise are charted in a matrix form showing the nature of the subjects over which authority exists and the organizational positions where decision-making authority rests.

Collegial management The case, as in universities, where the members of a group manage themselves through group meetings, committees, and consensus.

Commitment principle Logical planning encompasses a period of time in the future necessary to foresee, through a series of actions, the fulfillment of commitments involved in a current decision.

Committee A group of persons to whom, as a group, some matter is committed for purposes of information, advice, interchange of ideas, or decision.

Communication The transfer of information from one person to another that must be understandable to the receiver.

Completed staff work Implies presentation of a clear recommendation to a superior based upon full consideration of a problem, clearance with persons importantly affected, suggestions about avoiding any difficulties involved, and, often, the preparation of necessary implementing paperwork so that the receiving manager can accept or reject the proposal without further study, long conferences, or unnecessary work.

Composite strategies A group of strategies in various related areas that a company or other enterprises may have.

Concepts Mental images of anything formed by generalization from particulars; for example, a word or term.

Contingency approach to leadership A theory that leadership depends upon the group task situation and the degree to which the leader's style, personality, and approach fit the group.

Contingency management Managing which recognizes differences or contingencies in people, at various times and in actual situations; also referred to as "situational management"; an approach that emphasizes that there can be no "one best way" in all kinds of situations.

Contingency model of leadership effectiveness A leadership model developed by Fred Fiedler that postulates that a leader's effectiveness depends on three variables: (1) how well a leader is accepted by subordinates; (2) the degree to which subordinates' positions are routine and clearly spelled out in contrast to being vague and undefined; and (3) the formal authority in the position occupied by a leader.

Contingency planning Planning for possible future environments which are not expected to occur but which may occur; if this possible future is widely different from that premised, alternative premises and plans are required.

Contingency strategies Strategies developed to be used when unforeseen events or circumstances may make a selected strategy obsolete or unsuitable.

Controlling The managerial function of measuring and correcting performance of activities of subordinates in order to assure that enterprise objectives and plans are being accomplished.

Control of overall performance Control designed to measure the total performance of an enterprise, an integrated division of it, or a major program or project.

Control process In managing, the basic process involves (1) establishing standards, (2) measuring performance against standards, and (3) correcting for deviations.

Cooperative system A system, as perceived by Chester Barnard, as one whose purpose is cooperation and which is comprised of physical, biological, social, and psychological elements.

Coordination Achieving harmony of individual effort with group effort toward the accomplishment of group purposes and objectives.

Cost effectiveness That approach to problem solving which weighs alternatives and chooses an alternative, especially where advantages and costs cannot be accurately measured in numbers, by considering costs of other alternatives in comparison with benefits derived.

D

Decentralization of authority The tendency to disperse decision-making authority in an organization structure.

Decentralization of performance The geographic dispersal of operations in an enterprise.

Decision making The selection from among alternatives of a course of action; a rational selection of a course of action.

Decision trees An approach toward seeing risks and probabilities in a problem situation involving uncertainty, or chance events, by sketching in the form of a "tree" decision points, chance events, and the probabilities involved in various courses that might be undertaken.

Delegation of authority The vesting of decision-making discretion in a subordinate.

Delegation of authority, process of The determination of results expected from a subordinate, the assignment of tasks, the delegation of authority for accomplishing these tasks, and the exaction of responsibility for their accomplishment.

Delphi technique A technique normally used for forecasting such future events and conditions as technological developments by obtaining estimates of experts in a field and feeding back summaries of these estimates for additional estimates by those experts, until a reasonable degree of convergence is obtained.

Department A distinct area, division, or branch of an enterprise over which a manager has authority for the performance of specified activities and results.

Departmentation by customer The groupings of activities around customers.

Departmentation by function The grouping of activities in departments in accordance with the characteristic functions an enterprise undertakes; for example, in a manufacturing company—marketing, production, engineering, and finance.

Departmentation by marketing channels The grouping of activities around channels of marketing, that is, around the paths by which customers are reached.

Departmentation by markets Grouping of activities around markets served, often referred to as "market centering."

Departmentation by process or equipment The grouping of activities around a process or type of equipment used, such as electronic data processing or painting departments.

Departmentation by product The grouping of activities around a product or product line.

Departmentation by territory The grouping of activities by territorial segments; geographic departmentation.

Differentiation A characteristic of an open system, and a social system in particular, by which it tends to become more specialized in its structure and behavior patterns.

Direct control The concept that the most direct of all controls is to assure high-quality managers on the premise that qualified managers make fewer mistakes requiring other (or indirect) controls, perceive and anticipate problems, and initiate appropriate actions to avoid or correct for deviations.

Direct costing The technique of accounting for costs by dividing them between period costs (those which vary only with time or are fixed over a period of time regardless of changes in volume) and direct costs (those which vary to some extent with volume of output); also not carrying into inventory any period costs.

Directing and leading Clarifying, guiding, teaching, and encouraging participants in an enterprise to perform effectively and with zeal and confidence.

Distribution logistics An operations research optimizing model that treats the entire materials flow system of an enterprise—from sales forecasting through purchasing and processing of materials, inventorying them, to shipping of finished goods to sales warehouses—as a single system.

E

Elaboration The tendency of an open system, and a social system in particular, to enlarge its boundaries or create a new suprasystem with wider boundaries.

Enterprise self-audit The making by an enterprise of an audit, or appraisal, of its position, where it is heading under present programs, what its objectives should be, and whether revised plans are needed to meet these objectives.

Entrepreneurs People with the ability to see an opportunity, to obtain the necessary capital, labor, and other inputs, to know how to put together an operation successfully, and have the willingness to take the personal risk of success or failure.

Entropy The tendency of a system to "run down" as it utilizes systems energy or resources. *See* negative entropy.

Environment, managerial *See* managerial environment, economic; managerial environment, ethical; managerial environment, political; managerial environment, social; managerial environment, technological.

Environmental forecasting Forecasting the future environment—economic, technological, social, ethical, and political—as it may affect the enterprise.

Equifinality Especially with reference to social systems, the fact that goals can be accomplished in varying ways, with varying inputs and processes or methods.

Ethics Sets of generally accepted standards of social conduct.

Executives *See* managers.

Expectancy theory of motivation The theory that people will be motivated by their expectancy that a particular action on their part will lead to a desired outcome.

F

Feedback An informational input in a system transmitting messages of system operation to indicate whether the system is operating as planned; information concerning any type of planned operation relayed to the responsible person for evaluation.

Feedforward control A control system that attempts to identify future deviations from plans, early enough to take action before the deviations occur, by developing a model of system or process inputs, monitoring these inputs, and taking action in time to prevent undesired or unplanned system outputs.

Field theory of motivation Psychologist Lewin's theory that motivations depend on organizational climate and must be looked upon as an element in a larger field of restraining and driving forces.

Flexibility principle The more that flexibility (the ability to change direction without undue cost, embarrassment, or friction) can be built into plans, the less the danger of losses incurred by unexpected events.

Functional authority The right or power inherent in a position to issue instructions or approve actions of persons in positions not reporting directly to the person holding such authority; normally it is a limited line-type of authority applicable only to specialized areas and representing a delegation to a specialist by a superior manager with authority over both the position given functional authority and the position subjected to this authority. For example, a company controller is ordinarily given functional authority to prescribe the system of accounting throughout the company, but this specialized authority is really a delegation from the chief executive.

Functions of managers *See* managers, functions of, and managers, task of.

Gantt chart A technique for planning and control developed by Henry L. Gantt showing by bars on a chart the time requirements for the various tasks, or "events," of a production or other program.

Goal of managers See managers, goal of.

Goals See objectives.

Graicunas's theory A mathematical formula developed by V. A. Graicunas to calculate the number of human relationship situations involved in having various numbers of subordinates reporting to a single superior.

Guide-chart profile methods of position evaluation The point system developed by Edward H. Hay and Associates used for evaluating managerial positions based on evaluation in three areas: (1) know-how required; (2) problem solving involved; and (3) degree and extent of accountability or responsibility.

H

Hierarchy of needs Psychologist Abraham Maslow's theory that basic human needs exist in an ascending order of importance (physiological, security or safety, affiliation or acceptance, esteem, and self-actualization) and that once a lower-level need is satisfied, actions appealing to it cease to motivate.

Homeostasis, dynamic The characteristic of a system whereby it is constantly in motion with a tendency to seek equilibrium at various changing levels.

Human asset accounting Programs attempting to measure the value, and its changes, of investment in human assets of an enterprise.

Hygiene approach to motivation Psychologist Herzberg's theory that certain human needs motivate and others merely cause dissatisfaction if they are not met; in other words, the meeting of this latter class of needs is a "maintenance" or "hygiene" factor; these are such factors in a work situation as salary, company policy and administration, quality of supervision, working conditions, interpersonal relations, status, and job security.

I

Industrial dynamics An approach to planning and control in which flows of information, materials, manpower, capital equipment, and money are seen as an interacting system influencing enterprise growth, fluctuation, and decline.

Informal organization Any joint personal activity or relationship without conscious joint purpose; generally, patterns of human behavior and relationships existing in parallel with or lying outside the formal organization structure.

Input-output tables An approach to economic forecasting by development of tables that show the relationship of industries to one another and their sharing of gross national product by calculating the purchases and sales made between industries.

Instruction An action by managers which initiates, modifies, or stops an activity in the department under their control.

Intimate association, assignment by Assigning activities to a department where activities are diverse but are intimately associated with, or closely related to, the achievement of department or enterprise purposes.

J

Job enlargement Programs of expanding the job content with a view to making it less specialized and presumably more interesting and challenging.

Job enrichment Programs of building into jobs a high sense of meaning, challenge, and potential for accomplishment.

L

Leadership, definition of Influence, or the art or process of influencing people so that they strive willingly and enthusiastically toward the accomplishment of group goals.

Leadership continuum The concept advanced by Tannenbaum and Schmidt in which leadership is seen as involving a variety of styles ranging from highly boss-centered to highly subordinate-centered, depending on situations and personalities.

Leading The function of managers involving the process of influencing people so that they will strive willingly toward the achievement of group goals.

Limiting factor, principle of In choosing from among alternatives, the more individuals can recognize and solve for those factors which are limiting or critical to the attainment of the desired goal, the more clearly, accurately, and easily they can select the most favorable alternative.

Line An authority relationship in organizational positions where one person (a manager) has responsibility for the activities of another person (the subordinate). It is commonly erroneously thought of as a department or a person, and not a relationship; it is also commonly, but inaccurately, thought of as the major departments of an enterprise believed to be most closely contributing to the achieving of enterprise objectives, such as marketing and production in a manufacturing company.

Linear programming A technique for determining the optimum combination of limited resources to obtain a desired goal; it is based on the assumption that a linear relationship exists between variables and that the limits of variables can be determined.

Long-range planning Planning for a period of time in the future to foresee, as credibly as possible, the fulfillment of commitments being made today; planning to take into account the future impact of today's decisions.

Management as an art The use of underlying knowledge (science) and application of it to realities in a situation, usually with blend or compromise, to obtain practical results; managing is an art but management is more properly used to refer to the body of knowledge—science—underlying this art.

Management as a science Organized knowledge—concepts, theory, principles, and techniques—underlying the practice of managing; science systematically explains phenomena in managing, as it does in any field.

Management auditing Auditing the quality of managers through appraising them as individual managers and appraising the quality of the total system of managing in an enterprise.

Management development The process of individual growth in the full utilization of one's managerial capabilities.

Management inventory A technique, usually by use of a chart, whereby managers in an enterprise are designated as promotable now, promotable in one year, have potential for future promotion, are satisfactory but not promotable, or should be terminated.

Management techniques Ways of doing things in managing.

Management theory jungle The term applied by Harold Koontz in 1961 to identify the existence of a variety of schools of, or approaches to, management theory and knowledge. He found just six such schools or approaches in 1961, but in 1979 identified eleven. He found that the schools or approaches tended to vary in their semantics and their view of management, and approached the theory of management from different specialists' points of view.

Management training The provision of opportunities through various approaches and programs to improve a person's knowledge of, and proficiency in, the managerial task.

Managerial appraisal Evaluating the performance of managers in their positions, ideally evaluating performance in setting and achieving verifiable objectives and performance as a manager.

Managerial environment, economic That environment of managers which has to do with such elements as capital; materials; labor availability, quality, and price; price levels; productivity; availability of high-quality entrepreneurs and managers; government fiscal and tax policy; customers; and demands for goods and services.

Managerial environment, ethical That environment of managers which has to do with generally accepted sets of standards of personal conduct.

Managerial environment, political That environment of managers which has to do with the complex of laws, regulations, and government agencies and their actions.

Managerial environment, social That environment of managers which has to do with the attitudes, desires, expectations, degrees of intelligence, beliefs, and customs of people in any given group or society; social forces.

Managerial environment, technological That environment of managers which has to do with such elements as knowledge of ways of doing things; inventions; and techniques in the areas of processes, machines, and tools.

Managerial grid A way of analyzing leadership styles, developed by Blake and

Mouton, whereby leaders are classified on a grid with the two dimensions of concern for people and concern for production.

Managerial know-how Managerial knowledge applied effectively in practice; it includes both knowledge of the science underlying managing and the artful ability to apply it to realities.

Managers Those who undertake the task and functions of managing, at any level in any kind of enterprise.

Managers, functions of Planning, organizing, staffing, leading, and controlling.

Managers, goal of To so establish and maintain an environment for performance that individuals will contribute to group objectives with the least costs—whether money, time, effort, materials, discomfort, or dissatisfaction.

Managers, task of The design and maintenance of an environment for the effective and efficient performance of individuals working together in groups toward the accomplishment of preselected missions and objectives.

Managing by objectives Programs of basing much of managerial planning, operation, and appraisal on having each manager set objectives in verifiable terms (with the superior's approval) and assessing his or her performance against these objectives. Sometimes called management by objectives or "MBO."

Market centering See departmentation by markets.

Matrix organization A form of organization in which two or more basic types of departmentation are combined; in engineering and marketing this is likely to be a combination of project (or product) and functional departments with one overlaying the other; often referred to as "grid" organization structures or "product" management.

Milestone budgeting Budgeting by breaking down a program or project into identifiable and controllable pieces, or "milestones."

Missions, or purposes The basic function or task of an enterprise or agency or any department of it.

Motivators Forces that induce individuals to act or perform; forces that influence human behavior.

Motives The drives, desires, needs, wishes, and similar forces that channel human behavior toward goals. See expectancy theory of motivation, field theory of motivation, hierarchy of needs, hygiene approach to motivation, job enlargement, job enrichment.

Multinational corporations Corporations headquartered usually in one country, but having operations (usually at least manufacturing and marketing) in other countries.

N

Navigational change, principle of The more planning decisions commit for the future, the more important it is that a manager periodically check on events and expectations and redraw plans as necessary to maintain a course of action toward a desired goal; this implies flexibility in the planning process and a willingness to change plans.

Negative entropy The characteristic of a system whereby it imports more energy or resources from its environment than it uses or exports to its environment and thereby does not "run down"; a common characteristic of social systems.

O

Objectives, or goals The ends toward which activity is aimed—the end points of planning.

Objectives, verifiable An objective is verifiable if, at some target date in the future, a person can look back with certainty and determine whether or not it has been accomplished; goals or objectives may be verifiable if expressed quantitatively (i.e., in numbers) or qualitatively (a program with certain specific characteristics to be put into effect by a certain date).

Operational audit The regular and independent appraisal by a staff of internal auditors of the accounting, financial, and other operations of an enterprise.

Operational-management theory and science *See* approach to management, operational.

Operations research Ordinarily thought of as using optimizing models—the use of mathematical models to reflect the variables and constraints in a situation and their effect on a selected goal; the application of scientific method in a problem situation with a view to providing a quantitative basis for arriving at an optimum solution in terms of goals sought.

Organization A concept used in a variety of ways such as (1) a system or pattern of any set of relationships in any kind of undertaking; (2) an enterprise itself; (3) cooperation of two or more persons; (4) all behavior of all participants in a group; and (5) the intentional structure of roles in a formally organized enterprise.

Organization development A systematic, integrated, and planned approach to improve the effectiveness of people and groups in an enterprise through the use of techniques for problem discovery and various intervention techniques for solving these problems.

Organizational authority The degree of discretion in organizational positions conferring on persons occupying these positions the right to use their judgment in decision making.

Organizational behavior modification A motivational approach to organize behavior through defining and manipulating such internal states as desires, satisfactions, and attitudes.

Organizational development A development process embracing a wide variety of behavioral and management approaches designed to make human behavior and relationships in an organization more effective, primarily through probing behavior problems, attitudes, motives, and values of participants, and adopting such techniques as management by objectives and revision of task structure to make coordination more effective.

Organizational role An organizational post designed for individuals to fill; to be meaningful to people, it must incorporate (1) verifiable objectives; (2) a clear concept of the major duties or activities involved; (3) an understood area of discretion, or authority; (4) the availability of information and resources necessary to accomplish a task.

Organizing Establishing an intentional structure of roles in a formally organizied enterprise.

P

Parity of authority and responsibility *See* authority, parity with responsibility.

Partial controls Controls designed to measure performance in a specific activity, such as quality, cash, production, or sales.

Path goal approach to leadership effectiveness An approach that sees the most effective leadership style as one where leaders take various steps to design a situation where motivations of a group are responded to effectively, primarily by defining task roles clearly, removing obstacles to performance, and doing other things which will make it possible for people to perform and gain satisfactions thereby.

Peer rating Appraising of managers by other managers at the same organizational level.

PERT (Program Evaluation and Review Technique) A time-event network analysis system in which the various events in a program or project are identified, with the planned time for each, and are placed in a network showing the relationships of each event to other events; from the sequence of interrelated events, the path of those events in which there is the least "slack" time in terms of planned completion is the "critical path"; PERT/TIME systems deal only with time; PERT/COST systems introduce costs of each event and are usually combined with elapsed time of each event or series of events.

Peter Principle Principle enunciated by Laurence J. Peter and Raymond Hall that managers tend to be promoted until they reach the level of their incompetence.

Planning Selecting missions and objectives—and the strategies, policies, programs, and procedures for achieving them; decision making; the selection of a course of action from among alternatives.

Planning premises The planning assumptions—the expected environment in which plans will operate; they may be forecasts of the planning environment or basic policies and existing plans which will influence any given plan.

Planning premises, types of Premises may be internal or external to an enterprise, quantitative or qualitative, or controllable, uncontrollable, or semicontrollable.

Planning process A rational approach to setting and accomplishing an objective and evaluating alternatives in light of goals sought and against the environment of planning premises.

Plans, types of Purpose or missions, objectives, strategies, policies, procedures, rules, programs, and budgets.

Plural executive A committee, or group, which has the authority to execute, as a group, managerial functions.

Policies General statements or understandings which guide thinking in decision making; the essence of policies is the existence of discretion, within certain limits, in guiding decision making.

Positive reinforcement Psychologist Skinner's theory that people are best motivated by properly designing their work environment, giving them prompt feedback on performance, and finding ways to help them and praise them for the good things they do.

Preference, or utility, theory The theory that individual attitudes toward risk will vary from statistical probabilities, with some individuals being willing only to take lower risks than indicated by probabilities ("risk averters") and others taking greater risks ("gamblers").

Principles Fundamental truths, or what are believed to be truths at a given time, explaining relationships between two or more sets of variables, usually an independent variable and a dependent variable; may be descriptive, explaining what will happen, or prescriptive (or normative), indicating what a person should do; in the latter case, principles reflect some scale of values, such as efficiency, and therefore imply value judgments.

Procedures Chronological sequences of required actions detailing the exact manner in which an activity must be accomplished.

Profit The surplus of sales dollars over expense dollars.

Profit and loss control A control technique designed to measure a division or other part of a business enterprise by calculating the total profit (or loss) performance of that entity.

Program budgeting A budgeting approach, used primarily by government agencies, emphasizing goals, the programs to achieve them, and budgetary allocations designed to support such programs.

Programs A complex of goals, policies, procedures, rules, task assignments, steps to be taken, resources to be employed, and other elements necessary to carry out a given course of action and normally supported by capital and operating budgets.

Promotion based on open competition The policy of filling positions or making promotions from the most qualified people available whether inside or outside a given enterprise.

Promotion from within The practice of making all promotions in an enterprise from people within it if it is possible to do so.

R

Rationality Analysis requiring a clear goal, a clear understanding of alternatives by which a goal can be reached, an analysis and evaluation of alternatives in terms of the goal sought, needed information, and a desire to optimize.

Real-time information Information on events as they occur.

Recentralization of authority The recall of some or all authority previously delegated.

Responsibility The obligation owed by subordinates to their superiors for exercising authority delegated to them in a way to accomplish results expected.

Responsibility, absoluteness of The concept that, since responsibility is an obligation owed, it cannot be delegated.

Return-on-investment control A control technique designed to measure a division or other part of a business enterprise by looking on the profit made as a percentage of the investment in assets in that entity.

Risk analysis An approach to problem analysis which weighs risks in a situation by introducing probabilities to give a more accurate assessment of the risks involved.

Rules Required action or nonaction, allowing no discretion.

S

Sales forecast A prediction of expected sales, by product or service and price, for a period of time in the future; sales forecasts both are derived from plans and are major planning premises.

Satisfaction The contentment experienced when a want or need is satisfied.

Satisficing A term invented by Herbert A. Simon to denote the tendencies of managers, normally in instances of bounded rationality, in making decisions, to pick a course of action that is deemed "good enough" under the circumstances. See bounded rationality.

Scalar relationships Authority relationships are said to be scalar when subordinates report to their immediate superiors and when their superiors report directly, as subordinates, to their superiors (i.e., in "scales"). In other words, the chain of command that runs from the top of an organization to its lowest ranks.

Science Organized knowledge of pertinence to an area, usually an area of practice.

Scientific management A term originally used by F. W. Taylor and his associates as denoting their approach to management. It implies that the methods of scientific inquiry, analysis, and summary can be applied to the activities of managers. It later implied time study and similar methods used by Taylor and his followers to analyze activities of people in organizations. Basically, it sought to develop (1) ways of increasing productivity by making work easier to perform and (2) methods for motivating people to take advantage of labor-saving techniques it developed. Basically, it may be summarized as (1) replacing rules of thumb with rules of science, (2) obtaining harmony rather than discord, (3) achieving cooperation rather than chaotic individualism, (4) working for maximum rather than restricted output, (5) developing workers to the fullest extent possible.

Sensitivity training A form of training based on behavior of persons in groups and, through undirected group interchange, designed to make these persons more aware of their own feelings and the feelings of others toward them.

Service departments A grouping of activities that might be carried on in other departments but are brought together in a specialized department for purposes of efficiency, control, or both; as such, service departments are operating departments, but because they comprise specialists, they are often also used for staff advice and are often given functional authority.

Similarity, assignment by Assigning activities to a department where similar activities are being performed.

Situational approach to leadership The approach that studies leadership on the premise that it is strongly influenced by the situation from which the leader emerges and in which he or she operates.

Situational management *See* contingency management.

Social audit An audit of the performance of an enterprise in those areas which have a significant social impact and importance.

Social responsibility of managers The responsibility of managers, in carrying out their socially approved missions, to be responsive to, congruent with, and interact and live within the forces and elements of their social environment.

Social system A system viewed as including only social elements, that is, the interaction and behavior patterns of people.

Sociotechnical system A system viewed as an interconnection of physical and social elements in an organization.

Span of control *See* span of management.

Span of management The phenomenon that there is a limit to the number of persons a manager can supervise, even though this limit varies depending on situations and the competence of a manager; the various situations, or underlying variables, include time available for supervision; training possessed by, and required of, subordinates; clarity of authority delegations; clarity of plans; rate of change in an enterprise; effectiveness of managerial controls; effectiveness of communications techniques; and the extent to which a situation requires personal face-to-face contact. Often referred to as "span of control".

Splintered authority The situation where the total authority to accomplish a given result rests in more than one position and must be pooled, or combined, to make the required decision.

Staff A relationship in an organizational position where an incumbent's task is to give some other person advice or counsel.

Staffing Filling positions in the organization structure through defining workforce requirements, inventorying workforce, appraising, selecting, compensating, and training.

Strategies General programs of action and deployment of emphasis and resources to attain comprehensive objectives; the program of objectives of an organization and their changes, resources used to attain these objectives, and policies governing the acquisition, use, and disposition of these resources; the determination of the basic long-term objectives of an enterprise and the adoption of courses of action and allocation of resources necessary to achieve these goals.

Strategies, composite *See* composite strategies.

Strategies, contingency *See* contingency strategies.

Supervisors Same as managers, but ordinarily used to apply to managers at the lowest level, or first line, of managing.

System, definition of A set or assemblage of things connected, or interdependent and interacting so as to form a complex unity; a whole composed of parts in orderly arrangement according to some scheme or plan. For any system there must be boundaries that separate it from its environment. *See* cooperative system; differentiation; elaboration; entropy; equifinality; feedback; homeostasis, negative entropy; social system, sociotechnical system.

Systems, boundaries The demarcation lines or area definition separating a given system from its environment.

Systems, closed Not having interactions with the system's environment.

Systems, open Having interactions with the system's environment and exchanging information, energy, or material with that environment.

T

Tactics Action plans by which strategies are executed.

Task of the manager See managers, task of.

Technological forecasting Forecasting the future technology that may affect the operations of an enterprise.

Technology The sum total of knowledge of ways of doing things; it includes inventions, techniques, and the vast store of organized knowledge of how to do things.

Theory A systematic grouping of interrelated principles and concepts which provides a framework for significant knowledge.

Time-span of discretion method of position evaluation Developed by Elliott Jaques, this method is based on evaluating positions on the basis of the longest period that must elapse before it can be known whether an occupant of a position is exercising discretion accurately.

Trait appraisals Appraising people, whether managers or nonmanagers, on the basis of personal traits and work-oriented characteristics.

Transactional analysis A technique developed by Eric Berne and Thomas Harris which is designed to improve human relations and communication by identifying behavior patterns derived from the "Parent," "Adult," or "Child" ego states.

U

Unity of command Having each subordinate report to only one superior. The principle of unity of command implies only that the more an individual reports to a single superior, the less the problem of conflict in instructions and the greater the feeling of personal responsibility for results.

Universality of management The concept that essential, or basic, management science, theory, principles, and concepts are applicable to any culture even though applications in practice may vary depending on cultural differences, contingencies, or situations.

V

Variable budgets Budgets constructed by distinguishing between period costs

(costs that vary only with time or remain fixed over time) and variable costs (costs that vary to some extent with the volume of enterprise output) and showing budgeted expenses of an organizational unit as they vary with volume.

Verifiable objectives *See* objectives, verifiable.

Z

Zero-based budgeting Budgeting in which enterprise programs are divided into "packages," comprising goals, activities, and needed resources, and costs are calculated for each package from the ground up.

Name Index

Subject Index